Civilization Past & Present

FIFTH EDITION · SPECIAL PRINTING · VOLUME 1

T. WALTER WALLBANK
Emeritus Professor of History, University of Southern California

ALASTAIR M. TAYLOR
Professor of Political Studies and Geography, Queens University

NELS M. BAILKEY
Professor of History, Tulane University

GEORGE F. JEWSBURY
Associate Professor of History, Oklahoma State University

Civilization Past & Present

FIFTH EDITION · SPECIAL PRINTING · VOLUME 1

Scott, Foresman and Company
Glenview, Illinois • London, England

Library of Congress Cataloging in Publication Data
Main entry under title:

Civilization past & present.

  Includes bibliographies and indexes.
    1. Civilization—History. I. Wallbank, T. Walter
(Thomas Walter).   II. Title: Civilization past and present.
CB57.C556 1984   909   84-23525
ISBN 0-673-18165-0

Preface

Civilization Past and Present, originally published in 1942, was the first text of its kind. Its objective was to present a survey of world cultural history, treating the development and growth of civilization not as a unique European experience but as a global one through which all great culture systems have interacted to produce the present-day world.

This Special Printing in two softbound volumes of the Fifth Single-Volume Edition of *Civilization Past and Present* continues to present a global survey of humanity's experiences and accomplishments. It maintains the various strengths that have made the Fifth Edition the most successful version of an already widely popular introductory textbook.

Among the popular features of *Civilization Past and Present* are the seven sections of color plates which, in themselves, constitute a capsule history of world art and the nine Family Profiles depicting the daily life of individuals in different historical periods. Each of these features provides an extra dimension of social and cultural relevance.

The Special Printing of the Fifth Single-Volume Edition (published in 1983) reflected a careful updating of the text. The changes, while less comprehensive than those in a major revision, went considerably beyond those that would be expected in a normal reprinting. In keeping with the objective of providing essential background for understanding contemporary problems, this updating focused special attention on coverage of the decades since World War II. The chapters in Part Eight were reworked to incorporate the most recent happenings, not only in the political sphere, but in the cultural as well. Four-color reference maps 11 through 14 were also brought up to date. This softbound two-volume version of the Special Printing incorporates further updating of the text material in Chapters 34 through 36, as well as of the chronological tables at the end of Volume 2.

This Special Printing of *Civilization Past and Present* places particular emphasis on the fundamental forces that are speeding up change in this penultimate decade of the twentieth century. The need is greater than ever to understand these changes in their historical perspective.

Note to the Student

This book has been developed with the dual purpose of helping you acquire a solid knowledge of past events and, equally important, of helping you think more constructively about the significance of those events for the difficult times in which we live. In the Prologue you will learn more about studying the meaning of history. This note is intended to acquaint you with the principal features of the text.

THE INTERCHAPTERS

Aid in the organization and review of your reading will be provided by the interchapters, which outline the material to be covered in each unit.

THE FAMILY PROFILES

Appearing at the end of each Part (with an additional one following Chapter 17), are Family Profiles. These concisely written descriptions look into the world of individuals living during the period of history covered in the preceding section. Each Family Profile tells about living conditions, social activities, occupations, religious attitudes, political loyalties, aspirations, and constraints of the family members depicted. In Volume 1 we get a good insight into the lives of a working-class Roman family, a medieval Chinese family, an Aztec family, and an English family in the Tudor period.

SUGGESTIONS FOR READING

At the conclusion of each chapter, you will find an annotated bibliography, pertaining especially to what has been covered in that chapter. The readings list special historical studies, biographies, reputable historical fiction, and some collections of source materials. As indicated in the listings, many of these works can be purchased in less expensive paperbound editions. These bibliographies will provide you with ample readings from which to develop special reports or with which to improve your understanding of a given subject.

THE COLOR PLATES

Seven inserts of full-color art reproductions appear throughout the two volumes. The works of art have been carefully selected and faithfully reproduced to illustrate, in every case, some facet of a culture pattern discussed in the text. These reproductions, with the accompanying commentary, constitute a capsule history of world art.

THE CHRONOLOGICAL CHARTS

At the end of each volume are chronological charts showing the sequence of events discussed within the text. By studying these charts, you can fix in your mind the relationship of events in the various parts of the world.

THE MAPS

Two-color maps are liberally distributed throughout both volumes of this book. Some are designed to make clear the nature of a single distinctive event or idea discussed in the text; others illustrate larger trends. At the end of each volume are sixteen pages of full-color reference maps, showing all the major areas of the world and virtually every town, political subdivision, and geographic feature mentioned in the text. Most of the reference maps and several of the two-color maps appear in relief.

THE PRONUNCIATION KEY

In the index the correct pronunciation is given for many proper names. Thus you will find it easy, as well as extremely helpful, to look up the correct pronunciation of the names of persons and places referred to in the text.

Contents

Civilization Past & Present

FIFTH EDITION • SPECIAL PRINTING • VOLUME 1

Perspective on Humanity

If the time span of our planet—now estimated at some five billion years—were telescoped into a single year, the first eight months would be devoid of any life. The next two months would be taken up with plant and very primitive animal forms, and not until well into December would any mammals appear. In this "year" members of *Homo erectus*, our ancient predecessors, would mount the global stage only between 10 and 11 P.M. on December 31. And how has the human species spent that brief allotment? Most of it—the equivalent of more than half a million years—has been given over to making tools out of stone. The revolutionary changeover from a food-hunting nomad to a farmer who raised grain and domesticated animals would occur in the last sixty seconds. And into that final minute would be crowded all of humanity's other accomplishments: the use of metal, the creation of civilizations, the mastery of the oceans, the harnessing of steam, then gas, electricity, oil, and, finally, in our lifetime, atomic energy. And now humankind's technological genius has enabled it to escape from age-old bondage to the earth and to initiate an interplanetary age. Brief though it has been, man's time on the globe reveals a rich tapestry of science, industry, religion, and art. This accumulated experience of the human species is available for study. We call it *history*.

THE PAST AS PAST

The Koster site. The Koster family farms its land in the lower Illinois River valley, some forty-five miles north of St. Louis. A neighbor with an interest in archaeology had been impressed by large numbers of artifacts lying about in the Kosters' fields, and reported his finds to an archaeologist at Northwestern University. Dr. Stuart Struever investigated and, in 1969, began to excavate in a cornfield close to a stream which runs all year and to 150-foot-high bluffs that would protect the site from severe weather. The "dig" revealed twenty-three "horizons" (the archaeologist's term for strata bearing traces of human habitation), each excellently preserved, together with thousands of items that were washed, analyzed, catalogued (with the aid of a computer), and stored. The Koster site—which possessed the greatest potential yet found for unfolding the story of ancient human existence in North America—has shown that prehistoric humans lived in this valley for more than 9000 years, and further excavation might have uncovered signs of the Paleo-Indian, who inhabited this continent from 10,000 to 8000 B.C.

It may be asked: What is the "use" of all this painstaking effort? The Koster site unearthed no sarcophagus, gold mask, or jeweled scarab like those discovered in King Tut's tomb in Egypt. Yet its seemingly prosaic evidence can yield something no less exciting: information about the lives and environmental challenges met by men and women who lived at Koster on twenty-three different occasions during nine millennia. Thus the middle levels contained the remains of hearths and food-storage pits dating back to 6500 B.C. Found, too, were nine human burials placed by radiocarbon dating to the same time. Archaeologists' discoveries included the skeleton of a human infant (whose body had been covered for burial with powdered hematite, a yellowish-red ore of iron) and those of domesticated dogs that had been buried. Other evidence indicates that the Indians at Koster had domesticated squash, pumpkins, and gourds by 800 B.C.; the domestication of corn has been placed at 600 A.D., although the Indians did not become agriculturalists until 900 A.D. Why the delay, compared with societal transformations in other parts of the world? Koster archaeologists determined, also, that for thousands of years—from the period of Horizon 11 through that of Horizon 2—the population grew very little. Yet before and after Horizon 1 came into existence (100 B.C.), large population increases occurred. The Horizon 1 years also saw the appearance of organized violence, which is defined here as collective conflict against other peoples in a struggle, perhaps for survival.

Thus the scientists at the Koster site have augmented and altered our knowledge of North American preliterate history. The interest displayed by the thousands of visitors who came to the site while work was in progress and the enthusiasm of the student archaeologists trained there attest to the curiosity that we all share about the past. Our resulting satisfaction is enhanced, moreover, when we use this knowledge as a yardstick to measure our own age and experiences within a global time-space perspective.

PAST AND PRESENT

"The more things change . . ." Obviously, the cultural horizons revealed by the archaeologist's spade are very different from the "horizon" in which we live. The Koster farm has electricity and modern farm implements; it is near a state-highway system and within an hour's drive of a metropolis, itself a microcosm of twentieth-century science, technology, education, soaring buildings, and complex institutions. From their cars and trailers parked near the "dig," visitors disgorged cameras, transistor radios, and camping equipment that would have mystified the original inhabitants. They breakfasted on Florida grapefruit, Brazilian coffee, and meats and cereals of a variety and quality far beyond the capability of the Archaic hunters and farmers. Those differences in technology, societal structure, and world-view are further demonstrated as the campers' radios report news from all parts of the globe.

". . . the more they remain the same." And yet, we are linked by more than mere curiosity to these archaic Illinois River valley inhabitants. Why? Because we are of the same species, and we share a fundamental invariance which connects present with past: the man-environment nexus. Ultimately speaking, it is the dynamic interplay of environmental factors and human activities that accounts for the terrestrial process known as history. Because of the biological continuity of our species, coupled with mankind's unflagging inventiveness, each generation has been able to build upon the experiences and contributions of its predecessors—so that continuity and change in human affairs proceed together. Hence, the two groups of *Homo sapiens* at the Koster site—ancient and modern—are at once dissimilar and similar.

The universal culture pattern. In this interplay of men and women with their environment and fellow-beings, they have always expressed certain fundamental needs. These form the basis of a "universal culture pattern" and deserve to be enumerated.

1. *The need to make a living.* Men and women must have food, shelter, clothing, and the means to provide for their offsprings' survival.

2. *The need for law and order.* From earliest times, communities have had to keep peace among their members, defend themselves against external attack, and protect community assets.

3. *The need for social organization.* For people to make a living, raise families, and maintain law and order, a social structure is essential. Ideologies may hold different views about the relative importance of the group and the individual within any such social structure.

4. *The need for knowledge and learning.* Since earliest times, humankind has transmitted the knowledge acquired from experience, first orally and then by means of writing systems. As societies grow more complex, there is increasing need to preserve knowledge and transmit it through education to as many people as possible.

5. *The need for self-expression.* People have responded creatively to their environment even before the days when they decorated the walls of Paleolithic caves with paintings of the animals they hunted. The arts appear to have a lineage as old as man himself.

6. *The need for religious expression.* Equally old is humanity's attempt to answer the "why" of its existence. What primitive peoples considered supernatural in their environment could at a later time often be explained by science in terms of natural phenomena. Yet today, no less than in archaic times, men and women continue to search for answers to the ultimate questions of existence.

These six needs have been common to people at all times and in all places. They apply equally to

10,000 Years Of Koster Life

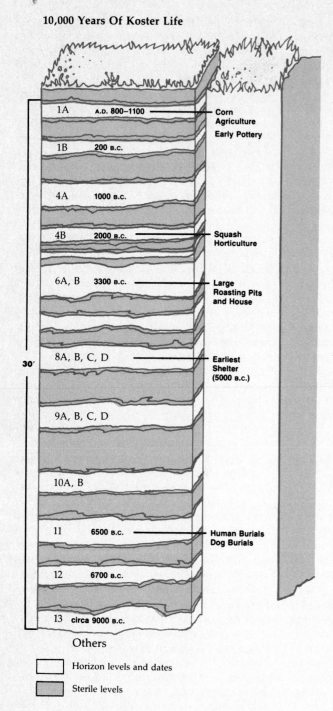

1A   A.D. 800–1100 — Corn Agriculture / Early Pottery

1B   200 B.C.

4A   1000 B.C.

4B   2000 B.C. — Squash Horticulture

6A, B   3300 B.C. — Large Roasting Pits and House

8A, B, C, D — Earliest Shelter (5000 B.C.)

9A, B, C, D

10A, B

11   6500 B.C. — Human Burials / Dog Burials

12   6700 B.C.

13   circa 9000 B.C.

30′

Others

☐ Horizon levels and dates

▨ Sterile levels

the ancient and present-day inhabitants of the Koster site. For example, archaeologists discovered stone tools, postholes for dwelling supports, and foodstuffs as part of the response to the need to make a living. Examination of the twenty-three horizons suggests a peaceful continuity and, eventually, recourse to collective conflict, either to defend the site against external aggressors or, again, to attack other communities. The presence of ancient villages underscores the organization of the species at a level more complex than the primary family unit, while the phenomenon of a stable population for millennia suggests societal behavior patterns and perhaps even regulations of some kind. Knowlege of how to make tools, weapons, and pottery had to be acquired, systematized as learning, and transmitted from one generation to the next. Although the designs displayed on pottery fragments found at Koster did not serve any "practical" purpose, they satisfied the potter's aesthetic needs. The elaborate burial rite for the infant found at Horizon 11 can hardly be divorced from a religious significance.

Culture traits and diffusion. Carrying the concept of a universal culture pattern one step further: When a group of people behave similarly and share the same institutions and ways of life, they can be said to have a common culture. Each person born into that group will derive from it his basic way of life. It follows that the basic differences between the first residents at the Koster site and those of the present-day Koster family are due mainly to the fact that their culture traits are at different stages of development or that they worked out different methods of solving the same problems of existence. In the succeeding chapters, we shall be looking at a number of different cultures, some of which are designated as *civilizations*. (If *all* tribes or societies have culture, then civilization is a particular *kind* of culture.) "A culture is the way of life of a human group; it includes all the learned and standardized forms of behavior which one uses and others in one's group expect and recognize. . . . Civilization is that kind of culture which includes the use of writing, the presence of cities and of wide political organization, and the development of occupational specialization."[1]

Cultures are never static or wholly isolated. A particular culture may have an individuality which sets it off sharply from other cultures, but invariably it has been influenced by external contacts—and this process would have applied to every "horizon" at the Koster site. Such contacts may be either peaceful or warlike, and they meet with varying degrees of acceptance or resistance. The early American colonists took from the Indians the use of corn and tobacco, while the latter obtained the horse and firearms from the newcomers. On the other hand, the Second World War saw the Nazis and Japanese force their cultures upon subjugated peoples with little or no permanent result.

Environment and invention in culture change. Geography has profoundly influenced the development of cultures, but we should not exaggerate its importance. Although riverine civilizations evolved along the Nile and the Tigris-Euphrates, for example, none emerged in the physically comparable valleys of the Jordan and Rio Grande.[2] Moreover, environmental influences tend to become less marked as people gain increasing technological skill, as shown by the transformation of arid regions in southwestern United States into rich citrus areas and the extension of the grain-growing belt in the Canadian prairies further north through the development of frost- and rust-resistant types of wheat.

Invention is therefore another important source of culture change. The domestication of animals and cereals, for example, took place in both the old and new worlds, albeit the animals and grains were different because of dissimilar ecological factors — yet so far as we know, there was no physical contact at the time between the two cultural heartlands. To what extent, then, is physical contact required in the process of invention? Or, is it possible for men and women in different times and places to hit upon similar solutions to the challenges posed by their respective environments — resulting in the phenomenon known as "parallel invention"?

Culture lag. Some parts of a culture pattern change more rapidly than others, so that one institution sometimes becomes outmoded in relation to others in a society. When different parts of a society fail to mesh harmoniously, the condition is often called *culture lag.* Numerous examples of this lag could be cited: the failure to give women the vote until this century; the tragedy of hunger in the midst of plenty during the 1930's; in our own day, the repeated inability of the United Nations to limit atomic energy to peaceful uses because of the insistence by national states to arm themselves as they please.

PAST AND PRESENT AS PROLOGUE

Toward tomorrow's world. While time can be regarded as a continuum, we experience it only in a single direction. The Koster "dig" was an excavation into yesterday; our "present" must become tomorrow's "past" in turn. And thus is "history" created. Past and present conjoin to become the prologue for tomorrow's world, precisely because cultural and environmental processes must bring about continued transformations within societies and cultural patterns alike.

What can the past and present — as history — suggest to us for tomorrow's world? In the first place, changes in the physical and social environments will probably accelerate as a result of continued technological innovation. These changes can result in increased disequilibrium and tensions among the various segments comprising the universal culture pattern — in other words, in increased culture lag. To some observers, this culture lag has assumed dangerous proportions in the apparently widening gap in communications and outlook between science and the technological sector on the one hand and our traditional humanistic culture and value system on the other. These two major segments of our culture pattern appear to be advancing, and changing, at the speeds of a supersonic jet and of a horse-and-buggy respectively.

Just what dynamic factors are at work that bring about different rates of speed in the processes of change? Because our modern age derives its particular world outlook in ever-growing measure from the discoveries of science and the changes wrought by technology, we shall have a greater need than we have ever had before to understand the dynamics involved in the process and how they are already shaping the pattern of our culture for the decades ahead.

Today we are having to pay the price of environmental and societal disequilibrium — as is evidenced by the energy crisis, the rapid depletion of many nonreplenishable minerals and fossil fuels, the deterioration of our physical environment from pollution, and a population explosion in the underdeveloped regions of the world. Throughout its long planetary experience, mankind has had to endure shortages. Today, however, those shortages result from causes very different from anything that has happened hitherto in history. Our scarcities stem not from a traditional inability to do much more than scratch the earth's riches, but from our technological genius at converting and consuming those resources on a scale both prodigious and prodigal.

From exponential growth to steady-state? Has the past anything to tell the future about the consequences of cultural disequilibrium — anything which we might profitably utilize in present-day planning for the decades ahead? The evidence found in the Koster horizons is relevant. It tells us that for 8000 years or more, men and women were able to lead what Dr. Struever terms the "good life." Archaic man "had plenty of leisure time in which to domesticate pets. It's sheer folklore that primitive people had to struggle from dawn to dusk simply to survive. How hard a man works depends a lot on what he considers necessary goals in life, and there was no environmental imperative in the valley requiring man to work hard. . . . Man lived in a land of milk and honey, with tremendous food resources all around him in this valley, and the taking was easy."[3] During that long period of successive habitations, the Indians at Koster maintained a stable equilibrium with an environment which in turn underwent no apparent deterioration.

Again, for much the longest part of that time, when the economy was still at the food-collecting stage, the Indians maintained their numbers with little change. True, prior to Horizon 1, there occurred a large increase in population, and this increase may either have occasioned, or in turn been occasioned by, a shift to agriculture. Yet in any case, it would appear that a new overall balance was struck between environmental factors and population growth—an equilibrium that would have resulted at some point in a "steady-state" condition.

The experience at the Koster site is far from unique. The historical record shows that all societies, previous to the present, have tended to shift from open-ended increase of physical size, population, and social complexity toward steady-state. Because our planet and its resources are finite, at some point, too, our society in turn must expect to shift from exponential growth to no-growth. By that term, we mean the setting of maximal levels upon the numbers of humans who can inhabit this planet with an assured minimal standard of life, and upon the exploitation of the earth's resources required to provide that standard. Otherwise, environmental disaster on an unprecedented scale could result in the decades ahead. But here we are talking about quantitative, not qualitative, no-growth. Too often, we have confused mere size and expansion with quality of life—which is about as logical as comparing a lump of coal with a diamond (though they both derive from carbon). Past and present conjoin to alert us to the need not only to engage in new forms of planning for the years ahead, but no less to rethink our existing social goals and value system. We shall require as long and accurate a perspective as possible from our global experience in order to make realistic analyses and take the right kinds of action to improve our quality of life.

THE "HOW" OF HISTORY

Definition of history. History is the record of the past actions of humankind, based upon surviving evidence. The historian uses this evidence to reach conclusions which he believes are valid. In this way he becomes an interpreter of the development of humanity. History shows that all patterns and problems in human affairs are the products of a complex process of growth. By throwing light on that process, history provides a means for profiting from human experience. In this connection it is salutary to recall the words of the philosopher George Santayana when he declared, "Those who cannot remember the past are condemned to repeat it."

Is history a science? There is more than one way of treating the past. In dealing with the American Revolution, for example, the historian may describe its events in narrative form. Again, he may prefer to analyze its general causes or perhaps compare its stages with the patterns of revolutions in other countries. But the historian does not aim for the same kind of results as the scientist. The latter can verify his conclusions by repeating his experiment under controlled conditions in his laboratory, and he also seeks to classify the phenomenon in a general group or category. For his part, the historian has to pay special attention to the *uniqueness* of his data, because each event takes place at a particular time and in a particular place. And since that time is now past, he cannot verify his conclusions by duplicating the circumstances in which the event occurred. Moreover, since history is concerned fundamentally with the lives and actions of men and women, the causes involved are bound to be relatively subjective.

Nevertheless, historians insist that history be written as scientifically as possible and that evidence be analyzed with the same objective attitude employed by the scientist when he examines natural phenomena. This scientific spirit requires the historian to handle his evidence according to established rules of historical analysis, to recognize his own biases and attempt to eliminate their effects from his work, and to draw only such conclusions as the evidence seems to warrant.

Historical method. To meet these requirements, historians have evolved the "historical method." The first step is the search for *sources*, without which there can be no history. They may consist of material remains—such as the bones, tools, weapons, and pottery found at the Koster site; oral traditions such as myths, legends, and songs; pictorial data such as drawings and maps; and, of course, written records ranging from ancient manuscripts to treaties, diaries, books, and yesterday's newspaper.

Having acquired his sources, the historian must next infer from them the facts. This process has two parts. *External criticism* tests the genuineness of the source. Its importance was demonstrated dramatically in recent years by the unmasking of a hoax—Piltdown Man—which had long duped scientists. For the most part however, the historian has to deal with less spectacular problems, such as checking ancient documents for errors that have crept into the text through faulty copying or translating.

The second step in the analytical process is called *internal criticism.* In evaluating written materials, the historian must ascertain the author's meaning and the accuracy of his work. To do so may require study of the language of the era or the circumstances in which the author's statement was made. A politician's memoirs may be suspect because of an almost universal tendency to present oneself in the most favorable light, while official documents must in turn be examined for what they may conceal as well as what a government wishes to reveal.

The final step in historical method is *synthesis.* Here the historian must determine which factors in a given situation are most relevant to his purpose, since obviously he cannot include everything that occurred. This delicate process of selection underscores the role that subjectivity plays in the writing of history. Furthermore, the more complex the events involved, the more crucial becomes the historian's judgment.[4]

The problem of periodization. Can we really categorize history as "ancient," "medieval," and "modern"? When we reflect upon this question, it becomes clear that what is "modern" in the twentieth century could conceivably be considered "medieval" in the twenty-fifth century, and eventually "ancient" in the thirty-fifth century A.D. Yet not to break up the account would be akin to reading this book without the benefit of parts, chapters, paragraphs, or even separate sentences. Like time itself, history would then become a ceaseless flow of consciousness and events. To simplify his task and to manage his materials more easily, the historian divides time into periods. The divisions he chooses, the lines he draws, reveal the distinctive way in which he regards the past—namely, in terms of patterns which appear to him logical and meaningful. Needless to add, no two historians see the past in an identical pattern; thus the division of the past into periods is necessarily arbitrary—and, like airline schedules subject to change without prior notice.

THE "WHY" OF HISTORY

Historical analysis. The historian seeks to describe not only *what* has happened and *how* it happened, but also *why* society undergoes change. Any search of this kind raises a number of fundamental questions: the roles of Providence, the individual, and the group in history; the extent to which events are unique or, conversely, can fit into patterns; and the problem of progress in human affairs. The answers vary with different philosophical views of the universe and man's role therein.

Providence or the individual. Those who hold the teleological view see in history the guidance of a Divine Will, directing human destinies according to a cosmic purpose. This concept was accepted as self-evident in ancient theocratic societies and medieval times, but lost ground after the Renaissance, when the spread of rationalistic doctrines and scientific triumphs seemed to forecast unlimited progress in human affairs. Other thinkers have exalted the role of the individual in the historical process—such as Thomas Carlyle, who contended that major figures, or "Great Men," chiefly determined the course of human events. In our own day, there has been a reaction against the nineteenth century's comfortable assumption that man is virtually a free agent.

"Laws" and "forces" in history. Opponents of Carlyle's thesis often contend that history is determined by "forces" and "laws" and by the actions of entire societies. Sociologists approach history primarily by analyzing the origins, institutions, and functions of groups. Like the sociologist, the economist tends to look at the historical record from the standpoint of group action and especially the impact of economic forces such as that of, say, supply and demand or diminishing returns.

The most explosive interpretation of history in modern times was made by Karl Marx. To him, irresistible economic forces governed human beings and determined the trend of events. Marx contended that the shift from one economic stage to another—such as from feudalism to capitalism—is attained by upheavals, or revolutions, which occur because the class controlling the methods of production eventually resists further progress in order to maintain its vested interests. He predicted that the proletariat would overthrow the exploiting capitalists and that the end result would be a classless society, followed by a gradual withering away of the state itself. These predictions, however, have proved considerably less than "scientific" in their accuracy.

Theories of civilization. Numerous other attempts have been made to explain societal processes according to a set of principles. Oswald Spengler, a disillusioned German, maintained that civilizations were like organisms; each grew with the "superb aimlessness" of a flower and passed through a cycle of spring, summer, autumn, and winter. He declared that western civilization was in its winter period and had already entered into a state of rapid decline. Like Spengler, other thinkers have sought to explain societal behavior in terms of biological growth and decay. Charles Darwin's evolutionary hypothesis made a strong impact upon nineteenth-century thought and gave rise to the concept that the principle of "survival of the fittest" must also apply to human societies. This line of thought—known as social Darwinism—raises social and ethical questions of major importance.

Does history obey impersonal laws and forces so that its course is inevitable? Or, at the other extreme, since every event is a unique act, is history simply the record of unforeseen and unrelated episodes? Can this apparent dilemma be avoided? We believe it can. Though all events are in various respects unique, they also contain elements which invite comparison—as in the case of the origin and course of revolutions in different countries. The comparative approach permits us to seek relationships between historical phenomena and to group them into movements or patterns or civilizations. For our part, we eschew any single "theory" of history, preferring to see merit in a number of basic concepts. These include the effects of physical environment on social organization and institutions; the roles played by economic, political, and religious factors; and the impact exerted by men and women occupying key positions in various societies.

Progress and growth is a continuous factor. It depends on, and contributes to, the maintenance of peace and security, the peaceful settlement of international disputes, and worldwide improvement in economic and social standards.

THE CHALLENGE

The role of history today. The archaeologists at the Koster site have added to our understanding about humanity's life on this planet, its challenges and creative responses. The evidence from Koster suggests that there is no single, predestined road along which humanity must travel, or a set pattern of responses to its environmental problems and opportunities. Societal development is a creative, open-ended process, whether at Koster or any other location on this planet. The archaeologists as they sift and evaluate the unearthed evidence from the ancient past, the historians as they analyze the written records of classical civilizations, and the social scientists as they investigate present-day societal phenomena—all share a common interest and concern: to learn more about the human condition.

And we shall need to know all we can about that condition. While human technology is at present moving ahead at supersonic speed, there has been no corresponding increase in man's own mental or physical capacity. He has probably no more native intelligence than his predecessors at the Koster horizons—and just as probably less muscle. So we come to a fundamental challenge: how is twentieth-century man to cope with the ever widening disparity between what he *is* and what he *has?* How can he control and utilize his tremendous technological powers for happiness and not for nuclear self-annihilation? Today he seeks to conquer other planets before he has learned to govern his own.

Surely an indispensable step toward solving contemporary humanity's dilemma—technology without the requisite control, and power without commensurate wisdom—must be a better understanding of how man and all his works became what they are today. Only by understanding the past can we assess both the perils and the opportunities of the present—and move courageously and compassionately into the uncharted future.

PART ONE
The Ancient World

■ How old the universe is and how the planet earth came into being may never be known precisely, but modern scientists believe that our world has been circling the sun for four and one-half to five billion years. During that incredibly long time, the earth changed from a gaseous to a liquid state and finally solidified; waters formed on the earth's shell, and in their depths life took form. As one geological epoch succeeded another, first single-celled and then multicelled organisms evolved, and some of them learned to live on land. Eventually this ceaseless process of adaptation to environment brought forth the mammal class, of which man is a member.

Remains of early manlike creatures unearthed in Africa may be nearly three to four million years old. The time span from those remote days to about 3500 B.C. is usually referred to as prehistoric, or preliterate, times. By far the greater part of that time span was taken up by man's relentless struggle for survival—a struggle in which he learned to shape crude weapons and tools from stone, make fire, and domesticate certain plants and animals. The latter achievement was of revolutionary consequence, for it freed man of the necessity to hunt the migrant beasts. And a measure of control over plants and animals meant that he could settle down in one place and become a farmer and herdsman.

The stage was now set for a progressively rapid extension of man's control over his environment. Life became more complex and more rewarding. The discovery of metallurgy, progress in arts and crafts, the organization of larger social and political units, and the invention of writing heralded a new era of existence. These momentous advances did not occur over the entire earth but were concentrated in a few great river valleys. There the well-watered, fertile soil produced abundant harvests and food surpluses supported increased populations. Cities sprang up, inhabited by men with diverse talents: priests, potters, basket weavers, tool makers, and merchants.

Along the banks of rivers, then, we must look for the first civilizations. We shall find them widely scattered: Mesopotamia straddled the Tigris and the Euphrates; Egypt stretched along the Nile; India arose along the Indus and the Ganges; and China expanded eastward from the region of the Wei and the Huang Ho. Prolific in their gifts to mankind and so dynamic that two of them have retained unbroken continuity to our own day, these civilizations possessed similarities at least as arresting as their differences. In all four, political systems were developed, crafts flourished and commerce expanded, calendars and systems of writing were invented, art and literature of extraordinary beauty were created, and religions and philosophies came into being to satisfy men's inner yearnings.

Indebted to the Egyptians and Mesopotamians, the inhabitants of Crete and Mycenaean Greece fashioned a wealthy, sophisticated, commercial culture. Much of this Aegean civilization —the first advanced culture to appear in Europe —was destroyed by the end of the second millennium B.C., but enough remained to serve as the foundation for Greek civilization. Insatiably curious about man and man's world, the Greeks enjoyed a freedom of thought and expression unknown in earlier societies. Their fierce passion to remain untrammeled, however, was too often unrestrained. The failure of the Greek city-states to find a workable basis for cooperation doomed them to political disaster. Although the conquest of the city-states by King Philip of Macedonia ended the Hellenic Age, the influence of the Greeks was destined to increase. The establishment of a vast empire in the Near East by Philip's talented son, Alexander the Great, ushered in the Hellenistic Age and the widespread diffusion of Greek culture.

Meanwhile, a new power—Rome—had been evolving on the Italian peninsula. After five centuries of modest growth, this city-state embarked upon a career of unprecedented expansion. The splendor of Roman arms was matched by skill in administration, wisdom in law, and ingenuity in the practical arts of engineering and communication. These talents and abilities enabled the Romans to erect a Mediterranean empire which survived until the fifth century A.D. Probably the greatest achievement of the Roman Empire was the skillful maintenance of a diversity of cultures within a political unity. To the Romans we owe a debt for preserving and disseminating classical culture, for the legacy of Graeco-Roman culture is the foundation of western civilization.

In the first centuries of the Christian era we enter a brief but fascinating period in which the principal civilizations of West and East were in contact, engaged in a mutually beneficial exchange of wares and ideas. Unhappily, this process of culture contact and diffusion—which, had it been allowed to continue, might have had incalculable effects for good on world history— was brought to an untimely halt, largely as a result of a crisis in the West. The Graeco-Roman world was subjected to a series of shattering invasions which will be described in the next unit. The present unit surveys the classical age of civilization in both the West and the East—a period which must always remain one of the glorious epochs in human achievement.

CHAPTER 1

The Civilizations of the Ancient Near East

Along the Banks of Rivers

INTRODUCTION. As early as three million years ago or more, man's ancestors appeared on earth, naked in a world of enemies. The story of man's journey out of the darkness of ignorance and fear covers a period of hundreds of thousands of years during which he mastered the skills necessary for survival. Early man's most important achievements concern agriculture and the ways of life it engendered. Wild beasts were tamed as work animals or kept for their meat and hides. The first farmers scattered kernels of grain on the earth and waited patiently for harvest time. Because their fields and flocks could supply most of their wants, a settled existence became possible; men were no longer compelled to move on endlessly in search of food, as their food-gathering ancestors had done for countless generations. Where conditions were favorable, these ancient farmers were able to acquire more food than they needed for survival—surpluses to tide them over seasons of cold and drought. Thus, in green oases and on fertile plateaus, farming villages sprang up.

It was along the banks of great rivers that villages first grew into towns and cities. In early Egyptian picture writing a town is shown as a cross within a circle—the intersection of two pathways enclosed by a wall. The symbol is an appropriate one, for in the history of mankind the town——marks the spot where civilization as we know it began.

Within the towns the business of living took new turns. While the majority still farmed, there were now more craftsmen turning out specialized wares, merchants trading for metals and other needed raw materials, priests conducting religious ceremonies, and administrators planning and supervising the necessary cooperative effort for the common good. Time could be found also for intellectual and artistic pursuits that enriched the lives of the participants and developed a cultural heritage.

A culture can endure only if the knowledge necessary for its survival is passed on from generation to generation. Early peoples relied on information transmitted by word of mouth. But as towns and cities grew up and cultures became increasingly complex, methods for keeping records were devised and systems of writing were created. To most authorities, the development of writing is a prerequisite to civilization.

The four earliest civilizations—the Sumerian, the Egyptian, the Indian, and the Chinese—arose between c. 3500 B.C. and c. 1500 B.C., in each case in the valley of a great river system. In this chapter we shall trace the progress of civilization, including man's earliest advances in technology and his creation of written languages, in Mesopotamia and Egypt. In Chapter 4 we shall see the stirrings of civilization far to the east, in India and in China.

1 TOOLS AND ART OF EARLY MAN

Evolution: a major theory. Did God create humanity "in His own image," or was our species itself the product of physical change and adaptation no less than the rocks, plants, and animals of this planet? This question—so basic in nineteenth-century thought that it caused anguish and bitter controversy among theologians and scientists alike—came to the fore when Sir Charles Lyell's *The Principles of Geology* (1830) provided evidence that the earth was the product of a tremendously long period of change.

The issue became critical with the appearance of Charles Darwin's two treatises, *The Origin of Species* (1859) and *Descent of Man* (1871). The controversy surrounding the theory of human evolution has raged on into the twentieth century, although with decreasing intensity as more fossil evidence has come to light. Of course, the fossil record can probably never be complete, and paleontologists have only skeletal remains (usually partial ones) to analyze. The evidence for evolution appears overwhelming, but the theory by no means precludes the presence of a guiding intelligence ultimately responsible for a progressive development of organic life from simple to more complex forms, culminating thus far in the intelligence and creativity of our own species.

Evolution of the hominids. Who the ancestors of early humans were and when and where tools were first made are much debated questions in scholarly circles. According to the theory of evolution, a crucial development occurred when the ape family became differentiated into the tree-dwelling apes and the ground-dwelling types known as *hominids* ("prehumans" or "protohumans"). The remains of Australopithecines ("Southern Apes"), the earliest known hominids, were discovered in Africa in 1924. *Australopithecus* had a fully erect posture but an apelike brain with a cranial volume no greater than 500 cubic centimeters, as compared to 1300 to 1600 cubic centimeters in modern humans.

Since World War II, and especially during the 1970s, our knowledge of the hominids has been rapidly growing. It involves three major sites in East Africa. Between 1972 and 1977, a joint American-French expedition, including C. D. Johanson, working at Hadar in Ethiopia amassed a remarkable collection of hominid specimens. The biostratigraphic evidence dates the Hadar formation as between 2.6 and 3.3 million years old. The collection comprises at least thirty-five individuals, with one skeleton—known as "Lucy"—being nearly 40 percent complete.

During this period, too, the British anthropologist Mary D. Leakey discovered at Laetolil, in northern Tanzania, the oldest reliably dated hominid remains. These were the fossil jaws and teeth of eight adults and three children, between 3.35 and 3.75 million years old. Subsequently, she uncovered fifty-seven footprints made by two individuals—the oldest known marks of human-like creatures on earth.

Meanwhile, in 1972 at a site on the east side of Lake Rudolph, Kenya, Mary Leakey's son Richard had made yet another major discovery. He found two intact thigh bones, quite similar to those of modern man, which showed in turn that this hominid had walked erect. Of special interest was his discovery of a skull (labeled KNM-ER 1470), probably 2.9 million years old. Its cranial volume exceeded 800 cubic centimeters—much larger than the Hadar and Laetolil crania. But, surprisingly, it was also much larger than the cranial capacity of the famous find made by his father, L. S. B. Leakey, in 1964, which the elder Leakey claimed to be the earliest representative of our own genus, *Homo*.

L. S. B. Leakey had made his discovery at Olduvai Gorge, in Tanzania, at a site some 1.75 million years old. The remains possessed a cranial capacity of 656 cubic centimeters. *Homo habilis* ("mentally skillful man") was about four feet tall, walked erect, and had a well-developed thumb. Significantly, these fossil remains were found in association with crude tools. With the advent of a hominid capable of making tools, Leakey felt confident in assigning his find to the genus *Homo*.

Homo erectus. The first evidence of the more advanced group known as *Homo erectus* was discovered in Java in 1891. Peking man and other members of this group, whose earliest fossils are about 1.5 million years old, have been discovered in Asia, Africa, and Europe. *Homo erectus* had a brain size averaging 1046 cubic centimeters, larger than

Homo habilis but smaller than our own. The members of this group were about five feet tall, had heavy brows, and a receding forehead. They knew the use of fire and produced tools, including the first true hand-ax. About 300,000 years ago *Homo erectus* became extinct.

Neanderthal man and Homo sapiens. From about 85,000 to 40,000 years ago, just before and during the early part of the last glaciation of the Ice Age, *Homo neanderthalensis* was the principal inhabitant of Europe and adjacent parts of Asia and Africa. About five feet tall, Neanderthal people possessed a brain capacity averaging 1438 cubic centimeters (equal to our own), a thick-set body, short forearms, and a slouching posture. They invented tools of advanced design, were able hunters, and adapted to extreme cold by using fire and living in caves.

The culminating stage in the development of the genus *Homo* occurred during the last glaciation of the Ice Age, when *Homo sapiens* displaced *Homo neanderthalensis* in Europe. *Homo sapiens* may have been living in Western Europe as early as 70,000 years ago, probably as a contemporary of *Homo neanderthalensis*. By 20,000 B.C. *Homo sapiens* inhabited Europe, Asia, Africa, and Australia, and had begun to move across the Bering Strait to America. Today, *Homo sapiens* is the only existing member of the genus *Homo*.

The dawn of Paleolithic culture. Benjamin Franklin is credited with first defining man as a "tool-making animal." The making and using of tools is the first evidence of man's ability to use reason to solve problems. Since the use of stone implements was the most distinctive feature of early human culture, this first cultural stage is known as the Paleolithic or Old Stone Age. It is a food-collecting stage, characterized by hunting, fishing, and the collecting of wild fruits, nuts, and berries. (Paleolithic culture survives among a few primitive peoples today.)

Australopithecine sites in South Africa indicate that although the Australopithecines did not fashion tools, they occasionally used objects as improvised tools and weapons. This simple *utilization* has been described as the first of three major steps in the formative history of toolmaking. "The second step would have been *fashioning* — the haphazard preparation of a tool when there was a need for it. The third step would have been *standardization*. Here, men began to make tools according to certain set traditions."[2]

The haphazard fashioning of tools is associated with pebble tools, the earliest of which are made of split pebbles or shattered chunks of stone about the size of one's fist or a bit larger. Such occasional toolmaking is found in early Pleistocene geological beds in Africa, including the Olduvai Gorge. Standardized toolmaking includes the later and better made pebble tools having sharp edges. Richard Leakey's finds in Kenya indicate that *Homo*'s toolmaking capability is older and more sophisticated than previous evidence had suggested. Some 600 knifelike tools unearthed by Leakey had been carefully fashioned from smooth volcanic rock, had edges that were still sharp, and have been dated as 2.6 million years old.

Hand-axes were the first major standardized, all-purpose implement. They were equipped with a sharp cutting edge on both sides and were probably used both for hunting and for chopping, cutting, scraping, and digging up grubs and roots. Hand-axes are associated with *Homo erectus* and possess such uniformity of design that specimens from Madras, Kenya, and London are nearly identical as regards form.

Homo sapiens developed a technique of pressure flaking to produce a long, slender, sharp-edged blade which made an excellent projectile point and a useful chisel, the burin. The invention of the spearthrower made hunting more efficient.

To withstand the cold, late Paleolithic peoples made garments from skins and erected buildings in areas where natural caves did not exist. The reindeer and mammoth hunters of present-day Czechoslovakia and Russia lived in tents and huts made of hides and brush or in communal houses partially sunk into the ground with mammoth's ribs for roof supports. There is evidence that they used coal for fuel.

The first artists. One of the highest achievements of late Paleolithic culture was art. Man was an artist endeavoring to give expression to his creative imagination long before he could write or fashion a metal knife. Animated, realistic paintings of animals, colored in shades of black, red, yellow, and brown, have been found in caves in Spain and France (see Color Plate 2). Paleolithic people also modeled clay and chiseled pictures on rock and bone. Cave art rivals that of civilized man both stylistically and as an expression of significant human experience. It represents Paleolithic man's dependence on an abundance of game animals and success in hunting them.

Mesolithic or Transitional cultures. With the final retreat of the glaciers about 10,000 B.C., Europe became covered with dense forests. Because of their highly specialized adaptation to cold weather, many animals hunted by late Paleolithic peoples became extinct. Man, however, adjusted to postglacial conditions by developing new cultures called Mesolithic or Transitional. Many of these Mesolithic groups lived along the coast, fishing and gathering shellfish. Others lived inland, where they made bows and arrows for hunting and devised skis, sleds, and dugout canoes. Our Mesolithic forebears also domesticated the dog.

The Neolithic revolution. By 7000 B.C. the people in the Near East, north of the area called the Fertile Crescent (see map, p. 17), had shifted from food gathering to food producing. Men in this region had domesticated wheat, barley, sheep, goats, and pigs and lived in village communities near their herds and fields. This was the most important breakthrough in the relationship of man to his environment and ushered in the Neolithic or New Stone Age.

One of the oldest Neolithic village sites to be excavated is Jarmo in northern Iraq. The 150 people of the village lived in twenty mud-walled houses, reaped their grain with stone sickles, stored their food in stone bowls, and possessed domesticated goats, sheep, and dogs. The later levels of settlement contain evidence of domesticated pigs and clay pottery. Since many tools were made of obsidian, a volcanic rock from beds 300 miles away, a primitive form of commerce must have existed.

The best preserved early village so far uncovered is Catal Hüyük in southern Turkey, excavated in 1961. The large, 32-acre site, first occupied shortly before 6000 B.C., contains some of the most advanced features of Neolithic culture: pottery, woven textiles, mud-brick houses, shrines honoring a mother goddess, and plastered walls decorated with murals and carved reliefs.

The Neolithic revolution spread to the Balkan Peninsula by 5000 B.C., Egypt and central Europe by 4000 B.C., and Britain and northwest India by 3000 B.C. The Neolithic cultures of Middle America and the Andes are independent developments, while a possible relationship between China and the Near East remains an open question.

II PRIMITIVE THOUGHT AND CUSTOM

Analysis of primitive societies. Perhaps it is natural for most of us, living as we do in a highly complex machine-age society, to assume that primitive men, prehistoric or modern, would possess few laws, little education, and only the simplest codes of conduct. But this is far from true. The organization of a primitive society may be as complex as our own. Rules regarding the role of parents, the treatment of children, the punishment of the evildoer, the conduct of business, the worship of the gods, and the conventions of eating and recreation have existed for thousands of years, along with methods to compel the individual to do "the correct thing."

How can we know about those features of early man's culture which are not apparent from the remains of tools and other objects? The early myths and epics which originated in prehistoric times reflect the ideas and customs of early peoples. Studies of present-day primitive societies have given scholars hints about the culture of prehistoric man, but caution must be used in applying the findings of such studies to prehistoric primitive societies: the fact that the general level of technological development appears to be similar in both groups does not mean that all aspects of the two societies are comparable. Further-

more, it is difficult to measure the impact of advanced civilization on modern primitive societies.

Forms of social organization. Among all peoples, the basic social unit appears to be the elementary family group—parents and their offspring. Anthropologists do not know what marriage customs were prevalent in the earliest societies, but monogamy was probably most common. Other social groupings found in primitive societies include the extended family, the clan, and the tribe.

The extended family is an individual family together with a circle of related persons who usually trace their descent through their mothers and are bound together by mutual loyalty. The extended family strengthens the elementary unit in obtaining food and in protecting its members against other groups. Land is communally owned but allocated to separate families. Weapons, tools, and utensils are individually owned.

A clan is a group of extended families whose members believe that they have a common ancestor. A clan is patrilineal if its members trace their relationship through the male line and matrilineal if through the female. Many primitive peoples identify their clans by a totem—an animal or other natural object—which is revered and made the subject for amulets of various sorts. Totemism exists today in military insignia and the emblems of fraternal organizations.

A tribe comprises a number of clans, both related and unrelated. It is a community characterized by a common speech or distinctive dialect, a common cultural heritage, a specific inhabited territory, and a tribal chief. Group loyalty is strong and is often accompanied by a contempt for the people and customs of other tribes.

Collective responsibility in law and government. In primitive societies ethical behavior consists in not violating custom. The close relationships that exist in extended families and clans encourage conformity. Justice in a primitive group operates to maintain equilibrium. Theft disturbs economic equilibrium, and justice is achieved by a settlement between the injured man and the thief. The victim is satisfied and the

The Venus of Laussel is a stone seat from the Laussel shelter in Dordogne, France. Like many similar statuettes of the Paleolithic period, it is visibly a fertility symbol with obvious female characteristics.

thief is not punished. Murder and wounding are also private matters to be avenged by the next of kin. On the other hand, certain acts, such as treason, witchcraft, and incest, are considered dangerous to the whole group and require punishment by the entire community. If a member of a clan gets into trouble too often, his fellows may outlaw or execute him.

As a general rule, government in primitive societies is of a democratic character. The older tribal members—the council of elders—play a dominant role in decision making because of their greater experience and knowledge of the group's customs and lore. Serious decisions, such as going to war or electing a chief, require the consent of a general assembly of all adult males. The elected chief of the tribe is pledged to rule in accordance with custom and in consultation with the council of elders. Due to the strong element of representation present, this early form of government has been called "primitive democracy."

Religion, magic, and science. Religion is a strong force in the lives of primitive people. One form of religious belief among primitive peoples was animism, the belief that all things in nature—wind, stones, trees, animals, and man—were inhabited by spirits. Many spirits became objects of reverence,

with man's own spirit being one of the first. Neanderthal man placed food and implements alongside his carefully buried dead, an indication that he believed in an afterlife and held his ancestors in awe. We know also that late Paleolithic man revered the spirits of the animals he hunted for food as well as the spirit of fertility upon which both human and animal life depended. This led to totemism and to the worship of a fertility goddess who is known to us from many carved and modeled female figures with exaggerated sexual features.

Closely associated with primitive religion is the practice of magic. In addition to revering the spirits, primitive man wants to compel them to favor him. For his purpose he employs magic to ward off droughts, famines, floods, and plagues. There may have been an element of magic in the paintings of primitive peoples, who may have believed that through their paintings they could wield power over the spirits of animals.

Traditionally, magic has been regarded as diametrically opposed to science. Magic claims supernatural powers over natural forces, whereas science rejects any such determinism and studies natural phenomena by open-ended methods in its search for general laws. Yet, as scholars are increasingly recognizing, both primitive man and the scientist believe that nature is orderly and that what is immediately apprehended by the senses can be systematically classified. The great contributions of Stone Age men and women—domestication of plants and animals, invention of tools, pottery, and weaving—involved centuries of methodical observation and oft-repeated experiments, few of which could have yielded immediate results. Early man must therefore be credited with a desire for knowledge for its own sake.

Further indications of this desire have been provided by studies of the large stone monuments (megaliths) constructed by Neolithic peoples. An engineering professor, Alexander Thom, surveyed 300 megalithic sites in Britain; he discovered a widespread use of a uniform measure of length, the "megalithic yard," which is 2.72 feet. Some sites were set out with an accuracy approaching 1 in 1000, and the builders of the sites had knowledge of practical geometry. The megalithic complex of Stonehenge had traditionally been considered a religious structure. However, an American astronomer, Professor Gerald Hawkins, using a computer, found an "astonishing" number of correlations between the alignments of recognized Stonehenge positions—stones, stone holes, mounds—and the solar and lunar declinations as of 1500 B.C. when Stonehenge was built.[3] The alignments made possible an accurate calendar and the prediction of the rising and setting of the sun and moon. Hawkins also saw in these Neolithic structures the joy of achievement by man the problem-solver as he searches for order in the cosmos.

III MESOPOTAMIA: THE FIRST CIVILIZATION

Prelude to civilization. About 5000 B.C., after the agricultural revolution had begun to spread from its place of origin on the northern fringes of the Fertile Crescent, Neolithic farmers started filtering into the Fertile Crescent itself. Although this broad plain received insufficient rainfall to support agriculture, it was watered by the Tigris and Euphrates rivers. Known in ancient days as Mesopotamia (Greek for "between the rivers"), the lower reaches of this plain, beginning near the point where the two rivers nearly converge, was called Babylonia. Babylonia in turn encompassed two geographical areas—Akkad in the north and Sumer, the delta of this river system, in the south.

Broken by river channels teeming with fish and refertilized every year by alluvial silt laid down by uncontrolled floods, Sumer had a splendid agricultural potential—provided the environmental problems were solved. "Arable land had literally to be created out of a chaos of swamps and sandbanks by a 'separation' of land from water; the swamps . . . drained; the floods controlled; and lifegiving waters led to the rainless desert by artificial canals."[4] In the course of the several successive cultural phases that followed the arrival of the first Neolithic

farmers, these and other related problems were solved by large-scale cooperative effort. By 3500 B.C. the foundations had been laid for a type of economy and social order markedly different from anything previously known. This far more complex culture, based on large urban centers rather than simple villages, is what we associate with the term *civilization.*

Authorities do not all agree about the definition of *civilization.* Most would accept the view that "a civilization is a culture which has attained a degree of complexity usually characterized by urban life"[5]—that it is capable, in other words, of sustaining a substantial number of specialists to cope with the economic, social, political, and religious needs of a populous society. Other characteristics usually present in a civilization include a system of writing to keep records, monumental architecture in place of simple buildings, and an art that is no longer merely decorative but representational of man and his activities. Moreover, an urban environment is important because of the self-consciousness and pride which it generates.

During the millennium preceding 3500 B.C. some of the most significant discoveries and inventions in human history were achieved. By discovering how to use metals to make tools and weapons, Neolithic man effected a revolution nearly as far-reaching as that wrought in agriculture. By 4500 B.C. Neolithic artisans had discovered how to extract copper from oxide ores by heating them with charcoal. Shortly before 3000 B.C. metalworkers discovered that copper was improved by the addition of tin. The resulting alloy, bronze, was harder than copper and provided a sharper cutting edge.

Thus the advent of civilization in Sumer is associated with the beginning of the Bronze Age in the West, which in time spread to Egypt, Europe, and Asia. The Bronze Age lasted until about 1200 B.C., when iron weapons and tools began to replace those made of bronze.

The farmer's first plow was probably a stick which he pulled through the soil with a rope. In time, however, the cattle that his forebears had domesticated for food and milk were harnessed to drag the hoe in place of his mate or himself. Yoked, harnessed animals pulled plows in the Mesopotamian alluvium by 3000 B.C. As a result, farming advanced from the cultivation of small plots to the tilling of extensive fields. "By harnessing the ox man began to control and use a motive power other than that furnished by his own muscular energy. The ox was the first step to the steam engine and gasoline motor."[6]

Since the Mesopotamian plain had no stone, no metals, and no timber except its soft and inadequate palm trees, there was great need of an economical means of transporting these materials from Syria and Asia Minor. Water transport down the Tigris and Euphrates solved the problem. The oldest sailing boat known is represented by a model found in a Sumerian grave of about 3500 B.C. Soon after this date wheeled vehicles appear in the form of ass-drawn war chariots. For the transport of goods overland, however, men continued to rely on the pack ass.

Another important invention was the potter's wheel, first used in Sumer soon after 3500 B.C. Earlier, men had fashioned pots by molding or coiling clay by hand, but now a symmetrical product could be produced in a much shorter time. A pivoted clay disk heavy enough to revolve of its own momentum, the potter's wheel has been called "the first really mechanical device."

The emergence of civilization in Sumer. By 3500 B.C. the population of Sumer had increased to the point where people were living in small cities and had developed a preponderance of those elements previously noted as constituting civilization. Since these included the first evidence of writing, this first phase of Sumerian civilization, to about 2800 B.C., is called the Protoliterate period.[7]

New settlers appeared in Sumer at the beginning of the Protoliterate period, and another migration occurred shortly before 3000 B.C. Scholars cannot agree on which, if either, of these newcomers were the Sumerians, whose language is not related to those major language families of mankind that later appear in the Near East—Semites and Indo-Europeans. (The original home of the Semitic-speaking peoples is thought to have been the Arabian peninsula, while the Indo-Euro-

peans migrated from the region north of the Black and Caspian seas. A third, much smaller language family is the Hamitic, which included the Egyptians and other peoples of northeastern Africa.)

How would life in Protoliterate Sumer have appeared to a visitor seeing it for the first time? As he approached Ur, one of about a dozen Sumerian cities, he would pass farmers working in their fields with ox-drawn plows. He might see some of the workers using bronze sickles. The river would be dotted by boats carrying produce to and from the city. Dominating the flat countryside would be a ziggurat, a platform (later a lofty terrace, built in the shape of a pyramid) crowned by a sanctuary, or "high place." This was the "holy of holies," sacred to the local god. Upon entering the city, the visitor would see a large number of specialists pursuing their appointed tasks as agents of the community —some craftsmen casting bronze tools and weapons, others fashioning their wares on the potter's wheel, and still others, merchants, arranging to trade grain and manufactures for the metals, stone, lumber, and other essentials not available in Sumer. Scribes would be at work incising thin tablets of clay with picture signs. Some tablets might bear the impressions of cylinder seals, small stone cylinders engraved with a design. Examining the clay tablets, the visitor would find that they were memoranda used in administering the temple, which was at once the warehouse and workshop of the entire community. Some of the scribes might be making an inventory of the goats and sheep received that day for sacrificial use; others might be drawing up wage lists. They would be using a system of counting based on the unit 60, still used today, over five thousand years later, in computing divisions of time and angles.

Certain technical inventions of Protoliterate Sumer eventually made their way to both the Nile and the Indus valleys. Chief among these were the wheeled vehicle and the potter's wheel. The discovery in Egypt of cylinder seals similar in shape to those used in Sumer attests to contact between the two areas toward the end of the fourth millennium B.C. Certain early Egyptian art motifs and

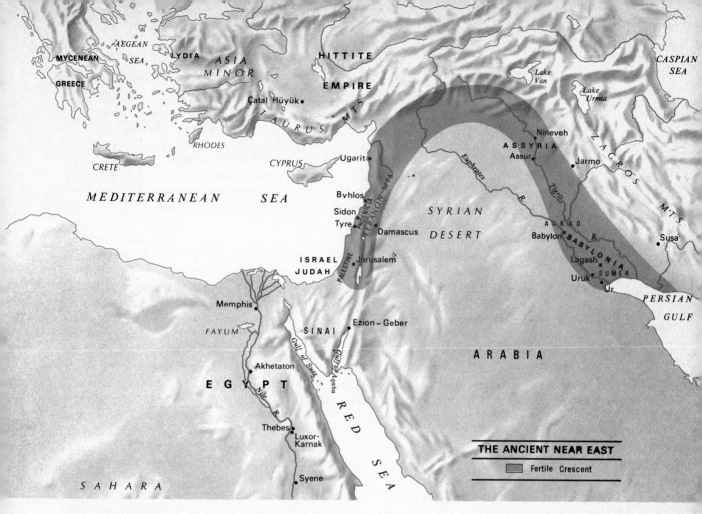

MYCENEAN
GREECE
AEGEAN SEA
LYDIA
ASIA MINOR
HITTITE EMPIRE
CASPIAN SEA
Çatal Hüyük
TAURUS MTS.
RHODES
CRETE
CYPRUS
Ugarit
MEDITERRANEAN SEA
Byblos
Sidon
Tyre
PHOENICIA
LEBANON MTS.
Damascus
SYRIAN DESERT
Lake Van
Lake Urmia
Nineveh
ASSYRIA
Assur
Jarmo
ZAGROS MTS.
Euphrates R.
Tigris R.
AKKAD
Babylon
BABYLONIA
Susa
Lagash
Uruk
SUMER
Ur
ISRAEL
JUDAH
PALESTINE
Jerusalem
Memphis
FAYUM
SINAI
Ezion–Geber
Gulf of Suez
Gulf of Aqaba
PERSIAN GULF
ARABIA
EGYPT
Akhetaton
Nile R.
Thebes
Luxor-Karnak
RED SEA
Syene
SAHARA

THE ANCIENT NEAR EAST

Fertile Crescent

architectural forms are also thought to be of Sumerian origin. And it is probable that the example of Sumerian writing stimulated the Egyptians to develop a script of their own. These are examples of how cultures during their most formative stages may influence one another yet continue to develop unique features which stamp them as distinctive civilizations.

Sumerian writing. As we have noted, the symbols on the oldest Sumerian clay tablets were primarily pictures. However, many matters, including thought processes, cannot be depicted conveniently by pictures. Sumerian scribes overcame this problem by arbitrarily adding marks to the picture signs to denote new meanings. During the Proto-literate period some two thousand signs were in use. This cumbersome system could have been still further enlarged and complicated by the creation of more pictures and modifying marks. Fortunately, the Sumerians adopted an alternative solution whereby the signs represented sounds rather than ob-

jects or ideas. By giving the signs a phonetic value, the Sumerians could spell out names and compound words instead of inventing new signs. The use of syllabic signs reduced the number of signs to some six hundred by 2800 B.C.

In writing, a scribe used a reed stylus to make impressions in soft clay tablets. The impressions took on a wedge shape, hence the term *cuneiform* (Latin *cuneus*, "wedge"). The cuneiform system of writing was adopted by many other peoples of the Near East, including the Babylonians, Assyrians, Hittites, and Persians.

The Old Sumerian period. By 2800 B.C. the Sumerian city-states had emerged into the light of history. This first historical age, called the Old Sumerian (or Early Dynastic) period, was characterized by incessant warfare as each city sought to protect or enlarge its land and water rights. Each city-state was a theocracy, for the local god was believed to be the real sovereign. His earthly representative was the *ensi*, the high priest and city governor, who acted as the god's steward in both religious and secular functions. Though endowed with divine right by virtue of being the human agent of the god, the *ensi* was not considered divine.

Like life on a medieval manor, early Sumerian society was highly collectivized, with the temples of the city god and subordinate deities assuming the central role. "Each temple owned lands which formed the estate of its divine owners. Each citizen belonged to one of the temples, and the whole of a temple community—the officials and priests, herdsmen and fishermen, gardeners, craftsmen, stonecutters, merchants, and even slaves—was referred to as 'the people of the god X.'"[8] That part of the temple land called "common" was worked by all members of the community, while the remaining land was divided among the citizens for their support at a rental of from one third to one sixth of the crop. Priests and temple administrators, however, held rent-free lands.

In time, priests, temple administrators, and *ensis* became venal, usurping temple

These Old Sumerian period statues from the Abu Temple, Tell Asmar, are fashioned of limestone with inlaid shell and lapis lazuli eyes. These statues sometimes represented family groups and found their way into the temples often as a "substitute" for the actual persons. They possess some individuality between them as noted between the bearded man, shaven priest, and tunic-clad woman, but all hold the same rigidly frontal pose of religious concentration and have similar expressions.

property and oppressing the common people. This frequently led to the rise of despots called *lugals* (literally "great man" but usually translated "king") who rode to power on a wave of popular discontent. These secular rulers made the general welfare their major domestic concern. Best known is Urukagina, who usurped power at Lagash at the end of the Old Sumerian period. His reform inscriptions state that when he "had received the lugalship . . . he removed from the inhabitants of Lagash usury, forestalling, famine, robbery, attacks; he established their freedom . . . [and] protected the widow and the orphan from the powerful man."[9]

Akkadian dominance. Immediately north of Sumer lay the narrow region of Akkad, inhabited by Semites who had absorbed Sumerian culture. Appearing late in the fourth millennium B.C., the Akkadians were the earliest of the Semitic peoples who filtered into Mesopotamia from Arabia. A generation after Urukagina, Sargon I (2370-2315 B.C.), an energetic Akkadian ruler, conquered Sumer and went on to establish the world's first empire which, he claimed, extended "from the lower sea to the upper sea" (the Persian Gulf to the Mediterranean Sea).

Very proud of his lower-class origins, Sargon boasted that his humble, unwed mother had been forced to abandon him: "She set me in a basket of rushes . . . [and] cast me into the river."[10] Rescued and brought up by a gardener, Sargon rose to power through the army. As *lugal*, Sargon looked after the welfare of the lower classes and aided the rising class of private merchants. At the latter's request he once sent his army to far-off Asia Minor to protect a colony of merchants from interference by a local ruler. We are told that Sargon "did not sleep" in his efforts to promote prosperity; trade moved as freely "as the Tigris where it flows into the sea, . . . all lands lie in peace, their inhabitants prosperous and contented."[11]

Sargon's successors, however, were unable either to withstand the attacks of semibarbaric highlanders or to overcome the desire for independence of the priest-dominated Sumerian cities. As a result, the house of Sargon collapsed about 2230 B.C.

The Neo-Sumerian period. Order and prosperity were restored a century later by the *lugals* of the Third Dynasty of Ur (c. 2113-2006 B.C.). By creating a highly centralized administration in Sumer and Akkad, these rulers solved the problem of internal rebellion that had plagued Sargon and his successors. The formerly temple-dominated cities became provinces administered by governors who were watched closely by a corps of "messengers." The "church" became an arm of the state; the high priests were state appointees, and the temple economic organization was used as the state's agent in rigidly controlling the economy.

At the head of this bureaucratic state stood the now-deified ruler, celebrated in hymns as a heaven-sent messiah who "brings splendor to the land, . . . savior of orphans whose misery he relieves, . . . the vigilant shepherd who conducts the people unto cooling shade."[12] Much of what we now call social legislation was passed by these "vigilant shepherds." Such laws were called "rightings" (Sumerian *nig-si-sa*, usually translated "equity"), since their object was the righting of wrongs that were not covered by the old customary law (*nig-ge-na*, "truth"). The prologue to the law code of Ur-Nammu, founder of the dynasty, declared that it was the king's purpose to see that "the orphan did not fall a prey to the wealthy" and that "the man of one shekel did not fall a prey to the man of one mina (sixty shekels)."[13]

Disaster struck Ur about 2006 B.C., when Elamites from the highlands to the east destroyed the city. The Sumerians were never again a dominant element politically, but their culture persisted as the foundation for all subsequent civilizations in the Tigris-Euphrates valley.

For more than two centuries following the destruction of Ur, disunity and warfare again plagued Mesopotamia, along with depression, inflation, and acute hardship for the lower classes. Merchants, however, utilized the lack of state controls to become full-fledged capitalists who amassed fortunes which they invested in banking operations and in land. (These merchants used a form of double-entry bookkeeping which they called "balanced accounts." Their word for capital, *qaqqadum,* meaning "head," influenced later peoples; our word *capital* is derived from the Latin form, *caput*). The stronger local rulers of the period freed the poor from debt slavery and issued a variety of reform laws which are best illustrated by the legislation of Hammurabi.

Hammurabi and the Babylonian empire. Semitic Amorites (from *Amurru*, the "West"), under the rule of their capable king, Hammurabi of Babylon (c. 1792-1750 B.C.), again brought most of Mesopotamia under one rule by 1760 B.C.

Hammurabi is best known for his code of nearly three hundred laws whose stated objective was "to cause justice to prevail in the land, to destroy the wicked and the evil, to prevent the strong from oppressing the weak . . . and to further the welfare of the people."[14] Hammurabi's legislation reestablished a state-controlled economy in which merchants were required to obtain a "royal permit," interest was limited to 20 percent, and prices were set for basic commodities and for fees charged by physicians, veterinarians, and builders. Minimum wages were established, and debt slavery was limited to three years. Other laws protected wives and children, although a wife who had "set her face to go out and play the part of a fool, neglect her house, belittle her husband"[15] could be divorced without alimony, or the husband could take another wife and compel the first to remain as a servant. Punishments were graded in their severity; the higher the culprit in the social scale, the more severe the penalty.

In the epilogue to the code, Hammurabi eloquently summed up his efforts to provide social justice for his people.

Let any oppressed man, who has a cause, come before my image as king of righteousness! Let him read the inscription on my monument! Let him give heed to my weighty words! And may my monument enlighten him as to his cause and may he understand his case! May he set his heart at ease! (and he will exclaim): "Hammurabi indeed is a ruler who is like a real father to his people. . . ."[16]

Mathematics and science. Carrying on the work of the Sumerians, the Babylonians made advances in arithmetic, geometry, and algebra. For ease of computation with both whole numbers and fractions, they compiled tables for multiplication and division and for square and cube roots. They knew how to solve linear and quadratic equations, and their knowledge of geometry included the theorem later made famous by the Greek philosopher Pythagoras: the square of the hypotenuse of a right-angled triangle is equal to the sum of the squares of the other two sides. Perhaps their greatest achievement was the principle of place-value notation which gave numbers a value according to their position in a series.

The Babylonians achieved little that today deserves to be called science. They did observe nature and collect data, which is the first requirement of science; but in seeking intelligible explanations of natural phenomena, they did not go beyond the formulation of myths which explained things in terms of the unpredictable whims of the gods. The sun, the moon, and the five visible planets were thought to be gods who were able to influence men's lives; accordingly, their movements were watched, recorded, and interpreted.

Literature and religion. The Babylonians took over from the Sumerians a body of literature ranging from heroic epics that compare favorably with the *Iliad* and the *Odyssey* to wisdom writings that have their counterparts in the Old Testament books of Job, Proverbs, and Ecclesiastes. Longest and most famous is the *Epic of Gilgamesh*, which recounts the exploits of a heroic ruler of Uruk who lived about 2700 B.C. The central theme of the epic is Gilgamesh's hope of immortality. This leads him to seek out and question Ut-napishtim, the Babylonian Noah who was granted eternal life because he saved all living creatures from the flood. Ut-napishtim's story has many remarkable similarities with the Hebrew account of the flood. But Gilgamesh's quest is hopeless, and he is so informed on several occasions:

Gilgamesh, whither rovest thou?
The life thou pursuest thou shalt not find.
When the gods created mankind,
Death for mankind they set aside,

Life in their own hands retaining.
Thou, Gilgamesh, let full be thy belly,
Make thou merry by day and by night.
Of each day make thou a feast of rejoicing,
Day and night dance thou and play! . . .
Pay heed to the little one that holds on to thy hand,
Let thy spouse delight in thy bosom!
For this is the task of mankind![17]

The ancient Mesopotamians never went beyond this early view that immortality was reserved for the gods. Unlike the Egyptians (see p. 25), the Babylonians did not go on to develop a belief in an attractive life after death as a reward for good behavior on earth. They did come to believe in divine rewards for moral conduct, but these were rewards to be enjoyed in this life—increased worldly goods, numerous offspring, and many years of life. Thus, the sun-god Shamash was celebrated in hymns which proclaimed that "the honest merchant . . . is pleasing to Shamash, and he will prolong his life. He will enlarge his family, gain wealth . . . and his descendants will never fail."[18]

Fall of the Babylonian empire. The pattern of disunity and warfare, all too familiar in Mesopotamia, reasserted itself following Hammurabi's death. In 1595 B.C. the Hittites, an Indo-European people who had established themselves in Asia Minor (see p. 28), mounted a daring raid down the Euphrates, capturing and plundering Babylon. The next five centuries is a dark age about which little is known; yet it did preserve the cultural heritage left by the Sumerians and Babylonians. Meanwhile, in a neighboring river valley, another civilization had emerged.

EGYPT: GIFT OF THE NILE

Predynastic Egypt. Egypt is literally "the gift of the Nile," as the ancient Greek historian Herodotus observed. The Nile valley, extending 750 miles from the first cataract to the Mediterranean, is a fertile oasis cut out of a limestone plateau. Its soil is renewed annually by the rich silt deposited by the flood water of the river, which rises and falls with unusual precision. The rise begins early in July and continues until the banks are overrun, reaching its crest in September. By the end of October the river is once more contained within its banks.

By 4000 B.C. Neolithic villagers had begun to build dikes to catch and hold the Nile flood and to construct ditches and wells for irrigation. Population grew and social organization advanced, leading to the formation of two distinct kingdoms late in the fourth millennium: Lower Egypt comprised the broad Nile delta north of Memphis, while Upper Egypt extended southward along the narrow ten- to twenty-mile-wide valley as far as the first cataract at Syene (Aswan). Each kingdom contained about a score of districts, or *nomes*, which had formerly been ruled by independent chieftains.

The Predynastic period ended about 3100 B.C. when Menes (also known as Narmer), ruler of Upper Egypt, united the two kingdoms and founded the First Dynasty with its capital at Memphis. Because little is known of these first two dynasties, the period is called Egypt's archaic age.

The Old Kingdom (c. 2700-2200 B.C.). The pharaohs of the Third through the Sixth Dynasties—the period called the Old Kingdom or Pyramid Age—firmly established order and stability and the essential elements of Egyptian civilization. The nobility lost its independence, and all power was centered in the pharaoh (*Per-ao*, "Great House"). The pharaoh was considered a god rather than the human agent of a god, as was the rule in Mesopotamia. As the god of Egypt, the pharaoh owned all the land (although frequent grants were made to temples and private persons), controlled the irrigation system, decided when the fields should be sown, and received the surplus from the crops produced on the huge royal estates. This surplus supported a large corps of specialists—administrators, priests, scribes, artists, artisans, and merchants—who labored in the service of the pharaoh. The people's welfare was thought to rest on absolute fidelity to the god-king. "If you want to know what to do in life," advised one Egyptian writer, "cling to the pharaoh and be loyal. . . ."[19] As a consequence, the Egyptian felt a sense of security that was rare in Mesopotamia.

The belief that the pharaoh was a god led

to the practice of mummification and the construction of colossal tombs—the pyramids—to preserve the pharaoh's mummy for eternity. The pyramid tombs, in particular those of the Fourth Dynasty at Gizeh near Memphis which are the most celebrated of all ancient monuments, reflect the great power and wealth of the Old Kingdom pharaohs. Their construction provided employment during the months when the land was inundated by the Nile.

Toward the end of the Sixth Dynasty the centralized authority of the pharaohs was undermined when the nobles assumed the prerogatives of the pharaohs, including the claim to immortality, and the *nomes* again became independent. For about a century and a half, known as the First Intermediate Period (c. 2200-2050 B.C.), civil war raged, and outsiders raided and infiltrated the land. The lot of the common people became unbearable as they faced famine, robbery, and oppression by petty tyrants. "The land trembled," wrote a contemporary, "all the people were in terror, the villages were in panic, fear entered into their limbs."[20]

The Middle Kingdom (c. 2050-1800 B.C.). Egypt was rescued from anarchy by the pharaohs of the Eleventh and Twelfth Dynasties, who reunited the country and ruled from Thebes. Stressing their role as watchful shepherds of the people, the Middle Kingdom pharaohs promoted the welfare of the downtrodden. One of them claimed: "I gave to the destitute and brought up the orphan. I caused him who was nothing to reach [his goal], like him who was [somebody]."[21] No longer was the nation's wealth expended on huge pyramids, but on public works. The largest of these, a drainage and irrigation project in the marshy Fayum district south of Memphis, resulted in the reclamation of 27,000 acres of arable land. Moreover, a concession that has been called "the democratization of the hereafter" gave the lower classes the right to have their bodies mummified and thereby to enjoy immortality.

Following the Twelfth Dynasty, Egypt again was racked by civil war as provincial governors fought for the pharaoh's throne. During this Second Intermediate Period (c.

1800-1570 B.C.), the Hyksos, a mixed but preponderantly Semitic people, invaded Egypt from Palestine about 1720 B.C. They easily conquered the deltà and made the rest of Egypt tributary. It was probably at this time that some Hebrews entered Egypt, accepting the invitation of Joseph, who rose to high position under a friendly Hyksos king.

The New Kingdom or Empire (c. 1570-1090 B.C.). The Egyptians viewed the Hyksos conquest as a great humiliation imposed on them by detestable barbarians. An aggressive nationalism emerged, promoted by the native prince of Thebes who proclaimed: "No man can settle down, when despoiled by the taxes of the Asiatics. I will grapple with him, that I may rip open his belly! My wish is to save Egypt and to smite the Asiatics!"[22] Adopting the new weapons introduced by their conquerors—the composite bow, constructed of wood and horn, and the horse-drawn chariot—the Egyptians expelled the Hyksos and pursued them into Palestine. The pharaohs of the Eighteenth Dynasty, who reunited Egypt and founded the New Kingdom, made Palestine the nucleus of an Egyptian empire in western Asia (see Reference Map 1).

The outstanding representative of the aggressive state that Egypt now became was Thutmose III (c. 1490-1436 B.C.). This "Napoleon of Egypt" led his professional standing army on seventeen campaigns into Syria, where he set up his boundary markers on the banks of the Euphrates. Nubia and northern Sudan were also brought under his sway. The native princes of Palestine, Phoenicia, and Syria were left on their thrones, but their sons were taken to Egypt as hostages. Here they were brought up and, thoroughly Egyptianized, eventually sent home to rule as loyal vassals. Thutmose III erected obelisks—tall, pointed shafts of stone—to commemorate his reign and to record his wish that "his name might endure throughout the future forever and ever." Four of his obelisks now adorn the cities of Istanbul, Rome, London, and New York.

Under Amenhotep III (c. 1398-1361 B.C.) the empire reached its peak. Tribute flowed in from conquered lands; and Thebes, with its temples built for the sun-god Amon east of the Nile at Luxor and Karnak, became the most magnificent city in the world. The Hittites and the rulers of Babylonia and Crete, among others, sent gifts, including princesses for the pharaoh's harem. In return, they asked the pharaoh for gold, "For gold is as common as dust in your land."

During the reign of the succeeding pharaoh, Amenhotep IV (c. 1369-1353 B.C.), however, the Empire went into sharp decline as the result of an internal struggle between the pharaoh and the powerful and wealthy

The step-pyramid of Zoser at Sakkara was erected during the Third Dynasty (c. 2600 B.C.), and is a magnificent early example of Egyptian pyramid building.

priests of Amon. The pharaoh undertook to revolutionize Egypt's religion by proclaiming the worship of the sun's disk, Aton, in place of Amon and all the other deities. Often called the first monotheist (although, as Aton's son, the pharaoh was also a god), Amenhotep changed his name to Akhenaton ("Devoted to Aton"), left Amon's city to found a new capital (Akhetaton), and concentrated upon religious reform. Most of Egypt's vassal princes in Asia defected when their appeals for aid against invaders went unheeded. Prominent among these invaders were groups of people called the Habiru, whose possible identification with the Hebrews of the Old Testament has interested modern scholars. At home the army leaders joined with the Amon priesthood to encourage dissension. When Akhenaton died, his weak successor, Tutankhamen (c. 1352-1344 B.C.)—famed for his small but richly furnished tomb discovered in 1922—returned to Thebes and the worship of Amon.

One of the army leaders who succeeded Tutankhamen founded the Nineteenth Dynasty (c. 1305-1200 B.C.), which sought to reestablish Egyptian control over Palestine and Syria. The result was a long struggle with the Hittites, who in the meantime had pushed south from Asia Minor into Syria. This struggle reached a climax in the reign of Ramses II (c. 1290-1224 B.C.), the pharaoh of the Hebrew Exodus from Egypt. Ramses II regained Palestine, but when he failed to dislodge the Hittites from Syria, he agreed to a treaty. Its strikingly modern character is revealed in clauses providing for non-aggression, mutual assistance, and extradition of fugitives.

The long reign of Ramses II was Egypt's last period of national grandeur. The number and size of Ramses' monuments (see illustration, p. 22) rival those of the Pyramid Age. Outstanding among them are the great Hypostyle Hall, built for Amon at Karnak, and the temple at Abu Simbel, with its four colossal statues of Ramses, which has recently been raised to save it from inundation by the waters of the new High Dam at Aswan. (Syene). After Ramses II, royal authority gradually declined as the power of the priests of Amon rose.

Period of Decadence (1090-332 B.C.). During the early part of the Period of Decadence the Amon priesthood at Thebes became so strong that the high priest was able to found his own dynasty and to rule over Upper Egypt. Civil war grew increasingly common, and Egypt became, in the words of the Old Testament, a "broken reed," with the result that in 671 B.C. the Assyrians made Egypt a province of their empire.

Egypt enjoyed a brief Indian summer of revived glory during the Twenty-Sixth Dynasty (663-525 B.C.), which expelled the Assyrians with the aid of Greek mercenaries. The revival of ancient artistic and literary forms proved sterile, and after attempts to regain Palestine failed, "the king of Egypt came not again any more out of his land" (II Kings 24:7). Only the commercial policies of these rulers were successful. In about 600 B.C., to facilitate trade, Pharaoh Necho ordered a canal dug between the Nile mouth and the Red Sea (it was later completed by the Persians), and he commissioned a Phoenician expedition which circumnavigated Africa in three years—a feat not to be duplicated until 1497 A.D.

Egypt passed under Persian rule in 525 B.C., and two hundred years later this ancient land came within the domain of Alexander the Great. Persian rule marked the end of thirty Egyptian dynasties which had existed for nearly three thousand years.

Egyptian society and economy. Although most Egyptians were serfs and subject to forced labor, class stratification was not rigid, and people of merit could rise to a higher rank in the service of the pharaoh. The best avenue of advancement was education. The pharaoh's administration needed many scribes, and young men were urged to attend a scribal school: "Be a scribe, who is freed from forced labor, and protected from all work. . . . he directeth every work that is in this land." Yet then as now the education of a young man was beset with pitfalls: "I am told thou forsakest writing, that thou givest thyself up to pleasures; thou goest from street to street, where it smelleth of beer, to destruction. Beer, it scareth men from thee, it sendeth thy soul to perdition."[23]

Largely because all landed property de-

An Egyptian lord and his party are bird hunting, in this detail from a New Kingdom wall-painting found on a tomb at Thebes (c. 1400 B.C.). In addition to the visual background of hieroglyphics, the artist has painted the abundant vegetation and wildlife of the Nile Valley in realistic and loving detail.

scended from mother to daughter, the status of Egyptian women was exceptionally favorable. Upon the death of his wife a husband lost the use of the property, which was then inherited by the daughter and her husband. Brother and sister marriages often took place within the Egyptian ruling family to ensure the right of succession to the throne, which was always through the female line.

The economy of Egypt has been called "theocratic socialism" because the state, in the person of the divine pharaoh, owned the land and monopolized commerce and industry. Because of the Nile and the proximity to the Mediterranean and Red seas, most of Egypt's trade was carried on by ships. During the Old Kingdom boats plied regularly up and down the Nile, which, unlike the Tigris and the Euphrates, is easily navigable in both directions up to the first cataract at Aswan (Syene). The current carries ships downstream and the prevailing north wind enables them to sail upstream easily. Trade reached its height during the Empire, when commerce traveled along four main routes: the Nile River; the Red Sea, which was connected by caravan to the Nile bend near Thebes; a caravan route to Mesopotamia and southern Syria; and the Mediterranean Sea, connecting northern Syria, Cyprus, Crete, and Greece with the delta of the Nile. Egypt's

indispensable imports were lumber, copper, tin, and olive oil, paid for with gold from its rich mines, linens, wheat, and papyrus rolls —the preferred writing material of the ancient world.

Mathematics and science. The Egyptians were much less skilled in mathematics than were the Mesopotamians. Their arithmetic was limited to addition and subtraction, which also served them when they needed to multiply and divide. They could cope with only simple algebra, but they did have considerable knowledge of practical geometry. The obliteration of field boundaries by the annual flooding of the Nile made land measurement a necessity. Similarly, a knowledge of geometry was essential in computing the dimensions of ramps for raising stones during the construction of pyramids. In these and other engineering projects the Egyptians were superior to their Mesopotamian contemporaries. Like the Mesopotamians, the Egyptians had acquired a "necessary" technology without effecting a conceptual breakthrough to a truly scientific method.

Yet, what has been called the oldest known scientific treatise was composed during the Old Kingdom. Its author described forty-eight cases requiring surgery, drawing conclusions solely from observation and re-

2. Painted bichrome cow, Lascaux (c. 15000–14,500 B.C.). Dating back to the Upper Paleolithic period, this painting is found high on the wall in the interior of the Lascaux cave in central France. Discovered in 1940, Lascaux contains some of the finest examples of animal cave painting in existence. Paleolithic artists used paints prepared from natural deposits found in the soil, ground to a fine powder, and mixed with water. Pigment was applied with fingers, pointed tools, or pads of moss and fur. The lifelike images have been taken as evidence that Paleolithic art may express, in abstract form, a complex system of fecundity myths.

3. Egypt: Back of the throne of Tutankhamen (New Kingdom, c. 1350 B.C.). Fashioned of gold, and inlaid with enamel and semi-precious stones, this throne is an outstanding example of the treasures discovered in 1922 in the only intact tomb remaining in the Valley of the Kings. The scene portrayed is that of Tutankhamen and his young queen, Ankhesenamen, who appears to be anointing him with oil from a vessel she holds in her hand. In his brief nine-year reign, Tutankhamen restored Egypt back to its ancient belief in a multitude of gods. It was probably for this reason that he was buried along with many objects of incredible wealth and splendor.

4. Greece: Temple of Apollo at Delphi (c. fourth century B.C.). Delphi was famous throughout ancient Greece as the site of the temple and oracle of Apollo. It was considered by the Greeks to be the center of the earth and the place where the god Apollo communicated to man through oracles his knowledge of the future. As part of a religious ritual, a prophetess would deliver Apollo's message while in a trance-like state. Though now in ruins, the site was built in a sacred area and contained several temples, treasuries, and monuments. There were also stadiums, gymnasiums, theatres, and even a hotel to house visitors.

5. Room in a villa at Boscoreale, near Pompeii (first century B.C.). Rome's singular accomplishment in architecture included an attention to domestic buildings that reflected a traditional concern for home and family. Since the Roman country house had few doors and windows, a large amount of wall space was available for the lavish decoration that is a mark of so much Roman art. Wall paintings were often intended to create the illusion of space beyond the room and, as is evident here, the realistic Roman style convincingly achieved the illusion.

jecting supernatural causes and treatments. In advising the physician to "measure for the heart" which "speaks" in various parts of the body, he recognized the importance of the pulse and approached the concept of the circulation of the blood. This text remained unique, however, for in Egypt as elsewhere in the ancient Near East, thought failed to free itself permanently from domination by priests and bondage to religion.

The Old Kingdom also produced the world's first known solar calendar, the direct ancestor of our own. In order to plan their farming operations in accordance with the annual flooding of the Nile, the Egyptians kept records and discovered that the average period between inundations was 365 days. They also noted that the Nile flood coincided with the annual appearance of the Dog Star (Sirius) on the eastern horizon at dawn, and they soon associated the two phenomena. (Since the Egyptian year was six hours short of the true year, Julius Caesar in Roman times corrected the error by adding an extra day every four years.)

Egyptian religion. Early Egyptian religion had no strong ethical character. Relations between men and gods were based largely on material considerations, and the gods were thought to reward those who brought them gifts of sacrifice. But widespread suffering during the First Intermediate Period led to a revolution in religious thought. It was now believed that instead of propitiatory offerings the gods were interested in good character and love for one's fellow man: "More acceptable [to the gods] is the character of one upright of heart than the ox of the evildoer. . . . Give the love of thyself to the whole world; a good character is a remembrance."[24]

The cult of Osiris became very popular when it combined the new emphasis on moral character with the supreme reward of an attractive afterlife. "Do justice whilst thou endurest upon earth," men were told. "A man remains over after death, and his deeds are placed beside him in heaps. However, existence yonder is for eternity. . . . He who reaches it without wrongdoing shall exist yonder like a god."[25] Osiris, according to an ancient myth, was the god of

the Nile, and the rise and fall of the river symbolized his death and resurrection. The myth recounted that Osiris had been murdered by Seth, his evil brother, who cut the victim's body into many pieces. When Isis, the bereaved widow, collected all the pieces and put them together, Osiris was resurrected and became immortal. Osiris was thus the first mummy, and every mummified Egyptian was another Osiris.

But only a soul free of sin would be permitted to live forever in what was described as the "Field of the Blessed, an ideal land where there is no wailing and nothing evil; where barley grows four cubits high, and emmer wheat seven ells high; where, even better, one has to do no work in the field oneself, but can let others take care of it."[26] At the time of soul testing, Osiris weighed the candidate's heart against the Feather of Truth. If the ordeal was not passed, a horrible creature devoured the rejected heart. During the Empire the priesthood of Osiris became corrupt and claimed that it knew clever methods of surviving the soul testing, even though a man's heart were heavy with sin. Charms and magical prayers and formulas were sold to the living as insurance policies guaranteeing them a happy outcome in the judgment before Osiris. They constitute much of what is known as the Book of the Dead, which was placed in the tomb.

Akhenaton's religious reformation was directed against the venal priests of Osiris as well as those of the supreme god Amon. As we have seen, Akhenaton failed to uproot Amon and the multiplicity of lesser gods; his monotheism was too cold and intellectual to attract the masses who yearned for a blessed hereafter.

Monumentalism in architecture. Because of their impressive and enduring tombs and temples, the Egyptians have been called the greatest builders in history. The earliest tomb was the mud-brick mastaba, so called because of its resemblance to a low bench. By the beginning of the Third Dynasty stone began to replace brick, and an architectural genius named Imhotep constructed the first pyramid by piling six huge stone mastabas one on top of the other. Adjoining this Step Pyramid was a temple complex whose stone columns were not freestanding but attached to a wall, as though the architect was still feeling his way in the use of the new medium.

The most celebrated of the true pyramids were built for the Fourth Dynasty pharaohs Khufu, Khafre, and Menkaure. Khufu's pyramid, the largest of the three, covers thirteen acres and originally rose 481 feet. It is composed of 2,300,000 limestone blocks, some weighing fifteen tons, and all pushed and pulled into place by human muscle. This stupendous monument was built without mortar, yet some of the stones were so perfectly fitted that a knife cannot be inserted in the joint. The Old Kingdom's eighty pyramids are a striking expression of Egyptian civilization. In their dignity, massiveness, and repose, they reflect the religion-motivated character of Egyptian society.

As the glory and serenity of the Old Kingdom can be seen in its pyramids, constructed as an act of faith by its subjects, so the power and wealth of the Empire survives in the temples at Thebes, made possible by the booty and tribute of conquest. On the east side of the Nile stand the ruins of the magnificent temples of Karnak and Luxor. The Hypostyle Hall of the temple of Karnak, built by Ramses II, is larger than the cathedral of Notre Dame. Its forest of 134 columns is arranged in sixteen rows, with the roof over the two broader central aisles (the nave) raised to allow the entry of light. This technique of providing a clerestory over a central nave was later used in Roman basilicas and Christian churches.

Sculpture and painting. Egyptian art was essentially religious. Tomb paintings and relief sculpture depict the everyday activities that the deceased wished to continue enjoying in the afterlife, and statues glorify the god-kings in all their serenity and eternity. Since religious art is inherently conservative, Egyptian art seldom departed from the traditions established during the vigorous and self-assured Old Kingdom. Sculptors idealized and standardized their subjects, and the human figure is shown either looking directly ahead or in profile (see illustration, p. 24), with a rigidity very much in keeping with the austere architectural settings of the statues.

Yet on two occasions an unprecedented naturalism appeared in Egyptian sculpture. The faces of some of the Middle Kingdom rulers appear drawn and weary, as though they were weighed down by the burden of reconstructing Egypt after the collapse of the Old Kingdom. An even greater naturalism is seen in the portraits of Akhenaton and his beautiful queen, Nefertete. The pharaoh's brooding countenance is realistically portrayed, as is his ungainly paunch and his happy but far from god-like family life as he holds one of his young daughters on his knee or munches on a bone. The "heretic" pharaoh, who insisted on what he called "truth" in religion, seems also to have insisted on truth in art.

Painting in Egypt shows the same precision and mastery of technique that are evident in sculpture. However, no attempt was made to show objects in perspective, and the scenes give an appearance of flatness. The effect of distance was conveyed by making objects in a series or by putting one object above another. Another convention employed was to depict everything from its most characteristic angle. Often the head,

In contrast to conventional Egyptian art, this representation of Akhenaton is so naturalistic that it borders on caricature.

arms, and legs were shown in side view and the eye, shoulders, and chest were shown in front view.

Writing and literature. In Egypt, as in Sumer, writing began with pictures. But unlike the Mesopotamian signs, Egyptian hieroglyphs ("sacred signs") remained primarily pictorial. At first the hieroglyphs represented only objects, but later they came to stand for ideas and syllables. Early in the Old Kingdom the Egyptians began to use alphabetic characters for twenty-four consonant sounds. Although they also continued to use the old pictographic and syllabic signs, this discovery was of far-reaching consequence. It led to the development of the Semitic alphabet, from which our present alphabet is derived.

Egypt's oldest literature is the Pyramid Texts, a body of religious writing found inscribed on the walls of the burial chambers of Old Kingdom pharaohs. Their recurrent theme is a monotonous insistence that the dead pharaoh is really a god.

The troubled life that followed the collapse of the Old Kingdom produced the highly personal literature of the First Intermediate Period and Middle Kingdom. It contains protests against the ills of the day, demands for social justice, and praise for the romantic excitements of wine, women, and song. The universal appeal of this literature is illustrated by the following lines from a love poem, in which the beloved is called "sister":

I behold how my sister cometh, and my heart is in gladness.
Mine arms open wide to embrace her; my heart exulteth within me: for my lady has come to me. . . .
She kisseth me, she openeth her lips to me: then am I joyful even without beer.[27]

A classic of Egyptian literature is Akhenaton's *Hymn to the Sun*, which is similar in spirit to Psalm 104. A few lines will indicate its lyric beauty and its conception of one omnipotent and beneficent Creator.

How manifold are thy works!
They are hidden before men,
O sole god, beside whom there is no other.
Thou didst create the earth according to thy heart
While thou wast alone.[28]

The Rosetta Stone, discovered in Egypt in 1799 by an officer in Napoleon's army, supplied the means by which Jean Champollion was able in 1822 to decipher Egyptian writing. On the stone a decree, dated 196 B.C., is inscribed in three different scripts, as is shown by the section reproduced here. The bottom layer of writing is Greek, which Champollion could read. Working from the Greek he was able to decipher the hieroglyphic writing in the top layer. The middle layer is a simplified form of hieroglyphic writing, called demotic.

By the fifth century A.D. the ability to read ancient Egyptian writing had been lost. Not until fourteen hundred years later, when the Rosetta Stone was deciphered by Jean François Champollion (1790-1832), could modern man appreciate this ancient literature.

THE HITTITES

The Hittite empire. Except for brief mention in the Bible, very little was known about the Hittites until archaeologists began to unearth the remains of their civilization in Asia Minor in 1906. By 1920 their writing had been deciphered, and it proved to be the earliest example of a written Indo-European language. The Hittites are thought to have entered Asia Minor from the north about 2000 B.C., and their superior military means—particularly the horse-drawn chariot—enabled them to conquer the native people of central Asia Minor.

After 1450 B.C. a series of energetic Hittite kings created a more centralized government and an empire that included Syria, lost by the Egyptian pharaoh Akhenaton. Pharaoh Ramses II moved north from Palestine in a vain attempt to reconquer Syria. Ambushed and forced back to Palestine after a bloody battle, Ramses agreed to a treaty of "good peace and good brotherhood" in 1269 B.C. (see p. 23). The Hittites may have been eager for peace with Egypt because of the threat posed by a new movement of Indo-European peoples. Shortly after 1200 B.C. these barbarians, chief among whom were the Phrygians, destroyed the Hittite empire. Darkness settled over Asia Minor until after 800 B.C.

Hittite civilization. The Hittite state under the empire was modeled after the older oriental monarchies of the Near East. The king claimed to represent the sun god and was deified after death. The nobles held large estates from the king and in return provided warriors armed increasingly with iron weapons. The Hittites are credited with being the first people to work iron from local deposits, which afforded them a jealously guarded monopoly. Not until after 1200 B.C. did iron metallurgy become widespread.

The Hittites adopted the Mesopotamian cuneiform script together with some works of Babylonian literature. While their law code shows some similarity to the code of Hammurabi, it differed in prescribing more humane punishments. Instead of retaliation ("an eye for an eye"), the Hittite code made greater use of restitution and compensation.

The chief importance of Hittite culture lies in the legacy it left to the Phrygians and Lydians and, through them, to the Greeks who settled along the Aegean coast of Asia Minor. The Hittite goddess Kubaba, for example, became the great Phrygian goddess Cybele, the "Great Mother" whose worship became widespread in Roman times.

After 1200 B.C., with the Hittite empire de-stroyed and Egypt in decline, the Semitic peoples of Syria and Palestine ceased being pawns in a struggle between rival imperialisms. For nearly five hundred years, until they were conquered by the Assyrians, these peoples were able to play an independent and significant role in history.

THE ERA OF SMALL STATES *V/*

The Phoenicians. *Phoenician* is the name the Greeks gave to those Canaanites who dwelt along the Mediterranean coast of Syria, an area that is today the state of Lebanon. Hemmed in by the Lebanon Mountains to the east, the Phoenicians turned to the sea and by the eleventh century B.C. had become the greatest traders, shipbuilders, navigators, and colonizers before the Greeks. To obtain silver and copper from Spain and tin from Britain, Gades (Cadiz) was founded on the Atlantic coast of Spain. Carthage, one of a number of Phoenician trading posts around the shores of the Mediterranean, was destined to become Rome's chief rival in the third century B.C.

Although the Phoenicians were essentially traders, their home cities—notably Tyre, Sidon, and Byblos—also produced manufactured goods. Their most famous export was woolen cloth dyed with the purple dye obtained from shellfish found along their coast. They were also skilled makers of furniture (made from the famous cedars of Lebanon), metalware, glassware, and jewelry.

Culturally the Phoenicians were not creative. They left behind no literature and little art. Yet they made one of the greatest contributions to human progress, the perfection of the alphabet, which, along with the Babylonian sexagesimal system of notation, they carried westward. The origin of the alphabet is still a moot question. Between 1800 and 1600 B.C. various Canaanite peoples, influenced by Egypt's semialphabetical writing, started to evolve a simplified method of writing. The Phoenician alphabet of twenty-two consonant symbols (the Greeks later added the vowel signs) is related to the thirty-character alphabet of Ugarit, a Canaanite city (see map, p. 17) which, like the Hittite empire, was destroyed about 1200 B.C.

The half-dozen Phoenician cities never united to form a strong state, and in the last half of the eighth century B.C. all but Tyre were conquered by the Assyrians. When Tyre finally fell to the Chaldeans in 571 B.C., the Hebrew prophet Ezekiel spoke what reads like an epitaph to the once great role played by the Phoenicians:

When your wares came from the seas, you satisfied many peoples; with your abundant wealth and merchandise you enriched the kings of the earth. Now you are wrecked by the seas, in the depths of the waters; your merchandise and all your crew have sunk with you. [29]

The Arameans. Closely related to the Hebrews were the Arameans, who occupied Syria east of the Lebanon Mountains. The most important of their little kingdoms was centered on Damascus, one of the oldest continuously inhabited cities of the world. The Arameans dominated the camel caravan trade connecting Mesopotamia, Phoenicia, and Egypt and continued to do so after Damascus fell to the Assyrians in 732 B.C. The Aramaic language, which used an alphabet similar to the Phoenician, became the international language of the Near East. In Judea it displaced Hebrew as the spoken language and was used by Jesus and his disciples.

The Hebrew kingdoms. In war, diplomacy, inventions, and art, the Hebrews made little splash in the stream of history. In religion and ethics, however, their contribution to world civilization was tremendous. Out of their experience grew three great religions: Judaism, Christianity, and Islam.

Hebrew experience is recorded in the Holy Writ of Israel, the Old Testament of the Christian Bible, whose present content was approved about 90 A.D. by a council of rabbis. All of us are familiar with the power and beauty of some of its many great passages. As a work of literature it remains unsurpassed; but it is more than that. "It is Israel's life story—a story that cannot be told adequately apart from the conviction that

God had called this people in his grace, separated them from the nations for a special responsibility, and commissioned them with the task of being his servant in the accomplishment of his purpose." [30]

The Biblical account of the history of the Hebrews (later called Israelites and then Jews) begins with the patriarchal clan leader Abraham. About 1800 B.C. Abraham led his people out of Ur in Sumer, where they had settled for a time in their wanderings, and eventually they arrived in the land of Canaan, later called Palestine.

About 1700 B.C., driven by famine, some Hebrews followed Abraham's great-grandson Joseph, the son of Israel (also called Jacob), into Egypt. Joseph's rise to power in Egypt, and the hospitable reception of his people there, is attributed to the presence of the largely Semitic Hyksos, who had conquered Egypt about 1720 B.C. (see p. 22). Following the expulsion of the Hyksos by the pharaohs of the Eighteenth Dynasty, the Hebrews were enslaved by the Egyptians. Shortly after 1300 B.C. Moses led them out of bondage and into the wilderness of Sinai, where they entered into a pact or covenant with their God, Yahweh. The Sinai Covenant bound the people as a whole—the nation of Israel, as they now called themselves—to worship Yahweh before all other gods and to obey his Law. In return, Yahweh made the Israelites his chosen people whom he would protect and to whom he granted Canaan, "a land flowing with milk and honey." The history of Israel from this time on is the story of the working out of this covenant.

The Israelites had to contend for Palestine against the Canaanites, whose Semitic ancestors had migrated from Arabia early in the third millennium B.C. Joined by other Hebrew tribes already in Palestine, the Israelites formed a confederacy of twelve tribes (clans of the twelve sons of Israel) and, led by war leaders called judges, in time succeeded in subjugating the Canaanites. In the meantime, however, a far more formidable foe had appeared. The Philistines, from whom we get the word *Palestine*, settled along the coast about 1175 B.C., having been uprooted from Asia Minor by the invasions that destroyed the Hittite empire (see p. 28).

Aided by the use of iron weapons, which were new to Palestine, the Philistines were well on their way to dominating the entire land by the middle of the eleventh century.

It became apparent that the loose twelve-tribe confederacy could not cope with the Philistine danger. "Give us a king to govern us," the people demanded, "that we also may be like all the nations, and that our king may govern us and go before us and fight our battles."[31] Saul, the first king of Israel (1020-1000 B.C.), died while fighting the Philistines, but his successor David (1000-961 B.C.) not only restricted the Philistines to a narrow coastal strip but became the ruler of the largest state in the ancient history of the area, stretching from the Euphrates to the Gulf of Aqaba.

The work of David was completed by his son Solomon, in whose long reign (961-922 B.C.) Israel reached a pinnacle of wordly power and splendor as an oriental-style monarchy. In the words of the Bible:

Solomon ruled over all the kingdoms from the Euphrates to the land of the Philistines and to the border of Egypt; they brought tribute and served Solomon all the days of his life. . . . And Judah and Israel dwelt in safety, from Dan even to Beer-sheba, every man under his vine and under his fig tree, all the days of Solomon. . . . And God gave Solomon wisdom and understanding beyond measure, and largeness of mind. . . . Now the weight of gold that came to Solomon in one year was six hundred and sixty-six talents of gold, besides that which came from the traders and from the traffic of the merchants, and from all the kings of Arabia and from the governors of the land. . . . The king also made a great ivory throne, and overlaid it with the finest gold. . . .[32]

But the price of Solomon's vast bureaucracy, building projects (especially the palace complex and the Temple at Jerusalem), standing army (1400 chariots and 12,000 horses), and harem (700 wives and 300 concubines) was great. High taxes, forced labor, and the loss of tribal independence led to dissension, and on the death of Solomon in 922 B.C. the realm was split into two kingdoms—Israel in the north and Judah in the south. These two weak kingdoms were in no position to defend themselves when new, powerful empires rose again in Mesopotamia. In 721 B.C. the Assyrians captured Samaria, the capital of the northern kingdom, taking 27,900 Israelites into captivity and settling foreign peoples in their place. The resulting mixed population, called Samaritans, made no further contribution to Hebrew history or religion.

The southern kingdom of Judah held out until 586 B.C. when Nebuchadnezzar, the Chaldean ruler of Babylonia, destroyed Jerusalem and carried away ten thousand captives; "none remained, except the poorest people of the land."[33] Thus began the famous Babylonian Exile of the Jews (Judeans), which lasted until 538 B.C. when Cyrus the Persian, having conquered Babylon, allowed them to return to Jerusalem where they rebuilt the Temple destroyed by Nebuchadnezzar.

Persian rule was followed by that of the Hellenistic Greeks and Romans. In 66-70 A.D. the Jews rebelled against Rome, and Jerusalem was totally destroyed in the savage

ANCIENT ISRAEL
8TH CENTURY B.C.

Damascus

Tyre
PHOENICIA
Kadesh

KINGDOM
OF
ARAM

MEDITERRANEAN
SEA

Sea of
Galilee

Megiddo

KINGDOM
OF
ISRAEL

Samaria

Joppa
Shiloh
Bethel
Jericho

Jordan R.

AMMON

Jerusalem
Bethlehem

KINGDOM
OF
JUDAH

Hebron

Gaza
PHILISTIA

DEAD
SEA

MOAB

Beersheba

NEGEV
(DESERT)

EDOM

Uncertain   Boundary

fighting that ensued. The Jews were again driven into exile, and the Diaspora—the "scattering"—was at its height.

Hebrew religion. From the time of Abraham the Hebrews worshiped one god, a stern, warlike tribal deity whose name Yahweh (Jehovah) was first revealed to Moses. Yahweh differed from the many Near Eastern nature gods in being completely separate from the physical universe which He had created. This view of Yahweh as the Creator of all things everywhere was inevitably to lead to the monotheistic belief that He was the sole God in the universe.

After their entrance into Palestine, many Hebrews adopted the fertility deities of the Canaanites as well as the luxurious Canaanite manner of living. As a result prophets arose who "spoke for" (from the Greek word *prophetes*) Yahweh in insisting on strict adherence to the Sinai Covenant and in condemning the "whoring" after other gods, the selfish pursuit of wealth, and the growth of social injustice.

Between roughly 750 and 550 B.C. appeared a series of great prophets who wrote down their messages. They sought to purge the religion of Israel of all corrupting influences and to elevate and dignify the concept of Yahweh. As summed up by Micah in a statement often cited as the essence of all higher religion, "He has shown you, O man, what is good; and what does the Lord require of you but to do justice, and to love kindness, and to walk humbly with your God?"[34] The prophets viewed the course of Hebrew history as being governed by the sovereign will of Yahweh, seeing the Assyrians and the Chaldeans as "the rod of Yahweh's anger" to chastise His stubborn, wayward people. They also developed the idea of a coming Messiah, the "anointed one" from the family of King David, who would inaugurate a reign of peace and justice.

Considered the greatest of the prophets are Jeremiah and the anonymous Second Isaiah, so-called because his message was incorporated in the Book of Isaiah (chapters 40-55). Jeremiah witnessed the events that led to Nebuchadnezzar's destruction of Jerusalem and the Temple and to the Babylonian Captivity of the Jews. He prepared the people for these calamities by affirming that Yahweh would forgive their sins and restore "a remnant" of his people and by proclaiming a "new covenant." The old covenant had been between Yahweh and the nation, which no longer existed, and it had become overlaid with ritual and ceremony and centered in the Temple, which had been destroyed. The new covenant was between Yahweh and each individual; religion was now a matter of a man's own heart and conscience, and both the nation and the Temple were considered superfluous. Second Isaiah, who lived at the end of the Babylonian Captivity, capped the work of his predecessors by proclaiming Israel to be Yahweh's "righteous servant," purified and enlightened by suffering and ready to guide the world to the worship of the one, eternal, supreme God. Thus were the Jews who returned from the Exile provided with a renewed faith in their destiny and a new comprehension of their religion which would sustain them through the centuries to come.

LATER EMPIRES OF WESTERN ASIA

Assyrian expansion. By 700 B.C. the era of small states was at an end. For two hundred years the Assyrians had been bidding to translate the growing economic unity of the Near East—evidenced by Solomon's trading operations and even more by the activities of Aramean merchants—into political unity. The Assyrian push toward the Mediterranean began in the ninth century and, after a lapse, was resumed in the eighth century, during which Babylon was also subdued. By 721 B.C. the Assyrians were the masters of the Fertile Crescent.

A Semitic people long established in the hilly region of the upper Tigris, the Assyrians had been schooled for a thousand years by constant warfare. But their matchless army was only one of several factors that explain the success of Assyrian imperialism: a

The militaristic nature of the Assyrians is reflected in this relief sculpture of sling-carrying warriors.

policy of calculated terrorization, an efficient system of political administration, and the support of the commercial classes that wanted political stability and unrestricted trade over large areas.

The Assyrian army, with its chariots, mounted cavalry, and sophisticated siege engines, was the most powerful yet seen in the ancient world. Neither troops or walls could long resist the Assyrians who, in Byron's well-known phrase, "came down like a wolf on the fold." Conquered peoples were held firmly in control by systematic terrorization. "From some I cut off their noses, their ears and their fingers, of many I put out the eyes. . . . I bound their heads to tree trunks round about the city"[35] is a characteristic statement from the Assyrian royal inscriptions. In addition, mass deportations were employed as an effective means of destroying national feeling.

The well-coordinated Assyrian system of political administration was another factor in the success of the empire. Conquered lands became provinces ruled by governors who exercised extensive military, judicial, and financial powers. Their chief tasks were to ensure the regular collection of tribute and the raising of troops for the permanent army that eventually replaced the native militia of sturdy Assyrian peasants. An efficient system of communications carried the "king's word" to the governors as well as the latter's reports to the royal court—including one prophetic dispatch reading: "The king knows that all lands hate us. . . ."[36] Nevertheless, the Assyrians must be credited with laying the foundations for the later more humane administrative systems of the Persians and Alexander the Great and his successors.

Assyrian culture. Culturally the Assyrians were not creative; their role was rather one of borrowing from the superior cultures of other peoples and unifying the best elements into a new product. This is evident in Assyrian architecture and sculpture, the work of subject artisans and artists. Both arts glorified the power of the Assyrian king. The palace, serving both as residence and administrative center, replaced the temple as the characteristic architectural form. A feature of Assyrian palace architecture was the structural use of the arch and the column, both borrowed from Babylonia. The palaces were decorated with splendid relief sculptures that glorified the king as warrior and hunter. Assyrian sculptors were especially skilled in portraying realistically the ferocity and agony of charging and dying animals.

Assyrian kings were interested in preserving written as well as pictorial records of their reigns. King Ashurbanipal (d. 631 B.C.) left a record of his great efforts in collecting the literary heritage of Sumer and Babylon, and the 22,000 clay tablets found in the ruins of his palace at Nineveh provided modern scholars with their first direct knowledge of this literature.

Downfall of the Assyrian empire. Revolt against Assyrian terror and tribute was inevitable when Assyria's strength waned and effective opposition arose. By the middle of the seventh century B.C. the sturdy Assyrian stock had been decimated by wars, and the Assyrian kings had to rely on unreliable mercenary troops and subject levies. Egypt regained its independence under the Twenty-

Sixth Dynasty, and the Medes refused further tribute. Then the Chaldeans, a new group of Semites who had filtered into Babylonia, revolted in 626 B.C. In 612 they joined the Medes in destroying Nineveh, the Assyrian capital. From one end of the Fertile Crescent to the other people rejoiced: "Nineveh is laid waste: who will bemoan her?"[37]

The Lydians and the Medes. The fall of Assyria left four states to struggle over the crumbs of empire: Chaldea and Egypt vied over Syria-Palestine, while Media and Lydia clashed over eastern Asia Minor.

After the collapse of the Hittite empire about 1200 B.C., the Lydians had followed the Phrygians, whose last king was the semi-legendary Midas (d. c. 680 B.C.), in establishing a kingdom in western Asia Minor. When Assyria fell, the Lydians expanded eastward until stopped by the Medes at the Halys River. Lydia profited from being astride the commercial land route between Mesopotamia and the Aegean and from the possession of valuable gold-bearing streams. As a result, the Lydians invented coinage (about 675 B.C.), which replaced the silver bars hitherto in general use. Lydia's most famous king was Croesus, and the phrase "rich as Croesus" is a reminder of Lydian opulence. With his defeat by the Persians (see p. 34), Lydia ceased to exist.

The Medes were an Indo-European people who by 1000 B.C. had established themselves on the Iranian plateau east of Assyria. In the seventh century B.C. they had created a strong kingdom with Ecbatana as capital and with the Persians, their kinsmen to the south, as vassals. Following the collapse of Assyria, the Medes expanded into Armenia and eastern Asia Minor, but their short-lived empire ended in 550 B.C. when they, too, were absorbed by the Persians.

The Chaldean empire. While the Median kingdom controlled the highland region, the Chaldeans, with their capital at Babylon, were masters of the Fertile Crescent. Nebuchadnezzar, becoming king of the Chaldeans in 604 B.C., raised Babylonia to another epoch of brilliance after more than a thousand years of eclipse. By defeating the Egyptians in Syria, Nebuchadnezzar ended their hopes of re-creating their empire. As we have seen

earlier (p. 30), he destroyed Jerusalem in 586 B.C. and carried several thousand Jews captive to Babylonia.

Nebuchadnezzar built Babylon into the largest and most impressive city of its day. The tremendous city walls were wide enough at the top to have rows of small houses on either side; between the rows of houses was a space wide enough for the passage of a chariot. In the center of Babylon ran the famous Procession Street, which passed through the Ishtar Gate. This arch, which was adorned with brilliant tile animals, is the best remaining example of Babylonian architecture. The immense palace of Nebuchadnezzar towered terrace upon terrace, each resplendent with masses of ferns, flowers, and trees. These roof gardens, the famous Hanging Gardens of Babylon, were so beautiful that they were regarded by the Greeks as one of the seven wonders of the ancient world.

Nebuchadnezzar also rebuilt the great

THE ASSYRIAN EMPIRE
ABOUT 670 B.C.

temple-tower or ziggurat, the Biblical "Tower of Babel," which the Greek historian Herodotus viewed a century later and described as

a tower of solid masonry, a furlong in length and breadth, upon which was raised a second tower, and on that a third, and so on up to eight. The ascent to the top is on the outside, by a path which winds round all the towers.[38]

Nebuchadnezzar was the last great Mesopotamian ruler, and Chaldean power quickly crumbled after his death in 562 B.C. The Chaldean priests—whose interest in astrology greatly added to the fund of Babylonian astronomical knowledge—continually undermined the monarchy. Finally, in 539 B.C., they opened the gates of Babylon to Cyrus the Persian, thus fulfilling Daniel's message of doom upon the notorious Belshazzar, the last Chaldean ruler: "You have been weighed in the balances and found wanting."[39]

The Persian empire. Cyrus the Persian was the greatest conqueror in the history of the ancient Near East. In 550 B.C. he had ended Persian vassalage to the Medes by capturing Ecbatana and ousting the Median dynasty. The Medes readily accepted their vigorous new ruler, who soon demonstrated that he deserved to be called "the Great." When King Croesus of Lydia moved across the Halys River in 547 B.C. to pick up some of the pieces of the Median empire, Cyrus defeated him and annexed Lydia, including those Greek cities on the coast of Asia Minor which were under the nominal control of Lydia. Then he turned east, establishing his power as far as the frontier of India. Babylon and its empire, as we have seen, was next on his list. Following the death of Cyrus, his son Cambyses conquered Egypt. The next ruler, Darius I (522-486 B.C.), began a conflict with the Greeks that continued intermittently for more than 150 years until the Persians were conquered by Alexander the Great. Long before this event the Persian nobility had forgotten Cyrus the Great's answer to their suggestion that they "leave this small and barren country of ours" and move to fertile Babylonia:

Do so if you wish, but if you do, be ready to find yourselves no longer governors but governed; for soft lands breed soft men; it does not happen that the same land brings forth wonderful crops and good fighting men.[40]

Persian government. Although built upon the Assyrian model, the Persian administrative system was far more efficient and humane. The empire was divided into twenty provinces, or satrapies, each ruled by a governor called a satrap. To check the satraps, a secretary and a military official representing the "Great King, King of Kings" were installed in every province. Also, special inspectors, "the Eyes and Ears of the King," traveled throughout the realm.

Imperial post roads connected the important cities of the empire. Along the Royal Road between Sardis and Susa there was a post station every fourteen miles, where the king's couriers could obtain fresh horses, enabling them to cover the 1600-mile route in a week. "Nothing mortal travels so fast as these Persian messengers," wrote Herodotus. "These men will not be hindered . . . , either by snow, or rain, or heat, or by the darkness of night."[41]

The Persian empire was the first to attempt governing many different racial groups on the principle of equal responsibilities and rights for all peoples. So long as his subjects paid their taxes and kept the peace, the king did not interfere with local religion, customs, or trade. Indeed, Darius was called the "shopkeeper" because he stimulated trade by introducing a uniform system of gold and silver coinage on the Lydian model.

Persian religion and art. The humaneness of the Persian rulers may have stemmed from the ethical religion founded by the prophet Zoroaster, who lived in the early sixth century B.C. Zoroaster sought to replace what he called "the lie"—ritualistic, idol-worshiping cults and their Magi priests—with a religion centered on the sole god Ahura-Mazda ("Wise Lord"), who demanded "good thoughts of the mind, good deeds of the hand, and good words of the tongue" from those who would attain paradise (a Persian word). The new religion made little progress

THE CHALDEAN AND
PERSIAN EMPIRES

▨ Chaldean Empire
About 586 B.C.

▨ Persian Empire
About 500 B.C.

0 100 200 300 400 500
1" = 430 MILES

until first Darius and then the Magi adopted it. The Magi revived many old gods as lesser deities, added much ritual, and replaced monotheism with dualism by transforming what Zoroaster had called the principle or spirit of evil into the powerful god Ahriman, rival of Ahura-Mazda. The complicated evolution of Zoroastrianism is revealed in its holy writ, the *Avesta* ("The Law"), assembled in its present form between the fourth and the sixth centuries A.D. Zoroastrian eschatology—"the doctrine of final things" such as the resurrection of the dead and a last judgment—influenced Judaism. Following the Muslim conquest of Persia in the seventh century A.D., Zoroastrianism gradually died out in its homeland. It exists today among the Parsees in India.

In art the Persians borrowed largely from their predecessors in the Fertile Crescent, especially the Assyrians. Their most important work was in palace architecture, the best remains of which are at Persepolis. Built on a high terrace, the royal residences were reached by a grand stairway faced with beautiful reliefs. Instead of the warfare and violence that characterized Assyrian sculpture, these reliefs depict hundreds of soldiers, courtiers, and representatives of twenty-three nations of the empire bringing gifts to the king for the festival of the new year.

SUMMARY

This chapter has recounted the evolution of human affairs from primitive culture to civilization. The first great period in man's prehistory, during which man was a hunter and food-gatherer whose chief all-purpose tool was the hand-ax, is called the Paleolithic or Old Stone Age. Evidence indicates that the Paleolithic cultural stage may have begun in Africa over two million years ago. Some nine thousand years ago the Neolithic stage was initiated with the appearance of food-producing villages in western Asia. This revolutionary change from a food-gathering to a food-producing economy, quite probably the most momentous development in human history, made possible the rise of civilization.

Civilization rose in Mesopotamia and Egypt during the second half of the fourth millennium B.C. Both these civilizations were river-made, one by the Tigris and Euphrates and the other by the Nile. In each case the complex society we call a civilization was the result of human cooperation in taming the rivers to make them work for man.

The words *monumental* and *timeless* best describe Egyptian culture. The Egyptians built colossal statues and huge tombs; their burial customs were designed to outwit time itself. The state centered upon the absolute rule of the pharaohs—god-kings who eventually extended their rule from Nubia to the Euphrates River.

The story of ancient Mesopotamia is primarily concerned with the achievements of the Sumerians and the later adoption of their civilization by various invaders. The most important of these new states was the Babylonian empire created by Hammurabi. Babylon was sacked by the Indo-European Hittites of Asia Minor, who went on to duel with Egypt over Syria and Palestine.

By 1200 B.C. the first great Near Eastern empires—Babylonian, Egyptian, and Hittite —had collapsed, allowing the small Semitic peoples of Syria and Palestine freedom to make their own contributions—the greatest being the ethical monotheism of the Hebrews. Political diversity was ended by the rise of the Assyrian empire, which unified all of the ancient Near East for the first time. After the fall of Assyria, the Chaldean Nebuchadnezzar erected a new Babylonian empire, but it was soon terminated by the expansion of Persia. Stretching from India to Europe, the Persian empire gave the Near East its greatest extension and power—which produced an inevitable conflict with the Greeks. The next major phase in the history of civilization was to be centered on Greece.

SUGGESTIONS FOR READING

The Cambridge Ancient History, Vols. I-II, 3rd ed. (Cambridge Univ., 1975) incorporates the latest research on prehistory and the ancient Near East. R. Braidwood, **Prehistoric Men,** 8th ed. (Scott, Foresman, 1975) is the best short survey. Also recommended: Grahame Clark, **World Prehistory: An Outline,** 2nd ed. (Cambridge Univ.); D. Roe, **Prehistory: An Introduction** (Univ. of California); L. S. B. Leakey, **Adam's Ancestors: The Evolution of Man and His Culture** (Torchbooks); and J. H. Coles and E. S. Higgs, **The Archaeology of Early Man** (Penguin, 1976).

C. W. Ceram, **Gods, Graves, and Scholars** (Bantam, 1972) and L. Cottrell, **The Anvil of Civilization** (Mentor) are popular archaeological surveys. J. Deetz, **Invitation to Archaeology** (Anchor) describes the techniques of the archaeologist. See also Evan Hadingham, **Circles and Standing Stones** (Walker, 1975) which accounts riddles of archaeology in Britain.

W. Hallow and W. Simpson, **The Ancient Near East** (Harcourt Brace Jovanovich, 1971) is comprehensive. Other short surveys are M. Covensky, **The Ancient Near Eastern Tradition** (Harper & Row); G. Childe, **What Happened in History** (Penguin); H. Frankfort, **The Birth of Civilization in the Near East** (Anchor); and S. Moscati, **The Face of the Ancient Orient** (Anchor).

H. Saggs, **The Greatness That Was Babylon** (Mentor) is a brief general history of Ancient Mesopotamia. See also S. N. Kramer, **The Sumerians** (Univ. of Chicago, 1971) and the same author's popular **History Begins at Sumer** (Anchor).

Jon M. White, **Everyday Life in Ancient Egypt** (Capricorn) and L. Casson, **Ancient Egypt** (Time-Life) are brief surveys. A. Gardiner, **Egypt of the Pharaohs** (Galaxy) is a detailed political history. On the Empire period see G. Steindorff and K. Steele,

When Egypt Ruled the East (Phoenix); C. Aldred, **Akhenaton and Nefertiti** (Viking, 1973); and C. Desroaches-Noblecourt, **Tutankhamen** (New York Graphic Society, 1976).

H. Frankfort *et al.*, **Before Philosophy** (Penguin) is a notable interpretation of Mesopotamian and Egyptian thought. John A. Wilson, **The Culture of Ancient Egypt** (Phoenix) is recommended. O. Neugebauer, **The Exact Sciences in Antiquity** (Torchbooks) is an authoritative work.

O. R. Gurney, **The Hittites** (Penguin) and D. Harden, **The Phoenicians** (Praeger) are authoritative surveys. See also Gerhard Herm, **The Phoenicians: The Purple Empire of the Ancient World** (Morrow, 1975) about the great mariners and traders.

J. A. Hexter, **The Judaeo-Christian Tradition** (Harper & Row, 1966) is a succinct overview of Hebrew history and religion. Excellent longer surveys are H. M. Orlinsky, **Ancient Israel** (Cornell); E. Ehrlich, **A Concise History of Israel** (Torchbooks); B. W. Anderson, **Understanding the Old Testament,** 3rd ed. (Prentice-Hall, 1975); and O. Eissfeldt, **The Old Testament: An Introduction** (Harper & Row, 1965).

A. Olmstead, **History of Assyria** (Univ. of Chicago) and **History of the Persian Empire** (Phoenix) are the standard accounts. See also R. Zaehner, **The Dawn and Twilight of Zoroastrianism** (Putnam).

H. Frankfort, **The Art and Architecture of the Ancient Orient** (Penguin, 1971) and I. E. S. Edwards, **The Pyramids of Egypt** (Penguin, 1975) give methods and reasons for the construction of the pyramids.

*Indicates a less expensive paperbound edition.

CHAPTER 2

Aegean, Hellenic, and Hellenistic Civilizations

The Glory That Was Greece

INTRODUCTION. Scarred by time and weather, the ruins of the Athenian Acropolis stand against a vivid blue sky and overlook the trees and buildings of a modern city sprawled beneath. These ruins are striking symbols of a departed civilization—the democracy of Athens at its height.

In the fifth century B.C. the temples and statuary of the Acropolis were gleaming and new, fresh from the hands of builders and sculptors. Five hundred years later Plutarch wrote:

The works are . . . wonderful: because they were perfectly made in so short a time, and have continued so long a season. . . . [The Acropolis looks] at this day as if it were but newly done and finished, there is such a certain kind of flourishing freshness in it . . . that the injury of time cannot impair the sight thereof. As if every one of those . . . works had some living spirit in it, to make it seem young and fresh: and a soul that lived ever, which kept them in their good continuing state.[1]

Today the Acropolis bears the heavy "injury of time"; yet for us no less than for Plutarch, ancient Athens has retained a "flourishing freshness." This quality, together with a refined sense of symmetry and proportion, is characteristic of the Greek spirit and the dazzling achievements of Greek civilization. The ancient Greeks repeatedly demonstrated an ability to regard the world about them from a "young and fresh" perspective and to inject a love of proportion not only into their architecture but into almost everything they attempted. Yet in the crucial sphere of politics, their sense of proportion failed them. Instead of compromising their differences, the city-states quarreled continually, and that fervid individualism which moved them to brilliant creative efforts blinded them to the necessity of cooperation. Thus the political life of the Greeks was marked by conflicts between the city-states until they were at last subjugated by King Philip of Macedonia and his son, Alexander the Great.

Yet Alexander, out of genuine admiration of the Greek cultural achievement, strove to perpetuate the learning of the city-states as he set forth to forge a world-state. Greece's accomplishment was to prove so enduring that its magnificent legacy of knowledge and art would provide much of the cultural heritage of the West and, to a lesser extent, of the East. Thus the English poet Shelley could say with justification, "We are all Greeks." Probably no other people has made so lasting an impression on man's intellectual history.

I BACKGROUND FOR GREEK CULTURE

Aegean civilization. Greek civilization was unique in so many ways that a student of history might infer that Greek culture developed in a vacuum or, free from outside influences, sprang full-blown from the rocky hills of this small land. The Greek achievement, however, was preceded by an advanced civilization located on the lands surrounding the Aegean Sea. This Aegean civilization, which came into full flower about 2000 B.C. and collapsed suddenly following 1200 B.C., developed through two major periods. The first and longer period, which ended about 1450 B.C., is called "Minoan" after the legendary Cretan King Minos. Crete was the center of Minoan civilization, which spread to the Aegean Islands, the coast of Asia Minor, and mainland Greece. The last period of Aegean civilization, the two and one half centuries following 1450 B.C. when the center of Aegean political power and culture lay on the Greek mainland, is called "Mycenaean" after its most important site at Mycenae.

The Minoans. The narrow, 160-mile-long island of Crete was a stepping stone between Europe, Asia, and Africa. Stimulated by contacts with Mesopotamia and Egypt, a brilliant civilization emerged here by 2000 B.C.

Minoan prosperity was based on large-scale trade that ranged from Troy to Egypt and from Sicily to Syria and employed the first ships capable of long voyages over the open sea. Chief exports were olive oil, wine, metalware, and magnificent pottery. This trade was the monopoly of an efficient bureaucratic government under a powerful ruler whose administrative records were written on clay tablets, first in a form of picture writing and later in a syllabic script known as Linear A. Neither script can be read, but Linear A appears to contain some borrowed Semitic words, the result of Cretan trade with the coastal cities of Syria. Our knowledge of Minoan civilization is therefore scanty and imprecise; most of it is derived from the material remains uncovered by archaeologists.

It was the epoch-making discoveries of the English archaeologist Sir Arthur Evans that first brought to light this civilization, whose existence had previously only been hinted at in Greek legends and the epics of Homer. Between 1900 and 1905 Evans unearthed the ruins of a great palace at Knossos, the dominant city in Crete after 1700 B.C. Rising at least three stories high and sprawl-

THE AEGEAN WORLD

THRACE

MACEDONIA

EPIRUS

THESSALY

AETOLIA

ACHAIA

ARCADIA

PELOPONNESUS

MESSENIA

LACONIA

BOEOTIA

ATTICA

EUBOEA

Byzantium

SEA OF MARMARA

PHRYGIA

MYSIA

LYDIA

Pergamum

Sardis

Hermus R.

Ephesus

Meander R.

Miletus

Halicarnassus

RHODES

SAMOS

SPORADES

AEGEAN SEA

CRETAN SEA

MEDITERRANEAN SEA

Hellespont

Ilium (Troy)

LESBOS

CHIOS

SAMOTHRACE

LEMNOS

CYCLADES

NAXOS

PAROS

IOS

THERA

MELOS

CRETE

Knossos

OLYMPUS

Delphi

Thebes

Corinth

Mycenae

Argos

Athens

Piraeus

Sparta

Olympia

Pylos

LEUCAS

CEPHALLENIA

ZACYNTHUS

CORCYRA

CYTHERA

0   25   50   75

The Lion Gate at Mycenae was built about 1250 B.C. Mycenaean palaces served as hilltop fortresses and were enclosed by defensive walls of mammoth stone blocks. The Lion Gate is the most impressive remnant of these massive fortifications.

ing over nearly six acres, this "Palace of Minos," built of brick and limestone and employing unusual downward-tapering columns of wood, was a maze of royal apartments, storerooms, corridors, open courtyards, and broad stairways. Walls were painted with elaborate frescoes in which the Minoans appear as a gay, peaceful people with a pronounced liking for dancing, festivals, and athletic contests. Women are shown enjoying a freedom and dignity unknown elsewhere in the ancient Near East or classical Greece. Furnished with running water, the palace had a sanitation system surpassing anything constructed in Europe until Roman times and, after that, until the nineteenth

century. The palace was linked to other parts of Crete by well-paved roads lined with the luxurious dwellings of the nobility.

The glory of Minoan culture was its art—gay, spontaneous, and full of rhythmic motion. Art was an essential part of everyday life and not, as in the ancient Orient, an adjunct to religion and the state. What little is known of Minoan religion also contrasts sharply with conditions in the Near East: there were no great temples, powerful priesthoods, or large cult statues of the gods. The principal deity seems to have been the Mother Goddess, and a number of recovered statuettes show her dressed like a fashionable Cretan lady with flounced skirts, a tightly laced, low-cut bodice, and an elaborate coiffure. It is also noteworthy that the later classical Greeks believed that Zeus and other deities came from Crete.

The Mycenaeans. About 2000 B.C., or shortly thereafter, the first Indo-European Greek tribes, collectively called Achaeans, entered Greece, where they absorbed the earlier settlers and ruled from strongly fortified citadels at Mycenae, Pylos, Thebes, and other sites. By 1600 B.C. the Achaeans—or Mycenaeans, as they are usually called—had evolved their own civilization, based largely on borrowings from the Minoans, and were plying the seas both as pirates and as traders.

Some of the wealth accumulated by the kings of Mycenae—the greatest single hoard of gold, silver, and ivory objects found anywhere before the discovery of Tutankhamen's tomb—was unearthed in 1876 by Heinrich Schliemann, fresh from his even more sensational discoveries at Troy (see p. 41). The royal palace on the acropolis, or citadel, of Mycenae had well-proportioned audience rooms and apartments, fresco-lined walls, floors of painted stucco, and large storerooms. Noteworthy also were the royal "beehive" tombs, constructed of cut stone and covered with earth.

The expansive force of this hitherto unimagined Mycenaean civilization led to the planting of colonies in the eastern Mediterranean (Hittite sources refer to Achaeans in Asia Minor) and to the conquest of Knossos about 1450 B.C. The latter event was made possible by the destruction of the labyrinthian palace at Knossos by fire—the after-effect, it is now conjectured, of a great tidal wave caused by the eruption of the small volcanic island of Thera (Santorini) eighty miles north of Crete. The palace at Knossos was rebuilt by the Mycenaeans (to be finally destroyed about 1380 B.C. by earthquake and fire), and the center of Aegean civilization shifted to the Greek mainland.

This story of Achaean-Cretan relations was unclear until after 1952 when a young English architect, Michael Ventris, startled the scholarly world by deciphering a type of Cretan script known as Linear B, many examples of which had been found by Evans at Knossos and by later archaeologists at Pylos, Mycenae, and Thebes. When Linear B turned out to be an early form of Greek written in syllabic characters, it followed that the rulers of Knossos after 1450 B.C. must have been Achaean Greeks who had adopted the Cretan script to write their own language.

The Linear B texts, which are administrative documents and inventories, greatly add to our knowledge of Mycenaean life. The Mycenaean centers were fortified palaces and administrative centers and not, as in Crete, true cities. The bulk of the population lived in scattered villages where they worked either communal land or land held by nobles or kings. The nobles were under the close control of the kings, whose administrative records were kept daily by a large number of scribes. Prominent in these records are details of the disbursement of grain and wine as wages and the collection of taxes in kind. The most important item of income was olive oil, the major article in the wide-ranging Mycenaean trade which was operated as a royal monopoly. Perhaps it was their role as merchant-monopolists that led the Achaean kings late in the thirteenth century B.C. to launch the famous expedition against Troy in order to eliminate a powerful commercial rival.

Troy, site of the Homeric epics. The city of Troy occupied a strategic position on the Hellespont (the strait from the Aegean to the Black seas now known as the Dardanelles). Thus Troy could command both sea traffic through the straits and land caravans going between Asia and Europe. For many years scholars thought this city existed only in the epic poems of Homer. Heinrich Schliemann (1822-1890), a German romantic dreamer and amateur archaeologist, believed otherwise. As a boy, he had read Homer's *Iliad,* and thereafter he remained firmly convinced that Troy had actually existed. At the age of forty-eight, having amassed a fortune in the California gold rush and in world-wide trade, Schliemann retired from business to put his persistent dream of ancient Troy to the test.

In 1870 Schliemann began excavations at the legendary site of Troy, where he unearthed several cities, built one on top of the other. He discovered a treasure of golden earrings, hairpins, and bracelets in the second city, which led him to believe that this was the city of Homer's epics. Excavations in the 1930's, however, showed that the seventh city, over a thousand years more recent than the second, was the one made famous by Homer.

Neither the view that Troy was the victim of commercial rivalry nor the other widely held theory that it was destroyed by Achaean pirates seeking booty corresponds to Homer's view that the Trojan War was caused by the abduction of the beauteous Helen, queen of Sparta, by the Trojan prince Paris. Led by Agamemnon, king of Mycenae, the

This vase, discovered at Mycenae in 1876 by Heinrich Schliemann, shows both the adventurous and martial nature of the Mycenaeans.

wrathful Achaeans besieged Troy for ten long years. Homer's *Iliad* deals only with a few weeks during the tenth year of the siege.

The fall of Mycenaean civilization. About 1200 B.C., not long after the fall of Troy, a new wave of Indo-Europeans, the Dorian Greeks, materially aided by weapons made of iron instead of bronze, burst upon Greece. First of the Mycenaean strongholds to fall was Pylos, whose Linear B archives contain numerous references to hastily undertaken preparations to repel the invaders. We find orders directing women and children to places of safety; instructions to armorers, "rowers," and food-suppliers; and a report entitled "how the watchers are guarding the coastal regions."[2] The preparations were in vain, however. Pylos was sacked and burned, and the destruction of the other major Mycenaean citadels soon followed. Mycenaean refugees found a haven at Athens and in Ionia on the western coast of Asia Minor.

The next four centuries, the Greek Dark Ages, were marked by the disappearance of the major characteristics of the relatively advanced Mycenaean civilization—political centralization, wide-ranging commerce, sophisticated art forms (including monumental architecture), and writing. Yet while the Dorian invasion was an undoubted catastrophe, it was also vital to the ultimate rise of a unique Hellenic (from *Hellas*, the Greek name for Greece) civilization that was not largely an offshoot of the Near East, as was Aegean civilization.

THE RISE OF HELLENIC CIVILIZATION

The influence of geography. Geographical factors played an important part in shaping the events of Greek history. The numerous mountain ranges which crisscross the peninsula severely hampered internal communications and led to the development of fiercely independent, autonomous political units—the city-states. Furthermore, the Greeks had every incentive to go down to the sea in ships. The numerous islands and indented coastlines of the Greek peninsula and of Asia Minor stimulated seagoing trade, and the rocky soil (less than a fifth of Greece is arable) and limited natural resources encouraged the Greeks to establish colonies abroad.

The Homeric Age. Most of our information about the Greek Dark Ages (c. 1150-750 B.C.) which followed the Dorian invasion is derived from the epics composed during the last century of this period and attributed to the blind Ionian poet Homer. Controversy surrounds the problem of Homer's existence and whether he or several poets composed the *Iliad* and the *Odyssey*. The Homeric epics retain something of the material side of the bygone Mycenaean period; yet in filling in the details of political, economic, and social life, the religious beliefs and practices, and the ideals that gave meaning to life, the poet could only describe what was familiar to him in his own age.

The values that gave meaning to life in the Homeric Age were predominantly heroic values—the strength, skill, and valor of the preeminent warrior. Such was the earliest meaning of *aretē*, "excellence" or "virtue," a key term throughout the course of Greek culture. To obtain *aretē*—defined by one Homeric hero as "to fight ever in the forefront and outvie my peers"—and the imperishable fame that was its reward, men welcomed hardship, struggle, and even death. Honor, like fame, was a measure of *aretē*, and the greatest of human tragedies was the denial of honor due to a great warrior. Homer makes such a denial the theme of the *Iliad*: "The ruinous wrath of Achilles that brought countless ills upon the Achaeans" when Achilles, insulted by Agamemnon, withdraws from battle.

To the Homeric Greeks, the gods were plainly human: Zeus, the king of the gods, was often the undignified victim of the plots of his wife Hera and other deities, and he asserted his authority through threats of violence. Hades, the abode of the dead, was a subterranean land of dust and darkness, and Achilles, as Homer tells us in the *Odyssey*, would have preferred to be a slave on earth than a king in Hades.

Society was clearly aristocratic—only the *aristoi* ("aristocrats") possessed *aretē*—and the common man was reviled and beaten when he dared to question his betters. Yet the common man had certain political rights as a member of the assembly that was summoned whenever a crisis, such as war, required his participation. Two other instruments of government described by Homer were the tribal king and his council. The king was hardly more than a chief among his peers, his fellow nobles, who sat in his council to advise him and to check any attempt he might make to exercise arbitrary power. Economic conditions were those of a simple, self-sufficient agricultural system much like that of the early Middle Ages in western Europe.

C **The city-state: origin and political evolution.** The *polis*, or city-state, the famed Greek political unit consisting of a city and its surrounding plains and valleys, did not exist in the Greek Dark Ages. The nucleus of the *polis* was the elevated, fortified site—the *acropolis* —where people could take refuge from attack. With the revival of commerce in the eighth and seventh centuries B.C., a trading center developed below the acropolis. The two parts combined, forming the *polis*, from which our word *politics* is derived.

The political development of the *polis* was so rich and varied that it is difficult to think of a form of government not experienced— and given a lasting name—by the Greeks. Four major types of government evolved: (1) monarchy limited by an aristocratic council and a popular assembly, as described in the Homeric epics; (2) oligarchy ("rule of the few"), arising when the aristocratic council ousted the king and abolished or restricted the popular assembly; (3) tyranny, imposed by one man who rode to power on the discontent of the lower classes; (4) democracy ("rule of the people"), the outstanding political achievement of the Greeks, which emerged after the tyrant was deposed and the popular assembly revived and made the chief organ of government. After dissatisfaction with democratic government became widespread in the fourth century B.C., many of the city-states returned either to oligarchy or to one-man rule.

D **The Age of Oligarchy.** By the middle of the eighth century B.C., the nobles, who resented the power wielded by the tribal kings, had taken over the government, ushering in the Age of Oligarchy. Ruthlessly exercising their superior power, the nobles acquired a monopoly of the best land, reducing many commoners to virtual serfdom and forcing others to seek a living on rocky, barren soil.

The hard lot of the common man under oligarchy produced the anguished protest of Hesiod's *Works and Days* (c. 700 B.C.). A commoner who had been cheated out of his parcel of land by his evil brother in league with "bribe-swallowing" aristocratic judges, Hesiod was the prophet of a more exalted conception of the gods and a new age of social justice. To establish a just society, Hesiod argued, men must learn to pursue moderation (*sophrosynē*) in all things—apparently the first expression of this famous Greek ideal—and realize that "far-seeing" Zeus and the other gods punish evildoers and reward the righteous. He redefined human excellence, or *aretē*, in a way to make it attainable for the common man. Its essential ingredients were righteousness and work— honest work in competition with one's fellows being a form of strife in moderation. "Gods and men hate him who lives without work," Hesiod insisted. "His nature is like the drones who sit idle and eat the labor of the bees." Furthermore, "work is no shame, but idleness is a shame," and "esteem," "glory," and "riches" follow work.[3]

Hesiod's new ideals of moderation and justice took root slowly, and the poor found relief only by emigrating to new lands overseas. As Plato later noted, the wealthy promoted colonization as a safety valve to ward off a threatened political and economic explosion:

When men who have nothing, and are in want of food, show a disposition to follow their leaders in an attack on the property of the rich—these, who are the natural plague of the state, are sent away by the legislator in a friendly spirit as far as he is able; and this dismissal of them is euphemistically termed a colony.[4]

From 750 to 550 B.C. the Greeks planted colonies throughout much of the Mediterranean world, a development often compared with the expansion of Europe in modern

Examples of Greek painting have totally disappeared except for what has survived through vase-painting. This has become an invaluable source of what everyday life was like in ancient Greece. An affectionate domestic scene is depicted on this water-jug from the fifth century B.C.

times. Settlements sprang up along the northern coast of the Aegean and around the Black Sea. So many Greeks migrated to southern Italy and eastern Sicily that the region became known as *Magna Graecia*, or Great Greece. Colonies were also founded as far west as present-day France—at Massilia, modern Marseilles—and Spain and on parts of the African coast. Unique was Naucratis in Egypt, not a true colony but a trading post whose residents gained extraterritorial rights (their own magistrates and law courts) from the Egyptians.

In time colonization ameliorated Greece's economic and social problems. By 600 B.C. the use of coined money, learned from the Lydians, had created the beginnings of a middle class. The Greek home states gradually became "industrialized" as a result of concentrating upon the production of specialized wares—vases, metal goods, textiles, olive oil, and wine—for export in exchange for foodstuffs and raw materials. But before this economic revolution was completed, the continuing land hunger of the peasants con-

tributed to a political revolution. After 650 B.C. tyrants arose in many Greek states and, supported by the aggrieved peasantry and the rising merchant class, seized the reins of government from the nobility. These tyrants (the word meant simply "master" and did not at first have the unfavorable meaning it now possesses) not only distributed land to the peasants but, by promoting further colonization, trade, and industry, accelerated the rise of a mercantile class and the completion of the Greek economic revolution.

Athens to 500 B.C. Athens and Sparta, the city-states destined to dominate the history of Greece during the classical period (the fifth century and most of the fourth), underwent markedly different developments during the period prior to 500 B.C. While Athens' political, economic, and social evolution was typical of most other Greek states, Sparta's development produced a unique way of life that elicited the wonder and often the admiration of other Greeks.

During the course of the seventh century B.C. at Athens, the council of nobles became supreme. The popular assembly no longer met, and the king was replaced by nine aristocratic magistrates, called archons, chosen annually by the council to exercise the king's civil, military, and religious powers. The nobility acquired the good land on the plain; the peasants either stayed on as sharecroppers, who were often reduced to debt slavery, or took to the hills.

When the Athenian nobles finally realized that their failure to heed the cry for reform would result in the rise of a tyrant, they agreed to the policy of compromise advocated by the liberal aristocrat Solon. In 594 B.C. Solon was made sole archon with broad authority to reconcile the lower classes. Inspired by the new ideals of moderation and justice promoted by Hesiod, Solon instituted middle-of-the-road reforms that have made his name a byword for wise statesmanship.

Solon provided a new start for the lower classes by canceling all debts and forbidding future debt bondage, but he rejected as too radical their demand for the redivision of the land. His long-range solution to the economic problem was to seek full employment by stimulating trade and industry. To achieve this goal, Solon required fathers to teach their sons a trade, granted citizenship to foreign artisans who settled in Athens, and encouraged the intensive production of olive oil for export.

Moderation also characterized Solon's political reforms—the common people were granted important political rights, but not equality. While laws continued to originate in the new aristocratic Council of Four Hundred, they now had to be ratified by the popular assembly, which Solon revived. And since wealth, not birth, became the qualification for membership in the Council and for the archonships, wealthy commoners acquired full political equality. Furthermore, the assembly could now act as a court to hear appeals from the decisions of the archons and to try them for misdeeds in office.

Unfortunately, Solon's moderate reforms satisfied neither party. The poor had received neither land nor political equality, while the nobles thought Solon a radical who had betrayed his class. Deeply discouraged, Solon described what is too often the lot of moderate reformers: "Formerly their eyes sparkled when they saw me; now they coldly scorn me, no longer friends but enemies."[5]

Solon had warned the Athenians to accept his reforms lest "the people in its ignorance comes into the power of a tyrant." He lived to see his prediction fulfilled. In 560 B.C., after a period of civil strife, Pisistratus, a military hero and champion of the commoners, usurped power as tyrant. He solved the economic problem by banishing many nobles, whose lands he distributed among the poor, and by promoting commerce and industry. Together with extensive public works and the patronage of culture—thus starting Athens on the road to cultural leadership in Greece—these reforms gave rise to a popular saying that "Life under Pisistratus was paradise on earth."

Pisistratus was succeeded by his two sons, one of whom was assassinated and the other exiled. When the nobles, aided by a Spartan army, took this opportunity to restore oligarchy, Cleisthenes temporarily seized power in 508 B.C. and put through constitutional reforms that destroyed the remaining power of the nobility. He disregarded the old noble-dominated tribes and created ten new ones, each embracing citizens of all classes from widely scattered districts. The popular assembly acquired the right to initiate legislation, while the new and democratic Council of Five Hundred, selected by lot from the ten tribes, advised the assembly and supervised the administrative actions of the archons. A final reform of Cleisthenes was the peculiar institution of *ostracism*, an annual referendum in which a quorum of six thousand citizens could vote to exile for ten years any individual thought to be a threat to the new Athenian democracy.

Sparta to 500 B.C. In sharp contrast to Athens was the rival city-state Sparta. Sparta had not joined the other Greek cities in trade and colonization but had expanded instead by conquering and enslaving its neighbors. To guard against revolts by the state slaves (helots), who worked the land for their conquerors, Sparta was forced to deviate from the normal course of Greek political development and transform itself into a militaristic totalitarian state. Aristotle called the government of Sparta a "mixed constitution"; for the small minority of ruling Spartans, it was a democracy, but for the great mass of subjected people it was an oligarchy. The government included two kings, a small Council of Elders, and an assembly of all Spartan citizens. True power resided in five overseers, the ephors, who were elected by the assembly and wielded more influence than the dual monarchs.

The state enforced absolute subordination of the individual to its will. Throughout his life every Spartan was first of all a soldier. Sickly infants were left to die on lonely mountaintops; boys were taken from their families when they were seven years old to live under rigorous military discipline for the rest of their lives; girls were trained to become healthy mothers of warrior sons. As their men marched off to war, Spartan women bid them a laconic farewell: "Come back with your shield or on it."

While Sparta developed the finest military machine in Greece, it remained backward culturally and economically. Trade and travel were prohibited because the city fathers feared that alien ideas might disturb the status quo. A self-imposed isolation forbade those cultural contacts without which no balanced civilization can develop. Sparta is a classic example of how intellectual stagnation accompanies rigid social conformity and military regimentation.

To provide additional assurance that its helots remain uncontaminated by democratic ideas, Sparta allied itself with oligarchic parties in other Peloponnesian states and aided them in suppressing their democratic opponents. The resulting Spartan League of oligarchic states, in operation by the end of the sixth century B.C., was shortly to be faced by an Athenian-led union of democratic states (see map, p. 48).

UNITY AND STRIFE IN THE HELLENIC WORLD

The Persian Wars. The leaders of the Greek economic and cultural revival after 750 B.C. were the Ionian Greeks, descendants of the Mycenaeans who had fled to the Aegean coast of Asia Minor and its offshore islands. Influenced by contacts with Phoenician traders (from whom they borrowed the alphabet in the eighth century), neighboring Lydia, and Egypt, the Ionians "first kindled the torch of Hellenism."

We have seen in Chapter 1 that when the Persians conquered Lydia in 547 B.C. they also annexed Ionia, which had been under nominal Lydian rule. Chafing under Persian-appointed tyrants, the Ionian cities revolted in 499 B.C., established democratic regimes, and appealed to the Athenians, who were also Ionians, for aid. Athens sent twenty ships, but to no avail. By 494 B.C. Darius I had crushed the revolt, burning Miletus in revenge.

The battle of Marathon. Darius knew that Ionia was insecure as long as Athens remained free to incite her kinsmen to revolt, and thus in 490 B.C. a Persian force of about twenty thousand men sailed across the Aegean and debarked on the plain of Marathon near Athens. Darius' aim of forcing the Athenians to accept the exiled son of Pisistratus as a pro-Persian tyrant was frustrated when the Athenian army, half the size of the Persian, won an overwhelming victory, killing 6400 of the foe while losing only 192.

The battle of Marathon was one of the most decisive in history. It destroyed the belief in Persian invincibility and demonstrated, in the words of the Greek historian Herodotus, that "free men fight better than slaves." The victory also gave the Athenians the self-confidence that would soon make their city the leading Greek state.

End of the Persian Wars. Ten years later the Greeks were well prepared for a new Persian invasion under Xerxes, Darius' successor, whose objective was the subjection of all of Greece. Athens now had two hundred ships, the largest fleet in Greece, and Sparta had agreed to head a defensive alliance of thirty-one states.

The Persian army—reckoned by Herodotus at 1,700,000 but more likely 150,000 or so—was too huge to be transported by ship. Crossing the swift-flowing, mile-wide Hellespont on two pontoon bridges—a notable feat of engineering—the army marched along the Aegean coast accompanied by a great fleet carrying provisions. The Spartans wanted to abandon all of Greece except the Peloponnesus to the invaders but finally agreed to a holding action at the narrow pass of Thermopylae. Here three hundred Spartans and a few thousand other Greeks held back the Persians for three days, until a Greek traitor led them over a mountain path to the rear of the Greek position. The Spartans fought magnificently until all were slain, together with seven hundred other Greeks. The Spartan dead were immortalized on a monument erected at the pass: "Go tell the Spartans, thou that passeth by, / That here, obedient to their laws, we lie."

The Persians then burned Athens, whose inhabitants had fled, for they placed their faith in "wooden walls"—their fleet. Their faith was not misplaced; in the Bay of Salamis the Greek fleet, largely Athenian, turned the tide of victory with the shout: "On, sons of the Greeks! Set free your country, set your children free, your wives, the temples of your country's gods, your fathers' tombs;

now they are all at stake."[6] With 200 of his 350 ships destroyed and his lines of communication cut, Xerxes had no alternative but to retreat to Asia, although he left a strong force in Greece. The following summer (479 B.C.) the Greek army, with the Spartan contingent in the van, routed the Persian force at Plataea, and Greece was for the time being safe from invasion.

Culmination of Athenian democracy. Following the expulsion of the Persians, the Athenians "felt themselves suddenly to be 'on top of the world,' and from this in a large measure sprang the reckless confidence and boundless energy which now carried them forward to the greatest phase of their history. Athens' heyday lasted less than eighty years, and the number of her adult male citizens scarcely exceeded fifty thousand. Yet this handful of men attempted more and achieved more in a wider variety of fields than any nation great or small has ever attempted or achieved in a similar space of time."[7]

For more than thirty years (461-429 B.C.) during this Golden Age of Greece, the great statesman Pericles guided Athenian policy. In Pericles' time the actual executive power no longer resided in the archonship, which was filled by lot, but in a board of ten elected generals. This board operated much like a modern-day governmental cabinet. The generals urged the popular assembly to adopt specific measures, and the success or failure of their policies determined whether or not they would be reelected at the end of their annual term. Pericles failed of reelection only once, and so great was his influence on the Athenians that, in the words of the contemporary historian Thucydides, "what was in name a democracy was virtually a government by its greatest citizen."[8]

To enable even the poorest citizen to participate in government, Pericles extended payment to jurors (a panel of six thousand citizens chosen annually by lot) and to members of the Council. While his conservative opponents called this political bribery, Pericles insisted that it was essential to the success of democracy:

Our constitution is named a democracy, because it is in the hands not of the few but of the many.

But our laws secure equal justice for all in their private disputes, and our public opinion welcomes and honours talent in every branch of achievement, not as a matter of privilege but on grounds of excellence alone. . . . [Athenians] do not allow absorption in their own various affairs to interfere with their knowledge of the city's. We differ from other states in regarding the man who holds aloof from public life not as "quiet" but as useless; we decide or debate, carefully and in person, all matters of policy, holding, not that words and deeds go ill together, but that acts are foredoomed to failure when undertaken undiscussed.[9]

The majority of the inhabitants of Athens, however, were not recognized as citizens. Women, slaves, and resident aliens were denied citizenship and had no voice in the government. Nor did they have any standing in the law courts. If a woman desired the protection of the law, she had to seek out a citizen to plead for her in court.

Athenian imperialism. The victory over Persia had been made possible by a partial unity of Hellenic arms; but that unity quickly dissolved when Sparta, fearful of helot rebellion at home, recalled its troops and resumed its policy of isolation. Because the Persians still ruled the Ionian cities and another invasion of Greece seemed probable, Athens in 478 B.C. invited the city-states bordering on the Aegean to form a defensive alliance called the Delian League. To maintain a two-hundred-ship navy that would police the seas, each state was assessed ships or money in proportion to its wealth. From the beginning, Athens dominated the League. Since almost all of the 173 member states paid their assessments in money, which Athens was empowered to collect, the Athenians furnished the necessary ships.

By 468 B.C., after the Ionian cities had been liberated and the Persian fleet destroyed, various League members thought it unnecessary to continue the confederacy. In suppressing all attempts to secede, the Athenians were motivated by the fear that the Persian danger still existed and by the need to maintain and protect the large free-trade area so necessary for Greek—and especially Athenian—commerce and industry. The Athenians created an empire because they dared not unmake a confederation. By aiding in

the suppression of local aristocratic factions within its subject states, Athens both eased the task of controlling its empire and emerged as the leader of a union of democratic states.

To many Greeks—above all to the members of the oligarchic Spartan League and the suppressed aristocratic factions within the Athenian empire—Athens was a "tyrant city" and an "enslaver of Greek liberties." Pericles, on the other hand, justified Athenian imperialism on the ground that it brought "freedom" from fear and want to the Greek world:

We secure our friends not by accepting favours but by doing them. . . . We are alone among mankind in doing men benefits, not on calculations of self-interest, but in the fearless confidence of freedom. In a word I claim that our city as a whole is an education to Hellas. . . .[10]

The Peloponnesian War. In 431 B.C. the Peloponnesian War broke out between the Spartan League and the Athenian empire. While commercial rivalry between Athens

and Sparta's ally Corinth was an important factor, the conflict is a classic example of how fear can generate a war unwanted by either side. The historian Thucydides wrote:

The real but unavowed cause I consider to have been the growth of the power of Athens, and the alarm which it inspired in Lacedaemon [Sparta]; this made war inevitable.[11]

Several incidents served to ignite the underlying tension, and Sparta declared war on the "aggressors."

Sparta's hope for victory lay in its army's ability to besiege Athens and lay waste its fields. Pericles, on the other hand, relied on Athen's unrivaled navy to import foodstuffs and to harass its enemies' coasts. Fate took a hand in this game, however. In the second year of the war a plague carried off a third of the Athenian population, including Pericles. His death was a great blow to Athens, for leadership of the government passed to demagogues. In the words of Thucydides:

Pericles, by his rank, ability, and known integrity, was able to exercise an independent control over the masses—to lead them instead of being led by them. . . . With his successors it was different. More on a level with one another, and each grasping at supremacy, they ended by committing even the conduct of state affairs to the whims of the multitude. This, as might have been expected in a great imperial state, produced a host of blunders. . . .[12]

Eight more years of indecisive warfare ended in 421 B.C. with a compromise peace. During the succeeding period Athenian imperialism manifested itself in its worst form through the actions of Pericles' unworthy successors. In 416 B.C. an expedition embarked for Melos, a neutral Aegean island, to force it to join the Athenian empire. Thucydides reported the specious logic the Athenians employed to justify their naked imperialism on this occasion:

We believe that Heaven, and we know that men, by a natural law, always rule where they are stronger. We did not make that law nor were we the first to act on it; we found it existing, and it will exist forever, after we are gone; and we know that you and anyone else as strong as we are would do as we do.[13]

The Athenians put all Melians of military age to death and sold the women and children into slavery.

The war was resumed in 415 B.C. with an Athenian expedition against Syracuse that was destined to end in disaster. Acting on the invitation of states that feared Syracusan expansion, the Athenians hoped to add Sicily to their empire and so become powerful enough "to rule the whole of the Greek world."[14] But ill luck and incompetent leadership resulted in two Athenian fleets and a large army being destroyed by the Syracusans, supported by Sparta. The war dragged on until 404 B.C., when Athens capitulated after its last fleet was destroyed by a Spartan fleet built with money received from Persia in exchange for possession of the Greek cities in Ionia. At home, Athens had been weakened by the plots of oligarchic elements to whom Sparta now turned over the government. The once great city was also stripped of its possessions and demilitarized.

Aftermath of the war. Anarchy and depression were the political and economic legacies of the Peloponnesian War. Having ended the "tyranny" of Athens over Greece, the Spartans substituted their own form of rule which made the Athenian empire seem mild in comparison. Everywhere democracies were replaced by oligarchies supported by Spartan troops. The bloody excesses of these oligarchs soon led to democratic revolutions at Athens and elsewhere. As one of their generals admitted, the Spartans did not know how to govern free men. Incessant warfare filled the early fourth century as a bewildering series of shifting alliances, usually financed by Persia which wanted to keep Greece disunited and weak, sought to keep any state from predominating.

Political disintegration in turn contributed to the economic and social ills that plagued Greece during the fourth century B.C. Commerce and industry languished, and the unemployed who did not go abroad as soldiers of fortune supported demagogues and their radical schemes for the redivision of wealth. The wealthy, for their part, became increasingly reactionary and uncompromising. Even most intellectuals—including Plato and Aristotle—lost faith in democracy and joined with the wealthy in looking for "a champion powerful in action" who would bring order and security to Greece. They found him, finally, in the person of the king of Macedonia.

The Macedonian unification of Greece. To the north of Greece lay Macedonia, inhabited by hardy peasants and nobles who were related to the Greeks but were culturally inferior to them. Macedonia became a centralized, powerful state under the able and crafty Philip II (359-336 B.C.), who created the most formidable army yet known by joining the crack Macedonian cavalry of nobles with the infantry phalanx used by the Greeks. In his youth, Philip had been a hostage at Thebes, where he acquired an appreciation of Greek culture, an understanding of Greek political weakness, and a desire to win for Macedonia a place in the Hellenic world.

After unifying Macedonia—including a string of Greek colonies that had been established along its coast during the earlier centuries of Macedonia's weakness—Philip turned to the Greek city-states, whose wars afforded him the opportunity first to intervene, then to dominate. In vain did Demosthenes, the great Athenian orator and democratic leader, warn that "democracies and dictators cannot exist together" and urge the Athenians and other Greeks to stop Philip before it was too late. Belatedly, Athens and Thebes acted, but their combined forces were shattered at Chaeronea in 338 B.C. Philip then forced the Greeks into a federal league in which each state, while retaining self-government, swore to "make war upon him who violates the general peace" and to furnish Philip with men and supplies for a campaign against Persia. On the eve of setting out for Asia Minor, Philip was assassinated by a noble with a personal grudge, leaving the war against Persia as a legacy for his brilliant son Alexander.

Incapable of finding a solution to the anarchy that tore their world to shreds, the Greeks ended as political failures and at the mercy of a great outside power, first Macedonia and then Rome. They retained their cultural leadership, however, and the culture of the new Hellenistic Age and its successor, the world of Rome, was to be largely Greek.

IV THE GREEK GENIUS

The Greek character. The Greeks were the first to formulate many of the western world's fundamental concepts in philosophy, science, and art. How was it that a relative handful of people could bequeath such a legacy to civilization? The definitive answer may always elude the historian, but a good part of the explanation lies in environmental and social factors.

Unlike the Near Eastern monarchies, the *polis* was not governed by a "divine" ruler, nor were the thoughts and activities of its citizens limited by powerful priesthoods. Many Greeks, and most notably the Athenians, were fond of good talk and relished debate and argument. The nature of the universe and of man, a person's duty to the state and to his fellow citizens, law and freedom, the purpose of art and poetry, the standards of a good life—these were a few of the numerous problems they discussed brilliantly and with pertinence for our times as much as theirs.

The Greeks felt a deep-seated need to discover an order in the flux of human life and in nature. This quest for order produced exceptional results in science, art, and philosophy. Beginning with Hesiod (see p. 43), the Greeks stressed the virtue of *sophrosynē* (moderation, self-control) as the key to happiness and right living. Its opposite was *hubris*, meaning pride, arrogance, and unbridled ambition. The result of human excesses and lying at the root of personal misfortune and social injustice, *hubris* invariably provoked *nemesis*, or retribution. According to the Greeks, an inexorable law would cause the downfall or disgrace of anyone guilty of *hubris*. The Athenian dramatists often employed this theme in their tragedies, and Herodotus attributed the Persian defeat by the Greeks to Xerxes' overweening pride, for "Zeus tolerates pride in none but himself."[15]

The Greeks exhibited human frailties and failings—at times they were irrational, vindictive, and cruel. But at their best they were guided by the ideals that permeate their intellectual and artistic legacy. The philosopher Protagoras is credited with the statement, "Man is the measure of all things"—a saying which sums up the outstanding feature of Greek thought and art. In short, the Greeks were humanists.

Greek religion. Early Greek religion abounded in gods and goddesses who personified physical elements. Thus Demeter was the earth and giver of grain, Apollo, the sun and giver of light, and Poseidon, who dwelled in the sea, was the ruler of the waters. Other deities had special functions, such as Aphrodite, the goddess of love, Dionysus, the god of fertility and wine, and Athena, the goddess of wisdom and the guardian of Athens. The Greeks of Homeric times believed in manlike deities, capable of malice, favoritism, and jealousy, and differing from ordinary men only in their immortality and their possession of supernatural powers. Zeus, the king of sky, earth, and men, supposedly ruled the world from Mount Olympus with the aid of lesser deities.

By the time of Hesiod, as we have seen (p. 43), a religious reformation had begun which changed the vengeful and capricious gods of Homer into austere arbiters of justice who rewarded the good and punished the wicked. Demeter and Dionysus gained prominence as the central figures of "mystery" cults whose initiates (*mystae*) were promised an afterlife of bliss in Elysium—formerly the abode of heroes only. And from the famous oracle at Delphi the voice of Zeus' son Apollo urged all Greeks to follow the ideal of moderation: "Nothing in excess" and "Know thyself" (meaning "Know your limitations").

Early Greek philosophy and science. Philosophy arose from the insatiable Greek curiosity about nature. As we noted in Chapter 1, the Mesopotamians were skilled observers of astronomical phenomena such as eclipses, which they attributed to magical and supernatural causes. The early Greek philosophers, beginning with Thales of Miletus (c. 636-546 B.C.), changed the course of human knowledge by insisting that the phenomena of the universe can be explained by natural causes. This rejection of the supernatural and the application of reason to discern universal principles in nature has been called the "Greek miracle." It led men to the threshold of today's world of science and technology.

Called "the father of philosophy," Thales speculated on the nature of the basic substance from which all else in the universe is composed. He concluded that it was water, which exists in different states or forms and is indispensable to the maintenance and growth of organisms. Thales' successors in Ionia proposed elements other than water as the primal substance in the universe. One called it the "boundless," apparently a general concept for "matter"; another proposed "air," out of which all things come by a process of "rarefying and condensing"; a third asserted that fire was the "most mobile, most transformable, most active, most life-giving" element. This search for a material substance as the first principle or cause of

all things culminated two centuries after Thales in the atomic theory of Democritus (c. 460-370 B.C.). To Democritus, reality was the mechanical motion of indivisible atoms, which differed in shape, size, position, and arrangement but not in quality. Moving about continuously, atoms combined to create objects. Scientists have used this theory to the present day, although we are now aware that the atom is neither indivisible nor indestructible.

While these and other early Greek philosophers were proposing some form of matter as the basic element in nature, Pythagoras of Samos (c. 582-500 B.C.) countered with the profoundly significant notion that the "nature of things" was something nonmaterial—numbers. By experimenting with a vibrating cord, Pythagoras discovered that musical harmony is based on arithmetical proportions, and he intuitively concluded that the universe was constructed of numbers and their relationships. His mathematical interpretation of nature greatly influenced Plato, and modern mathematical physicists have continued along the path he was the first to trod.

An important consequence of early Greek philosophical speculation was the undermining of conventional beliefs and traditions. In religion, for example, Xenophanes ridiculed the traditional view of the gods: "If oxen and lions had hands, . . . they would make portraits and statues of their gods in their own image." The eroding of traditional views caused Greek inquiry to turn away from nature to man—to a consideration of human values and institutions. During the last half of the fifth century B.C., the Sophists —"men of wisdom" who taught public speaking and prepared men for public life— submitted all conventional beliefs to the test of rational criticism. Concluding that truth was relative, they denied the existence of universal standards to guide human actions.

Socrates, a martyr to truth. The outstanding opponent of the Sophists was the Athenian Socrates (c. 470-399 B.C.), a snub-nosed, plain man but a fascinating conversationalist. Like the Sophists, Socrates turned from cosmic to human affairs; in the words of the Roman statesman Cicero, Socrates was "the first to call philosophy down from the heavens and to set her in the cities of men, bringing her into their homes and compelling her to ask questions about life and morality and things good and evil."[16] But unlike the Sophists, Socrates believed that by asking salient questions and by subjecting the answers to logical analysis, agreement could be reached about ethical standards and rules of conduct. And so he would question passers-by in his function of midwife assisting in the birth of correct ideas (to use his own figure of speech). Taking as his motto the famous inscription on the temple of Apollo at Delphi, "Know thyself," he insisted that "the unexamined life is not worth living." To Socrates, human excellence or virtue (*aretē*) is knowledge, and evil and error are the result of ignorance.

In time Socrates' quest for truth led to his undoing, for the Athenians, unnerved by the Peloponnesian War, arrested him on the charge of impiety and corrupting youth. By a slim majority a jury of citizens condemned Socrates to die, a fate he accepted without rancor and with a last request:

When my sons are grown up, I would ask you, my friends, to punish them, and I would have you trouble them, as I have troubled you, if they seem to care about riches, or anything, more than about virtue; or if they pretend to be something when they are really nothing, then reprove them, as I have reproved you, for not caring about that for which they ought to care, and thinking that they are something when they are really nothing. And if you do this, both I and my sons will have received justice at your hands.

The hour of departure has arrived, and we go our ways—I to die, and you to live. Which is better God only knows.[17]

Plato and his Theory of Ideas. After Socrates' death, philosophical leadership passed to his most famous disciple, Plato (427-347 B.C.). Like Socrates, Plato believed that truth exists, but only in the realm of thought, the spiritual world of Ideas or Forms. Such universals as Beauty, Good, and Justice exist apart from the material world, and the beauty, good, and justice that we encounter in the world of the senses are only imperfect re-

flections of eternal and changeless Ideas. Man's task is to come to know the True Reality—the eternal Ideas—behind these imperfect reflections. Only the soul, and the "soul's pilot," reason, can accomplish this, for the human soul is spiritual and immortal, and in its prenatal state it existed "beyond the heavens" where "true Being dwells."[18]

Disillusioned with democracy, Plato expounded his concept of an ideal state in the *Republic*, the first systematic treatise on political science. The state's basic function, founded on the Idea of Justice, was the satisfaction of the common good. Plato described a kind of "spiritualized Sparta" in which the state regulated every aspect of life, including thought. The family and private property, for example, were abolished on the grounds that both bred selfishness, and marriage was controlled in order to produce strong, healthy children. Individuals belonged to one of three classes and found happiness only through their contribution to the community: workers by producing the necessities of life, warriors by guarding the state, and philosophers by ruling in the best interests of all the people.

Plato founded the Academy in Athens, the famous school which existed from about 388 B.C. until 529 A.D. Here he taught and encouraged his students, whom he expected to become the intellectual elite who would go forth and reform society.

Aristotle, the encyclopedic philosopher. Plato's greatest pupil was Aristotle (384-322 B.C.), who set up his own school, the Lyceum, at Athens. Reacting against the other-worldly tendencies of Plato's thought, Aristotle insisted that Ideas have no separate existence apart from the material world; knowledge of universal Ideas is the result of the painstaking collection and organization of particular facts. Aristotle's Lyceum, accordingly, became a center for the analysis of data from many branches of learning.

To us today, Aristotle's most significant treatises are the *Ethics* and the *Politics*. They deal with what he called the "philosophy of human affairs," whose object is the acquisition and maintenance of human happiness. Two kinds of virtue (*aretē*), intellectual and moral, which produce two types of happiness, are described in the *Ethics.* Intellectual virtue is the product of reason, and only such men as philosophers and scientists ever attain it. Much more important for the good of society is moral virtue—for example justice and temperance—which is the product less of reason than of habit and thus can be acquired by all. In this connection Aristotle introduced his Doctrine of the Mean as a guide for good conduct. He considered all virtues to be means between extremes; thus courage, for example, is the mean between cowardice and rashness.

In the *Politics* Aristotle viewed the state as necessary "for the sake of the good life," because its laws and educational system provide the most effective training needed for the attainment of moral virtue and hence happiness. Thus to Aristotle the viewpoint that the state stands in opposition to the individual would be unthinkable.

Aristotle's writings on formal logic, collectively known as the *Organon* ("Instrument"), describe two ways in which new truths can be acquired. The first, induction, moves from particular facts to general truths. Deductive logic, on the other hand, moves from the general to the particular. To facilitate deductive reasoning from general truths, Aristotle devised the syllogism, a logical structure requiring a trio of propositions. The first two propositions (the major and minor premises) must be plainly valid and logically related so that the third proposition, the conclusion, inevitably follows. For example, (1) all Greeks are human; (2) Socrates is a Greek; (3) therefore Socrates is human.

There has probably never been another man whose interests were so widespread or whose knowledge was so encyclopedic as Aristotle's. He investigated such diverse fields as biology, mathematics, astronomy, physics, psychology, rhetoric, logic, politics, ethics, and metaphysics. His accomplishments won him renown, and he was ultimately requested to tutor the young prince of Macedonia, who became his most famous pupil—Alexander the Great.

Medicine. Preconceived and false ideas about the human body blocked the development of medical science until 420 B.C., when Hippocrates, the "father of medicine," founded a school in which he emphasized the value of observation and the careful interpretation of symptoms. The members of this school were firmly convinced that disease resulted from natural, not supernatural, causes. Writing of epilepsy, considered at the time a "sacred" or supernaturally inspired malady, one Hippocratic writer observed:

It seems to me that this disease is no more divine than any other. It has a natural cause just as other diseases have. Men think it supernatural because they do not understand it. But if they called everything supernatural which they do not understand, why, there would be no end of such things![19]

Despite their empirical approach, the Hippocratic school adopted the theory that the body contained four liquids or humors—blood, phlegm, black bile, and yellow bile—whose proper balance was the basis of health. This doctrine was to impede medical progress until modern times.

The writing of history. History for the Hellenic Greeks was not an account of legendary events and mythical figures, nor were the forces of history attributable simply to the whims of the gods. The Greeks viewed history as a humanistic study by which historians sought to learn about the actions and characters of men. As such, history could be subjected to rational standards and critical judgment.

If history be defined as an "honest attempt first to find out what happened, then to explain why it happened," Herodotus of Halicarnassus (484?-425? B.C.) deserves to be called the "father of history." In his highly entertaining history of the Persian Wars he discerned the clash of two distinct civilizations, the Hellenic and the Near Eastern. His portrayal of both the Greeks and the Persians was eminently impartial, but his fondness for a good story often led him to include tall tales in his work.

The first truly scientific historian was Thucydides (460-400? B.C.), who wrote a notably objective chronicle of the Peloponnesian War. Although he was a contemporary of the events and a loyal Athenian, a reader can scarcely detect whether he favored

Athens or Sparta. Thucydides' belief that his history would become "an everlasting possession" for those who desire a clear picture of what has happened and, mankind being as it is, is likely to be repeated in the future, is based on his remarkable ability to analyze and explain individual behavior. (Two examples—his definition of statesmanship and his account of Athenians justifying their empire on grounds of power alone—have been quoted on page 49.) In describing the character and purpose of his work, Thucydides probably had Herodotus in mind:

The absence of romance in my history will, I fear, detract somewhat from its interest; but I shall be content if it is judged useful by those inquirers who desire an exact knowledge of the past as an aid to the interpretation of the future, which in the course of human things must resemble if it does not reflect it. My history has been composed to be an everlasting possession, not the show-piece of an hour.[20]

Hellenic poetry and drama. Greek literary periods can be classified according to dominant poetic forms which reflected particular stages of cultural evolution in Greece. First came the time of great epics, followed by periods in which lyric poetry and drama flourished.

Sometime during the eighth century B.C. in Ionia, the *Iliad* and the *Odyssey*, the two great epics attributed to Homer, were set down in their present form. The *Iliad*, describing the clash of arms between the Greeks and the Trojans "on the ringing plains of windy Troy," glorifies heroic valor and physical prowess against a background of divine intervention in human affairs. The *Odyssey*, relating the adventure-filled wanderings of Odysseus on his return to Greece after Troy's fall, places less stress on divine intervention and more on the cool resourcefulness of the hero in escaping from danger and in regaining his kingdom. These stirring epics have provided inspiration and source material for generations of poets in the western world.

As Greek society became more sophisticated, a new type of poetry, written to be sung to the accompaniment of the lyre, arose among the Ionian Greeks. Its authors sang not of legendary events but of present delights and sorrows. This new note, personal and passionate, can be seen in the following examples, in which the contrast between the new values of what is called the Greek Renaissance and those of Homer's heroic age is sharply clear. Unlike Homer's heroes, Archilochus of Paros (seventh century B.C.) unashamedly throws away his shield and runs from the battlefield:

My trusty shield adorns some Thracian foe;
I left it in a bush—not as I would!
But I have saved my life; so let it go.
Soon I will get another just as good.[21]

And in contrast to Homer's view of an unromantic, purely physical attraction between Paris and Helen, Sappho of Lesbos (sixth century B.C.), the first and one of the greatest of all woman poets, saw Helen as the helpless victim of romantic love:

She, who the beauty of mankind
Excelled, fair Helen, all for love
The noblest husband left behind;
Afar, to Troy she sailed away,
Her child, her parents, clean forgot;
The Cyprian [Aphrodite] led her far astray
Out of the way, resisting not.[22]

Drama, which developed from the religious rites of the Dionysian mystery cult, filled a civic-religious function in Greek society. In Athens, by the fifth century B.C., two distinct forms—tragedy and comedy—had evolved. Borrowing the old familiar legends of gods and heroes for their plots, the tragedians reinterpreted them in the light of the changing spirit of the times.

By depicting man in conflict with destiny, Aeschylus (525-456 B.C.) expressed the new concern for achieving harmony and avoiding the excesses which led to suffering. In his trilogy, the *Oresteia*, for example, he concerned himself with *hubris*, as applied to the murder of the hero Agamemnon by his false queen, and then proceeded to work out its ramifications—murder piled on murder until men through suffering learn to substitute the moral law of Zeus for the primitive law of the blood feud. Like the prophets of Israel, Aeschylus taught that while "sin brings misery," misery in turn leads to wisdom:

The Persian invasion made Athens a heap of ruins, but the withdrawal of the invaders left the Athenians free to reconstruct the Acropolis into a treasury of temples and statues. In the Parthenon, which housed Phidias' huge gold and ivory statue of Athena, great care was taken to design a structurally and visually perfect building. The tops of the Doric columns lean toward the center of each colonnade, the steps curve upward at the center, and the columns are more widely spaced in the middle of each row than at the ends—all these refinements create an illusion of perfect regularity which would be lacking if the parts were actually perfectly proportioned. The Parthenon was originally brightly painted, and painted sculpture adorned the gables and parts of the frieze, while another sculptured and painted frieze ran around the walls inside the colonnade. A reconstruction of the entire Acropolis appears at the right.

Zeus the Guide, who made man turn
Thought-ward, Zeus, who did ordain
Man by Suffering shall Learn.
So the heart of him, again
Aching with remembered pain,
Bleeds and sleepeth not, until
Wisdom comes against his will.[23]

A generation later, Sophocles (c. 496-406 B.C.) largely abandoned the problem of how to justify the ways of god to man and concentrated upon character. To Sophocles, a certain amount of suffering was inevitable in life. No man was perfect; there was a tragic flaw in the character of the best of men which caused them to make mistakes. Sophocles dwelled mainly on the way in which men react to suffering. Like his contemporary, the sculptor Phidias, Sophocles viewed man as an ideal creature—"Many are the wonders of the world, and none so wonderful as Man"—and he displayed man's greatness by depicting him experiencing great tragedy without whimpering.

Euripides (c. 480-406 B.C.), the last of the great Athenian tragedians, reflects the rationalism and critical spirit of the late fifth century. To him, the life of man was pathetic, the ways of the gods ridiculous. His recurrent theme was "Since life began, hath there in God's eye stood one happy man?" and for this he has been called "the poet of the world's grief." Euripides has also been called the first psychologist, for he looked deep into the human soul and described what he saw with intense realism. Far more than Aeschylus or even Sophocles, Euripides strikes home to modern man.

Comedies were bawdy and spirited. There were no libel laws in Athens, and Aristophanes (c. 445-385 B.C.), the famous comic-dramatist and a conservative in outlook, brilliantly satirized Athenian democracy as a mob led by demagogues, the Sophists (among whom he included Socrates) as subversive, and Euripides as an underminer of civic spirit and traditional faith.

The Greeks as builders. In the sixth century B.C. architecture flourished in Ionia and Greece with the construction of large temples of stone, the form having developed from earlier wooden structures which had been influenced by the surviving remains of Mycenaean palaces. Architecture reached its zenith in fifth-century Athens, then at the height of its power and wealth.

The Parthenon, the Erechtheum, and the other temples on the Athenian Acropolis exhibit the highly developed features that make Greek structure so pleasing to the eye. All relationships, such as column spacing and height and the curvature of floor and roof lines, were calculated and executed with remarkable precision to achieve a perfect balance, both structurally and visually. The three orders, or styles, usually identified by the characteristics of the columns, were the Doric, which was used in the Parthenon; the Ionic, seen in the Erechtheum; and the later and more ornate Corinthian.

Located where all men could see and enjoy them, the Greek temples afford an interesting comparison with those of Egypt. Whereas the Egyptian temple was enclosed and mysterious, the Greek temple was open, with a colonnade porch and an inside room containing a statue of the god. Sacrifice and ritual took place outside the temple, where the altar was placed.

Other types of buildings, notably the theaters, stadiums, and gymnasiums, also express the Greek spirit and way of life. In the open-air theaters the circular shape of the spectators' sections and the plan of the orchestra section set a style which has survived in principle to the present day.

Sculpture and pottery. Greek sculpture of the archaic period (c. 625-480 B.C.), although crude in its representation of human anatomy, has the freshness and vigor of youth. Influenced partly by Egyptian models, the statues of nude youths and draped maidens usually stand stiffly with clenched fists and with one foot thrust awkwardly forward (see photo, p. 57). The fixed smile and formalized treatment of hair and drapery also reveal how the sculptor is struggling to master the technique of his art.

The achievement of mastery of technique by 480 B.C. ushered in the classical period of fifth-century Greek sculpture whose "classic" principles of harmony and proportion have shaped the course of western art. Sculpture from this period displays both the end of technical immaturity and the beginning of

Between the sixth and fourth centuries B.C. Greek art developed from the rigid stylization, reminiscent of Egyptian art, of the *kouros* ("boy") figure (left) to the more complex, naturalistic, yet idealized Hermes by Praxiteles, shown holding the young Dionysus.

idealization of the human form which reached its culmination in the dignity and poise of Phidias' figures in the continuous frieze and pediments of the Parthenon. Carved with restraint and "calm exaltation," the frieze depicts the citizens of Athens participating in the Panathenaic procession in honor of Athena which took place every four years.

The more relaxed character of fourth-century B.C. Hellenic sculpture contrasts with the grandeur and dignity of fifth-century art. Charm, grace, and individuality characterize the work of Praxiteles, the most famous sculptor of the century. These qualities can be seen in his supple statues of the god Hermes holding the young Dionysus and of Aphrodite stepping into her bath.

The making of pottery was a highly developed art in Greece. The earliest vases were decorated with abstract geometric designs, then came paintings of scenes from mythology and daily life. From the surviving Greek pottery, we can get an inkling of what Greek painting, now lost, was like (see illustration, p. 44).

THE HELLENISTIC AGE

Alexander the Great. When Philip of Macedonia was assassinated in 336 B.C., his crown fell to his gifted twenty-year-old son, Alexander, who crushed rebellion in Greece and proved himself a resolute, ambitious king from the beginning of his reign.

Like his father, the youthful Alexander was alive to the glories of Hellenic culture, having as a youth been tutored by Aristotle. Reveling in the heroic deeds of the *Iliad*, Alexander may have seen himself as a second Achilles waging war against barbarians when he planned to revenge the Persian attacks on Greece. Two years after Philip's death, he set out with an army of 35,000 soldiers recruited from Macedonia and the Greek League that his father had organized (see p. 50). In quick succession he subdued Asia Minor, Syria, Palestine, and Egypt. Then the young leader marched into Mesopotamia and there, in 331 B.C., defeated the last powerful army of Darius III, the Persian monarch. Alexander was now master of Persia,

This mosaic from Pompeii is a copy of a fourth-century B.C. Greek painting depicting the defeat of Darius (at the right) by Alexander (at the left) at the Battle of Issus. While this mosaic can only be an imperfect realization of the original painting, the intricacy and vitality of the composition attest to the skill of the Greeks at painting, an art at which they themselves believed they excelled.

the proud empire that had controlled the Near East. He ventured as far east as the rich river valleys of India (see Chapter 4), where his weary soldiers forced him to turn back. In 323 B.C., while he was planning the circumnavigation of Arabia, Alexander died at the age of thirty-two, the victim of malaria. With the Greeks now masters of the ancient Near East, a new and distinctly cosmopolitan period in their history and culture began— the Hellenistic Age.

Alexander's legacy to political thought was the vision of a unified world and the brotherhood of mankind. Various of his military and administrative policies sought to unify the lands he conquered and to promote what he himself called "concord and partnership in the empire" between orientals and westerners. He blended Persians with Greeks and Macedonians in his army and administration; he founded numerous cities—seventy, according to tradition—in the East and settled many of his followers in them; and he married two oriental princesses and encouraged his officers and men to take foreign wives. Finally, for personal as well as political reasons, Alexander ordered the Greek city-states to accord him "divine honors."

The division of Alexander's empire. For several decades following Alexander's sudden death, his generals vied for the spoils of empire. Three major Hellenistic kingdoms emerged and maintained a precarious balance of power until the Roman conquests of the second and first centuries B.C.: Egypt, ruled by Ptolemy and his successors; Asia, comprising most of the remaining provinces of the Persian empire and held together with great difficulty by the dynasty founded by Seleucus; and Macedonia and Greece, ruled by the descendants of Antigonus the One-Eyed.

While the Antigonids in Macedonia followed the model of Alexander's father Philip in posing as national kings chosen by the army, the Ptolemies ruled Egypt as divine pharaohs, and some of the Seleucids became deified "saviors" and "benefactors." Ptolemaic and Seleucid administrations were centralized in bureaucracies staffed by Greeks, an arrangement which created a vast gulf between a ruler and his native subjects.

Plagued by native revolts, dynastic troubles, and civil war, the Hellenistic kingdoms soon began to crumble. Macedonia lost effective control of Greece when Athens asserted its independence and most of the other Greek states formed two federal leagues, the Aetolian in the north and the Achaean in the Peloponnesus, which successfully resisted Macedonian domination. The eastern reaches of Alexander's empire—India, Bactria, and Parthia—gradually drifted out of the Seleucid sphere of influence. Pergamum, in northwestern Asia Minor, renounced its allegiance to the Seleucids and became an independent kingdom famous for its artists and scholars. In the year 200 B.C. the new power of Rome entered upon the scene, and by 30 B.C. Rome had annexed the last remaining Hellenistic state, Egypt.

Hellenistic economy and society. The Hellenistic Age was a time of economic expansion and social change. In the wake of Alexander's conquests, thousands of Greeks flocked eastward to begin a new era of Greek colonization. An economic union between East and West permitted the free flow of trade, and prosperity was stimulated further when Alexander put into circulation huge hoards of Persian gold and silver and introduced a uniform coinage. The result was a much larger and more affluent middle class than had hitherto existed.

By the third century B.C. the center of trade had shifted from Greece to the Near East. Largest of the Hellenistic cities, and much larger than any cities in Greece itself, were Antioch in northern Syria and Alexandria in Egypt. The riches of India, Persia, Arabia, and the Fertile Crescent were brought by sea and land to these Mediterranean ports.

Alexandria outdistanced all other Hellenistic cities as a commercial center. Its merchants supplied the ancient world with wheat, linen, paper, glass, and jewelry. Boasting a population of about a million, the city had a double harbor in which a great lighthouse, judged one of the wonders of the ancient world, rose to a height estimated at 370 feet. Its busy streets were filled with a

mixture of peoples—Greeks, Macedonians, Jews, and Egyptians. As in all other Hellenistic cities in the Near East, the privileged Greeks and Macedonians were at the top of the social scale and the mass of natives at the bottom. Harsh social and economic differences separated the rich from the poor, and the exploited workers frequently went on strike.

Hellenistic philosophy. Developments in philosophy reflected the changed environment of the Hellenistic Age. With the growing loss of political freedom and the prevalence of internal disorder, philosophers concerned themselves less with the reform of society and more with the attainment of happiness for the individual. This emphasis on peace of mind in an insecure world led to the rise of four principal schools of thought.

The Skeptics and Cynics reflected most clearly the doubts and misgivings of the times. The Skeptics achieved imperturbability by denying the possibility of finding

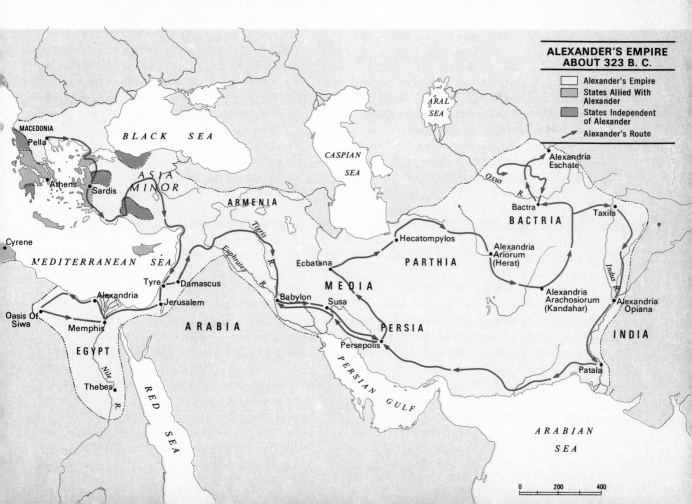

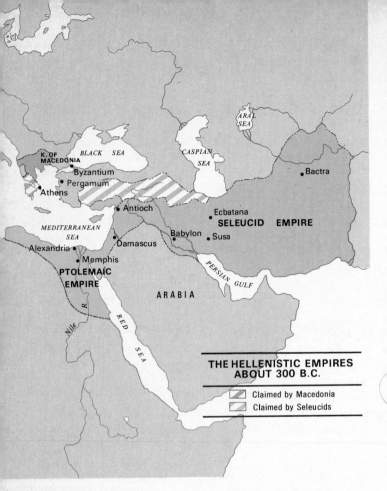

THE HELLENISTIC EMPIRES
ABOUT 300 B.C.

☐ Claimed by Macedonia
◨ Claimed by Seleucids

fall apart at death. Thus, beyond death there is no existence and nothing to fear. Epicurus maintained that the finest pleasures were intellectual, but many of his followers later distorted his teachings so that Epicureanism appeared to be concerned only with the gratification of sensual desires.

The Stoics, followers of Zeno (c. 336-c. 264 B.C.), a Semite from Cyprus, argued in contrast to Epicureanism that the universe is controlled by some power—variously called Reason, World Soul, Fortune, and God—which determines everything that happens. Fortified by this knowledge, the Stoic wise man conforms his will to the World Will and "stoically" accepts whatever part fortune allots him in the drama of life. With its insistence on duty and on the brotherhood of man in One Great City, Stoicism was particularly attractive to the Romans.

Science and mathematics. The Greek concern for rational, disinterested inquiry reached a zenith in the Hellenistic period, particularly at Alexandria where the Ptolemies subsidized a great research institute, the Museum, and a library of more than half a million books. Emphasizing specialization and experimentation, and enriched by Near Eastern astronomy and mathematics, Greek science in the third century B.C. achieved results unmatched until early modern times.

The expansion of geographical knowledge incited scientists to make accurate maps and to estimate the size of the earth, which had been identified as a globe through observation of its shadow in a lunar eclipse. Eratosthenes, the outstanding geographer of the century, drew parallels of latitude and longitude on his map of the inhabited world and calculated the circumference of the globe with only 1 percent error by measuring the difference in the angles of the noonday sun at Aswan and Alexandria.

In astronomy, Aristarchus put forward the radical theory that the earth rotates on its axis and moves in an orbit around the sun. Most of his contemporaries adhered, however, to the prevailing geocentric theory, which stated that the earth was stationary and the sun revolved around it. This view not only was supported by the powerful authority of Aristotle, but it also seemed to ex-

truth. The wise man, they argued, will suspend his judgment and not dogmatize; he has learned that sensory experience, man's only source of knowledge, is deceptive. The Cynics carried negativism further; their ideal was nonattachment to the values and conventions of society. Cynic philosophers wandered from city to city, haranguing the public to pursue a concept of virtue that is echoed by modern hippies: "Look at me, I am without house or city, property or slave. I sleep on the ground. I have no wife, no children. What do I lack? Am I not without distress or fear? Am I not free?"[24]

More practical and popular were Epicureanism and Stoicism. The Athenian Epicurus (342-270 B.C.) taught that the wise man could achieve happiness simply by freeing his body from pain and his mind from fear—particularly the fear of death. To reach this goal, men must avoid bodily excesses, including those of pleasure, and accept the scientific teaching of Democritus that both body and soul are composed of atoms which plain all the known facts of celestial motion. This was particularly true after Hipparchus in the next century added the new idea of epicycles—each planet revolves in its own small orbit while moving around the earth. Aristarchus' heliocentric theory was not revived until the sixteenth century A.D.

Mathematics also made great advances. Euclid systematized the theorems of plane and solid geometry, and Archimedes of Syracuse, who had studied at Alexandria, calculated the value of π, invented a terminology for expressing numbers up to any magnitude, and laid the foundations of calculus. Archimedes also discovered specific gravity by noticing the water he displaced in his bath. And despite his disdain for making practical use of his knowledge, he invented the compound pulley, the windlass, and the endless screw for raising water.

The Hellenistic Greeks extended the advances in medicine made earlier by Hippocrates and his school. By dissecting bodies of dead criminals, they were able to trace the outlines of the nervous system, to understand the principle of the circulation of the blood, and to ascertain that the brain, not the heart, was the true center of consciousness.

Architecture, sculpture, and literature. The host of new cities that sprang up in Hellenistic times served as a tremendous impetus to architecture. The new cities benefited from town planning: the streets were laid out according to a rectangular plan. The great public edifices were elaborate and highly ornamented; this was an age which preferred the more ornate Corinthian to the simple Doric and Ionic orders.

Hellenistic sculptors continued and intensified the realistic, dramatic, and emotional approach that began to appear in Hellenic sculpture during the fourth century B.C. Supported by rulers and other rich patrons in Alexandria, Antioch, Rhodes, and Pergamum, they displayed their technical virtuosity by depicting violent scenes, writhing forms, and dramatic poses—all with a realism which could make stone simulate flesh. Little evidence remained of the balance and restraint of classical Greek sculpture. The famous Laocoön group (see illustration) and the frieze from the altar of Zeus at

Pergamum, with their twisted poses, contorted faces, and swollen muscles, remind one of the Baroque sculpture of seventeenth-century Europe which replaced the classical art of the Italian Renaissance.

The quality of literature from the Hellenistic Age was generally inferior to that of the Hellenic Age, although the historian Polybius, who lived in the second century B.C. and described Rome's eastward expansion, ranks second only to Thucydides as an exponent of scientific history. Scholarship flourished, and we are indebted for the preservation of much of Greek classical literature to the subsidized scholars at the Alexandrine library—"fatted fowls in a coup," as a Skeptic philosopher called them. Yet, paradoxically, these sophisticated scholars produced superb pastoral poetry extolling the simple life of shepherds. The best was written by the scholar Theocritus at Alexandria in the third

The trend toward realism and increased complexity in sculpture begun in the fourth century B.C. culminated in the art of the Hellenistic period, which produced such intricate sculptures as the contorted Laocoön group.

century B.C. The following short example, written by a contemporary, well illustrates its character and appeal:

Would that my father had taught me the craft of a
    keeper of sheep,
For so in the shade of the elm-tree, or under the
    rocks on the steep,
Piping on reeds I had sat, and had lulled my
    sorrow to sleep.[25]

The Hellenistic contribution: the East. The greatest contribution of the Hellenistic Age was the diffusion of Greek culture throughout the ancient East and the newly rising Roman West. In the East, the cities that Alexander and his successors built were the agents for spreading Hellenistic culture from the Aegean Sea to India. Literate Asians learned Greek to facilitate trade, become members of the ruling circles of the Hellenistic states, and read Hellenic classics.

For a time the Seleucid empire provided the peace and economic stability necessary to ensure the partial Hellenization of a vast area. But with an insufficient number of Greeks to colonize so large an area as the Near East, the Greek city-states remained only islands in an Asian ocean. As time elapsed, this ocean encroached more and more upon the Hellenized areas.

The gradual weakening of the loosely knit Seleucid empire eventually resulted in the creation of independent kingdoms on the edge of the Hellenistic world. Bactria achieved independence in the middle of the third century B.C. Its Greek rulers, descendants of Alexander's veterans, were remarkably successful in enlisting native cooperation; and their prosperous state, which controlled the caravan route to India, lasted for over a century (see also p. 100).

Also in the middle of the third century, a nomad chieftain founded the kingdom of Parthia, situated between the Seleucid and Bactrian kingdoms. Claiming to be the heirs of the Persians, the Parthians expanded until by 130 B.C. they had wrested Babylonia from the Seleucids. Although Parthia was essentially a native Iranian state, its inhabitants absorbed some Hellenistic culture.

The Hellenistic contribution: the West. In the history of western civilization there is little of greater significance than Rome's absorption of Greek civilization and its transferance of that heritage to modern Europe. The stage on which this story began was the cosmopolitan Hellenistic Age, which "longed and strove for *Homonoia*, Concord, between man and man . . . [and] proclaimed a conception of the world as One Great City."[26] The process by which the Roman West was Hellenized will be described in the following chapter.

SUMMARY

The two most important centers of the Aegean maritime civilization were Knossos on the island of Crete and Mycenae on the Greek mainland. Aegean civilization reached its zenith first in Crete (2000-1450 B.C.), where the island dwellers fashioned a sophisticated urban culture, synthesizing cultural elements from the Near East. After 1450 B.C. the center of Aegean culture shifted to Mycenae on the Greek mainland. The Mycenaean phase lasted until the warlike Dorians invaded the Peloponnesus and forced the Mycenaeans to flee eastward to Ionia in Asia Minor. There, by the eighth century B.C., fiercely independent city-states evolved a distinctly Hellenic culture which was to come to fruition in the Hellenic Age (the eighth to fourth centuries B.C.).

Achilles, the hero of Homer's *Iliad*, would have lived forever had not a Trojan arrow pierced him fatally in the heel, the only vulnerable part of his body. Like Achilles, the Greek city-states of the Hellenic period had one fatal defect—in their case, an inability to submerge individual differences for the sake of common survival. The city-states failed to adapt themselves to the political realities of the fifth century B.C., which had resulted from the colonial expansion and economic revolution of previous centuries and which linked the destinies of Athens and other Greek cities with those of a larger Mediterranean community. Instead of developing the Delian League into a true Greek federation, Athens placed its own interests first and converted the League into an Athenian maritime empire, thus plunging the Greeks into the disastrous Peloponnesian War.

Fortunately for the Greeks, Philip II, the Macedonian ruler who conquered the city-states sixty years after the Peloponnesian War, sincerely admired Hellenic culture—an admiration which was shared by his son, Alexander the Great. It was the ambitious and gallant Alexander who conquered the Near East and laid the boundaries for three large empires carved from his conquered lands. The Hellenistic Age, which began after Alexander's death, was a period of economic expansion, cosmopolitanism, striking intellectual and artistic achievements, and the wide diffusion of Greek culture.

What is it about the Greeks that leads us to speak so admiringly? The secret lies in the originality with which they met every situation. Free of Near Eastern superstitions and traditions, they examined each problem in a spirit of critical inquiry and sought for an explanation that accorded with the natural world rather than supernatural law. Thus their view of life, something entirely new in the world's history, tended to be secular rather than religious, rational instead of credulous. This clear-cut, straightforward approach to life may have been the most lasting contribution of the Greeks to human history.

SUGGESTIONS FOR READING

P. MacKendrick, **The Greek Stones Speak*** (Mentor) is an account of the great archaeological discoveries in the Aegean area. See also R. W. Hutchinson, **Prehistoric Crete*** (Peter Smith); C. W. Blegen, **Troy and the Trojans** (Praeger); E. Vermeule, **Greece in the Bronze Age*** (Univ. of Chicago, 1972); and John Chadwick, **The Decipherment of Linear B*** (Vintage). M. Renault, **The King Must Die*** (Bantam, 1974) is an absorbing novel set in Mycenaean times.

A. R. Burn, **The Pelican History of Greece*** (Penguin); M. I. Finley, **The Ancient Greeks*** (Compass); and C. E. Robinson, **Hellas: A Short History of Ancient Greece*** (Beacon) are valuable analyses. Other good surveys include M. Bowra, **The Greek Experience*** (Mentor); H. Kitto, **The Greeks** (Peter Smith); and H. Lloyd-Jones, **The Greek World*** (Penguin). J. B. Bury, **A History of Greece to the Death of Alexander the Great,** 4th ed. (St. Martin's, 1975) is a standard detailed history. D. Kagan, ed., **Problems in Ancient History,** Vol. I, **Ancient Near East and Greece** (Macmillan, 1975) is a good survey of the formative centuries of Greek civilization. On Greek colonization see J. Boardman, **The Greeks Overseas*** (Peter Smith). On the transition from oligarchy to democracy see A. Andrewes, **The Greek Tyrants*** (Torchbooks); and W. G. Forrest, **The Emergence of Greek Democracy, 800-400 B.C.*** (McGraw-Hill).

Valuable special studies on politics, economics, and society include A. R. Burn, **Persia and the Greeks: The Defense of the West, 546-478 B.C.** (Funk & Wagnalls, 1968); H. Mitchell, **Sparta*** (Cambridge); A. E. Zimmern, **The Greek Commonwealth: Politics and Economics in Fifth-Century Athens*** (Galaxy); G. Glotz, **Ancient Greece at Work*** (Norton); V. Ehrenberg, **The Greek State*** (Norton); T. B. Webster, **Everyday Life in Classical Athens*** (Capricorn); Frank Frost, **Greek Society*** (Heath, 1971); and A. H. M. Jones, **Athenian Democracy** (Barnes & Noble). Plutarch, **The Rise and Fall of Athens*** (Penguin, 1975) contains nine biographies from the *Parallel Lives*.

Edith Hamilton, **The Greek Way*** (Avon) is a popular appreciation of the beauty and values of Hellenic literature. A. Lesky, **A History of Greek Literature*** (Crowell) is a detailed treatment, as is J. B. Bury, **Ancient Greek Historians*** (Dover).

C. Seltman, **The Twelve Olympians*** (Apollo) recounts myths about the Olympian gods and goddesses. See also M. Grant, **Myths of the Greeks and Romans*** (Mentor); W. K. Guthrie, **The Greeks and Their Gods*** (Beacon); and A. W. Adkins, **Moral Values and Political Behavior in Ancient Greece*** (Norton, 1973).

Good introductions to Greek philosophy and science include W. K. Guthrie, **Greek Philosophers from Thales to Aristotle*** (Torchbooks); F. M. Cornford, **Before and After Socrates*** (Cambridge); and G. E. R. Lloyd, **Early Greek Science: Thales to Aristotle*** (Norton, 1974) and **Greek Science After Aristotle*** (Norton, 1973). G. Majno, **The Healing Hand: Man and Wound in the Ancient World** (Harvard, 1974) is a major work describing ancient man's attempts to conquer pain and disease.

Recommended for fine arts students are J. Pollitt, **Art and Experience in Classical Greece*** (Cambridge, 1972); J. Boardman, **Greek Art*** (Praeger, 1973); Martin Robertson, **A History of Greek Art,** 2 vols. (Cambridge, 1976); and A. W. Lawrence, **Greek Architecture,*** rev. ed. (Penguin, 1975).

W. W. Tarn, **Hellenistic Civilization*** 3rd ed. (Meridian) is a detailed survey. Brief and well illustrated is J. Ferguson, **The Heritage of Hellenism: The Greek World From 323 to 31 B.C.*** (Harcourt Brace Jovanovich, 1973). On the career and motives of Alexander the Great see Robin Lane-Fox, **Alexander the Great** (Dial, 1974), a serious history and biography; W. W. Tarn, **Alexander the Great*** (Beacon); and A. R. Burn, **Alexander the Great and the Hellenistic World*** (Collier).

*Indicates a less expensive paperbound edition.

CHAPTER 3

The Roman World:
509 B.C. to 180 A.D.

The Grandeur That Was Rome

INTRODUCTION. As the Athenian saw the symbol of his city-state's democracy and culture in the rock-jutting Acropolis, so the Roman viewed the Forum as the symbol of imperial grandeur. Temples were to be found there, but in contrast to the Acropolis, the Forum was dominated by secular buildings —basilicas, the nearby Colosseum, and the great palaces of the emperors rising on the neighboring Palatine Hill. While the Acropolis was crowned with statues to Athena, the Forum gloried in triumphal arches and columns commemorating military conquests. Rome was the capital of a world-state, extending from the Rhine to the Euphrates, and its citizens were proud of their imperial mission.

Although the buildings in the Forum appear fundamentally Greek in style, they are more monumental and sumptuous. Here, then, are two clues to an understanding of the Romans: they borrowed profusely from the Greeks, and they modified what they took. *Adoption* and *adaptation* are key words in the study of Roman civilization.

Rome was the great intermediary—the bridge over which passed the rich contributions of the Fertile Crescent, Egypt, and especially Greece to form the basis of modern western civilization. The Romans replaced the anarchy of the Hellenistic Age with law and order and embraced the intellectual and artistic legacy of the conquered Greeks. As Rome's empire expanded, this legacy was spread westward throughout Europe.

Yet Rome was more than an intermediary, for it made many important and original contributions to our western culture. Throughout a history which led from a simple farming community in the plain of Latium to a strong state which became the master of the Mediterranean world as well as Gaul, Britain, and part of Germany, the Romans met one challenge after another with practicality and efficiency. In the shadows of its marching legions went engineers and architects, so that today, scattered throughout the lands that once were part of the Roman world, the remains of roads, walls, baths, basilicas, amphitheaters, and aqueducts offer convincing evidence of the Romans' technical prowess. Most lasting and far reaching of all were their administrative institutions—the legal codes and governmental systems they developed and modified to meet changing needs—which have served as the framework of western political life for many centuries.

ROME TO 509 B.C.

Early settlers of Italy. The Greeks and Romans were offshoots of a common Indo-European stock, and settlement of the Greek and Italian peninsulas followed broadly parallel stages. Between 2000 and 1000 B.C., when Indo-European peoples invaded the Aegean world, a western wing of this nomadic migration filtered into the Italian peninsula, then inhabited by indigenous Neolithic tribes. The first invaders, skilled in the use of copper and bronze, settled in the Po valley. Another wave of Indo-Europeans, equipped with iron weapons and tools, followed; and in time the newer and older settlers intermingled and spread throughout the peninsula. One group, the Latins, settled in the lower valley of the Tiber River, a region that became known as the plain of Latium.

For ages history had bypassed the western Mediterranean, but it was henceforth to become an increasingly significant area. During the ninth century B.C. the Etruscans, a non-Indo-European people who probably came from Asia Minor, brought the first city-state civilization to Italy. Expanding from the west coast north to the Po valley and south to the Bay of Naples, the Etruscans organized the backward Italic peoples into a loose confederation of Etruscan-dominated city-states. After 750 B.C. Greek colonists migrated to southern Italy and Sicily, where they served as a protective buffer against powerful and prosperous Carthage, a Phoenician colony established in North Africa about 800 B.C. Yet the future was not to belong to these various invaders, but to an insignificant village on the Tiber River, then in the shadow of Etruscan expansion. This was Rome, destined to be ruler of the ancient world.

Rome's origins. According to ancient legend, Rome was founded in 753 B.C. by the twin brothers Romulus and Remus, who were saved from death in their infancy by a she-wolf who sheltered and suckled them. Virgil's *Aeneid* preserves a different tradition that the founder of the Roman race was Aeneas, a Trojan who after the fall of Troy founded a settlement in Latium. Turning from fable to fact, modern scholars believe that in the eighth century B.C. the inhabitants of some small Latin settlements on hills in the Tiber valley united and established a common meeting place, the Forum, around which the city of Rome grew. Situated at a convenient place for fording the river and protected by the hills and marshes from invaders, Rome was strategically located. Nevertheless, the expanding Etruscans conquered Rome about 600 B.C., and under their tutelage Rome first became an important city-state.

Some aspects of Etruscan culture were borrowed from the Greek colonies in southern Italy, and much of this, including the alphabet, was passed on to the conquered

Romans. (Etruscan writing can be read phonetically but not understood.) From their Etruscan overlords, the Romans acquired some of their gods and goddesses and the practice of prophesying by examining animal entrails. From the conquerors, too, the conquered learned the art of building—especially the arch. Even the name *Roma* appears to be an Etruscan word.

The Roman monarchy. Rome's political growth followed a line of development similar to that of the Greek city-states: limited monarchy of the sort described by Homer, oligarchy, democracy, and, finally, the permanent dictatorship of the Roman emperors. We shall see that in moving from oligarchy to democracy, the Romans, unlike the Greeks, succeeded in avoiding the intermediate stage of tyranny.

According to tradition, early Rome was ruled by kings elected by the people. After the Etruscan conquest, this elective system continued, although the last three of Rome's seven kings were Etruscan. The king's executive power, both civil and military, was

called the *imperium*, which was symbolized by an eagle-headed scepter and an ax bound in a bundle of rods (*fasces*). The *fasces* symbol is found on the United States dime, and in the 1930's it provided both the symbol and the name for Mussolini's political creed of fascism.

Although the *imperium* was conferred by a popular assembly made up of all arms-bearing citizens, the king turned for advice to a council of nobles called the Senate. Each senator had lifelong tenure, and the members of this group and their families constituted the patrician class. The other class of Romans, the plebeians, or commoners, included small farmers, artisans, and many clients, or dependents, of patrician landowners. In return for a livelihood, the clients gave their patrician patrons political support in the assembly.

EARLY REPUBLIC, 509-133 B.C.: DOMESTIC AFFAIRS

Establishment of the Republic. In 509 B.C., according to tradition, the patricians expelled the last Etruscan king, claiming that he had acted despotically, and established what they called a republic (*res publica*, "commonwealth"), in which they held the reins of power. The *imperium* was transferred to two new magistrates, called consuls. Elected annually from the patrician class, the consuls invariably exercised their power in its interest. In the event of war or serious domestic emergency, a dictator could be substituted for the two consuls, but he was given absolute power for six months only.

Struggle for equal rights. For more than two centuries following the establishment of the Republic, the plebeians struggled for political and social equality. Outright civil war was averted by the willingness, however reluctant and delayed, of the patricians to compromise. This largely explains why it was unnecessary for the plebeians to resort to tyrants to help them gain their goals, as had happened in the Greek city-states. Much of the plebeians' success in this struggle was

Cheerful artwork frequently adorned Etruscan tombs. In this painting the youth at the right is playing a double flute, an instrument the music-loving Etruscans particularly enjoyed.

due to their having been granted the right to organize themselves as a corporate body capable of collective action. (Rome's constant wars gave the plebeians, who were indispensable in filling the ranks of Rome's conscript army, great bargaining power.) This concession, granted by the Senate early in the fifth century after the plebeians threatened to leave Rome and found a city elsewhere, established a sort of state within a state known as the *Concilium Plebis,* which was presided over by plebeian leaders called tribunes. The tribunes had the right to stop unjust or oppressive acts of the patrician consuls with the word *veto* ("I forbid").

The next major concession was in the field of law. Because the consuls often interpreted Rome's unwritten customary law to suit patrician interests, the plebeians demanded that it be written down and made available for all to see. As a result, about 450 B.C. the law was inscribed on twelve tablets of bronze and set up publicly in the Forum. The Law of the Twelve Tables was the first landmark in the long history of Roman law, and Cicero tells us that Roman schoolchildren were required to memorize it.

The plebeians in time acquired other fundamental rights and safeguards: they secured the right to appeal a death sentence imposed by a consul and to be retried before the popular assembly; the tribunes gained a veto power over any legislation or executive act that threatened the rights of the plebeians; and marriage between patricians and plebeians, prohibited by the Law of the Twelve Tables, was legalized. Important also was the abolition of the enslavement of citizens for debt.

Little by little the plebeian class acquired more power in the functioning of the government. In 367 B.C. one consulship was reserved for the plebeians, and before the end of the century plebeians were eligible to hold other important magistracies which the patricians had in the meantime created. Among these magistracies, whose powers originally had been held by the consuls, were the praetor (in charge of the law courts), quaestor (treasurer), and censor (supervisor of public morals and the letting of state contracts). The right to hold high political offices proved to be a stepping stone to the Senate, and some plebeians succeeded in gaining entry to that august body.

The long struggle for equality ended in 287 B.C. when the *Concilium Plebis* was recognized as a constitutional body, henceforth known as the Tribal Assembly, with the right to pass laws that were binding on all citizens, patricians as well as plebeians. The plebeians demanded this right because of the undemocratic organization and procedure of the older popular assemblies, which the patricians had been able to control. The Roman Republic was now technically a democracy, although in actual practice a senatorial aristocracy of patricians and rich plebeians continued to control the state. Having gained political and social equality, the plebeians were willing to allow the more experienced Senate to run the government during the remainder of this period of almost constant warfare down to 133 B.C.

After 287 B.C. conflict in Roman society gradually assumed a new form. Heretofore, the issue had been primarily social and political between hereditary classes. When equality was achieved, many plebeians were able to profit from new opportunities and amass prestige and wealth in the state's expanding economy. As a result, wealth instead of aristocratic descent was most important, and the old distinction between patrician and plebeian became much less fundamental than a new conflict between rich and poor which arose after 133 B.C.

The early Roman citizen. The basic unit of early Roman society was the family. The father's power was absolute, and strict discipline was imposed to instill in children those virtues to which the Romans attached particular importance—loyalty, courage, self-control, and respect for laws and ancestral customs. The Romans of the early Republic were stern, hard-working, and practical. Man's relationship to the universe and the possibilities of immortal life did not concern them unduly, and religious practices were confined to placating the spirits (*numina*) of the family and the state. Under Etruscan influence the major spirits were personified. Thus the sky-spirit Jupiter became god of the universe; Mars, spirit of vegetation, became god of war; and Janus, whose temple doors remained open when the army was away at war, was originally the spirit of the city gate.

EARLY REPUBLIC, 509-133 B.C.: FOREIGN AFFAIRS

Roman conquest of Italy. The growth of Rome from a small city-state to the dominant power in the Mediterranean world in less than four hundred years (509-133 B.C.) is a remarkable success story. By 270 B.C. the first phase of Roman expansion was over. Ringed about by hostile peoples—Etruscans in the north, predatory hill tribes in central Italy, and Greeks in the south—Rome had subdued them all after long, agonizing effort and found itself master of all Italy south of the Po valley. Roman expansion was not deliberately planned; rather, it was the result of dealing with unsettled conditions, first in Italy and then abroad, which were thought to threaten Rome's security. Rome always claimed that its wars were defensive.

Rome's position was favored by geography. While the Italian peninsula has a great mountainous backbone, the Apennines, running down most of its length, the country is not so rugged as Greece. Consequently the mountains did not constitute a barrier to political unification. Also, the Alps in the north kept all but the most intrepid barbarian tribes from entering the Italian peninsula. In addition, the Latins occupied a central position on the peninsula, which made it difficult for their enemies to unite against them successfully.

Soon after ousting their Etruscan overlords in 509 B.C., Rome and the Latin League, composed of Latin peoples in the vicinity of Rome, entered into a defensive alliance against the Etruscans. This new combination was so successful that by the beginning of the fourth century B.C. it had become the chief power in central Italy. But the members of the Latin League grew alarmed at Rome's increasing strength, and war broke out between the former allies. With the victory of

Rome in 338 B.C., the League was dissolved, and the Latin cities were forced to sign individual treaties with Rome. Thus the same year which saw the rise of Macedonia over Greece (see p. 50) also saw the rise of a new power in Italy.

Border clashes with aggressive highland Samnite tribes led to three fiercely fought Samnite wars and the extension of Rome's frontiers to the Greek colonies in southern Italy by 290 B.C. Fearing Roman conquest, the Greeks prepared for war and called in the Hellenistic Greek king, Pyrrhus of Epirus, who dreamed of becoming a second Alexander the Great. Pyrrhus' war elephants, unknown in Italy, twice routed the Romans, but at so heavy a cost that such a triumph is still called a "Pyrrhic victory." When a third battle failed to induce the Romans to make peace, Pyrrhus is reported to have remarked, "The discipline of these barbarians is not barbarous," and returned to his homeland. By 270 B.C. the Roman army had subdued the Greek city-states in southern Italy.

Treatment of conquered peoples. Instead of slaughtering or enslaving their defeated foes, the Romans treated them fairly, in time creating a strong loyalty to Rome throughout the peninsula. Roman citizenship was a prized possession and was not extended to all peoples on the peninsula until the first century B.C. Most defeated states were required to sign a treaty of alliance with Rome which bound them to adhere to Rome's foreign policy and to supply troops for the Roman army. No tribute was required, and each allied state retained local self-government. Rome did, however, annex about one fifth of the conquered lands, on which nearly thirty Roman colonies were established by 250 B.C.

The First Punic War. After 270 B.C. only Carthage remained as Rome's rival in the West. Much more wealthy and populous than Rome, with a magnificent navy that controlled the western Mediterranean and with a domain that included the northern coast of Africa, Sardinia, western Sicily, and parts of Spain and Corsica, Carthage seemed more than a match for Rome. But Carthage was governed by a commercial aristocracy which hired mercenaries to do the fighting. In the long run, the lack of a loyal body of free

Rhine R.

Danube

A L P S

Rhone

Drava

VENETIA

Sava

TRANSPADANE GAUL

_R._

_Po_ _R._

•Parma

LIGURIA

CISPADANE GAUL

_R._

ADRIATIC

•Genoa

A P E N N I N E

Rubicon R.

SEA

Pisa•

Arno R.

•Florentia

U M B R I A

M O U N T A I N S

E T R U R I A

Tiber R.

•Spoletium

C O R S I C A

S A M N I U M

A P U L I A

Rome•

Ostia•

L A T I U M

C A M P A N I A

MT. VESUVIUS

•Brundisium

Pompeii•

•Tarentum

S A R D I N I A

LUCANIA

T Y R R H E N I A N   S E A

B R U T T I U M

M E D I T E R R A N E A N

•Messina

S I C I L Y

MT. ETNA

S E A

•Syracuse

•Carthage

A F R I C A

ROMAN ITALY BEFORE AUGUSTUS

0   50   100

citizens and allies, such as Rome had, proved to be Carthage's fatal weakness.

The First Punic War (from *punicus*, Latin for "Phoenician") broke out in 264 B.C. when Rome sought to oust a Carthaginian force that had occupied Messina on the northeastern tip of Sicily just across from Roman Italy. According to Polybius, a Hellenistic Greek historian, the Romans "felt it was absolutely necessary not to let Messina fall, or allow the Carthaginians to secure what would be like a bridge to enable them to cross into Italy."[1] Rome lost 200,000 men in disastrous naval engagements before Carthage sued for peace in 241 B.C. Sicily, Sardinia, and Corsica were annexed as the first provinces of Rome's overseas empire, governed and taxed by Roman proconsuls.

The contest with Hannibal. Thwarted by this defeat, Carthage concentrated upon enlarging its empire in Spain. Rome's determination to restrict the Carthaginian sphere of influence led to the greatest and most difficult war in Roman history. While both powers jockeyed for position, a young Carthaginian general, Hannibal, precipitated the Second Punic War by attacking Saguntum, a Spanish town claimed by Rome as an ally. Rome declared war, and Hannibal, seizing the initiative, in 218 B.C. led an army of about 40,000 men, 9000 cavalry troops, and a detachment of African elephants across the Alps into Italy. Although the crossing had cost him nearly half of his men and almost all of his elephants, Hannibal defeated the Romans three times within three years.

Hannibal's forces never matched those of the Romans in numbers. At Cannae, for example, where Hannibal won his greatest victory, some 70,000 Romans were wiped out by barely 50,000 Carthaginians. On the whole Rome's allies remained loyal—a testimony to Rome's generous and statesmanlike treatment of its Italian subjects—and because the Romans controlled the seas, Hannibal received little aid from Carthage. Thus Hannibal was unable to inflict a mortal blow against the Romans.

The Romans finally found a general, Scipio, who was Hannibal's match in military strategy and who was bold enough to invade Africa. Forced to return home after fifteen years spent on Italian soil, Hannibal clashed with Scipio's legions at Zama, where the Carthaginians suffered a complete defeat (see map, p. 71). The power of Carthage was broken forever by a harsh treaty imposed in 201 B.C. Carthage was forced to pay a huge indemnity, disarm its forces, and turn Spain over to the Romans. Hannibal sought asylum in the kingdom of the Seleucids where he stirred up anti-Roman sentiment.

Roman intervention in the East. The defeat of Carthage left Rome free to turn eastward and settle a score with Philip V of Macedonia, who, fearing Roman expansion, had allied himself with Hannibal during the darkest days of the war. Now, in 200 B.C., Rome was ready to act, following an appeal from Pergamum and Rhodes for aid in protecting the smaller Hellenistic states from Philip, who was advancing in the Aegean, and the Seleucid emperor, who was moving into Asia Minor. The heavy Macedonian phalanxes were no match for the mobile Roman legions, and in 197 B.C. Philip was soundly defeated and his dreams of empire were ended when Rome deprived him of his warships and military bases in Greece. The Romans then proclaimed the independence of Greece and were eulogized by the grateful Greeks:

There was one people in the world which would fight for others' liberties at its own cost, to its own peril, and with its own toil, not limiting its guaranties of freedom to its neighbours, to men of the immediate vicinity, or to countries that lay close at hand, but ready to cross the sea that there might be no unjust empire anywhere and that everywhere justice, right, and law might prevail.[2]

A few years later Rome declared war on the Seleucid emperor who had moved into Greece, urged on by Hannibal and a few greedy Greek states that resented Rome's refusal to dismember Macedonia. The Romans forced him to vacate Greece and Asia Minor, pay a huge indemnity, and give up his warships and war elephants. The Seleucids were checked again in 168 B.C. when a Roman ultimatum halted their invasion of Egypt, which became a Roman protectorate, and a year later Rome supported the Jews in their successful revolt against the Seleucids (see p. 122).

Roman Territories
Allies Of Rome By Treaty

Most of the East was now a Roman protectorate, the result of a policy in which Roman self-interest was mingled with idealism. But Roman idealism turned sour when anti-Romanism became widespread in Greece, particularly among the radical masses who resented Rome's support of conservative governments and the status quo in general. (The Romans, for example, helped crush a socialist revolution in Sparta.) The new policy was revealed in 146 B.C. when, after many Greeks had supported an attempted Macedonian revival, Rome destroyed Corinth as an object lesson, supported oligarchic factions in all Greek states, and placed Greece under the watchful eye of the governor of Macedonia, which was made a Roman province.

Destruction of Carthage. In the West, meanwhile, Rome's hardening policy led to suspicion of Carthage's reviving prosperity and to a demand by extremists for war—*Carthago delenda est* ("Carthage must be destroyed"). Treacherously provoking the Third Punic War, the Romans besieged Carthage, which resisted heroically for three years, destroyed the city in 146 B.C.—the same year of Corinth's destruction—and annexed the territory as a province.

Rome, supreme in the ancient world. In 133 B.C. the king of Pergamum, dying without heir, bequeathed his kingdom to Rome. Apparently he feared that the discontented masses would revolt after his death unless Rome, with its reputation for maintaining law and order in the interest of the propertied classes, took over. Rome accepted the bequest and then spent the next three years suppressing a proletarian revolution in its first Asian province.

With provinces on three continents—Europe, Africa, and Asia (see map above)—the once obscure Roman Republic was now supreme in the ancient world. But the next century, during which Rome's frontiers reached the Euphrates and the Rhine, would witness the failure of the Republic to solve the problems that were the by-products of the acquisition of an empire.

LATE REPUBLIC, 133-30 B.C.

Effects of Roman expansion. The political history of Rome thus far consists of two dominant themes: the gradual liberalization of the government and the expansion of Roman dominion over the Mediterranean world. Largely as a result of this expansion, important social and economic problems faced Rome by roughly the midpoint of the second century B.C.

One of the most pressing problems was the disappearance of the small landowner, whose energy and spirit had made Rome great. Burdened by frequent military service, his farm buildings destroyed by Hannibal, and unable to compete with the cheap grain imported from the new Roman province of Sicily, the small farmer sold out and moved to Rome. Here he joined the unemployed, discontented proletariat, so called because their only contribution was *proles*, "children."

On the other hand, improved farming methods learned from Greeks and Carthaginians encouraged rich aristocrats to buy more and more land and, abandoning the cultivation of grain, introduce large-scale scientific production of olive oil and wine, or of sheep and cattle. This trend was especially profitable because an abundance of cheap slaves from the conquered areas was available to work on the estates. These large slave plantations, called *latifundia*, were now common in Italy, while small farms were the exception.

The land problem was further complicated by the government's earlier practice of leasing part of the territory acquired in the conquest of the Italian peninsula to anyone willing to pay a percentage of the crop or animals raised on it. Only the patricians or wealthy plebeians could afford to lease large tracts of this public land, and in time they treated it as if it were their own property. As early as the fourth century B.C. plebeian protests had led to an attempt to limit the holdings of a single individual to 320 acres of public land, but the law devised for that purpose was never enforced.

Corruption in the government was another mark of the growing degeneracy of the Roman Republic. Provincial officials seized opportunities for lucrative graft, and a new class of Roman businessmen scrambled selfishly for the profitable state contracts to supply the armies, collect taxes in the provinces, and lease mines and forests. Although in theory the government was a democracy, in practice it remained a senatorial oligarchy, as we have seen (p. 67). The tribunes, guardians of the people's rights, had become mere yes-men of the Senate.

Thus by the middle of the second century B.C., the government was in the hands of the wealthy, self-seeking Senate, which was unable to cope with the problems of governing a world-state. Ordinary citizens were for the most part impoverished and landless; and Rome swarmed with fortune hunters, imported slaves, unemployed farmers, and discontented war veterans. The poverty of the many, coupled with the opulence of the few, hastened the decay of the old Roman traits of discipline, simplicity, and respect for authority.

The next century (133-30 B.C.) saw Rome convulsed by civil war, even while engaged in occasional foreign wars. The Senate was noticeably inefficient in carrying on foreign conflicts, but its most serious weakness was its inability to solve the economic and social problems following in the wake of Rome's conquests. This led to the establishment of a dictatorship and the end of the Republic.

Reform movement of the Gracchi. An awareness of Rome's profound social and economic problems led to the reform program of an idealistic young aristocrat named Tiberius Gracchus. Supported by a few liberal Senators, Tiberius was elected tribune for the year 133 B.C. at the age of twenty-nine. His reforming zeal was the product of the newly imported liberal learning of Greece and an awareness that the old Roman character and way of life was fast slipping away. He sought to arrest Roman decline by restoring the backbone of the old Roman society—the small landowner.

Tiberius proposed to the Tribal Assembly that the act limiting the holding of public land to 320 acres per person be reenacted.

Much of the public land would in the future be held by the present occupants and their descendants as private property, but the surplus was to be confiscated and allotted to landless Roman citizens. In his address to the assembly Tiberius noted that

it is with lying lips that their commanders exhort the soldiers in their battles to defend sepulchres and shrines from the enemy; . . . they fight and die to support others in wealth and luxury, and though they are styled masters of the world, they have not a single clod of earth that is their own.[3]

Although the Tribal Assembly adopted Tiberius' proposal by a wide majority, the Senate induced one of the other tribunes to veto the measure. On the ground that a tribune who opposed the will of the people thereby forfeited his office, Tiberius took a fateful—and, the Senate claimed, unconstitutional—step by having the assembly depose the tribune in question. The agrarian bill was then passed.

To ensure the implementation of his agrarian reform, Tiberius again violated custom by standing for reelection after completing his one-year term. On the pretext that he sought to make himself king, partisans of the Senate murdered Tiberius and three hundred of his followers. The Republic's failure at this point to solve its problems without bloodshed stands in striking contrast to its previous development by peaceful means.

Tiberius' work was taken up by his younger brother, Gaius Gracchus, who was elected tribune for 123 B.C. In addition to the reallocation of public land, Gaius proposed establishing Roman colonies in southern Italy and on the site of Carthage. To protect the poor against speculation in the grain market (especially in times of famine), Gaius committed the government to the purchase and storage of wheat and to its subsequent distribution to the urban masses at about half the former market price. Unfortunately, what Gaius intended as a relief measure later became a dole, whereby free food was distributed—all too often for the advancement of astute politicians—to the entire proletariat.

Another of Gaius' proposals would have granted citizenship to Rome's Italian allies, who were now being mistreated by Roman officials. This proposal cost Gaius the support of the Roman proletariat, which did not wish to share the privileges of citizenship or endanger its control of the Tribal Assembly. Consequently, in 121 B.C. Gaius failed to be reelected to a third term and the Senate was emboldened to resort to force again. Martial law was declared and three thousand of Gaius' followers were arrested and executed, a fate Gaius avoided by committing suicide.

The Senate had shown that it had no intention of initiating needed domestic reforms, or of allowing others to do so, and the Gracchi's deaths were ominous portents of the manner in which the Republic was henceforth to decide its internal disputes.

In foreign affairs, too, the Senate soon demonstrated its incapability. Rome was forced to grant citizenship to its Italian allies after the Senate's failure to deal with their grievances goaded them into revolt (99-88 B.C.). Other blunders led to the first of the civil wars that destroyed the Republic.

The first civil war: Marius vs. Sulla. Between 111 and 105 B.C. Roman armies, dispatched by the Senate and commanded by senators, failed to protect Roman capitalists in North Africa and to prevent Germanic tribes from overrunning southern Gaul, now a Roman province, and threatening Italy itself. Accusing the Senate of lethargy and incompetence in directing Rome's foreign affairs, the people elected Gaius Marius to the consulship in 107 B.C., and the Tribal Assembly commissioned him to raise an army and deal with the foreign danger. Marius first pacified North Africa and then crushed the first German threat to Rome. In the process he created a new-style Roman army that was destined to play a major role in the turbulent history of the late Republic.

In contrast to the old Roman army, which was composed of conscripts who owned their own land and who thought of themselves as loyal citizens of the Republic, the new army created by Marius was recruited from landless citizens for long terms of service. These professional soldiers identified their own interests with those of their commanders, to whom they looked for bonuses of land or money, and were ready to follow them in any undertaking. Thus the character of the army changed from a militia to a career service in which loyalty to the state was no longer paramount. Aspiring generals would soon use their military power to seize the government.

In 88 B.C. the ambitious king of Pontus in Asia Minor, encouraged by the growing anti-Roman sentiment in Asia Minor and Greece caused by corrupt governors and tax collectors, declared war on Rome. The Senate ordered Cornelius Sulla, an able general and a staunch supporter of the Senate's prerogatives, to go east. As a countermove, the Tribal Assembly chose Marius for the eastern command. In effect both the Senate and the Tribal Assembly, whose power the Gracchi had revived, claimed to be the ultimate authority in the state. The result was a series of civil wars between rival generals, each claiming to champion the cause of either the Senate or the Tribal Assembly. The first of the civil wars ended in a complete victory for Sulla, who in 82 B.C. had himself appointed dictator for an unlimited period with power to "issue edicts and reorganize the Republic."

Sulla set out to restore the preeminence of the Senate. He drastically curtailed the powers of the tribunes and the Tribal Assembly, giving the Senate the control of legislation which it had enjoyed two hundred years before. Convinced that his work would be permanent, Sulla voluntarily resigned his dictatorship in 79 B.C. His reactionary constitutional changes were not to last.

The second civil war: Pompey vs. Caesar. The first of the civil wars and its aftermath increased factionalism and discontent and nursed the ambitions of individuals eager for personal power. The first to come forward was Pompey, who had won fame as a military leader. In 70 B.C. he was elected consul, and, though he was a former partisan of Sulla, courted the populace by repealing Sulla's laws against the tribunes and the Tribal Assembly. Pompey then put an end to anarchy in the East caused by piracy, the protracted ambitions of the king of Pontus, and the death throes of the Seleucid empire. New Roman provinces and client states brought order eastward to the Euphrates and southward to Palestine (see map, p. 77).

Still another strong man made his appearance in 59 B.C., when Julius Caesar allied himself politically with Pompey and was elected consul. Following his consulship, Caesar spent nine years conquering Gaul, where he accumulated a fortune in plunder and trained a loyal army of peerless veterans. During his absence from Rome, he cannily kept his name before the citizens by publishing a lucidly written account of his military feats, *Commentaries on the Gallic War.*

Caesar's conquest of Gaul was to have tremendous consequences for the course of western civilization, for its inhabitants quickly assimilated Roman culture. Consequently, when the Roman Empire collapsed in the West in the fifth century A.D., Romanized Gaul—or France—emerged before long as the center of medieval civilization.

Jealous of Caesar's achievements in Gaul and fearful of his growing power, Pompey conspired with the Senate to ruin him. When the Senate demanded in 49 B.C. that Caesar disband his army, he crossed the Rubicon, the river in northern Italy which formed the boundary of Caesar's province. By crossing the Rubicon—a phrase employed today for any step that commits a person to a given course of action—Caesar in effect declared war on Pompey and the Senate. He marched on Rome while Pompey and most of the Senate fled eastward. Pompey was soon killed in Egypt where he sought refuge, but the last Pompeian army was not defeated until 45 B.C.

Caesar assumed the office of dictator for life, and during his brief period of autocratic rule he initiated far-reaching reforms. He granted citizenship liberally to non-Italians and packed the Senate with many new provincial members, thus making it a more truly representative body as well as a rubber stamp for his policies. In the interest of the poorer citizens, he reduced debts, inaugurated a public works program, established colonies outside Italy, and decreed that one third of the laborers on the slave-worked estates in Italy be persons of free birth. As a result, he was able to reduce from 320,000 to 150,000 the number of people receiving free grain. His most enduring act was the reform of the calendar in the light of Egyptian knowledge; with minor changes, this calendar of 365¼ days is still in use today.

Caesar realized that the Republic was, in fact, dead. In his own words, "The Republic is merely a name, without form or substance." He believed that benevolent despotism alone could save Rome from continued civil war and collapse. But Caesar incurred the enmity of many, particularly those who viewed him as a tyrant who had destroyed the Republic. On the Ides (the fifteenth) of March, 44 B.C., a group of conspirators, led by ex-Pompeians whom Caesar had pardoned, stabbed him to death in the Senate, and Rome was once more plunged into conflict.

Caesar's assassins had been offended by his trappings of monarchy—his purple robe, the statues erected in his honor, the coins bearing his portrait—and they assumed that with his death the Republic would be restored to its traditional status. But the people of Rome remained unmoved by the conspirators' cry of "Liberty! Freedom! Tyranny is dead!" The majority of them were prepared to accept a successor whose power and position stopped just short of a royal title. The real question was: Who was to be Caesar's successor?

The third civil war: Antony vs. Octavian. Following Caesar's death, his eighteen-year-old heir, Octavian, allied himself with Caesar's chief lieutenant, Mark Antony, against the conspirators and the Senate. Although he was not a conspirator, Cicero, the renowned orator and champion of the Senate, was put to death for his hostility to Antony, and the conspirators' armies were routed. Then for more than a decade Octavian and Antony exercised dictatorial power and divided the Roman world between them. But the ambitions of each man proved too great for the alliance to endure.

Antony, who took charge of the eastern half of the empire, became infatuated with Cleopatra, the last of the Egyptian Ptolemies. He even went so far as to transfer Roman territories to her dominions. Octavian took advantage of this high-handedness to arouse Rome and Italy against Antony. When Octavian's fleet met Antony's off Actium in Greece, first Cleopatra and then Antony deserted the battle and fled to Egypt. There Antony committed suicide, as did Cleopatra soon afterwards when Alexandria was captured in 30 B.C. At the end of a century of civil violence Rome was at last united under one ruler, and the Republic gave way to the permanent dictatorship of the Empire. Two centuries of imperial greatness, known as the *Pax Romana* (the Roman Peace), followed.

THE PAX ROMANA: 30 B.C. TO 180 A.D.

Reconstruction under Augustus. Following his triumphal return to Rome, Octavian in 27 B.C. announced that he would "restore the Republic." But he did so only outwardly by blending republican institutions with strong personal leadership. He provided the Senate with considerable authority, consulted it on important issues, allowed it to retain control over Italy and half of the provinces, and gave it the legislative functions of the nearly defunct Tribal Assembly. The Senate in return bestowed upon Octavian the title *Augustus* ("The Revered," a title previously used for gods), by which he was known thereafter.

Augustus never again held the dictatorship, and he seldom held the consulship. Where, then, did his strength lie? Throughout his career he kept the power of a tribune (which gave him the right to initiate and to veto legislation) and the governorship of the frontier provinces, where the armies were stationed. Augustus' control of the army meant that his power could not be successfully challenged. From his military title, *imperator* ("victorious general"), are derived our modern terms of *emperor* and *empire*.

Augustus thus effected a compromise "between the need for a monarchical head of the empire and the sentiment which enshrined Rome's republican constitution in the minds of his contemporaries."[4] He preferred the modest title of *princeps*, "first citizen" or "leader," which he felt best described his position, and his form of disguised monarchy is therefore known as the Principate. At the beginning of the Empire, then, political power was divided between the Senate and the *princeps*, and this *dyarchy* ("rule of two") lasted for more than two centuries, although the Senate slowly faded into the background.

Augustus faced the problems of curing a sick society and removing the scars resulting from a century of civil strife. The aristocracy was too decadent to be patriotic, and in the cities an unemployed mob favored with free bread and circuses had long since lost interest in hard work. Accordingly, Augustus concentrated on internal reform, although he did extend the Roman frontier to the Danube as a defense against barbarian invasions while failing in an attempt to conquer Germany up to the Elbe River (see map, p. 77). His thorough reconstruction of government and society laid the foundation for two centuries of order and prosperity. For example, he created a professional civil service, open to all classes—which greatly reduced the corruption and exploitation that had flourished in the late Republic—and a permanent professional army, stationed in the frontier provinces and kept out of politics. By means of legislation and propaganda, he also sought with some success to check moral and social decline and to revive the old Roman ideals and traditions. Augustus' reforms engendered a new optimism and patriotism which

The Gemma Augustea celebrates some of the great events of Augustus' reign. Holding the imperial staff, Augustus and the goddess Roma rest their feet on the weapons of conquered peoples. The emperor is receiving a laurel crown, the symbol of civilization. Tiberius, Augustus' successor, steps from a chariot at the left. Victorious Roman soldiers occupy the lower panel.

were reflected in the art and literature of the Augustan Age (discussed later in chapter).

The Julio-Claudian and the Flavian emperors. Augustus was followed by four descendants of his family, the line of the Julio-Claudians, who ruled from 14 to 68 A.D. Tiberius, Augustus' stepson whom the Senate accepted as his successor, and Claudius were fairly efficient and devoted rulers; in Claudius' reign the Roman occupation of Britain began in 43 A.D. The other two rulers of this imperial line were of a different stripe: Caligula was a madman, who demanded to be worshiped as a god and made his favorite horse a senator; Nero was infamous for his immorality, the murder of his wife and his mother, and his persecution of Christians in Rome.

During Nero's reign, in 64 A.D., a great fire raged for nine days, destroying more than half of the capital. The Roman historian Tacitus has left us a vivid account of how Nero made the unpopular Christians scapegoats for the fire:

... large numbers ... were condemned—not so much for incendiarism as for their anti-social tendencies. Their deaths were made farcical. Dressed in wild animals' skins, they were torn to pieces by dogs, or crucified, or made into torches to be ignited after dark. ... Nero provided his Gardens for the spectacle, and exhibited displays in the Circus .... Despite their guilt as Christians, and the ruthless punishment it deserved, the victims were pitied. For it was felt they were being sacrificed to one man's brutality rather than to the national interest.[5]

The Julio-Claudian line ended in 68 A.D. when Nero, faced by army revolts, committed suicide. In the following year four emperors were proclaimed by rival armies, with Vespasian the final victor. For nearly thirty years (69-96 A.D.) the Flavian dynasty (Vespasian followed by his two sons) provided the Empire with effective, if autocratic, rule. The fiction of republican institutions gave way to a scarcely veiled monarchy as the Flavians openly treated the office of emperor as theirs by right of conquest and inheritance.

The Antonines: "five good emperors." An end to autocracy and a return to the Augustan principle of an administration of equals— emperor and Senate—characterized the rule

THE GROWTH OF THE ROMAN EMPIRE
44 B.C. TO 180 A.D.

- Acquired before the Death of Caesar, 44 B.C.
- Acquired before the Death of Augustus, 14 A.D.
- Acquired before the Death of Marcus Aurelius, 180 A.D.

0   250   500

of the Antonine emperors (96-180 A.D.), under whom the Empire reached the height of its prosperity and power. Selected on the basis of proven ability, these "good emperors" succeeded, according to Tacitus, in "reconciling things long incompatible, supreme power and liberty." Two of these emperors are especially worthy of notice.

Hadrian reigned from 117 to 138 A.D. His first important act was to stabilize the boundaries of the Empire. He gave up as indefensible recently conquered Armenia and Mesopotamia and erected protective walls in Germany and Britain, the latter an imposing structure of stone and turf twenty feet high. Hadrian traveled extensively, inspecting almost every province of the Empire. New towns were founded, old ones restored, and many public works were constructed, among them the famous Pantheon in Rome (see illustration, p. 83).

The last of the "five good emperors," Marcus Aurelius, who ruled from 161 to 180 A.D., approached Plato's ideal of the "philos-

opher king" and preferred the quiet contemplation of his books to the blood and brutality of the battlefield. Yet, ironically, he was repeatedly troubled by the invasions of Germanic tribes across the Danube. While engaged in his Germanic campaigns, he wrote his *Meditations*, a philosophical work notable for its lofty Stoic idealism and love of humanity.

The "immense majesty of the Roman peace." In the finest period of the Empire, a vast area stretching from Britain to the Euphrates and from the North Sea to the Sahara and containing upwards of 100 million people was welded together into what Pliny the Elder, in the first century A.D., termed the "immense majesty of the Roman peace." Non-Romans were equally conscious of the rich benefits derived from Roman rule. To a Greek writer of the second century, it was

a world every day better known, better cultivated, and more civilized than before. Everywhere roads are traced, every district is known, every country opened to commerce. . . . There are now as many cities as there were once solitary cottages. . . . Wherever there is a trace of life there are houses and human habitations, well-ordered governments and civilized life.[6]

This quotation throws significant light upon the period known as the *Pax Romana*. While the economy remained predominantly agricultural, the Empire became progressively more urban in character as cities increased in number, particularly in the frontier provinces. The cities formed vital nerve centers linked together by a vast network of roads and waterways. The Empire lay secure behind natural frontiers guarded by well-trained armies, the roads were cleared of brigands and the seas of pirates. The *Pax Romana* also witnessed the creation of a cosmopolitan world-state where races and cultures intermingled freely.

The Graeco-Roman cultural synthesis. Writing during the rule of Augustus, the Roman poet Virgil was the spokesman for what enlightened Romans felt to be the mission of the Empire:

Others, doubtless, will mould lifelike bronze with greater delicacy, will win from marble the look of life, will plead cases better, chart the motions of the sky with the rod and foretell the risings of the stars. You, O Roman, remember to rule the nations with might. This will be your genius —to impose the way of peace, to spare the conquered and crush the proud.[7]

By "others," Virgil was referring to the Greeks, to whom the Romans willingly acknowledged a cultural debt. The Romans learned the Greek language, copied Greek architecture, employed Greek sculptors, and identified their gods with Greek deities. Although Greek ways of life introduced sophisticated habits which were often corrupting to the Roman virtues of self-reliance, personal integrity, family cohesion, and discipline, Greek influences made the Romans on the whole less harsh and insensitive. Largely because of their admiration for Greek culture, the Romans helped perpetuate the legacy of Greece. The *Pax Romana* was the acme of Graeco-Roman civilization.

Governing the diverse state. At the head of this huge world-state stood the emperor, its defender and symbol of unity as well as an object of veneration. The major theme of the many encomiums written to celebrate the enlightened, beneficent government of the Principate was that liberty had been exchanged for order and prosperity. The Empire was said to represent a new kind of democracy—"a democracy under the one man that can rule and govern best." "The whole world speaks in unison, more distinctly than a chorus; and so well does it harmonize under this director-in-chief that it joins in praying this Empire may last for all time."[8] Nevertheless, during the Principate the cities of the Empire continued to exercise a large measure of self-government, and although the central government increasingly intervened in their affairs, this was usually the result of the failure of city authorities to solve local problems.

Economic prosperity. Rome's unification of the ancient world had far-reaching economic consequences. The *Pax Romana* was responsible for the elimination of tolls and other artificial barriers, the suppression of piracy and brigandage, and the establishment of a reliable coinage. Such factors, in addition to the longest period of peace the West has ever enjoyed, explain in large measure the great expansion of commerce that occurred in the first and second centuries A.D. Industry also was stimulated, but its expansion was hindered since wealth remained concentrated and no mass market for industrial goods arose. Industry remained organized on a small-shop basis with producers widely scattered, resulting in local self-sufficiency.

Although the cities were the centers of political and cultural life, most of them, particularly in the West, were of secondary importance economically. They consumed much more than they produced and flourished only because the economy of the Empire remained prosperous enough to support them. Most were like Rome itself, into which so much revenue poured from the provinces that its citizens had the necessary purchasing power to buy immense quantities of goods from other parts of the Empire and even from regions far beyond the imperial frontiers.

The economy of the Empire remained basically agrarian, and the huge estates, or *latifundia*, prospered. On these tracts, usually belonging to absentee owners, large numbers of *coloni*, free tenants, tilled the soil as sharecroppers. The *coloni* were gradually replacing slave labor, which was becoming increasingly hard to secure with the disappearance of the flow of captives from major wars.

Despite the general prosperity, the Empire under the Antonines had already entered upon its "Indian summer." Once the Empire had ceased to expand geographically, its economy in turn became progressively more static. Late in the first century A.D. Italian agriculture began to suffer from the loss of its markets in the western provinces, which were becoming self-sufficient in the production of wine and olive oil. To aid the wine producers the Flavian emperor Domitian created an artificial scarcity by forbidding the planting of new vineyards in Italy and ordering the plowing under of half the existing vineyards in the provinces. This was followed by a program of state subsidies, inaugurated by the Antonine emperors. Loans at 5 percent interest were made to ailing landowners, with the interest to be paid into the treasuries of declining Italian municipalities and earmarked "for girls and boys of needy parents to be supported at public expense." This system of state subsidies to both producers and consumers was soon extended to the provinces. Also contributing to Roman economic stagnation was the continuing drain of money into the oriental luxury trade (see p. 117). This early evidence of declining prosperity foreshadowed the economic crisis of the third century A.D., when political anarchy and monetary inflation caused the economy of the Empire to decline rapidly (see Chapter 5).

Rome, imperial capital. At the hub of the sprawling Empire was Rome, with about a million inhabitants. Augustus boasted that he had found a city of brick and had left one of marble. Nonetheless, Rome presented a striking contrast of magnificence and tawdriness, of splendid public buildings and squalid tenements which often collapsed or caught fire. The crowded narrow streets, lined with apartment houses and swarming with all manner of people, are described by the satirist Juvenal early in the second century A.D.:

. . . Hurry as I may, I am blocked
By a surging crowd in front, while a vast mass
Of people crushes onto me from behind.
One with his elbow punches me, another
With a hard litter-pole; one bangs a beam
Against my head, a wine-cask someone else.
With mud my legs are plastered; from all sides
Huge feet trample upon me, and a soldier's
Hobnails are firmly planted on my toes.[9]

Social life. At the top of the social order were the old senatorial families who lived as absentee owners of huge estates and left commerce and finance to a large and wealthy middle class. In contrast to the tenements of the poor, the homes of the rich were palatial, as revealed by excavations at Pompeii, which was buried by the eruption of Vesuvius in 79 A.D. These elaborate villas contained courts and gardens with fountains, rooms furnished with marble walls, mosaics on the floors, and numerous frescoes and other works of art. An interesting feature of Roman furniture was the abundance of couches and the scarcity of chairs. People usually reclined, even at meals—a custom which may have had its value during the sumptuous dinners served by the wealthy gourmands, who were not above administering emetics to permit disgorging and starting afresh on more food and wine.

The lower classes in the cities found a refuge from the dullness of their existence in social clubs, or guilds, called *collegia*, each comprising the workers of one trade. The activity of the *collegia* did not center on economic aims, like modern trade unions, but on the worship of a god and on feasts, celebrations, and decent burials for members.

The living conditions of slaves varied greatly. Those in domestic service were often treated humanely, and their years of efficient service frequently rewarded by emancipation. Nor was it uncommon for freed slaves to rise to places of eminence in business, letters, and the imperial service. On the other hand, conditions among slaves on the large estates could be indescribably harsh. Beginning with Augustus, however, numer-

The Colosseum, built by the Flavian emperors, uses arch construction both to light the interior and to disperse weight. Largest of the Roman amphitheaters, it was used for gladiatorial combats, animal fights, and even for naval exhibitions—water pipes for flooding still exist in some arenas.

ous enactments protected slaves from mistreatment; Hadrian, for example, forbade private prisons and the killing of a slave without judicial approval.

Recreation played a key role in Roman social life. Both rich and poor were exceedingly fond of their public baths, which in the capital alone numbered eight hundred during the early days of the Empire. The baths served the same purpose as our modern-day athletic clubs. The larger baths contained enclosed gardens, promenades, gymnasiums, libraries, and famous works of art as well as a wide variety of types of baths. An old Roman inscription expresses an interesting philosophy: "The bath, wine, and love ruin one's health but make life worth living."

Foot races, boxing, and wrestling were minor sports; chariot racing and gladiatorial contests were the chief amusements. The cry for "bread and circuses" reached such proportions that by the first century A.D. the Roman calendar had 159 days set aside as holidays, 93 of which were given over to games furnished at public expense. The most spectacular sport was chariot racing. The largest of six race courses at Rome was the Circus Maximus, a huge marble-faced structure seating about 150,000 spectators. The games, which included upwards of twenty-four races each day, were presided over by the emperor or his representative. The crowds bet furiously on their favorite charioteers, whose fame equaled that of the all-American football heroes of our own day.

Scarcely less popular, but infinitely less civilized, the gladiatorial contests were also organized by the emperors as a regular feature on the amusement calendar. These cruel spectacles, which have no exact counterpart in any other civilization, were held in arenas, the largest and most famous of which was the Colosseum. The contests took various forms. Ferocious animals were pitted against armed combatants or occasionally even against unarmed men and women who had been condemned to death. Another type of contest was the fight to the death between gladiators, generally equipped with different types of weapons but matched on equal terms. It was not uncommon for the life of a defeated gladiator who had fought courageously to be spared at the request of the spectators. Although many Romans decried these blood-letting contests, there persisted a streak of cruelty in Roman public amusements which can scarcely be comprehended, far less condoned, today.

THE ROMAN CONTRIBUTION

The Roman spirit. The Roman spirit was compounded of many factors. Never completely lost was the tradition of plain living. Geography was another factor; for centuries the Romans were faced with the need to conquer or be conquered, and they had to stress discipline and duty to the state. But the Roman spirit also had another side. It could be arrogant and cruel, and its deep-rooted sense of justice was too often untempered with mercy.

By and large, the Romans lacked the creative fire of the Greeks, but they knew superbly well how to preserve, adapt, and disseminate civilization. Therefore we might characterize the Romans as synthesists rather than innovators—and at the same time pay respect to their recognition of cultural indebtedness. For all their limitations, the Romans had greatness as a people. The *Pax Romana* could have been fashioned and maintained only by a people grave in nature, mature in judgment, and conscious of their responsibilities to others.

Contributions in government. Roman political thinkers such as Cicero contributed the germinal ideas for many governmental theories destined to be influential in later centuries. Some of these deserve mention: the social-contract theory (that government originated as a voluntary agreement among citizens); the idea of popular sovereignty (that all power ultimately resides with the people); and the concept that law must be the paramount rule in government. Although the growing despotism of the Roman emperors corroded these concepts, they were never lost sight of and ultimately were transmitted to modern times. Important, too, was the Roman tradition of unity and order within a great imperial structure. As we will see in later chapters, this concept was to play an important role in the politics of medieval Europe.

The Romans laid the foundations for the political framework of modern Europe in still other ways. Many current administrative divisions, such as the county and province, are derived from Roman practice. In some instances European boundaries are little altered from those existing under the Caesars. The medieval Church also modeled its organization, administrative units, and much of its law after that of the Empire.

Evolution of Roman law. Of the contributions made by the Romans in government and politics, Roman law is preeminent. Two great legal systems, Roman law and English common law, are the foundation of jurisprudence in most modern western nations. Roman law is the basis for the law codes of Italy, France, Scotland, and the Latin American countries. Where English common law is used, as in the United States, there is also a basic heritage of great legal principles originated by ancient Roman jurists. In addition, Roman legal principles have strongly affected the development of the canon law of the Roman Catholic Church; and international law has borrowed principles inherent in the Roman system.

Roman law evolved slowly over a period of about a thousand years. At first, when Rome was a struggling city-state, the law was unwritten, mixed with religious custom, and harsh in its judgments. In the fifth century B.C., as we have seen (p. 67), the law was written down in the Law of the Twelve Tables. During the remainder of the Republic the body of Roman law (*jus civile*, "law of the citizen") was enlarged by legislation passed by the Senate and the assembly and, equally important, by judicial interpretation of existing law to meet new conditions. By the second century A.D. the emperor had become the sole source of law, a responsibility he entrusted to scholars "skilled in the law" (*jurisprudentes*). Holding to the idea of equity ("follow the beneficial interpretation"), and influenced by Stoic philosophy with its concept of a "law of nature" common to all men and ascertainable by means of human reason, these jurists humanized and rationalized Roman law to meet the needs of a world-state. Finally, in the sixth century A.D., the enormous bulk of Roman law from all sources was codified (see p. 151) and thus easily preserved for posterity.

Roman engineering and architecture. The Empire's needs required a communication system of paved roads and bridges as well as huge public buildings and aqueducts for the cities. Pride in the Empire led also to the erection of ostentatious monuments symbolizing Rome's dignity and might.

As road builders, the Romans surpassed all previous peoples. Constructed of layers of stone according to sound engineering principles, their roads were planned for the use of armies and messengers and were kept in constant repair. The earliest and best known main Roman highway was the Appian Way, running from Rome to the Bay of Naples, which was built about 300 B.C. to facilitate Rome's expansion southward. It has been said that the speed of travel possible on Roman highways was not surpassed until the early nineteenth century.

In designing their bridges and aqueducts, the Romans placed a series of stone arches next to one another to provide mutual support. At times several tiers of arches were used, one above the other. Fourteen aque-

ducts, stretching a total of 265 miles, supplied some fifty gallons of water daily for each inhabitant of Rome. The practical nature of the Romans and their skill and initiative in engineering were demonstrated also in the many dams, reservoirs, and harbors they constructed.

At first the Romans copied Etruscan architectural models, but later they combined basic Greek elements with distinctly Roman innovations. The structural simplicity of Hellenic buildings was too restrained for the Romans who, by utilizing brick and concrete as new building materials, developed new methods for enclosing space. The static post and lintel system of the Greeks was replaced with the more dynamic techniques of vaulting.

The barrel vault, basically a series of adjoining arches forming a structure resembling a tunnel, was a new method of enclosing space. In the barrel vault the piers, or supports, of the arches became heavy masonry walls to bear the weight of the vaulted roof. The Romans next developed the cross vault by intersecting two barrel vaults at right angles. Cross vaults were employed to great effect in public baths and basilicas.

Another important advance in architectural engineering was the Romans' success in constructing concrete domes on a magnificent scale. The weight of the dome was transferred directly to the walls, and since there was no sidewise thrust, no other support was necessary. The largest of the domed structures was the Pantheon (temple of "all

In the barrel vault, essentially a Roman contribution, the walls support the sideways and downward pressure of the material above. The walls of the cross vault, an advance in architectural engineering, did not need to be as thick as those of a barrel vault, because the weight of the material was spread over a larger area. Also, openings in the supporting walls furnished window space.

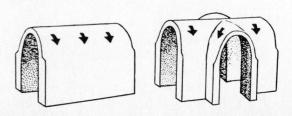

the gods"), which still stands (see illustration).

The standard type of Roman public building was the basilica, a colonnaded structure that became a model for early Christian churches (see illustration, p. 127). Rows of columns divided the interior into a central nave and side aisles, with the roof over the nave raised to admit light, creating a clerestory like those found in Egyptian temples. Perhaps the most famous Roman edifice is the Colosseum (see illustration, p. 80), a huge amphitheater about one quarter of a mile around on the outside and with a seating capacity of about 45,000. Its three stories of arches are decorated with Doric, Ionic, and Corinthian columns.

Roman buildings were built to last, and their size, grandeur, and decorative richness aptly symbolized the proud imperial spirit of Rome. Whereas the Greeks evolved the temple, theater, and stadium, the Romans contributed the triumphal arch, bath, basilica, amphitheater, and the multistoried apartment house. Many modern public buildings show the influence of Rome's bold new architecture.

Sculpture and painting. After the conquest of Greece thousands of statues and other art pieces were brought to Rome. Many Romans acquired a passion for art, and the homes of the wealthy were filled with all kinds of Greek art.

Although strongly influenced by Etruscan and Greek models, the Romans developed a distinctive sculpture of their own which was remarkably realistic, secular, and individualistic. Lifelike portraiture flourished particularly during the Republic, probably originating in the early practice of making and preserving wax images of the heads of important families. During the Principate, on the other hand, portraiture and relief sculpture tended to idealize the likenesses of the emperors (see illustrations, pp. 76, 84). Portraits on coins also served to glorify the Empire and particular emperors. Equestrian statues, sculptured coffins, or sarcophagi, and the reliefs found on imperial monuments were exceptionally fine works of art. The Romans developed a great fund of decorative motifs, such as cupids, garlands of flowers, and scrolls of various patterns, which are still used today.

What little Roman painting has been preserved clearly reflects the influence of Hellenistic Greek models. The Romans were particularly skilled in producing floor mosaics—often copies of some Hellenistic painting (see p. 58)—and in painting frescoes. The frescoes still to be seen in Pompeii and elsewhere show that the artist drew the human figure accurately and showed objects in clear though imperfect perspective.

Literary Rome. In literature as in art the Romans turned to the Greeks for their models. Roman epic, dramatic, and lyric poetry forms were usually written in conscious imi-

The Pantheon, built by the emperor Hadrian, is one of the best preserved buildings of Imperial Rome. It impressively harmonizes the Greek-style colonnaded porch with the Roman-style dome.

Sculpture, during the Augustan age, expressed itself best in portraiture—the finest examples combining expressive realism with the classical insistence on serenity. One of the most frequent subjects is the emperor Augustus Caesar, here presented in an idealized, militaristic pose.

tation of Greek masterpieces. Compared with Greek literature, however, Latin writing was more moralistic and less speculative and imaginative. But it remains one of the world's great literatures largely because of its influence upon medieval, Renaissance, and modern culture.

Formal Latin literature did not begin until late in the third century B.C. when a Greek slave named Livius Andronicus translated Homer's *Odyssey* and several Greek plays into Latin. By the end of the same century the first of a series of Latin epics dealing with Rome's past was composed.

The oldest examples of Latin literature to survive intact are the twenty-one comedies of Plautus (c. 254-184 B.C.), which were adapted from Hellenistic Greek originals but with many Roman allusions, colloquialisms, and customs added. Plautus' comedies are bawdy and vigorously humorous, and their rollicking plots of illicit love and stock characters of the shrewish wife, henpecked husband, lovelorn youth, clever slave, and swashbuckling soldier reveal the level of culture and taste in early Rome. The works of Plautus suggest many of the types that modern comedy has assumed—the farce, burlesque, and the comedy of manners. From him Shakespeare got ideas for his *Comedy of Errors* and *The Merry Wives of Windsor*.

The Golden Age of Latin literature. Latin literature entered its first great period of creative activity in the first century B.C., when an outpouring of intellectual effort coincided with the last years of the Republic. This period marks the first half of the Golden Age of Latin literature, known as the Ciceronian period because of the stature of Marcus Tullius Cicero (106-43 B.C.), the greatest master of Latin prose and perhaps the outstanding intellectual influence in Roman history.

Acclaimed as the greatest orator of his day, Cicero found time during his busy public life to write extensively on philosophy, political theory, and rhetoric. Some nine hundred of his letters still exist, and these, together with his speeches, give us insight into Cicero's personality, as well as into the problems and manners of republican Rome. Much of the value of Cicero's letters lies in the fact that most were not intended for publication and thus he spoke his mind freely. Cicero also made a rich contribution to knowledge by passing on to later ages much of Greek thought—especially that of Plato and the Stoics—and at the same time interpreting it from the standpoint of a Roman intellectual and practical man of affairs. He did more than any other Roman to make Latin a great literary language.

The Ciceronian period also produced the personal lyrical poetry of Catullus (c. 87-54 B.C.), a young man about town who wrote intensely of his loves and hates:

I hate and love—the why I cannot tell,
But by my tortures know the fact too well.[10]

Catullus' contemporary, Lucretius (99-55 B.C.), found in the philosophy of Epicurus an antidote to his profound disillusionment with his fellow citizens who, he wrote, "in their greed of gain . . . amass a fortune out of civil bloodshed: piling wealth on wealth, they heap carnage on carnage. With heartless glee they welcome a brother's tragic death."[11] His long philosophical poem, *On the Nature of Things*, will be discussed later in this chapter.

Augustus provided the Roman world with a stability that was conducive to a further outpouring of literary creativeness. The second phase of the Golden Age of Latin literature, the Augustan Age, was notable particularly for its excellent poetry. Virgil (70-19 B.C.) was probably the greatest of all Roman poets. His masterpiece, a great national epic called the *Aeneid*, glorifies the work of Augustus and eloquently asserts Rome's destiny to conquer and rule the world (see quotation, p. 78). Using Homer's *Iliad* and *Odyssey* as his models, Virgil recounted the fortunes of Aeneas, the legendary founder of the Latin people, who came from his home in Troy to Italy. The *Aeneid* breathes Virgil's deep and enthusiastic patriotism and is as much a piece of imperial symbolism as Rome's triumphal arches.

Horace (65-8 B.C.) was famous for both lyrical odes and satirical verse. Succeeding generations have turned to Horace because of his urbane viewpoint and polished style:

Happy the man, and happy he alone,
He, who can call to-day his own:
He who secure within, can say,
To-morrow do thy worst, for I have lived to-day.[12]

Quite a different sort was Ovid (43 B.C.-17 A.D.), a poet akin to Catullus in spirit and personal life, who combined a predilection for themes on sensual love with first-rate storytelling. In fact, it is largely through his *Metamorphoses,* a collection of Greek stories about the life of the gods, that classical mythology was transmitted to the modern world.

The Silver Age. The literature of the so-called "Silver Age," the period between the deaths of Augustus and Hadrian (14-138 A.D.), substitutes a more critical and negative spirit for the patriotism and optimism of the Augustan Age. Despite a great emphasis upon artificial stylistic devices, the Silver Age was memorable for its moral emphasis (seen in Tacitus, Plutarch, and Seneca) and its brilliant satirical poetry which reached its peak in Juvenal (55?-130 A.D.). This master of poetic invective flayed the shortcomings of contemporary Roman society (see also quotation, p. 79):

Whatever passions have the soul possessed,
Whatever wild desires inflamed the breast
(Joy, Sorrow, Fear, Love, Hatred, Transport, Rage),
Shall form the motley subject of my page.
For when could Satire boast so fair a field?[13]

The writing of history. Two Roman historians produced notable works during the Golden and Silver Ages. The first, Livy (59 B.C.-17 A.D.), was a contemporary of Virgil; his immense *History of Rome*, like the latter's *Aeneid*, is of epic proportions and glorifies Rome's conquests and ancestral ways. By assembling the legends and traditions of early Roman history and welding them into a continuous narrative, Livy, like Virgil, sought to advance Augustus' program of moral and social regeneration. He glorified the virtues of the ancient Romans—their heroism, patriotism, and piety—and sought to draw moral lessons from an idealized past.

Tacitus (55-117 A.D.), like his contemporary Juvenal, was concerned with improving society, but he used history rather than poetry to serve his ends. In his *Germania* Tacitus contrasted the life of the idealized, simple Germanic tribes with the corrupt and immoral existence of the Roman upper classes. In the *Annals* and *Histories* he used his vivid, epigrammatic prose to depict the shortcomings of the emperors and their courts from the death of Augustus to 96 A.D. Some of his brief, trenchant statements have been quoted for centuries; for example, "Tyrants merely procure infamy for themselves and glory for their victims"; "The more corrupt the state, the more numerous the laws"; and (in his description of Roman conquest) "They make a solitude and call it peace." Tacitus suffered from the bias of his own senatorial class; he looked upon the emperors as tyrants and thus could not do justice to the positive contributions of imperial government.

The most famous Greek author in the Empire was Plutarch (46?-120? A.D.). He lectured on philosophy at Rome before retiring to his small hometown to pursue research on the outstanding figures in Roman and Greek history in order to discover what qualities make men great or ignoble. His *Parallel Lives*, containing forty-six biographies of famous Greeks and Romans arranged in pairs for the purpose of comparison, is one of the eminently readable classics of Greek literature. Because many of the sources Plutarch used have been lost, his *Lives* is a mine of invaluable information for the historian.

Stoicism and Epicureanism. The Romans contributed no original philosophical theories, preferring to adapt existing Greek systems of thought to suit their needs. As men of action with grave governmental responsibilities, the Romans paid scant attention to such abstract problems as the nature of the universe and of human knowledge. But the corrupting effects of life in the late Republic on the old Roman virtues and traditions caused thoughtful Romans to be concerned over problems of behavior. As a consequence, they were attracted to the two chief Hellenistic ethical philosophies, Epicureanism and Stoicism.

Epicureanism made its greatest impact during the last days of the Republic, since men found its tenets comforting in a period of political upheaval when no one knew what the morrow would bring. As young men, Virgil and Horace embraced Epicureanism, but Lucretius was the most important Roman interpreter of this philosophy. In his *On the Nature of Things*, Lucretius followed Epicurus (see p. 60) in basing his explanation of the "nature of things" on materialism and atomism. He called on men to free themselves from the superstitious fears of the gods and of death, which were causing them to become converts to the emotional mystery religions of Greece and the East. Lucretius exhorted his readers to "make the most of today," but to seek pleasure in philosophical serenity, rather than in sensuous gratification, and to have no fear of death since souls, like bodies, are composed of atoms that fall apart when death comes:

What has this bugbear Death to frighten man,
If souls can die, as well as bodies can? . . .
So, when our mortal frame shall be disjoin'd,
The lifeless lump uncoupled from the mind,
From sense of grief and pain we shall be free;
We shall not feel, because we shall not be.[14]

More enduring, especially in the days of the Empire, was the appeal of Stoicism to the Roman ruling classes. It had a humanizing effect on Roman law by introducing such concepts as the law of nature (see p. 82), the brotherhood of men—including slaves—and the view that a man is innocent until proved guilty. The main emphasis of Roman Stoicism was on a just life, constancy to duty, courage in adversity, and service to humanity.

One of the outstanding Roman Stoics was Seneca (4 B.C.-65 A.D.), Nero's tutor and a writer of moral essays and of tragedies meant to be read rather than performed. He was regarded with high favor by the leaders of the early Christian Church, for his Stoicism, like that of the ex-slave Epictetus (d. 135 A.D.) and the emperor Marcus Aurelius, was a kind of religious creed. He stressed an all-wise Providence, or fatherly god, and the immortality of the soul. Seneca occupies an important place in the development of moral theory in Europe because his essays enjoyed a wide reputation among thinkers during the Middle Ages and the Renaissance.

Science in the Roman Empire. The Romans had little scientific curiosity, but by putting the findings of Hellenistic science to practical use, they became masters in engineering, applied medicine, and public health.

The Romans pioneered in public health service and developed the extensive practice of hydrotherapy—the use of mineral baths for healing. Beginning in the early Empire, doctors were employed in infirmaries where soldiers, officials, and the poor could obtain free medical care. Great aqueducts and admirable drainage systems also indicate Roman concern for public health.

Characteristic of their utilitarian approach to science was the Romans' predilection for amassing immense encyclopedias. The most important of these was the *Natural History* compiled by Pliny the Elder (23-79 A.D.), an enthusiastic collector of all kinds of scientific odds and ends. In writing his massive work, Pliny is reputed to have read more than two thousand books. The result is an intriguing mixture of fact and fable thrown together with scarcely any method of classification. Nevertheless, it was the most widely read work on science during the Empire and the early Middle Ages.

Pliny was well aware of the lack of creative scientific activity in his day. "In these glad times of peace," he wrote, "no addition whatever is being made to knowledge by means of original research, and in fact even the discoveries of our predecessors are not being thoroughly studied." To Pliny, the cause of this state of affairs was "blind engrossment with avarice," and he cited this example: ". . . now that every sea has been opened up . . . , an immense multitude goes on voyages—but their object is profit not knowledge."[15] Pliny himself was suffocated by a rain of hot ashes while he was studiously observing the eruption of Mount Vesuvius at Pompeii.

The last great scientific minds of the ancient world were two Greeks, Claudius Ptolemy and Galen, both of whom lived in the second century A.D. Ptolemy resided at Alexandria, where he became celebrated as geographer, astronomer, and mathematician. His maps show a comparatively accurate knowledge of a broad section of the Old World, and he used an excellent projection system (see illustration, p. 367). But he exaggerated the size of Asia, an error which influenced Columbus to underestimate the width of the Atlantic and to set sail from Spain in search of Asia. His work on astronomy, usually called the *Almagest* ("the great work") from the title of the Arabic translation, summed up the geocentric, or earth-centered, view of the universe that was to rule men's minds until the sixteenth century. In mathematics, Ptolemy's work in improving and developing trigonometry became the basis for modern knowledge of the subject.

Born in Pergamum in Asia Minor, Galen was a physician for a school of gladiators. His fame spread and he was called to Rome where he became physician to Marcus Aurelius. Galen was responsible for notable advances in physiology and anatomy; for example, he was the first to explain the mechanism of respiration. Forbidden by the Roman government to dissect human bodies, Galen experimented with animals and demonstrated that an excised heart can continue to beat outside the body and that injuries to one side of the brain produce disorders in the opposite side of the body. The most experimental-minded of ancient physicians, he once wrote: "I confess the disease from which I have suffered all my life—to trust . . . no statements until, so far as possible, I have tested them for myself."[16] His medical encyclopedia, in which he summarized the medical knowledge of antiquity, remained the standard authority until the sixteenth century.

SUMMARY

The story of how Rome rose from an insignificant muddy village along the banks of the Tiber to the mighty ruler of the Mediterranean world will always remain one of the most fascinating stories in world history. Emerging from obscurity about the middle of the eighth century before Christ, the Latin people who clustered about Rome and its seven hills succeeded in 509 B.C. in ousting their Etruscan overlords and establishing a republic. The history of the Roman Republic can be divided into two distinct periods. During the first, from 509 to 133 B.C., two themes are dominant: the gradual democratization of the government and the conquest of the Mediterranean.

By 287 B.C., thanks to the reluctant willingness of the patricians to compromise, the plebeians had succeeded in breaking down the privileged position of the patricians by obtaining recognition of their fundamental rights as citizens and by acquiring a progressively more important share of political power. Having achieved these gains, the rank and file of the citizens allowed the aristocratic Senate to continue exercising full control of the Republic.

The other theme in the early history of the Roman Republic was the conquest of the Mediterranean. Between the years 509 and 270 B.C. the Romans crushed all resistance to their rule in Italy. They then clashed with Carthage, and after a herculean struggle, Carthage surrendered in 201 B.C. Having conquered the West, the Romans found themselves drawn to the East, and by 133 B.C. Macedonia and Greece were ruled by Roman governors, the Seleucid emperor in Asia had been defeated and humbled, and Rome had acquired its first province on the Asian continent. But as the Mediterranean world succumbed to the Roman legions, the Republic itself faced civil war and degeneration.

The second and last period in the history of the Roman Republic, from 133 to 30 B.C., began with the attempts of the Gracchi brothers to persuade the senatorial oligarchy to allow the enactment of necessary reforms, but to no avail. Marius, Sulla, Pompey, and Julius Caesar mark the appearance of one-man rule and the end of the Republic. Augustus, the heir of Caesar, ruled Rome wisely and well. On the surface the old republican institutions, such as the Senate, were preserved, but Augustus wielded the real power in the new government, which is called the early Empire, or Principate. For two hundred years, during the *Pax Romana*, many millions of people in Italy and the Empire's provinces enjoyed peace and prosperity.

Through the Roman achievement of a single empire and a cosmopolitan culture, the Greek legacy was preserved, synthesized, and disseminated—and the Romans were able to make important contributions of their own. The Romans excelled in political theory, governmental administration, and jurisprudence. While the Greeks were individualistic, the Romans put a higher value on conformity, and their essentially conservative and judicious attitude of mind compensated for their lack of creativity. Primarily synthesists rather than innovators, the Romans willingly admitted their cultural indebtedness and by doing so exhibited a magnanimity characteristic of the Roman spirit at its best.

SUGGESTIONS FOR READING

D. R. Dudley, **The Civilization of Rome*** (Mentor); R. Barrow, **The Romans*** (Penguin); M. Grant, **The World of Rome*** (Mentor); and P. Arnott, **The Romans and Their World*** (St. Martin's, 1970) are brief excellent surveys of Roman history and culture. M. Cary and H. Scullard, **A History of Rome Down to the Reign of Constantine,** 3rd ed. (St. Martin's, 1975) is a standard detailed account. Highly recommended and recent is Michael Grant, **History of Rome** (Scribner's, 1979).

M. Pallotino, **The Etruscans*,** rev. ed. (Penguin); and E. Richardson, **The Etruscans: Their Art and Civilization** (Univ. of Chicago) are detailed accounts. See also Raymond Bloch, **The Origins of Rome** (Praeger), an examination of the archaeological, historical, and legendary evidence. For an instructive survey of archaeological discovery in Italy, see P. MacKendrick, **The Mute Stones Speak*** (Mentor).

H. Scullard, **History of the Roman World from 753 to 146 B.C.** (St. Martin's, 1975) and F. B. Marsh, **History of the Roman World from 146 to 30 B.C.** (Methuen, 1971) are detailed accounts. H. Scullard, **From the Gracchi to Nero,** 3rd ed. (Barnes & Noble) covers the transition from the late Republic to the early Empire. E. Salmon, **History of the Roman World from 30 B.C. to A.D. 138,** 6th ed. (Methuen) details the history of the early Empire.

Recommended special studies: F. E. Adcock, **Roman Political Ideas and Practice*** (Univ. of Mich.); Richard E. Smith, **The Fail-**ure of the Roman Republic** (Arno, 1975); R. Syme, **The Roman Revolution*** (Oxford); G. Ferrero, **The Life of Caesar*** (Norton); Lily R. Taylor, **Party Politics in the Age of Caesar*** (Univ. of Calif.); L. Cottrell, **Hannibal: Enemy of Rome** (Holt, Rinehart & Winston); J. Buchan, **Augustus** (Verry); and T. Africa, **Rome of the Caesars** (Wiley).

W. W. Fowler, **Social Life at Rome in the Age of Cicero*** (St. Martin's); S. Dill, **Roman Society from Nero to Marcus Aurelius*** (Meridian); M. Johnston, **Roman Life** (Scott, Foresman); J. Balsdon, **Roman Women** (Greenwood, 1975); and F. C. Grant, ed., **Ancient Roman Religion*** (Bobbs-Merrill) are all interesting. See also F. R. Cowell, **Life in Ancient Rome*** (Capricorn, 1975).

Other books of interest are Martin L. Clarke, **The Roman Mind: Studies in the History of Thought from Cicero to Marcus Aurelius*** (Norton, 1968); M. Grant, **Roman Literature*** (Penguin); Edith Hamilton, **The Roman Way*** (Avon); M. Wheeler, **Roman Art and Architecture*** (Praeger); and H. J. Rose, **Religion in Greece and Rome*** (Torchbooks).

Recommended historical novels: W. Bryher, **The Coin of Carthage*** (Harvest); T. Wilder, **The Ides of March*** (Avon, 1975); R. Graves, **I Claudius*** (Vintage); M. Yourcenar, **Memoirs of Hadrian*** (Noonday).

*Indicates a less expensive paperbound edition.

CHAPTER 4

Ancient India and China to 220 A.D.

The Asian Way of Life

INTRODUCTION. Civilization had its genesis in four Afro-Asian regions: Egypt, Mesopotamia, and the valleys of the Indus and the Huang Ho rivers. For two thousand years, these areas charted the path for the civilized world. By 500 B.C., Western peoples began to make rapid progress in the civilized arts of life; and for a thousand years, both great segments of the human race were roughly in equilibrium.

This chapter will trace the genesis and development of the two oldest continuous civilizations now in existence—the Indian and the Chinese—in order to learn how their ancient ideas and institutions continue to affect the people of Asia. In addition, this chapter will examine the early trade and diplomatic exchanges between East and West. These exchanges provide us with our first view of historical development on a global scale.

A modern Indian scholar, A. Coomaraswamy, has said: "All that India can offer to the world proceeds from her philosophy." Indian thinkers have consistently held a fundamental belief in the unity of all life, establishing no dividing line between the human and the divine. This pervasive belief in the unity of life has made possible the assimilation and synthesis of a variety of ideas and customs from both native and foreign cultures. Thus, despite its almost continual political disunity, India has achieved and maintained a fundamental cultural unity.

While political disunity has characterized most of India's history, China has been united for more than 2000 years—the longest-lived political institution in world history. While religion has dominated the customs and attitudes of India's people, the Chinese have been much more humanistic and worldly. Their attitude toward life has led to a concern for the art of government, the keeping of historical records, and the formulation of down-to-earth ethical standards.

Despite these great cultural and political differences, however, India and China also have much in common. Having experienced poverty, both societies can look back to days of ancient glory. Now in control of their own affairs, both can remember foreign conquerors. Hemmed in by tradition and custom, both find themselves in a world of nuclear power and space-age technology. The course that these countries follow in the future will inevitably be conditioned by what they have experienced in the past.

EARLY INDIA

Geography of India. We can think of India* as a gigantic triangle, bounded on two sides by the warm waters of the Indian Ocean and on the third by the mountain wall of the Himalayas. The highest mountains in the world, the Himalayas and their western extensions cut India off from the rest of Asia, making it an isolated subcontinent as large as Europe. Through the Khyber and other mountain passes in the northwest have come the armed conquerors, restless tribes, and merchants and travelers who did much to shape India's turbulent history.

The Indian subcontinent comprises two other major geographical regions (see map, p. 91). In the north is the great plains known as Hindustan, which extends from the Arabian Sea to the Bay of Bengal. It forms the watersheds of two great river systems, the Indus and the Ganges, which have their sources in the Himalayas. South of this great plain rises a high plateau that covers most of the southern, or peninsular, part of India and is called the Deccan (the "South"). The sloping western and eastern sides of this highland zone are known as the Western and Eastern Ghats.

Our interest lies principally in Hindustan, where India's earliest civilization arose. This area is made up of an alluvial plain watered by the upper Indus and its tributaries (called the Punjab, or Land of the Five Rivers), and the region of the lower Indus (called Sind, from *sindhu,* meaning "river," and the origin of the terms *Hindu* and *India*).

The Indus Civilization (c. 2500–c. 1500 B.C.). The rise of civilization in the Indus valley around 2500 B.C. duplicates what occurred in Mesopotamia nearly one thousand years earlier. In both areas, Neolithic farmers lived in food-producing villages situated on the hilly flanks of a large river valley. Under pressure from increased population and the need for more land and water, they moved to the more abundant and fertile soil of the river valley. Here their successful adaptation to a new environment led to the more complex way of life that is called a civilization. In India's case, four or five of the farming villages had grown into large cities with as many as 40,000 inhabitants by 2300 B.C. Excavations of two of these cities, Mohenjo-Daro in Sind and Harappa in the Punjab, have provided most of our knowledge of this civilization.

Although Harappa and Mohenjo-Daro were four hundred miles apart, the Indus

*Until the text deals with the creation of the separate states of India and Pakistan in 1947, the word *India* will refer to the *entire* subcontinent.

River made possible the maintenance of a uniform administration and economy over the large area. The cities were carefully planned, with straight paved streets intersecting at right angles and an elaborate drainage system with underground channels. A standard system of weights was used throughout the area. The spacious two-storied houses of the well-to-do contained bathrooms and were constructed with the same type of baked bricks used for roads. A uniform pictographic script employing some 270 syllabic signs has not yet been deciphered. The only known use of the script was on engraved stamp-seals, which were probably used to mark property with the name of the owner.

The economy of the Indus civilization, like that of Babylonia and Egypt, was based on irrigation farming. Wheat and barley were the chief crops, and the state collected these grains as taxes and stored them in huge granaries. The importance of agriculture explains the presence of numerous mother-goddess figurines; representing the principle of fertility, they are adorned with elaborate headdresses. For the first known time in world history, cotton was grown and used in making textiles.

Copper and bronze were used for tools and weapons, but the rarity of weapons indicates that warfare was uncommon. Trade was sufficiently well organized to obtain needed raw materials—copper, tin, silver, gold, and timber—from the mountain regions to the west. There is also evidence of trade contacts with Mesopotamia, some 1500 miles to the west, as early as 2300 B.C. (time of Sargon of Akkad).

For centuries the people of the Indus valley pursued a relatively unchanging way of life. However, excavations at Mohenjo-Daro show clearly that decline had set in after about 1800 B.C. Street frontages were no longer strictly observed when houses were rebuilt after great floods, brickwork became shoddy, and the spacious homes of the wealthy were becoming tenements for the poor. Finally, groups of skeletons huddled together in their dwellings and on the streets suggest that the city and the civilization came to a sudden end at the hands of invaders who came through the northwest passes about 1500 B.C.

The Aryan invasion and the Early Vedic Age (c. 1500-1000 B.C.). The invaders who brought an end to the already tottering Indus civilization called themselves *Aryans*, meaning "nobles." They spoke Sanskrit, an Indo-European language, and were a part of the great Indo-European migrations of the second millennium B.C., whose profound effects on the ancient world we have noted in earlier chapters. The Aryans were pastoralists who counted their wealth in cattle and whose chief interests were war and cattle rustling. Their horse-drawn chariots, which were unknown to the native population of India, made them invincible.

We know more about the Aryans than we know about their Indus civilization predecessors. Our knowledge comes largely from the four *Vedas* ("Knowledge"), great collec-

ANCIENT INDIA

Indus Valley Civilization

tions of hymns to the gods and ritual texts composed and handed down orally between 1500 and 500 B.C. by the Aryan priests, the Brahmins. Hence this thousand-year period is commonly called the Vedic Age.

The earliest and most important of the *Vedas*, the *Rig-Veda* ("Royal Veda"), gives an insight into the institutions and ideas of the Early Vedic Age, which ended about 1000 B.C. Each tribe was headed by a war leader called *rajah*, a word closely related to the Latin word for king, *rex*. Like the early kings of Sumer, Greece, and Rome, the rajah was not an absolute monarch. Two tribal assemblies, one a small council of the great men of the tribe and the other a larger gathering of heads of families, approved his accession to office and advised him on important matters.

The native population, later called Dravidians, was either conquered by the Aryan invaders or driven south into the Deccan. The Aryans contemptuously referred to these conquered people as *Dasyu*, or slaves.

The earliest hymns in the *Rig-Veda* mention only two social classes, the Kshatriyas (nobility) and the Vaisyas (commoners). But by the end of the Early Vedic Age two addi-

tional classes were recognized: the Brahmins, or priests, who because of their specialized religious knowledge had begun to assume the highest social rank; and the Sudras, the non-Aryan conquered population of serfs at the bottom of the social scale. From these four classes the famous caste system of India was to develop during the Later Vedic Age.

The early Aryans had an unsophisticated premoral religion. It involved making sacrifices to the deified forces of nature in return for such material gains as victory in war, long life, and many offspring. The gods were conceived in the image of humans—virile and warlike, fond of charioteering, dancing, and gambling, and addicted to an intoxicating drink called *soma*, which was believed to make them immortal. The most popular god in the *Rig-Veda* was Indra, storm-god and patron of warriors, who is described leading the Aryans in destroying the forts of the Dasyu. Virile and boisterous, Indra personified the heroic virtues of the Aryan warrior aristocracy as he drove his chariot across the sky, wielded his thunderbolts, ate bulls by the score, and quaffed entire lakes of intoxicating *soma*. Another major Aryan god

Excavations at Mohenjo-Daro have unearthed mother-goddess figurines and seals which may have had religious significance. The seals bear Indus writing, essentially a pictographic script employing about 250 symbols and 400 characters, which is still undeciphered. Such seals have been found along the Iranian plateau trade routes and on an island in the Persian Gulf, indicating that trade existed between the Indus civilization and western civilizations. This seven-inch-high statue of a man also suggests contacts between the Mesopotamian and Indus valley civilizations because of its heavy beard, a common feature of contemporaneous Sumerian sculpture.

was Varuna, the sky-god. Viewed as the king of the gods, he lived in a great palace in the heavens where one of his associates was Mitra, known as Mithras to the Persians and widely worshiped in the Roman Empire. Varuna was the guardian of *rita,* which means "setting in motion" and refers to the cosmic order—the regularity of all nature such as day and night, the four seasons, and the life-cycle of living things.

The Later Vedic Age (c. 1000-500 B.C.). Most of our knowledge about the five hundred years following the composition of the *Rig-Veda* is gleaned from two great epics, the *Mahabharata* and the *Ramayana,* and from the religious compositions of the Brahmin priests. These compositions include the three later *Vedas,* containing many hymns along with spells and incantations designed to avoid harm or secure blessings to the worshiper; the *Brahmanas,* which describe and explain the priestly ritual of sacrifice and reflect the dominant position achieved by the Brahmin class in society; and the more philosophical speculations collectively known as the *Upanishads.*

The kernel of the two Indian epics, which glorify the Kshatriyan (noble or warrior) class, was originally secular rather than religious. The core of the *Mahabharata* is a great war between rivals for the throne of an Aryan state situated in the upper Ganges plain in the region of modern Delhi. As in the Greek *Iliad's* account of the Trojan War, all the rulers of India participate in a decisive battle, which raged for eighteen days near the beginning of the Later Vedic Age. The epic came to be used in royal sacrificial ritual, and a long succession of priestly editors added many long passages on statecraft, morals, and theology.

One of the most famous additions is the *Bhagavad-Gita (The Lord's Song),* a philosophical dialogue which stresses the performance of duty, or *dharma,* without passion or fear. It is still the most treasured piece in Hindu literature. *Dharma,* whose broad meaning is moral law and is often translated as "virtue," had by this time replaced the earlier Vedic term *rita* which, as noted above, originally meant premoral cosmic law.

The other great epic, the *Ramayana,* has been likened to the Greek *Odyssey.* It recounts the wanderings of the banished prince Rama and his faithful wife Sita's long vigil before they are reunited and Rama gains his rightful throne. In the course of time priestly editors transformed this simple adventure story into a book of devotion. Rama became the ideal man and the incarnation of the great god Vishnu, while Sita emerged as the perfect woman.

The two epics, together with the last three *Vedas* and the *Brahmanas,* reflect the many changes that occurred in Indian life during the Later Vedic Age. The Aryans had moved eastward from the Punjab, conquering the native population and forming larger and frequently warring states in the upper Ganges valley. These were territorial rather than tribal states. Although some were oligarchic republics, most were ruled by rajahs. Despite the presence of an advisory council of nobles and priests, the rajahs' powers were greater than those of the tribal leaders of the earlier period. The rajahs now lived in palaces and collected taxes—in the form of goods from the villages—in order to sustain their courts and armies. A few small cities arose, some as administrative centers connected with a palace, and some as commercial centers. Trade contacts with Mesopotamia were renewed, and merchants probably brought back from the West the use of coinage and the Aramaic alphabet, which was adapted to Sanskrit.

Village, caste, and family. In the Later Vedic Age, the three pillars of traditional Indian society—the autonomous village, caste, and the joint family—were established. India has always been primarily agricultural, and its countryside is still a patchwork of thousands of villages. The ancient village was made up of related families governed by a headman. Land was considered to be the property of the whole community and was distributed among the joint families by the headman, who also collected the rajah's taxes. Villages enjoyed considerable autonomy; the rajah's government hardly interfered at all as long as it received its quota of taxes.

The four classes, or castes—Kshatriyas (nobles), Vaisyas (commoners), Brahmins (priests), and Sudras (workers or serfs)—have remained constant throughout India's history. But during the Later Vedic Age, the Brahmins assumed the highest social rank. The four castes also began to subdivide into numerous subcastes, each with a special social, occupational, or religious character. For example, such new occupational groups as merchants and artisans became subcastes. Furthermore, another main social division was formed, consisting of those whose occupations were the most menial and degrading—scavengers, sweepers, tanners (because they handled the carcasses of dead animals),

The Kailasa Temple at Ellora, the largest and most elaborate of the Indian temples carved out of solid rock, contains intricate carvings of incidents and characters from the great epics, the *Mahabharata* and the *Ramayana*.

and carriers of human and animal waste. These outcasts were called Untouchables because their touch was considered defiling to the upper castes.

Although the inequalities of the caste system clearly contributed to the wealth and influence of the upper castes, the lower caste groups came to accept the system. One reason for this was the manner in which a caste performed the functions of a guild in maintaining a monopoly for the caste in its occupation and in securing other favorable conditions for its members. By maintaining discipline in accordance with caste rules, the caste leaders in each village also gave Indian society a stability that partially compensated for the lack of political stability over a wide area through much of Indian history.

Brahmanism: priestly power. Radical changes in Indian religion and thought occurred during the Later Vedic Age, producing what became one of the world's most complex religious and philosophical systems. The first phase of this development began about 1000 B.C. and is often called Brahmanism because it was the product of the emergence of the Brahmin priests to a position of supreme power and privilege in society. Since only the priests possessed the technical expertise to perform the complex and lengthy rites of sacrifice (some of which lasted for months), and since the slightest variation in ritual was thought to turn the gods against people, the Brahmins strengthened their position over the nobles and rulers of the Kshatriya class. The priests gave the caste system a religious sanction by extending the concept of *dharma,* moral duty, to include the performance of caste functions as social duty.

The Upanishads: philosophical speculation. The more than 250 *Upanishads* were composed between 800 and 600 B.C. by some members of the Brahmin and Kshatriya classes who rejected both the simple nature worship of the *Rig-Veda* and the complicated sacrificial system of the *Brahmanas.* Like their counterparts in the West at about the same time—the first Greek philosophers —they speculated on the nature of reality, the purpose of life, and God. The following beliefs became an integral part of Indian religion and philosophy:

1. The fundamental reality, the essence of all things, is not something material, as most of the early Greek philosophers concluded, but spiritual — the World Soul, or *Brahman.*

2. Each individual possesses a soul, which is a part of the World Soul.

3. The material world is an illusion *(maya)* and the cause of all suffering. As long as such earthly goals as fame, power, and wealth are sought, the result will be pain and sorrow.

4. Salvation, or deliverance from *maya,* can only come through the reabsorption of the individual soul into the World Soul.

5. This release from *maya* is part of a complicated process of reincarnation. The individual soul must go through a long series of earthly reincarnations from one body to another.

6. Intertwined with the doctrine of reincarnation is the immutable law called *karma* (meaning "deed"). This law holds that the consequences of one's deeds determine one's future after death. A person's status at any particular point is not the result of chance but depends on his or her soul's actions in previous existences. Together with the doctrine of *maya, karma* gives a satisfactory explanation to the question of why suffering exists, a question that has troubled thoughtful people all over the world. The Indian answer is that the wicked who prosper will pay later, while the righteous who suffer are being punished for acts committed in former existences.

Hinduism: a religious synthesis. Upanishadic thought became a part of Hinduism, the developing religion of India, when the Brahmin priests incorporated it into their teaching. In doing so they gave the caste system additional religious support by linking it to *karma* and the process of reincarnation. In effect, caste became the essential machinery for the educative process of the soul as it went through the long succession of rebirths from the lowest categories in caste to that of the Brahmin, who presumably is near the end of the cycle. But because Upanishadic doctrines were often too intellectual and remote for the average person to fully grasp, devotional cults grew up side by side with them. They centered on gods who, as manifestations of Brahman (the World Soul), stood in close relationship to their worshipers.

The major Aryan gods gradually faded away, and Hinduism acquired a trinity consisting of Brahma the Creator, Vishnu the Preserver, and Shiva the Destroyer. Brahma, the personification of the World Soul whose name is the masculine form of *Brahman,* never acquired the vast popular following achieved by Vishnu and Shiva, a position they continue to maintain. These two popular deities evolved from Vedic and Dravidian origins.

In the old Vedic pantheon of the Aryans, Vishnu the Preserver was a god associated with the sun. He evolved into the friend and comforter, the savior who works continuously for the welfare of humanity. "No devotee of mine is lost," is Vishnu's promise. His followers believe that he has appeared in ten major "descents" in human form to save the world from disaster. Two of Vishnu's incarnations are described in the great Indian epics. As Krishna in the *Mahabharata,* he is the friend and adviser of princes and the author of *The Lord's Song (Bhagavad-Gita;* see p. 93). As Rama, the hero of the *Ramayana,* he saves mankind from the oppressions of a great demon before returning to the "City of the Gods" and resuming the form of Vishnu.

Shiva the Destroyer, the other great popular god of classical and modern Hinduism, evolved from a minor Aryan Vedic god who was the guardian of healing herbs but whose arrows also brought disease. Another prototype of Shiva was a pre-Aryan fertility god who was worshiped in the cities of the Indus civilization. For this reason, Shiva is often associated with phallic symbols. His spouse is the pre-Aryan mother goddess who under various forms, from grossly sexual to gentle and benevolent, often plays a more important role than her husband.

With such a background, Shiva is a very different character from Vishnu. Shiva personifies the cosmic force of change which both destroys and creates — the principle that death and reproduction are inseparable aspects of change. Some representations portray Shiva in terrifying guise, garlanded with skulls; others show him as the Lord of Dancers, whose activities are the source of all movement within the cosmos.

Most Hindus are devotees of either Vishnu or Shiva and their respective emanations, wives, and children. However, animals—especially the cow—vegetation, water, and even stones are also worshiped as divine. In time literally thousands of deities, demigods, and lesser spirits came to form the Hindu pantheon, the world's largest. Hindus, however, do not think of their religion as polytheistic, for all gods and spirits are viewed as manifestations of *Brahman,* the World Soul, which pervades everything.

Hinduism is probably the world's most tolerant religion. It possesses no canon, such as the Bible or the Koran; no single personal founder, such as Christ or Muhammad; and no precise body of authoritative doctrine. Hindus can believe what they like, and they remain Hindus as long as they observe the rules of their caste. Depending on one's intellectual and spiritual needs and capacities, Hinduism can be a transcendental philosophy, or a devotional adherence to a savior god such as Vishnu, or simple idolatry. From its earliest origins, Hinduism has exhibited an unusual organic quality of growth and adaptation. The last major element in the Hindu synthesis was provided by Gautama Buddha.

The Middle Way of Gautama Buddha. By taking over Upanishadic thought, the Brahmins had laid the foundations of classical Hinduism, but they continued to place great emphasis upon the importance of sacrifice, priestly ritual, and magical spells. This led in the sixth century to the rise of ascetics and reformers who sought to pursue the goals of Upanishadic thought by bypassing the priests and their mechanical ceremonialism. To achieve salvation from the cycle of birth and death, most of these dissenters lived as hermits, meditating on the true nature of human beings as part of the World Soul. They demonstrated by their indifference to discomfort and worldly matters that they had realized their oneness with the underlying essence of all things. The most important of these ascetics, who soon rejected extreme asceticism and found his own "Middle Way" to salvation, was Gautama, who called himself the Buddha ("The Enlightened One").

Gautama (563?–483 B.C.) was the son of a leading noble in a small oligarchic republic located at the foot of the Himalayas. In his twenty-ninth year, according to tradition, Gautama was deeply shocked by the misery, disease, and sorrow that he saw as he walked through the streets of his native city. He renounced his wealth and position and, forsaking his wife and child, determined to seek a meaningful answer to the question of human suffering. For six years he lived in a forest, practicing the self-mortification rites of the ascetics he found there. Gautama almost died from fasting and self-torture and at last concluded that these practices did not lead to wisdom.

One day, while sitting beneath a sacred fig tree meditating on the problem of human suffering, Gautama received "enlightenment." The meaning, the cause, and the conquest of suffering became clear to him. From this insight, he constructed a religious philosophy that has affected the lives of millions of people for 2500 years.

Dressed in a simple yellow robe, with begging bowl in hand, he wandered through the plains of the Ganges, speaking with everyone regardless of caste, and attracting disciples. At last, when he was eighty years old and enfeebled, he was invited by a poor blacksmith to a meal. According to legend, the food was tainted, but Gautama ate it rather than offend his host. Later in the day the Buddha had severe pains, and he knew death was near. Calling his disciples together, he gave them this parting message: "Be ye lamps unto yourselves. Be a refuge to yourselves. Hold fast to the truth as to a lamp. Look not for refuge to anyone beside yourselves."

Buddhist teachings. What is "the truth" that the Buddha believed could be discovered by individual effort, without the need for priestly assistance? The answer had been revealed to him during the Great Enlightenment in the form of the Four Noble Truths:

1. "the truth of pain," because pain and suffering are universal;
2. "the truth of the cause of pain," which is desire;
3. "the truth of cessation of pain," by ceasing to desire; and
4. "the truth of the way that leads to the cessation of pain," which is the Middle Way between worldly pursuits and extreme asceticism.

Like so many reform movements in the history of religion, the Buddha's teaching aimed at restoring the purity of an existing creed. The Buddha sought to strip the Upanishadic teachings of the corruptions that had enveloped them. Thus he restored the ethical basis of the doctrines of *karma* and reincarnation, which the priests had made dependent on the performance of ritual rather than moral behavior. He also repudiated the belief that only members of the Brahmin caste could attain release from the wheel of birth and rebirth, insisting that release was possible for everyone regardless of caste. Nor was there any place in his system for the popular gods of Hinduism. Indeed, what the Buddha taught was more a philosophy than a religion. For such reasons Buddhism soon became a movement separate from Hinduism.

Like the Christians, the Buddhists came to form two groups—monks and laymen. The Buddha's close disciples, who included women as well as men, renounced the world, donned yellow robes, and lived for part of the year in the first known monastic communities, with staves and begging bowls as their only possessions. By means of a strict discipline of mind and body, they aspired to achieve "the supreme peace of *nirvana*"—release from the wheel of birth and rebirth. The literal meaning of *nirvana* is "to extinguish," and it refers to the extinguishing of desire, which feeds on sensual pleasures and is the cause of suffering. *Nirvana* is also a state of superconsciousness, attained by a type of yoga concentration in which the individual personality or ego dissolves and becomes united with the spirit of life, which the Buddha taught exists in all creatures.

To the ascetic monks, Buddhism's major purpose is the dissolution of the ego and the sense of release and spiritual joy that results. To ordinary Buddhist laymen, who continue to live in the world (although they often "retreat" to a monastery for short periods), the Buddha's ethical teachings serve as a guide to right living. The beauty and nobility of those teachings can be seen in the following excerpts:

Hatred does not cease by hatred at any time; hatred ceases by love.

All men trouble at punishment, all men love life. Remember that you are like unto them, and do not cause slaughter.

Not by birth does one become an outcaste, not by birth does one become a Brahmin. By deeds one becomes an outcaste, by deeds one becomes a Brahmin.[1]

The counterreformation of Hinduism. The Buddha was a reformer who censured the rites and dogmas of the Brahmins, broke with the rules of caste, taught that all people are equal, and proclaimed a code of ethics

A temple wall painting shows the many-armed Hindu god Shiva as the Lord of the Dancers. In his hands he holds symbols of the various aspects of his divine power.

whose purity is universally recognized. We shall see that Buddhism reached its height in India in the third century B.C. Soon thereafter Buddhism began to decline, and ultimately it disappeared in its homeland.

A major reason for this development was a successful counterreformation of Hinduism. For most people accustomed to elaborate ritual and the worship of benevolent personal gods, original Buddhism seemed stern and austere, and in time the Buddha's simpler followers began to worship him as a god and the savior of humanity. Temples were built and statues were erected honoring the savior, and *nirvana* was viewed as a sort of heaven. Then when the Brahmins proclaimed the Buddha to be the ninth incarnation of the great Hindu god Vishnu, Buddhism began to fade as an independent religion in India.

Buddhism's impact on Hinduism was nevertheless profound, for it served to rejuvenate and purify the older religion. More emphasis was henceforth placed on ethical conduct and less on sacrifices, ritual prayers, and magic spells.

THE FIRST INDIAN EMPIRE

Alexander the Great in India. In 326 B.C. Alexander the Great, continuing his conquest of the Persian Empire (see Chapter 2), brought his phalanxes into the easternmost Persian satrapy in the Indus valley, defeating local Punjab rulers. When his weary troops refused to advance further eastward into the Ganges valley, Alexander constructed a fleet and explored the Indus to its mouth. From there he returned overland to Babylon, while his fleet skirted the coast of the Arabian Sea and reached the Persian Gulf.

After Alexander's death in 323 B.C., the empire he had built so rapidly quickly disintegrated, and by 321 B.C. his domain in the Punjab had completely disappeared. But he had opened routes between India and the West that would remain open during the following Hellenistic and Roman periods, and by destroying the petty princedoms of the Punjab he facilitated the conquests of India's first emperor.

Chandragupta Maurya, India's first emperor. In 322 B.C., shortly after Alexander's death, a new era began in India. In that year Chandragupta Maurya seized the state of Magadha in the Ganges valley. In the next twenty-four years Chandragupta conquered much of northern India and founded the Maurya dynasty, which endured until about 185 B.C. At its height the empire included all the subcontinent except the extreme south.

India's first empire reflected the imperial vision of its founder. He created an administrative system whose efficiency was not surpassed until the advent of British rule in the nineteenth century. Chandragupta was also a brilliant general and administrator. He was responsible for the first military victory of the East over the West; in 305 B.C. he defeated Seleucus, the general who had inherited the major part of Alexander's empire and had crossed the Indus in an attempt to regain Alexander's Indian conquests. Seleucus gave up his Indian claims in return for five hundred elephants and established friendly diplomatic relations with the Indian emperor.

Life in the Mauryan empire. Seleucus' ambassador to the court of Chandragupta, whose name was Megasthenes, wrote a detailed account of India, fragments of which have survived. They give a fascinating picture of life in the empire. Pataliputra, Chandragupta's capital city known today as Patna, covered eighteen square miles. Outside its massive wooden walls was a deep trench used for defense and sewage disposal.

The remarkably advanced Mauryan empire was divided and subdivided into provinces, districts, and villages whose headmen were appointed by the state. The old customary law, preserved and administered by the Brahmin priesthood, was superseded by an extensive legal code which provided for royal interference in all matters. A series of courts ranging from the village court presided over by the headman to the emperor's imperial court administered the law. So busy was Chandragupta with the details of his surprisingly modern administration that, according to Megasthenes, he had to hear court cases during his daily massage.

Two other agencies were very important in holding the empire together. One was the professional army, which Megasthenes reports was an incredibly large force of 700,000 men, 9000 elephants, and 10,000 chariots. The other was the secret police, whose numbers were so great that the Greek writer concluded that spies constituted a separate class in Indian society. So great was the danger of conspiracy that Chandragupta lived in strict seclusion, attended only by women who cooked his food and in the evening carried him to his apartment, where they lulled him to sleep with music.

This picture of an efficient but harsh bureaucracy is added to by a remarkable book, *Treatise on Material Gain (Arthasastra)*, written by Chandragupta's chief minister, Kautilya, as a guide for the king and his ministers. Kautilya exalts royal power as the means of establishing and maintaining "material gain," meaning political and economic stability. The great evil is anarchy, such as had existed among the small states in northern India. To achieve the aims of statecraft, Kautilya argues, a single authority is needed that will employ force when necessary. Like Machiavelli, the Renaissance Italian author of a famous book on statecraft (*The Prince*), Kautilya advocates deception or unscrupulous means to attain desired ends.

The Mauryan state also controlled and encouraged economic life. Kautilya's treatise, which is thought to reflect much actual practice, advises the ruler to "facilitate mining operations," "encourage manufacturers," "exploit forest wealth," "provide amenities" for cattle breeding and commerce, and "construct highways both on land and on water." Price controls are advocated because "all goods should be sold to the people at favorable prices," and foreign trade should be subsidized: "Shippers and traders dealing in foreign goods should be given tax exemptions to aid them in making profits." Foreign trade did flourish, and in the bazaars of Pataliputra were displayed goods from southern India, China, Mesopotamia, and Asia Minor. Agriculture, however, remained the chief source of wealth. In theory, all land belonged to the state, which collected one-fourth of the produce as taxes. Irrigation and crop rotation were practiced, and Mesgasthenes states that there were no famines.

Ashoka, India's greatest king. Following Chandragupta's death in 297 B.C., his son and grandson expanded the empire southward into the Deccan Peninsula. However, Chandragupta's grandson Ashoka (273-232 B.C.), the most renowned of all Indian rulers, was more committed to peace than to war. His first military campaign was also his last; the cruelty of the campaign horrified him, and he resolved never again to permit such acts of butchery. Soon thereafter he was converted to Buddhism, whose teachings increased his aversion to warfare.

Throughout his empire, Ashoka had his edicts carved on rocks and stone pillars. They remain today as the oldest surviving written documents of India and are invaluable for

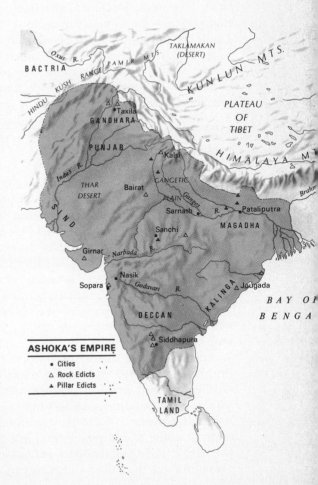

appreciating the spirit and purpose of Asho-ka's rule. For example, they contain his con-ception of the duty of a ruler:

He shall . . . personally attend the business . . . of earth, of sacred places, of minors, the aged, the afflicted, and the helpless, and of women. . . . In the happiness of his subjects lies his happi-ness. . . .[2]

Although a devout Buddhist, Ashoka did not persecute the Brahmins and Hindus but proclaimed religious toleration as official policy:

The king . . . honors every form of religious faith . . . ; whereof this is the root, to reverence one's own faith and never to revile that of others. Who-ever acts differently injures his own religion while he wrongs another's.[3]

Ashoka was a successful propagator of his faith. He sent Buddhist missionaries to many lands — the Himalayan regions, Tamil Land, Ceylon, Burma, and even as far away as Syria and Egypt — and transformed Bud-dhism from a small Indian sect to an ag-gressive missionary faith. Modern-day Indians revere his memory, and the famous lion on the capital of one of his pillars has been adopted as the national seal of the present Indian republic.

Fall of the Mauryan empire. Almost im-mediately after Ashoka's death in 232 B.C., the Mauryan empire began to disintegrate. The last emperor was assassinated about 185 B.C. in a palace revolution led by a Brah-min priest. Some five centuries of disintegra-tion and disorder followed. Northern India was overrun by a series of invaders, and the south broke free from northern control.

The sudden collapse of the powerful Mauryan state, and the grave consequences that ensued have provoked much scholarly speculation. Some historians have felt that the fall of the Mauryas can be traced to a hostile Brahmin reaction against Ashoka's patronage of Buddhism. Others believe that Ashoka's doctrine of nonviolence curbed the military ardor of his people and left them vulnerable to invaders. More plausible ex-planations for the fall of the Mauryan state

take into account the communications prob-lems facing an empire that included most of the Indian subcontinent, the difficulty of financing a vast army and bureaucracy, and the intrigues of discontented and ambitious elements within the empire.

NEW INVADERS OF INDIA

The Bactrian Greeks. The Mauryan empire was the first of two successful attempts to unify India in ancient times. The second — the work of the Gupta dynasty (320 – 500 A.D.) — will be described in Chapter 7. In the five centuries between these two eras of imperial splendor, a succession of foreign invaders entered from the northwest and added new racial and cultural elements to the Indian scene.

The first of the new invaders were Greeks from Bactria (see map, p. 99). They were descendants of the soldiers settled there by Alexander, who were the strong point of his empire in the east. After Alexander, Bactria continued on as a province of the Seleucid empire, a bastion against the at-tacks of wandering nomads from the north and a center for trade with India to the south-east. The decline of the Seleucid empire al-lowed the Bactrian Greeks to establish an independent kingdom about 245 B.C.

In 183 B.C., two years after the death of the last Mauryan emperor of India, the fourth Bactrian king, Demetrius, crossed the Hindu Kush mountains as Alexander had done 150 years earlier and occupied the northern Punjab. From their base at Taxila, Demetrius and his successors ruled an area stretching from Bactria to the upper Ganges valley, but soon after 150 B.C., Bactria itself was overrun by nomads. Thereafter Greek rule in India steadily declined until the last remnants disappeared late in the first century B.C.

The Greeks in India established the far-thest outpost of Hellenism in the Hellenistic Age. Demetrius and his successors came closer than any Hellenistic ruler to realizing Alexander's supposed goal of a union of races. Their cities were not artificial Greek enclaves in a hostile land, like Alexandria in

Egypt and Antioch in Syria. Indians were enrolled as citizens, a bilingual coinage was issued bearing Greek inscriptions on one side and Indian on the other, and at least one king, Menander, appears to have become a Buddhist.

The Kushans. Hordes of nomadic peoples, migrating out of central Asia, replaced the Greeks in Bactria and northwest India. First to arrive were the Indo-European Scythians, who had been pushed out of central Asia by nomads known in Chinese sources as the Yueh-chi. In their turn the Yueh-chi occupied Bactria, and about 40 A.D. they crossed the Hindu Kush and conquered the Punjab. The Kushans, as the Yueh-chi were called in India, expanded eastward to the Middle Ganges valley and southward perhaps as far as the borders of the Deccan. In contrast to the highly centralized Mauryan empire, the Kushan state was more feudal than bureaucratic—its kings were overlords rather than direct rulers—yet it gave northern India two centuries of peace and prosperity before collapsing soon after 200 A.D.

Hinayana and Mahayana Buddhism. Buddhism in the meantime had split into two major branches. The older branch was contemptuously called Hinayana or "Lesser Vehicle" (to salvation) by its opponents. It continued the early tradition of regarding the Buddha as a teacher who taught how the individual could achieve salvation by becoming an *arhat,* a saint who eliminated his ego and entered into *nirvana. Arhats* renounced the world to seek their own enlightenment and salvation. To the followers of the newer branch, the Mahayana or "Great Vehicle" (to salvation), the Hinayana goal was considered to be selfish and incomplete. They replaced the ideal of the *arhat* with that of the *bodhisattva* ("one whose essence is enlightenment"), a saint who postponed his own entry into *nirvana* in order to act as a savior to others in reaching that goal.

Mahayana Buddhism, with its message of hope and salvation for the masses, now spread rapidly along the overland trade route to Tibet and China, and from China to Korea, Japan, and Vietnam. The more austere Hinayana became the southern branch of Buddhism, spreading from India and Ceylon to Burma, Thailand, and Cambodia.

While Buddhism was becoming a world religion, Hinduism continued to maintain a strong hold on the Indian people. Unlike the Buddhists, who had disregarded caste and accepted both the Greeks and the Kushans, the Hindus rejected the foreign invaders as outcastes. Gradually the Indians came to consider Hinduism a more characteristically Indian movement than Buddhism, and the latter began to lose its popularity within India.

Buddhist sculpture and architecture. The most lasting Western influence on India in ancient times was on Buddhist sculpture. Before the Kushan period, Indian artists were influenced by the Buddha's prohibitions against idolatry and refrained from portraying the Buddha in human form. Beginning in the first century A.D., however, the Buddha himself was portrayed in numerous statues and reliefs. Most of these early Buddha figures come from Gandhara, the center of the Kushan empire and the earlier Graeco-Bactrian kingdom.

The primary inspiration for this Gandharan art came from Greece, but scholars dispute whether it was brought to India by the Bactrian Greeks or arrived later via the trade routes from the eastern provinces of the Roman Empire. The result was a subtle blending of Greek technique and Indian motifs.

A second inspiration for Gandharan art came from Mahayana Buddhism, which viewed the Buddha as a savior. This devotional form of Buddhism needed images for worship, and figures of the Buddha, as well as many *bodhisattvas,* were produced in large numbers. Mahayana Buddhism and Graeco-Buddhist images of the Buddha, both of which developed in the Kushan empire, spread together through eastern Asia.

The magnificent buildings of the Mauryan emperors have disappeared. All that remain are Buddhist *stupas,* dome-shaped monuments that were used as funeral mounds to enshrine the relics of saints or to mark a holy spot. Originally made only of earth, the mounds were later fashioned out

During the period of the Graeco-Bactrian kingdom, a prolific Graeco-Roman Buddhist school of art evolved from the fusion of Greek and Buddhist elements in Gandhara. Because of the Buddha's prohibitions against idolatry, artists had for centuries refrained from portraying the Buddha in human form, depicting instead only symbols of his life and teaching. In the capital from one of Ashoka's pillars, for example, the lion suggests Buddha's majesty and power while the wheel below is the Wheel of Law which was set in motion through his teachings. With the growth of the *Mahayana* school, however, artists began to create figures of the Buddha. Dating from the fifth century A.D., the head of Buddha from Gandhara shows Hellenistic influence in the modeling of the features and hair, while the elongated ear lobes, heavy-lidded eyes, mark on the forehead, knot of hair, and expression of deep repose are Indian. Eventually the *Mahayana* school of Buddhism and Graeco-Roman Buddhist art spread together throughout eastern Asia.

of earth faced with brick and surrounded by railings and four richly carved gateways of stone. On top of the dome was a boxlike structure surmounted by a carved umbrella, the Indian emblem of sovereignty that symbolizes the Buddha's princely birth. As centuries passed, the low dome was heightened into a tall, tapered structure more like a tower. Later, when Buddhism spread to other countries, the *stupa* type of architecture went along; its gateway was widely copied, and the *stupa* itself inspired the Buddhist pagodas that today dot East Asia (see illustration, p. 350).

South India. With the exception of a short period during the Mauryan empire, the vast tableland of south India—the Deccan—and its fertile coastal plains remained outside the main forces of political change in the north. The Dravidian peoples of this area, with their dark skin and small stature, differed in appearance, language, and culture from the Aryan-speaking peoples of the north. Gradually, however, as Brahmin priests and Buddhist monks infiltrated the south, Hinduism and Buddhism were grafted onto the existing Dravidian culture.

Politically the south remained divided into numerous warring states, the most interesting being three Tamil-speaking (a Dravidian dialect) kingdoms in the far south. Tamil folk poetry, which describes the people at work and at play, is justly famous. By the first century B.C. the Tamil land had become an intermediary in the maritime trade extending eastward to the East Indies and westward to the Hellenistic kingdoms.

When Augustus became head of the Roman world, the Tamil and Kushan rulers sent him congratulatory embassies. At least nine other embassies from India visited the Roman emperors, and Roman-Indian trade greatly increased. Indian birds became the pets of wealthy Roman ladies, and Indian animals (lions, tigers, and buffaloes) were used in the wild beast shows of Roman emperors. In view of these contacts, we can understand why Ptolemy's second-century-A.D. map of the world shows considerable knowledge of the geography of India (see illustration, p. 389).

The peace and prosperity that the Kushans brought to much of northern India ended about 220 A.D. The collapse of the Kushan state was followed by a century of chaos and almost total obscurity before a new era of unified imperial rule, which rivaled that of the Mauryas, began in India under the Guptas (see Chapter 7). In the meantime another great civilization had arisen in China.

CHINA: THE FORMATIVE CENTURIES

The land. Chinese civilization arose and developed in a vast area, one-third larger than the United States if such dependencies as Manchuria, Inner Mongolia, and Tibet are included. For centuries China was almost completely isolated from the other centers of civilization by mountains, deserts, and seas. This isolation helps explain the great originality of China's culture.

China proper is a vast watershed drained by three river systems that rise close together on the high Tibetan plateau and flow eastward to the Pacific. Three mountain systems also rise in the west, diminishing in altitude as they slope eastward between the river systems. The Yellow River (Huang Ho), traditionally known as "China's Sorrow" because of the misery caused by its periodic flooding, traverses the North China Plain. In this area, the original homeland of Chinese culture, the climate is like that of Western Europe. The Yangtze River marks the boundary between North and Central China, while the shorter rivers and valleys converging on present-day Canton in hot and humid South China form the third major river system.

This system of mountain ranges and river systems has, throughout China's history, created problems of political unity. At the same time, the great river valleys facilitated the spread of a homogeneous culture over a greater land area than any other civilization in the world.

China's prehistory. The discovery of Peking man in 1927 made it evident that ancient humanlike creatures with an early Paleolithic culture had dwelled in China. Certain physical characteristics of Peking man are thought to be distinctive marks of the Mongoloid branch of the human race. Skulls of modern humans *(Homo sapiens)* have also been found, providing evidence that late Paleolithic culture flourished in China between 70,000 and 20,000 years ago.

Neolithic farming villages first appeared about 4500 B.C. in the Yellow River valley. These people domesticated pigs, engaged in farming, and produced handmade red pottery decorated boldly in black. Scholars are divided over whether this earliest Neolithic culture reached China from the Near East or had a separate origin.

The people of a later Neolithic culture domesticated more varieties of animals than their predecessors and produced a wheel-made black pottery. Their culture spread widely in North China, including the Yangtze valley. Most scholars believe that this second Neolithic culture immediately preceded the Shang period, when civilization emerged in China about 1700 B.C. (or 1500, according to another tradition).

The Shang dynasty: China enters history. With the establishment of Shang rule over most of North China and the appearance of the first written texts, China completed the transition from Neolithic culture to civilization. Shang originally was the name of a nomadic tribe whose vigorous leaders succeeded in establishing themselves as the overlords of other tribal leaders in North China. The Shang capital, to which the tribal leaders came to pay tribute, changed frequently; the last capital was at modern Anyang (see map. p. 105).

The Shang people developed bronze metallurgy and carried it to heights hardly surpassed in world history. Bronze was used to cast elaborate ceremonial vessels and weapons that were intricately decorated with both incised and high-relief designs.

The Shang people also developed a distinctive writing system employing over two thousand characters, some of which are still in use today. These characters represent individual words, rather than sounds, and consist of three types: pictographs, recognizable as pictures of observable objects; ideographs, representing ideas; and compound characters, one part of which indicates the pronunciation.

Most Shang writing is found on "oracle bones," fragments of animal bones and tortoise shells on which were inscribed questions put to the gods and ancestral spirits. For example, the diviner would ask whether a particular member of the family would recover from an illness. The shell or bone would then be heated and the resulting cracks would be interpreted as an answer to the question.

Shang China was ruled by hereditary kings who were probably also priests acting as intermediaries between the people and the spirit world. Shang kings and nobles lived in imposing buildings, went to battle in horse-drawn chariots resembling those of Homer's Greece, and were buried in sumptuous tombs together with their chariots and still-living servants. Warfare was frequent, and the chariot, a new military weapon, facilitated the spread of Shang power through North China. The power of the kings and the nobles rested on their monopoly of bronze metallurgy, their possession of expensive

Shang artisans produced intricately detailed bronze vessels by a sophisticated casting process. This owl-like wine cup was used in religious ceremonies by the earliest emperors.

war chariots, and the king's religious functions.

Shang religion centered around the worship of ancestors and of the spirits of nature, such as the wind and the earth. The chief deity was called "Supreme Ancestor." There were regular animal sacrifices, and sometimes libations of a beerlike liquor were poured on the ground.

Farming methods were primitive, not having advanced beyond the Neolithic level. Bronze was used for weapons, not tools or implements, and the peasants continued to reap their grain with stone sickles and till their fields with sticks and wooden spades.

The Chou dynasty: the feudal age. Around 1122 (some scholars prefer 1027) B.C., the leader of the Chou tribe overthrew the Shang ruler, who, it was claimed, had failed to honor the ancestral spirits. The Chou leader announced that the spirit of heaven had given him a mandate to replace the Shang. A western frontier tribe, the Chou had maintained its martial spirit and fighting ability. The other Chinese tribes switched their loyalty to the Chou leader, who went on to establish the longest-lasting dynasty in Chinese history (1122-221 B.C.).

Comprising most of north China, the large Chou domain, like that of the Shang, made the establishment of a unified state impossible. Consequently, the Chou kings set up a feudal system of government by delegating local authority to relatives and noble magnates. These vassal lords, whose power was hereditary, recognized the overlordship of the Chou kings and supplied them with military aid.

The early Chou kings were vigorous leaders who were able to retain the allegiance of their vassals and fend off attacks from barbarian peoples on the frontiers. In time, however, weak kings succeeded to the throne, and the power and independence of their vassals increased. By the eighth century B.C., the vassals no longer went to the Chou capital for investiture by the Son of Heaven, as the Chou king called himself.

The remnants of Chou royal power disappeared completely in 771 B.C., when an alliance of dissident vassals and barbarians destroyed the capital and killed the king. Part of the royal family managed to escape eastward to Lo-yang, however, where the dynasty survived for another five centuries doing little more than performing state religious rituals. Seven of the stronger feudal princes gradually conquered their weaker neighbors. In the process they assumed the title *wang* ("king"), formerly used only by the Chou ruler, and began to extinguish the feudal rights of their own vassals and establish centralized administrations. Warfare among these emerging centralized states was incessant, particularly during the two centuries known as the Period of Warring States (403-221 B.C.). By 221 B.C. the ruler of Ch'in, the most advanced of the seven warring states, had conquered all his rivals, ended the Chou dynasty, and established a unified empire with himself as absolute ruler.

Chou economy and society. Despite its political instability, the Chou period is unrivaled by any later period in Chinese history for its material and cultural progress. These developments led the Chinese to distinguish between their own high civilization and the nomadic ways of the "barbarians" beyond their frontiers. A sense of the superiority of their own civilization became a lasting characteristic of the Chinese.

During the sixth century B.C., iron was introduced and came into general use by the end of the Chou. Iron weapons made warfare more efficient. The ox-drawn iron-tipped plow, together with the growth of large-scale irrigation and water-control projects, led to population growth based on increased agricultural yields. Canals were constructed to facilitate moving commodities over long distances. Commerce and wealth grew rapidly, and a merchant and artisan class emerged. Brightly colored shells, bolts of silk, and ingots of precious metals were the media of exchange; by the end of the Chou period small round copper coins with square holes were being minted. Chopsticks and finely lacquered objects, today universally considered as symbols of Chinese and East Asian culture, were also in use by the end of the period.

Class divisions and consciousness became

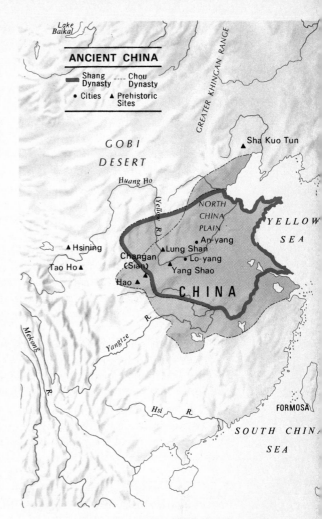

highly developed under Chou feudalism and have remained until modern times. The king and the aristocracy were sharply separated from the mass of the people on the basis of land ownership and family descent.

The customs of the nobles can be compared in a general way to those of Europe's feudal nobility (see Chapter 8). Underlying feudal society was a complex code of chivalry, called *li*, practiced in both war and peace. It became so important to the nobility as a symbol of gentility that men devoted years to its mastery. To display his martial skill and social grace, the Chinese noble "would come to the court of his seigneur to take part in tournaments of the noble sport of archery which was accompanied by musical airs and interspersed with elegant salutations, the whole regulated like a ballet."[4]

The art of horseback riding, developed among the nomads of central Asia, greatly influenced late Chou China. In response to the threat of mounted nomads, various rulers began constructing defensive walls, later joined together to become the Great Wall of China. Inside China itself, cavalry replaced the chariot in warfare.

The peasant masses worked as tenants of noble landholders, paying one-tenth of their crops as rent. Despite increased agricultural production resulting from large-scale irrigation and the ox-drawn iron-tipped plow, the peasants had difficulty eking out an existence. A major problem in the Chinese economy, evident by late Chou times, has been that the majority of farmers have worked fields so small that they could not produce a crop surplus to tide them over periods of scarcity.

The rise of philosophical schools. By the fifth century B.C., the increasing warfare among the feudal lords had destroyed the stability that had characterized Chinese society under the Shang and early Chou dynasties. Educated Chinese had become aware of the great disparity between the traditions inherited from their ancestors and the conditions in which they themselves lived. The result was the birth of a social consciousness that focused on the study of humanity and the problems of society. Some scholars have noted the parallel between the flourishing intellectual life of China in the fifth century B.C. and Greek philosophy and Indian religious thought at the same time. It has been suggested that these three great centers of world civilization stimulated and influenced each other. However, little or no historical evidence exists to support such an assertion. The birth of social consciousness in China, isolated from the other centers of civilization, can best be understood in terms of internal developments rather than external influences.

Confucianism: rational humanism. The first, most famous, and certainly most influential Chinese philosopher and teacher was K'ung-fu-tzu ("Master K'ung, the Sage"), known in the West by the Latinized form of his name, Confucius (551-479 B.C.).

Later Confucianists attributed to the master the role of composing or editing the Five Confucian Classics (two books of history and one book each on poetry, divination, and ceremonies), which were in large part a product of the Chou period. But the only work that can be accurately attributed to Confucius is the *Analects* ("Selected Sayings"), a collection of his responses to his disciples' questions.

Confucius, who belonged to the lower aristocracy, was more or less a contemporary of the Buddha in India, Zoroaster in Persia, and the early philosophers of Greece. Like the Buddha and Zoroaster, Confucius lived in a troubled time—an age of political and social turmoil—and his prime concern, like theirs, was the improvement of society. To achieve this, Confucius did not look to the gods and spirits for assistance; he accepted the existence of Heaven (*Ti'en*) and spirits, but he insisted it was more important "to know the essential duties of man living in a society of men." "We don't know yet how to serve men," he said, "how can we know about serving the spirits?" And, "We don't know yet about life, how can we know about death?" He advised a ruler to "respect the ghosts and spirits but keep them at a distance" and "devote yourself to the proper demands of the people."

Confucius believed that the improvement of society was the responsibility of the ruler and that the quality of government depended on the ruler's moral character: "The Way (*Tao*) of learning to be great consists in shining with the illustrious power of moral personality, in making a new people, in abiding in the highest goodness." Confucius' definition of the Way (*Tao*) as "moral personality" and "the highest goodness" was in decided contrast to the old premoral Way in which gods and spirits, propitiated by offerings and ritual, regulated human life for good or ill. Above all, Confucius' new Way meant a concern for the rights of others, the adherence to a Golden Rule:

Tzu-king [a disciple] asked saying, "Is there any single saying that one can act upon all day and every day?" The Master said, "Perhaps the saying about consideration: 'Never do to others what you would not like them to do to you.'[5]

Although Confucius called himself "a transmitter and not a creator," his redefinition of *Tao* was a radical innovation. He was, in effect, putting new wine into old bottles. He did the same with two other key terms, *li* and *chün-tzu. Li,* meaning "honorable behavior," was the chivalric code of the constantly fighting *chün-tzu,* the feudal "magnates" of the Chou period. As refined and reinterpreted by Confucius, *li* came to embody such ethical virtues as righteousness and love for fellow humans. The *chün-tzu,* under the influence of the new definition of *li,* became "gentlemen." His teachings have had a greater and longer-lasting influence on China, and much of East Asia, than those of any other philosopher.

Taoism: intuitive mysticism. A second philosophical reaction to the troubled life of the late Chou period was the teaching of Lao-tzu ("Old Master"), a semi-legendary figure who was believed to have been a contemporary of Confucius. As with Confucius, the key term in Lao-tzu's teaching is *Tao,* from which his philosophy derives its name. But while Confucius defined *Tao* as a rational standard of ethics in human affairs, Lao-tzu gave it a metaphysical meaning—the course of nature, the natural and inevitable order of the universe. The goal of Taoism, like Confucianism, is a happy life. Lao-tzu believed that this goal could be achieved by living a life in conformity with nature, retiring from the chaos and evils of contemporary feudal society and shunning human institutions and opinions as unnatural and artificial "outside things." Thus an important Taoist concept is *wu-wei,* or "nonaction" —a manner of living which, like nature itself, is nonassertive and spontaneous. Lao-tzu pointed out that in nature all things work silently; they fulfill their function and, after they reach their bloom, they return to their origins. Unlike Confucius' ideal gentleman, who is constantly involved in society in order to better it, Lao-tzu's sage is a private person, an egocentric individualist.

Taoism is a revolt not only against society

Courtesy, Museum of Fine Arts, Boston, Bigelow Collection

Buddha, Lao-tzu, and Confucius were three of the great leaders of East Asian thought. In this Japanese painting from the Kano period (1336-1558) they are depicted conversing together. Although the three philosophers were not contemporaries, their discussion symbolically represents the interaction of the three philosophical schools.

but also against the intellect's limitations. Indeed, one of the most famous Taoist philosophers, Chuang-tzu (fourth century B.C.), who made fun of Confucians as tiresome busybodies, even questioned the reality of the world of the senses. He said that he once dreamed that he was a butterfly, "flying about enjoying itself." When he awakened he was confused: "I do not know whether I was Chuang-tzu dreaming that I was a butterfly, or whether now I am a butterfly dreaming that I am Chuang-tzu."

Similar anecdotes and allegories abound in Taoist literature, as in all mystical teachings that deal with subjects that are difficult to put into words. But Taoist mysticism is philosophical, not religious; unlike Indian philosophy, it does not aim to extinguish the personality through the union with the Absolute or God. Rather, its aim is to teach how one can obtain happiness in this world by living a simple life in harmony with nature.

Confucianism and Taoism became the two major molds that shaped Chinese thought and civilization. Although these rival schools frequently sniped at one another, they never became mutually exclusive outlooks on life. Taoist intuition complemented Confucian rationalism; during the centuries to come Chinese would be Confucianists in their relations with their contemporaries and Taoists in their private life.

Mencius' contribution to Confucianism. The man whose work was largely responsible for the emergence of Confucianism as the most widely accepted philosophy in China was Mencius, or Meng-tzu (372-289 B.C.). Born a century after the death of Confucius, Mencius added important new dimensions to Confucian thought in two areas—human nature and government.

Although Confucius had only implied that human nature is good, Mencius emphatically insisted that all people are innately good and tend to seek the good just as water tends to run downhill. But unless people strive to preserve and develop their innate goodness, which is the source of righteous conduct, it can be corrupted by the bad practices and ideas existing in the environment. Mencius taught that the opposite of righteous conduct is selfishness, and he attacked the extreme individualism of the Taoists as a form of selfishness. He held that "all men are brothers"; he would have agreed with a later Confucian writer who summed up in one sentence the teaching of a famous Taoist: "He would not pluck so much as a hair out of his head for the benefit of his fellows."

The second area in which Mencius elaborated on Confucius' teaching was political theory. Mencius distinguished between good kings, who ruled benevolently, and the rulers of his day (the Period of Warring States), who governed by naked force and spread violence and disorder. Because good rulers are guided by ethical standards, he said, they will behave benevolently toward the people and provide for their well being. According to Mencius, the people have a right to rebel against bad rulers and even kill them if necessary, because they have lost the Mandate of Heaven.

As we have seen, this concept had been used by the Chou to justify their revolt against the Shang. On that occasion, the concept had had a religious meaning, being connected with the worship of ancestral spirits who supported the ruler as the Son of Heaven. Mencius, however, secularized and humanized the Mandate of Heaven by equating it with the people: "Heaven hears as the people hear; Heaven sees as the people see." By redefining the concept in this way, Mencius made the welfare of the people the ultimate standard for judging government; indeed, he even told rulers to their faces that the people were more important than they were.

Modern commentators, both Chinese and Western, have viewed Mencius' definition of the Mandate of Heaven as an early form of democratic thought. Mencius did believe that all people were morally equal and that the ruler needed the consent of the people, but he was clearly the advocate of benevolent monarchy rather than popular democracy.

Legalism. Another body of thought emerged in the fourth and third centuries B.C. and came to be called the School of Law, or Legalism. It had no single founder as did Confucianism and Taoism, nor was it ever a school in the sense of a teacher leading disciples. What it did have in common with Confucianism and Taoism was the desire to establish stability in an age of turmoil.

The Legalists emphasized the importance of harsh and inflexible law as the only means of achieving an orderly and prosperous society. They believed that human nature was basically bad and that people acted virtuously only when forced to do so. Therefore, they argued for an elaborate system of laws defining fixed penalties for each offense, with no exceptions for rank, class, or circumstances. Anyone who had knowledge of a crime and did not report it was considered as guilty as the criminal.

Since the enforcement of law required a strong state, the immediate goal of the Legalists was to enhance the power of the ruler at the expense of other elements, particularly the nobility. Their ultimate goal was the creation of a centralized state strong enough to unify all China and end the chaos of the Warring States period. The unification of China in 221 B.C. was largely the result of putting Legalist ideas of government into practice.

CHINA: THE FIRST EMPIRE

Rise of Legalist Ch'in. Throughout the two centuries of the Warring States period there was the hope that a king would emerge who would unite China and inaugurate a great new age of peace and stability. While the Confucians believed that such a king would accomplish the task by means of his outstanding moral virtue, the Legalists substituted overwhelming might as the essential element of effective government. The political philosophy of the Legalists, who liked to sum up and justify their doctrine in two words—"It works"—triumphed, and no state became more adept at practicing that pragmatic philosophy than the Ch'in.

The Ch'in's rise to preeminence began in 352 B.C., when its duke selected Lord Shang, a man imbued with Legalist principles, to be his chief minister. Recognizing that the growth of Ch'in's power depended on a more efficient and centralized bureaucratic structure than could exist under feudalism, Lord Shang undermined the old nobility by creating a new aristocracy based on military merit. He also introduced a universal draft beginning at approximately age fifteen. As a result, chariot and cavalry warfare, in which the nobility had played the leading role, was replaced by masses of infantry equipped with iron weapons and crossbows.

Economically, Lord Shang further weakened the old landowning nobility by abolishing the peasants' attachment to the land

and granting them ownership of the plots they tilled. The liberated peasants thereafter paid taxes directly to the state, thereby increasing its wealth and power. These reforms made Ch'in the most powerful of the Warring States. It soon began to extend the area of its political and social innovations.

Ch'in unites China. In the middle of the third century B.C., a hundred years after Lord Shang, another Legalist prime minister helped the king of Ch'in prepare and carry out the final conquests that unified China by 221 B.C. The king then declared himself the "First August Supreme Ruler" (Shih Huang-ti) of China, or "First Emperor," as his new title is usually translated. He also enlarged China—a name derived from the word Ch'in—by conquests in the south as far as the South China Sea.

The First Emperor gathered the aristocratic class—some 120,000 familes, according to tradition—at the capital, where they could be closely watched. To further forestall rebellion, the entire civilian population had to surrender its weapons to the state. A single harsh legal code, which replaced all local laws, was so detailed in its provisions that it was said to have been like "a fishing net through which even the smallest fish cannot slip out." The entire realm was divided into thirty-six provinces, administrative units drawn to obliterate traditional feudal units and to facilitate direct rule by the emperor's centrally controlled civil and military appointees. To destroy the source of the aristocracy's power and to permit the emperor's agents to tax every farmer's harvest, private ownership of land by peasants, promoted a century earlier in the state of Ch'in by Lord Shang, was decreed for all of China.

The First Emperor's most spectacular public work was repairing the remnants of walls built earlier by the northern feudal states and joining them into the Great Wall, extending from the sea into Central Asia for a distance of over 1400 miles. Constructed by forced labor, it was said that "every stone cost a human life." The wall was both a line of defense against the barbarians who habitually raided into China and a symbol of the distinction between China's agricultural society and the nomadic tribes of

Central Asia. It remains today one of the greatest monuments to engineering skill in the preindustrial age and one of the wonders of the world. It is said to be the only man-made structure on earth that can be seen from the moon.

The First Emperor tried to enforce intellectual conformity and make the Ch'in Legalist system appear to be the only natural political order. He suppressed all other schools of thought—especially the Confucians who idealized early Chou feudalism by stressing the obedience of sons to their parents, of nobles to their lord, and of lords to the king. To break the hold of the past, the emperor put into effect a Legalist proposal requiring all privately owned books reflecting past traditions to be burned and "all those who raise their voice against the present government in the name of antiquity [to] be beheaded together with their families."

When the First Emperor died in 210 B.C. while on one of his frequent tours of in-

spection, he was succeeded by an inept son who was unable to control the rivalry among his father's chief aides. Ch'in policies had alienated not only the intellectuals and the nobility but also the peasants, who were subjected to ruinous taxation and forced labor. Rebel armies rose in every province of the empire, some led by peasants, others by aristocrats. Anarchy followed, and by 206 B.C. the Ch'in dynasty, which the First Emperor had claimed would endure for "ten thousand generations," had completely disappeared. But the Chinese empire itself, which Ch'in created, would last for more than two thousand years, the longest-lived political institution in world history.

At issue in the fighting that continued for another four years was not only the question of succession to the throne but also the form of government. The peasant and aristocratic leaders, at first allied against the Ch'in, became engaged in a furious and ruthless civil war. The aristocrats sought to restore the oligarchic feudalism of pre-Ch'in times.

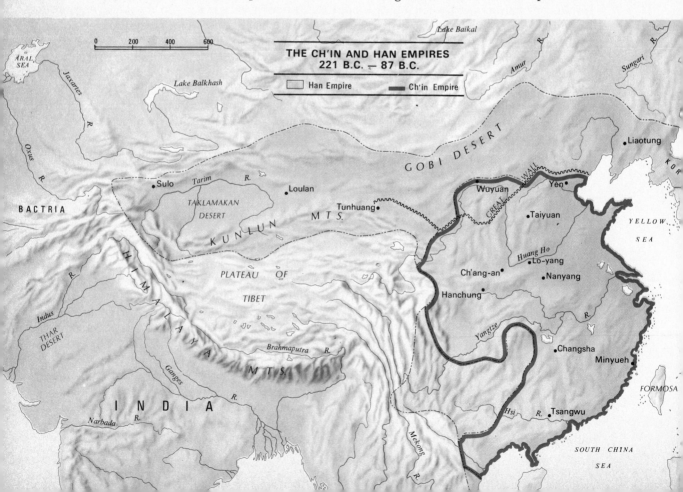

THE CH'IN AND HAN EMPIRES
221 B.C. — 87 B.C.

Han Empire   Ch'in Empire

An imperial bodyguard of over 7000 life-size terra cotta soldiers and horses, equipped with real chariots and bronze weapons, was arrayed in military formation in an underground chamber guarding the First Emperor's elaborate mausoleum. Excavation and restoration of the figures, which include archers and charioteers as well as full infantry and cavalry units, began in 1974.

Their opponents, whose main leader was Liu Pang, a peasant who had become a Ch'in general, desired a centralized state. In this contest between the old and the new, the new was the victor.

The Han dynasty: the empire consolidated. In 202 B.C., the year that the Romans defeated the Carthaginians at the battle of Zama, the peasant Liu Pang defeated his aristocratic rival and soon established the Han Dynasty. Named after the Han River, a tributary of the Yangtze, the new dynasty had its capital at Ch'ang-an (see map, p. 110). It lasted for more than four hundred years and is traditionally divided into two parts, the Earlier Han, from 206 B.C. to 8 A.D., and the Later Han, from 23 A.D. to 220 A.D. In time and importance, the Han corresponded to the late Roman Republic and early Roman Empire; modern Chinese still call themselves "Men of Han."

The empire and power sought by Liu Pang and his successors were those of the Ch'in, but they succeeded where the Ch'in had failed because they were tactful and gradual in their approach. Liu Pang reestablished for a time some of the vassal kingdoms and feudal states in regions distant from the capital. Peasant discontent was mollified by lessened demands for taxes and forced labor. But the master stroke of the Han emperors was to enlist the support of the Confucian intellectuals.

The Han emperors recognized that an educated bureaucracy was necessary for governing so vast an empire. The ban on the Confucian classics and other Chou literature was lifted, and the way was open for a revival of the intellectual life that had been suppressed under the Ch'in. Some older men were apparently able to write down from memory texts they had memorized in their youth; other texts were found in the walls of houses, where they had been hidden to escape the Ch'in book burning.

In accord with Legalist principles, now tempered by Confucian insistence on the ethical basis of government, the Han emperors established administrative organs staffed by a salaried bureaucracy to rule their empire. Talented men were chosen for government service through an examination system based on the Confucian classics, and they were promoted by merit.

The examinations were theoretically open to all Chinese except merchants. (The Han inherited both the Confucian bias against trade as an unvirtuous striving for profit and the Legalist suspicion of merchants, who could not be easily controlled like peasants.) But the bureaucrats were drawn largely from the landlord class because wealth was needed to obtain the education needed to pass the examinations. Consequently, the earlier division of Chinese society between aristocrats and peasants was now transformed into a division between landowner-bureaucrats and peasants.

Wu Ti and the Pax Sinica. After sixty years of consolidation, the Han empire reached its greatest extent and development during the long reign of Wu Ti ("Martial Emperor"), who ruled from 141 to 87 B.C. To accomplish his goal of territorial expansion, he raised the peasants' taxes but not those of the great landowners, who remained virtually exempt from taxation. In addition, he increased the amount of labor and military service the peasants were forced to contribute to the state.

The Martial Emperor justified his expansionist policies in terms of self-defense against Mongolian nomads, the Hsiung-nu, known to the West later as the Huns. Their attacks had caused the First Emperor to construct the Great Wall to obstruct their raiding cavalry. To outflank the nomads in the west, Wu Ti extended the Great Wall and annexed a large corridor extending through the Tarim River basin of Central Asia to the Pamir Mountains close to Bactria. Wu Ti failed in an attempt to form an alliance with the Scythians, who had recently occupied the territory, but the grape and alfalfa seeds his envoy brought back were the beginning of a commercial exchange between China and the West.

Wu Ti also outflanked the Hsiung-nu in the east by the conquest of southern Manchuria and northern Korea. In addition, he completed the conquest of South China, begun by the Ch'in, and added North Vietnam to the Chinese empire. Thus at a time when the armies of the Roman Republic were laying the foundations of the *Pax Romana* in the West, the Martial Emperor was establishing a *Pax Sinica* ("Chinese Peace") in the East.

Han decline. Wu Ti's conquests led to a fiscal crisis. As costs increased, taxes increased, and the peasants' burdens led to revolt. The end result was that the central government had to rely more and more on local military commanders and great landowners for control of the population, giving them great power and prestige at its own expense. This cycle of decline after an initial period of increasing prosperity and power has been the pattern of all Chinese dynasties. During the Han this "dynastic cycle," as Western historians of China call it, led to a succession of mediocre rulers after Wu Ti's death and a temporary usurpation of the throne (9-23 A.D.), which divided the Earlier from the Later Han.

The usurper, Wang Mang, was an ardent Confucian and humanitarian. Like his contemporary in the West, the Roman Emperor Augustus, his goal was the rejuvenation of society. By Wang Mang's day the number of large tax-free estates had greatly increased while the number of tax-paying peasant holdings had declined. More and more peasants became renters of plots belonging to great landowners. Falling behind in their rents, they were forced to sell themselves or their children into debt slavery. To remedy this situation and increase the government's tax income, Wang Mang decreed that the land was the property of the nation and should be portioned out to peasant families, who would pay taxes on their allotments.

Wang Mang sought to solve the long-standing problem of inflation, which had greatly increased since Wu Ti first began debasing the coinage when he found himself in financial difficulties, by setting maximum prices on basic commodities. He also sought to stabilize prices by instituting "leveling." According to this system, the government bought surplus commodities when prices fell and sold them when scarcity caused prices to rise. This remarkable reform program failed, however; officials bungled the difficult administrative task, and the powerful landowners rebelled against the ruler who proposed to confiscate their land. Even though Wang Mang rescinded his reforms, he was killed by the rebels in 23 A.D.

The Later Han Dynasty never reached the heights of its predecessor. Warlords who were members of the rich landowner class seized more and more power, and widespread peasant rebellions sapped the state's resources. Surviving in name only during its last thirty years, the Han Dynasty ended in 220 A.D., when the throne was usurped by the son of a famous warlord. Three-and-a-half centuries of disunity and turbulence followed—the longest in China's long history—as it did in Europe after the fall of the Roman Empire. But China eventually succeeded where Europe failed: in 589 A.D. China once again was united by the Sui Dynasty. With minor exceptions, it has remained united to this day. In Europe, unification remains even now a dream.

Han scholarship. Politically and culturally, the relation of the Han to the Chou paralleled that of ancient Rome to Greece. Politically, the disunity of Greece and the Chou was followed by the imperial unity and administrative genius of the Romans and the Han. Culturally, just as the Romans owed a great debt to the Greeks, so did the Han to the Chou. Furthermore, Greek and Chou intellectual creativity was not matched by the Romans and the Han.

Scholarship flourished under the Han, but it was mainly concerned with collecting and interpreting the classics of Chinese thought produced in the Chou period. As the basis of education for prospective bureaucrats,

Wu Ti established an imperial university in 124 B.C.; a century later it had three thousand students. The Han scholars venerated Confucius as the ideal wise man; Confucianism became the official philosophy of the state. Great respect for learning, together with the system of civil service examinations based on the Five Confucian Classics, became fundamental characteristics of Chinese civilization.

Han scholars started another scholarly tradition with their historical writings. Their antiquarian interest in researching the past produced a comprehensive history of China, the *Historical Records (Shih chi)*. This voluminous work of 130 chapters has been highly praised, in part for its inclusion of a vast amount of information about ancient China, but even more for its freedom from superstition and its careful weighing of evidence. In the Later Han, a scholar wrote the *History of the [Earlier] Han,* and thereafter it was customary for each dynasty to write the official history of its immediate predecessor. Another monument to Han scholarship was the world's first dictionary, *Explanation of Writing (Shuo wen),* produced during Wu Ti's reign.

Han art. In contrast to Han scholarship, Han art was clearly creative. The largely decorative art of the past, which served a religious purpose, was replaced by a realistic pictorial art portraying ordinary life. The result was the first great Chinese flowering of sculpture, both in relief and in the round.

Built as a defense against invaders, and extending for 1500 miles, the Great Wall symbolizes China's self-enforced isolation. It remains today one of the greatest monuments of engineering skill in the preindustrial age.

Some of the finer examples of this realistic secular art are the sculptured models of the tall and spirited horses that Wu Ti imported from Bactria. The Han greatly admired these proud "celestial" and "blood-sweating" horses from the West, and their artists brilliantly captured their high spirit.

Technological advances. During the Han period, China surpassed the level of technological development in the rest of the world. Notable inventions included a primitive seismograph capable of indicating earthquakes several hundred miles away; the use of water power to grind grain and to operate a piston bellows for iron smelting; the horse collar, which greatly increased the pulling power of horses; paper made from cloth rags, which replaced cumbersome bamboo strips and expensive silk cloth as writing material; and porcelain, or china. By the end of the first century B.C., the Han Chinese had recognized sunspots and had accurately determined the length of the calendar year.

Popular Taoism and Buddhism. By the time the First Emperor united China at the end of the third century B.C., a decadent or popular form of Taoism had emerged. Popular Taoism was a religion of spirits and magic that provided the spiritual comfort not found in either philosophical Taoism or Confucianism. Its goals were long life and personal immortality. These goals were to be achieved not so much as a reward for ethical conduct but through magical charms and spells and imbibing an "elixir of immortality." The search for such an elixir, which was thought to contain the vital forces of nature, led to an emphasis on diet.

Popular Taoism also became a vehicle for the expression of peasant discontent. In 184 A.D., the Yellow Turbans (one of the earliest of a long line of Chinese secret societies) led a widespread peasant revolt that was inspired by Taoists. It destroyed much of China and greatly contributed to the anarchy that fatally weakened the Later Han Dynasty.

Buddhism, which appeared in China during the first century A.D., provided another answer to the need for religious assurance. It was brought to China by missionaries and traders through Central Asia, and possibly also by sea to South China. About 184 A.D. a Buddhist missionary established a center for the translation of Buddhist writings into Chinese at the Later Han capital. However, relatively few Chinese were attracted to the religion during this period. Buddhism's great attraction of converts and influence on Chinese culture came after the fall of the Han Dynasty, when renewed social turmoil made its emphasis on otherworldly salvation appealing to many people.

This head of a horse, carved out of green nephrite jade, is characteristic of the work of the Han period.

THE MEETING OF EAST AND WEST IN ANCIENT TIMES

Beyond the Roman frontiers. During the first and second centuries A.D., the prosperous years of the *Pax Romana,* the peoples of the Roman Empire maintained trade contacts extending far beyond the imperial boundaries. Chinese silk, which the Romans believed was produced from the leaves of trees, was sold in the market quarter of Rome, and Indian cotton was converted into cloth at Alexandria. Contacts between West and East had progressively increased after 334 B.C., when Alexander the Great invaded Asia, until a chain of intercommunicating states stretched across Eurasia from the Atlantic to the Pacific.

After Alexander's death, the Seleucid and Ptolemaic kingdoms of the Hellenistic Age maintained trade contacts with India over two routes, one by land and the other by sea (see map, p. 116). The most frequented route was the caravan road that began in Syria or Asia Minor, crossed Mesopotamia, then skirted the Iranian plateau to either Bactra or Kandahar before crossing the Hindu Kush to reach Taxila in India. The sea route began either at the Red Sea ports of Egypt or at the head of the Persian Gulf and moved along the coast to India.

Sea traffic to India. By the late first century B.C., after Egypt and Syria had succumbed to Rome, Roman capital and appetite for the luxury goods of India—ivory, pearls, spices, dyes, and cotton—greatly stimulated eastern trade. By this time, however, the existing trade routes had serious disadvantages. The Parthians, whose kingdom extended from the Euphrates to the borders of Bactria, were levying heavy tolls on the caravan trade, and the Sabaean Arabs of southwest Arabia had cut off the Red Sea route at Aden and were in control of much of the overseas trade with India. From Aden, the Sabaeans sent Indian goods north by caravan to Petra, which grew rich as a distribution point to Egypt via Gaza and to the north via Damascus.

Augustus broke the hold of the Parthian and Arab middlemen on the eastern trade by establishing direct commercial connections by sea with India. By 1 B.C., he had reopened the Red Sea by forcing the Sabaeans out of Aden and converting it into a Roman naval base. Ships were soon sailing from Aden directly to India across the Arabian Sea, blown by the monsoon winds recently discovered by a Greek mariner named Hippalus. From May to October the monsoon blows from the southwest across the Arabian Sea, while the countermonsoon blows from the northeast between November and March.

Constructed with remarkable precision, this Chinese sundial from the Han period was superior to any devised in the West until the thirteenth century A.D. The base and vertical shaft have been reconstructed for this photograph.

Thus, direct roundtrip voyages, eliminating middlemen and the tedious journey along the coasts, could be made in eight months. Strabo, a Greek geographer during the time of Augustus, stated that 120 ships sailed to India every year from Egyptian ports.

Before the end of the first century A.D., Roman-financed ships had reached the rich markets of southern India and Ceylon. In 166 A.D., according to the Chinese *History of the Later Han Dynasty,* some merchants from Ta Ch'in ("Great Ch'in," the Chinese name for Rome), claiming to represent "King Antun" (the emperor Marcus Aurelius Antoninus), arrived in South China by sea across the Bay of Bengal and around the Malay Peninsula.

The silk trade with China. The Chinese made the first move to pierce the land barrier separating them from the West. In 138 B.C. the Han emperor Wu Ti dispatched an envoy to Bactria to seek allies against the Hsiungnu (Mongolian nomads). Although the envoy failed to secure an alliance, the information he brought back amounted to the Chinese discovery of the West.

Intrigued above all by his envoy's description of the magnificent western horses, Wu Ti resolved to open trade relations with the West. His armies pushed across the Pamir Mountains to a point close to Alexandria Eschate (Khojend), founded by Alexander the Great as the northern limit of his empire (see map, p. 59). Shortly after 100 B.C. silk began arriving in the West, transmitted by the Parthians. When the Chinese soon moved back across the Pamirs, the Kushans of India became middlemen, selling the silk to the Parthians and later to western merchants coming by sea to India.

It was not until about 120 A.D. that the Parthians allowed some western merchants to cross their land. The information they brought back on the Chinese was soon thereafter used by Ptolemy in constructing his map of the world.

The economic consequences for the West. To satisfy the Roman world's insatiable appetite for luxury goods, western trade with the East grew immensely in the first two centuries A.D. But because Roman exports of wool, linen, glass, and metalware to the East did not match in value the empire's imports of silk, spices, perfumes, gems, and other luxuries, the West suffered seriously from an adverse balance of trade. Gold and silver had to be continually exported to Asia. Late in the first century A.D., Pliny estimated that India, China, and Arabia drained away annually at least one hundred million sesterces (about five million noninflated dollars), declaring, "That is the sum which our luxuries and our women cost us." The discovery of large hoards of Roman coins in India supports Pliny's statement. We shall see that this serious drain was one of the factors in the general economic decline of the Roman world in the third century A.D.

Severance of East-West contacts. Beginning in the third century A.D., contacts between the East and the West gradually declined. With the overthrow of the Han dy-

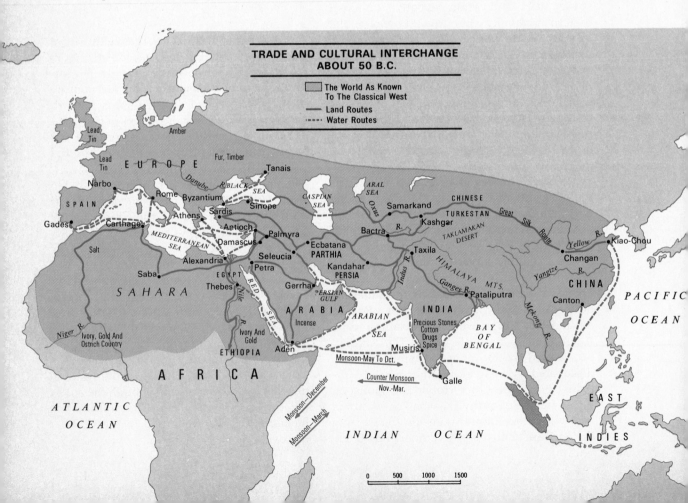

nasty in 220 A.D., China's power and prestige dwindled in Central Asia. By coincidence, the Kushan empire in northeast India fell at the same time, and India entered a period of change and transition. But probably the most significant factor in the disruption of East-West relations was the political and economic decline of the Roman world in the third century A.D., a topic that will be described in the following chapter.

SUMMARY

About 2500 B.C., the counterpart of the civilizations that developed along the Nile and the Tigris-Euphrates emerged along the Indus in India. Then about 1500 B.C., Aryan nomads invaded India, and a new culture developed. During this Vedic Age, the foundations of Hinduism's unique socio-religious system were laid, and the three pillars of Indian society—the autonomous village, the caste system, and the joint family—evolved. In the sixth century B.C., Gautama Buddha gave India a philosophy that has endured in Asia until the present.

In the late fourth and third centuries B.C., during the Hellenistic Age in the West, the Mauryan emperors in India presided over a progressive and prosperous realm in India. The most renowned Mauryan ruler, the pious and gentle Ashoka, sent missionaries throughout southern and eastern Asia, carrying the civilizing tenets of Buddhism.

The formative centuries of Chinese civilization began under the Shang Dynasty about 1700 B.C., near the end of Indus civilization in India. Building on this advance, the Chou period (1027 or 1122-256 B.C.) was one of remarkable dynamism and creativity. Its greatest achievement was the contribution to philosophy by Confucius, Mencius, and Lao-tzu. In the third century B.C., the state of Ch'in, which embraced the philosophy of Legalism, established the first unified empire in Chinese history. While the Ch'in Dynasty was short-lived, the imperial form of government it created was to endure for more than two thousand years. Its successor, the great Han Dynasty (206 B.C.-220 A.D.), gave China one of its most illustrious eras. Corresponding in time and achievement to the Romans in the West, the Han carved out an extensive empire, especially in Central Asia.

During the centuries immediately preceding and following the birth of Christ, the great civilizations of the world—Graeco-Roman, Indian, and Chinese—were connected by tenuous routes of commercial and diplomatic exchange. Although this contact between East and West began to decline in the third century A.D. and was eventually cut off, it continued long enough to establish a durable tradition in both the East and the West. Each civilization knew that beyond the mountains and the deserts to the east or to the west lay other great civilizations. This tradition incited adventurous spirits many centuries later to bring the "halves" of world civilization together once again.

SUGGESTIONS FOR READING

S. Wolpert, **A New History of India***** (Oxford, 1977) is an insightful account. A. L. Basham, **The Wonder That Was India***** (Taplinger, 1968) is comprehensive on Indian history and culture prior to the coming of the Muslims in the eleventh century. See also M. Wheeler, **The Indus Civilization,***** 3rd ed. (Cambridge Univ., 1968); and E. Lengyel, **Asoka the Great: India's Royal Missionary** (Watts, 1969).

K. Sen, **Hinduism***** (Penguin, 1962) describes the nature and function of Hinduism. S. Radhakrishnan, **The Hindu View of Life***** (Macmillan, 1939) compares Hinduism with western philosophy. W. T. De Bary, *et al.*, eds., **Sources of Indian Tradition,***** 2 vols. (Columbia, 1958) contains significant selections from Vedic and Upanishadic texts, with illuminating introductions. See also R. Narayan, **The Ramayana: A Shortened Modern Prose Version of the Indian Epic***** (Viking, 1972); and N. Frith, **The Legend of Krishna** (Schocken, 1976).

Edward J. Thomas, **The Life of Buddha as Legend and History***** (Routledge & Kegan Paul, 1975). See also C. Humphreys, **Buddhism***** (Penguin, 1951); and E. A. Burtt, ed., **The Teachings of the Compassionate Buddha***** (Mentor, 1955).

J. Fairbank and E. Reischauer, **China: Tradition and Transformation** (Houghton Mifflin, 1977) and Hilda Hookham, **A Short History of China***** (Mentor, 1972) are highly acclaimed histories. Shorter histories are R. Yang and E. Lazzerini, **The Chinese World***** (Forum, 1978); and L. C. Goodrich, **A Short History of the Chinese People,***** 5th ed. (Torchbooks). See also William Watson, **Ancient China: The Discoveries of Post-Liberation Archaeology***** (New York Graphic Society, 1974); and Li Chi, **Anyang** (Univ. of Washington, 1976).

Yu-lan Fung, **A Short History of Chinese Philosophy***** (Free Press, 1966) is an excellent introduction. A. Waley, **Three Ways of Thought in Ancient China***** (Anchor, 1956) is a concise introduction to Confucianism, Taoism, and Legalism. See also J. Ware, tr., **The Sayings of Confucius***** (Mentor); M. Granet, **The Religion of the Chinese People***** (Torchbooks); and R. Van Over, ed., **Taoist Tales***** (Mentor, 1973). W. T. De Bary, *et al.*, eds., **Sources of Chinese Tradition***** (Columbia, 1960) is an outstanding collection of translations with valuable commentaries. On Chinese science and technology see C. Ronan, **The Shorter Science and Civilization in China,** Vol. I (Cambridge Univ., 1978).

On Indian and Chinese art see A. Coomaraswamy, **History of Indian and Indonesian Art***** (Dover) and **The Dance of Shiva***** (Noonday, 1957); S. L. Weiner, **Ajanta: Its Place in Buddhist Art***** (California, 1977); Michael Sullivan, **The Arts of China,***** (California, 1978); and T. Froncek, ed., **The Horizon Book of the Arts of China** (American Heritage, 1969).

R. Wheeler, **Rome Beyond the Imperial Frontiers***** (Greenwood, 1972) is a study of Rome's trade with the East. See also P. C. Bagchi, **India and China: A Thousand Years of Cultural Relations,** 2nd ed. (Greenwood, 1971); and J. W. Sedlar, **India and the Greek World: An Essay in the Transmission of Culture** (Rowan and Littlefield, 1980).

*Indicates a less expensive paperbound edition.

The crowing of a cock awakened Marcus Ligustinus, who lived in the crowded, noisy, smelly working-class Subura district of Rome that stretched northward from the Forum. He knew that it was close to the first hour of the Roman twelve-hour day (and twelve-hour night), which began with sunrise. Since it was midwinter, the first hour began—in modern terms—at 7:30, and the twelfth hour would end with sunset at 4:30. (We follow the Romans in using the terms *ante meridiem*, "before midday," and *post meridiem*, "after midday," which we abbreviate as a.m. and p.m.) Marcus preferred the longer days and longer hours of midsummer, when the twelfth hour did not end until 7:30 and there was time for a siesta, even though sunrise came early. Most Roman commoners went to bed soon after sundown anyway, since both candles and the small olive oil lamps with their smoking wicks gave little light and were expensive.

The small bedroom was very stuffy and Marcus opened the tightly-closed window shutters and looked out on a large courtyard bounded by the wings of his four-story apartment building. Such apartment blocks were called *insulae* because they were "islands" surrounded on all four sides by streets. Flimsily built of wood by private capitalists in answer to the city's housing shortage, the *insulae* were one of Rome's gifts to civilization. They far outnumbered private homes and tenants could purchase their one- or two-room apartments (like modern condominiums), but renting was more common.

By our reckoning it was December 1, 107 B.C. To Marcus, too, it was December—the "tenth" month, so called because until 153 B.C., when it was changed to January 1, the Roman year had begun on March 1. The first day of the month was called the Kalends, from the verb *calo*, "to proclaim," since it was the day on which a priest announced which days had a religious significance. Marcus remembered it was also the day his rent was due and this made him angry, as it always did, at capitalist landlords.

Marcus awakened his two children, a boy of ten and a girl of eight. Back on their small five-acre farm his father had raised eight children, but in the city Marcus could not afford more than two. The number of Roman citizens was declining. Infant mortality had always been high—only one child in three reached the age of ten—and abortion had become common and would not be declared illegal until the end of the second century A.D. Marcus' wife, Turia, whom he had married when she was fourteen and he fifteen, had had two abortions (and several miscarriages) during

their ten-year marriage, but she was afraid to use the method of contraception favored by some of her friends—magical formulas and incantations. Some of Marcus' neighbors had also exercised their legal rights as heads of families to expose or abandon unwanted children.

The children rose from their cots and adjusted their woolen tunics, the basic garment worn day and night by all Romans. They followed their father to the adjoining room where Turia had just finished emptying the slop jar out of the one window onto the street three stories below. Before seating himself on one of the four stools beside the small table—the only furniture in the room—Marcus placed a bit of bread on a small boxlike shrine dedicated to the traditional spirits, the Lares and Penates, that guarded all Roman households. Then he addressed a prayer—taking great care not to stumble over the words lest the prayer lose its power—to Janus, the guardian spirit of the doorway for whom the month of January was named: "Father Janus, in offering to thee this sacrificial bread I make good prayers that thou be kind and favorable to me, my children, and my house and household."

A light breakfast was the first of the family's three daily meals, and Turia had taken from the cupboard a few olives, some wheat biscuits, and a round loaf of bread that Marcus had brought from the bakery where he worked as a miller. (Among lower-class Romans, men did all the shopping.) Marcus dipped his biscuit into a cup of warm wine to fortify himself against the long hours ahead before he returned for dinner at the ninth hour (1:30 in winter, 2:30 in summer). His dinner was always a thick porridge made from unground wheat, and supplemented by turnips, beans, olives, and figs. Sometimes honey, cheese, an egg, a bit of pork, or salted fish was added to the porridge. Marcus' third meal of the day, a light supper usually of bread and cheese, was eaten soon after sunset before retiring. Turia did all her cooking on a portable brazier filled with charcoal (coal was unknown), which also served as the sole source of heat in winter.

After breakfast Turia turned to her household chores, chiefly spinning woolen thread and weaving the rough cloth with which she made all the family's clothing. Marcus dropped his son off at the one-room school where he was learning reading, writing, and simple arithmetic with the aid of an abacus. Here a wealthy man had installed one of his Greek slaves as a teacher (*grammaticus*) of any boy whose father could afford the small fee. Marcus' son knew he was fortunate to be able to go to school, but he still looked forward to the long summer vacation from July 1 to October 15.

Like the school, the bakery where Marcus worked was located on the ground floor of his apartment building. Here the odor of freshly-baked bread mingled with that of a pig that served as a sort of vacuum cleaner to keep the floor clear of wheat husks. Marcus was in charge of the shop's stone flour mill which stood as high as a man and whose hollow top stone, into which the grain was poured, was rotated by a slave.

At midday all shops closed, and although they opened again after dinner, Marcus' working day was over. Throughout the year he usually worked six hours a day, and since the Roman work week consisted of seven days, he thus worked a 42-hour week. Marcus was a firm believer in the popular Roman slogan: "Six hours are enough for work: after that sample life."

Marcus "sampled life" in a variety of ways. Most exciting were the great state religious festivals called games (ludi). Each provided entertainment for a week or more for a total of 59 days during the year. On many days Greek and Roman tragedies and comedies were performed, but far more popular were coarse mimes which mimicked, usually without dialogue, the everyday life of the common people. Between acts jugglers, clowns, boxers, and wrestlers performed. A procession of nude girls served as a finale.

The most popular feature of the games was the chariot races held in the Circus Maximus. Marcus and his family, dressed in their formal togas, would leave home before dawn in order to find places on the wooden planks built up behind the stone seats that were reserved for senators and capitalists. Excitedly they would bet on a favorite charioteer and watch him risk life and limb as he whipped his horses around the oval course. Twelve races, each of seven laps (about five miles) were run each day. Sometimes the family would watch bloody fights to the death between gladiators (war prisoners and condemned criminals), animal fights (bulls against elephants, for example), and wild beast hunts, but these were privately promoted and not a part of the official games.

Other religious festivals that did not include games or other entertainment provided Marcus with another 45 public holidays during the year. Marcus' favorite was Anna Perenna on March 15, the festival of the first full moon during what had once been the first month of the Roman year. Held on the river bank north of the city, it was a veritable "pop festival" during which everyone drank much wine — a glass for every future year of one's life — and in the evening reeled homeward in a tipsy procession.

Rome had many wine shops catering to the lower classes, where heated wine and snacks were cheap and prostitutes charged six copper asses (the price of two loaves of bread), but Marcus seldom patronized such places. He was no puritan, but he could not be extravagant on his daily wage of 16 asses. He preferred the parties given by the miller's burial society (collegium), where he drank wine contributed by new members and munched on bread and sardines. The society's entrance fee was steep but it gave Marcus much satisfaction to know that when he died his body would not be thrown into a common pauper's grave outside the city walls. He would receive an honorable burial with his remains cremated and the ashes placed in an urn and set in one of the many niches of a wall-like tomb.

Marcus' favorite recreation was the public baths, where he spent most afternoons. The baths were privately owned, but the fee was nominal and often it was paid by some candidate for public office seeking votes. The baths provided Marcus many relaxing hours as he leisurely progressed through the sequence of rooms — the dry sweat room, the warm room where a slave scraped the sweat from his body (soap was unknown), the tepid room for cooling off, and the invigorating cold bath. Another popular room was the lavatory with its long row of marble toilets equipped with comfortable arm rests; here Marcus liked to sit for an hour or more chatting with other patrons.

When the baths closed at sundown, Marcus was usually in such a good mood that he would sometimes stop at a shop for some hot food to carry home for supper. And as he hurried homeward, he would break out in song: "Baths, sex, and wine our bodies undermine; Yet what is life but baths and sex and wine?"

6. (preceding page) **Hagia Sophia, Istanbul** (532-537 A.D.). By the sixth century the gradual decline of the Roman Empire had emptied the Graeco-Roman classical tradition of nearly all its strength. The imperial capital had been moved from Italy to Constantinople in 330. Christianity was now the state religion and already showing signs of becoming what it was destined to be: a primary force in shaping the world of the next 1000 years. Europe was on the brink of the Middle Ages. At this moment of climactic transition in western history, Hagia Sophia was erected, an immense stone symbol linking past and future. The grandeur of its construction — it is one of the greatest domed vaults of all time — recalls the glory of Rome, while its almost mystical illumination and spiritualized atmosphere prefigure the coming dominance of the Christian faith. After Constantinople was captured by the Turks in 1453, Hagia Sophia became an Islamic mosque, serving in this capacity until recently, when it was converted into a museum. 7. (above) **Muhammad Ascending to Paradise** (sixteenth century). Islam's meteoric rise to power and subsequent hegemony in the whole Middle East were attended by notable, often superb, achievements in the arts. This manuscript page from Persia was executed at a time when influences from both Christianity and the Far East relaxed the abhorrence Muslims traditionally felt toward making images of Muhammad. Note, however, that the Prophet's face is blank.

8. Ireland: "Christ Enthroned" from **Book of Kells** (c. 800). With the final dissolution of the Roman Empire, the pendulum of European civilization swung to the north where the barbarian peoples were gradually converted to Christianity. The Irish assumed the spiritual and cultural leadership of western Europe during this period and their monasteries were centers of Christian culture. Their manuscripts were considered sacred objects that contained the Holy Writ and much effort was put into decorative embellishment largely detached from physical reality.

9. The French town of Conques, with the Church of Ste. Foy (eleventh century).
By the eleventh century a wave of religious fervor swept across the Continent.
Hosts of pilgrims traveled set routes to sacred sites, and along these routes towns
sprang up. The towns erected churches, which were grander than ever before,
and whose complex floor plans could more readily accommodate the traffic of
the pilgrims. Christianity began to belong to the masses, and the flowering of the
Middle Ages grew increasingly evident in the stately towers and arches of the monumental Romanesque style.

PART TWO
The Middle Ages

■ When we speak of the "fall" of Rome, perhaps we forget that the great classical tradition was carried on for another thousand years without interruption in Constantinople, or "New Rome." Until it fell in 1453 the Byzantine empire acted as a buffer for western Europe, staving off attack after attack from the east. The culminating series of attacks, resulting in the collapse of the empire, was launched by the adherents of Islam—a dynamic way of life developed by the followers of Muhammad, an eloquent prophet who instilled in his people a vital sense of their destiny to rule in the name of Allah. With unbelievable swiftness, the followers of the Prophet became rulers of the Near East, swept across North Africa and surged into Spain, and expanded eastward to the frontiers of China. The Muslims, the great middlemen of medieval times, shuttled back and forth across vast expanses, trading the wares of East and West and acting as the conveyors of culture. Throughout most of the Middle Ages, the East outshone the West even as Constantinople and Baghdad outdazzled in material magnificence and intellectual and artistic triumphs any capital in western Europe.

In Europe, after the inundation of the Roman Empire by Germanic tribes in the fifth century brought disorder and fragmentation, a painful search for stability began. Centuries of confusion followed until Charlemagne established a new "Roman" empire. This ambitious and laudable experiment was premature, however, and after its collapse a new system had to be created— one which would offer at least a minimum of security, political organization, and law enforcement. This was feudalism. Under this system, the landed nobility acted as police force, judiciary, and army. Accompanying feudalism was the manorial system—an economic order which provided food and life's necessities and divided men into two great classes: the fighters or nobles and the workers or serfs.

Crude as it was, feudalism served to mitigate the chaos which followed the fall of Charlemagne's empire. Yet feudalism and the manorial system were inherently rural and rigid, and by the eleventh century new forces were at work. Shadowy outlines of new kingdoms—Germany, England, France, and Spain—began to emerge under the direction of vigorous monarchs. Europe went on the offensive, ejecting the Muslims from the southern part of the Continent, breaking Muslim control of the Mediterranean, and launching crusades to capture Jerusalem from the infidel. The "closed" economy of the feudal countryside gave way before the revival of trade and communications, the growth of towns, the increased use of money as a medium of exchange, and the rise of a new class in society—the bourgeoisie.

The greatest stabilizing force in Europe during the medieval period was the Church. The Middle Ages has sometimes been characterized as the Age of Faith; to an extent greater than in classical or modern times, the attention of men living in those days was directed toward a religious goal —the salvation of the soul—and the Church was the great arbiter of human destiny. With the authority that stemmed from its vital spiritual service, the Church provided the nearest approach to effective and centralized supervision of European life. All men were born, lived, and died under its protection. In the thirteenth century, when popes such as Innocent III bent proud monarchs to their will, the Church reached the zenith of its influence as a kind of international government as well as the focus of medieval society, arts, and scholarship. The Church was the chief patron of poets and artists; its monasteries were repositories for precious manuscripts; and it fostered a new institution of learning— the university.

During the ten centuries commonly referred to as the medieval period in the West, great civilizations in India and China experienced their golden ages while Europe was struggling to build a new and viable civilization on the debris of the defunct Roman Empire. In Gupta India the government was stable, and science and the arts flourished. Under the rule of the T'ang and Sung dynasties, Chinese life was enriched by notable creativity. Later, Mongol conquerors, symbolized by Genghis Khan, put together the largest empire in the world, stretching west from China as far as Russia and Mesopotamia. And influenced greatly by China, the proud and independent Japanese developed a unique culture pattern characterized best by the *samurai*, the knight, and the *bushido*, the code of the warrior.

CHAPTER 5

The Rise of Christianity and the Fall of Rome

The City of God

INTRODUCTION. To the inhabitants of the Graeco-Roman world, Rome was the "Eternal City"—a proud designation which is still used today. When, therefore, in 410 A.D. the barbarian Visigoths responded to its magnetic lure by entering Italy and sacking the city, a cry of anguish reverberated throughout the crumbling Empire. In distant Bethlehem St. Jerome cried, "The lamp of the world is extinguished, and it is the whole world which has perished in the ruins of this one city."[1]

This chapter completes the history of Rome—it tells of the fall of the City of the Caesars and the emergence, like the phoenix arising from the ashes, of the "City of God." It was St. Augustine who, in the wake of the Visigoths' capture of Rome, devised that phrase to represent the rise of a new Christian society on the ruins of paganism and a once invincible Empire—and to assure Christians that the "community of the Most High" would endure, although the greatest city on earth had fallen.

This period in history has several facets.

One concerns the national history of the Jews, the coming of Jesus in the midst of their turbulent relations with the Romans, and the eventual triumph of his teachings. Another is the story of the progressive decline of the Roman Empire during the time of Christianity's triumph. A third element is the migration of the Germanic peoples and their settlement in Europe—a movement which completed the disintegration of the western half of the Roman Empire. A final aspect (to be discussed in the next chapter) is the shift in civilization's center of gravity —from the West, overrun by barbarians, to the eastern shores of the Mediterranean and even beyond.

THE RISE AND TRIUMPH OF CHRISTIANITY

Post-exilic Jewish nationalism. At the very time when the Principate of Augustus was laying the foundations of Rome's imperial greatness, events were taking place in the distant Roman province of Judea that would one day alter the course of western history. Following the conquests of Alexander the Great in the Near East, Palestine was ruled first by the Ptolemies and then by the Seleucids. Since their return from exile in Babylonia in 538 B.C. (see p. 30), the Jews in Palestine had created a theocratic community, based upon the Torah, God's Law, originally revealed to Moses and contained in the Pentateuch (the first five books of the Old Testament), and later supplemented by the teachings of the prophets and the writings of scholars. Religious life centered on the Temple at Jerusalem, which echoed with the cry "Hallelujah" ("Praise ye Yahweh") in thanksgiving for Yahweh's gracious dealing with his people. The most powerful figure was the high priest, assisted by the Sanhedrin, the high court for the enforcement of the Law. Since there was no distinction between civil and religious law, the jurisdiction of the Sanhedrin covered all aspects of Jewish life.

The Hebrews, the "People of God," were tightly knit; even the Jewish groups outside Palestine were linked by spiritual bonds to the Temple and to a law which they believed to be divinely inspired. But, being unable to participate in the services of the Temple at Jerusalem, the Jews of the Diaspora met in local synagogues (from the Greek word for "assembly") for informal worship and instruction in the Scriptures. In the long run, the synagogue, which probably first arose during the Babylonian Exile, outlived the Temple to become the heart of Judaism. It also influenced the forms of worship in the Christian church and the Muslim mosque.

During the Hellenistic Age, Greek influences were constantly at work among the Jews. Most Jews outside Palestine spoke Greek, and a Greek translation of the Hebrew Scriptures became a necessity. Called the Septuagint (Latin for "seventy") from the tradition that it was the work of seventy scholars whose independent translations were miraculously identical, it was produced at Alexandria in the third century B.C.

Greek influences contributed to factionalism among the Jews in Judea. Eventually, one extremely pious group came to blows with the aristocratic pro-Greek Sadducees, as they came to be called, who were favored by the Seleucid rulers of Palestine. The internal conflict gave the Seleucid king an opportunity to intervene, and in 168 B.C., seeking to completely Hellenize the Jews, he ordered the Temple dedicated to the worship of Zeus. Viewing this decree as a blasphemous defilement, the Jews rebelled. Under their leader, Judas Maccabaeus, they rededicated the Temple to Yahweh and in 142 B.C. won their independence from the Seleucids.

Although Judas and his immediate successors contented themselves with the title of high priest, later members of the family were known as kings. In time these rulers became worldly and corrupt, and factionalism again flared up, resulting in persecution and bloodshed. It was in the midst of a civil war that the Roman legions appeared on the scene.

Roman occupation of Palestine. Adopting the practice habitually followed by eastern Mediterranean states, one Jewish faction appealed to Rome for aid. Pompey, who was then completing his pacification of Asia Minor and Syria (see p. 74), ended the civil war in 63 B.C. by making Judea subject to the governor of Syria.

Eventually, Herod the Great, a half-Jewish, half-Arab leader from Edom just south of Judea, rose to power as a tool of the Romans. Appointed by Mark Antony, Herod served as king of Judea from 37 to 4 B.C. He erected a magnificent palace, a theater, a hippodrome, and rebuilt the Temple on a lavish scale. To the Jews, however, Herod remained a detested usurper who professed Judaism as a matter of expediency. Soon after his death, Judea was made into a minor Roman province ruled by governors called procurators, the best known of whom is Pontius Pilate (26-36 A.D.), under whom Jesus was crucified.

The Jews themselves remained unhappy and divided. During centuries of tribulation the prophets had taught that God would one day create a new Israel when righteousness prevailed under a God-anointed leader, the Messiah. In time, many Jews lost hope in a political Messiah and an earthly kingdom and instead conceived of a spiritual Messiah who would lead all the righteous, including the resurrected dead, to a spiritual kingdom. But a group of ardent Jewish nationalists, called Zealots, favoring the use of force to drive the hated foreigner out of God's land, precipitated a fatal clash with Rome.

Destruction of Jerusalem. In 66 A.D. violence erupted when the Roman garrison at Jerusalem was massacred. After a five-year siege, Titus, son of the emperor Vespasian, laid waste the city. What came to be called the "Wailing Wall," a small part of the Temple complex, remained standing. The story is that it was protected by angels whose tears cemented the stones in place forever. It was later prophesied that a third Temple would be erected on the site when the Messiah came. (The Dome of the Rock, a mosque built by the Muslims, has occupied the site since the eighth century A.D.) The wholesale destruction of Jerusalem in 70 A.D. spelled the end of the ancient Hebrew state. The Jewish dream of an independent homeland was to remain unrealized for almost nineteen centuries, until the republic of Israel was proclaimed in 1948.

Development of Jewish religious thought. The destruction of Jerusalem did not destroy the most important single aspect of Jewish culture—its religion. Through centuries of suffering, captivity, and subjugation, the Jews had been taught by a succession of prophets to cleave to their covenant with Yahweh and to safeguard their religious inheritance.

In the centuries just preceding and following the birth of Christ, Judaism exhibited vigor and strength. While the aristocratic Sadducees, who controlled the office of high priest, stood for strict adherence to the written Law or Torah, the more numerous Pharisees believed that, with divine guidance, men could modify and amend the Law. For example, they accepted the belief in personal immortality and the Kingdom of Heaven. From their ranks came the rabbis, scholars who expounded the Law and applied it to existing conditions. The "oral law" propagated by the Pharisees became the core of the later Talmud. Moreover, following the destruction of the Temple and the end of the high priesthood, the rabbinical schools of the Pharisees did much to ensure that Judaism would endure.

The Dead Sea Scrolls. In recent years the discovery of the Dead Sea Scrolls has added greatly to our knowledge of another Jewish sect, the Essenes. While exploring caves about the desolate western shore of the Dead Sea in 1947, two Bedouin boys came across several clay jars containing long manuscripts wrapped in linen. Later, many more scrolls were found in other caves. Nearby were the ruins of a monastery built by the Essenes "to separate themselves," as the scrolls state, "from the abode of perverse men." Occupied between the second century B.C. and 68 A.D., the monastery was destroyed by the Romans during the great Jewish revolt. Prior to its destruction the Essenes hid their manuscripts in the caves.

Some scrolls are portions of the Old Testament dating from the first century B.C. and

The partially unrolled Thanksgiving Scroll, one of the Dead Sea Scrolls preserved at the Hebrew University in Jerusalem, is composed of religious hymns which poetically develop the Essenes' theological doctrines.

thus are centuries older than the earliest text previously known. Jewish and Christian scholars alike have been thrilled to read the Book of Isaiah in such ancient manuscript and to discover that the version we have been using, although based on much later sources, has been accurate except in some details.

Those scrolls which describe the Essene sect in the first century B.C.—that is, just prior to the appearance of Christianity—have been said to constitute "a whole missing chapter of the history of the growth of religious ideas between Judaism and Christianity."[2] Some scholars have attached much significance to common elements in the beliefs and practices of the Essenes and early Christians. The Essenes' founder, a shadowy figure known as the Teacher of Righteousness, suffered persecution and perhaps martyrdom late in the second century B.C. The sect considered itself the true remnant of God's people, preached a "new covenant," and waited patiently for the time when God would destroy the powers of evil and inau-

gurate His Kingdom. Similar views concerning the transition from the "Old Age" to the "New Age" were held by many other Jews as well as by Christians. For the Christians, however, the gap had been bridged. The Messiah had come, and his resurrection was proof that the New Age had arrived. "The New Testament faith was not a new faith, but the fulfillment of an old faith. . . . Lines of continuity between Moses and Jesus, Isaiah and Jesus, the Righteous Teacher and Jesus, John the Baptist and Jesus should occasion no surprise. On the contrary, a biblical faith insists on such continuities. . . . [The Bible is] a history of God's acts of redemption."[3]

The life of Jesus. Whatever its parallels with the Essene sect—including baptism and a communal meal—Christianity bears the unmistakable imprint of the personality of its founder, Jesus of Nazareth. According to the Biblical account, he was born in Bethlehem during the reign of Herod; therefore he may have been born by the time of Herod's death (4 B.C.) rather than in the year which traditionally begins the Christian era. After spending the first years of his life as a carpenter in the village of Nazareth, Jesus began his brief mission, preaching a gospel of love for one's fellow man and urging people to "Repent, for the kingdom of heaven is at hand" (Matthew 4:17).

The fame of Jesus' teaching and holiness spread among the Jews as he and his twelve disciples traveled from village to village in Palestine. When he came to Jerusalem to observe the feast of the Passover, he was welcomed triumphantly by huge crowds as the promised Messiah. But Jesus was concerned with a spiritual, not an earthly, kingdom, and when the people saw that he had no intention of leading a nationalistic movement against the Romans, they turned against him. His enemies then came forward—the moneylenders whom he had denounced, the Pharisees who resented his repudiation of their minute regulations of daily behavior, the people who considered him a disturber of the status quo, and those who saw him as a blasphemer of Yahweh. Betrayed by Judas, one of his disciples, Jesus was condemned by the Sanhedrin for blasphemy "because he claimed to be the Son of God" (John 19:7). Before the procurator Pontius Pilate, however, Jesus was charged with treason for claiming to be the king of Jews.

"Are you the king of Jews?" he [Pilate] asked him. Jesus answered, . . . "My kingdom does not belong to this world; if my kingdom belonged to this world, my followers would fight to keep me from being handed over to the Jews. No, my kingdom does not belong here. . . . You say that I am a king. I was born and came into the world for this one purpose, to speak about the truth. Whoever belongs to the truth listens to me." "And what is truth?" Pilate asked.[4]

Jesus was condemned to the death that Rome inflicted on criminals—crucifixion.

With Jesus' death it seemed as though his cause had been exterminated. No written message had been left behind, and his few loyal followers were disheartened. Yet in the wake of his martyrdom the Christian cause took on new impetus. Reports soon spread that Jesus had been seen after his crucifixion and had spoken to his disciples, giving them solace and inspiration. At first there were few converts within Palestine itself, but the Hellenized Jews living in foreign lands, in contact with new ideas and modes of living, were less firmly committed to traditional Jewish doctrines. The new religion first made real headway among the Jewish communities in such cities as Damascus, Antioch, Corinth, and Rome.

Paul's missionary work. As long as the followers of Jesus regarded him exclusively as a Messiah in the traditional Jewish sense, requiring his followers to observe the Jewish Law, the new religion could have no universal appeal. Largely through the missionary efforts of Paul, this obstacle was removed.

Born Saul, of strict Jewish ancestry, and raised in a Hellenistic city in Asia Minor, this Christian saint possessed a wide knowledge of Greek culture. Saul was also a strict Pharisee who considered Christians to be blasphemers against the Law and took an active part in their persecution. One day, on the road to Damascus—in Saul's own words:

And as I was traveling and coming near Damascus, about midday a bright light suddenly flashed from the sky around me. I fell to the ground and heard a voice saying to me, "Saul, Saul! Why do you persecute me?" "Who are you, Lord?" I asked. "I am Jesus of Nazareth, whom you persecute," he said to me. The men with me saw the light but did not hear the voice of the one who was speaking to me. I asked, "What shall I do, Lord?" and the Lord said to me, "Get up and go into Damascus, and there you will be told everything that God has determined for you."[5]

Saul, henceforth known as Paul, turned from being a persecutor into the greatest of Christian missionaries.

Paul taught that Jesus was the Christ (from *Christos*, Greek for "Messiah"), the Son of God, and that He had died to atone for the sins of mankind. Acceptance of this belief guaranteed salvation to Jews and gentiles alike. The Law, with its strict dietary regulations and other requirements that discouraged the conversion of gentiles, was unnecessary:

A man is put right with God only through faith in Jesus Christ, never by doing what the Law requires. . . . So there is no difference between Jews and Gentiles, between slaves and free men, between men and women: you are all one in union with Christ Jesus.[6]

Tradition states that after covering eight thousand miles teaching and preaching, Paul was beheaded at Rome about 65 A.D. (as was also Peter, founder of the church at Rome) during the reign of Nero. By this time Christian communities had already been established in all important cities of the Roman Empire.

Persecution of Christians. The Roman government tolerated any religion that did not threaten the safety or tranquility of the Empire. Christianity, however, clearly appeared to be a subversive danger to society and the state. The Christians refused to participate in the worship of the emperor which, although not an official state religion, was considered an essential patriotic rite uniting all Roman subjects in common loyalty to the imperial government. To Christians there was only one God; no other could share their loyalty to Him. In the eyes of the Roman officials this attitude branded them as traitors. In addition, the Christians seemed a secret, unsociable group forming a state within a state—"walling themselves off from the rest of mankind," as a pagan writer observed. Many were pacifists who refused to serve in the army, and all were intolerant of other religious sects and refused to associate with pagans or take part in social functions that they considered sinful or degrading.

During the first two centuries A.D. persecution was only sporadic and local, like that at Rome under Nero (see p. 76). But during the late third and early fourth centuries, when, as we shall see, the Empire was in danger of collapse, three organized empire-wide efforts were made to suppress Christianity. By far the longest and most systematic campaign against the Christians, who now comprised perhaps one tenth of the population, was instigated by the emperor Diocletian from 303 to 311. But the inspired defiance of the Christian martyrs, who seemed to welcome death—"The blood of the martyrs is the seed of the Church" are the words of a third-century Christian[7]—could not be overcome.

Official recognition and acceptance. In 311 the emperor Galerius recognized that persecution had failed and issued an edict of toleration making Christianity a legal religion in the East. In the following year the emperor Constantine was swayed toward Christianity during a desperate battle with the army of a rival for the throne. At the height of the conflict, tradition has it that he saw emblazoned across the sky a cross with the words *In hoc signo vinces* ("By this sign thou shalt conquer"). Constantine won the battle, and in 313 he issued the Edict of Milan, which legalized Christianity throughout the Empire and put it on a par with all the pagan cults. Constantine favored Christianity by granting many privileges to the Church, but he waited until he was on his deathbed before receiving baptism. His successors, with one exception, were Christians.

In his brief reign (361-363) the scholarly emperor Julian, Constantine's nephew, who had been raised a Christian, renounced his faith and sought to revive paganism; as a result, he was branded the Apostate. Julian did not persecute the Christians ("Those who are in the wrong in matters of supreme importance," he wrote, "are objects of pity rather than of hate"[8]), and his efforts to revive paganism failed dismally. On his deathbed he is supposed to have said, "Thou hast conquered, O Galilean."

The Church of St. Apollinare in Classe, outside Ravenna, is an early basilica (from the Greek, *basilikos*, meaning "kingly") which Justinian erected on the site of a temple of Apollo. The Church itself dates from the sixth century; the round bell tower at the right is a tenth-century addition.

The final step in the triumph of Christianity was taken during the reign of Theodosius I (379-395), who made Christianity the official religion of the Empire. Henceforth paganism was persecuted, and even the Olympic games were suppressed.

Reasons for the spread of Christianity. In its rise to preeminence Christianity competed with the philosophies and religions of the day. The philosophies were becoming more religious and other-worldly, however, which made it easy for their adherents to accept a Christianity whose doctrines, as we shall see, were becoming more philosophical. During the early Empire most Roman intellectuals had embraced Stoicism which, unlike Epicureanism with its unyielding materialism, had room for God (see p. 86). The dominant philosophy of the third century, Neo-Platonism, rejected human reason and taught that the only reality is spirit and that the soul's principal objective is to escape from the material world and, by union with God, return to its spiritual home.

There were also the popular mystery religions such as the worship of the Phrygian Great Mother (Cybele), the Egyptian Isis, the Greek Dionysus, and the Persian Mithras, god of light who fought against darkness (Mithras was especially popular with soldiers). All of these cults presented the comforting idea of a divine savior and the promise of everlasting life. Their followers found Christian beliefs and practices sufficiently familiar so as to make conversion easy.

But Christianity had far more to offer than did the mystery religions. Its founder was not a creature of myth, like the gods and goddesses of the mystery cults, but a real historic personality whose lofty ethical teachings and whose death and resurrection as the divine incarnation of God were preserved in detail in a unique record—the New Testament. Also unique was the Christian God—the omnipotent, jealous yet loving God of the Hebrew Scriptures now universalized as the God of all mankind. Moreover, Christianity was a dynamic, aggressive faith. It upheld the equality of all men—Jesus' ministry was chiefly to the poor and downtrodden—taught that a loving Father had

A view of the interior of the Church of St. Apollinare looking toward the apse. The fine mosaic work throughout dates from the second half of the sixth century and reflects strong Byzantine influence. The richly ornamented interior of St. Apollinare is in sharp contrast to the austere brick exterior (see photo, p. 126). This is a characteristic of early Christian architecture and may have been intended to greatly emphasize the difference between the everyday world as contrasted with the spiritual magnificence of the Kingdom of God.

sent His only Son to atone for men's sins, and offered a vision of immortality and an opportunity to be "born again" cleansed of sin. Its converts displayed enthusiasm and zeal, and the courage with which they faced death and persecution impressed even their bitterest enemies. In time, also, a Church organization was created that was far more united and efficient than any possessed by its competitors.

Church organization. The years immediately following Christ's death had passed with little organization in the Christian movement. Viewing the present world as something that would end quickly with the imminent Second Coming of their Lord, the earliest converts saw no necessity for organization. But after it became clear that the Second Coming had been postponed, a definite Church organization began to emerge.

At first there was little or no distinction

between laity and clergy. Traveling teachers visited Christian communities, preaching and giving advice where needed. But the steady growth in the number of Christians made necessary special Church officials who could devote all their time to religious work, clarifying the body of Christian dogma, conducting services, and caring for the funds. The earliest officials were called presbyters (elders) or bishops (overseers). By the second century the offices of bishop and presbyter had become distinct. Churches in the villages adjacent to the mother Church, which was usually located in a city, were administered by priests (a corruption of *presbyter*) responsible to a bishop. Thus evolved the diocese, a territorial administrative division under the jurisdiction of a bishop. Furthermore, the bishops were recognized as the successors of the apostles and, like them, the guardians of Christian teaching and tradition.

A number of dioceses made up a province; the bishop of the most important city in each province enjoyed more prestige than his fellows and was known as an archbishop or metropolitan. The provinces were grouped into larger administrative divisions called patriarchates. The title of patriarch was applied to the bishop of such great cities as Rome, Constantinople, and Alexandria.

Primacy of the bishop of Rome. A development of outstanding importance was the rise of the bishop of Rome to a position of preeminence in the hierarchy of the Church. At first only one of several patriarchs, the Roman bishop gradually became recognized as the leader of the Church in the West with the title of pope—from the Greek word meaning "father."

Many factors explain the emergence of the papacy at Rome. As the largest city in the West and the capital of the Empire, Rome had an aura of prestige that was transferred to its bishop. When the Empire in the West collapsed in the fifth century, the bishop of Rome emerged as a stable and dominant figure looked up to by all. The primacy of Rome was fully evident during the pontificate of Leo I, called the Great (440-461), who provided both the leadership that saved Italy from invasion by the Huns (see p. 135) and

the major theoretical support for papal headship of the Church—the Petrine theory. This doctrine held that since Peter, whom Christ had made leader of the apostles, was the first bishop of Rome, his authority over all Christians was handed on to his successors at Rome. The Church in the East, insisting on the equality of all the apostles, has never accepted the Petrine theory.

Foundations of Christian doctrine and worship. While the administrative structure of the Church was being erected, Christian beliefs were being defined and systematized. This process of fixing the dogma began with Paul, who stressed the divinity of Jesus and interpreted his death as an atonement for man's sins.

In time differences of opinion over doctrinal matters caused clashes. One of the most important controversies was over Arianism. At issue was the relative position of the three persons of the Trinity—God the Father, God the Son, and God the Holy Spirit. The view that the Father and the Son were equal was vigorously denied by Arius (256-336), a priest of Alexandria, who believed that Christ was not fully God because he was not of a substance identical with God and, as a created being, was not coeternal with Him. The controversy became so serious that in 325 the emperor Constantine convened the first ecumenical Church council, the Council of Nicaea, to resolve the problem. With Constantine presiding, the council branded the Arian belief a heresy—an opinion or doctrine contrary to the official teachings of the Church—and Christ was declared to be of the same substance as God, uncreated, and coeternal with Him. This mystical concept of the Trinity, without which the central Christian doctrine of the incarnation would be undermined, received official formulation in the Nicene Creed. Despite persecution, Arianism continued to flourish throughout the fourth century, and we shall see that some of the German tribes had been converted to this Christian heresy before they invaded the Empire.

The liturgy in the early churches was plain and simple, consisting of prayer, Scripture reading, hymns, and preaching. The early Christian worshiped God and sought salvation largely through his own efforts. Following the growth of Church organization and dogma, however, the Church was believed to be the indispensable intermediary between God and man. Without the Church the individual could not hope to approach God.

The development of the Church's dogma owed much to the Church Fathers of the second through fifth centuries. Since most of them were intellectuals who came to Christianity by way of Neo-Platonism and Stoicism, they maintained that Greek philosophy and Christianity were compatible. Because reason (*logos* in Greek) and truth come from God, "philosophy was a preparation," wrote Clement of Alexandria (d. 215), "paving the way towards perfection in Christ,"[9] the latest and most perfect manifestation of God's reason. Thus Christianity was viewed as a superior philosophy which could supersede all pagan philosophies and religions.

In the West three Church Fathers stand out. The scholarship of St. Jerome (340-420) made possible the famous Vulgate translation of the Bible into Latin, which in a revised form is still the official translation of the Roman Catholic Church. St. Ambrose (340-397) resigned his government post to become bishop of Milan, where he employed his great administrative skills to establish a model bishopric. By reproving the actions of the strong emperor Theodosius I and forcing him to do public penance, St. Ambrose was the first to assert the Church's superiority over the state in spiritual matters. St. Augustine (354-430) was probably the most important of all the Church Fathers. At the age of thirty-two he found in Christianity the answer to his long search for meaning in life, as he relates in his *Confessions*, one of the world's great autobiographies. As bishop of Hippo in North Africa, he wrote more than a hundred religious works which became the foundation of much of the Church's theology.

The regular clergy. So far we have discussed the secular clergy, who moved through the world (*saeculum*) administering the Church's services and communicating its teachings to the laity. But another type of churchmen also arose—the regular clergy, so called because they lived by a rule (*regula*) within monasteries. These monks sought seclusion from the distractions of this world in order to prepare themselves for the next.

The monastic way of life was older than Christianity, having existed in Judaism, for example, among the Essenes (see pp. 123–124). Christian ascetics, who had abandoned the worldly life and become hermits, could be found in the East as early as the third century A.D. Some went so far as to denounce even beauty as evil and, in pursuit of spiritual perfection by subordinating their flesh, tortured themselves and fasted to excess. In Syria, for example, St. Simeon Stylites lived for thirty-seven years on top of a pillar sixty feet high.

As a more moderate expression of asceticism, Christians in Egypt developed the monastic life, wherein men seeking a common spiritual goal lived together under a common set of regulations. St. Basil (330-379), a Greek bishop in Asia Minor, drew up a rule based on work, charity, and a communal life in which, however, each monk retained most of his independence. The Rule of St. Basil became the standard system in the eastern Church.

In western monasticism the work of St. Benedict (c. 480-543) paralleled St. Basil's efforts in the East. About 529 St. Benedict led a band of followers to a hill between Rome and Naples, named Monte Cassino, where they erected a monastery on the site of an ancient pagan temple. There he composed a rule which gave order and discipline to western monasticism. Benedictine monks took the three basic vows of poverty, chastity, and obedience to the abbot, the head of the monastery. Unlike eastern monks, the daily activities of the Benedictine monks were closely regulated: they participated in eight divine services, labored in field or workshop for six or seven hours, and spent about two hours studying and preserving the writings of Latin antiquity at a time when chaos and illiteracy had overtaken the western half of the Roman Empire. Benedictine monasticism was to be the most dynamic civilizing force in western Europe between the sixth and the twelfth centuries.

DECLINE AND DIVISION IN THE ROMAN WORLD

The crisis of the third century. In the third century A.D., while Christianity was spreading throughout the Roman world, internal anarchy and foreign invasion drastically transformed the nature of the Empire. What can be called the constitutional monarchy of the first and second centuries (see p. 75) changed to a despotic absolute monarchy in which the emperors made no attempt to hide the fact that they were "army made." By the late third century the emperor was no longer addressed as *princeps*, meaning first among equals, but as *dominus et deus*, "lord and god." The Principate had been replaced by absolute rule known as the Dominate.

The transformation of the Roman Empire in the third century was foreshadowed by the reign of Commodus, who succeeded his father, Marcus Aurelius, in 180 A.D. Commodus was an incompetent voluptuary whose dissipations, cruelties, and neglect of affairs of state motivated a group of conspirators to have him strangled in 192 A.D. Civil war followed as rival armies fought for the imperial throne—on one occasion troops holding Rome sold the throne to the highest bidder—until Septimius Severus emerged on top and established a dynasty that provided some measure of order.

The Severan dynasty (193-235), like the reign of Commodus and its aftermath, marks the approaching end of the Principate. The Senate was ignored and the army pampered and enlarged. Septimius Severus' dying words to his sons, "Enrich the soldiers and scorn all others," reflect the trend of the times.

The dire effects of this toadying to the soldiery became apparent after 235, when the last member of the Severan dynasty was murdered by mutinous troops. During the next fifty years the Empire was rent from within by bloody civil wars and lashed from without by foreign invaders. The imperial scepter was dragged in the gutter by generals who murdered emperors with no compunction, intimidated all opposition, and put themselves or their puppets on the throne. Of the twenty-six who claimed the title of emperor during this long period of military anarchy, only one died a natural death.

Meanwhile, German tribes breached the imperial frontiers: the Franks devastated Gaul and Spain, the Saxons attacked Britain, and the Goths occupied Dacia (modern Rumania). For the first time since Hannibal's invasion five centuries earlier, it was felt necessary to protect Rome itself with a wall twenty feet high and twelve feet wide, which still stands. In Asia a powerful new menace appeared after 226—a reinvigorated Persia under the rule of the Sassanid dynasty, which proceeded to attack Syria.

Economic decline. As deadly to the well-being of the Empire as military anarchy and foreign invasions was prolonged economic decline. The Empire was no longer expanding; the economy had become static. In the past military expansion had paid off in rich booty, and the tapping of new sources of wealth had justified a large army. Now, however, wars were defensive, and the army had become a financial liability rather than an asset. Gold and silver were also being drained away because of the one-sided trade with India and China (see pp. 116-117).

The trend toward the concentration of land ownership in a few hands was greatly accelerated by the turbulent conditions of the third century. Small farmers abandoned their lands, which were then bought up cheaply by large landowners, and the emperors added to their vast estates through confiscation. The number of tenant farmers, or *coloni* (see p. 79), increased as small farming decreased and men fled the insecurity of city life to find jobs and protection on the large estates with their fortified villas. There they cultivated their patches of land, paying rent to the landowner and providing him with free labor at sowing and reaping time. The condition of the *coloni* worsened as they fell behind in their rents and taxes and, by imperial order, were bound to their tenancies until they had discharged their debts. This was a first step toward serfdom and the social and economic pattern of the Middle Ages.

Frequent civil wars disturbed trade and thus helped undermine the prosperity of the cities, whose populations decreased correspondingly. To make matters worse, inflation spiraled because the government spent more than it took in. In order to meet their military and administrative expenses, the emperors repeatedly devalued the coinage by reducing its silver content. Ultimately the amount of alloy reached 98 percent, and prices soared as people lost confidence in the debased currency. The government later refused to accept its own money for taxes and required payment in goods and services.

Diocletian. A much-needed reconstruction of the Empire was accomplished by Diocletian (285-305), a rough-hewn soldier and administrative genius whose work of stabilization is often compared to that of Augustus after a similar period of turmoil. But while Augustus had established a form of constitutional monarchy, Diocletian founded an undisguised oriental despotism.

To increase the strength of the government, Diocletian completed the trend toward autocracy. The Senate was relegated to the status of a mere city council, while the person of the emperor was exalted. Adorned in robes laden with jewels, the emperor surrounded himself with all the splendor of an oriental despot. An imperial etiquette was established which transformed the emperor into a veritable god; rigid ceremonial demanded that men bow low before him and address him as "the most sacred lord."

The imperial administration was greatly enlarged. Diocletian realized that the Empire's problems had become too great for one man. He divided the Empire, retaining the eastern half for his own administration. In the West he created a coemperor who, like himself, was designated an Augustus. Each Augustus in turn was to entrust the direct rule of half his realm to an assistant, termed Caesar. Since each Caesar would succeed his Augustus when the senior official died or retired, the problem of succession was supposedly solved.

Next, Diocletian greatly increased the number and variety of administrative units

Diocletian and his co-Augustus, each with his appointed Caesar, are shown in an embrace symbolic of the unity which Diocletian hoped to maintain despite administrative division of the empire. This sculpture now adorns St. Mark's Cathedral in Venice.

within the four divisions of the Empire. The provinces were reduced in size and more than doubled in number. (Italy lost its hitherto favored position and was divided into provinces.) The 120 provinces were grouped into thirteen dioceses, each under a vicar. The dioceses in turn were grouped into four prefectures, each under a prefect who served directly under one of the four emperors. Paralleling this civil administration was a separate hierarchy of military officials. Finally, a large secret service was created to keep close watch over this vast bureaucracy. Even the Christian Church did not escape the spreading tentacles of the new regimented state, as Diocletian's ruthless persecution of Christianity demonstrates.

Diocletian also made strenuous efforts to arrest economic decay in the Empire. He gradually restored confidence in the debased currency by issuing new standard silver and gold coins. In the meantime, in an effort to stem the runaway inflation, he issued an edict fixing maximum prices for all essential goods and services, which were set to cover a wide range from peas to beer, and from haircuts to freight rates.

Head of the emperor Constantine, which was once part of an enormous statue.

Constantine. After Diocletian and his fellow Augustus retired in 305, his scheme for the succession collapsed, and civil war broke out once again. Within a few years Constantine (306-337), the only one of five rival emperors who favored Christianity (see p. 126), forged to the front, and after sharing the Empire for a few years with an eastern rival, became sole emperor in 324.

Constantine carried on Diocletian's work of reconstructing and stabilizing the Empire. We have already noted his solution of the Christian problem. To stabilize the manpower situation, necessary for the production of essential goods and services as well as the collection of taxes, Constantine issued a series of decrees which froze people to their occupations and places of origin. Henceforth no *colonus* could leave the soil, and the children of a *colonus* had to accept the same status as that of their father. In the cities the same restrictions were applied to members of those guilds whose activities were essential to the state, such as baking and transportation. Born into and bound to their occupations, members had to marry within the guild and train their sons to carry on the same line of work. Thus, to serve the interests of the state and to arrest further economic decline, a veritable caste system was established.

Division of the Empire. The Roman world's center of gravity shifted eastward during the age of Diocletian and Constantine. The administrative reforms swept away Italy's former primacy, and Rome even ceased to be a seat of imperial authority. Diocletian's coemperor in the West ruled from Milan, while Diocletian himself chose to govern the eastern half of the Empire and set up his court at Nicomedia in northwestern Asia Minor. His was a logical choice; the East had declined less than the West, and the greatest dangers to the Empire came from beyond the Danube River and from Persia. But even more strategic than Nicomedia was the old Greek colony of Byzantium, across the straits, selected by Constantine for a new capital. Reached only through a narrow, easily defended channel, Byzantium possessed a splendid harbor at the crossroads of Europe and Asia. Constantine dubbed his capital New Rome, but it soon became known as Constantinople.

The establishment of an eastern capital foreshadowed the impending division of the Empire into two completely separate states, the East and the West. For about fifty years following the death of Constantine in 337, the unity of the Empire was preserved, although there were often two joint emperors, one in the East and the other in the West. But after Theodosius I divided it between his two sons in 395, the Empire was never again governed as a single unit. Henceforth we can speak of a western Roman empire, which soon fell, and of an eastern Roman—or Byzantine—empire, which endured for another thousand years during which it adhered to the paternalistic and authoritarian pattern laid down by Diocletian and Constantine (see Chapter 6).

UPHEAVAL IN THE WEST

The Germanic tribes. Weakened by economic, social, and political decline, Rome had turned to the most extreme forms of absolutism in an effort to ride out the storm that threatened to engulf it. But its internal crisis was compounded by mounting external pressures that threatened to stave in its far-flung frontiers. The greatest danger lay to the north, the home of restless bands of fierce barbarians—the Germans. From the Franks on the Rhine to the Goths on the Black Sea, they were grouped into tribes (whose names will appear in the text as each makes its bid for the spoils of a tottering empire). Semi-nomads, the Germans were at a cultural stage midway between a pastoral and an agricultural economy. They engaged in so little commerce that cattle, rather than money, were sufficient as a measure of value.

According to the Roman historian Tacitus, the Germans were notorious as heavy drinkers and gamblers. On the other hand, Tacitus praised their courage, respect for women, and freedom from many Roman vices. A favorite amusement was listening to the tribal bards recite ancient tales of heroes and gods.

Each warrior leader had a retinue of followers, who were linked to him by personal loyalty. According to Tacitus:

On the field of battle it is a disgrace to the chief to be surpassed in valour by his companions, to the companions not to come up to the valour of their chief. As for leaving a battle alive after your chief has fallen, *that* means lifelong infamy and shame. To defend and protect him, to put down one's own acts of heroism to his credit—that is what they really mean by "allegiance". The chiefs fight for victory, the companions for their chief.[10]

This war band—called *comitatus* in Latin— had an important bearing on the origin of medieval feudalism, which was based on the personal bond between knights and their feudal lords. The heroic virtues associated with the *comitatus* also continued into the Middle Ages where they formed the basis of the value system of the feudal nobility.

In an effort to eliminate blood feuds, the Germanic system of justice was based on the principle of compensation. For the infliction of specific injuries a stipulated payment termed a *bot* was required. The amount of compensation varied according to the severity of the crime and the social position of the victim. For example, it cost forty times as much to kill a man of rank as a common man. Some crimes were botless—that is, so grave in character that compensation could not be paid. A person charged with such a crime had to stand trial and produce oath-helpers who would swear to his innocence. If unable to obtain oath-helpers, he was subjected to trial by ordeal, of which there were three kinds. In the first, the defendant had to lift a small stone out of a vessel of boiling water; unless his scalded arm had healed within a prescribed number of days, he was judged guilty. In the second, he had to walk blindfolded and barefooted across a floor on which lay pieces of red-hot metal; success in avoiding the metal was a sign of innocence. In the third, the bound defendant was thrown into a stream which had been blessed; only if the holy water accepted him and he sank was he believed innocent. Trial by ordeal, which was employed only where a strong presumption of guilt existed, lasted until the thirteenth century, when it was outlawed by Pope Innocent III and various secular rulers.

Roman-German contacts. During the many centuries that the Romans and Germans faced each other across the Rhine-Danube frontier, there was much contact—peaceful as well as belligerent—between the two peoples. Roman trade reached into Germany, and Germans entered the Empire as slaves. During the troubled third century many Germans were invited to settle on vacated lands within the Empire or to serve in the Roman legions. By the end of the fourth century the Roman army and its generals in the West had become almost completely German.

The Germans beyond the frontiers were kept in check by force of arms, by frontier walls, by diplomacy and gifts, and by employing the policy of playing off one tribe against another. In the last decades of the fourth century, however, these methods proved insufficient to prevent a series of great new invasions. A basic factor behind Germanic restlessness seems to have been land hunger. Their numbers were increasing, much of their land was forest and swamp, and their methods of tillage were inefficient.

Wholesale barbarian invasions. Meanwhile another restless people were on the move. The Huns, superb Mongolian horsemen and fighters, were nomads from Central Asia who had for centuries plundered and slain their Asian neighbors. In 372 they

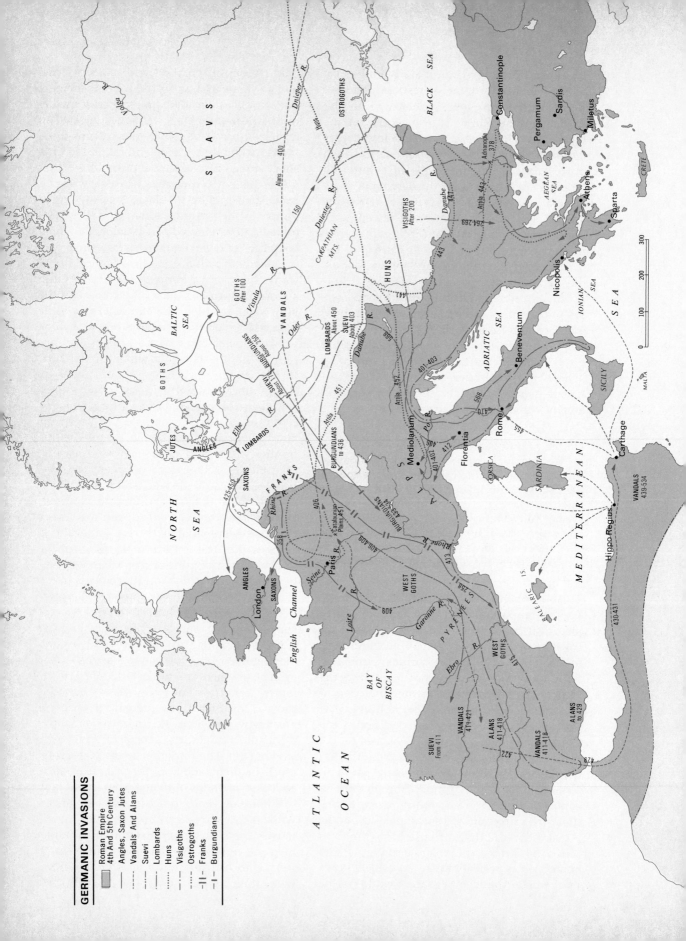

GERMANIC INVASIONS

Roman Empire
4th And 5th Century

———— Angles, Saxon Jutes
—·—·— Vandals And Alans
———— Suevi
—··—··— Lombards
············ Huns
—·—·— Visigoths
———— Ostrogoths
═╪═╪═ Franks
—╎—╎— Burgundians

·crossed the Volga and soon subjugated the easternmost Germanic tribe, the Ostrogoths. Terrified at the prospect of being conquered in turn by the advancing Huns, the Visigoths petitioned the Romans to allow them to settle as allies inside the Empire. Permission was granted, and in 376 the entire tribe crossed the Danube into Roman territory. But soon corrupt Roman officials cheated and mistreated the Visigoths, and the proud barbarians went on a rampage. The inept East Roman emperor sought to quell them, but he lost both his army and his life in the battle of Adrianople in 378.

Adrianople has been described as one of history's decisive battles: it destroyed the legend of the invincibility of the Roman legions and ushered in a century and a half of chaos. For a few years the capable emperor Theodosius I held back the Visigoths, but after his death in 395 they began to migrate and pillage under their leader, Alaric. He invaded Italy, and in 410 his followers sacked Rome. The weak West Roman emperor ceded southern Gaul to the Visigoths, who soon expanded into Spain. Their Spanish kingdom lasted until the Muslim conquest of the eighth century.

To counter Alaric's threat to Italy, the Romans had withdrawn most of their troops from the Rhine frontier in 406 and from Britain the following year. The momentous consequence of this action was a flood of Germanic tribes across the defenseless frontiers. The Vandals pushed their way through Gaul to Spain and, after pressure from the Visigoths, moved on to Africa, the granary of the Empire. In 455 a Vandal raiding force sailed over from Africa, and Rome was sacked a second time. Meanwhile the Burgundians settled in the Rhone valley, the Franks gradually spread across northern Gaul, and the Angles, Saxons, and Jutes invaded Britain. Although each of these several tribes set up a German-ruled kingdom within the confines of the Empire, only the Franks in Gaul and the Angles and Saxons in Britain managed to perpetuate their kingdoms longer than a few centuries.

While the Germans were taking over the western part of the Empire, the Huns pushed farther into Europe. Led by Attila, the "scourge of God," the mounted nomads crossed the Rhine in 451. The remaining Roman forces in Gaul, joined by the Visigoths, defeated the Huns near Troyes. Atilla then plundered northern Italy and planned to take Rome, but disease, lack of supplies, and the dramatic appeal of Pope Leo I— which was to give the papacy great prestige —caused him to return to the plains of Hungary. The Hunnic hordes disintegrated after 453, when Attila died on the night of his marriage to a Germanic princess whom legend immortalized as Krimhild of the *Nibelungenlied* (see p. 256).

The fall of Rome. What was happening to the imperial throne in the West during this turbulent period? As we have mentioned (p. 132), after the death of Theodosius I in 395, the Empire was divided between his two sons. Roman rule in the West grew increasingly impotent as a series of incompetent emperors sought safety behind marshes at Ravenna. The leaders of the mercenary soldiers, whose ranks were now mainly German, wielded the real power.

In 475 Orestes, the Germanic commander of the troops, forced the Senate to elect his young son Romulus Augustulus ("Little Augustus") as emperor in the West. In the following year another Germanic commander, Odovacar, slew Orestes and, seeing no reason for continuing the sham of an imperial line, deposed Romulus Augustulus and proclaimed himself head of the government. The deposition of the boy, who by a strange irony bore the names of the legendary founder of Rome and the founder of the Empire, marks the traditional "fall" of the Roman Empire.

Actually, no single date is accurate, for the fall of Rome was a long and complicated process. Yet 476 at least symbolizes the end of the Roman Empire in the West, for in this year the long line of emperors inaugurated by Augustus ended and the undisguised rule of Italy by Germanic leaders began.

Theodoric's kingdom in Italy. The disintegration of the Hunnic empire following the death of Attila freed the Ostrogoths to migrate as other tribes were doing. Under their energetic king, Theodoric (c. 454-526), who had spent some years as a hostage at Constantinople, the Ostrogoths were galvanized into action.

Theodoric accepted a commission from the emperor in the East to reimpose imperial authority over Italy, now in Odovacar's hands. In 488 he led his people into the Italian peninsula, where, after hard fighting, Odovacar sued for peace and was treacherously murdered. Theodoric then established a strong Ostrogothic kingdom in Italy with its capital at Ravenna. Because he appreciated the culture he had seen at Constantinople, Theodoric pursued a successful policy of maintaining classical culture on a high level. Following his death without a male heir in 526, civil war broke out in Italy, paving the way for a twenty-year war of reconquest (535-555) by the armies of the East Roman emperor Justinian. Italy was ravaged from end to end by the fighting, and the classical civilization that Theodoric had carefully preserved was in large part destroyed.

The Lombards. In 568, only three years after Justinian died, the last wave of Germanic invaders, the fierce Lombards, poured

Reminiscent of the classical architecture which the Ostrogothic king admired, Theodoric's tomb in Ravenna is remarkable for its dome, which is one enormous slab of stone, 35 feet in diameter and weighing 470 tons.

into Italy. The Eastern emperor held on to southern Italy, as well as Ravenna and Venice, and the pope now became the virtual ruler of Rome. Not until the late nineteenth century would Italy again be united under one government. The Lombard kingdom in Italy, weakened by the independent actions of many strong dukes, did not last long. In 774 it was conquered by the Franks, who, as we shall see in Chapter 8, had in the meantime established the most powerful and longest lasting of all the Germanic kingdoms that arose on the territory of the western empire.

The problem of the fall of Rome. The shock and dismay felt by contemporaries throughout the Roman world on learning of Alaric's sack of the Eternal City in 410 were to echo down the centuries, leaving the impression that the fall of Rome was a major calamity, one of the greatest in history.

Pagan writers attributed the sack of Rome to the abandonment of the ancient gods. In *The City of God* St. Augustine argued against this charge and put forth the theory that history unfolds according to God's design. Thus Rome's fall was part of the divine plan—"the necessary and fortunate preparation for the triumph of the heavenly city where man's destiny was to be attained."[11]

This view was challenged in the eighteenth century by Edward Gibbon, author of the famous *Decline and Fall of the Roman Empire*, who saw Rome's fall as the "triumph of barbarism and religion." Christianity, he argued, had played an important role in undermining the imperial structure: "The clergy successfully preached the doctrines of patience and pusillanimity; . . . the last remains of the military spirit were buried in the cloister."[12]

In our time some explanations of Rome's fall have been rooted in psychological theories. For example, the basic cause has been attributed to a weakening of morale in the face of difficulties, to a "loss of nerve." Or it has been argued that the ultimate failure of Rome came from its too complete success. The easy acquisition of power and wealth and the importing of ready-made cultures from conquered peoples led to "a changed attitude of men's minds" and indo-

lence and self-gratification among the ruling classes. Such subjective theories can scarcely be proven, however, or even fairly assessed.

Most historians account for Rome's decline in terms of a variety of interacting forces. On the political side, the failure of civil power to control the army following the death of Marcus Aurelius resulted in military anarchy, the disintegration of central authority, and the weakening of Rome's ability to withstand external pressures. Diocletian and his successors had to increase the military establishment despite a growing manpower shortage, caused in part by recurrent plagues from Asia (perhaps smallpox or measles). "Hence they found themselves on the horns of a dilemma. Either they could conscript Roman civilians for military service and so decrease still further production and the state revenues, or they could . . . make up the deficit with barbarians."[13] The decision they made led to Germanization of the army and to German colonization within the empire.

On the economic side, the small farmer class disappeared, and more and more land was consolidated into huge *latifundia*; civil war and barbarian attacks disturbed trade relations; a debased currency and a crushing tax burden undermined the confidence of the people. Eventually the rigid economic and social decrees of Diocletian and Constantine created a vast bureaucracy which only aggravated the existing ills in the western half of the Empire, already far gone along the road to decline.

Western Europe in the sixth century. In the West the Empire was no more than a memory by the sixth century. In its place were new states that foreshadowed the major political divisions of modern Europe: Visigothic Spain, Anglo-Saxon England, Frankish Gaul, and a divided Italy ruled by Lombard dukes, the Eastern emperor, and the pope.

Vast tracts of formerly cultivated land were left untilled, and the failure of communications and transportation, coupled with the flight of the labor force from the cities to the country, had brought on a progressive decentralization of the economy. With much industry transferred from cities to large country estates, scores of once flourishing towns near the frontiers ceased to exist, while those closer to the Mediterranean shrunk in size and importance. "Roman civilization had been essentially urban; medieval civilization was to be essentially rural. With the decline of the towns the general level of civilization was lowered and western Europe began to assume its medieval aspect."[14]

Yet the Germanic invasions were not as cataclysmic as was once thought. True, the invaders pillaged ruthlessly, and in certain sections of the empire, especially in Britain, Roman civilization was entirely wiped out. The Germans also seized a great deal of land, but most of this was either vacant or belonged to the emperors; few private landowners were displaced. In most areas the invaders still represented a minority of the population, and a gradual blending and fusing of the cultures and the blood of the two peoples began. Thus the barbarians in time lost their Germanic customs, religion, and speech; that is why hardly a trace of the Germanic languages remains in Italy, France, and Spain. The Church, under the dual leadership of Benedictine monasticism and the papacy, assisted the fusion between German and Roman.

By the sixth century the foundations for the spiritual and political power of the papacy, which would lead to the Church-state rivalry of the Middle Ages, had been laid. We have seen how Pope Leo the Great acquired the moral leadership of the West by successfully protecting Italy from the Huns, and how the Lombard conquests in Italy gave the papacy its opportunity to achieve independence. In addition, ready for future use was the doctrine of the supremacy of the Church over the state in spiritual matters, a doctrine implied by St. Augustine in his *City of God* and clearly expressed by St. Ambrose during his clash with the emperor Theodosius I.

By the sixth century, then, the three elements that were to create the pattern of western civilization in the Middle Ages were being interwoven: Graeco-Roman culture, the Christian Church, and the Germanic peoples and their institutions. Here, in a sense, were the mind, spirit, and muscle that were to work together in western man during the next thousand years.

Survival in the East. In our study of history thus far it is apparent that the most westerly focus of civilization was Rome, which was not only far removed from the "heartland" of civilization in the Fertile Crescent and Egypt but was also the cultural area most exposed at this time to counterforces. As a consequence, the western half of the Roman Empire was overwhelmed by those forces, while the eastern half, though seriously threatened, managed to ride out the storm.

Until 1453 the eastern—or Byzantine—empire maintained the Roman imperial tradition and administrative structure. Equally important was the preservation of Greek language and learning. The East also evolved its own Orthodox Church, which was to play a vital role in shaping the course of civilization in Russia and the Slavic world. For these reasons we must redirect our steps toward the East, where the Graeco-Roman legacy endured and from where it would one day be transmitted back to the West.

SUMMARY

Christianity's roots extend back into Jewish history long before the birth of Christ, and it is there that we find the concept of the Messiah, the divinely appointed leader who would create a new Israel. Under the rule of the Hellenistic Seleucid empire and later of Rome, many Jews hoped for such a Messiah to lead them to political independence; but when Jesus attacked the shortcomings of the established religion and refused to head a political revolt against the Romans, his enemies brought about his condemnation and execution. Yet his teachings did not die with his crucifixion. Interpreted through the efforts of St. Paul and the Church Fathers, they spread rapidly throughout the Roman Empire. Despite persecution, converts flocked to the new faith, and finally, with the Edict of Milan in 313, the emperor Constantine made Christianity a legal religion. Thereafter the Church grew and flourished, with an organization based on the imperial Roman pattern and a hierarchy of officials culminating in the pope at Rome.

From the death of Marcus Aurelius in 180 A.D., the Roman Empire declined as its rulers became pawns of the army. Only Diocletian and Constantine were able to check the downward trend, and in the long run their system of despotism failed to save the western half of the Empire from further deterioration. When the Visigoths, pushed by the Huns, defeated Roman forces at the battle of Adrianople in 378, the gates of the Empire burst open before the barbarian tribes. The date of the final collapse of Rome may be set at 476, when the last Roman emperor in the West was deposed.

The fall of Rome—one of the great dramatic developments in history—has been explained in a variety of ways by later historians. No single cause can be given; the collapse appears to have been the result of various interacting factors. Following the devastating invasions which overwhelmed the western half of the Empire, the gap left by the Caesars was filled by a powerful new agency, the Christian Church.

As the Roman Empire crumbled in the West, a new center of imperial strength arose in the East at Constantinople. To this city and its Byzantine civilization—a continuation of the Graeco-Roman but with original contributions of its own—we shall now turn.

SUGGESTIONS FOR READING

J. A. Hexter, **The Judaeo-Christian Tradition*** (Harper & Row) is a brief but highly valuable survey of the evolution of ancient Judaism and Christianity. On the late ancient history of the Jews see E. Bickermann, **From Ezra to the Last of the Maccabees: Foundations of Post-Biblical Judaism*** (Schocken); and D. S. Russell, **The Jews from Alexander to Herod** (Oxford).

Edmund Wilson, **The Dead Sea Scrolls, 1949-1969** (Oxford, 1969) is the most readable introduction to a fascinating subject. See also John Allegro, **The Dead Sea Scrolls: A Reappraisal*** (Penguin); G. Vermes, **The Dead Sea Scrolls in English*** (Penguin); and Frank M. Cross, **Qumram and the History of the Biblical Text*** (Harvard).

Albert Schweitzer, **The Quest of the Historical Jesus*** (Macmillan) surveys the attempts of scholars to discover the Jesus of history. See also E. J. Goodspeed, **A Life of Jesus*** (Torchbooks); M. Enslin, **Christian Beginnings*** (Torchbooks); R. Bultman, **Primitive Christianity*** (Collins-World) and H. Kee and F. Young, **Understanding the New Testament** (Prentice-Hall, 1973).

J. W. C. Ward, **A History of the Early Church to A.D. 500*** (Harper & Row, 1975); J. G. Davies, **The Early Christian Church*** (Anchor); and H. Chadwick, **The Early Church*** (Penguin) are excellent surveys of the first five centuries of Church history. See also Cyril Richardson, **Early Christian Fathers** (Macmillan, 1970); H. Mattingly, **Christianity in the Roman Empire*** (Norton); E. R. Dodds, **Pagan and Christian in an Age of Anxiety*** (Cambridge, 1965); and C. N. Cochrane, **Christianity and Classical Culture: A Study of Thought and Action from Augustus to Augustine*** (Galaxy).

On early monasticism see H. Waddell, **The Desert Fathers*** (Barnes & Noble, 1974); and E. Duckett, **The Gateway to the Middle Ages: Monasticism*** (Univ. of Michigan).

S. Katz, **The Decline of Rome and the Rise of Medieval Europe*** (Cornell) is a concise, clear account. A. H. M. Jones, **The Decline of the Ancient World*** (Longman, 1975) is a recent detailed survey. See also F. Lot, **The End of the Ancient World and the Beginning of the Middle Ages*** (Torchbooks); R. MacMullen, **Constantine** (Dial, 1969); and H. Doerries, **Constantine the Great*** (Torchbooks, 1972).

Edward Gibbon, **The Decline and Fall of the Roman Empire*** (Dell), ed. by F. C. Bourne, is an abridgment of this eighteenth-century classic. For modern scholarly opinion on Rome's decline see Lynn White, Jr., ed., **The Transformation of the Roman World: Gibbon's Problem After Two Centuries** (Univ. of Calif., 1966); F. Walbank, **The Awful Revolution: The Decline of the Roman Empire in the West*** (Univ. of Toronto, 1969); R. M. Haywood, **The Myth of Rome's Fall*** (Apollo); and D. Kagan, ed., **Decline and Fall of the Roman Empire: Why Did It Collapse?*** (Heath).

J. B. Bury, **The Invasion of Europe by the Barbarians*** (Norton) is the best general work on the nature and effect of the Germanic invasions. See also H. Moss, **The Birth of the Middle Ages, 395-814*** (Galaxy); E. A. Thompson, **The Early Germans** (Oxford); and O. J. Maenchen-Helfen, **The World of the Huns** (Univ. of Calif., 1973).

*Indicates a less expensive paperbound edition.

CHAPTER 6

The Byzantine Empire, Early Russia, and Muslim Expansion

Citadel and Conqueror

INTRODUCTION. When we speak of the fall of the Roman Empire, we sometimes forget that in fact only the western portion of that empire succumbed to the German invaders and entered into what has been described as its "Dark Ages." In the East, despite many vicissitudes, the east Roman or Byzantine empire stood for a thousand years as a citadel protecting an unappreciative West slowly emerging from semibarbarism.

Furthermore, the Byzantine empire made great contributions to civilization: Greek language and learning were preserved for posterity; the Roman imperial system was continued and Roman law codified; the Greek Orthodox Church converted the Slavic peoples and fostered the development of a splendid new Graeco-oriental art that was dedicated to the glorification of the Christian religion. Situated at the crossroads of East and West, Constantinople acted as the disseminator of culture for all peoples who came in contact with the empire. Called with justification "The City," this rich and turbulent metropolis was to the early Middle

Ages what Athens and Rome had been to classical times. By the time the empire collapsed in 1453, its religious mission and political concepts had borne fruit among the Slavic peoples of eastern Europe and especially among the Russians. The latter were to lay claim to the Byzantine tradition and to dub Moscow the "Third Rome."

The only rival of Byzantine civilization close at hand was the culture developed by followers of the Prophet Muhammad, who united the Arabian peninsula under the banner of his new religion, Islam, with its fundamental teachings of monotheism. The dynamic faith of Muhammad spread so rapidly that within a hundred years after the Prophet's death his followers had established a vast empire stretching from the Pyrenees to the Indus. This breathtaking religious and political expansion was followed by a flowering of Islamic culture that rivaled the achievements of the Byzantine empire and far surpassed those of western Europe at this time. The Muslims share with the Byzantines chief credit for preserving and disseminating learning in the Middle Ages.

THE PRECARIOUS FORTUNES OF THE EASTERN EMPIRE

Constantine's city. At the southern extremity of the Bosporus stands a promontory that juts out from Europe toward Asia, with the Sea of Marmora to the south and a long harbor known as the Golden Horn to the north. On this peninsula stood the ancient Greek city of Byzantium, which Constantine enlarged considerably and formally christened "New Rome" in 330 A.D.

Constantine had chosen his site carefully. The city commanded the waterway connecting the Mediterranean and the Black seas and separating Europe and Asia. Moreover, the site favored defense; it enabled Constantinople not only to become the great warehouse for East-West commerce but above all to be a buffer protecting Europe from attack.

In Chapter 5 we saw how, during the fourth and fifth centuries, both the eastern and western provinces of the Roman Empire were beset by dangers from beyond the northern frontier. Storming into the Empire, Visigoths, Huns, and Ostrogoths pillaged the Balkans and threatened Constantinople. But the more populous eastern provinces, with their greater military and economic strength, were saved from the fate that befell Rome.

As the western half of the Roman Empire crumbled, Constantinople turned eastward for its livelihood and culture, becoming gradually less Roman and western and more Greek and oriental. A panorama of triumphs and defeats, Byzantine history for the next one thousand years can be divided into four main periods—expansion, peril, recovery, and disintegration.

Justinian's reconquests. The history of the empire in the sixth century focuses upon the reign of Justinian (527-565), whose ambition was to restore the Roman Empire to its ancient scope and grandeur. Much of his success he owed to his wife, Theodora, who had been a dancer and was said to be the daughter of a circus animal trainer. Theodora proved to be a brave empress and a wise counselor. In 532, early in Justinian's reign, occurred the Nike rebellion (named after the victory cry of the rioters), the most famous of many popular revolts that have led historians to characterize Byzantine history as a despotism tempered by revolution. Theodora's coolness and bravery inspired her hard-pressed husband to remain in the capital and crush the rebellion:

May I never be separated from this purple, and may I not live that day on which those who meet me shall not address me as mistress. If, now, it is your wish to save yourself, O Emperor, there is no difficulty. For we have much money, and there is the sea, here the boats. . . . as for myself, I approve a certain ancient saying that royalty is a good burial-shroud.[1]

To carry out his plan for recovering the lost half of the Roman Empire from the Germans, Justinian first bought off the Persian

Sassanid kings, who threatened Syria and Asia Minor (see p. 130). Then in 533 he seized North Africa and the islands of the western Mediterranean from the Vandals. But it took twenty years of exhausting warfare for his generals to regain Italy from the Ostrogoths. Rome and other great Italian cities lay in ruins, and the classical civilization that the Ostrogothic king Theodoric had taken care to preserve was virtually annihilated. Justinian also wrested the southeastern portion of Spain from the Visigoths. Yet his empire was still much smaller than the Roman Empire at its height. Only a small part of Spain was his; nor had he recovered Gaul, Britain, or southern Germany. Furthermore his reconquests had been accomplished at the price of exhausting the empire, both militarily and financially. Nor were Justinian's reconquests permanent; three years after his death most of devastated Italy fell to the Germanic Lombards, and the Persians made inroads into Syria.

In domestic affairs as in warfare, Justinian sought to restore the dignity and splendor of the Roman Empire. In this area are found his greatest accomplishments—the codification of Roman law and the erection of the great Church of Hagia Sophia, both described later in this chapter.

Three centuries of peril, 565-867. With Justinian's death, the first and perhaps the greatest period of Byzantine history ended. The exhausted empire now entered an era of peril lasting from the middle of the sixth to the middle of the ninth century. By the time Heraclius (610-641) ascended the throne, the empire was in a desperate position. Slavic tribes had invaded the Balkans, a new wave of Asiatic nomads, the Avars, were being kept beyond the Danube only by the payment of tribute, and the Persians were in the process of conquering Syria, Palestine, and Egypt. Jerusalem fell in 614, and various sacred relics, including what was reputed to be the Holy Cross, were carried off to the Persian capital. While one Persian army conquered Egypt, another advanced to a point in Asia Minor opposite Constantinople. In three brilliant campaigns Heraclius virtually destroyed the Persian empire and regained Syria, Palestine, and Egypt, along with the Holy Cross.

Although the centuries-old menace of the Persians had now been removed, the Eastern empire was soon confronted with a new danger. The early part of the seventh century saw in Arabia the birth of a new faith—Islam. With fanatical zeal the Arabs attacked the weakened Persian and Byzantine empires, and by the middle of the century they had subjugated Palestine, Syria, Persia, Egypt, and much of North Africa (see map, p. 159). An Arab fleet even besieged Constantinople annually for several years, and the distracted empire was also threatened by a new Hunnish menace, the Bulgars, who in 680 settled

In this detail from a mosaic from the Church of San Vitale at Ravenna, the emperor Justinian prepares to present a gold plate to the archbishop of Ravenna. The mosaics of this period emphasize individuality in facial features along with magnificently patterned costumes.

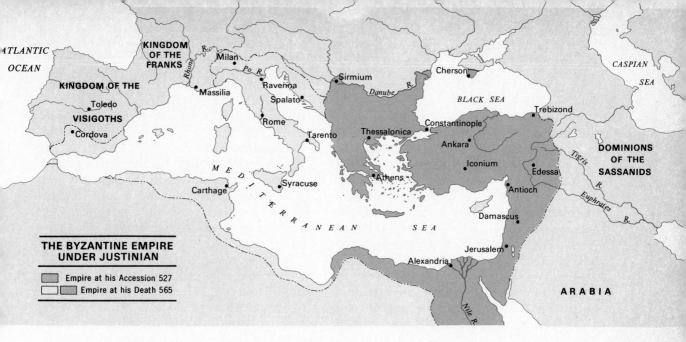

THE BYZANTINE EMPIRE UNDER JUSTINIAN

- ▨ Empire at his Accession 527
- □▨ Empire at his Death 565

in what is now Bulgaria. By 700 the Eastern empire stood on the brink of disintegration. In the Middle East it held only Asia Minor, while in the West it maintained a precarious hold on Sicily, southern Italy, Venice, and the exarchate of Ravenna, which extended from Ravenna southward through Rome.

The able Emperor Leo III (717-741) saved the hard-pressed empire. With the aid of a secret weapon, Greek fire (see p. 146), Leo repulsed the last great Arab assault on Constantinople in 718. He then turned to administrative and military reform. Civil and military authority in the provinces, separated by Diocletian (see p. 131), were reunited in the hands of provincial generals. Land was granted to the peasants in exchange for military service, and these free soldier-farmers, led by the powerful provincial generals, became the backbone of the Byzantine army. In contrast to the West, where the peasants were fast becoming serfs, a free peasantry continued to exist in the Eastern empire. Leo's religious policy, however, produced the iconoclastic controversy (see p. 147), which for over a hundred years caused widespread dissension.

Last days of grandeur, 867-1057. A little more than a century after Leo III's reforms had restored order to the hard-pressed empire, the strong Macedonian dynasty (867-1057) ushered in the third period of Byzantine history during which the empire went on the offensive. South Italy, which along with Sicily had recently been lost to the Muslims, was regained. The powerful Bulgarians, now Christianized and seeking to possess all the Balkans, were conquered, and the power of the Muslims in the East was shattered as the Byzantines regained the island of Cyprus and Antioch in Syria, both lost since the seventh century. It is also noteworthy that during this period of resurgence the emperors forged a new sphere of Byzantine influence in Russia.

The empire reached a high level of power under the energetic Basil II (976-1025). Byzantine military forces finally crushed their Bulgarian foes with great severity. On one occasion fifteen thousand Bulgars were blinded and only a handful, each with a single eye, were left to guide the rest home. The Bulgarian king is said to have died of shock when this sightless multitude returned. Basil the "Bulgar-slayer" incorporated the Bulgarian kingdom into the empire and the Byzantine frontier again reached the Danube.

Basil II was friendly with Vladimir, the prince of Kiev in southern Russia, and was instrumental in bringing about that ruler's conversion to Christianity. Other Russians also began to adopt Christian beliefs and various aspects of Byzantine culture. Trade augmented these relations.

Four centuries of decline: Part I, 1057-1204. At the end of the Macedonian dynasty in 1057, the Byzantine empire entered its last tempestuous period, one of decline, at times obvious and rapid, then again imperceptible and gradual. During these four centuries the foundations of Byzantine strength—a strong government, a prosperous economy, and a stable social order—suffered irreparable damage, and the weakened empire was shattered by both Christian and Muslim invaders.

During the tenth century a powerful landed nobility had begun to threaten the emperor's power. By absorbing the lands of the free peasants and reducing them to dependency, these landed magnates, whose interests were usually opposed to those of the central government, greatly increased their wealth and power. Since the free peasants had been the state's best taxpayers and the backbone of its armies, the empire's revenues and defenses became seriously undermined. At the end of the century Basil II twice had to repress the revolts of generals who represented the hostile aristocracy. Basil's successors held the great magnates in check until 1081, when one of them usurped the imperial throne.

In the meantime, within the orbit of Byzantine commerce a dangerous rival was emerging—the city of Venice, founded in the fifth and sixth centuries by refugees who fled the barbarian invasions of northern Italy and found safety on a cluster of small islands off the northern Adriatic coast. The island city of Venice was relatively safe from the barbarian hordes and thus remained under Byzantine sovereignty when most of the Italian peninsula was overrun. As subjects of the Byzantine empire, the Venetians enjoyed access to the eastern Mediterranean trade, but they were far enough away from Constantinople to run their own affairs. By the eleventh century Venice had acquired undisputed supremacy in the Adriatic, and ambitious Venetian merchants were dreaming of supplanting Byzantine commercial supremacy over all the eastern Mediterranean.

In the eleventh century also, the Byzantines were confronted with two new foes. The formidable Seljuk Turks (see p. 161) threatened Asia Minor; and the adventurous Normans, led by Robert Guiscard (see p. 207), began to carve out possessions for themselves in southern Italy. The Byzantine army was defeated by the Turks at the critical battle of Manzikert in 1071, and all of Asia Minor was soon lost. By an unfortunate coincidence, Bari, the empire's last stronghold in southern Italy, was captured by the Normans in the same year that the battle of Manzikert took place.

In 1081, when the empire stood deprived of rich possessions, sapped by growing commercial rivalry, and torn by the struggle with the landed aristocracy, a powerful landowner, Alexius Comnenus, became emperor by a coup d'état. Soon afterwards, in 1096, the first crusaders from the West appeared on the scene. Hoping to obtain some European mercenary forces to help defeat the

THE BYZANTINE EMPIRE
ABOUT 814

Latin Empire

Venetian Possessions

Seljuk Turks, Alexius had appealed to Pope Urban II for assistance, but he was dismayed to find a host of crusaders, including the dreaded Normans, approaching the capital. The western response to Urban's appeal to save the Eastern empire and the Holy Land from the Seljuks was met with suspicion on the part of the Byzantines, who viewed the pope as heretical and the crusaders as potentially dangerous to the Eastern empire. Adroitly, Alexius encouraged the crusaders to forgo his hospitality as quickly as possible and attack his Seljuk enemies. The successful weakening of Muslim power by the First Crusade enabled Alexius to recover valuable portions of Asia Minor.

With the Fourth Crusade (1202-1204), the envy and enmity which had been building up for decades in the West against the Byzantine empire were converted into violence. Dependent upon the Venetians for ships and money, the crusaders were persuaded to attack first the Christian city of Zara in Dalmatia, a commercial rival of Venice, and then Constantinople. The Venetian goal was to obtain a monopoly on Byzantine trade.

Constantinople was so rent by factional strife that the crusaders had little trouble in capturing it. A French noble among the crusaders described the resulting sacking of the city:

[I saw] . . . the great churches and the rich palaces melting and falling in, and the great streets filled with merchandise burning in the flames. . . . The booty gained was so great that none could tell you the end of it: gold and silver, and vessels and precious stones, and samite, and cloth of silk, and robes vair [squirrel] and grey, and ermine, and every choicest thing found upon the earth . . . . never, since the world was created, had so much booty been won in any city.[2]

Priceless works of art were destroyed, yet many art treasures and sacred relics did find their way to the West.

The Fourth Crusade irreparably weakened the Byzantine empire. A tiny empire in exile held out around Nicaea in Asia Minor, while a Latin emperor ruled at Constantinople and Venice took over islands and coastal ports which enabled her to monopolize the eastern trade.

Four centuries of decline: Part II, 1204-1453. The Latin empire of Constantinople, hated by the native population upon whom it imposed the Roman Church, lasted only until 1261. In that year Michael Palaeologus of Nicaea, allying himself with Genoa, which was jealous of Venetian commercial supremacy in the eastern Mediterranean, reconquered Constantinople. Amid the rejoicing of the populace, a Greek patriarch was reinstated in Hagia Sophia.

The rule of the Palaeologi lasted until the demise of the Byzantine empire—a span of two centuries of decline. Internally, the empire lost strength and resiliency. A form of feudalism developed in which the great landed magnates resisted the authority of the emperor and the imperial bureaucracy. Taxes and customs duties diminished, coinage was debased, and the military and naval forces, composed increasingly of mercenaries, grew fatally weak. Bitter religious disputes arose between the clergy and the emperors who sought western aid in return for a promise to unite the Eastern and Roman churches.

Externally, the situation was critical. The empire held only a small portion of its former territory and was surrounded by ambitious rivals and foes. The Latins still retained southern Greece; the Venetians and Genoese each possessed coastal cities and island territories of the empire; and in the fourteenth century a powerful Serbian kingdom developed in the Balkans and menaced Constantinople.

In the meantime a new and ultimately fatal menace had arisen across the Straits in Asia Minor. In the late thirteenth century the Ottoman or Osmanli Turks, named after their early leader Osman, had received from the Seljuk sultan at Ankara a military fief along the Byzantine border south of Nicaea. The prospect of booty from raids across the border attracted swarms of recruits, with the result that Nicaea was taken in 1331. In 1356 the Ottomans crossed over to Europe and soon captured Adrianople, which became their capital. By 1390 they had overrun Bulgaria and Serbia and reached the Danube. The Ottoman Turks also expanded eastward in Asia Minor, until they were defeated in 1402 by the Mongol marauder Timur the Lame, or Tamerlane (see p. 173).

This defeat and the lack of a strong navy delayed the Turkish conquest of Constantinople. The end came in 1453. After a heroic defense of seven weeks, in which Constantine XI confronted the Turkish army of nearly 160,000 soldiers with only 9000 fighting men (half of whom were foreign mercenaries), the great eastern bulwark of Christian civilization collapsed before the might of Islam. As the Turks stormed the walls of the city, the emperor rushed to meet them, crying out as he was cut down: "God forbid that I should live an Emperor without an Empire! As my city falls, I will fall with it."[3]

The fall of Constantinople reverberated throughout the contemporary world. The last direct link with the classical era was shattered. First Rome had perished, now New Rome; an epoch that had seemed eternal had passed into history.

Reasons for endurance of the Byzantine empire. As the preceding résumé of Byzantine history attests, the empire's political life had always been stormy. During its thousand years of existence it experienced some sixty-five revolutions and the abdications or murders of more than sixty emperors. How did the empire manage to survive for such a long period?

One reason lay in its continuous use of a money economy, in contrast to the primitive barter economy then prevailing in the West. The use of money facilitated trade and the payment of taxes and enabled the empire to maintain standing military and naval forces. Until the latter days of the empire Byzantine military science was relatively advanced and the armed forces effective. Surviving military manuals indicate the efficiency of army organization, which included engineering and medical units. Also, the Byzantines had a secret weapon called "Greek fire," an inflammable chemical mixture whose main ingredient, saltpeter, made it a forerunner of gunpowder. As from a modern flamethrower,

As heirs of the Romans, the Byzantines were fierce and disciplined fighters. A detail from an illuminated manuscript shows their prowess in a naval battle.

Greek fire was catapulted out of tubes onto the decks of enemy ships.

Of great significance for the endurance, as well as the character, of the empire was the wholesale loss of African, Italian, and eastern territory by the year 700. The lands still under the emperor's control were now more homogeneous; most of the population was Greek. Thus historians speak of the seventh century as the period when the eastern Roman empire was transformed into the "Byzantine" empire—that is, transformed into a Hellenized civilization, taking its name appropriately from the original Greek settlement on which Constantinople had been built.

Another reason for the empire's endurance was its centralized system of administration. Where the West was broken up into numerous feudal principalities, the Byzantines were governed by a strong monarchy, aided by a well-trained bureaucracy. The emperor was the supreme military commander, the highest judge, the only legislator, and the protector of the Church. His authority rested on the claim that he was chosen by God to rule the Christian empire entrusted to him by God. So absolute was the emperor's control that his title *Autokrator* has been carried over into the English word *autocracy*, meaning "absolute supremacy." Only a successful revolution could depose him.

The Orthodox Church was another factor in the endurance of the empire. Linked closely to the state, the Church usually was the staunchest ally of the throne.

THE ORTHODOX CHURCH

Collaboration between Church and state. The Byzantine, or Orthodox, Church not only dominated religious and cultural life in the empire but was also interwoven with the political fabric. Whereas the Roman Church did not identify itself with the Roman Empire or any other state in the West but became an international body, the Orthodox Church was a state church ruled by God's vicar on earth—the king-priest who, surrounded by splendid pomp and ceremony, ruled the Byzantine empire. In essence, the Church was a department of the state, and the emperor at times even intervened in spiritual matters. In many respects the patriarch of Constantinople had a position analogous to that of the pope in Rome, but with a significant difference—the patriarch, although elected by the bishops, was nominated by the emperor. Such blending of authority over Church and state in the office of emperor has been termed *Caesaropapism* (combining the functions of Caesar and pope).

The iconoclastic controversy. Relations between the eastern and western branches of the Church, continually undermined by what Constantinople viewed as Rome's excessive claims of primacy (see p. 128), deteriorated sharply in the eighth century as a result of the policies of the emperor Leo III. Although Leo had no use for Islam as a religion, he agreed with its contention that the employment of images and pictures in worship eventually led to idolatry. Therefore, in 726 Leo issued an edict forbidding the use of images (icons) of the sacred personages of Christianity, including Christ and all the saints. Statues were removed from churches, and church walls were whitewashed to cover all pictures.

In Constantinople rioting in protest against iconoclasm, or image breaking, broke out immediately. The demonstration was put down by troops, who killed some of the rioters. When the patriarch of Constantinople objected, he was replaced by another man more agreeable to the emperor's will. Riots continued to break out in Greece and Italy, and the pope at Rome, Gregory II, called a council of bishops who read out of the Church all those who had accepted iconoclasm. This caused an open breach between the papacy and the Eastern emperor.

Final separation of the churches. In 843 the iconoclastic controversy was finally settled by the restoration of images, but other sources of friction made permanent reunion of the Byzantine and Roman churches impossible. Exactly when the final breaking point was reached is difficult for scholars to determine. The traditional date is 1054, when doctrinal and liturgical disputes (the use of leavened vs. unleavened bread in the communion service, for example) caused the pope and the patriarch of Constantinople to excommunicate each other, thus creating a schism that was never to be healed. The important fact is that for centuries the papacy in the West and the Orthodox Church in the East steadily grew apart until they came to maintain distinctly separate existences, each viewing the other with suspicion and intolerance.

Missionary activity of the Church. The credit for converting many Slavic tribes to Christianity goes to the Orthodox Church. About 863 two monks who were also brothers, Cyril and Methodius, set out from Constantinople to bring the gospel to the pagan Moravians, a Slavic group living in what is now Czechoslovakia. They took with them translations of the Bible and the divine service written in an alphabet of modified Greek characters adapted to the Slavic languages. (The Cyrillic alphabet, used even now in Bulgaria, Serbia, and Russia, is named after Cyril, who invented it.) Although the Moravians and others of the westernmost Slavs eventually came under the sway of the Roman Church, the work begun by the two brothers triumphed among the Slavs to the east and south, so that ultimately the Orthodox Church extended throughout much of eastern Europe.

BYZANTINE ECONOMY, SOCIETY, AND CULTURE

Byzantine prosperity. During the early Middle Ages, Constantinople was called "The City"—with good reason. Visitors were fascinated by the pomp and pageantry of the court and Church, the scholarly and artistic endeavors, and the wealth, which far surpassed anything to be found in the West.

The complex urban civilization of the Byzantine world rested upon a foundation of strong and well-diversified economic activities. For centuries a stable agricultural system provided city and country folk with adequate food, and a varied industrial and commercial economy successfully supported large urban populations. The decline of population which had contributed to the collapse of the Roman Empire in the West did not occur in the East.

Geography was another major factor responsible for Byzantine prosperity. Constantinople stood at the crossroads of Europe and Asia, and its site ensured its being a port of transit for a great marine trading basin extending from the Adriatic to southern Russia. The merchants of Constantinople exported luxury goods, wines, spices, and silks to Russia and in turn imported furs, fish, caviar, beeswax, honey, and amber. Metalwork, leather goods, and other products manufactured in the empire went to India and China, while back to Constantinople came spices, precious stones, costly woods, and perfumes, some of which were transported on to the few western Europeans who could afford the luxuries of the Orient.

Trade supported, and was in turn stimulated by, the existence of a sound gold currency. In the West a decline in commerce had been attended by a shrinkage in the supply and use of money. The Byzantine empire, on the other hand, retained a currency of such excellence that its gold bezant was a medium of international exchange, remaining free of debasement until the eleventh century—far longer than any other coinage in history.

Besides being the greatest trading center of the early Middle Ages, Constantinople had industries that supplied Christendom with many products. The city specialized in luxury goods, and was famous for the manufacture of armor, weapons, hardware, and textiles. Until the time of Justinian, all raw silk for manufacturing fabrics had been imported from China, but after silkworms were smuggled out of China about 550 A.D., silk production began to flourish within the empire. Silken fabrics embroidered with gold and silver thread and fashioned into costly vestments for Church services or court attire were eagerly sought all over Europe. The silk industry was a profitable state monopoly.

The state controlled the economy through a system of guilds to which all tradesmen and members of the professions belonged. Wages, profits, hours of labor, and the price of foodstuffs—all were controlled "so that," as stated in a Byzantine handbook detailing such regulations, "men, being well directed thereby, should not shamelessly trample upon one another and the stronger should not do violence to the weaker."[4]

Constantinople, city of contrasts. The colorful social life of the empire was concentrated in Constantinople. The city itself had three centers: the imperial palace, the Church of Hagia Sophia, and the giant Hippodrome.

Court ceremonial was arranged to impress both foreigners and Byzantines with the emperor's exalted nature and his remoteness from mundane matters. An envoy to the palace was escorted through great lines of uniformed guards and dignitaries into a resplendent hall. At the appointed time a curtain was raised, disclosing the emperor clad in his imperial robes on his throne. Golden lions flanked the throne and golden birds perched in pomegranate trees. While the envoy prostrated himself, the throne would be raised aloft, symbolizing the unapproach-ability of the heir of the Caesars. During the audience the emperor remained motionless, silent, and aloof, while a court official spoke in his name.

Seating perhaps eighty thousand spectators, the Hippodrome was the scene of hotly disputed chariot races between the two major factions of the populace, the Blues and the Greens. Organized for political purposes as well as for sports, these factions used the Hippodrome as a forum to voice their opinions. The Blues tended to reflect the views of the great landowners, the Greens those of the merchants and the bureaucracy. In the Nike rebellion (see p. 141), Blues and Greens united in opposition to Justinian's costly policies.

Byzantine art: a unique synthesis. While Byzantine art was basically Roman in character during the reigns of the first Constantine and his immediate successors, the new capital's eastern location could not fail to bring additional artistic forces into play. Greek tradition had persisted in Alexandria and Antioch, and Constantinople was exposed also to influences from Persia. By the sixth century these elements were fused with the strong Christian spirit that had motivat-

This oldest known view of Constantinople, drawn in 1420, shows both its wealth of monumental architecture and its outstanding fortifications.

ed New Rome since its inception; the result was a new style of a uniquely Byzantine character.

Byzantine painting, for example, displays a synthesis of different—and even conflicting—cultural influences. The Greek tradition provided a graceful and idealistic approach; art historians point out, however, that while classical elements remained in Byzantine art, oriental influences—with their emphasis upon a more abstract and formalized style, vivid coloring, and ornamentation—eventually predominated.

Church architecture. The first great age of Byzantine art was associated with Justinian, who commissioned the magnificent Church of Hagia Sophia (Holy Wisdom), as well as many other churches and secular buildings. No other Byzantine church equaled Hagia Sophia in size or magnificence. According to Procopius, the historian of Justinian's reign, it was "a church, the like of which has never been seen since Adam, nor ever will be" (see Color Plate 6). The effect of light playing upon its multicolored marbles and bright mosaics moved Procopius to declare:

On entering the church to pray one feels at once that it is the work, not of man's effort or industry, but in truth the work of the Divine Power; and the spirit, mounting to heaven, realizes that here God is very near and that He delights in this dwelling that He has chosen for Himself.[5]

The dome is the crowning glory of Hagia Sophia both because of its beauty and because it represents a major advance in architecture. With forty windows piercing its base, Procopius described it as

marvellous in its grace, but by reason of the seeming insecurity of its composition altogether terrifying. For it seems somehow to float in the air on no firm basis, but to be poised aloft to the peril of those inside it.[6]

The Romans had been able to construct a huge dome on the Pantheon but had erected it upon massive circular walls which limited the shape of the building. The dome of Hagia Sophia was supported by pendentives, four triangular segments which received the weight of the dome and distributed it to four supporting piers. The use of pendentives made it possible to place a dome over a square area.

Over the centuries many other fine structures employed the pendentive principle. A favorite design, with symbolic appeal, was a church in the shape of a cross, surmounted by a dome. A still further development was the five-domed church, which was cross-shaped, with a central dome at the crossing and a smaller dome on each of the four arms. The most famous existing example of this design is St. Mark's in Venice, constructed in the eleventh century.

Vivid mosaics and decorative arts. The second outstanding period of Byzantine art began in the middle of the ninth century with the settling of the iconoclastic controversy and lasted until the sack of Constantinople in 1204. This age is notable for producing the finest examples of Byzantine decorative art.

In the decoration of churches, Byzantine artists made extensive use of mosaics—small pieces of multicolored glass or stone cemented into patterns to form brilliant decorations. Not only did the rich colors of the mosaics increase the splendor of the church interiors and heighten the emotional appeal of the rituals, but the representations also served as useful teaching devices by presenting the viewer with scenes from the Bible and with images of Christ, the Virgin, and the saints.

With their penchant for vivid colors and elaborate detail, Byzantine artists also excelled in such decorative arts as carving in ivory, the illumination of manuscripts, and the decoration of book covers, chests, thrones, and altars. Constantinople was renowned for its cloisonné technique, by which enamel was inlaid between thin gold bands to form the design.

Wall and panel painting. The third important period of Byzantine artistic activity took place during the fourteenth and fifteenth centuries when Byzantium was no longer wealthy. This revival expressed itself in brilliant paintings on walls and panels, a form of art necessitated in some measure by

In this late tenth-century mosiac over the south door of Hagia Sophia, Constantine is offering his city and Justinian is presenting his church to the Virgin. The combination of oriental style and Christian subject matter is characteristic of Byzantine art.

the need to find cheaper substitutes for expensive mosaics and enamels.

Like mosaics, Byzantine wall paintings were employed to decorate churches. In addition, icons—panel paintings of sacred personages—were used in daily worship. As in mosaics, the subject matter of Byzantine painting was treated symbolically rather than realistically: "like much of the art of today, which is not easy to understand at first glance, its significance lies below the surface; it is an art of the spirit rather than of the flesh, and must be approached from that point of view."[7]

The preservation of classical learning. The official adoption of the Greek language in the formative centuries of the Byzantine empire proved a stimulus to the preservation of classical works in philosophy, literature, and science. The scholars who perpetuated the Greek tradition were not clerics, as in the West, but members of the civil service; Byzantine monasteries produced many saints and mystics but showed little interest in learning or teaching. Byzantine scholars, concerned chiefly with recovering and classifying Hellenic and Hellenistic learning, were imitative rather than creative, and their own contributions tended to be a rehash of classical works. Yet when in the twelfth century the West began absorbing Greek science and Aristotelian philosophy from the Muslims in Spain, it was to Byzantine scholarship that the latter were indebted. Moreover, most of the West's knowledge of Greek literature and Platonic philosophy came from Constantinople in the fourteenth and fifteenth centuries.

One of the great achievements of Byzantine scholarship was the codification of Roman law. In 528 Justinian convoked a commission of scholars to gather and classify the vast, disorganized, and often contradictory mass of law that had accumulated during centuries of Roman government. The result was a great legal work popularly known as the Justinian Code and formally titled the *Corpus Juris Civilis*. It organized the imperial law of the last four centuries into the *Codex* and included as well the *Digest* of the writings of republican and imperial jurists, and the *Institutes*, a commentary on the principles

The Transfiguration of Christ is a twelfth-century example of Byzantine enamel work. The combination of oriental style and Christian subject matter is an important characteristic of Byzantine art.

underlying the laws. Appended to the main text were the *Novels*, the laws promulgated by Justinian and written in Greek, now the dominant language of the empire.

By this codification, Rome's priceless legal heritage was preserved and passed on to posterity. In holding that the will of the emperor is the source of law, that the judge is the emperor's representative in interpreting law, and that equity is the basic principle of law, Justinian's Code stands in sharp contrast to Germanic folk law (see p. 133). The Code was unknown in the West during the early Middle Ages, but in the twelfth century it slowly began to have a notable influence on the improvement of medieval justice and the emergence of strong monarchs, who borrowed for their own use the Roman doctrine of the emperor as a source of law.

EARLY RUSSIA

The Slavs. While the fortunes of the Byzantine empire had been ebbing and flowing, its culture had exercised continuous and substantial influence upon the development of Russia in its formative centuries.

The ancestors of the Russians were the Slavic tribes, whose original home is thought by some scholars to have been the wooded area of the Pripet Marshes (see map, p. 153). Moving into the lands vacated by the migrating Germans, in time three main groups developed. The Western Slavs—Poles and Bohemians—reached the Elbe and came under Latin Christian influences. Both the Southern Slavs, who moved into the Balkans, and the Eastern Slavs, the ancestors of the Russians who occupied the lands between the Carpathians and the Don, were subjected to Greek Christian influences.

Founding of a Russian state. About the time when their Viking brethren from Denmark and Norway were plundering and conquering throughout western Europe (see p. 194), Swedish Norsemen, called Varangians by the Byzantines, combined piracy with trade and began to venture along the waterways from the eastern Baltic to the Black and Caspian seas. The Slavic settlements along the rivers often hired the fierce Varangians as protectors. In 862 the people of Novgorod employed one such warrior, the half-legendary Rurik, who became prince of the city. His brothers and companions established themselves in other cities, one being Kiev.

By the late ninth century the Varangian ruler of Kiev had succeeded in establishing his supremacy over a large area which gradually became known as Russia, a name derived from *Rus* (meaning "seafarers"), by which the Slavs knew the Norse. The Kievan state operated as a loose confederation, with the prince of Kiev recognized as senior among his kinsmen who ruled the other Russian city-states. By the end of the tenth century the Norse minority had merged with the Slavic population.

Kievan Russia was less a political entity than a commercial entity, a coordinated group of princely states with a common interest in maintaining trade along the river routes. Kievan military expeditions against Constantinople itself began as early as 860, partly as typical Viking raids for plunder and partly to extort treaties which opened up a profitable Russian-Byzantine trade. Every spring after the ice had melted on the Dnieper, cargoes of furs, wax, honey, and slaves were floated down to Kiev. From there a great flotilla would descend the Dnieper and proceed along the Black Sea shore to Constantinople. Returning with silks, spices, jewelry, wines, and metalwares, the Kievans would pass these goods on to northeastern Europe via Novgorod and the Baltic.

Christianity in Kievan Russia. The official conversion of the Russians to Christianity took place about 989 under Prince Vladimir of Kiev. According to an early Russian chronicle, Vladimir shopped around before making his choice of religions. He rejected Islam because of its injunctions against the use of strong drink, Judaism because the God of the Jews could not be considered very powerful since He had allowed them to be ejected from their Holy Land, and Roman Christianity because the pope entertained dangerous ideas about his superiority to all secular rulers. There remained the Orthodox Church of the Byzantines, which was presented to Vladimir's subjects as his choice.

From the outset the Kievan princes followed the Byzantine example and kept the Church dependent on them, even for its revenues, so that the Russian Church and state were always closely linked. The Russians also copied the Byzantines in Church ritual, theology, and such practices as monasticism.

Apogee and decline of Kiev. Kiev reached its greatest splendor in the reign of Yaroslav the Wise (1019-1054 A.D.), who issued Russia's first law code (based on the customary law of the Eastern Slavs) and was a patron of art and learning. Byzantine architects and artists were brought to Kiev to build the cathedral of Hagia Sophia, named after its prototype in Constantinople. Yaroslav negotiated marriage alliances for his children with the royal families of Poland, Norway, Hungary, and France.

Following the death of Yaroslav, however, the princes of the various cities fought increasingly among themselves for possession of the Kievan state; and to these disruptions was added the devastation of the nomads who roamed uncomfortably close to the capital and cut the trade route to Constantinople. The trading and farming population around Kiev could not sustain such hardships, and they sought refuge in flight. Many fled northeastward to city-states in the neighborhood of present-day Moscow. When the Asiatic Mongols destroyed Kiev in 1240 (see p. 277), it had already lost much of its power, wealth, and population.

Byzantine aspects of Kievan culture. The commercial contacts between Constantinople and Kiev and the power of the Orthodox Church during the Kievan period were the chief factors responsible for the Byzantine influences in Russia. Architecture, for ex-

ample, came within the province of the Church. The outstanding churches built at Kiev, Novgorod, and other cities show strong Byzantine influence. In time architects developed a distinctly Russian style, including the characteristic "onion dome," which is merely a fanciful "helmet" covering the dome. The decoration of churches also followed Byzantine models. In fact, the earliest mosaics, as well as mural and icon paintings, appear to have been the work of Byzantine artists who were brought to Russia. At Hagia Sophia in Kiev, some of these wall paintings still remain.

The adaptation of the Greek alphabet to the Slavic tongue and the translation of Church liturgy into Slavic stimulated the growth of Russian literature. Although at first Kievan literature consisted of translations of Byzantine works—chiefly sermons, saints' lives, and condemnations of Roman Catholicism—in time a literature of the Russian people emerged, as epics of their strug-

The Byzantine influence on Russian architecture is evident in Hagia Sophia in Kiev, originally built in the eleventh century by Yaroslav the Wise.

gles to resist the barbaric nomads from the steppes appeared. But the use of Slavic in the Church caused many churchmen to remain ignorant of Latin and to lack even a good knowledge of Greek; hence the majority of the learned had no direct contact with the literature in those two languages. Much of Russia's cultural isolationism in the past has been ascribed to this factor.

By the eleventh century, however, and particularly during the reign of Yaroslav the Wise, Kievan Russia could boast of a culture and an economy that were superior to what then existed in western Europe; for these achievements Kiev was primarily obligated to the Byzantine empire, which at the time enjoyed the highest cultural level in Christendom. In the wake of the fall of Constan-

tinople in 1453, the Russians would appropriate even more of the Byzantine tradition, dubbing the new Russian center of Moscow the "Third Rome."

MUHAMMAD AND HIS FAITH

Pre-Islamic Arabia. In our examination of the Byzantine empire, we had occasion to mark the swift rise of a rival religious culture, Islam, imbued with expansionist aims. In 1453, adherents of that faith succeeded in conquering the eastern citadel of Christianity. We shall now trace the genesis and meteoric expansion of Islam, together with the splendid civilization it fostered.

The term *Islam*, meaning "submission to God," is derived from the Muslim holy book, the Koran. The followers of Muhammad, the founder of the faith, are known as Muslims. (This faith is often referred to as Muhammadanism, but Muslims frown on this term, which implies the worship and deification of Muhammad.)

The story begins in Arabia, a peninsula one third the size of the continental United States. Much of it is desert, and rainfall is scarce in the rest of the peninsula. Thus vegetation is scant and very little land is suitable for agriculture. Throughout much of Arabia, particularly in the interior, nomadism was the only way of life.

The nomads, or Bedouins, lived according to a tribal pattern; at the head of the tribe was the sheik, elected and advised by the heads of the related families comprising the tribe. Driven from place to place in their search for pastures to sustain their flocks, the Bedouins led a precarious existence. Aside from their flocks, they relied on booty from raids on settlements, on passing caravans, and on one another. The Bedouins worshiped a large number of gods and spirits, many of whom were believed to inhabit trees, wells, and stones. Each tribe had its own god, symbolized generally by a sacred stone which served as an altar where communal sacrifices were offered.

Although the Bedouins of the interior led a primitive and largely isolated existence, some parts of Arabia were influenced by neighboring—and more advanced—cultures. By the latter half of the sixth century Christian and Jewish groups were found throughout the Arabian peninsula. Their religious convictions and moral principles had a strong effect on the indigenous population, and their monotheistic beliefs were later incorporated into Islamic doctrine.

Mecca. Several of the more advanced cities were in Hejaz, among them Mecca, destined to be the key city in the Islamic religion. Fifty miles inland from the port of Jiddah, Mecca was favorably located for trade. Its merchants carried on business with southern Arabia, with Abyssinia across the Red Sea, and with the Byzantine and Persian empires. Mecca was controlled by the Quraysh, an Arab tribe whose members formed trading companies that cooperated in dispatching large caravans north and south.

The Quraysh merchants were also concerned with protecting a source of income derived from the annual pilgrimage of tribes to a famous religious sanctuary at Mecca. Known as the Kaaba (cube), this square temple contained the sacred Black Stone, by legend brought to Abraham and his son Ishmael by Gabriel. According to tradition, the stone was originally white but had been blackened by the sins of those touching it. The Kaaba supposedly housed the images of some 360 local deities and fetishes

Muhammad, founder of Islam. Into this environment at Mecca was born a man destined to transform completely the religious, political, and social organization of his people. Muhammad (570-632) came from a family belonging to the Quraysh tribe. Left an orphan in early life, he was brought up by an uncle and later engaged in the caravan trade. Muhammad's formative years are known to us by legend only, but his first biographer relates that he was influenced by a monotheist named Zayd, who may have been either a Jewish or a Christian convert. When he was about twenty years old, Muhammad entered the service of a wealthy widow, Khadija, whose caravans traded with Syria. In his twenty-fifth year he married his employer, who was some fifteen years his senior. Despite the difference in their

ages, the marriage was a happy one; and they had four daughters.

According to tradition, Muhammad frequently went into the foothills near Mecca to meditate. One night he dreamed that the archangel Gabriel appeared with the command, "Recite!" When Muhammad asked, "What shall I recite?" he was told:

Recite in the name of thy Lord who created
Man from blood coagulated.
Recite! Thy Lord is wondrous kind
Who by the pen has taught mankind
Things they knew not (being blind).[8]

This was the first of a series of visions and revelations.

Far from regarding himself as a prophet, Muhammad was at first afraid that he had been possessed by a spirit, and he even contemplated suicide. During his periods of doubt and anguish Muhammad was comforted by Khadija, and finally he became certain that he was a divinely appointed prophet of Allah, "*The* God." He became convinced that Allah was the one and only God—the same God worshiped by the Jews and Christians—who had chosen him to perfect the religion revealed earlier to Abraham, Moses, the prophets, and Jesus.

At first Muhammad had little success in attracting followers. His first converts were his wife, his cousin Ali, and Abu Bakr, a leading merchant of the Quraysh tribe who was highly respected for his integrity. Abu Bakr remained the constant companion of the Prophet during his persecution and exile and eventually became the first caliph of Islam. Most other early converts were slaves or oppressed persons. Opposition came from the leading citizens ("Shall we forsake our gods for a mad poet?"), who either ridiculed Muhammad's doctrine of resurrection (pre-Islamic Arabs had only vague notions concerning the afterlife) or feared that his monotheistic teaching might harm the city's lucrative pilgrimage trade to the Kaaba.

The Hijra and triumphal return to Mecca. The first encouraging development occurred when a group of pilgrims from Medina, a prosperous trading rival of Mecca with a large Jewish population, accepted the Prophet's teachings. Meanwhile, increased persecu-

Mecca as it very likely looked in the Middle Ages. Each year thousands of Muslims make a pilgrimage to Mecca to worship at the Kaaba, a temple housing the sacred Black Stone that the angel Gabriel, according to legend, gave to Abraham and his son.

tion of the Muslims in Mecca encouraged the Prophet to migrate with his band to Medina.

Carried out in secrecy, this move took place in 622 and is known as the *Hijra*, which means "flight" or, in this context, "the breaking of old ties." The Hijra was such a turning point in Muhammad's career that the year in which it occurred is counted as the first in the Muslim calendar. In Mecca, Muhammad's own kinsmen had persecuted him, but in Medina he came to be acknowledged as a leader with divine authority in spiritual and temporal matters. He commanded the Muslims to turn toward Mecca when praying. This practice served to recognize the city as the spiritual capital of Islam and also emphasized the need for its conquest from the pagan trading oligarchy that governed it.

In the year 630 Muhammad marched on Mecca with an army. His old enemies were forced to surrender to the Prophet, who acted with magnanimity toward them. His first act was to cast out of the Kaaba its multitude of idols and fetishes; but the temple itself, together with the Black Stone, was preserved as the supreme center of Islam, the "Mecca" to which each devout Muslim should make a pilgrimage during his lifetime.

With Mecca and Medina both under his control, Muhammad became the undisputed master of Hejaz. In the two remaining years of his life tribe after tribe of Bedouins throughout Arabia offered him their loyalty. Upon his death in 632 the Prophet left behind a faith which had united Arabia and which was to astound the world with its militant expansion.

The Koran, the Muslim bible. Muslims believe that the Koran contains the actual word of God as revealed to Muhammad. The Prophet's revelations occurred over a period of more than twenty years, and before his death many of the messages had been written down. Abu Bakr, Muhammad's successor as head of the community, ordered the compilation of all these materials, including the passages that had only been committed to memory. Twenty years after the death of the Prophet, an authorized version was promulgated, which has remained the official text to the present day.

Because the Koran must never be used in translation for worship, the spread of Islam created a great deal of linguistic unity. Arabic supplanted many local languages as the language of daily use, and that part of the Muslim world which stretches from Morocco to Iraq is still Arabic-speaking. Furthermore, this seventh-century book remains the last word on Muslim theology, law, and social institutions and is therefore still the most important textbook being used in Muslim universities.

Theology of Islamic faith. Within the Koran one finds the central tenet of Islam— monotheism. There is only one God, Allah; this is proclaimed five times daily from the minaret of the mosque as the faithful are called to prayer:

God is most great. I testify that there is no God but Allah. I testify that Muhammad is God's Apostle. Come to prayer, come to security. God is most great.⁹

While Allah is the only God, many other supernatural figures are acknowledged, as in Christianity. Islamic angels, for example, are similar to those described in the Bible. In addition, there exist *jinn*, who are spirits midway between angels and men. Some *jinn* are good, while others are evil. Islam recognizes the existence of prophets who preceded Muhammad. The Koran mentions twenty-eight, of whom four are Arabian, eighteen are found in the Old Testament, three in the New Testament (including Jesus), and one of the remainder has been identified as Alexander the Great. But to Muslims the greatest prophet is, of course, Muhammad. He is ascribed no superhuman status, although he was chosen to proclaim God's message of salvation. That message included the belief in the Last Judgment and the existence of paradise and hell.

Geography played an important role in the Prophet's concepts of heaven and hell: both are described in terms that incite an immediate reaction in people living in the desert. Those who have submitted to Allah's rule—the charitable, humble, and forgiving —and those who have fought for His faith, shall dwell in a Garden of Paradise, reposing in cool shades, eating delectable foods, attended by "fair ones with wide, lovely eyes like unto hidden pearls," and hearing no vain speech or recrimination but only "Peace! Peace!" This veritable oasis is far different from the agonies of the desert hell that awaits the unbelievers, the covetous, and the erring. Cast into hell with its "scorching wind and shadow of black smoke," they will drink of boiling water.

Islam imposes on all Muslims five obligations, known as the "Pillars of Faith"—belief in only one God and in Muhammad as His Prophet, prayer, almsgiving, fasting, and a pilgrimage to Mecca. Prayers are said five times a day, and each occasion calls for a sequence of recitations coordinated with a sequence of postures. They are to be repeated either alone or, preferably, in a mosque. The Muslim is required to give alms, a practice regarded as expressing piety and contributing to one's salvation. During the month of Ramadan, the ninth month of the lunar year, Muslims fast. Since food and drink are pro-hibited between sunrise and sunset, this is a very strenuous observance, although sick persons and travelers are exempted providing they fast for an equal length of time later. The second chapter of the Koran commands Muslims to make a pilgrimage to Mecca, where they go through traditional ceremonies, such as kissing the Black Stone in the Kaaba. Each Muslim should make the pilgrimage to Mecca at least once during his lifetime if he has the means.

The Koran also provides Muslims with a body of ethical teachings. Idolatry, infanticide, usury, gambling, the drinking of wine, and the eating of pork are all prohibited. Similarly, Islam encouraged the humane treatment of slaves and regulated such matters as the guardianship of orphans and divorce. Muslim men were allowed four wives (and an unspecified number of concubines), but if he could not treat them all with equal kindness and impartiality, a husband should retain but one.

Pervading Islam was the principle of religious equality. There was no priesthood— no intermediaries between man and God. There were leaders of worship in the mosques as well as the *ulema,* a class of learned experts in the interpretation of the Koran; but they were all laymen. In this way Islam was spared the priestly tyranny such as arose in India, where the Brahmins considered themselves superior to all other classes in the rigid caste system.

Islamic law. In addition to being a religion, Islam offered a system of government, law, and society. The Islamic community was an excellent example of a theocratic state, one in which all power resides in God in whose behalf political, religious, and other forms of authority are exercised.

Especially in the period of expansion after the Prophet's death, the Islamic state required detailed rules covering a variety of new situations. The code that was developed was based partly on pre-Islamic legal customs. Before Muhammad's time each tribe had its own *sunna*, or body of custom, which served as a law code. After the Prophet's death his followers prepared a Sunna based upon the "traditions" (*hadith*) of what he had said and done. Using the Koran and the Sunna as their sources, Islamic jurists developed a body of religious law which regulated all aspects of Muslim life. Its development and interpretation were in the hands of the *ulema*. Agreement among these scholars set the seal of orthodoxy on questions of text and doctrine, with the result that Islamic law became progressively authoritarian and static.

THE SPREAD OF ISLAM

Expansion under the first four caliphs. Upon the Prophet's death in 632 the question arose as to who should direct the fortunes of Islam. This was a dangerous moment. Muhammad left no son to succeed him; and, even if he had, neither his unique position as the Prophet nor Arab custom permitted any such automatic succession. Acting swiftly, Muhammad's associates selected the Prophet's most trusted friend and advisor, Abu Bakr, as his official successor, the caliph (from *khalifa*, meaning "deputy"). The second caliph was also one of Muhammad's companions, while the fourth was his cousin and son-in-law.

During the reigns of the first four caliphs (632-661) Islam spread rapidly. Their wars of conquest were aided by the Prophet's belief that any Muslim dying in battle for the faith was assured entrance into paradise. This concept of holy war (*jihad*) bred in the Arabs, already a fierce fighting people, fanatical courage. Moreover, the prospect of rich and fertile territory, as well as plunder, proved a strong incentive to a people who had been eking out a bare existence from the desert.

The Islamic cause was also aided by political upheavals occurring outside of Arabia. The Muslim triumphs in the Near East can be partly accounted for by the long series of wars between the Byzantine and Persian empires. Earlier Byzantine victories had left both sides exhausted and open to conquest. Moreover, the inhabitants of Syria and Egypt, alienated by religious dissent, were anxious to be free of Byzantine rule. In 636 Arab forces conquered Syria. The Muslims then wrested Iraq from the Persians and, within

ten years after Muhammad's death, subdued Persia itself. The greater part of Egypt fell with little resistance in 640 and the rest shortly afterward. Thus, by the end of the reigns of the first four caliphs, Islam had vastly increased its territory (see map, p. 159).

The imposition of a head tax on all non-Muslims encouraged many to become converts to Islam. Contrary to exaggerated accounts in the West of the forceful infliction of Islam upon conquered peoples, the Jews and Christians outside of Arabia enjoyed toleration because they worshiped the same God as the Muslims.

Islam is one of the most effective religions in removing barriers of race and nationality. Apart from a certain privileged position allowed the Arabs, distinctions were mostly those of class. The new religion converted and embraced peoples of many colors and cultures. This egalitarian feature of Islam undoubtedly aided its expansion.

Arab domination under the Umayyads. The expansion of Islam under the first four caliphs produced a new type of claimant to the caliphate—powerful generals and governors of provinces. In 661 the governor of Syria proclaimed himself caliph, made Damascus his capital, and founded the Umayyad dynasty which lasted until 750. Thus the caliphate became in fact, although never in law, a hereditary office, not, as previously, a position filled by election.

The Umayyad navy held Cyprus, Rhodes, and a string of Aegean islands, which served as a base for annual sea-borne attacks on Constantinople from 674 to 678. With the aid of Greek fire, Constantinople was saved, and the Arab advance was checked for the first time. Westward across North Africa, however, the Umayyad armies had great success. The Berbers, a warlike Hamitic-speaking people inhabiting the land between the Mediterranean and the Sahara, resisted stubbornly until converted to Islam. The next logical jump was across the Strait of Gibraltar into the weak kingdom of the Visigoths in Spain. The governor of Muslim North Africa sent his general, Tarik, and an army across the Strait into Spain in 711. Seven years later the kingdom of the Visigoths had completely crumbled. The Muslims swept across the

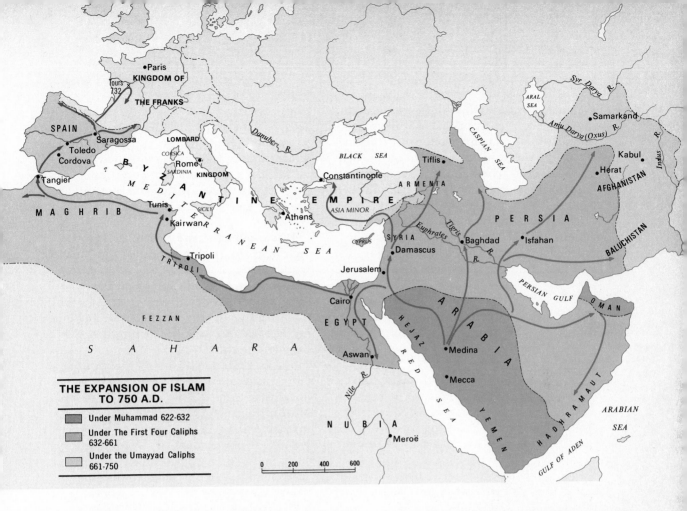

THE EXPANSION OF ISLAM
TO 750 A.D.

Under Muhammad 622-632

Under The First Four Caliphs
632-661

Under the Umayyad Caliphs
661-750

Pyrenees and gained a foothold in southwest France, where they carried out a major raid to explore the possibility of a further northward advance. However, they were defeated by Charles Martel near Tours in 732 (see p. 190), in a battle which, together with their defeat by the Byzantine emperor Leo III in 718 (see p. 143), proved decisive in halting their westward expansion. Meanwhile the Muslims had been expanding eastward into Central Asia, and by the eighth century they could claim lands as far as Turkestan and the Indus valley.

The mainstay of Umayyad power was the ruling class of Arabs, who formed a privileged aristocracy greatly outnumbered by non-Arabic converts to Islam—Egyptians, Syrians, Persians, Berbers, and others. Many of these possessed cultures much more advanced than that of the Arabs, and the economic and cultural life of the Arab empire depended on these people. But because they were not Arab by birth, they were treated as second-class Muslims. They were not per-

mitted to marry Arab women, and as soldiers they received less pay and booty than the Arabs. Resentment grew among the non-Arabic Muslims and eventually helped bring about the downfall of the Umayyads.

Shia movement against the ruling group. This resentment also found expression in the religious sphere, where large numbers of the non-Arabic Muslims joined the sect known as the Shia, formed when Ali, Muhammad's son-in-law and fourth caliph, was deposed by the Umayyads. The Shia continued to regard Ali and his descendants as the rightful rulers of the Islamic community. They believed that in every age a messiah-like leader would appear and that he must be obeyed. The Shia also rejected the Sunna, the body of later tradition concerning Muhammad that was not contained in the Koran; they insisted on the Koran as the sole authority on the life and teachings of the Prophet. Though originally an Arab party, the Shia in time became a general Islamic movement that stood for opposition to the ruling dynasty. The Shia evolved into one of the two major groups in Islam. The majority, named Sunnites because they were the "orthodox" perpetuators of Muhammad's Sunna, or tradition, upheld the principle that the caliph owed his position to the consent of the Islamic community. The numerical superiority of the Sunnites has continued to this day.

The Abbasids, high tide of Islamic civilization. In 750 the Umayyad dynasty was crushed by rebels, and a new dynasty, the Abbasid, ruled most of the Muslim world from 750 to 1258. The city of Baghdad was built in 762 as the capital of the new dynasty. The Abbasids owed their success to the discontent of the non-Arabic Muslims, who were the chief elements in the towns and in the Shia.

The fall of the Umayyad dynasty marked the end of Arab predominance; henceforth all Muslims were treated as equals. The Arab aristocracy had led the forces of conquest during the great period of Islamic expansion, but with the advent of more stable political conditions, the important status thus far held by the Arab soldier was given to non-Arab administrators and merchants. The traditional Arabic patterns of nomadism and tribal war were giving way before economic prosperity, the growth of town life, and the rise of a merchant class. The Abbasid caliph who built Baghdad forecast that it would become the "most flourishing city in the world"; and indeed it rivaled Constantinople for that honor, situated as it was on the trade routes linking West and East. Furthermore, Abbasid patronage of scholarship and the arts produced a rich and complex culture far surpassing that then existing in western Europe.

The location of a new capital at Baghdad resulted in a shift of Islam's center of gravity to the province of Iraq, whose soil, watered by the Tigris and Euphrates, had nurtured man's earliest civilization. Here the Abbasid caliphs set themselves up as potentates in the traditional style of the ancient East—and more particularly of Persia—so that they were surrounded by a lavish court that contrasted sharply with the simplicity of the Prophet.

The Abbasid dynasty marked the high tide of Islamic power and civilization. The empire ruled by these caliphs was greater in size than the domain of the Roman Caesars; it was the product of an expansion during which the Muslims had assimilated peoples, customs, cultures, and inventions on an unprecedented scale. This Islamic state, in fact, drew on the resources of the entire known world.

Trade, industry, and agriculture. From the eighth to the twelfth centuries the Muslim world enjoyed a prosperity such as post-Roman Europe did not experience until early modern times. In close contact with three continents, the Muslims could shuttle goods back and forth from China to western Europe and from Russia to central Africa. Trade was facilitated also by the absence of tariff barriers within the empire and by the tolerance of the caliphs, who allowed non-Muslim merchants and craftsmen to reside in their territories and carry on commerce with their home countries. The presence of such important urban centers as Baghdad, Cairo, and Cordova stimulated trade and industry throughout the Muslim world.

The cosmopolitan nature of Baghdad was evident in its bazaars, which contained goods from all over the known world. There were spices, minerals, and dyes from India; gems and fabrics from Central Asia; honey and wax from Scandinavia and Russia; and ivory and gold dust from Africa. One bazaar in the city specialized in goods from China, including silks, musk, and porcelain. In the slave marts the Muslim traders bought and sold Scandinavians, Mongolians from Central Asia, and Africans. Joint-stock companies flourished along with branch banking, and checks (an Arabic word) drawn on one bank could be cashed elsewhere in the empire.

Muslim textile industries turned out excellent cottons (muslins), silks, and linens. The steel of Damascus and Toledo, the leather of Cordova, and the glass of Syria became world famous. Notable also was the art of papermaking, learned from China. Under the Abbasids, vast irrigation projects in Iraq increased cultivable land which yielded large crops of fruits and cereals. Wheat came from the Nile valley, cotton from North Africa, olives and wine from Spain, wool from eastern Asia Minor, and horses from Persia.

The opulent reign of Harun al-Rashid. Just as the Abbasid was the most brilliant of Muslim dynasties, so the rule of Harun al-Rashid (786-809) was the most spectacular of the Abbasid reigns. He was the contemporary of Charlemagne, who had revived the Roman Empire in the West (see Chapter 8), and there can be no doubt that Harun was the most powerful ruler of the two and the symbol of the more highly advanced culture. The two monarchs were on friendly terms, based on self-interest. Charlemagne wanted to exert pressure on the Byzantine emperor to recognize his new imperial title. Harun, on the other hand, saw Charlemagne as an ally against the Umayyad rulers of Spain, who had broken away from Abbasid domination. The two emperors exchanged embassies and presents. The Muslim sent the Christian rich fabrics, aromatics, and even an elephant named Abu-Lababah, meaning "the father of intelligence." An intricate water clock from Baghdad seems to have been looked upon as a miracle in the West.

Relations between the Abbasid caliphate and the Byzantine empire were never very cordial, and conflicts often broke out along the constantly shifting border that separated Christian and Muslim territories. Harun al-Rashid once replied to a communique from the Byzantine emperor in the following terms:

In the name of God, the Merciful, the Compassionate. From Haroun, Commander of the Faithful, to Nicephorus, the dog of the Greeks. I have read your letter, you son of a she-infidel, and you shall see the answer before you hear it.[10]

Whereupon the irate caliph sent forth expeditions to ravage Asia Minor.

In the days of Harun al-Rashid, Baghdad's wealth and splendor equaled that of Constantinople, and its chief glory was the royal palace. With its annexes for eunuchs, officials, and a harem, the caliph's residence occupied a third of Baghdad. Resplendently furnished, the caliph's audience chamber was the setting for an elaborate ceremonial which continued that of the Byzantines and Persians.

Disintegration of the Abbasid empire. Despite the unprecedented prosperity of the far-flung Islamic world, the political unity of Islam began to disappear soon after the accession of the Abbasid dynasty. The first sign of political disintegration appeared in 756 when a member of the deposed Umayyad family founded his own dynasty at Cordova in Spain; in 929 his descendant assumed the title of caliph. Also in the tenth century the Fatimids—Shiites who claimed descent from Muhammad's daughter Fatima who had married Ali, the fourth caliph—proclaimed themselves the true caliphs of all Islam. From their capital at Cairo, which they founded, their rule eventually extended from Morocco to northern Mesopotamia.

Meanwhile, in the latter part of the tenth century Turkish nomads, called Seljuks, had migrated from Central Asia into the Abbasid lands, where they accepted Islam. After annexing most of Persia, the Seljuks gained control of Baghdad in 1055 and absorbed Iraq. Subsequently they conquered Syria and Palestine at the expense of the Fatimids and proceeded to annex most of Asia Minor from the Byzantines. It was the Seljuk's great advance that prompted the First Crusade in 1095. The Seljuks permitted the Abbasids to retain nominal rule, but a new and terrible enemy was now to appear and change everything.

Early in the thirteenth century Genghis Khan succeeded in uniting the nomads of Mongolia; he and his successors conquered eastern and central Asia (see Chapters 7 and 10) and swept into Persia and Iraq. In 1258 a grandson of Genghis Khan captured Baghdad and had the caliph put in a sack and trampled to death. Not only did the Abbasid dynasty come to an end, but so did most of the vast irrigation system that had supported the land since the beginning of civilization; Iraq was not to recover until modern times. The dynasty established by the Mongols survived for only a short time, and the Mongol ruling class was eventually absorbed into the native population of Persia and Iraq.

Muslim Egypt was saved from the Mongol advance by the Mamluks, captured slaves trained to become good Muslims and soldiers. They took over Palestine and Syria, ejecting the last of the crusaders in 1291. Ultimately they fell before the onslaught of another offshoot of the once great Seljuk empire, the Ottomans.

The Ottoman Turks. Having settled in northwestern Asia Minor in the thirteenth century as vassals of the Seljuks, the Ottoman Turks had organized their own aggressive state of Muslim frontier fighters by the end of the century (see p. 146). The Ottomans pitted their strength against the crumbling power of the Byzantines, and after capturing Constantinople in 1453 they pressed on into southeastern Europe. Driving as far as Vienna, they were turned back with difficulty in 1529 and again in 1683. Meanwhile, in 1517, the Ottomans had conquered the Mamluk territories, and within a few years they had added Iraq, much of Arabia, and all of the North African coastal belt to the borders of Morocco.

We have reviewed the expansion of Islam into western Asia and areas around the Mediterranean. In later chapters we shall trace its expansion as a missionary faith into India and Southeast Asia, and Chapter 17 will describe the medieval Afro-Muslim kingdoms of equatorial Africa. Although political solidarity was not maintained in the Islamic world, a form of unity was perpetuated by a common religion and culture. As a result, that world emerged in modern times as an almost solid ribbon of peoples stretching from Morocco in the west through Indonesia in the east. Today about one seventh of the world's population is composed of Muslim peoples, whose religious solidarity and cultural heritage provide the basis for a program of political resurgence.

ISLAMIC CULTURE

Borrowing the best from other cultures. The high attainment of the Muslims in the intellectual and artistic fields can be attributed not only to the Arabs, who as a group remained primarily concerned with religion, politics, and commerce, but also to those peoples who had embraced Islam in Persia, Mesopotamia, Syria, Egypt, North Africa, and Spain. Muslim learning benefited both from Islam's ability to absorb other cultures and from the native genius of the Islamic peoples. The cosmopolitan spirit permeating the Abbasid dynasty supplied the tolerance necessary for a diversity of ideas, so that the science and philosophy of ancient Greece and India found a welcome in Baghdad. Under Harun al-Rashid and his successors the writings of Aristotle, Euclid, Ptolemy, Archimedes, Galen, and other great Greek scientific writers were translated into Arabic. This knowledge formed the basis of Muslim learning, which in turn was later transmitted to scholars in western Europe (see p. 252). In addition to being invaluable transmitters of learning, the Muslims also made some original contributions of their own to science.

Advances in medicine. The two hundred years between 900 and 1100 can be called the golden age of Muslim learning. This period was particularly significant for advances made in medicine. In spite of a ban against the study of anatomy and a few other limitations imposed on Muslims by their religion, their medical men were in most ways far superior to their European contemporaries. Muslim cities had excellent pharmacies and hospitals, and both pharmacists and physicians had to pass state examinations to be licensed. Physicians received instruction in medical schools and hospitals.

Perhaps the greatest Muslim physician was the Persian al-Razi (d. 925), better known to the West as Rhazes. He wrote more than a hundred medical treatises in which he summarized Greek medical knowledge and added his own acute clinical observations. His most famous work, *On Smallpox and Measles*, is the first clear description of the symptoms and treatment of these diseases. The most influential Muslim medical treatise is the vast *Canon of Medicine* of the Persian scholar Avicenna (d. 1037), in which all Greek and Muslim medical learning is systematically organized. In the twelfth century the *Canon* was translated into Latin and was so much in demand in the West that it was issued sixteen times in the last half of the fifteenth century and more than twenty times in the sixteenth. It is still read and used in the Orient today.

Progress in other sciences. Muslim physicists were no mere copyists. Alhazen (d. 1039) of Cairo developed optics to a remarkable degree and challenged the view of Ptolemy and Euclid that the eye sends visual rays to its object. The chief source of all medieval western writers on optics, he interested himself in optic reflections and illusions and examined the refraction of light rays through air and water.

Although astronomy continued to be astrology's handmaiden, Muslim astronomers built observatories, recorded their observations over long periods, and achieved greater accuracy than the Greeks in measuring the length of the solar year and in calculating eclipses. Interest in alchemy—the attempt to transmute base metals into precious ones and to find the magic elixir for the preservation of human life—produced the first chemical laboratories in history and an emphasis on the value of experimentation. Muslim alchemists prepared many chemical substances (sulphuric acid, for example) and developed methods for evaporation, filtration, sublimation, crystallization, and distillation. The process of distillation, invented around 800, produced what was called *al-kuhl* (alcohol), a new liquor that has made Geber, its inventor, an honored name in some circles. Others claim that "Geber" became the etymological root of "gibberish."

In mathematics the Muslims were indebted to the Hindus as well as to the Greeks. From the Greeks came the geometry of Euclid and the fundamentals of trigonometry which Ptolemy had worked out. From the Hindus came arithmetic and algebra and the nine signs, known as Arabic numerals, whose value depends on their position in a series. The Muslims invented the all-important zero, although some scholars assign this honor to the Indians. Two Persians deserve mention: al-Khwarizmi (d. about 840), whose *Arithmetic* introduced Arabic numerals and whose *Algebra* first employed that mathematical term; and Omar Khayyám (d. 1123?), whose work in algebra went beyond quadratics to cubic equations. Other scholars developed plane and spherical trigonometry.

Muslim scholars devoted themselves to the study of science and medicine. In an observatory in Constantinople some astronomers make mathematical computations with the assistance of a variety of instruments, while others gather around a globe showing Asia, Africa, and Europe.

In an empire that straddled continents, where trade and administration made an accurate knowledge of lands imperative, the science of geography flourished. The Muslims added to the geographical knowledge of the Greeks, whose treatises they translated, by producing detailed descriptions of the climate, manners, and customs of many parts of the known world.

Islamic literature and scholarship. To westerners, whose literary tastes have been largely formed by Graeco-Roman classics, Arab literature may seem strange and alien. Where we are used to restraint and simplicity, "the Muslim writer excels . . . in clothing the essential realism of his thought with the language of romance."[11] Consequently, Arabic poetry abounds in elegant expression, subtle combinations of words, fanciful and even extravagant imagery, and witty conceits.

Westerners' knowledge of Islamic literature tends to be limited to the *Arabian Nights* and to the hedonistic poetry of Omar Khayyám. The former is a collection of often erotic tales told with a wealth of local color; although it professedly covers different facets of life at the Abbasid capital, it is in fact often based on life in medieval Cairo. The fame of Omar Khayyám's *Rubáiyát* is partly due to the musical (though not overaccurate) translation of Edward Fitzgerald. The following stanzas indicate the poem's beautiful imagery and gentle pessimism:

A Book of Verses underneath the Bough,
A Jug of Wine, a Loaf of Bread—and Thou
  Beside me singing in the Wilderness—
Oh, Wilderness were Paradise enow!

Some for the Glories of This World; and some
Sigh for the Prophet's Paradise to come;
  Ah, take the Cash, and let the Credit go,
Nor heed the rumble of a distant Drum! . . .

The Moving Finger writes; and, having writ,
Moves on: nor all your Piety nor Wit
  Shall lure it back to cancel half a Line,
Nor all your Tears wash out a Word of it.

And that inverted Bowl they call the Sky,
Whereunder crawling coop'd we live and die,
  Lift not your hands to *It* for help—for It
As impotently moves as you or I.[12]

The same rich use of imagery is found in much Islamic prose. As the first important prose work in Arab literature, the Koran set the stylistic pattern for Arabic writers even down to modern times. The holy book was designed particularly to be recited aloud; anyone who has listened to the chanting of the Koran can testify to its cadence, melody, and power.

Muslim philosophy, essentially Greek in origin, was developed by laymen and not, as in the West, by churchmen. Like the medieval Christian philosophers (see Chapter 11), Muslim thinkers were largely concerned with reconciling Aristotelian rationalism and

This map, made for Roger II of Sicily (note the size of Sicily in comparison to the rest of Europe), represents a direct contact between medieval Arab and European cartography. Arabia was placed near the top of the world; thus for clarity the map should be viewed upside down. Based on classical Ptolemaic models, the map uses a grid system of horizontal and vertical lines to divide the world into seventy geographical areas, thus producing a forerunner of the modern rendering of longitude and latitude.

religion. The earlier Muslim thinkers, including Avicenna, the physician with many talents, sought to harmonize Platonism, Aristotelianism, and Islam. Avicenna's work was widely read in the West, where it was translated in the twelfth century. The last great Islamic philosopher, Averroës (d. 1198), lived in Cordova where he was the caliph's personal doctor. In his commentaries on Aristotle's works, which gave the Christian West its knowledge of Aristotle long before the original Greek texts were obtained from Constantinople, Averroës rejected the belief in the ultimate harmony between faith and reason along with all earlier attempts to reconcile Aristotle and Plato. Faith and reason, he argued, operate on different levels; a proposition can be true philosophically but false theologically. On the other hand, Moses Maimonides, Averroës' contemporary who was also born in Muslim Spain, sought, in his still influential *Guide to the Perplexed*, to harmonize Judaism and Aristotelian philosophy. When St. Thomas Aquinas in the next century undertook a similar project for Christianity, he was influenced by these earlier attempts to reconcile faith and reason.

Islamic historiography found its finest expression in the work of ibn-Khaldun of Tunis (d. 1406), who has also been called "a father of sociology." Despite his busy life in public affairs, he found time to write a large general history dealing particularly with man's social development, which he held to be the result of the interaction of society and the physical environment. Ibn-Khaldun defined history as follows:

It should be known that history, in matter of fact, is information about human social organization, which itself is identical with world civilization. It deals with such conditions affecting the nature of civilization as, for instance, savagery and sociability, group feelings, and the different ways by which one group of human beings achieves superiority over another. It deals with royal authority and . . . with the different kinds of gainful occupations and ways of making a living, with the sciences and crafts that human beings pursue as part of their activities and efforts, and with all the other institutions that originate in civilization through its very nature.[13]

Artistry and precise observation combine to make this illustration from a thirteenth-century Islamic natural history text both graceful and accurate. Persian painters and book illustrators often ignored the prohibition about representing people and animals.

Ibn-Khaldun conceived of history as an evolutionary process, in which societies and institutions change continually.

Art and architecture. Religious attitudes played an important part in Muslim art. Because the Prophet inveighed strongly against idols and their worship, there was a prejudice against pictorial representation of human and animal figures. The effect of this prejudice was to encourage the development of stylized and geometrical design. Muslim art, like Muslim learning, borrowed from many sources. Islamic artists and craftsmen followed chiefly Byzantine and Persian models and eventually integrated what they had learned into a distinctive and original style (see Color Plate 7).

The Muslims excelled in two fields—architecture and the decorative arts. That Islamic architecture can boast of many large and imposing structures is not surprising, because it drew much of its inspiration from the Byzantines and Persians, who were monumental builders. In time an original style of building evolved; the great mosques

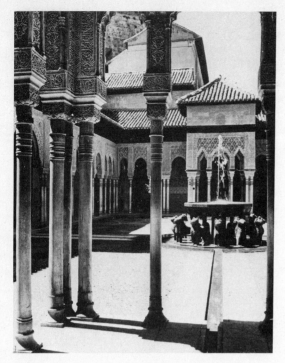

Graceful columns and arches frame the Court of the Lions, in the center of the Alhambra palace in Granada, Spain. This is the ultimate stage of refinement of Moorish architecture which combines both Spanish and Islamic elements.

SUMMARY

We have examined two rival but equally fascinating civilizations: first, the Byzantine, a citadel of classical and Christian culture; second, a dynamic Islam, conqueror alike of kingdoms and of the spiritual allegiance of populations stretching from Gibraltar to Java. With the conquest of Constantinople in 1453, this second civilization overwhelmed its rival.

When Constantine chose the site for New Rome, he picked a location that was geographically excellent for defense and trade. Constantinople's tradition as the eastern capital of the Roman empire encouraged Justinian to attempt to recover the western territory that had been under Roman rule; but these efforts failed, and in the long run Byzantium had to fight continually against invasions that diminished its empire on all sides. In 1453 the Ottoman Turks conquered "The City," and the empire of a thousand years was destroyed.

For a millennium the empire had acted as a buffer state, repulsing attacks while the weak, divided West grew in strength. And while learning was all but lost in medieval western Europe, the Byzantine world remained the custodian of classical knowledge and ideals until a resurgent West was able to assimilate its classical heritage. But Constantinople did much more than all this. Roman, Greek, and oriental elements were fused into a distinct and original culture; Slavic peoples were converted to Christianity; and the benefits of civilization were brought to Russia and neighboring lands.

The Norsemen who founded Kievan Russia also set up trade with Constantinople which continued for centuries. Through this medium, culture and religion were imported into Russia from the Eastern empire. While Constantinople itself fell, its heritage was in many ways maintained in the new Slavic state that was spreading across the vast Russian plain.

Muhammad (570-632), the founder of the Islamic religion, was born into a desert area populated by nomadic Bedouins and a

embody such typical features as domes, arcades, and minarets, the slender towers from which the faithful are summoned to prayer. The horseshoe arch is another graceful and familiar feature of Muslim architecture.

On the walls and ceilings of their buildings, the Muslims gave full rein to their love of ornamentation and beauty of detail. The Spanish interpretation of the Muslim tradition was particularly delicate and elegant (see p. 208). Other outstanding examples of Islamic architecture are to be found in India; the Taj Mahal, for example, is based largely on Persian motifs.

Being restricted in their subject matter, Muslim craftsmen conceived beautiful patterns from flowers and geometric figures. Even the Arabic script, the most beautiful ever devised, was used as a decorative motif. Muslim decorative skill also found expression in such fields as carpet and rug weaving, brass work, and the making of steel products inlaid with precious metals.

few scattered groups of townsmen. Soon after Muhammad's death, his monotheistic teachings were compiled in the Koran, the Muslim bible.

During the reigns of the first four caliphs and the century of the Umayyad dynasty (661-750), great strides were made in annexing new territories and peoples. But the Umayyad dynasty was based on a ruling hierarchy of Arabs, and the resentment of the non-Arabs produced a revolution which set the Abbasid dynasty (750-1258) on a new throne in Baghdad.

During the early Abbasid period Islam reached the high point of its geographical expansion and cultural achievements, and a ribbon of Muslim peoples extended from Spain across three continents to the Far East. Unparalleled prosperity evolved from a combination of successful trade, industry, and agriculture. But the Muslims were not able to maintain an integrated empire; despite a religious unity, which still exists (though without formal organization), politically the empire broke up into smaller Muslim states.

The Muslims were especially gifted in science, literature, and philosophy. Muslim intellectual life was in good part the product of a genius for synthesizing varying cultures, and their diffusion of this knowledge was a tremendous factor in the revival of classical learning and the coming of the Renaissance in Europe.

Ironically, while the arts and learning were beginning to thrive in the West, Islamic civilization itself entered a period of cultural decline. Various reasons have been advanced for this phenomenon, including the influx of semibarbarous peoples into Islamic lands, intellectual stagnation resulting from rigid adherence to the Koran's sacred law, and the despotic and eventually corrupt rule of such Muslim dynasties as the Ottomans in Turkey, who destroyed all progressive political and economic movements.

SUGGESTIONS FOR READING

Charles Diehl, **Byzantium: Greatness and Decline*** (Rutgers) is highly recommended as a brief introduction. Also brief is R. Guerdan, **Byzantium: Its Triumphs and Tragedy*** (Capricorn). For greater detail see G. Ostrogorsky, **History of the Byzantine State** (Rutgers, 1969); **The Cambridge Medieval History**, Vol. IV, rev. ed., **The Byzantine Empire**, Pt. I, **Byzantium and Its Neighbors;** Pt. II, **Government, Church and Civilization.**

D. A. Miller, **The Byzantine Tradition*** (Torchbooks, 1966) is a brief perceptive survey of Byzantine civilization. See also J. Hussey, **The Byzantine World*** (Torchbooks); and S. Runciman, **Byzantine Civilization*** (Meridian).

John W. Barker, **Justinian and the Later Roman Empire** (Univ. of Wisconsin, 1966) is clear and lively, as is R. Browning, **Justinian and Theodora** (Praeger). See also G. Downey, **Constantinople in the Age of Justinian** (Oklahoma, 1968); and Dean A. Miller, **Imperial Constantinople*** (Wiley, 1969).

C. M. Brand, **Byzantium Confronts the West, 1184-1204** (Harvard, 1968); and D. Queller, ed., **The Latin Conquest of Constantinople*** (Wiley, 1971) describe the events marking the beginning of the disintegration of the Byzantine empire. See also M. Donald Nicol, **The Last Centuries of Byzantium, 1261-1453** (St. Martin's).

H. Magoulias, **Byzantine Christianity: Emperor, Church, and the West** (Rand McNally, 1970); and T. Ware, **The Orthodox Church*** (Penguin) are two good surveys. S. Runciman, **The Eastern Schism*** (Oxford) disentangles fact from legend.

See D. Talbot Rice, **Art of the Byzantine Era*** (Oxford); and A. Grabar, **Art of the Byzantine Empire** (Crown, 1966). For superb color reproductions of Byzantine mosaics see H. Newmayer, **Byzantine Mosaics*** (Crown).

F. Dvornik, **The Slavs in European History and Civilization** (Rutgers, 1975) emphasizes Byzantine influences. G. Vernadsky, **Kievan Russia,** 2nd ed. (Yale, 1973) is detailed and authoritative. M. Florinsky, **Russia: A History and an Interpretation,** Vol. I (Macmillan) is excellent on early Russia. See also G. Fedotov, **The Russian Religious Mind: Kievan Christianity, the Tenth to the Thirteenth Centuries*** (Torchbooks).

P. K. Hitti, **The Arabs: A Short History*** (Gateway) is an abridgment of a scholarly general history. See also C. Brockelmann, **History of the Islamic Peoples*** (Capricorn); and A. G. Chejne, **Muslim Spain** (Minnesota, 1974).

W. M. Watt, **Muhammad: Prophet and Statesman*** (Galaxy) is short and excellent. See also T. Andrae, **Mohammed: The Man and His Faith*** (Torchbooks); and M. Rodinson, **Mohammed** (Vintage, 1974). For an interpretation and translation of the Koran, see M. Pickthall, **The Meaning of the Glorious Koran*** (Mentor); H. A. R. Gibb, **Mohammedanism: An Historical Survey*** (Galaxy) is outstanding.

P. Coles, **The Ottoman Impact on Europe*** (Harcourt Brace Jovanovich) is a lucid survey. See also S. Runciman, **The Fall of Constantinople, 1453*** (Cambridge); and N. Itkowitz, **The Ottoman Empire and Islamic Tradition*** (Knopf, 1972).

R. A. Nicholson, **A Literary History of the Arabs*** (Cambridge, 1969) traces the growth of Arab thought and culture through its literature, as does H. A. R. Gibb, **Arabic Literature,** 2nd ed. (Oxford, 1974). See also P. Hitti, **Makers of Arab History*** (Torchbooks) and D. Talbot Rice, **Islamic Art*** (Praeger).

*Indicates a less expensive paperbound edition.

CHAPTER 7

India, China, and Japan:
200-1350

The Guptas and the T'ang: Two Golden Ages

INTRODUCTION. The span of little more than a thousand years from the fifth to the fifteenth century was characterized in most parts of the world by numerous ethnic migrations and significant intercultural impacts. Later chapters will describe the ebb and flow of peoples—Vikings, Mongols, Magyars, and Germanic tribes—in medieval Europe; this chapter discusses the movement of peoples and cultural diffusion in Asia. During this period Indian culture expanded throughout Southeast Asia, enriching indigenous societies in what are now Burma, Indochina, the Malay peninsula, and Indonesia, while Buddhism exerted a profound influence upon China and Japan. Similarly, there was a continuous flow of Chinese culture eastward to the Korean peninsula and Japan. In the later part of this period, Muslim conquest appreciably influenced Indian society, and the repeated invasions by the Mongols and other nomadic peoples wrought important political and social changes in China.

The events related in this chapter point up a significant theme in history—the important role played by restless, nomadic peoples in the rise and fall of civilizations. In the decline of the Roman Empire, as treated in Chapter 5, we witnessed a classic example of this recurring phenomenon—nomad tribes pressing and probing "softer," more civilized, less dynamic groups, discovering the weak spots in their defenses, and finally overwhelming them. Again, in Chapter 6, we saw Byzantium assailed continuously for a thousand years until it at last fell victim to inexorable outside pressures. Perhaps the most awesome of all the nomads were the Mongols ruled by Genghis Khan, who led his hordes into China in search of booty and went on to create the greatest empire the world had yet seen—a vast realm extending all the way from the China Sea to eastern Europe. But if the assault of nomads is an important concern of this chapter, a corollary is how, once victorious, the predatory invader usually becomes respectable and sedentary, ceasing to be a menace to neighboring peoples.

In spite of these seemingly confused migrations and confrontations between peoples—or perhaps in part because of them—Asian civilizations reached a high peak during this period. In India the Gupta rulers came to power, and the subcontinent bene-

fited from their enlightened government. Hindu culture entered a period of flourishing growth marked by important advances in mathematics, medicine, chemistry, textile production, and imaginative literature. In fact, in the realm of culture diffusion and creative thought, India played the major role in Eurasia during the four centuries from 200 to 600 A.D. In the following period, from the seventh through the tenth centuries, the T'ang dynasty held sway in China, reviving the greatness of Chinese civilization after a period of disorder and division. For the most part, the Chinese enjoyed prosperity and good government, and there was a flowering of scholarship and the arts. It was during the T'ang and Sung dynasties that such revolutionary inventions as printing, explosive powder, and the compass were devised. The Japanese archipelago, after being occupied by ancestors of the present inhabitants, was never successfully invaded until the twentieth century. Influenced greatly by China, the proud and independent Japanese gradually developed a unique culture pattern best symbolized by the *samurai*, the knight, and *bushido*, the code of the warrior. Here, too, was a development which centuries later affected world history.

INDIA: THE IMPERIAL GUPTAS

The Gupta empire. As we recall from Chapter 4, the Kushan dynasty, which had witnessed one of the richest periods in Indian civilization, crumbled about 220 A.D. Subsequent events in northern India followed a pattern that has recurred time and again in the history of the subcontinent: an epoch of distinction followed by an era of political disintegration and comparative cultural darkness.

With the advent of the Gupta empire in the fourth century, northern India came out of its dark era and entered upon another epoch of greatness. In about 320 A.D., the first ruler of the Gupta dynasty, Chandragupta I (not related to Chandragupta Maurya, p. 98), established himself as monarch of the Ganges valley; and his successor ex-

tended the imperial boundaries in all directions. As a result, much of northern India from the Himalayas south to the Narbada River was included within the Gupta empire, thus making it the most extensive and powerful Indian state since the days of Ashoka six centuries earlier. Nor had its limits been reached. The grandson of the dynasty's founder, Chandragupta II, extended the empire still farther west until it stretched from sea to sea (see map, p. 171). During his reign (c. 380-c. 413), the Gupta empire reached its zenith. In all its long history before the British conquest India probably came closest to political unity during the reigns of Ashoka, Chandragupta II, and the Mughuls (see Chapter 16).

Under the Gupta dynasty, India exhibited

a state of cultural integration and social harmony such as it has never since achieved. By comparison with the Roman Empire, which was nearing its demise, and China, which was enduring a troubled interim period between the two great eras of the Han and the T'ang, India was probably the most civilized region of the world at this time.

Dominance of Hinduism. Although religious tolerance was characteristic of the Gupta period, the Gupta rulers preferred Hinduism to Buddhism, and the Brahmin caste enjoyed imperial patronage. While Buddhism as a distinct faith became practically extinct, certain of its teachings—for example, *ahimsā*, nonviolence and respect for life—were incorporated into Hinduism. From about 185 B.C. to about 800 A.D., Hinduism not only became dominant in India but also gradually crystallized into its present form.

By recognizing all varieties of religious experience, Hinduism is capable of absorbing different and often even contradictory points of view—a factor that helps account for its tremendous tenacity. Names mean very little; God may be worshiped in many forms and by many names. Hinduism stresses conduct and ceremony rather than rigid belief. To be a Hindu it is only necessary to accept the leadership of the Brahmins and one's status in caste, thereby implying acceptance of the belief of reincarnation.

Notwithstanding the many invasions into India, all of the intruders—excluding the Muslims and later the British—were absorbed and found a place in Hinduism.

The caste system. By the Gupta period the caste system was rapidly assuming its basic features. Each caste was usually related to a specific occupation, was endogamous (a man was expected to select his bride from within his own group), and had its own *dharma*—rules regulating the types of food eaten, the manner of consumption, and with what other castes there could be social contact. The untouchables, the lowest rung in the caste ladder, had a degraded status.

In the light of modern democratic ideology, caste is a reprehensible system and indeed is so regarded by many of India's present leaders. Defenders of the institution, however, point out that a caste forms a kind of brotherhood in which all members are equal. Furthermore, within his caste the Hindu enjoys a sense of security that makes him feel part of a cosmic process in which no mistakes are made.

Achievements in Sanskrit literature. The Gupta period has been called the golden age of Sanskrit, the classical language of India. Court poetry was zealously produced, and the kings were generous patrons of many writers. The most famous writer, Kalidasa (c. 400-455), excelled as both a lyric and an epic poet and has been termed the "Indian

The best examples of Gupta painting are found in the caves at Ajanta in the Deccan. Hollowed out of solid rock and adorned with sculpture and murals, these twenty-nine worship halls and dwelling places served as a hermitage for Buddhist monks. Some of the paintings, which depict scenes from the life of Buddha and from Buddhist stories, date from the second century B.C.; the finest, however, were painted during the Gupta period. Presenting a brilliant panorama of contemporary life, the murals portray beggars, princes, peasants, women, children, beasts, and birds. This painting depicts the temptation of Buddha.

Shakespeare" because of his superb dramas. Characterized by a lack of action unfamiliar to western audiences, his plays abound in splendid imagery.

India presented an unusually fertile soil for the creation of fables and folklore. Since its religions stressed the unity of all life and the cycle of transmigration, it was not difficult for storytellers to reverse the positions of the animal and human kingdoms and to conceive of beasts acting like men and vice versa. Many Indian stories were eventually carried to Europe by the Muslims. Perhaps the most famous is the story of Sindbad, which found its way into the *Arabian Nights*. Boccaccio, Chaucer, La Fontaine, the Grimm brothers, and Kipling have all been indebted to Indian folklore.

Gupta science and technology. Scholarship and science were of a very high caliber during Gupta times. Students from all over Asia came to India's foremost university, situated at Nalanda. The most famous scientist was the astronomer and mathematician Aryabhata, who lived in the fifth century. In verse he discussed quadratic equations, the value of π, solstices and equinoxes, the spherical shape of the earth, and the earth's rotation. Other Indian astronomers predicted eclipses accurately, calculated the moon's diameter, and expounded on gravitation.

In astronomy and mathematics (except for geometry) the Hindus surpassed the achievements of any ancient western people. The Arabic numerals and the decimal system we use today appear to have come originally from India. Even the zero may have come from Indian rather than Arabic sources.

The Hindus were also remarkably advanced in chemistry; they discovered how to make soap and cement and were the finest temperers of steel in the world. Indian industry was famous for its superior dyes and fine fabrics; the methods of production were taken over by the Arabs, and from them by Europeans. The Arabs named one Indian cloth *quittan*—hence the word *cotton*. *Calico*, *cashmere*, *chintz*, and *bandanna* are also of Indian origin.

The development of Indian medicine was due to various factors, including an interest in physiology which resulted from Yoga. Some Gupta physicians were surprisingly modern in their techniques; they prepared carefully for an operation and sterilized wounds by fumigation. Caesarean operations, bone setting, and plastic surgery were all attempted. The Indians also used many drugs then unknown in Europe.

A period of instability. By 413, when Chandragupta II died, the Gupta empire had reached the zenith of its power. In the last half of the fifth century, while their kinsmen were ravaging Europe under Attila, "The Scourge," Huns invaded the Punjab. They soon gained control of northwestern India but were prevented from advancing into eastern India by a confederacy of Hindu princes.

In the seventh century the various states in the Ganges valley fought constantly with one another until at last a strong man arose. In the short space of six years (606-612) Harsha, rajah of one of the northern kingdoms, mastered much of the territory formerly

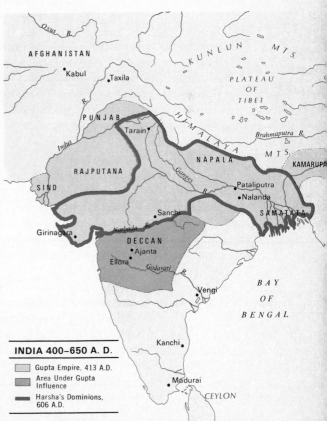

INDIA 400–650 A. D.

Gupta Empire, 413 A.D.

Area Under Gupta Influence

Harsha's Dominions, 606 A.D.

ruled by the Guptas. With his death in 647, northern India reverted to confusion and warfare which lasted for centuries.

Particularly warlike were the descendants of Central Asian peoples who had followed the Huns into northwest India in the fifth century and had intermarried with the local population. In time these people assumed the privileges of "blue-blooded" Hindus, haughtily called themselves Rajputs (Sons of Kings), and carved out kingdoms for themselves in parts of north India, especially in what became known as Rajputana, a strategic area between the Indus and Ganges valleys. The Rajputs possessed a code of chivalry not unlike that which existed in medieval Europe. Youths were brought up with the privileges and obligations of the warrior caste (the Kshatriya) and taught to respect women, spare the fallen, and demand fair play.

Expansion of Indian culture. For nearly one thousand years India sent her art, religious ideas, literature, and traders to many parts of Asia. The diffusion of *Mahayana* Buddhism into Central Asia, China, Korea, and finally Japan during this period was the most striking sign of the dynamic power of Indian culture. The relationship between India and China was especially strong, and many Chinese scholars made pilgrimages to the former. The most celebrated was Hsüan-tsang (or Yuan-chuang), who spent thirteen years (630-643) in Buddha's holy land. Returning to his native land, Hsüan-tsang brought back 657 manuscripts, together with many Buddhist relics, and devoted the remainder of his life to translating his treasures. His journal is one of the most valuable sources of information on medieval India.

Resulting mainly from peaceful trading activities, Indian cultural expansion in what has been called "Greater India" in Southeast Asia began about the second century A.D. and continued until the ninth or tenth century. The impact of Indian culture was not equally strong or enduring over all sections. One scholar has divided Greater India into two segments: the western zone (including Ceylon, Burma, the central part of Siam, and the Malay peninsula) received the full force of Indian colonizing activity and conse-quently developed a culture that was largely a colonial imitation of the original; the eastern zone (comprising mainly Java, Cambodia, and Champa in Indochina) experienced Indianization that was very definite but not strong enough to prevent the indigenous peoples from developing their own distinctive cultures and ways of life.

From the second century A.D. on, the kingdoms established in Greater India were ruled by monarchs with Indian names. Some of these kingdoms endured more than a thousand years, persisting, in fact, after India itself had been overwhelmed by foreign invaders. Two monuments attest to the splendor of these states.

About 1100 one of the greatest architectural edifices in history was erected in Cambodia —Angkor Wat (see Color Plate 15). Long forgotten and swallowed up by the jungle, this vast complex was accidentally discovered by a French naturalist in 1861. It is surrounded by a stone enclosure measuring half a mile from north to south and two thirds of a mile from east to west. Nearby lay the Cambodian capital city, which may have had a population of close to one million.

In central Java one of the most imposing Buddhist shrines in the world is located: the immense monument of Borobudur. Erected on the top of a hill in nine successive terraces, Borobudur is covered with images of the Buddha, sculptures illustrating Buddhist texts, and carved scenes of everyday life. The art of Southeast Asia was unmistakably influenced by Indian styles and techniques, but in Angkor Wat and Borobudur the works created were larger than anything found in India itself.

THE MUSLIM CONQUEST OF INDIA

The Muslim invasions. In 711, the same year in which they invaded Spain, Arabs appeared in India. They made the southern valley of the Indus a province of the vast Umayyad empire, but the Rajput princes soon halted further Arab penetration of India.

At the end of the tenth century more Muslim invaders swept through the northwest passes. The newcomers were Turks and Afghans who, in 1022, annexed the Punjab. Despite destructive forays by various Muslim sultans, the Rajput and other Hindu kingdoms of the interior remained independent. Not until the closing years of the twelfth century did the Muslims establish a large Indian dominion.

The Delhi sultanate. The first important Muslim ruler was a former general who in 1206 established himself as sultan at Delhi, ruling a strong Muslim kingdom covering much of north India. The Delhi sultanate existed until the early years of the sixteenth century, and during the period of its greatest power (1206-1388), it gave northern India political unity. The early Delhi sultans also pushed Muslim authority and religion southward into the Deccan and in the first decades of the fourteenth century reached southernmost India. The Delhi sultanate, however, soon lost control in southern India to a rival sultanate in the Deccan and to other Muslim and Hindu states.

Tamerlane. In 1398 the Punjab was invaded by a Mongol who had already conquered Central Asia—Timur the Lame (Tamerlane). Defeating all armies sent against him, Timur looted wealthy Delhi, killing perhaps 100,000 prisoners. Afterwards, he departed westward for Samarkand, leaving Delhi's few surviving inhabitants to perish of famine and plague. After Timur's terrible visitation, nearly all semblance of political unity was destroyed in north India, and Muslim sultans maintained independent principalities in defiance of the ineffectual authority at Delhi.

Effects of Muslim rule. The Muslim conquest of India was unusually ruthless. To the Muslims, Hinduism with its many deities, elaborate ritual, powerful priestcraft, and fondness for images was the opposite of all that Islam held sacred. Hindu forces desperately resisted their Muslim conquerors and, after defeat, often suffered wholesale massacre. Many people clung tenaciously to their Hindu faith—the upper classes in particular—but a fairly large number of Hindus were converted to Islam. In some cases it was a choice between Allah or the sword; in others it was a voluntary matter: poor men sought to avoid the heavier taxes levied on infidels, low-caste Hindus became Muslims to escape their degraded status, and ambitious administrators accepted Islam in order to succeed in the official service of the Muslim rulers. One result of the Muslim intrusion was the emergence of a common spoken language—Urdu. This language was a combination of Persian, Turkish, and Arabic words which utilized the grammatical constructions of the Hindu languages. Urdu and the native Hindi became the languages most commonly used in northern India, and they are today the dominant languages of Muslim Pakistan and Hindu India.

The injection of the Islamic way of life into the pattern of Hindu society was to have profound effects upon the history of the Indian subcontinent. Fiercely proud of their own faith, and disdainful of Hinduism, the Muslims jealously retained their religion and ways of life. After the establishment of the powerful Delhi sultanate in 1206, therefore, the life of India was divided into two streams, the Hindu and the Muslim, which mingled only superficially and never really united. This division was to have momentous consequences in the twentieth century, when India, freed from British rule, split into two nations, India and Pakistan.

CHINA: THE MEN OF T'ANG

An age of political division. After the fall of the Han empire in 220 A.D., China was destined to suffer three and a half centuries of disorder and division before another great dynasty arose and reunited the country. The internal collapse of the Han empire —as with the breakdown of the Mauryan and Gupta regimes in India and of Rome in the West—allowed various nomadic peoples to penetrate the frontiers and raid and pillage. In North China these barbarians set up various petty states, especially after the opening of the fourth century.

Central and South China escaped these

barbarian intrusions and were now more intensively developed than before, especially by émigrés from the north. Hence the literate classical tradition was preserved in the south; and a sequence of regimes, with capitals at Nanking, kept alive the notion of a unified state under a "Son of Heaven."

Buddhism adapts itself. Although Buddhism had been introduced into China during Han times, this religion made its most important gains from the third century A.D. on. As the sober, balanced social order inculcated by Confucianism came to make less sense in a world run by warlords, all classes of Chinese were touched by Buddhism. Part of Buddhism's appeal resembled that of the mystery religions and of Christianity in the decaying Roman world: the assurance of inner consolation through faith and of salvation in a glorious afterlife even for humble folk. The monastic aspects of Buddhism appealed to many thousands of Chinese seeking seclusion and protection in the face of contemporary social chaos.

Political and economic conditions under the T'ang. After internal collapse and barbarian invasion, neither the Indian nor the Graeco-Roman world-state was ever able fully to regenerate itself politically. But in the late sixth and early seventh centuries the Chinese did just that, re-creating and improving on the Han model. After a short-lived reign of the Sui dynasty, the T'ang emperors (618-906) provided a long period of stable growth and cultural flowering, giving China renewed preeminence in all East Asia. As the Gupta empire represents tthe golden age of Hindu culture, the T'ang dynasty represents the golden era of China. Even today many Chinese like to consider themselves not only "Sons of Han" but also "Men of T'ang" in reference to these great ages.

The second emperor of the T'ang dynasty, T'ai Tsung ("Grand Ancestor"), reigned from 627 to 650 and is considered one of China's greatest emperors. After defeating the northern Turks decisively in 630, he took advantage of internal dissension in Turkestan to reestablish Chinese dominance over the Tarim Basin. Under his son, a successful war was undertaken against Korea, which was made a tributary vassal state. At this point China stood at the zenith of its power. The T'ang empire extended from Korea and Manchuria through Tibet and Central Asia to the borders of India and Persia (see map, p. 175).

A statesman as well as a great soldier, T'ai Tsung was energetic in instituting reforms. One of his major reforms was to strengthen the administrative system of the country. The emperor governed the center of his empire by means of a bureaucracy recruited through a civil service program rooted in Han precedent but now more elaborated. T'ang improvements also extended to land reform; laws were passed to curb the growth of large estates and to ensure equitable amounts of land for the peasants. Economic prosperity resulted from these reforms as well as from the more efficient transportation system which the T'ang developed by completing the Sui canal system. A thriving foreign commerce also contributed to the economic boom. Caravans arrived frequently from West and Central Asia; and great quantities of luxury goods were exported to such far-distant points as Jerusalem and Cairo.

T'ang scholarship. The T'ang period was outstanding in scholarly achievements. Two encyclopedias were compiled to assist bureaucrats in their work, and Buddhist scholars translated sacred texts into Chinese. T'ai Tsung ordered the publication of an elaborate edition of the Five Classics of Confucianism and also stressed the value of historical writings.

. . . by using a mirror of brass you may see to adjust your cap; by using antiquity as a mirror, you may learn to foresee the rise and fall of empires.[1]

Li Po and Tu Fu, masters of T'ang poetry. An eighteenth-century anthology of T'ang poetry included hundreds of scrolls containing 48,900 poems by 2300 poets. The astonishing literary output of the T'ang era would almost appear to justify the remark: "[At this age,] whoever was a man was a poet."[2]

The two greatest poets of this era, Li Po (701?-762) and Tu Fu (712-770), were good friends who occasionally twitted each other in their works. Tu Fu summed up his fellow poet—a Taoist hedonist whose heavy drinking prevented his entrance into government service—in this fashion:

As for Li Po, give him a jugful of wine,
And he will write a hundred poems.[3]

And Li Po once addressed these witty lines to Tu Fu:

Here! is this you on the top of Fan-Ko
   Mountain,
Wearing a huge hat in the noon-day sun?
How thin, how wretchedly thin, you have
   grown!
You must have been suffering from poetry
   again.[4]

The poetry of Li Po exerted a great appeal for his countrymen. But the majority of Chinese scholars and poets today consider Tu Fu the greater poet, perhaps China's greatest.

T'ang art. The T'ang dynasty was the formative period of Chinese painting. Wu Tao-tzu, considered by the Chinese their greatest master, lived at this time. Landscape, called "mountain-and-water" painting by the Chinese, now became the most typical form of expression. Through the ages to come, the Chinese artist would express his sense of cosmic forces and deep spirituality in mountain-and-water pictures (see Color Plate 14).

Buddhism, establishing itself under the T'ang, brought with it the need to represent its gods and saviors visually, and for the first time in Chinese history sculpture became an important art. Although sculptors used Buddhist subject matter, they gave their work a distinctively Chinese interpretation.

The invention of printing. In the first century A.D. the Chinese had discovered how to make paper, and in the fifth century they put ink stampings on documents by using seals fashioned from metal and stone. These

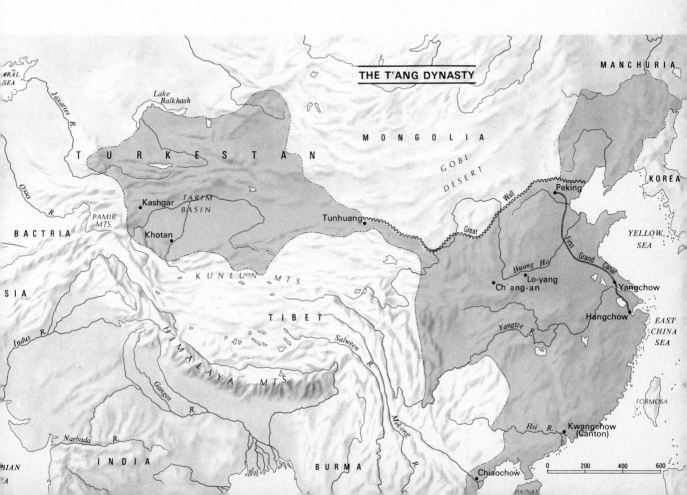

THE T'ANG DYNASTY

The Chinese invented block printing in about 600, and the earliest existing book printed by this method is the *Diamond Sutra*, dating from about 868.

technical discoveries paved the way for the culminating invention—printing.

Evidence would indicate that the process of block printing—printing from an image cut in a wooden block—was invented in China by about 600, although the earliest surviving examples come from Japan and date from 764 to 770. The first extant printed book is the *Diamond Sutra*, which was discovered in a cave in northwestern China. Printed in 868, the *Diamond Sutra* consists of six sheets of text pasted together to form a roll some sixteen feet long; the sheets are each two and a half feet by almost one foot in size and must have been printed from very large blocks.

Because the Chinese language is written not by means of an alphabet but by means of separate characters that represent entire words, the Chinese found block printing satisfactory. Nevertheless, they were the first to invent movable type, probably in the first half of the eleventh century.

T'ang decline: the end of an epoch. In the seventh century the T'ang dynasty still enjoyed a suzerainty that stretched from the Pamir Mountains in the west into Korea in the east, but during the next century divisive political forces arose. From mid-century on, the imperial boundaries contracted, and within the empire, decadence and disorder held sway. In 755 a revolt broke out, and the emperor was forced to flee, abdicating in

favor of his son. When the rebellion was finally put down, the weakened dynasty survived for a century and a half; in 906 the T'ang dynasty came to an end.

The Sung dynasty. The fall of the T'ang dynasty left China vulnerable to external attack and in another of its periods of internal disorder. This upheaval was followed by the founding of the Sung dynasty (960-1279). Early in the eleventh century the Sung emperors adopted the practice of "buying protection" by paying the Khitan Tatars in North China an annual tribute of 100,000 ounces of silver and 200,000 pieces of silk. In time the Sung were forced to increase these amounts and to begin paying tribute to other border kingdoms. Even though such payments did not represent a large percentage of the total state revenues, they were a drain on the imperial finances.

The unprecedented development of large estates whose owners managed to evade paying their share of taxes resulted in an increasingly heavy burden of taxation falling on the small farmers. The drop in the state revenues, a succession of budget deficits, and widespread inflation caused the emperor to seek advice from one of China's most fascinating statesmen and economists, Wang An-shih (1021-1086).

Wang An-shih believed that the ruler was responsible for providing his subjects with the necessities of life. He expressed his social philosophy thus:

The state should take the entire management of commerce, industry, and agriculture into its own hands, with a view to succoring the working classes and preventing them from being ground into the dust by the rich.[5]

To this end, he initiated an agricultural loans measure to relieve the farming peasants of the intolerable burden of interest which callous moneylenders exacted from them in difficult times and to ensure that lack of capital would not hinder the work of agriculture. To destroy speculation and break up the monopolies, he initiated a system of fixed commodity prices; and he appointed boards to regulate wages and plan pensions for the aged and unemployed. Wang An-shih also revamped the state examination system so that less emphasis was placed on literary style and memorization of the classics and more on practical knowledge.

In the next generation opposition from vested interests, difficulties in maintaining reforming zeal and efficiency among officials, the impracticality of some reform projects, and renewed foreign crises led to the victory of the conservative opposition and to the rescinding of most of Wang's "new laws." It is remarkable, nonetheless, to see how modern his theories were; the concepts of the welfare state and a planned economy are apparently not quite so new as we may have supposed.

The Neo-Confucian synthesis. The failure of Wang's reforms was viewed by many Confucianists as proof of their contention that immediate practical reforms were doomed to fail unless their acceptance by rulers and subjects had been prepared for by a long period of moral rehabilitation. The result was a revival of Confucianism, often called Neo-Confucianism, which culminated in the teachings of Chu Hsi (1130-1200). His con-

cern with achieving the goal of moral perfection led him to provide Confucian ethics with a metaphysical foundation which it had hitherto lacked. Influenced by Buddhist and Taoist metaphysics, Chu Hsi's voluminous commentaries on the Confucian Classics developed an elaborate synthesis that postulated a single universal principle—eternal moral law—which men could perceive by meditation and education and whose cultivation would lead to moral perfection. Despite its debt to Buddhist and Taoist metaphysics, Neo-Confucianism emphasized the this-worldly teachings of Confucius and Mencius.

Neo-Confucianism, as shaped by Chu Hsi, became the dominant intellectual force in China until the revolutionary political and social changes of the twentieth century.

Buddhism came into disfavor under the Sung as an alien religion and lost its old prestige and intellectual respectability among the upper classes. It survived principally as one of several popular cults among the masses.

The empirical sciences. Chu Hsi contended that self-cultivation required the extension of knowledge, best achieved by the "investi-

During the T'ang and Sung dynasties Chinese science and technology were far in advance of European science of the same era. One of the most complicated Chinese mechanical and scientific creations, this astronomical observatory, dating from about 1090, used a water-powered clock to rotate the instruments in time with the motion of the stars. It had previously been thought that the mechanical clock was a western achievement of the fourteenth century.

gation of things." As a consequence, Neo-Confucianism was accompanied by significant advances in experimental and applied sciences. The Sung period witnessed the production of large numbers of works concerning chemistry, zoology, and botany. Algebra was developed until it was the most advanced in the world. In medicine, inoculation against smallpox was introduced. Progress was also notable in astronomy, geography, and cartography; at this time, the earliest relief maps were constructed. By the end of the eleventh century the magnetic compass was employed as an aid to navigation. Another major development was the use of explosive powder—first in fireworks, then in warfare.

Excellence in Sung art. Many critics assert that "at its best Chinese painting is one of the outstanding expressions of man's ability to create beauty."[6] The Chinese painter believed that only days spent in meditation of a vista would reveal to him the scene's essential mood. When he had observed nature as long as he thought necessary, he would then paint the scene without looking at it. The awe and love felt for nature by Chinese painters was the force behind much of their work (see Color Plate 14).

Chinese paintings were not publicly displayed but were mounted on heavy scrolls and kept hidden away. Only on special occasions were they taken out for a short period of concentrated esthetic enjoyment. The painter was highly esteemed, for his techniques required years of intensive training. The use of ink on silk meant that he had to be sure of every line, for once the brush stroke had been made, no changes were possible. Calligraphy, or the use of the brush in writing the intricate Chinese word symbols, also provided excellent training.

Sung pottery—especially porcelain—was also of unsurpassed excellence. The Chinese loved the delicacy and beauty of the elegant porcelain pieces produced in this period.

The Southern Sung. During the eleventh century a group of people from Manchuria took northern China, ruling as the Chin dynasty (not related to the earlier Ch'in, p. 110). From 1127 on, the Sung had no control over northern China. They established a capital in the south of China, first at Nanking and then at Hangchow, and for the next one hundred years China was thus divided into two empires, the Sung and Chin.

Although militarily weak, the Southern Sung was economically and socially one of the greatest periods in Chinese history. Increased population, together with marked improvements in production, led to vastly increased internal and external trade. Commerce broke out of the controlled marketplaces, and shops began to line the streets of the towns and cities. More and more of the upper classes began to reside permanently in the urban centers rather than in the countryside. As Chinese foreign trade grew, large communities of foreign merchants settled inside China.

The growth of commerce required a more efficient monetary system. At first copper cash was used, but the advance of trade created such a money shortage that bank drafts and other forms of commercial paper were introduced in the ninth century. By 1024 the government began to issue paper money. This commercial revolution strongly resembled that which was to take place in Europe several centuries later. In the latter, however, feudalism was too rigid to develop within itself the new institutions required by commerce. In China very significant changes in society and culture did accompany the great economic growth and increased mercantile activity that took place from the eighth to the thirteenth centuries.

During the Southern Sung the bureaucracy, recruited more and more by examination and from the Yangtze valley area, began to replace the northern aristocracy as the main support of dynastic power. This professionalization of government service was an important factor in the early modernization of Chinese society. A change in the landholding and tax system, which occurred earlier in the eighth century, had weakened the power of the aristocracy and great landholders because it permitted the appearance of small- and medium-sized landholdings. The new "gentry" class which arose exerted its influence through the government bureaucracy, which drew most of its members from this class.

THE BARBARIAN CHALLENGE TO CIVILIZATION

China and the "barbarians." At the end of the twelfth century, with China split between the rule of the Chin and the Southern Sung, East Asian civilization faced a new threat from the north, greater than any in its previous history. By this time a recognizable pattern had emerged in China's relations with the nomadic peoples who surrounded her from the northeast to the southwest. Dynastic weakness encouraged "barbarian" invaders. The "barbarians" usually obtained the advice of Chinese administrators and military specialists, and they had superior military power based on the cavalry of the Central Asian steppe and use of the iron stirrup, which enabled an archer to shoot from the back of his horse without falling off. It was their excellent horsemanship that caused them to maintain military superiority over the peasant foot-soldiers.

As they acquired control over more and more settled Chinese territory, the "barbarians" usually adopted a policy of tolerance over the captured villages. They frequently employed the conquered Chinese in administration and tax collection, and also often employed other foreigners, feeling they could be trusted more than the Chinese.

All "barbarian" dynasties faced two great problems in their relationship with the Chinese. First, they sought to maintain their own identity by keeping their original homeland separate and by preserving their own language and customs. Always a small minority, they constantly faced the problem of losing their "barbarian" vigor by adopting the sedentary and "cultured" ways of the Chinese. Second, they had to control their new territories and alien population by military means. This meant stationing their forces at strategic locations throughout the country and defending major urban centers and economic regions from other "barbarians" and from internal revolt. Their resources were often not sufficient to accomplish this.

Rise of the Mongol onslaught. Up to the middle of the twelfth century the Mongol peoples had no national organization or identity but lived in scattered tribes spread over large areas. The majority lived as nomads, depending on animals for their needs; the protection of grazing routes through land as opposed to permanent domination of the land was a major nomadic concern. These nomads were never wholly independent from the sedentary civilizations like the Chinese, because they could not themselves produce the grains, metal goods, and other items they needed or desired.

This silk painting of barbarian royalty worshiping Buddha gives some indication of the extent of Chinese interaction with the outside world during the T'ang and Sung periods. Notice the many different kinds of dress and facial expression among the foreigners and the quality of caricature in their depiction, as compared with the portrayal of the serene and very Chinese Buddha with his disciples and guardians.

At the time of the birth of Genghis (also spelled Chinggis) Khan about 1162, no one leader had yet emerged to unite the Mongols as a whole. During Genghis' youth his father was killed. Brought up in a spirit of revenge, he slowly built up a personal following and overpowered his own overlord and other clans and tribes. At last, at a great meeting of the Mongol tribes in 1206, he was recognized as the ruler of all the Mongols and given the title by which he is known to history, Genghis Khan, which probably meant "ocean ruler" or "universal ruler."

Genghis was one of the greatest organizational geniuses of all time. Out of a population of a little over a million Mongols, he fashioned a war machine based on units of ten and trained in the most sophisticated cavalry techniques. With this machine he and his people conquered most of the known world from the Pacific to the Danube and the Mediterranean, terrorized the rest, and established a *Pax Tatarica* in eastern Europe, the Middle East, Central Asia, and the Far East that permitted the greatest development of travel and trade between the continents that the world was to witness before the seventeenth century.

Leading his magnificent army, Genghis campaigned against the Chin empire. In 1215 the Chin capital near Peking was sacked and its inhabitants massacred. Following this victory, the attack on the Chin slowed down because Genghis sent much of his army westward on a campaign through Central Asia and on into Russia. But the conquest of northern China was later renewed, and city after city was subdued. The Great Khan himself was killed, probably by assassination, in 1227. A Mongol legend claims that he will return one day to lead the Mongols to world conquest once more.

Genghis' death did not slow down the Mongol war machine. By 1234 the last remnants of the Chin empire were extinguished by his son, who then embarked on the slow process of conquering the Southern Sung. After years of heroic resistance the Chinese were subdued in 1279 by Genghis' grandson, Kublai Khan, founder of the Yüan dynasty — the first "barbarian" dynasty to rule all China. Although China was now incorporated into an empire that stretched across the world, it did not lose its separate identity. On the death of Genghis, portions of the empire had been administered by his sons and grandsons under the general leadership of one son elected as khan of all the Mongols. After 1260 the unity of an empire divided into a suzerain khanate and four vassal khanates was becoming a fiction, and Mongol China was a distinct state. The unity of the empire weakened after Kublai Khan, who from 1260 to 1294 held the suzerain khanate comprising China and Mongolia, moved his capital to Peking.

China under the Mongols. Instead of turning all of North China into one vast pasture land, the khans were taught the art of governing the sedentary Chinese and the advantages of maintaining a stable society in China from which the Mongols might obtain great benefits through taxation. While separating themselves from the Chinese by custom and law, the Mongols adopted most of the T'ang and Sung administrative institutions and even instituted an examination system to recruit bureaucrats. The Yüan also employed many foreigners in high positions, including Marco Polo. They set up a hierarchical system in which they were at the top and the Southern Chinese, the most numerous group, were at the very bottom.

The arts flourished during this "barbarian" dynasty. The drama, which was probably influenced by Central Asian dance performances, was popular, and what we now know as the "Chinese opera," a combination of singing, dancing, and acting accompanied by music, achieved its classical development during the Yüan. Growing out of the prompting books used by professional storytellers, the novel also developed rapidly.

The reign of Kublai Khan. For knowledge of Kublai Khan's reign, we are indebted to the famous Venetian traveler Marco Polo, author of probably the world's outstanding travelogue and what has been called the finest European account of Chinese civilization at this time. As a youth, Marco Polo accompanied his father and uncle, two Venetian merchants, eastward to Kublai Khan's court, arriving there about 1275. Received with honor and given posts in the imperial service, the Polos remained seventeen years in China. Marco Polo reported that the Great Khan maintained order throughout his dominions, improved the roads, constructed canals, revised the calendar, built granaries to store food surpluses, and aided the sick, orphans, and old scholars by means of state care.

After Marco Polo returned to Italy, he wrote of his travels. But his fellow Venetians were so incredulous of the figures he used in describing the wealth and power of China, whose civilization was superior to that of thirteenth-century Europe, that they dubbed him "Messer Millions." His account of black stones (coal) used for heating purposes and the people's habit of taking frequent baths seemed fabulous to them, since coal was unknown in medieval Europe and Europeans in the Middle Ages seldom, if ever, took baths.

Pax Tatarica: relinking of East and West. In the first centuries of the Christian era the West had been linked with India and China by the spice and silk trades. The subsequent centuries of mutual isolation were broken during the T'ang dynasty when its court attracted such diverse groups as Muslims, Christians, and Persians. With the advent of the nomadic Mongols, East and West were again linked together along the ancient silk routes. The resumption of this trade had permanent consequences. By making the trade routes across Asia safe and by tolerating diverse religions, the Mongol dynasty attracted European traders and missionaries to China.

With the unification, however temporary, of almost all Asia and the restoration of roads, communication was restored to the point where the Polos were far from being the only travelers to cross the great spaces separating East and West. One monk, from a Christian community in Peking, traveled in the thirteenth century as an envoy of Mongol Persia to the pope and also met the kings of England and France. The papacy sent various missions to the Far East in the same century, with the result that in the early fourteenth century a Roman Catholic community of several thousand persons existed in China.

Cultural interchange between China and the West was also considerable during medieval times. One authority believes that the Mongols and other Central Asian peoples conveyed gunpowder to Europe, and we know that the Muslims transmitted westward such invaluable Chinese inventions as the arts of papermaking and printing and the magnetic compass. China itself was enriched by its imports. One of the most important was a new food, sorghum, which was brought to China by way of India in the thirteenth century. By that time the abacus, a familiar sight in Far Eastern shops today, had also made its appearance. Ceramics and bronzes were affected by influences from civilizations to the west, especially Persia, while the cloisonné technique was undoubtedly borrowed from the Byzantines.

These are but random examples of a cultural interchange which certainly enriched East and West alike. Yet the profound psychological effect created in Europe by the accounts of Marco Polo and other travelers was perhaps even more far-reaching in the evolution of world history. Travelers' accounts had revealed that the Far East not only equaled but exceeded Europe in population, wealth, and luxury. Europeans now realized that the Mediterranean was neither the central nor the most important area of the world, and they began to develop new attitudes to fit this knowledge.

Decline of Mongol China. Actually, the prosperous appearances which Marco Polo described were largely deceptive. Kublai Khan's ambitious foreign wars and domestic works necessitated heavy government spending. Tax rates rose, and many peasants were dispossessed of their land and forced to work for greedy landowners of vast estates. Large issues of paper money depreciated in value, while hard currency diminished. Kublai Khan's projected invasion of Japan was a disastrous failure (see p. 184).

The seven other Yüan emperors who succeeded Kublai Khan all proved to be inadequate rulers. The Mongols allowed their armed strength to lapse; and the exclusion of Chinese from the imperial administration continued to fan the resentment of the people against the rule of foreigners. By 1368, less than a century after Kublai's final conquest of the Sung, rebellious forces from South China, led by an ex-Buddhist novice, took Peking and founded the Ming dynasty.

The nomad challenge of the Mongols was thus rebuffed in East Asia, but its scourge was longer felt elsewhere. Remnants of West Asian Mongols, converted to Islam, were part of continuing steppe-world invasions into India. Older Muslim centers in Mesopotamia never fully recovered. That segment of Mongols who had settled as overlords in southern Russia continued for more than two centuries to affect and condition Russian development.

THE EVOLUTION OF JAPAN

The geography of Japan. In the mountainous Japanese archipelago of over three thousand islands, only four are relatively large: Honshu, Hokkaido, Shikoku, and Kyushu (see map, p. 183). The oceanic sides of Kyushu and Honshu receive abundant rain and are warmed by the Japan Current (the Pacific's analog to the Gulf Stream); here have been the centers of Japanese life, past and present. Earthquakes, typhoons, and tidal waves are frequent catastrophes; yet the Japanese in all ages have expressed love for their native land and a sensitive appreciation of its scenic beauties.

Japan's distance from the major centers of older continental cultures has meant that while there have been crucial periods of close cultural borrowing (usually based on Japanese initiative), there have also been long periods of relatively isolated development. Japanese culture has been notably homogeneous, partly because in historic times there were no notable additions of new peoples—nothing equivalent to the British Isles' successive experience of Romans, Angles, Saxons, Danes, and Normans.

Origins of the Japanese people. In prehistoric times there must have been many strands of migration, particularly from Northeast Asia and the Asian mainland by way of Korea and from Southeast Asia and its adjacent islands by way of the island chain south of Japan. No precise theories concerning the origins of the Japanese people are possible, but the evidence points to a mixed origin. In time there developed a common ethnic community—predominantly Mongoloid though darker and hairier than Mongoloid types on the Asian mainland—with a single basic language belonging to the same Altaic family as Korean.

Early Japanese society. In ancient times the mountainous islands of Japan facilitated the growth of numerous small tribal states, each ruled by a hereditary chieftain who claimed descent from a tribal deity. According to Japanese folklore, the first emperor of Japan—Jimmu Tenno—descended from the Sun Goddess and became emperor in 660 B.C. Ever since, the same family has reigned in Japan, and thus the Japanese claim with justice to have the oldest unbroken dynastic line in the world. Historians believe that the ruling family of Japan originated with the most important tribal group —the Yamato clan—which occupied a fertile plain on Honshu.

The religion of the Japanese, known as *Shinto*, or "Way of the Gods," included the worship of forces and objects of nature and of ancestral spirits. With the growth of Yamato power, Shinto centered primarily on the Sun Goddess as the divine ancestress of the Yamato and, eventually, of all the Japanese people.

Agriculture was the foundation of the economy, with the clan rulers and nobles controlling the land. With the clans engaged in constant struggles for land, warfare was the order of the day. The rigid social structure was well suited for purposes of warfare; the subservient lower orders had to cater to the warrior nobles and their divinely descended chieftain. Thus the warrior in Japan has from earliest times tended to enjoy a social position and political power greater than that of his Chinese counterpart.

During the first few centuries A.D. the Yamato clan extended its power in central Japan. Its chieftain began to regard himself as a kind of emperor, while the chieftains of clans brought under the control of the Yamato attached themselves to the imperial court. Still, however, the Yamato had only nominal suzerainty over some of the more powerful clans.

Influence of China. While the Japanese archipelago is sufficiently removed from the Asian mainland to make invasion extremely difficult, it is close enough to allow commercial and cultural contacts. Thus much of Japan's history is the story of the influx of external ideas and institutions and adaption by the Japanese to form a unique culture pattern. During the Han dynasty (202 B.C.-220 A.D.) Chinese rule was extended to part of Korea, and elements of Chinese culture were transmitted from there to Japan. In the succeeding centuries the influx of Chinese and Korean artisans, potters, weavers, painters, and farmers enriched Japanese culture. In addition, Chinese medicine and military science were introduced and the Chinese calendar adopted. Educated scribes brought to Japan the Chinese language with its character script and also the riches of Chinese literature. Transplanted from Korea in the

sixth century A.D., Buddhism was promoted by the rulers both as a means of weakening the clans with their allegiance to native Shinto and as a vehicle for the importation of Chinese ways and ideas.

The Taika reform: emulation of China. Faced by continued clan power and strife, the emperor and his advisers turned to T'ang China, probably the world's best-governed state in the seventh century, as a model for reforms that would change Japan from a clan and tribal society to a strongly centralized state. Inaugurated in 646, this "Great reform" (Taika) created a centralized bureaucracy and adopted the T'ang system of landholding and taxation. Law codes of the Chinese type were also drawn up. The Japanese state slowly began to take on the image of the T'ang government. Unlike the Chinese model, the emperor of Japan was claimed to be a divine personage and given the title of *Tenno* (heaven sovereign) so that rebellion against the throne constituted a religious crime. A court

aristocracy was set up where officials owed their positions to imperial appointment which quickly became hereditary.

The Fujiwara regents (857-1160). In 784 the capital was removed from Nara, where a Chinese-type court had been established in 710, and ten years later settled upon Kyoto— then called Heian-kyo—where it remained until 1868. The early centuries at Kyoto are identified politically as the Fujiwara period.

The Fujiwara family had been prominent in the government at Nara and soon rose to dominate the imperial government at Kyoto. Holding vast provincial estates, this family acquired so much power that the emperors were reduced to the status of puppet rulers whose wives were chosen for them from Fujiwara women. Once a royal son had been born, the emperor would frequently be forced to abdicate and retire to a Buddhist monastery, leaving a Fujiwara grandfather or uncle to rule the country as regent for the new infant emperor. Between the ninth and twelfth centuries, the tradition was thus established that the emperor reigned but did not rule, for his powers were delegated to hereditary officials of an aristocratic civil bureaucracy.

At Kyoto, Japanese culture, hitherto an unashamed imitation of Chinese culture, began to develop its own distinctive character. A refined appreciation of beauty in all its forms emerged from the gay, sophisticated ceremonial of Fujiwara court life, in which women played a major role. This preoccupation with the esthetic inspired a sudden flowering of literature and art that established the classic canons of Japanese artistic tradition.

In time the hereditary bureaucracy of the Fujiwara grew inefficient and the government became impoverished. Taxable property steadily decreased, due to the exemption of temple lands and of estates that originally had been given to officials as payment for their services and which then remained hereditary. Eventually most of the land in the kingdom ceased to be a source of revenue for the imperial government.

The bankruptcy of the government finances was accompanied by an increase of disorder and lawlessness in the provinces.

To protect their estates, the provincial lords hired bands of professional soldiers, and a feudal society began to develop. By the twelfth century, power and authority had shifted from the civil aristocracy to a military nobility, who were destined to dominate Japanese history for the next seven centuries.

The Kamakura shogunate and the samurai. After the two leading military clans had battled from one end of the country to the other—a brutal struggle celebrated in present-day Japanese movies, television series, and historical fiction—one of Japan's outstanding soldier-statesmen, Yoritomo of the Minamoto clan, emerged victorious in 1185. He soon forced the emperor to grant him the office of *shogun* (generalissimo) and effectively ruled Japan through a feudal hierarchy of warrior nobility. From his residence at Kamakura, Yoritomo appointed constables and stewards in every province to prevent rebellion. Although he continued to pay the utmost respect to the emperor and governed at a discreet distance from the imperial court at Kyoto, the shogun, not the emperor, was the real ruler in Japan.

Following Yoritomo's death in 1199, control passed to the leaders of the Hojo clan who, copying the Fujiwara technique of rule, governed in the name of puppet shoguns. The outstanding event in the Hojo period was the repulse of invasions by Kublai Khan of Mongol China in 1274 and 1281, the only such external attacks the Japanese experienced until World War II. On both occasions nature in the form of a typhoon (thenceforth called *Kamikaze*, or "the Divine Wind") aided the Japanese by shattering the invading armadas.

The establishment of the shogunate gave prominence to the growing strength and importance of the *samurai* or *bushi*, the warrior nobility. Official recognition was now given to *Bushido* ("The way of the warrior"), the unwritten *samurai* code of conduct that resembled the western code of chivalry, but lacked its religious inspiration and idealization of women. This stern code was instilled in childhood with such injunctions as:

What a coward to cry for a little pain! What will you do when your arm is cut off in battle, or when, for the sake of honor, you must rip your stomach open with your sword?[7]

Stressing courage, fortitude, loyalty, and discipline, the code of *Bushido* approved the custom of ceremonial suicide—*seppuku*—which is generally known to westerners as *hara-kiri*. By means of *seppuku*, a warrior could atone for his crimes, escape disgrace if he had "lost face," or prove his loyalty to his lord.

The *samurai* spirit infused and strengthened the tightly knit system of noble privilege, military government, and national loyalty. It persisted long after the overthrow of the shogunate in 1868—until, in fact, the defeat of Japan in World War II.

Joined with the *samurai* spirit was Shinto's glorification of the nation and the emperor's sacred position, together with Zen Buddhism's stress on strict mental and physical discipline as the means of achieving enlightenment. Imported from China late in the twelfth century, the Zen sect discarded not only emphasis on ritual and learning but also the simple piety and devotionalism of the savioristic sects of Buddhism that were followed by the humbler folk.

The Ashikaga shogunate. In 1333 Kamakura, the seat of the shogunate since its establishment in 1192, was destroyed by the Ashikaga family, which succeeded in founding a new shogunate five years later with headquarters at the imperial city of Kyoto. The Ashikaga shoguns failed to establish effective control over the other great barons (*daimyos*) and the *samurai* retainers, and the whole country drifted into disorder. By 1500 Japanese society was completely feudalized in a fashion comparable to western Europe during the same period.

SUMMARY

At the very time when Europe was beset by the tribulations following the collapse of the Graeco-Roman world, Asia was being enriched by what were probably its most splendid centuries of cultural development. The first of these centuries saw the emer-

This Japanese Buddhist temple guardian figure illustrates both the unusual nature of Japanese Buddhism and the more salient aspects of Kamakura sculpture. Kamakura sculpture, influenced by contemporaneous Chinese Sung art, abounded in vivid realism.

gence of a golden age in India. With the Guptas, the zenith of Hindu culture was reached. Artists produced paintings of contemporary life and sculpture characterized by dignity and restraint; the Gupta poet Kalidasa wrote dramas which have been compared favorably with those of Shakespeare. In mathematics, the so-called Arabic numerals, the decimal system, and many of the basic elements of algebra came into use; and there were important discoveries in chemistry and medicine. So powerful was Gupta civilization that it diffused to many parts of Asia, thereby raising the cultural level of a large segment of mankind.

The Gupta age was followed in India by a period of internal dissolution and external invasion, culminating in the subjugation of the country by the forces of an uncompromisingly antagonistic religious culture, Islam. The consequences of that impact were in our own century to split the Indian subcontinent into two separate states: India and Pakistan.

China's outstanding achievement was the successful re-creation of a unitary centralized state on classical lines that had no analogy in India or the West. Barbarians were domesticated in the T'ang period, which also saw a rich flowering of poetry, painting, and sculpture, and the invention of printing.

The Sung period, despite its weakness in dealing with barbarian states, brought to perfection the bureaucratic civil service system, saw Buddhism lose ground to a secular Neo-Confucian philosophy among the upper classes, and refined many traditional arts and crafts, especially painting and ceramics. The invention of explosive powder for warfare, the magnetic compass, and paper money bear witness to the range of Chinese creative ability.

The short period of Mongol rule in China, through briefly uniting China with the West by trade routes, confirmed the growing Chinese tendency to be contemptuous of foreign ways and to accept despotic rule. Economic disorders and popular rebellion ended the Mongols' regime in China sooner than in other parts of their far-flung empire.

Japan was brought within the world of civilized communities by impulses radiating from the T'ang. The Japanese blended continental forms of government, social organization, religion, and the arts with their own native traits. They preferred patterns of hereditary aristocratic privilege to the social mobility found in China. Embracing Buddhism, they also retained their native Shinto in both public life and popular cult. While China was perfecting its centralized civilian administrative system, Japan was increasingly divided by the controls and ideals of a hereditary feudal military nobility.

SUGGESTIONS FOR READING

Sir Percival Spear, **India: A Modern History,** rev. ed., (Univ. of Michigan, 1972) contains one of the best introductory accounts of Gupta India and the coming of the Muslims. R. C. Majumdar and A. D. Pulsaker, eds., **The Classic Age** (Verry), Vol. III of **The History and Culture of the Indian Peoples** is the most comprehensive history of the Gupta period. See also B. G. Gokhale, **Samudra Gupta** (Asia, 1962).

For a well-illustrated account of the influence of India's art on neighboring countries, see B. Rowland, **The Art and Architecture of India*** (Penguin, 1971).

For the Islamic impact upon India the following are authoritative: K. S. Lal, **Twilight of the Sultanate** (Asia); and S. M. Ikram, **Muslim Civilization in India** (Columbia).

For the expansion of Hindu culture see D. G. Hall, **History of South-East Asia,*** 3rd ed. (St. Martin's, 1968); and G. Coedes, **The Indianized States of Southeast Asia** (East-West Center Press, 1975).

C. P. Fitzgerald, **China: A Short Cultural History,*** 3rd ed., (Praeger) contains an excellent account of the intellectual and artistic activities of the T'ang and Sung periods. See also John Meskill, **An Introduction to Chinese Civilization*** (Heath, 1973).

An excellent biographical study of a leading personality under the T'ang is C. P. Fitzgerald, **Son of Heaven: A Biography of Li Shih-min, Founder of the T'ang Dynasty** (AMS Pr.). The lives and works of the two greatest T'ang poets are treated authoritatively in A. Waley, **The Poetry and Career of Li Po: 701-762 A.D.** (Humanities); and W. Hung, **Tu Fu, China's Greatest Poet,** 2 vols. (Russell, 1969).

T. F. Carter and L. C. Goodrich, **The Invention of Printing in**

China and Its Spread Westward (Ronald) is the best detailed study. E. Kracke, **Civil Service in Early Sung China, 960-1067** (Harvard) is useful for an understanding of the Chinese political system.

John Meskill, **Wang An-Shih: Practical Reformer?*** (Heath) is an introduction, through readings and discussion, to the greatest premodern Chinese social theorist. See also H. R. Williamson, **Wang An-Shih: Chinese Statesman and Educationalist of the Sung Dynasty,** 2 vols. (Hyperion, 1973).

L. Kwanten, **Imperial Nomads: A History of Central Asia, 500-1500** (Univ. of Pennsylvania, 1979), is excellent and up to date on the Mongols.

Jacques Gernet, **Daily Life in China on the Eve of the Mongol Invasion*** (Stanford) has vivid descriptions of all facets of life, as does his **Daily Life in China in the Thirteenth Century** (Macmillan).

L. Olschki, **Marco Polo's Asia** (Univ. of Calif., 1960) is an exhaustive study of the life and times of Marco Polo. See also the same author's **Marco Polo's Precursors** (Octagon, 1971); and Henry Hart, **Marco Polo: Venetian Adventurer** (Univ. of Oklahoma).

G. B. Sansom, **A History of Japan,** 3 vols., (Stanford Univ., 1958-1963) is the best history in English. Also extremely valuable is E. O. Reischauer and J. K. Fairbank, **East Asia: Tradition and Transformation** (Houghton Mifflin, 1973). E. O. Reischauer, **The United States and Japan*** (Compass) is a synthesis of modern scholarship on Japanese history and culture. The relinking of East and West under the *Pax Tatarica* is treated in G. F. Hudson, **Europe and China** (Gordon Pr., 1976).

*Indicates a less expensive paperbound edition.

CHAPTER 8

The Rise and Fall of the Carolingian Empire; Feudalism and the Manorial System: 500-1050

Europe's Search for Stability

INTRODUCTION. We last surveyed the fortunes of Europe at a crucial turning point in western civilization—the fifth century (see Chapter 5). The mighty Roman Empire in the West was breaking apart under the pressure of incoming Germanic tribes, and unity and stability gave way to fragmentation and disorder. What was the future of western Europe to be?

The first indication of the new forms that life and politics would take in the West came from the Germanic Franks in alliance with the Church. In the single century from 714 to 814, covering the reigns of the Frankish rulers from Charles Martel to Charlemagne, the Carolingian House of the Franks gave Europe an interim of stability and progress. A great empire was fashioned, Christianity was extended to barbarian tribes, and law and order were maintained.

This accomplishment of the Carolingians was premature, however. Charlemagne's empire could not endure, partly because it lacked the economic basis that had supported the Romans. By the ninth century

Muslim conquests had cut off what remained of European trade in the Mediterranean; inland trade shriveled up and urban life almost disappeared. In addition, the empire had no strong administrative machinery to compensate for the weak Carolingian rulers who followed the dominating figure of Charlemagne on the throne; the empire disintegrated amid civil wars and invasions.

Out of the ruins of the Carolingian empire emerged a new form of government known as feudalism. Based on local authority, feudalism was a poor and primitive substitute for a powerful, comprehensive central government; but it was better than no authority at all, and it survived for several hundred years. Also appropriate to the times was the rural, self-sufficient economy known as the manorial system. In sum, the poverty and localism of western Europe in the tenth century contrasts sharply with the contemporary societies of Byzantium and Islam.

NEW EMPIRE IN THE WEST

The kingdom of the Franks under Clovis. In the blending of the Roman and Germanic peoples and cultures, the Franks played an especially significant part. The kingdom of the Franks was not only the most enduring of all the Germanic states established in the West, but it became, with the active support of the Church, the center of the new Europe that arose upon the ruins of the western Roman empire.

Before the Germanic invasions the several tribes that made up the Franks lived along the east bank of the Rhine close to the North Sea. Late in the fourth century the Franks began a slow movement south and west across the Rhine into Gaul. By 481 they occupied the northern part of Gaul as far as the old Roman city of Paris, and in this year Clovis I of the Merovingian House became ruler of one of the petty Frankish kingdoms. By the time of his death in 511, Clovis had united the Franks into a single kingdom that stretched southward to the Pyrenees.

Clovis achieved his goal with the aid of an arsenal of weapons that included marriage alliances, treachery, assassination, and religion. As a first step, Clovis allied himself with other petty Frankish kings to dispose of Syagrius, the last Roman general in Gaul. The victor then turned against his Frankish allies and subdued them.

According to the sixth-century Gallo-Roman bishop and historian Gregory of Tours, whose *History of the Franks* is the fullest account of any Germanic people, Clovis became converted to Christianity in 496 as a result of a battle against the Alemanni, a pagan Germanic tribe whose name became the French word for Germany, *Allemagne*. On the verge of being defeated, Clovis called upon Christ for help:

"For I have called on my gods, but I find they are far from my aid. . . . Now I call on Thee. I long to believe in Thee. Only, please deliver me from my adversaries."[1]

Clovis won the battle and was baptized together with his whole army. He became the only orthodox Christian ruler in the West, for the other Germanic tribes were either pagan or embraced the heretical form of Christianity known as Arianism (see pp. 128, 242).

The conversion of the Franks must be considered a decisive event in European history. Ultimately it led to an alliance of the Franks and the papacy, and immediately it assured Clovis the loyalty of the Gallo-Roman bishops, the leaders of the native Christian population of Gaul. This was a political advantage not open to the heretical Arian Visigothic and Burgundian kings. Thus with the help of the native population of Gaul, Clovis was able to expand his realm in the name of Christian orthodoxy.

In 507 Clovis attacked the Visigoths, who ruled Gaul south of the Loire River and all of Spain (see map, p. 137). "Verily it grieves my soul," Clovis told his troops, "that these Arians should hold a part of Gaul."[2] The Visigothic king was killed, and his people abandoned most of their Gallic territory. Clovis died four years later at the age of forty-five—a ripe old age for a barbarian. Although never hardly more than a Germanic chieftain, he had created France.

Decline of the Merovingians. Clovis' sons and grandsons conquered the Burgundian kingdom and extended the Frankish domain to the Mediterranean and further into Germany. At the same time, however, the Merovingian House began to decay from inner weaknesses. The Germanic practice of treating the kingdom as personal property and dividing it among all the king's sons resulted in constant and bitter civil war. The royal heirs plotted murders and became adept at intrigue and treachery. The Merovingian princes also engaged in all manner of debaucheries, the least unpleasant of which was excessive drinking. Soon the Frankish state broke up into three separate kingdoms; in each, power was concentrated in the hands of the chief official of the royal household, the mayor of the palace, a powerful noble who desired to keep the king weak and ineffectual. The Merovingian rulers were mere puppets, the *rois fainéants* ("do-nothing kings").

A dark age. By the middle of the seventh century western Europe had lost most of the essential characteristics of Roman civilization. The Roman system of administration and taxation had completely collapsed, and the dukes and counts who represented the Merovingian king received no salary and usually acted on their own initiative in commanding the fighting men and presiding over the courts in their districts. International commerce had ceased except for a small-scale trade in luxury items carried on by adventurous Greek, Syrian, and Jewish traders, and the old Roman cities served mainly to house the local bishop and his retinue. The virtual absence of a middle class meant that society was composed of the nobility, a fusion through intermarriage of aristocratic Gallo-Roman and German families who owned and exercised authority over vast estates, and, at the other end of the social scale, the semi-servile *coloni*, who were bound to the land. These serfs included large numbers of formerly free German farmers.

The abstract transfigured Christ carved on a seventh-century Frankish tomb shows Jesus holding a spear. Even in a spiritual image, a militant Savior may have seemed most appropriate to the warlike Franks. (Courtesy of Rheinisches Landesmuseum, Bonn.)

Only about 10 percent of the peasant population of Gaul maintained a free status.

Coinciding with Merovingian decay, new waves of invaders threatened. A great movement of Slavic people from the area that is now Russia had begun about 500 A.D. (see p. 152). From this nucleus the Slavs fanned out, filling the vacuum left by the Germanic tribes when they pushed into the Roman Empire. By 650 the western Slavs had reached the Elbe River, across which they raided German territory. Another danger threatened western Europe from the south; in the late seventh century the Muslim Moors prepared to invade Spain from North Africa.

Charles Martel and the rise of the Carolingians. A new period dawned when Charles Martel became mayor of the palace in 714. His father, one of the greatest Frankish landowners, had eliminated all rival mayors, and Charles ruled a united Frankish kingdom in all but name. For the time being, however, the Merovingian kings were kept as harmless figureheads at the court.

Charles is best remembered for his victory over the Muslim invaders of Europe, which earned him the surname Martel, "The Hammer." In 711 an army of Moors from North Africa had invaded Spain, and by 718 the weak kingdom of the Visigoths had collapsed. With most of the peninsula under control, the Muslims began making raids across the Pyrenees. In 732 Charles Martel met them near Tours, deep within the Frankish kingdom. Muslim losses were heavy, and during the night they retreated toward Spain.

A major military reform coincided with the battle of Tours. For some time before this conflict, the effectiveness of mounted soldiers had been growing, aided by the introduction of the stirrup, which gave the mounted warrior a firm seat while wielding his weapons. To counteract the effectiveness of the quick-striking Muslim cavalry, Charles recruited a force of professional mounted soldiers whom he rewarded with sufficient land to enable each knight to maintain himself, his equipment, and a number of war horses. Such grants of land later became an important element in feudalism.

Pepin the Short. Charles Martel's son, Pepin the Short, who ruled from 741 to 768, was a worthy successor to his father. To legalize the regal power already being exercised by the mayors of the palace, he requested and received from the pope a ruling which stipulated that whoever had the actual power should be the legal ruler. In this maneuvering, St. Boniface (p. 242) was the intermediator, and in 751 Pepin was elected king by the Franks and crowned by St. Boniface. The last Merovingian was quietly shelved in a secluded monastery. In 754 the pope reaffirmed the usurpation by crossing the Alps and personally anointing Pepin, in the Old Testament manner, as the Chosen of the Lord.

Behind the pope's action lay his need for a powerful protector. In 751 the Lombards had conquered the exarchate of Ravenna, the seat of Byzantine government in Italy, and were demanding tribute from the pope and threatening to take Rome. Following the coronation, the pope secured Pepin's promise of armed intervention in Italy and his pledge to give the papacy the exarchate of Ravenna, once it was conquered. In 756 a Frankish army forced the Lombard king to relinquish his conquests, and Pepin officially conferred the exarchate of Ravenna upon the pope. Known as the "Donation of Pepin," the gift made the pope a temporal ruler over the Papal States, a strip of territory that extended diagonally from coast to coast (see map, p. 192).

The alliance between the Franks and the papacy affected the course of politics and of religion for centuries. It accelerated the separation of Latin from Greek Christendom by providing the papacy with a dependable western ally in place of the Byzantines, hitherto its only protector against the Lombards; it created the Papal States which played a major role in Italian politics until the late nineteenth century; and, by the ritual of anointment, it provided western kingship with a religious sanction that would in time contribute to the rise of monarchs strong enough to pose a threat to the papacy.

Charlemagne: the man and his conquests. Under Pepin's son, Charlemagne (Charles the Great), who ruled from 768 to 814, the

KINGDOM OF CLOVIS I

NORTH SEA

Elbe R.

Cologne

Tournai

Rhine R.

Seine R.

Paris

Strasbourg

Danube R.

Loire R.

Tours

Bordeaux

Garonne R.

Toulouse

Rhône R.

ALPS

Po R.

PYRENEES

MEDITERRANEAN SEA

Frankish state and the Carolingian House reached the summit of their power. Einhard, in his famous biography of Charlemagne, pictured his king as a natural leader of men—tall, physically strong, and a great horseman who was always in the van of the hunt. Although he was preeminently a successful warrior-king, leading his armies on yearly campaigns, Charlemagne also sought to provide an effective administration for his realm. In addition, he had great respect for learning and was proud of the fact that he could read Latin.

Taking advantage of feuds among the Muslims in Spain, Charlemagne sought to extend Christendom southward into that land. In 778 he crossed the Pyrenees with indifferent success. As the Frankish army headed back north, it aroused the antagonism of the Christian Basques, who attacked its rear guard. In the melee the Frankish leader, a gallant count named Roland, was killed. The memory of his heroism was later enshrined in the great medieval epic, the *Chanson de Roland (Song of Roland)*. On later expeditions the Franks drove the Muslims back to the Ebro River and established a frontier area known as the Spanish March, or Mark, centered around Barcelona. French immigrants moved into the area, later called Catalonia, giving it a character distinguishable from the rest of Spain.

Charlemagne conquered the Bavarians and the Saxons, the last of the independent Germanic tribes. It took thirty-two campaigns to subdue the staunchly pagan Saxons, who lived between the Rhine and Elbe rivers. Charlemagne divided Saxony into bishoprics, built monasteries, and proclaimed harsh laws against paganism. Eating meat during Lent, cremating the dead (an old pagan practice), and pretending to be baptized were offenses punishable by death.

Like his father before him, Charlemagne intervened in Italian politics. Expansionist ambition drove the Lombard king to invade again the territories of the papacy. At the behest of the pope, Charlemagne defeated the Lombards in 774 and proclaimed himself their king. While in Italy, he cemented his father's alliance with the Church by confirming the Donation of Pepin.

The interior of the Chapel of Charlemagne in Aachen. Built as his tomb, it was modeled in an octagonal design after San Vitale in Ravenna and imported materials from Italy were used in the construction. The interior shows a conscious attempt to revert to arched Roman forms; it emphasized Charlemagne's desire to initiate an artistic renaissance.

The empire's eastern frontier was continually threatened by the Avars, Asiatic nomads related to the Huns, and the Slavs. In six campaigns Charlemagne decimated the Avars and then set up his own military province in the valley of the Danube to guard against any possible future plundering by eastern nomads. Called the East Mark, this territory later became Austria.

Charlemagne's coronation in Rome. One of the most important single events in Charlemagne's reign took place on Christmas Day in the year 800. The previous year the unruly Roman nobility had ousted the pope, charging him with moral laxity. Charlemagne came to Rome and restored the pope to his office. Then, at the Christmas service while Charlemagne knelt before the altar at St. Peter's, the pope placed a crown on his head amid the cries of the assembled congregation: "To Charles Augustus crowned of God, great and pacific Emperor of the Romans, long life and victory!"

This ceremony demonstrated that the memory of the Roman Empire still survived as a vital tradition in Europe and that there was a strong desire to reestablish political unity. In fact, Charlemagne previously named his capital at Aix-la-Chapelle (Aachen)

CHARLEMAGNE'S EMPIRE

- At His Accession, 768
- At His Death, 814

ATLANTIC OCEAN

IRELAND
NORTHUMBRIA
WALES MERCIA EAST ANGLIA
WESSEX ESSEX
SUSSEX

Magdeburg
Aix-la-Chapelle (Aachen)
Fulda
Rhine R.
Elbe R.
Oder R.
Prague
Seine R.
Paris
Verdun
TRIBUTARY SLAVIC STATES
Loire R.
CAROLINGIAN
EMPIRE
Tours
St. Gall
EAST MARCH
Danube R.
Lyons
Rhone R.
AVARS
A L P S
KINGDOM OF ASTURIAS
Bordeaux
PYRENEES
SPANISH MARCH
Ebro R.
Po R.
KINGDOM OF ITALY
Ravenna
PAPAL STATES
KHANATE OF BULGARIA
UMAYYAD EMIRATE OF CORDOVA
Tagus R.
Toledo
Barcelona
CORSICA
Rome
DUCHY OF BENEVENTO
Constantinople
Cordova
SARDINIA
B Y Z A N T I N E   E M P I R E
MEDITERRANEAN SEA
Athens
SICILY
Carthage

0   200   400

"New Rome" and was about to take the title of emperor and revive the Roman empire in the West. By seizing the initiative and crowning Charlemagne by the Grace of God, the pope assumed a position of superiority as the maker of emperors. A future clash between these two powers was inevitable, but it was postponed by the collapse of both the empire and the papacy in the ninth and tenth centuries, which came to be known as the age of feudalism.

Charlemagne's administration. The extent of Charlemagne's empire was impressive. His territories included all of the western area of the old Roman Empire except Africa, Britain, southern Italy, and most of Spain (see map). Seven defensive provinces, or marks, protected the empire against hostile neighbors.

The Carolingian territories were divided into some three hundred administrative divisions, each under a count (*graf*) or, in the marks along the border, a margrave (*mark graf*). In addition, there were local military

officials, the dukes. In an effort to solve the problem of supervising the local officials, a problem that plagued all German rulers, Charlemagne issued an ordinance (capitulary) creating the *missi dominici*, the king's envoys. Pairs of these itinerant officials, usually a bishop and a lay noble, traveled throughout the realm to check on the local administration. To make the *missi* immune to bribes, they were chosen from men of high rank, were frequently transferred from one region to another, and no two of them were teamed for more than one year.

The Carolingian Renaissance. Charlemagne also fostered a revival of learning and the arts. His efforts in this area were destined to be far more lasting than his revival of the Roman Empire in the West, and they have prompted historians to speak of this period as one of cultural rebirth.

In 789 Charlemagne decreed that every monastery must have a school for the education of boys in "singing, arithmetic, and grammar." As he stated in a letter to the abbot of Fulda, Charlemagne was greatly concerned over the illiteracy of the clergy:

Since in these years there were often sent to us from divers monasteries letters in which . . . , owing to neglect of learning, the untutored tongue could not express [itself] without faultiness. Whence it came that we began to fear lest, as skill in writing was less, wisdom to understand the Sacred Scriptures might be far less than it ought rightly to be.[3]

At Aix-la-Chapelle, his capital, the emperor also sponsored a palace school for the education of the royal household and the stimulation of learning throughout the realm. Alcuin, an Anglo-Saxon scholar in charge of the school, began the arduous task of reviving learning by undertaking the first step of writing textbooks on grammar, spelling, rhetoric, and logic. "Ye lads," Alcuin exhorted his students, "whose age is fitted for reading, learn! The years go by like running water. Waste not the teachable days in idleness!"[4]

The reform of handwriting and the preservation of classical manuscripts were significant achievements of the Carolingian revival. Copyists labored in monasteries to preserve the classics of pagan and Christian thought with the result that the oldest manuscripts of most of the Latin classics that have come down to us date from the age of Charlemagne. The corrupt and almost illegible script of the Merovingian period was replaced by a more legible style of writing, known as Carolingian minuscule—"little letters," in contrast to the capitals used by the Romans—which became the foundation for the typeface still used in present-day printing.

At Aix-la-Chapelle Charlemagne also strove to recapture something of the grandeur of ancient Rome by building a stone palace church modeled after a sixth-century church in Ravenna. Its mosaics were probably the work of Byzantine artisans, and its marble columns were taken from ancient buildings in Rome and Ravenna.

Charlemagne's work on balance. Charlemagne must be considered one of the great constructive figures of world history. He extended Christian civilization in Europe, set up barriers against incursions of the Slav and Avar, and created a new Europe whose center was in the north rather than on the Mediterranean and in which a measure of law and order was again enforced after three centuries of disorder. Furthermore, his patronage of learning left a cultural heritage that later generations would build upon in producing a European civilization distinct from the Byzantine to the east and the Muslim to the south.

Charlemagne's empire afforded no more than a breathing space, however, for its territories were too vast and its nobility too powerful to be held together under existing conditions after the dominating personality of its creator had passed from the scene. Charlemagne had no standing army; his foot soldiers were essentially the old Germanic war band summoned to fight by its war leader, and his mounted warriors served him, as they had Charles Martel, in return for grants of land. Nor did Charlemagne have a bureaucratic administrative machine comparable to that of Roman times. The Frankish economy was agricultural and localized, and there was no system of taxation adequate to maintain an effective and permanent administration. Under Charlemagne's weak successors the empire disintegrated amid the confusion of civil wars and devastating new invasions. Progress toward an advanced civilization in the new Europe founded by Charlemagne was delayed for two centuries.

The division of the empire. Before his death in 814, Charlemagne himself, ignoring the pope, placed the imperial crown on the head of his only surviving son, Louis the Pious. Louis subsequently partitioned his realm among his sons, and bitter rivalry and warfare broke out among the brothers and their father. In 840 Louis the Pious died, a well-meaning man who was loved by the clergy, ignored by the nobility, and mistreated by his sons.

Strife continued among Louis' three surviving sons. Lothair, the elder, was opposed by the two younger—Louis the German and Charles the Bald. In 842 the younger brothers joined forces in the famous Strasbourg Oaths. The text of these oaths is significant in that one part was in an early form of French, the

both Latin and Teutonic cultures, and although it was divided in 870 between Charles and Louis, the area was disputed for centuries. Lorraine remained one of the cockpits of Europe, a land drenched with the blood of countless French and German peoples.

The rival Carolingian houses produced no strong leaders worthy of being called "Hammer" (Martel) or "Great"; instead, we find kings with such revealing names as Charles the Fat, Charles the Simple, Louis the Child, and Louis the Sluggard. The last of the East Frankish Carolingians died in 911. In West Frankland the nobles, ignoring the eighteen-year-old Carolingian prince, chose Odo, the count of Paris, as king in 887.

The new invasions. During the ninth and tenth centuries the remnants of Charlemagne's empire were also battered by new waves of invaders. Scandinavians attacked from the north, Muslims from the south, and a new wave of Asiatic nomads, the Magyars, struck from the east. Christian Europe had to fight for its life against these plundering and murdering raiders, who did far more damage to life and property than the Germanic invaders of the fifth century.

From bases in North Africa, Muslim corsairs in full command of the sea plundered the coasts of Italy and France. In 827 they began the conquest of Byzantine Sicily and southern Italy. From forts erected in southern France they penetrated far inland to attack the caravans of merchants in the Alpine passes. What trade still existed between Byzantium and western Europe, except for that of Venice and one or two other Italian towns, was now almost totally cut off, and the great inland sea became a Muslim lake.

The most widespread and destructive raiders came from Scandinavia. During the ninth and tenth centuries Swedes, Danes, and Norwegians—collectively known as Vikings—stormed out of their remote forests and fiords. The reason for this expansion is not clear. Some historians stress overpopulation and a surplus of young men. Other scholars view these raiders as defeated war bands expelled from their homeland by the gradual emergence of strong royal power. Still others see a clue in the fact that the Vikings had developed seaworthy ships ca-

other in German. The first could be understood by Charles' followers, who lived mainly west of the Rhine; the other by Louis' followers, who lived east of the Rhine. These oaths are evidence that the Carolingian empire was splitting into two linguistic parts—East Frankland, the forerunner of modern Germany, and West Frankland, or France.

In 843 the brothers met at Verdun, where they agreed to split the Carolingian lands three ways. Charles the Bald obtained the western part and Louis the German the eastern; Lothair, who retained the title of emperor, obtained an elongated middle kingdom which stretched a thousand miles from the North Sea to central Italy (see map).

The importance of the Treaty of Verdun is that it began the shaping of modern France and Germany by giving political recognition to the cultural and linguistic division shown in the Strasbourg Oaths. Lothair's middle kingdom soon collapsed into three major parts, Lorraine in the north and Burgundy and Italy in the south. Lorraine encompassed pable of carrying a hundred men and powered by long oars or by sail when the wind was favorable. Viking sailors also had developed expert sailing techniques; without benefit of the compass, they were able to navigate by means of the stars at night and the sun during the day.

The range of Viking expansion was amazing. The Vikings went as far as North America to the west, the Caspian Sea to the east, and the Mediterranean to the south. Few areas seemed immune from their lightning raids, which filled civilized Europeans with a fear that is reflected in a new prayer in the litany of the Church: "From the fury of the Northmen, O Lord deliver us."

Three main routes of Viking expansion can be identified. The outer path, which was followed principally by the Norwegians, swung westward to Ireland and the coast of Scotland. Between 800 and 850 Ireland was ravaged severely. Monasteries, the centers of the flourishing culture attained by the Irish Celts, were destroyed. By 875 the Norwegians were beginning to occupy remote Iceland, and it was here rather than in their homeland that the magnificent Norse sagas were preserved, little affected by either classical or Christian influences. During the tenth century the Icelandic Norsemen ventured on to Greenland and, later, to North America (see Chapter 18).

Another route, the eastern line, was followed chiefly by the Swedes, who went down the rivers of Russia as merchants and soldiers of fortune and, as has been described in Chapter 6, forged the nucleus of a Russian state.

The Danes took the middle passage, raiding England and the shores of Germany, France, and Spain. By the 870's they had occupied most of England north of the Thames. Also in the middle of the ninth century their fury broke upon the Continent, where their long boats sailed up the Rhine, Scheldt, Seine, and Loire. In particular the Danes devastated northwest France, destroying dozens of abbeys and towns. Unable to fend off the Viking attacks, the weak Carolingian king Charles the Simple arranged an epoch-making treaty with a Norse chieftain named Rollo in 911. This agreement created a Viking buffer state, later called Normandy, and recognized Rollo as duke and vassal of the French king. Like Viking settlers elsewhere, these Northmen, or Normans, soon adopted Christian civilization. By the eleventh century, as we shall see later, Normandy was a powerful duchy, and the Viking spirit of the Normans was producing the most vigorous crusaders, conquerors, and administrators in Europe.

Europe in 900. Europe's response to the invasions of the ninth and tenth centuries was not uniform. In England by 900 Viking occupation initiated a strong national reaction which soon led to the creation of a united English kingdom. Similarly, Germany in 919 reacted to the Magyar danger by installing the first of a new and able line of kings who went on to become the most powerful European monarchs since Charlemagne. The response to the invasions in France, however, is a different story.

The Viking attacks on France had the effect of accelerating the trend toward politi-

An example of the animal style common in the Celtic-Germanic art of the early Middle Ages, this wooden animal head of the early ninth century is the terminal of a post of a buried Viking ship found at Oseberg in southern Norway. It combines realistic details (nostrils, teeth, and gums) with the imaginative use of abstract geometric patterns derived from metalwork.

cal fragmentation that began under the Merovingians but was temporarily halted by the strong personal leadership provided by the Carolingians. When Charlemagne's weak successors were unable to cope with the incessant Viking assaults, people increasingly surrendered both their lands and their persons to the many counts, dukes, and other local lords in return for protection. The decline of trade further strengthened the aristocracy, whose large estates, or manors, became economically self-sufficient. In addition, the old Germanic levy of foot soldiers, who provided their own arms when called to battle, was dying out in favor of a professional force of heavily armed mounted knights, who received land grants from the king in return for military service.

Out of all these elements—the disintegration of central power, the need for protection, the decrease in the class of freemen, the rise of a largely independent landed aristocracy, and the creation of the mounted knight—new patterns of society, feudalism and the manorial system, took shape. Reaching their height in France during the tenth and eleventh centuries, feudalism and manorialism were the culmination of earlier trends that had been accelerated by the Viking attacks.

FEUDALISM

Nature and origins of feudalism. Feudalism can be defined as a type of government in which political power is exercised locally by private individuals rather than by the agents of a centralized state. It is often a transitional stage which follows the collapse of a unified political system; it serves as a stopgap until conditions permit the emergence of a centralized government. Feudalism has appeared in various areas and times in world history—in ancient Egypt and in modern Japan, for example—but the most famous of all feudal systems emerged in France following the collapse of Charlemagne's empire.

Fully developed feudalism was a fusion of three basic elements: (1) the personal element, called lordship or vassalage, by which one nobleman, the vassal, became the loyal follower of a stronger nobleman, the lord or suzerain; (2) the property element, called the fief (usually land), which the vassal received from his lord in order to enable him to fulfill the obligations of vassalage; and (3) the governmental element, meaning the private exercise of governmental functions over vassals and fiefs. The roots of these three elements run back to late Roman and early Germanic times.

By the fifth century the ability of the Roman emperor to protect his subjects had disappeared, and citizens had to depend on the patronage system, by which a Roman noble organized a group of less fortunate citizens as a personal bodyguard and in return looked after their wants and interests. A similar arrangement existed among the Germans—the war band or *comitatus*, described by Tacitus (see p. 133). Vassalage, the personal element in feudalism, arose from the combination of patronage and the *comitatus*.

The roots of the property element in feudalism, the fief, go back to Roman practices mainly. In the late Roman Empire the owners of great estates (*latifundia*) were steadily adding to their already extensive holdings. Unable to manage their tracts, the nobles granted the temporary use of portions to other people in exchange for dues and services. Such land was called a *beneficium*, or benefice (literally, a "benefit"). In late Merovingian times, when mounted warriors rather than old-style foot soldiers were needed to deal effectively with Muslim raiders from Spain, Charles Martel granted numerous benefices to compensate his mounted followers for this added expense. During the civil wars and foreign invasions of late Carolingian times, the competition among Charlemagne's successors for the available supply of mounted knights led not only to the wholesale granting of benefices but also to making the benefice hereditary. On the death of the vassal, the benefice now passed to his heir instead of reverting to the king. Hereditary benefices were commonly called fiefs.

The third basic element in feudalism, the exercise of governmental power by private individuals, also had antecedents in late Roman times. As the imperial government weakened, the powerful Roman landowners organized their own private armies to police their estates and fend off governmental agents, particularly tax collectors. The emperors also favored certain estates with grants of immunity from their authority, a practice which the Germanic kings often followed and which became the rule with Charlemagne's successors in their competitive efforts to fill their armies with mounted fief-holding vassals. And where immunity from the king's authority was not freely granted, it was often usurped.

With the coalescing of these three elements, feudalism can be said to have emerged as a definable—although highly complex and variable—governmental system in France by the end of the ninth century. To a greater or less degree the feudal system spread throughout most of western Europe, but our description of it applies particularly to the form it took in northern France.

The feudal hierarchy. In theory feudalism was a vast hierarchy. At the top stood the king, and theoretically all the land in his kingdom belonged to him. He kept large areas for his personal use (royal or crown lands) and, in return for the military service of a specified number of mounted knights, invested the highest nobles—such as dukes and counts (in England, earls)—with the remainder. Those nobles holding lands directly from the king were called tenants-in-chief. They in turn, in order to obtain the services of the required number of mounted warriors (including themselves) owed to the king, parceled out large portions of their fiefs to lesser nobles. This process, called *subinfeudation*, was continued until, finally, the lowest in the scale of vassals was reached—the single knight whose fief was just sufficient to support one mounted warrior.

Subinfeudation became a problem when a conflict of loyalties arose. Since the Count of Champagne, for example, was vassal to nine different lords, on whose side would he fight should two of his lords go to war against one another? This dilemma was partially solved by the custom of liege homage. When a vassal received his first fief, he pledged liege or prior homage to that lord. This obligation

was to have top priority over services that he might later pledge to other lords.

Except for the knight with a single fief, a nobleman was usually both a vassal and a lord. Even a king might be a vassal; John of England was vassal to King Philip of France for certain French lands, yet he in no way thought himself inferior to Philip.

By maintaining a king at the head of the hierarchy, feudalism kept intact the vestiges of monarchy, which would in time reassert itself and restore centralized government. As one historian put it, feudalism "contained in its bosom the weapons with which it would be itself one day smitten."[5]

Relation of lord and vassal: the feudal contract. Basic to feudalism was the personal bond between lord and vassal. In the ceremony known as the act of *homage*, the vassal knelt before his lord, or suzerain, and promised to be his "man." In the oath of fealty which followed, the vassal swore on the Bible or some other sacred object that he would remain true to his lord. Next, in the ritual of *investiture*, a lance, glove, or even a bit of straw was handed the vassal to signify his jurisdiction (not ownership) over the fief.

The feudal contract thus entered into by

Warfare was a normal occupation for gentlemen during the feudal age, and even the more brutal aspects of combat were not considered ignoble subjects for art.

lord and vassal was considered sacred and binding upon both parties. Breaking this tie of mutual obligations was considered a felony, because it was the basic agreement of feudalism and hence of early medieval society. The lord for his part was obliged to give his vassal protection and justice. The vassal's primary duty was military service. He was expected to devote forty days' service each year to the lord without payment. In addition, the vassal was obliged to assist the lord in rendering justice in the lord's court. At certain times, such as when he was captured and had to be ransomed, the lord also had the right to demand money payments, called *aids*. Unusual aids, such as defraying the expense of going on a crusade, could not be levied without the vassal's consent.

The lord also had certain rights, called feudal *incidents*, regarding the administration of the fief. These included *wardship*—the right to administer the fief during the minority of a vassal's heir—and *forfeiture* of the fief if a vassal failed to honor his feudal obligations.

Feudal warfare. The final authority in the feudal age was force, and the general atmosphere of the era was one of violence. Recalcitrant vassals frequently made war upon their suzerains. But warfare was also considered the normal occupation of the nobility, for success offered glory and rich rewards. If successful, warfare enlarged a noble's territory; and, if they produced nothing else, forays and raids kept a man in good mettle. To die in battle was the only honorable end for a spirited gentleman; to die in bed was a "cow's death."

The Church and feudalism. Another unhappy result of feudalism was the inclusion of the Church in the system. The unsettled conditions caused by the Viking and Magyar invasions forced Church prelates to enter into close relations with the only power able to offer them protection—the feudal barons in France and the kings in Germany. Bishops and abbots thus became vassals, receiving fiefs for which they were obligated to provide the usual feudal services. The papacy fared even worse; during much of the tenth and early eleventh centuries the papacy fell into decay after becoming a prize sought after by local Roman nobles.

On the positive side, however, the Church in time sought to influence for the better the behavior of the feudal warrior nobility. In addition to attempting to add Christian virtues to the code of knightly conduct called chivalry, which will be described later in this chapter, the Church sought to impose limitations on feudal warfare. In the eleventh century bishops inaugurated the Peace of God and Truce of God movements. The Peace of God banned from the sacraments all persons who pillaged sacred places or refused to spare noncombatants. The Truce of God established "closed seasons" on fighting: from sunset on Wednesday to sunrise on Monday and certain longer periods, such as Lent. These peace movements were generally ineffective, however.

Class structure. Medieval society conventionally consisted of three classes: the nobles, the peasants, and the clergy. Each of these groups had its own task to perform. The nobles were primarily fighters, belonging to an honored society distinct from the peasant workers—freemen and serfs. In an age of physical violence, society obviously would accord first place to the man with the sword rather than to the man with the hoe. The Church drew on both the noble and the peasant classes for the clergy. Although most higher churchmen were sons of nobles and held land as vassals under the feudal system, the clergy formed a class that was considered separate from the nobility and peasantry.

THE MANORIAL SYSTEM

The manor in relation to feudalism. Having discussed feudalism, the characteristic political system of the ninth, tenth, and eleventh centuries, let us turn to the economic organization of the period, the manorial system. The feudal system was the means whereby protection was obtained for society; the manor was the agency that provided the necessary food for society's members. Feudalism and the manorial system evolved independently, but they were intimately connected.

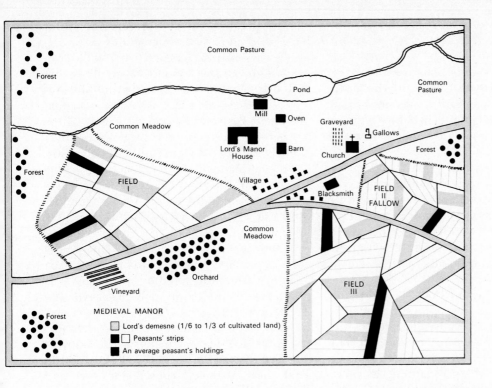

MEDIEVAL MANOR
- ☐ Lord's demesne (1/6 to 1/3 of cultivated land)
- ■☐ Peasants' strips
- ■ An average peasant's holdings

As the self-contained economic unit of early medieval life, the manor operated on a system of reciprocal rights and obligations based on custom. In return for protection, strips of arable land, and the right to use the nonarable common land, the peasant paid dues and worked on the lord's demesne. Under the three-field system, one third of the land lay fallow so that intensive cultivation did not exhaust the soil.

The term manorial system refers to the economic and social system that centered on the manors, the great estates whose origins go back to the Roman *latifundia* with their *coloni* workers (see p. 79). In Gaul, in particular, these estates survived the Germanic invasions. During the early Middle Ages they were held either by the descendants of their Roman owners or by Frankish kings, nobles, and the Church. The medieval serf was the direct descendant of the Roman *colonus* who worked the land, paid rent in kind, and could not leave the estate without the owner's permission.

Agriculture, the chief function of the manor. The manor varied in size from one locality to another. A small one might contain only about a dozen households. Since the allotment to each family averaged about thirty acres, the small manors probably included about 350 acres of tillable land, not counting the meadows, woods, wasteland, and the lord's demesne land. A large manor might contain fifty families and a total area of 5000 acres.

The center of the manor was the village, with the thatched cottages of the peasants grouped together along one street. Around each cottage was a space large enough for a vegetable patch, chicken yard, haystack, and stable. An important feature of the landscape was the village church, together with the priest's house and the burial ground. The lord's dwelling might be a castle or a more modest manor house.

Distribution of the land. Every manor contained two types of land, arable and nonarable. Part of the arable land, called the *demesne*, was reserved for the lord and was cultivated for him by his serfs. The remainder of the arable land was held by the villagers. The nonarable land, consisting of meadow, wood, and wasteland, was used in common by the villagers and the lord.

From one third to two fifths of the arable land was given over to the lord's demesne. The demesne might be either sharply set off from the tenures of the villagers or distributed among the lands of the tenants. The land not held in demesne was allotted among the villagers under the open-field system, whereby the fields were subdivided into strips. The strips, each containing about an acre, were separated by narrow paths of uncultivated turf. The serf's holding was not all in one plot, for all soil throughout the manor was not equally fertile, and a serious attempt was made to give each of the villagers land of the same quality.

Each tenant was really a shareholder in the village community, not only in the open fields but also in the meadow, pasture, wood, and wastelands. His rights in these common lands were determined by the number of acres he held in the open fields.

The wooded land was valuable as a place to graze pigs, the most common animal on the manor. Again the tenant was limited in the number of pigs that he might turn loose there. The tenant could also gather dead wood in the forest, but cutting down green wood was prohibited unless authorized by the lord.

Medieval farming methods. It is dangerous to generalize too sweepingly about agricultural methods, because differences in locality, fertility of soil, crop production, and other factors resulted in a variety of farming methods. But if we study farming as practiced in northwestern Europe, we can discover some common factors. The implements which the peasants used were extremely crude; the plow was a cumbersome instrument with heavy wheels, often requiring as many as eight oxen to pull it. (By the twelfth century plow horses were common.) There were also crude harrows, sickles, beetles for breaking up clods, and flails for threshing. Inadequate methods of farming soon exhausted the soil. It has been estimated that the average yield per acre was only six to eight bushels of wheat, a fourth of the modern yield.

In classical times farmers had learned that soil planted continually with one crop rapidly deteriorated. To counteract this, they employed a two-field system, whereby half of the arable land was planted while the other half lay fallow to recover its fertility. Medieval farmers learned that wheat or rye could be planted in the autumn as well as in the spring. As a result, by the ninth century they were dividing the land into three fields, with one planted in the fall, another in the spring, and the third left lying fallow. This system not only kept more land in production but also required less plowing in any given year.

Administration of the manor. Though the lord might live on one of his manors, each manor was administered by such officials as the steward, the bailiff, and the reeve. The steward was the general overseer who supervised the business of all his lord's manors and presided over the manorial court. It was the bailiff's duty to supervise the cultivation of the lord's demesne, collect rents, dues, and fines, and inspect the work done by the peasants. The reeve was the "foreman" of the villagers, chosen by them and representing their interests.

In status and function the various social classes that made up the manor community differed not only from locality to locality but from period to period. However, they can be roughly divided into three major categories: the lord and his officials, the free peasants, and the unfree peasants (serfs).

There often were freemen on the manor, however small a proportion of its population they may have represented. They possessed personal freedom and were not subject to the

In this fourteenth-century illumination peasants reap grain under the direction of the reeve.

same demands as the unfree peasants. The freeman did not have to work in the lord's fields himself but could send substitutes. He paid rent for his holding and, if he wanted to leave, could locate a new tenant for the land, provided the transfer took place in open court and the new man was acceptable to the lord. Aside from these privileges, however, the freeman was little different from the unfree man. His strips in the open field adjoined those of the servile worker, and he lived in a cottage in the same village.

The unfree peasants, the serfs, were bound to the manor and could not leave without the lord's consent. Serfdom was a hereditary status; the children of a serf were attached to the soil as their parents were. The lord of the manor was bound by the force of custom to respect certain rights of his serfs. So long as they paid their dues and services, serfs could not be evicted from their hereditary holdings. Although a serf could not appear in court against his lord or a freeman, he could appeal to the manor court against any of his fellows.

Whereas the peasants found their economic, political, legal, and social life in the manor, to the lord the manor was essentially a source of income from three obligations imposed on the peasantry: (1) services in the form of labor, (2) dues levied on the peasant, and (3) manorial monopolies.

The most important service was *week-work*. The peasant had to donate two or three days' work each week to the lord. The week-work included such jobs as repairing roads or bridges or carting manure to the fields. Because the lord's demesne "had always to be plowed first, sowed first, and reaped first," the peasant also had to perform extra *boon-work* at these times.

Various dues or payments—usually in produce, in money if it was available—were made to the lord. The *taille* (or tallage), a tax on whatever property a peasant managed to accumulate, was the most common. It was levied on all peasants one or more times a year. Another burdensome tax was imposed when a peasant died; before a son could inherit his father's cottage and strips, the lord claimed the best beast or movable possession as inheritance tax.

In addition to services and dues, the lord profited from certain monopolies. He operated the only grain mill, oven for baking bread, and wine and cider press on the manor, and he collected a toll each time these services were needed.

The weary round of peasant life. On the manors of the Middle Ages the margin between starvation and survival was narrow, and the life of the peasant was not easy. Famines were common; warfare and wolves were a constant threat; grasshoppers, locusts, caterpillars, and rats repeatedly destroyed the crops. Men and women alike had to toil long hours in the fields. A medieval poem vividly describes the life of a peasant family:

I saw a poor man o'er the plough bending. . . .
All befouled with mud, as he the plough followed. . . .
His wife walked by him with a long goad, . . .
Barefoot on the bare ice, so that the blood followed.
And at the field's end lay a little bowl,
And therein lay a little child wrapped in rags,
And twain of two years old upon another side;
And all of them sang a song that sorrow was to hear,
They cried all a cry, a sorrowful note,
And the poor man sighed sore, and said 'Children, be still.'[6]

The difficulties of the peasant's life were reflected in his home, a cottage with mud walls, clay floor, and thatched roof. The fire burned on a flat hearthstone in the middle of the floor; and unless the peasant was rich enough to afford a chimney, the smoke escaped through a hole in the roof. The windows had no glass and were stuffed with straw in the winter. Furnishings were meager, consisting usually of a table, a kneading trough for dough, a cupboard, and a bed, often either a heap of straw or a box filled with straw, which served the entire family. Pigs and chickens wandered about the cottage continually, while the stable was frequently under the same roof, next to the family quarters.

The peasant, despite his hard, monotonous life, was not without a few pleasures. Wrestling was exceedingly popular, as were cock-fighting, a crude type of football, and fighting with quarterstaves, in which both the con-

Into this medieval print the artist has crowded the whole life of the manorial village. A hunting party is shown in the foreground, the ladies riding behind the knights. The castle, with its moat and drawbridge, dominates the countryside. In the midst of the village houses, which are surrounded by a fence, stands the church. Note also the mill and the millrace at the left and what appears to be a wine or cider press to the right of the mill. In the upper right corner a serf is using the heavy plow common to northwestern Europe (the artist has shown only two draft animals). The nets were apparently set to catch hares, and below them stands a wayside shrine. Visible on the horizon is a gibbet with buzzards wheeling over it.

testants stood an excellent chance of getting their heads bashed in. Around the porch of the parish church the peasants often congregated to dance and sing on the numerous holy days. The Church preached in vain against "ballads and dancings and evil and wanton songs and such-like lures of the Devil." The peasants refused to give up these amusements, a small enough compensation for the constant exploitation they suffered. Yet medieval serfs also possessed a large degree of economic security, and in this respect they were perhaps better off than the factory workers of the early nineteenth century.

THE AGE OF CHIVALRY

Chivalry in feudal society. One of the most interesting and significant legacies of the Middle Ages is its concept of chivalry, a code which governed the behavior of all truly perfect and gentle knights. Such a paragon was Sir Galahad—"the gentlest man that ever ate in hall among the ladies." Early chivalry,

however, which emerged during the heyday of feudalism in the eleventh century, was rough and masculine. It stressed the warrior virtues that were essential in a feudal society: prowess in combat, courage, and loyalty to one's lord and fellow warriors. The virtues of early chivalry are best expressed in early medieval epics, such as the eleventh-century *Song of Roland*, where they are summed up in the words of the hero who, surrounded by foes, cries: "Better be dead than a coward be called."

The later chivalry of the twelfth and thirteenth centuries contained new virtues which the Church and the ladies sought to impose upon the generally violent and uncouth behavior of feudal warriors. The chivalric romances that began to be written in the twelfth century mirror these new influences. In Chrétien de Troyes' *Perceval*, for example, the hero's mother sends him off to be dubbed a knight with these words of advice:

Serve ladies and maidens if you would be honored by all. If you capture a lady, do not annoy her. Do nothing to displease her. He has much from a maiden who kisses her if she agrees to give a kiss. You will avoid greater intimacy if you wish to be guided by me. . . . Above all I wish to beg you to go to churches and abbeys and pray to our Lord so that the world may do you honor and you may come to a good end.[7]

In sum, fully developed chivalry was a combination of three elements: warfare, religion, and reverence toward women. It required the knight to fight faithfully for his lord, champion the Church and aid the humble, and honor womankind. Unfortunately, practice often differed from theory. The average knight was more superstitious than religious, and he continued to fight, plunder, and abuse women, especially those of the lower class. The ideals of chivalry, however, have affected manners in later eras, and even today they color our concept of a gentleman.

Women in general shared the characteristics of the menfolk. They lived in a crude and often brutal age devoid of many of our modern refinements. Like their husbands, medieval women were heavy drinkers and eaters. It is said that a common compliment to a member of the fair sex was that she was "the fairest woman who ever drained a bottle."

Training for knighthood. From the time they were boys, men of the nobility underwent a rigid training for knighthood. At the age of seven, a boy was sent to the household of a relative, a friend, or the father's suzerain. There he became a page, learning the rudiments of religion, manners, hawking, and hunting. When about fifteen or sixteen, he became a squire and prepared himself seriously for the art of war. He learned to ride a war horse with dexterity and to handle the sword, the shield, and the lance correctly. The squire also waited on his lord and lady at the table and learned music, poetry, and games.

If not already knighted on the battlefield for valor, the squire was usually considered eligible for knighthood at twenty-one. By the twelfth century the Church claimed a role in the ceremony, investing it with impressive symbolism. The candidate took a bath to symbolize purity and watched his weapons before the altar in an all-night vigil, confessing and making resolutions to be a worthy knight. During the solemn Mass that followed, his sword was blessed on the altar by a priest. The climax of the ceremony came when the candidate, kneeling before his lord, received a light blow on the neck or shoulder (the *accolade*), as the lord pronounced these words: "In the name of God, Saint Michael, and Saint George, I dub thee knight. Be valiant." The ceremony was designed to impress upon the knight that he must be virtuous and valiant, loyal to his suzerain and to God.

Heraldry. With its unique decorative designs, worn proudly by each noble family on its armor, heraldry was one of the more colorful aspects of chivalry. The popularity of heraldry began to sweep through Europe in the twelfth century. The use of the closed helmet, which hid the face, required that some means of identification be developed. Ingenious feudal artists devised 285 variations of the cross and decorated the nobles' shields with such real and fictitious animals as the lion, leopard, griffin, dragon, unicorn, and a host of others in fanciful postures. A man's social position was evident in his coat of arms, for its quarterings, or divisions, showed to which noble families its owner was related.

Castles as fortresses and homes. The life of the nobles centered about the castle. The earliest of these structures, mere wooden blockhouses, were built in the ninth century. Not until the twelfth and thirteenth centuries were massive castles constructed entirely of stone.

The donjon, or central tower, was the focal point of the castle; it was surrounded by an open space that contained storerooms, workshops, and a chapel. The outside walls of the castle were surmounted by turrets from which arrows, boiling oil, and various missiles might be showered upon the attackers. Beyond the wall was the moat, a steep-sided ditch filled with water to deter the enemy. The only entrance to the castle lay across the drawbridge. The portcullis, a heavy iron grating which could be lowered rapidly to protect the gate, was a further barrier against unwanted intrusion.

A French manuscript illumination of a knight entering the lists to fight in a tournament gives some idea of the splendor with which such contests were frequently invested. These often brutal battles were considered suitable entertainment for noble ladies and gentlemen.

Life in the castle was anything but comfortable or romantic. The lord at first dwelt in the donjon, but by the thirteenth century he had built more spacious quarters. Because the castle was designed for defense, it possessed no large windows; and the rooms were dark and gloomy. The stone walls were bare except for occasional tapestries to allay the draft and dampness, and a huge fireplace provided the only warmth.

Amusements of the nobles. The average noble derived his pleasures primarily from outdoor sports, among which he included warfare. In peacetime the joust and tournament substituted for actual battle. The joust was a conflict between two armed knights, each equipped with a blunted lance with which he attempted to unseat the other. The tournament was a general melee in which groups of knights attacked each other. Often fierce fighting ensued, with frequent casualties.

The nobles were very fond of hunting, and the constant demand for fresh meat afforded a legitimate excuse for galloping over the countryside. Most hunting was done in the nearby forests, but at times an unlucky peasant's crops might be ruined during the chase.

A similar outdoor pastime, which lords, ladies, and even high church dignitaries delighted in, was falconry, a method of hunting with predatory birds. The hawks were reared with the utmost care, and large companies of lords and ladies spent many afternoons eagerly wagering with one another as to whose falcon would bring down the first victim. Nobles often attended Mass with hooded falcons on their wrists.

Indoor amusements included the universally popular diversions of backgammon, dice, and chess. The long, monotonous nights were sometimes enlivened by the quips of jesters. At other times a wandering minstrel entertained his noble hosts in exchange for a bed and a place at the table.

The decline of chivalry. The development of national governments under strong kings who enforced tranquility and order changed the whole basis of feudal society (see Chapter 10). Knights were no longer needed to fight for their lords, to rush to the succor of helpless maidens, or to take the law into their own hands in defense of personal honor. Yet chivalry continued on as an ideal, reaching its culmination in the fourteenth and fifteenth centuries. By the sixteenth century its code had become fantastic and even ridiculous, as is pointed out so cleverly in Cervantes' *Don Quixote*. Some knights continued to live in the past and obtained their excitement by becoming robbers, picking needless quarrels with their neighbors, or inventing imaginary females who had to be rescued from a fate worse than death.

SUMMARY

This chapter has surveyed the political, economic, and social history of the early Middle Ages (500-1050), during which the axis of European civilization was centered in France. The conversion of Clovis to Christianity and the subsequent Frankish alliance with the papacy meant that the most energetic of the Germanic tribes had united with the greatest existing force for civilization in western Europe—the Christian Church. The foundation of the new Europe whose center was no longer the Mediterranean was completed by Charlemagne, but his empire depended too heavily on the forceful personality of its founder and did not survive his inferior successors. After the Carolingian collapse, new political and economic patterns evolved to meet the turbulent conditions of the time.

Feudalism was a bridge between the centralized governments of the Romans and Carolingians and the national states of modern Europe. Like so many things in medieval civilization, feudalism was a blend of German and Roman customs, enriched and humanized by the ideals of Christianity. The people who held land under feudal tenure were a privileged caste of landed aristocrats whose main function was military service. Set apart from the feudal nobles but forming the backbone of economic life was the vast majority of the people—the peasants. On the manors, the economic units of early medieval life, the unfree peasants or serfs grew the food for all medieval people and performed the heavy labor needed. They were politically inarticulate, tied to the soil, and seldom masters of their own destinies.

One aspect of feudalism which has come down to the twentieth century as a highly romanticized tradition is chivalry. Although its practice in the Middle Ages fell far beneath its principles, its idealism became part of the medieval legacy to the twentieth century.

SUGGESTIONS FOR READING

M. Keen, **The Pelican History of Medieval Europe*** (Penguin); D. Hay, **The Medieval Centuries*** (Torchbooks); and H. Trevor-Roper, **The Rise of Christian Europe*** (Harcourt Brace Jovanovich) are valuable surveys of the Middle Ages. See also N. Zacour, **An Introduction to Medieval Institutions,** 2nd ed. (St. Martin's, 1976); and C. Erickson, **The Medieval Vision: Essays in History and Perception*** (Oxford, 1976).

J. Wallace-Hadrill, **The Barbarian West, 400-1000*** (Torchbooks); R. E. Sullivan, **Heirs of the Roman Empire*** (Cornell); and A. R. Lewis, **Emerging Medieval Europe, A.D. 400-1000*** (Knopf) are excellent brief surveys of the early Middle Ages. See John Morris, **The Age of Arthur** (Scribner's, 1973) for a history of the British Isles to 650 A.D. For greater detail see H. Moss, **The Birth of the Middle Ages, 395-814*** (Oxford); C. Dawson, **The Making of Europe*** (Meridian); M. Deanesley, **History of Early Medieval Europe, 476-911*** (Barnes and Noble); and G. Barraclough, **The Crucible of Europe: The Ninth and Tenth Centuries** (Univ. of California, 1976).

H. Fichtenau, **The Carolingian Empire: The Age of Charlemagne*** (Torchbooks) is the best work on the subject. See also R. Winston, **Charlemagne: From the Hammer to the Cross*** (Peter Smith); and P. Munz, **Life in the Age of Charlemagne*** (Capricorn). On the Carolingian Renaissance see F. Heer, **The World of Charlemagne** (Macmillan, 1975) which is scholarly and readable; E. Duckett, **Alcuin, Friend of Charlemagne: His World and His Work** (Shoe String); and M. Laistner, **Thought and Letters in Western Europe, A.D. 500 to 900*** (Cornell).

J. Brondsted, **The Vikings*** (Penguin); and Gwyn Jones, **A History of the Vikings** (Galaxy, 1973) are outstanding on Viking activities. G. Turville-Petre, **The Heroic Age of Scandinavia** (Greenwood, 1976) describes the Norse way of life as reflected in their heroic legends.

Carl Stephenson, **Mediaeval Feudalism*** (Cornell) is a clear introduction. See also F. Ganshof, **Feudalism*** (Torchbooks); and M. Bloch, **The Feudal Society,*** 2 vols., (Phoenix). S. Painter, **French Chivalry*** (Cornell) is a delightful essay on the feudal, religious, and courtly aspects of chivalry.

On rural life and the manorial system see **The Agrarian Life of the Middle Ages,** Vol. I in **The Cambridge Economic History of Europe,** 2nd ed. (Cambridge, 1967); and G. Duby, **Rural Economy and Country Life in the Medieval West** (So. Carolina, 1968). G. G. Coulton, **Medieval Village, Manor, and Monastery** (Peter Smith); H. S. Bennett, **Life on the Medieval Manor*** (Cambridge); and E. Power, **Medieval People*** (Barnes and Noble) are worthwhile accounts.

*Indicates a less expensive paperbound edition.

CHAPTER 9

The Crusades and
the Rise of Trade, Towns,
and a New Society:
1050-1450

The West Takes the Offensive

INTRODUCTION. Following the collapse of Charlemagne's empire, Europeans probably felt that the future held little promise. No longer was there an effective central government to maintain peace and enforce laws over large territories, and with political fragmentation had come economic localism in the form of the self-sufficient manorial system.

In this chapter we shall trace the rise of a new Europe—a Europe which in the eleventh century was to emerge from what is sometimes called the "dark ages." With the ejection of the Muslims from Sicily and the successful challenge to Muslim control of the Mediterranean, Christian Europe ceased to be on the defensive and took the offensive instead.

In northern Spain a few bands of Christians sparked a long struggle against the Muslims in a movement known as the *Reconquista*, meaning "reconquest"; but the most dramatic manifestation of Europe's new dynamism was the crusades. Spurred on by religious fervor, love of adventure, and hopes of personal gain, the crusaders set out to drive the Muslims from the Holy Land and free Jerusalem from the infidel. These expansive movements helped the recovery of international trade and the rise of flourishing towns. New markets stimulated the growth of industry and crafts; and the development of banking and the use of money, which superseded the old exchange by barter, made everyday business transactions more efficient. At the same time, men cleared and drained forests and swamps, and new lands went under the plow. All these factors—particularly the revival of urban life—sounded the death knell for the manorial system in western Europe.

Above all, the forces transforming the western world led to the growth of a new class in society—townsmen, the bourgeoisie or middle class. The status of a member of the middle class was based not on ancestry or ownership of large estates, as was the case with the feudal aristocrat, but on possession of goods and money. Gradually the bourgeoisie gained influence as well as wealth and began to exert a growing impact on history.

EUROPE AGAINST THE MUSLIMS

Norman conquests in Italy and Sicily. About the year 1000 southern Italy was a battleground for rival Lombard dukes, the Byzantine empire, and the Muslims. The Lombards ruled several duchies; the Eastern empire controlled the "heel and toe" of the peninsula, all that remained of Justinian's reconquest of Italy; and across the Strait of Messina Muslim princes ruled the island of Sicily.

In 1016 adventurers of Viking ancestry from Normandy plunged into this maelstrom of continual warfare. At first the Norman knights fought for hire, but soon they began to carve out large estates for themselves. The obscure house of Tancred of Hauteville was burdened with twelve husky sons, all of whom made their way to southern Italy. One blond giant of this family, Robert Guiscard, established his authority over his fellow Normans and by 1071 extinguished the last Byzantine foothold in southern Italy (see p. 144). Meanwhile Robert had allied himself with the pope, and in return the papacy recognized him as the ruler of southern Italy and of Sicily, still in Muslim hands. Under the leadership of Robert and his brother Roger, the Normans crossed the Strait of Messina and gained a footing in Sicily just a few years before another Norman, William the Conqueror, crossed the Channel to invade England. In 1072 these land-hungry Normans captured Palermo, and twenty years later the entire island of Sicily was theirs.

Venice, Genoa, and Pisa battle the Muslims. While the Normans had been ejecting the Muslims from Sicily, similar offensives had been going on elsewhere in the Mediterranean. Venice, still nominally a part of the Byzantine empire, had cleared the Adriatic Sea and in 1002 had won a great naval victory over a Muslim fleet. This enhanced Venetian trade with Byzantium. Genoa and Pisa also began to fight the Muslims, and by 1090 the western Mediterranean had been cleared of Muslim pirates and traders. The crusades to the Holy Land would shortly do the same for the eastern Mediterranean.

Muslim civilization in Spain. Although the offensive of the West had cleared the Muslims from the waters of the western Mediterranean, Muslim power remained in Spain. We will recall that with the fall of Rome in the fifth century, Visigothic tribes had settled in Spain; but they in turn had fallen to the Muslim invasion (see p. 190). Muslim Spain was ruled from Damascus until 756, when it became an independent Muslim state under the last remaining member of the Umayyad dynasty.

From their center at Cordova, the ancient capital of Roman Spain, the Umayyad rulers (756-1031) inaugurated a brilliant era. The Caliphate of Cordova, as Muslim Spain was called after 929, made many economic and cultural advances. Water power was harnessed to drive mills, new crops such as rice and sugar cane were introduced, and

The Great Mosque at Cordova is a fine example of the Islamic art that flourished in Spain during the Muslim rule of that country.

grain cultivation flourished. Other important products included wine, olive oil, leather goods, weapons, glass, and tapestries. Cordova's Great Mosque held 5500 worshipers, and its library held 400,000 volumes.

The Muslims of Spain were the most cultured people of the West. Literature and art became their glories, and learning flourished when the rulers, often men of letters themselves, invited some of the best scholars of the Muslim East to settle in Spain (see p. 165). By the twelfth century scholars from northern Europe were flocking to Spain to study, and through them much of the learning of the Arabs passed to Christian Europe.

The lot of the conquered Christians was not especially bad. Christian worship continued, and, generally speaking, tolerance was granted to all people—including Christians and Jews. The latter, who had been persecuted under the Visigoths, flourished in the professions and as officials of the state. Many Jews came from Christian Europe and the East, and the Talmudic school at Cordova became a leading center of Hebrew learning. Christians were converted to Islam, there was much intermarriage, and many of the later Muslim leaders were of Gothic or Hispano-Roman descent.

Politically, Muslim Spain was usually weak and disunited. Spain had been conquered by a medley of Arabs, Syrians, and Berbers who were often in discord and outnumbered by the native population. The Caliphate reached the height of its power in the tenth century but thereafter the caliphs were a mediocre lot, unable to withstand the pressures of factionalism. In 1031 the Umayyads were overthrown, and the Caliphate of Cordova was replaced by twenty-three small, warring states.

Early Christian victories in the Reconquista. During the period of Muslim dominance the following Christian states survived in the north of Spain (see map, p. 233): the county of Barcelona, nucleus of later Aragon, in the east; Leon in the west; and in between, Navarre, peopled by the fiercely independent Basques whom neither the Romans nor the Visigoths had wholly subdued.

Slowly gathering strength and resolution, these Christian states expanded south through the hills, with Leon leading the way. An offshoot of Leon was the county of Castile, named after the many castles built to defend it. In the mid-tenth century Castile became strong enough to throw off the rule of the king of Leon. The disintegration of the Caliphate of Cordova into small Muslim states after 1031 opened the way for further Christian advances: Castile captured a large part of what was to become Portugal, and the southern border of Castile was pushed from the Douro to the Tagus River. In 1063, a generation before the first crusade to the Holy Land, the pope proclaimed the *Reconquista* to be a holy crusade, and the first of many northern knights flocked to Spain to fight the Muslims. In 1085 the mighty bastion of Toledo fell to the king of Castile, and the end of the Muslim occupation seemed in sight. But Muslim resistance in southern Spain continued for another four centuries, and militant expansion in the name of Christianity would continue to color the formative years of Spain and Portugal.

THE CRUSADES: "GOD WILLS IT!"

The call to a crusade. The most dramatic expression of Europe on the offensive was the crusades. For hundreds of years peaceful pilgrims had been traveling from Europe to worship at the birthplace of Christ. By the tenth century bishops were organizing mass pilgrimages to the Holy Land; the largest of these, which set out from Germany in 1065, included about seven thousand pilgrims.

During the eleventh century, however, Christian pilgrims to the Holy Land became especially concerned and aggravated when the Seljuk Turks, who were new and fanatical converts to Islam, came sweeping and plundering into the Near East. The Seljuks seized Jerusalem from their fellow Muslims and then swept north into Asia Minor. Byzantine forces desperately tried to bar the invader, but at the battle of Manzikert (1071) the eastern emperor was captured and his army scattered. Within a few years Asia Minor, the chief source of Byzantine revenue and troops, was lost, and the emperor was writing to western princes and to the pope seeking mercenaries with which to regain lost territories. In addition, tales of alleged Turkish mistreatment of Christian pilgrims circulated throughout Europe, and though there is evidence that these stories were propaganda, men's minds became inflamed.

In 1095 Pope Urban II proclaimed the First Crusade to regain the Holy Land. Preaching at the Council of Clermont in that year, he exhorted Christians to take up the cross and strive for a cause that promised not merely spiritual rewards but material gain as well:

For this land which you inhabit . . . is too narrow for your large population; nor does it abound in wealth; and it furnishes scarcely food enough for its cultivators. Hence it is that you murder and devour one another. . . . Enter upon the road to the Holy Sepulchre; wrest that land from the wicked race, and subject it to yourselves.[1]

At the end of his impassioned oration the crowd shouted "God wills it"—the expression which the crusaders later used in battle.

Although the pope saw in the crusade an outlet for the restless energy of pugnacious nobles—their warring fervor would be channeled for the glory of God—the primary impetus behind the crusade was undoubtedly religious. It was viewed as a holy war, and following Pope Urban's appeal, there was a real and spontaneous outpouring of religious enthusiasm. The word *crusade* itself is derived from "taking the cross," after the example of Christ. (On the way to the Holy Land, the crusader wore the cross on his breast; on his journey home, he wore the cross on his back.) Pope Urban promised the crusaders that they would enjoy indulgence for their past sins. He also hoped that the religious enthusiasm following in the wake of the crusades would strengthen his claim to the moral leadership of Europe.

The First Crusade gains the Holy Land. From the end of the eleventh century to the end of the thirteenth, there were seven major crusades, as well as various small expeditions which from time to time tried their hands against the Saracen.

The First Crusade, composed of feudal nobles from France, parts of Germany, and Norman Italy, proceeded overland to Constantinople. Having expected the help of European mercenaries against the Seljuks, the emperor Alexius Comnenus was taken aback when confronted by an unruly horde of what Pope Urban himself had called "aforetime robbers." He hastily directed the crusaders out of Constantinople to fight the Turks. The First Crusade was the most successful of the seven; with not more than five thousand knights and infantry, it overcame the resistance of the Turks, who were no longer united. Above all, it captured the Holy City—Jerusalem. A contemporary account of the Christian entrance into Jerusalem reads:

But now that our men had possession of the walls and towers, wonderful sights were to be seen. Some of our men . . . cut off the heads of their enemies; others shot them with arrows, so that they fell from the towers; others tortured them longer by casting them into the flames. Piles of heads, hands, and feet were to be seen in the streets of the city. It was necessary to pick one's way over the bodies of men and horses. But these were small matters compared to what happened at the Temple of Solomon [where] . . . men rode in blood up to their knees and bridle reins. Indeed it was a just and splendid judgment of God that this place should be filled with the blood of the unbelievers, since it had suffered so long from their blasphemies.[2]

The First Crusade conquered a narrow strip of land stretching from Antioch to Jerusalem (see map, p. 143) and created the Latin kingdom of Jerusalem, which lasted until its last remnant fell to the Muslims in 1291.

When the kingdom of Jerusalem became endangered, the eloquent St. Bernard induced the kings of France and Germany to lead the Second Crusade in 1147. It never reached Jerusalem, having turned aside to attack Damascus where its forces were routed.

The "Crusade of Kings." The fall of Jerusalem in 1187 to the Muslims, reinvigorated under the leadership of Saladin, the Kurdish sultan of Egypt and Syria, served to provoke the Third Crusade (1189). Its leaders were three of the most famous medieval kings—Frederick Barbarossa of Germany, Richard the Lion-Hearted of England, and Philip Augustus of France. Frederick was drowned in Asia Minor; and, after many quarrels with Richard, Philip returned home. Saladin and Richard remained the chief protagonists.

To keep the Muslims united, Saladin proclaimed a *jihad*, or holy war, against the Christians, but he remained a patient statesman and chivalrous warrior. "Abstain from the shedding of blood," he once said, "for blood that is spilt never slumbers."[3] His commonsense approach to a settlement was evidenced when he proposed that Richard should marry his sister and be given Palestine as a wedding present, a proposal which shocked the Europeans.

Richard and Saladin finally agreed to a three-year truce and free access to Jerusalem for Christian pilgrims. Since Saladin would have granted this concession at any time, the truce scarcely compensated for the cost of such an expensive crusade.

The Fourth Crusade. The Fourth Crusade (1202-1204) reflects the decline of a religious ideal. No kings answered Pope Innocent III's call and the knights who did were unable to pay the Venetians the agreed-upon transport charges (see p. 145). The Venetians persuaded them to pay off the sum by capturing the Christian town of Zara on the Adriatic coast, which had long proved troublesome to Venetian trading interests. Then, in order to absorb all Byzantine commerce, the Venetians pressured the crusaders into attacking Constantinople. After conquering and sacking the greatest city in Europe, the crusaders set up the Latin empire of Constantinople (see map, p. 145) and forgot about recovering the Holy Land.

In this manuscript illumination Saladin wrests the cross, symbol of Christianity, from one of the leaders of the crusades.

Later crusades fail. The thirteenth century saw other crusades. The youngsters of the ill-fated Children's Crusade in 1212 fully expected the waters of the Mediterranean to part and make a path to the Holy Land, which they would take without fighting, but thousands of them were sold into slavery by Marseilles merchants. The Fifth Crusade in 1219 failed in its attack on Egypt, the center of Muslim power in the Near East. The unique Sixth Crusade in 1228 was organized and led by the excommunicated enemy of the pope, the emperor Frederick II, who by skillful diplomacy succeeded in acquiring Jerusalem, Bethlehem, and Nazareth from the sultan of Egypt without striking a blow. This arrangement ended in 1244 with the Muslim reconquest of the Holy City. The loss inspired the saintly Louis IX of France to organize the Seventh Crusade in 1248, but despite his zeal it ended in a fiasco when Louis was captured in Egypt and forced to pay an enormous ransom. This was the last major attempt to regain Jerusalem, and the era of the crusades ended in 1291 when Acre, the last stronghold of the Christians in the Holy Land, fell to the Muslims.

The crusader states. Altogether four crusader principalities, with the kingdom of Jerusalem dominant, had been established along the eastern Mediterranean coast. By the time Jerusalem fell to Saladin in 1187, however, only isolated pockets of Christians remained, surrounded by a vast hinterland of hostile Muslims. They were able to survive only by reason of frequent transfusions of strength from Europe in the form of supplies and manpower. It was natural for the European nobles who sought a permanent home in the Holy Land to adopt the customs of their Muslim neighbors and dress in light, flowing robes and turbans. Their houses were like Moorish villas, decorated and furnished with divans of brocade, Persian rugs, mosaic floors, and silk hangings. These transplanted Europeans became tolerant and easygoing, trading and even hunting with Muslims. Frequently there was bad blood between them and the newly arrived crusaders who had come for a short stay and a dash against the infidel.

The crusader states were defended by three semi-monastic military orders: the Templars, or Knights of the Temple, so called because their first headquarters was on the site of the old Temple of Jerusalem; the Hospitalers, or Knights of St. John of Jerusalem, who were founded originally to care for the sick and wounded; and the Teutonic Knights, exclusively a German order. Combining monasticism and militarism, these orders had as their aims the protection of all pilgrims and perpetual war against the Muslims. These men of the cross could put five hundred armed knights into the field, and their great castles guarded the roads and passes against Muslim attack. For two centuries the uniforms of these orders were a common sight in the crusader states; the Templars wore a white robe decorated with a red cross, the Hospitalers a black robe with a white cross, and the Teutonic Knights a white robe with a black cross.

The crusades evaluated. Even though the crusades failed to achieve their specific objective permanently, they cannot be written off as mere adventures. On the contrary, their influence extended over a much wider geographical field than just the Holy Land. Much of the crusading fervor carried over to the fight against the Muslims in Spain and the pagan Slavs in eastern Europe. Politically the crusades weakened the Byzantine empire and accelerated its fall (see Chapter 6). Although the early crusades strengthened the moral leadership of the papacy in Europe, the ill-success of the later crusades, together with the preaching of crusades against Christian heretics and political opponents lessened both the crusading ideal and respect for the papacy.

The contact with the East widened the scope of the Europeans, ended their isolation, and exposed them to a vastly superior civilization. Although it is easy to exaggerate the economic effects of the crusades, they did complete the reopening of the eastern Mediterranean to western commerce, which in turn stimulated the rise of cities and the emergence of a money economy in the West. The crusades as a movement were a manifestation of the dynamic vitality and expansive spirit of Europe, evident in many fields by the end of the eleventh century.

THE RISE OF TRADE
AND TOWNS

Revitalized trade routes. Although scholars have long debated the extent of trade and urban life that existed during the early Middle Ages, there is general agreement that fresh trade activity was evident even before the crusades. With the ending of Viking and Magyar attacks in the tenth century, a northern trading area developed which extended from the British Isles to the Baltic Sea. Closely related to this northern trade area was the route established by the Vikings as early as the ninth century, when they settled in Russia and created the lucrative Varangian route from the eastern Baltic down the rivers of Russia to the Black Sea and Constantinople (see p. 152).

The center of this northern trade system was the county of Flanders. By 1050 Flemish artisans were producing a surplus of woolen cloth of such fine quality that it was in great demand. Baltic furs, honey and forest products, and British tin and raw wool were exchanged for Flemish cloth. From the south by way of Italy came oriental luxury goods—silks, sugar, and spices.

Equally important as a catalyst of the medieval commercial revolution—whose impact on the Middle Ages deserves to be compared to that of the Industrial Revolution on the modern world—was the opening up of the Mediterranean trading area. In the eleventh century the Normans and Italians broke the Muslim hold on the eastern Mediterranean and the First Crusade inaugurated trade with the Near East. Arab vessels brought luxury goods from the East to ports on the Persian Gulf and Red Sea. From there they were shipped by caravan to Alexandria, Acre, and Joppa, and from those ports the merchants of Venice, Genoa, and Pisa transported the goods to Italy on their way to the markets of Europe. Other trade routes from Asia came overland, passing through Baghdad and Damascus and on to ports, such as Tyre and Sidon, in the crusader states. The easiest route north from the Mediterranean was via Marseilles, up the Rhone valley.

Early in the fourteenth century two more major trade lanes developed within Europe. An all-sea route connected the Mediterranean with northern Europe via the Strait of Gibraltar. The old overland route from northern Italy through the Alpine passes to central Europe was also developed. From Venice and other north Italian cities, trade flowed through such passes as the Brenner, sharply reducing the business of the Rhone valley route and the famous fairs of Champagne.

Fairs, centers of European trade. Along the main European trade routes, astute lords set up fairs, where merchants and goods from Italy and northern Europe met. During the twelfth and thirteenth centuries the fairs of Champagne in France (see Reference Map 4) functioned as the major clearing house for this international trade.

Fairs were important and elaborate events held either seasonally or annually in specified areas of each European country. The feudal law of the region was set aside during a fair, and in its place was substituted a new commercial code called the "law merchant." Special courts, with merchants acting as judges, settled all disputes which arose. In England such courts were called "pie-powder courts," from the French *pied-poudré*, meaning "dusty foot." Fairs also greatly stimulated the revival of a money economy and early forms of banking and credit.

Factors in the rise of towns. The resurgence of trade in Europe was the prime cause of the revival of towns. Trade and towns had an interacting effect on each other; the towns arose because of trade, but they also stimulated trade by providing greater markets and by producing goods for the merchants to sell.

In the revival of cities, geography played a significant role. Rivers, which were important in the evolution of ancient civilizations, were also important in the development of medieval towns. They were natural highways on which articles of commerce could be easily transported. Many communities developed at the confluence of two important streams; others arose where a river might be easily crossed by a ford or bridge, "Oxford" or "Cam-bridge," for example.

Often at a strategic geographic location a feudal noble had already erected a fortified castle, or *burg* (*bourg* in French, *borough* in English). Such a stronghold offered the merchants a good stopping place. The inhabitants of the burg were likely to buy some of the merchant's wares, and the castle offered him protection. In time a permanent merchant settlement, called a *faubourg*, grew up outside the walls of the burg. Frequently, too, merchants settled at an old Roman episcopal city like Cologne (Colonia Agrippina) or a fortified abbey or cathedral. Munich grew up around a monastery, and Durham was "half cathedral and half fortress against the Scot."

Another factor contributing to the rise of towns was the growth of population. In England, for example, the population more than tripled between 1066 and 1350. The reasons for this rapid increase in population are varied. The ending of bloody foreign invasions and, in some areas, the stabilization of feudal society were contributing factors. More important was an increase in food production brought about by the cultivation of wastelands, the clearing of forests, and the draining of marshes. Technological innovations such as the three-field system of crop rotation also increased production.

Interacting with the growth of towns was the decline of serfdom. Many serfs escaped from the manors and made their way to the towns. After living a year and a day in the town, a serf was considered a freeman.

The Hanseatic League. Sometimes a group of towns joined forces for mutual protection and to win special privileges. This was particularly true in Germany where by the thirteenth century a strong state capable of maintaining order did not exist. Most famous was the Hanseatic League, whose nucleus was Lübeck, Hamburg, and Danzig, but which by the fourteenth century comprised more than seventy cities. The League built up a lucrative monopoly on Baltic and North Sea trade. Its wealth came primarily from its control of the Baltic herring fisheries, its corner on Russian trade, and its rich business with England and Flanders. It established permanent trading stations in such leading European centers as London, Bruges, and Novgorod. Until the fifteenth century, when it began to lose its privileges and

A guild warden examines the work of an apprentice mason and carpenter before their admission as master craftsmen.

monopolies, the Hanseatic League remained the great distributor of goods to northern Europe. Its navy safeguarded its commerce from pirates and even waged a successful war with the king of Denmark when he threatened its Baltic monopoly.

Merchant and craft guilds. In each town the merchants and artisans organized themselves into guilds, which were useful not only for business but also for social and political purposes. There were two kinds of guilds: merchant and craft.

The merchant guild ensured a monopoly of trade within a given locality. All alien merchants were supervised closely and made to pay tolls. Disputes among merchants were settled at the guild court according to its own legal code. The guilds also tried to make sure that the customers were not cheated: they checked weights and measures and insisted upon a standard quality for goods. To allow only a legitimate profit, the guild fixed a "just price," which was fair to both producer and consumer.

When guilds first appeared, there was no adequate central government to protect merchants as they carried on their trading activities throughout the land. As a result the guilds assumed some functions which would otherwise have been governmental. If a merchant was imprisoned in another town, the guild tried to secure his release at its own expense. If a merchant of a London guild refused to pay a debt owed to a merchant of a guild in Bristol, the merchant guild in the latter town would seize the goods of any London merchant coming to Bristol.

The guild's functions stretched beyond business and politics into charitable and social activities. If a guildsman fell into poverty, he was aided. The guild also provided financial assistance for the burial expenses of its members and looked after their dependents. Members attended social meetings in the guildhall and periodically held processions in honor of their patron saints.

The increase of commerce brought a quickening of industrial life in the towns so that, as early as the eleventh century, the artisans began to organize. Craftsmen in each of the medieval trades—weaving, cobbling, tanning, and so on—joined forces. The result was the craft guild, which differed from the merchant guild in that membership was limited to artisans in one particular craft.

The general aims of the craft guilds were the same as those of the merchant guilds— the creation of a monopoly and the enforcement of a set of trade rules. Each guild had a monopoly of a certain article in a particular town, and every effort was made to prevent competition between members of the same guild. The guild restricted the number of its members, regulated the quantity and quality of the goods produced, and set prices. It also enforced regulations to protect the consumer from bad workmanship and inferior materials.

The craft guild also differed from the merchant guild in its recognition of three distinct classes of workers—apprentices, journeymen, and master craftsmen. The apprentice was a youth who lived at the master's house and was taught the trade thoroughly. Although he received no wages, all his physical needs were supplied. His apprenticeship commonly lasted seven years. When his schooling was finished, the youth became a journeyman (from the French *journée*, meaning "day's work"). He was then eligible to receive wages and to be hired by a master.

When about twenty-three, the journeyman sought admission into the guild as a master. To be accepted he had to prove his ability. Some crafts demanded the making of a "master piece"—for example, a pair of shoes that the master shoemakers would find acceptable in every way.

In the fourteenth century, when prosperity began to wane, the master craftsmen drastically restricted the number of journeymen who were allowed to become masters. The guilds either admitted only the relatives of masters or imposed excessively high entrance fees. When the journeymen then set up their own journeyman organizations, they were crushed by the wealthy guild masters, who usually controlled the town governments. By the fifteenth century most journeymen could not hope to become more than wage earners, and they bitterly resented the restrictions of the guild system.

Acquiring urban freedom. The guilds played an important role in local government. Both artisans and merchants, even though freemen, were subject to the feudal lord or bishop upon whose domain the city stood. The citizens of the towns resented the fact that their overlord collected tolls and dues as though they were serfs. The townsmen demanded the privileges of governing themselves—of making their own laws, administering their own justice, levying their own taxes, and issuing their own coinage. Naturally the overlord resented the impertinent upstarts who demanded self-government. But the towns won their independence in various ways.

One way was to become a commune, a self-governing town. The merchant guilds took the lead in acquiring charters of self-government for the towns. Often a charter had to be won by a revolt; in other circumstances it could be purchased, for a feudal lord was always in need of money. By 1200 the Lombard towns of northern Italy, as well as many French and Flemish towns, had become self-governing communes.

Where royal authority was strong, we find "privileged" towns. In a charter granted to the town by the monarch, the inhabitants won extensive financial and legal powers. The town was given management of its own

The horses pulling grain uphill in this illumination are wearing improved horseshoes which permit greater traction and collars which, by relieving pressure on their windpipes, greatly increase their pulling power.

finances and paid its taxes in a lump sum to the king. It was also generally given the right to elect its own officials. The king was glad to grant such a charter, for it weakened the power of his nobles and won him the support of the townsmen.

Founding new towns was still another way in which feudal restrictions were broken down. Shrewd lords and kings, who recognized the economic value of having towns in their territories, founded carefully planned centers with well-laid-out streets and open squares. As a means of obtaining inhabitants, they offered many inducements in the form of personal privileges and tax limitations. Among such new towns were Newcastle, Freiburg, and Berlin.

Technological advances. While in ancient societies men and animals were almost the only source of power, our medieval ancestors succeeded in greatly maximizing the muscle power of draft animals by three major developments. First, for the traditional horse collar which fastened around the animal's neck and choked him when pulling a heavy load, they substituted a harness fitted so that the shoulders bore the weight. Second, they developed a tandem harness in order to utilize the strength of several horses; and finally, they improved traction with a new type of horseshoe. These inventions are said to have done for the eleventh and twelfth centuries what the steam engine did for the nineteenth. In addition, our medieval forebears increased the number of

prime movers beyond sheer human and animal muscle power. They developed watermills (known but little used in the ancient world) and invented windmills for use in flat lands where waterfalls did not exist. Useful not only for grinding grains, these water- and windmills provided power for draining marshlands, for reclaiming areas from the sea (as in the Low Countries), and for fulling woolen cloth, which the West exported in quantity to the Byzantine and Muslim East.

The use of money, banking, and credit. All the aspects of Europe's expansion—the crusades, and the revival of trade, cities, and industry—had far-reaching effects on the financial structure. The first big change came with the reappearance of money as a medium of exchange. Coins were made from silver dug from old and new mines throughout Europe, but during the whole of the Middle Ages silver bullion was in short supply. In the thirteenth century silver coins were superseded in international trade by gold, especially the florin of Florence, which became a monetary standard for Europe.

When the English king Henry III invaded France in 1242, he carried with him thirty barrels of money, each containing 160,000 coins, to defray the expenses of the expedition. This incident graphically illustrates the need for instruments of credit and other forms of banking. All-important was the technique of "symbolic transfer." By this system a man deposited his money in a bank

In this representation of the Wat Tyler uprising, John Ball is shown at the head of a well-disciplined group of helmeted peasants bearing the banners of England and of St. George.

and received in return a letter of credit which, like a modern check, could later be cashed at any of the offices of the same bank. Letters of credit were common at fairs and very useful during the crusades, when the Templars arranged a system whereby crusaders could deposit money in the Paris office and withdraw it from the office in the Holy Land.

Banking also sprang from the activities of moneychangers at fairs and other trading centers. In addition to exchanging the coin of one region for another, these moneychangers would also accept money on deposit for safekeeping. The most important bankers, however, were Italian merchants from Florence and the Lombard cities, who by the middle of the thirteenth century were loaning their accumulated capital to kings and prelates. They found various ways of circumventing the Church's disapproval of all interest as usury. For example, if a sum was not repaid by a certain date, a penalty charge was levied.

THE EMERGENCE OF A NEW SOCIETY

The typical town. Medieval towns, which by the twelfth century were centers of an advanced culture as well as of trade and industry, were not large by modern standards. Before 1200 no town contained 100,000 inhabitants, and one of 20,000 was a metropolis.

Since the area within the walls was at a premium, medieval towns were more crowded than the average modern city. Shops were even built on bridges (as on the Ponte Vecchio, which still stands in Florence), and buildings were erected to a height of seven or more stories. The houses projected over the street with each additional story so that it was often possible for persons at the tops of houses opposite one another to touch hands.

The streets below were dark and narrow and almost invariably crooked, although they were often designed to be wide enough "to give passage to a horseman with his lance across his saddle-bows." The streets were full of discordant sounds—drivers yelled at pedestrians to get out of the way of the horses and oxen; dogs, pigs, and geese added their alarms; merchants bawled out their wares; people of every description jostled past one another, and unoiled signs above inns and shops creaked ominously in the wind, constantly threatening to crash down on some innocent passerby.

The bourgeoisie. The triumph of the townsmen in their struggle for greater self-government meant that a new class had evolved in Europe, a powerful, independent, and self-assured group, whose interest in trade was to revolutionize social, economic, and political history. The members of this class were called burghers or the bourgeoisie. Kings came to rely more and more on them in combating the power of the feudal lords, and their economic interests gave rise to a nascent capitalism. Also associated with the rise of towns and the bourgeoisie were the decline of serfdom and the manorial system and the advent of modern society.

A medieval townsman's rank was based on money and goods rather than birth and land. At the top of the social scale were the great merchant and banking families, the princes of trade, bearing such names as Medici, Fugger, and Coeur. Then came the moderately wealthy merchants and below them the artisans and small shopkeepers. In the lowest slot was the unskilled laborer, whose miserable lot and discontent were destined to continue through the rest of the Middle Ages and most of modern history.

The decay of serfdom. Attracted by the freedom of town life, many serfs ran away from their manors and established themselves in a town. As a result the remaining serfs became unreliable. Sometimes they secured enough money to buy their freedom by selling food surpluses in the towns, but often the lords freed their serfs and induced them to remain on the manor as tenants or hired laborers. As a first step in the emancipation of the serfs, the lords accepted a money payment from them as a substitute for their old obligations of labor and produce. The final step was for the lord to become a landlord in the modern sense, renting the arable land of the manor to free tenants. Thus former serfs became satisfied tenants or, on occasion, members of the yeoman class who owned their small farms. Serfdom had largely died out in England and France by 1500, although in the latter country many of the old and vexatious obligations, such as payment for the use of the lord's mill and oven, were retained. In eastern Europe serfdom persisted until the nineteenth century.

The depression of the late Middle Ages. While the twelfth and thirteenth centuries had been a boom period, during the late Middle Ages—the fourteenth and fifteenth centuries—the economy leveled off and then stagnated. By 1350 a great economic depression, which lasted approximately a century, was underway. Its causes are difficult to ascertain, but one of its symptoms, population decline, was probably also a major cause.

By 1300 the population of western Europe had ceased increasing, probably because it had expanded up to the limits of the available food supply. Famines had once again become common by the time of the Black Death, a bubonic plague from Asia carried by fleas on rats. The Black Death struck western Europe in 1347, decimating and demoralizing society. It is estimated that about one third of the population was wiped out. Hardest hit were the towns; the population of Florence, for example, fell from 114,000 to about 50,000 in five years. Coupled with this blow was the destruction and death caused by the Hundred Years' War between France and England (1337-1453).

Another symptom of economic stagnation was social unrest and tension. Individual folk heroes such as Robin Hood robbed the rich to benefit the poor, but more important was concerted group action. For the first time since the fall of Rome the common people organized themselves into pressure groups. Organized textile workers in the Flemish cities and in Florence, who resented the restrictions of the guild system (see p. 214), waged class war against guild masters and rich merchants, while peasant unrest flamed into revolt in France and England. A famous example of the latter was the Wat Tyler uprising in England in 1381. The decimation of the peasant population by the Black Death caused a rise in the wages of the day laborers and an increased demand for the abolition of serfdom. Parliament tried to legislate against the pay raise but succeeded only in incurring the anger of the peasants. This resentment was fanned by the sermons of a priest, John Ball, known as the first English socialist:

Ah, ye good people, the matter goeth not well to pass in England, nor shall not do so till everything be common, and that there be no villains or gentlemen, but that we may be all united together and that the lords be no greater masters than we be. What have we deserved or why should we be thus kept in serfdom; we be all come from one father and one mother, Adam and Eve.[4]

As in the case of other revolts, this uprising was crushed amid a welter of blood and broken promises.

Depression and economic stagnation began to be eased by 1450. A new period of economic expansion was at hand, promoted by a new breed of strong monarchs and stimulated by geographical discovery and expansion over the face of the globe (see Chapter 18).

SUMMARY

Constructive forces fashioning a new Europe became apparent in the period between 1050 and 1300. The great achievement of the eleventh century was expansion and offensive action by the forces of western Europe. The Muslims lost naval supremacy in the Mediterranean, and a Christian reconquest was initiated in Spain. Above all, a great movement, the crusades, was initiated in 1095. While the objective was to push the Muslims out of the Holy Land and particularly from Jerusalem, the crusades opened new doors for the narrow, ingrown Europeans.

During the eleventh century Europe was transformed by new forces: increased food production and population, revitalized trade, new towns, expansion of industry, and a money economy. A new society began to take shape; the bourgeoisie emerged and serfdom declined. (From 1350 to 1450, however, economic depression produced unrest among peasants and urban workers.) In the political realm, the tradition of kingship persisted in spite of feudalism with its many local sovereignties. Aided substantially by the new economic forces, the kings were to impose their will on the nobles and become masters of new nations. The beginnings of this movement, which were contemporary with the developments described in this chapter, will be set forth in Chapter 10.

SUGGESTIONS FOR READING

C. H. Haskins, **The Normans in European History*** (Norton); and D. C. Douglas, **The Norman Achievement, 1050-1100** (Univ. of Calif., 1969) are excellent studies of Norman power.

S. Runciman, **A History of the Crusades,*** 3 vols. (Cambridge) is highly recommended for both its literary and historical merit. R. A. Newhall, **The Crusades*** (Peter Smith) is a brief, lucid introduction to the subject. Also recommended are Hans E. Meyer, **The Crusades*** (Oxford, 1973); Zoé Oldenbourg, **The Crusades*** (Ballantine); G. Hundley, **Saladin** (Barnes and Noble, 1976); R. Dozy, **Spanish Islam: A History of the Muslims in Spain** (Barnes and Noble, 1969); and W. M. Watt, **A History of Islamic Spain** (Edinburgh).

R. M. Smail, **Crusading Warfare: 1097-1193** (Cambridge, 1967) describes the weapons, organization, and tactics of both the Latin and Muslim armies together with the nature and function of the Crusaders' castles. See also Smail's **The Crusaders in Syria and the Holy Land** (Praeger, 1974); and J. Beeler, **Warfare in Feudal Europe, 730-1200*** (Cornell, 1971). C. Oman, **The Art of War in the Middle Ages: A.D. 378-1515*** (Cornell) is the standard work.

R. Latouche, **The Birth of Western Economy: Economic Aspects of the Dark Ages*** (Torchbooks); and Robert Lopez, **The Commercial Revolution of the Middle Ages*** (Prentice-Hall, 1971)

throw new light on economic history. See also M. M. Postan, **The Medieval Economy and Society*** (Penguin); and G. Hodgett, **A Social and Economic History of Medieval Europe*** (Torchbooks, 1974). N. J. Pounds, **An Economic History of Medieval Europe** (Longman, 1974) is an excellent survey.

H. Pirenne, **Economic and Social History of Medieval Europe** (Harvest) and **Medieval Cities*** (Princeton) are two small classics on the revival of trade and growth of cities. F. Rörig, **The Medieval Town*** (Univ. of Calif.) treats urban life from the eleventh to the sixteenth centuries. See also A. R. Lewis, **Naval Power and Trade in the Mediterranean, A.D. 500-1100;** S. Baldwin, **Business in the Middle Ages** (Cooper Square, 1968); **Trade and Industry in the Middle Ages,** Vol. 2 of **The Cambridge Economic History of Europe** (Cambridge). More specialized accounts are A. Sapori, **The Italian Merchant in the Middle Ages*** (Norton) and S. Thrupp, **The Merchant Class of Medieval London*** (Univ. of Michigan).

D. M. Stenton, **English Society in the Early Middle Ages, 1066-1307*** (Penguin) is a brief, comprehensive, and readable account. See also A. Luchaire, **Social France at the Time of Philip Augustus** (Gannon); P. Ziegler, **The Black Death*** (Torchbooks); and Jeffrey B. Russell, **Witchcraft in the Middle Ages** (Cornell, 1972).

*Indicates a less expensive paperbound edition.

CHAPTER 10

Medieval Political History: 1050-1300

Nations in the Making

INTRODUCTION. Between 1050 and 1300, a period sometimes called the High Middle Ages, political as well as economic and social change was manifest in Europe. Not only did trade revive, cities grow, and a new bourgeois social class emerge, but kings developed their power at the expense of the feudal nobility. Inadequate to meet the demands of a new and progressive society in the making, feudalism was on the wane.

Perhaps the greatest weakness of feudalism was its inability to guarantee law and order. Too often feudalism meant anarchy in which robber barons, in the words of a twelfth-century observer, "levied taxes on the villages every so often, and called it 'protection money'" (see p. 224). Feudalism provided no consistently effective agency to deal with such ruffians. As a result, confusion, inefficiency, and injustice often prevailed.

The inefficiency inherent in the feudal system also hindered economic progress. Trade and commerce spread over ever larger areas, but the boundaries of many tiny feudal principalities acted as barriers to this expansion. Along the Seine River, for example, there were tolls every six or seven miles. Only by welding the confusing multiplicity of fiefs and principalities into a large territorial unit—the nation—could the irritating tolls and tariffs imposed by local barons be removed, trade advanced, the lack of a uniform currency be remedied, and justice established. In other words, the ills of feudalism could be cured only by the creation of unified and centralized national states. We shall see in this chapter how monarchs in England and France expanded their power and improved the machinery of government, thus laying the foundations for such states. In Germany and Italy, however, efforts to create a national state ended in failure, and in Spain unification was retarded by the formidable task of ousting the Muslims.

THE GENESIS OF MODERN ENGLAND

Britain after the Romans. When the Roman legions withdrew from Britain to Italy at the beginning of the fifth century, they left the Romanized Celtic natives at the mercy of the Anglo-Saxon invaders. These Germanic tribes devastated Britain so thoroughly that little remained of Roman civilization other than a splendid system of roads. Proof of the force with which the invaders struck is the fact that almost no traces of the Celtic language remain in modern English. Not only did the Anglo-Saxons push most of the Celts out of Britain, but they also fought among themselves. At one time there were more than a dozen little tribal kingdoms, all jealous and hostile, on the island.

The Anglo-Saxon monarchy. Gradually peace and a semblance of order came to the distracted island as rivalries among the kingdoms diminished and the overlordship of the island was held in turn by the different rulers. In the ninth century the kingdom of Wessex (see map, p. 192) held the dominant position. The famous Wessex king, Alfred the Great (871-899), was confronted with the task of turning back a new wave of invaders, the Danes, who overran all the other English kingdoms. After a series of disheartening reverses, Alfred defeated the Danes and forced them into a treaty whereby they settled in what came to be called the Danelaw (see map, p. 194) and accepted Christianity.

In addition to being a successful warrior, Alfred the Great made notable contributions in government in order, as he wrote, that he "might worthily and fittingly steer and rule the dominion that was entrusted to me."[1] He reorganized the militia of freemen (*fyrd*) so that part was always ready for battle while the rest tilled the soil, and the ships he built to repel future Viking attacks have won him the title of founder of the English navy. He also issued a set of laws, which reflect his desire to see the average man protected from wrongdoing and violence.

Following the example of Charlemagne, Alfred also advanced the intellectual life of his country. He invited learned men from abroad and founded a palace school. Since Latin was virtually unknown in England, Alfred urged the bishops to have translated into English the books "which are most necessary for all men to know." He also encouraged monks to keep an account of current affairs, the *Anglo-Saxon Chronicle*, which continued to be written for hundreds of years afterward.

Alfred's successors were able rulers who conquered the Danelaw and created a unified English monarchy. Danes and Saxons intermarried, and soon all differences between the two people disappeared. After 975, however, a decline set in. The power of the central government lagged and with it the ability to keep order at home and repel outside attacks. The impotence of the kingdom is well illustrated in the unhappy reign of Ethelred the Unready (978-1016), who was unable to keep a firm hand on the great nobles or to cope with a new attack by the Danes.

In its political structure, the major defect

of Anglo-Saxon England was the weakness of its central government: the inability of the king to control the great nobles, the earls, who were the king's deputies in their districts. But as a positive contribution to political history, the Anglo-Saxons developed local government to a strong degree. They left us a valuable legacy: the tradition of the people's participation in their government. In the local political divisions—the shires and their subdivisions, the hundreds—numerous assemblies or courts (moots) existed. Presided over by a royal official, the reeve, and composed of freemen of the area, the moots dispensed justice according to local custom and helped administer the realm. Here was one of the seeds of later democratic government. It is an interesting carry-over that American law students call their trial cases "moot court cases" and that our modern title of sheriff is derived from the shire's most important official, the shire reeve.

Following the reign of Ethelred, the Anglo-Saxons were again overrun by the Danes, and King Canute of Denmark ruled England as well as Norway. Canute proved to be a wise and civilized king and was well liked by his Anglo-Saxon subjects because he respected their rights and customs. Canute's empire fell apart after his death in 1035, and in 1042 the English crown was secured by Ethelred's son, Edward the Confessor. So pious that he remained a virgin all his life, Edward was a weak ruler who had little control over the powerful earls who had usurped most of the king's authority in their regions. This decline in government was reversed after the Normans conquered the island in 1066.

The Norman Conquest. The Norman Conquest of England really began in the reign of Edward the Confessor. Edward had spent most of his early life in Normandy, and as king of England he showed a strong pro-Norman bias. On his death without heir in 1066 the *Witan*—the council of the kingdom—selected Harold Godwinson, a powerful English earl, as the new ruler. Immediately William, duke of Normandy, claimed the English throne, basing his demand on a flimsy hereditary right and on the assertion that Edward had promised him the crown.

An outstanding statesman and soldier, William as duke of Normandy had subdued the rebellious nobles and established a new kind of centralized feudal state. William effectively controlled his vassals, and his feudal army of one thousand knights made him the most powerful ruler west of Germany. His centralized authority in Normandy contrasted sharply with the situation in England, where the powerful earls were continually embarrassing the king.

By promising to promote Church reform in England, William secured the sanction of the pope, which gave his invasion the flavor of a crusade. His well-equipped army of hard-fighting Norman knights and landless nobles from Brittany and Flanders looked upon the conquest of England as an investment that would pay them rich dividends in the form of lands and serfs.

The cross-Channel maneuver was hazardous; five thousand knights, bowmen, and supporting infantry, as well as many horses, had to be transported in open boats. On October 14, 1066, at Hastings, William's mounted knights broke the famed shield-wall of the English infantry, and resistance ceased when King Harold was slain. The defeat ended Anglo-Saxon rule and brought a new pattern of government that would make England the strongest state in Europe.

William the Conqueror's centralized feudal monarchy. As king of England, William directed all his policies at a single goal—the increase of his own power within the context of feudalism. And, sensibly, he utilized some of the institutions existing in England. He retained the Anglo-Saxon shires and hundreds as administrative divisions, along with the system of local courts and sheriffs. But the long arm of royal power also reached the local level through the king's commissioners, who occasionally toured the shires, and the sheriffs, who became the effective local agents of the king in collecting the feudal dues and in presiding over the shire courts.

Most important, William introduced the Norman system of centralized feudalism into England. As owner of all England by right of conquest, William retained some land as his royal domain and granted the remainder as fiefs to royal vassals called tenants-in-chief, among whom were bishops and abbots. In return for their fiefs, the tenants-in-chief provided William with a stipulated number of knights to serve in the royal army. To furnish the required knight service, the great vassals—most of whom were French-speaking Normans—subinfeudated parts of their fiefs among their own vassals. But from all the landholders in England, regardless of whether or not they were his immediate vassals, William exacted homage and an oath that they would "be faithful to him against all other men." Hence, both the tenants-in-chief holding fiefs directly from the king and the lesser tenants holding fiefs as vassals of the tenants-in-chief swore loyalty to the king, their feudal suzerain. This meant that a disgruntled noble could not call out his own vassals against the king, because every man owed his first allegiance to William.

William did not depend solely upon feudal levies, however; he retained the old Anglo-Saxon militia, in which every freeman was required to serve, and he hired mercenaries.

Thus the king had in readiness an independent fighting force to crush a rebellious baron. Furthermore, private feudal warfare was forbidden, and no castle could be built without royal permission.

The Domesday Survey is another example of the energetic and methodical manner in which William took over full control of England. Because William, like all medieval kings, constantly needed money, he ordered an accurate census of the property and property holders in his realm as a basis for collecting all the feudal "aids" and "incidents" (see p. 198) owed to him. Royal commissioners gathered testimony from local groups of older men who were put under oath and questioned. The complaints and even riots which the inventory caused are reflected in the *Anglo-Saxon Chronicle:*

So very narrowly did he cause the survey to be made that there was not a single hide nor a rood of land, nor—it is shameful to relate that which he thought no shame to do—was there an ox or a cow or a pig passed by that was not set down in the accounts. . . .[2]

The Bayeux tapestry, actually a woolen embroidery on linen, dates from the eleventh century. Over 230 feet long and 20 inches wide, it both depicts and narrates (in Latin) the events of the Norman Conquest of England in 1066. This section shows the English shield wall being attacked by the mounted French knights.

This seal was struck during the reign of William the Conqueror. The Latin inscription on the face reads "Know by this sign William, chief of the Normans"; the reverse reads "By this sign know the same William, king of the English."

In line with his policy of controlling all aspects of the government, William revamped the old Anglo-Saxon *Witan*, which had elected and advised the kings. The new Norman ruler changed its title to the Great Council—also called *curia regis*, the king's council or court—and converted it into a feudal body composed of his tenants-in-chief. The Great Council met at least three times a year as a court of justice for the great barons and as an advisory body in important matters. At other times a small permanent council of barons advised the king.

William also dominated the English Church. He appointed bishops and abbots and required them to provide military service for their lands. Although he permitted the Church to retain its courts, he denied them the right to appeal cases to the pope without his consent. Nor could the decrees of popes and Church councils circulate in England without royal approval.

Thus William formed the conquered island into one of Europe's most advanced states. In his determination to be master of his own house, he ruthlessly oppressed any opposition to his will. The nobility and the Church were burdened with feudal services, and the Anglo-Saxon freemen, oppressed by the exactions of their Norman lords, were in time reduced to serfdom. William advanced political feudalism and the manorial system and fused the two into a highly centralized feudal structure.

William's sons. William II, who succeeded his father in 1087, was a disappointing namesake. Utilizing his father's methods, but without his ability, William II stirred up several baronial revolts before being shot in the back—accidentally, it was said—while hunting. Succeeding him was his brother, Henry I (1100-1135), a more able and conciliatory monarch who met with only one baronial revolt.

While the Great Council, made up of the chief nobles, occasionally met to advise the king, the small permanent council of barons grew in importance. From it now appeared the first vague outlines of a few specialized organs of government. The exchequer, or treasury, supervised the collection of royal revenue, now greatly increased with the revival of a money economy. Notable was *scutage* or "shield money," a fee which the king encouraged his vassals to pay in lieu of personal military service. The well-trained "barons of the exchequer" also sat as a special court to try cases involving revenue. At times members of the small council were sent throughout the realm to judge serious crimes which endangered what was called the King's Peace.

Henry I's achievements in strengthening the monarchy were largely undone by the nineteen years of chaos that followed his death. Ignoring their promise to recognize Henry's only surviving child, Matilda, wife of Geoffrey Plantagenet, count of Anjou in France, many barons supported Henry's weak nephew Stephen. During the resulting civil war the nobility became practically independent of the crown and, secure in their strong castles, freely pillaged the land. According to the *Anglo-Saxon Chronicle:*

They levied taxes on the villages every so often, and called it "protection money." . . . If two or three men came riding to a village, all the villagers fled, because they expected they would be robbers. The bishops and learned men were always excommunicating them, but they thought nothing of it. . . .[3]

Henry II. Anarchy ceased with the accession of Matilda's son, Henry II (1154-1189), the founder of the Plantagenet, or Angevin, House in England. As a result of his inheritance (Normandy and Anjou) and his marriage to Eleanor of Aquitaine, the richest heiress in France, Henry's possessions stretched from Scotland to the Pyrenees. The English holdings in France far exceeded the land directly ruled by the French kings, who eyed their vassal rival with jealousy and

The White Tower, the oldest part of the Tower of London, was erected during the reign of William the Conqueror. This fortress was long used as a prison for those accused of crimes against the English throne.

fear. Henry's reign marks the outbreak of the strife between England and France, which runs like a red thread throughout the tapestry of medieval and modern history.

Stephen, Henry's weak predecessor, had left a sorry heritage. The judicial system was confused and corrupt. The royal courts administered by the king's justices faced strong competition from both the baronial courts, run independently by feudal lords, and the Church courts, which threatened to extend their supremacy over the whole realm.

Henry's chief contribution to the development of the English monarchy was to increase the jurisdiction of the royal courts at the expense of the feudal courts. This produced three major results: a permanent system of circuit courts presided over by itinerant justices, the jury system, and a body of law common to all England.

Itinerant justices on regular circuits were sent out once each year to try breaches of the King's Peace. To make this system of royal criminal justice more effective, Henry employed the method of inquest used by William the Conqueror in the Domesday Survey. In each shire a body of important men were sworn (*juré*) to report to the sheriff all crimes committed since the last session of the king's circuit court. Thus originated the modern-day grand jury which presents information for an indictment.

Henry's courts also used the jury system as a means of settling private lawsuits. Instead of deciding such civil cases by means of oath-helpers or trial by ordeal (see p. 133), the circuit judges handed down decisions based upon evidence sworn to by a jury of men selected because they were acquainted with the facts of the case. This more attractive and efficient system caused litigants to flock to the royal courts, a procedure facilitated by the sale of "writs," which ordered a sheriff to bring the case to a royal court. Not only was the king's income greatly increased by fees from the sale of writs, but the feudal courts of the nobility were greatly weakened.

This petit or trial jury eventually evolved into the modern trial jury whose members, no longer witnesses, determine guilt or innocence. Trial by jury became the most characteristic feature of the judicial system of all English-speaking nations and was carried to the far corners of the earth as a hallmark of justice.*

Henry's judicial reforms promoted the growth of the common law—one of the most important factors in welding the English people into a nation. The decisions of the royal justices became the basis for future decisions made in the king's courts, superseded the many diverse systems of local justice in the shires, and became the law common to all Englishmen.

Thomas à Becket, victim of Church-state rivalry. While Henry skillfully diminished the activities of the baronial courts by making the royal courts more powerful, he was not so successful against his other legal rival —the Church courts. When he appointed Thomas à Becket archbishop of Canterbury, the king assumed that his former boon companion and royal chancellor could easily be persuaded to cooperate, but Becket proved to be stubbornly independent, stoutly upholding the authority of the Church.

In 1164 Henry stipulated that clergymen found guilty by a Church court of committing heinous crimes, such as murder and grand larceny, were to be unfrocked and handed over to a royal court where punishments were more severe than in the Church courts. Henry's idea was to prevent the abuses resulting from "benefit of clergy"— the principle that the Church alone had legal jurisdiction over its clergy, among whom were included all who claimed to be students, crusaders, and even servants of clergymen. Becket refused to yield, claiming that clergymen would suffer unjust "double punishment" for a crime—unfrocked by the Church and punished by the state.

When Becket received no support from the English clergy, he fled to France and

THE DOMINIONS OF HENRY II

- Inheritance
- Suzerainty
- Acquisitions by Marriage to Eleanor of Aquitaine
- French Royal Domain

Henry II was king, feudal suzerain, and vassal—all in one. He was king of England, feudal overlord of Scotland, Wales, Ireland, and Brittany, and vassal to the French king for the English holdings in France (although he held more territory there than the French monarch).

appealed to the pope for aid. After a few years the pope patched up the quarrel, and the archbishop returned to England. His first act, however, was to excommunicate the bishops who, in his absence, had crowned the eldest prince heir to the throne. When this news reached Henry, in a fit of passion he roared: "What a pack of fools and cowards I have nourished in my house, that not one of them will avenge me of this turbulent priest."[5] Responding to this tirade, four knights went to Canterbury and murdered Becket before the high altar of the cathedral. An eyewitness wrote that Becket "fell on his knees and elbows, offering himself a living victim, and saying in a low voice, 'For the name of Jesus and the protection of the church I am ready to embrace death.'"[6]

The resulting uproar destroyed all chance of reducing the power of the Church courts.

*The workings of Roman law offer an interesting contrast. "Under Roman law, and systems derived from it, a trial in those turbulent centuries, and in some countries even today, is often an inquisition. The judge makes his own investigation into the civil wrong or the public crime, and such investigation is largely uncontrolled. The suspect can be interrogated in private. He must answer all questions put to him. His right to be represented by a legal adviser is restricted. The witnesses against him can testify in secret and in his absence. And only when these processes have been accomplished is the accusation or charge against him formulated and published. Thus often arise secret intimidation, enforced confessions, torture, and blackmailed pleas of guilty."[4]

Becket became a martyr and, after miracles were reported to have occurred at his tomb, was canonized a saint. Although Becket was without much doubt a Norman, legend soon made him the symbol of English resistance to the yoke of Norman tyranny.

Richard the Lion-Hearted, knight-errant. As was the case after William the Conqueror's reign, the good beginning made by Henry II was marred by the mistakes of his successors. Having no taste for the prosaic tasks of government, Richard the Lion-Hearted wasted his country's wealth in winning a great reputation as a crusader (see p. 210) and in fighting the king of France. Richard spent only five months of his ten-year reign (1189-1199) in England, which he regarded as a source of money for his overseas adventures. The royal bureaucracy worked so well, however, that the king's absence made little difference.

John's powers limited by Magna Carta. Richard's successor, his brother John (reigned 1199-1216), was an able ruler who worked hard to promote his father's governmental system but who lacked his brother's chivalrous qualities. His cruelty and unscrupulousness cost him the support of his barons at the very time he needed them most in his struggles with the two ablest men of the age, Philip II of France and Pope Innocent III. As feudal overlord for John's possessions in France, Philip found the occasion to declare John an unfaithful vassal and his fiefs forfeit. John put up only feeble resistance, and after losing more than half his possessions in France he became involved in a struggle with Innocent III in which he was forced to make abject surrender (see pp. 245-246). In the meantime, John had completely alienated the English barons by attempting to collect illegal feudal dues and committing other infractions of feudal law. The exasperated barons rebelled and in 1215 forced John to affix his seal to Magna Carta, which bound the king to observe all feudal rights and privileges. People in later centuries, however, looked back upon Magna Carta as one of the most important documents in the story of human freedom.

To Englishmen of the time, this document did not appear to introduce any new constitutional principles. It was merely an agreement between the barons and the king, the aristocracy and the monarchy. But the seeds of political liberty were to be discovered in Magna Carta. Certain provisions were later used to support the movement toward constitutional monarchy and representative government:

Clause XII. [Taxation or feudal aids except those sanctioned by custom] . . . shall be levied in our kingdom only by the common consent of our kingdom [i.e., by the king's Great Council].

Clause XXXIX. No free man shall be taken or imprisoned or dispossessed, or outlawed, or banished, or in any way destroyed . . . except by the legal judgment of his peers or by the law of the land.

Clause XL. To no one will we sell, to no one will we deny, or delay right or justice.[7]

In 1215 these limitations upon the king's power applied only to freemen—that is, to the clergy, the barons, and a relatively small number of rural freeholders and burghers—not to the majority of the population, who were still serfs. As serfdom gradually disap-

A detail from a medieval illuminated manuscript depicts the murder of Thomas à Becket.

peared, however, the term *freeman* came to include every Englishman.

The importance of Magna Carta does not lie in its original purpose but rather in the subsequent use made of it. Two great principles were potential in the charter: (1) the law is above the king; and (2) the king can be compelled by force to obey the law of the land. This concept of the rule of law and the limited power of the crown was to play an important role in the seventeenth-century struggle against the despotism of the Stuart kings; Clause XII was interpreted to guarantee the principle of no taxation without representation and Clause XXXIX to guarantee trial by jury.

The origins of Parliament. The French-speaking Normans commonly used the word *Parlement* (from *parler*, "to speak") for the Great Council, or *curia regis*, composed of the king's feudal tenants-in-chief. Anglicized as *Parliament*, the term was used interchangeably with Great Council and *curia regis*. Modern historians, however, generally apply the term to the Great Council only after 1265, when its membership was radically enlarged.

The first meeting of Parliament—the enlarged Great Council—took place in the midst of a baronial rebellion against Henry III, the son of King John. In an effort to gain the widest possible popular support, Simon de Montfort, the leader of the rebellion, summoned not only the barons but also two knights from every shire and two burghers from every borough to the Great Council in 1265.

Parliament gains stature. Parliament first became important during the reign of Henry III's son, Edward I (1272-1307), one of England's half-dozen outstanding monarchs. Beginning with the "Model Parliament" of 1295, Edward followed the pattern set by Simon de Montfort in summoning representatives of shires and towns to meetings of the Great Council. In calling Parliaments, Edward had no idea of making any concession to popular government. His aim was to enhance royal power by, in essence, packing his Great Council with representatives who would tend to support him rather than his opponents, the powerful barons. He could

Probably the earliest authentic view of Parliament in session, this picture shows a meeting called by Edward I. The dignitaries occupying the center benches are Church officials and secular lords. In the center are members of the judiciary seated on woolsacks to remind them that wool was vital to the English economy. Just below them are representatives from the towns and shires.

then expect to more easily obtain consent for new taxation, and he could use Parliament as an easy way of informing the country about royal policy. His utilization of the growing wealth and influence of the burghers to support royal power was soon copied by the king of France, Philip IV, who in 1302 began the practice of including representatives of the French bourgeoisie in his feudal council.

Early in the fourteenth century the representatives of the knights and the burghers, called the "Commons," adopted the practice of meeting separate from the lords spiritual and temporal. Thus arose the divisions of Parliament that came to be called the House of Commons and the House of Lords.

Parliament, particularly the Commons, soon discovered its power as a major source of money for the king. It gradually became the custom for Parliament to exercise this "power of the purse" by withholding its financial grants until the king had redressed grievances, made known by petitions. Parliament also presented petitions to the king with the request that they be promulgated as statutes, as the laws drawn up by the king and his council and confirmed in Parliament were called. Gradually the right to initiate legislation through petition was obtained. Again, Parliament's "power of the purse" turned the trick.

Edward I's statutes. Edward issued through Parliament a series of great statutes, many aimed at curtailing the power of the nobility that had greatly increased during the baronial revolts of his father's reign. The statute known as *Quo Warranto*, which demanded of a lord that he prove "by what warrant" he exercised certain rights and privileges, led to the recovery of lost royal rights. Another statute established the entail system which enabled a landowner to will his entire estate to his eldest son on condition that the property remain forever undivided. The younger brothers were thus forced to shift for themselves in governmental service, in the professions, or in commerce. By contrast, estates on the Continent were usually divided among all the sons in a family, a practice which encouraged the growth of a large and parasitic class of landowners. Edward also restricted the power of the Church, grown exceedingly rich through gifts of land. The Statute of Mortmain forbade the giving of more land to the Church without royal approval.

Widening the boundaries of the realm. Edward I was the first English king who was determined to be master of the whole island of Britain—Wales, Scotland, and England. In 1284, after a five-year struggle, English law and administration were imposed on Wales. As a concession to the Welsh, Edward gave his oldest son the title of Prince of Wales.

A dispute over the succession to the Scottish throne in the 1290's gave Edward his opportunity to intervene in the land to the north. After calling upon Edward to settle the dispute, the Scots accepted him as their overlord. Then Edward unwisely demanded that the Scots furnish him with troops to fight in England's wars. Under the coura-

geous William Wallace, rebellion quickly flared up. After winning several victories against the English, Wallace was defeated and hanged as a traitor. But the fires of Scottish nationalism continued to burn despite numerous attempts to put out the flames. Edward II, the next English king, attempted to humble the Scots, but at the battle of Bannockburn (1314) the Scots, led by Robert Bruce, won their independence. The two peoples remained bitter enemies, with the Scots often joining the French in their wars against the English. Not until 1603 were the two kingdoms united under a common monarch.

THE BEGINNINGS OF THE FRENCH NATIONAL STATE

Political fragmentation. At the time William the Conqueror set sail, the monarchy in France barely existed. As we saw in Chapter 8, the later Carolingian rulers were generally weak and unable to defend the realm from Viking incursions. This task fell to the local counts and dukes, who built castles to protect the countryside and exercised the powers of the king in their territories. In France by the beginning of the tenth century there were more than thirty great feudal princes who were nominally vassals of the king but who gave him little or no support. Nevertheless, except for the short reign of Odo (see p. 194), the Carolingian kings maintained their precarious grasp on the throne. When the last Carolingian, Louis the Sluggard, died in 987, the nobles elected as his successor Hugh Capet, count of Paris and descendant of Odo.

The "kingdom" that Hugh Capet theoretically ruled was roughly comparable to, but smaller than, modern France. The territory Hugh actually controlled was a small feudal county extending from Paris to Orléans. It was almost encircled by rivers—hence, perhaps, its name: the Ile de France. The royal domain was surrounded by many independent duchies and counties, such as Flanders, Normandy, Anjou, and Champagne, which were a law unto themselves.

The early Capetians. Starting with little power and limited territory under their direct rule, the Capetian monarchs gradually extended their control over the great magnates. France was literally made by its kings, for ultimately the royal domain, in which the king's word was law, came to coincide with the boundaries of the realm.

In the late tenth and eleventh centuries, however, there was little tangible evidence that the Capetian kings would fulfill their destiny. They were weaker than many of their own vassals, and they had no hand in the stirring events of their time. While they remained historical nonentities, one of their vassals, the duke of Normandy, seized the throne of England; another, the count of Flanders, became a leader of the First Crusade and ruler of the kingdom of Jerusalem; and another vassal became the founder of the kingdom of Portugal.

The major accomplishment of the first four Capetian kings was their success in keeping the French crown within their own family. The nobles who elected Hugh Capet to the kingship had no thought of giving the Capetian family a monopoly on the royal office. But the Capetian kings, with the support of the Church, which nurtured the tradition of kingship as a sacred office, cleverly arranged for the election and coronation of their heirs. Before the king died, the young prince was crowned by the Church and became "associated" with his father in his rule. For three hundred years the House of Capet never lacked a male heir, and by the end of the twelfth century the hereditary principle had become so ingrained that French kings no longer took the precaution of crowning their sons during their own lifetime.

Louis the Fat pacifies the Ile de France. The advent of the fifth Capetian king, Louis VI (1108-1137), also known as Louis the Fat, heralded the end of Capetian weakness. Louis' pacification of the royal domain, the Ile de France, paralleled on a smaller scale the work of William the Conqueror in England.

With the support of the Church (which supplied him with able advisers), Louis determined to crush the lawless barons who were defying royal authority in the Ile de France. According to Abbot Suger, his chief adviser and biographer:

A king, when he takes the royal power, vows to put down with his strong right arm insolent tyrants whensoever he sees them vex the state with endless wars, rejoice in rapine, oppress the poor, destroy the churches, give themselves over to lawlessness which, and it be not checked, would flame out into ever greater madness. . . .[8]

In the end the castles of the defiant vassals were captured and in many cases torn down. "And this," writes Abbot Suger, "they deserved who had not feared to raise their hand against the Lord's anointed."[9] Louis had made his word law in the Ile de France, established a solid base from which royal power could be extended, and so increased the prestige of the monarchy that the great duke of Aquitaine deigned to marry his daughter Eleanor to Louis' son. Unfortunately, Eleanor's behavior so scandalized Louis' pious son ("I thought I married a king," Eleanor

FEUDAL FRANCE
ABOUT 1000

Ile de France

once exclaimed, "but instead I am the wife of a monk") that he had the marriage annulled, and Aquitaine passed to Eleanor's second husband, Henry II of England.

Philip Augustus extends royal rule. The first great expansion of the royal domain was the work of the next Capetian, Philip II Augustus (1180-1223), during whose reign the French king for the first time became more powerful than any of his vassals and France replaced Germany as the strongest monarchy in continental Europe.

Philip Augustus' great ambition was to wrest from the English Plantagenets the vast territory they held in France. Philip made little headway against Henry II, except to make Henry's life wretched by encouraging his faithless sons, Richard the Lion-Hearted and John, to revolt. As we have seen, Philip took Normandy, Maine, Anjou, and Touraine from John, thereby tripling the size of the royal domain.

Philip also greatly strengthened the royal administrative system by devising new agencies for centralized government and tapping new sources of revenue, including a money payment from his vassals in lieu of military service. New salaried officials, called bailiffs, performed duties similar to those carried out in England by itinerant justices and sheriffs. A corps of loyal officials, like the bailiffs recruited not from the feudal nobility but from the ranks of the bourgeoisie, was collected around the king. As in England, special administrative departments were created: the *parlement*, a supreme court of justice (not to be confused with the English Parliament, which became primarily a legislative body); the chamber of accounts, or royal treasury; and the royal or privy council, a group of advisers who assisted the king in the conduct of the daily business of the state.

In this early phase of consolidation of royal power, the papacy, which was struggling with the German emperors, usually allied itself with the French monarchy. As in England and Germany, however, the kings sometimes collided with the popes. Philip II defied Innocent III by having French bishops annul his marriage; but when the pope imposed an interdict on France, Philip backed down, and his wife again became his queen.

On the other hand, the Church inadvertently helped expand the royal domain. In southern France, particularly in Toulouse, the heretical Albigensian sect flourished. Determined to stamp out this sect, Innocent III in 1208 called the Albigensian Crusade, discussed in Chapter 11. Philip, faced with the enmity of King John and the German emperor, did not take part, but he allowed his vassals to do so. After Philip's death his son Louis VIII led a new crusade to exterminate the remnants of Albigensian resistance. Later in the century Toulouse escheated to the French crown when its count died without heir. The royal domain now stretched from the chilly coast of the

The *Très Riches Heures du Duc de Berry* is a devotional book containing prayers for each day of the year. The months are illustrated by full-page miniatures. This one, of October, depicts peasants sowing grain in fields on one bank of the Seine, while on the far bank is the Louvre as it appeared in the time of Philip II, who built the fortress as a storage place for his records and money.

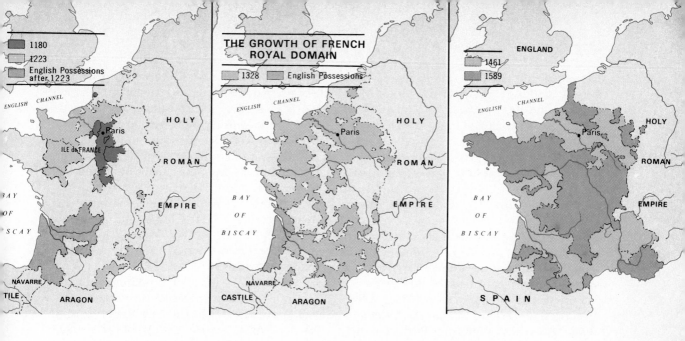

THE GROWTH OF FRENCH ROYAL DOMAIN

English Channel to the warm shores of the Mediterranean.

Louis IX dignifies the throne. After the brief reign of Louis VIII, France came under the rule of Louis IX (1226-1270), better known as St. Louis because of his piety and noble character. In contrast to the cunning opportunism of his grandfather, St. Louis' ideal was to rule justly, and he made some sacrifices to that end. For example, special officials were created to check on the bailiffs, who were forbidden to encroach on the feudal rights of the nobility. On the other hand, St. Louis believed himself responsible only to God, who had put him on the throne to lead his people out of a life of sin. Accordingly, St. Louis was the first French king to issue edicts for the whole kingdom without the prior consent of his council of great vassals. He also ordered an end to trial by battle and the time-honored feudal right of private warfare. Certain matters, such as treason and crimes on the highways, were declared to be the exclusive jurisdiction of the royal courts. Furthermore, St. Louis insisted on the right of appeal from the feudal courts of his vassals to the high royal court of *parlement* at Paris.

St. Louis' passion for justice impressed his contemporaries. He endeavored to hear personally his subjects' problems and complaints, and Joinville, his friend and biographer, whose *St. Louis, King of France* is a medieval masterpiece, has left us this sketch:

Many a time it happened that in summer time he would go and sit down in the wood at Vincennes, with his back to an oak, and make us take our seats around him. And all those who had complaints to make came to him without hindrance from ushers or other folk. Then he asked them with his own lips: "Is there any one here who has a cause?" Those who had a cause stood up when he would say to them: "Silence all, and you shall be dispatched [judged] one after another."[10]

Just, sympathetic, and peace-loving, St. Louis convinced his subjects that the monarchy was the most important agency for assuring their happiness and well-being.

Climax of Capetian rule under Philip IV. The reign of Philip IV, the Fair (1285-1314), climaxed three centuries of Capetian rule. The antithesis of his saintly grandfather, Philip was a man of craft, violence, and deceit. He took advantage of the growing anti-Semitism that had appeared in Europe with the crusades to expel the Jews from France and confiscate their possessions. (Philip's English contemporary, Edward I, had done the same.) Again, heavily in debt to the Knights Templars, who had turned to banking after the crusades, Philip had the order suppressed on trumped-up charges of heresy.

Philip's need of money also caused him to clash with the last great medieval pope. As we shall see in Chapter 12, Pope Boniface VIII refused to allow Philip to tax the French clergy and made sweeping claims to supremacy over secular powers. But the national state had reached the point where such leaders as Philip IV would not brook interference with their authority no matter what the source. The result of this controversy was the humiliation of Boniface, a blow from which the medieval papacy never recovered.

In domestic affairs the real importance of Philip's reign lies in the increased power and improved organization of the royal government. Philip's astute civil servants, recruited mainly from the middle class, concentrated their efforts on exalting the power of the monarch. Trained in Roman law, and inspired by its maxim that "whatever pleases the prince has the force of law," they sought to make the power of the monarch absolute.

Like Edward I in England, Philip enlarged his feudal council to include representatives of the third "estate" or class—the townsmen. This Estates-General of nobles, clergy, and burghers was used as a means of obtaining popular support for Philip's policies, including the announcement of new taxes. Significantly, Philip did not need to ask the Estates-General's consent for his tax measures, and it did not acquire the "power of the purse" that characterized the English Parliament. Philip had sown the seeds of absolutism in France, but their growth was to be interrupted by the Hundred Years' War between France and England, which broke out twenty-three years after his death (see Chapter 12).

CHRISTIAN RECONQUESTS IN SPAIN

The Reconquista. The unification of Spain was a more complex process than that of either France or England. The customary rivalry between the feudal aristocracy and the royal authority was complicated by another significant element—a religious crusade. Unification required the ejection of the Muslims, with their alien religion and civilization. Unity also called for the integration of several distinct Christian states.

In Chapter 9 we noted the beginning of the *Reconquista*, or reconquest of Spain, up to the year 1085, when the Muslim strong-

hold of Toledo was captured. During this long struggle a mounting patriotism blended with a fanatical religious spirit. As early as the ninth century northern Spain became suffused with a religious zeal centering around Santiago de Compostela, reputed to be the burial site of the apostle St. James. His bones were enshrined in a great cathedral which thousands of pilgrims visited. Banners were consecrated there, and the battle cry of the Christian soldiers became "Santiago" (a contraction of *Sante Iago*, St. James' name in Spanish).

The Poem of My Cid. Another symbol of national awakening was an eleventh-century soldier of fortune, El Cid (Arabic for "lord"). His exploits against the Muslims thrilled Europe, and he became the hero of the great Spanish epic, *Poema de Mio Cid*. In the epic El Cid appears as a perfect Christian knight, although in reality he was an adventurer seemingly more interested in booty and power than in religion. The following characteristic lines begin with a reference to a victory over the Moors near Valencia:

His fame goes re-echoing even beyond the sea;
My Cid rejoiced, and all his company,
because God had given him aid and he had routed
    them there.
He sent out raiders, all night they rode; . . .
They destroyed the lands of the Moors as far as
    the seashore. . . .
Seizing and despoiling, riding at night,
sleeping in the daytime, taking those towns,
My Cid spent three years in the lands of the
    Moors. . . .
He sent forth a herald to Aragón and Navarre;
he sent his messages to the lands of Castile:
"Whoever would leave his toil and grow rich,
let him come to My Cid, whose taste is for battle.
He would now lay siege to Valencia to give it to
    the Christians."[11]

In 1212, at Las Navas de Tolosa, the Christians achieved one of the decisive victories of the Middle Ages. A few years later they captured first Cordova, whose great mosque was reconsecrated as a cathedral (see illustration, p. 208), and then Seville. By the end of the thirteenth century, when the reconquest halted until the latter part of the fifteenth century, Moorish political control was confined to Granada.

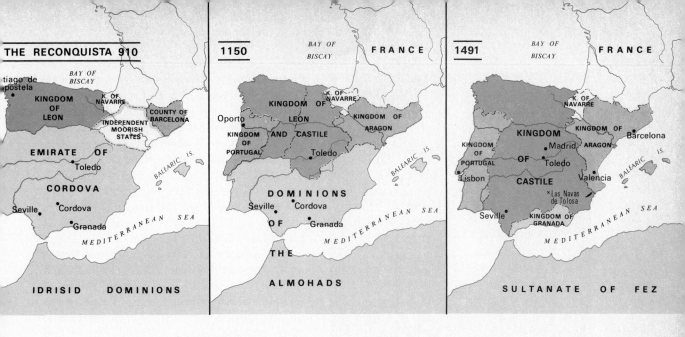

THE RECONQUISTA 910

1150

1491

It was usual for the Christian victors to allow their new Muslim subjects to enjoy their own religion and traditions. Muslim traders and artisans were protected because of their economic value, and Muslim culture—art in particular—was often adapted by the Christians.

FAILURES OF THE NATIONAL STATE: GERMANY AND ITALY

German tribal duchies. Following the collapse of the Carolingian empire, the tribal consciousness of its people kept Germany from falling into the extreme political fragmentation that characterized feudal France. When the successors of Louis the German, who received East Frankland in the Treaty of Verdun in 843 (see p. 194), proved incapable of coping with the attacks of savage Magyar horsemen in the late ninth and early tenth centuries, the task was taken over by the tribal leaders of the Saxons, Bavarians, Swabians, and Franconians who assumed the title of duke. The dukes of the five German duchies —including Lorraine, which Louis the German had acquired on the breakup of Lothair's middle kingdom—usurped the royal power and crown lands in their duchies and also took control over the Church.

When the last Carolingian, Louis the Child, died in 911, the dukes elected the weakest among them, Conrad of Franconia, to be their king. The new monarch ruled just eight years and proved himself incapable of meeting the menace of the Magyar raids. On his deathbed he recommended that the most powerful of the dukes, Henry the Fowler, duke of Saxony, be chosen as his successor. Henry founded the illustrious Saxon dynasty, which ruled until 1024 and made Germany the most powerful state in western Europe.

Henry the Fowler. After some initial opposition, Henry I (919-936) obtained recognition of his kingship from the other dukes. He exercised little authority outside of his own duchy, however, and his kingdom was hardly more than a confederation of independent duchies.

Against Germany's border enemies, Henry was more successful. He pushed back the Danes and established the Dane Mark as a protective buffer. Inroads were also made against the Slavs across the Elbe, where in 928 Brandenburg was set up as another defensive mark. Thus began the *Drang nach Osten* ("push to the East"), which became a permanent feature of German history. Further to the southeast, in Bohemia, Henry forced the Slavic Czechs to recognize his overlordship.

More spectacular was Henry's great victory over the Magyars in 933, following his refusal to pay the annual tribute demanded by these marauders. By this victory Henry

The crown of Otto I, which was probably made for his coronation, consists of eight gold plaques held together by hinges which open or close by means of pearl-headed pins. The crown was constructed in this portable fashion because Otto traveled a good deal and needed to have his crown with him for state occasions in various countries. Four of the plaques consist of pearls and gems held together by gold filigree. The other four plaques contain enamel panels showing God, David, Hezekiah with Isaiah, and (in the plaque visible here) Solomon. The upper part of the crown is an eleventh-century addition.

earned the gratitude of the German people, and when he died no one disputed the election of his son Otto to succeed him.

Otto the Great. Realizing that the great hindrance to German unity was the truculence of the dukes, Otto I, the Great (936-973), initiated a policy of gaining control of the unruly duchies by setting up his own relatives and favorites as their rulers. As an extra precaution he appointed, as supervising officials, counts who were directly responsible to the king. This policy was only temporarily successful, however, for both the counts and Otto's relatives and favorites proved unreliable. Even Otto's son, who was made duke of Swabia, rebelled against his father.

In the long run it was by means of an alliance with the Church that Otto constructed a strong German monarchy. The king protected the bishops and abbots and

granted them a free hand over their vast estates; in return the church prelates furnished him with the officials, the income, and the troops that he lacked. Otto appointed the bishops and abbots, and since their offices were not hereditary, he could be sure that their first obedience was to his royal person. These prelates replaced the counts as the chief agents of the king in the duchies and furnished as much as three quarters of his military forces.

This alliance of crown and Church was a natural one at the time. At his coronation at Aachen, Otto had insisted on being anointed *rex et sacerdos* ("king and priest"), thus reviving the Carolingian concept of the theocratic ruler and the alliance between crown and Church. Furthermore, both partners feared the unruly and arrogant dukes whose usurpations included the right to appoint bishops and abbots in their duchies.

Otto also put an end to the Magyar menace, thereby enhancing his claim that the king, and not the dukes, was the true defender of the German people. In 955 Otto crushed the Magyars at Lechfeld, near Augsburg (see map, next page), another decisive battle of the Middle Ages. The people of the time compared Lechfeld to the battle of Tours more than two centuries earlier; and Otto the Great, like Charles Martel, was hailed as the savior of Europe. The remaining Magyars settled quietly in Hungary, and by the year 1000 they had accepted Christianity.

The eastward movement. Otto continued German expansion eastward against the Slavs, and the region between the Elbe and the Oder became more and more Germanized. Like Charlemagne earlier, Otto relied on the Church to Christianize the stubborn heathens, and Magdeburg and other bishoprics were established in the conquered lands.

This expansion has been called the greatest achievement of the medieval Germans. Had it not been for this move eastward, modern Germany would have been a narrow strip of land wedged in between the Rhine and the Elbe; it has been estimated that 60 percent of German territory before the First World War had been taken from the Slavs. On the other hand, because the borders between the German colonists and the Slav natives were never clearly defined, pockets of Slavs and Germans intermingled. This ethnic admixture has caused serious disputes and conflicts in modern times.

The German empire. Like so many men of the Middle Ages, Otto the Great tended to revere the past, and he regarded the Roman and Carolingian empires as golden ages. As one historian succinctly put it: "His objective was Empire, and his model was Charlemagne." This pursuit of an empire characterized the German monarchy until the middle of the thirteenth century and was a major factor in its collapse.

Italy in the tenth century, having split into warring fragments, was a tempting field for an invader. In the north the old Lombard realm, which had been a part of Lothair's middle kingdom, became the object of various rival contenders. In central Italy were the Papal States, ruled by the pope. During this century, however, the popes were ap-

GERMANY ABOUT 1000
☐ Holy Roman Empire

pointed and controlled by the Roman nobility, and the power and prestige of the papacy was at its lowest ebb. Further south were two Lombard duchies; and, finally, at the extreme tip of the peninsula, the Byzantine empire retained a shaky foothold on the Italian mainland. Dotted here and there were cities, such as Venice, which had never become completely depopulated.

In deciding to invade Italy, Otto the Great was initially motived by defense. The dukes of the south German duchies of Swabia and Bavaria were hopeful of seizing Burgundy and Lombardy, and Otto believed that his position as German king would be endangered if those large remnants of Lothair's old middle kingdom fell into the hands of his German rivals. He first placed Burgundy and its weak ruler under his "'protection." Then he turned to Italy, where not only politics but, as chivalrous contemporary accounts explained it, romance also beckoned. Queen Adelaide, the widow of the former king of Lombardy, had been imprisoned by a usurper. Her plight suited Otto's political ambitions. In 951 he crossed the Alps, met Adelaide, who had escaped, and married her. He then dethroned her captor and proclaimed himself king of Italy.

On his second expedition to Italy in 962, Otto was crowned emperor by the pope, whose Papal States were threatened by an Italian duke. No doubt Otto thought of himself as the successor of the imperial Caesars and Charlemagne; and, in fact, his empire later became known as the Holy Roman Empire. But Otto also needed the imperial title to legitimatize his claim to Lombardy, Burgundy, and Lorraine, which had belonged to the middle kingdom of Lothair, the last man to hold the imperial title. Otto's coronation was a momentous event that brought Italy and Germany, pope and emperor, into a forced and unnatural union.

The distracting, even malevolent, effect of the German pursuit of empire in Italy is demonstrated by the reign of Otto III (983-1002), who eagerly promoted his grandiose scheme for "the renewal of the Roman Empire." Ignoring Germany, the real source of his power, he made Rome his capital, built a palace there, and styled himself "emperor of the Romans." As the "servant of Jesus Christ," another of his titles, Otto installed non-Italian popes in Rome and conceived of the papacy as a partner in ruling an empire of Germans, Italians, and Slavs. But notwithstanding Otto's love for Italy, the fickle Roman populace revolted and forced him to flee the city. He died a year later while preparing to besiege Rome.

Despite the distractions in Italy, the Saxon rulers were the most powerful in Europe. They had permanently halted Magyar pillaging and, by utilizing the German Church as an ally, had curbed the divisive tendencies toward feudalism. Economically, too, there was progress. German eastward expansion had begun, and the Alpine passes had been freed of Muslim raiders and made safe for the Italian merchants who by the year 1000 were ready to act as middlemen linking western Europe with the eastern Mediterranean.

The Salian emperors vs. the papacy. Pioneers in nation-making, the Saxon kings were succeeded by a new royal line, the Salian House (1024-1125), whose members set about with increased vigor to establish a centralized monarchy. To the dismay of many nobles, a body of lowborn royal officials was recruited; and the power of the dukes was weakened further when the crown won the allegiance of the lesser nobles.

The reign of Henry IV (1056-1106) was a watershed in German history. The monarchy reached the height of its power, but it also experienced a major reversal. For a century the Ottonian system, by which the king had governed his kingdom through the clergy, whom he appointed, had functioned smoothly. Under Henry IV, however, the revival of a powerful papacy led to a bitter conflict, centering on the king's right to appoint Church officials who were at the same time his most loyal supporters. This conflict, known as the Investiture Struggle (see p. 244), resulted in the loss of the monarchy's major sources of strength: the loyalty of the German Church, now transferred to the papacy; and the chief material base of royal power, the king's lands, which were dissipated by grants to loyal nobles.

The real victors in the Investiture Struggle were the German nobles, many of whom allied themselves with the papacy and continued to wage war against the monarchy long after the reign of Henry IV. From the time of Henry's death in 1106 until the accession of Frederick Barbarossa in 1152, the Welfs of Bavaria and the Hohenstaufens of Swabia, along with other noble factions, fought over the throne, which they made elective rather than hereditary. The outcome was that the structure of a strong national state was wrecked and Germany became extensively feudalized. The great nobles usurped royal rights, built strong castles, and forced lesser nobles to become their vassals. On the other hand, the great nobles acknowledged no feudal relationship to the king. Many free peasants, in turn, lost their freedom and became serfs. The evil effects of this period were to hinder the development of a unified Germany until modern times.

Prosperity in divided Italy. Italy was even less unified than Germany. Jealous of one another and of their independence, the prosperous city-states in northern Italy joined the struggle between the German emperors and the papacy. The Welf-Hohenstaufen rivalry in Germany was reflected in Italy, where the rival factions were known as Guelphs and Ghibellines—the latter name derived from Waiblingen, the chief Hohenstaufen stronghold in Swabia. The former were usually pro-papal; the latter strongly favored the German monarchy's imperial claims in Italy. Yet, amidst the turmoil, the vitality, wealth, and culture of the northern Italian cities increased.

A brilliant civilization also flourished on the island of Sicily. By 1127 the Norman conquests (see p. 207) resulted in the establishment of the kingdom of Naples and Sicily which, under the able rule of Roger II (1130-1154), became one of the strongest and wealthiest states in Europe. Scholars from all over the East and Europe traveled to Roger's court, which ranked next to Spain's in the translation of Arabic documents. Life and culture in the Sicilian kingdom, which included Norman, Byzantine, Italian, and Arabic elements, was diverse and colorful. In the thirteenth century the history of Naples and Sicily became fatally entwined with the history of the German empire and hinged on the rise and fall of the powerful royal house of Hohenstaufen.

Frederick Barbarossa. The second Hohenstaufen emperor, Frederick I Barbarossa ("Red-beard"), who reigned from 1152 to 1190, realistically accepted the fact that during the preceding half century Germany had become thoroughly feudalized; his goal was to make himself the apex of the feudal pyramid by forcing the great nobles to acknowledge his overlordship. Using force when necessary, he was largely successful, and Germany became a centralized feudal monarchy not unlike England in the days of William the Conqueror.

To maintain his hold over his German tenants-in-chief, Frederick needed the resources of Italy—particularly the income from taxes levied on wealthy north Italian cities, which, encouraged by the papacy, joined together in the Lombard League to resist him. Frederick spent about twenty-five years fighting intermittently in Italy, but although some of the cities submitted to his authority, the final result was failure. The opposition from the popes and the Lombard League was too strong. Frederick did score a diplomatic triumph, however, by marrying his son to the heiress of the throne of Naples and Sicily. The threat of Hohenstaufen encirclement made it vital to the papacy that this royal house be destroyed.

Frederick Barbarossa died in Asia Minor while en route with the Third Crusade, and in time he became a folk hero in Germany. It was believed that he still lived, asleep in a cave in the mountains near Berchtesgaden in Bavaria. Some day, awakened by a flight of ravens, he would emerge and bring unity and strength back to Germany. "In the late nineteenth century, the artists of the Prussian court delighted to paint pictures of his last, and joyful, awakening in 1871, when the sky was full of ravens since a second German Empire had been called into existence. Statues of Frederick Barbarossa and Kaiser Wilhelm I were placed side by side to symbolize the 'fact' that where one had left off, the other had begun."[12]

Frederick II, a brilliant failure. It fell to the lot of Frederick Barbarossa's grandson,

Frederick Barbarossa is shown here with his two sons in a miniature dated around 1180. He is credited with originating the title "Holy Roman Empire" for the lands he claimed in Germany and Italy while seeking to centralize royal power in his empire.

Frederick II (1194-1250), to meet the pope's challenge to the threat of Hohenstaufen encirclement. Orphaned at an early age, Frederick was brought up as the ward of the most powerful medieval pope, Innocent III. During Frederick's minority the empire fell on evil days; the Welf and Hohenstaufen factions resumed their struggle over the throne, and the strong feudal monarchy created by Frederick Barbarossa collapsed. In 1215, one year before Innocent died and with his support, Frederick was elected emperor. Faced by a resurgent nobility in Germany, he soon turned his attention to wealthy Italy.

The papacy and the north Italian cities successfully defied Frederick throughout his reign, and in the end he experienced the same failure as had Frederick Barbarossa. Frederick also clashed with the papacy in another sphere. Embarking on a crusade at the pope's insistence, he turned back because of illness and was promptly excommunicated. A few months later Frederick resumed his crusade and was again excommunicated, this time for crusading while excommunicated. When Frederick acquired Jerusalem by negotiation (see p. 211) and agreed to allow Muslims to worship freely in the city, the pope called him "this scorpion spewing poison from the sting of its tail" and excommunicated him a third time.

Frederick sacrificed Germany in his efforts to unite all Italy under his rule. He transferred crown lands and royal rights to the German princes in order to keep them quiet and to win their support for his inconclusive Italian wars. Born in Sicily, he remained at heart a Mediterranean monarch. He shaped his kingdom of Sicily into a modern state. Administered by paid officials who were trained at the University of Naples, which he founded for that purpose, his kingdom was the most centralized and bureaucratic in Europe. Economically, too, it was far in advance of other states; Frederick minted a uniform currency and abolished interior tolls and tariffs, and his powerful fleet promoted and protected commerce.

As long as he lived, this brilliant Hohenstaufen held his empire together, but it quickly collapsed after his death in 1250. In Germany his son ruled ineffectively for four years before dying, and soon afterward Frederick's descendants in Sicily were killed when the count of Anjou, brother of St. Louis of France, was invited by the pope to annihilate what remained of what he called the "viper breed of the Hohenstaufen."

Significance of the fall of the Hohenstaufens. The victory of the papacy was more apparent than real, for its struggle against the emperors lost it much of its prestige. Men had seen popes using spiritual means to achieve earthly ambitions—preaching a crusade against Frederick II and his descendants, for example. More and more, popes acted like Italian princes, playing the game of diplomacy amid shifting rivalries. This involvement in worldly concerns and the accompanying decay in religious ideals help explain the increasing attacks on the papacy that would culminate in the Protestant revolt.

The Hohenstaufen kingdom of Naples and Sicily might have become the nucleus of a unified Italy. Unfortunately, the count of Anjou's seizure of the kingdom initiated a long period of bitter rivalry between Spaniards of the House of Aragon, who had married into the Hohenstaufen family, and Frenchmen representing Anjou. Beset by this interference, southern Italy and Sicily precipi-

tously declined amid alien rule, corruption, and, at times, horrible cruelty.

The Holy Roman Empire never again achieved the brilliance it last enjoyed during the reign of Frederick Barbarossa. The emperors usually did not try to interfere in Italian affairs, and they ceased going to Rome to receive the imperial crown from the pope. In German affairs the emperors no longer even attempted to assert their authority over the increasingly powerful nobles. After the fall of the Hohenstaufens, Germany lapsed more and more into the political disunity and ineffectual elective monarchy that remained characteristic of its history until the late nineteenth century.

SUMMARY

During the period from 1050 to 1300, England and France arose as pioneers in national unification and centralization. The essential pattern of historical development was similar in both nations, although each had its distinctive problems. (1) At first the kings were faced with serious competitors to their royal authority, the feudal nobility and the Church; (2) the kings became more powerful than their competitors, first by strengthening their power within the context of the feudal system, then by gradually establishing some of the military, judicial, and administrative agencies of a modern state; (3) the kings in effect made alliances with the rising middle class in the cities against their common enemy, the nobility. From the middle class came most of the money that the king needed to maintain a professional civil service, including a standing army that gradually replaced the often unreliable feudal levies.

In England William the Conqueror secured a unified kingdom in 1066 as a result of the Conquest, and successive English kings managed to keep their competitors under control and build up the machinery of royal administration. English development is also noteworthy for its legal and constitutional achievements: the common law, the jury system, circuit judges, and the first steps in the creation of representative government through Parliament.

In France the movement toward the consolidation of royal power started from a small area—the minuscule Ile de France. Each of the many counties and duchies that constituted feudal France had to be subordinated and brought within the framework of royal authority. It took the French kings three centuries to accomplish what William the Conqueror had done in one generation.

Nation-making in Spain was unique, since it was suffused with the religious fervor of a crusade. In the mid-eleventh century the Christian Spanish states began the *Recon-*

quista in earnest, but not until the end of the fifteenth century would the task be completed.

Although they had initial success in building a strong state at home, the German kings dissipated their energies by seeking the prize of empire over the Alps. For hundreds of years German rulers pursued this imperial phantom in Italy. In the face of resistance from the Italian cities, the treachery of the German nobles, and the opposition of the papacy, the German kings failed to achieve their goal. In both Germany and Italy after 1250, disunity and weakness prevailed; national unification was delayed until the nineteenth century.

SUGGESTIONS FOR READING

F. Heer, **The Medieval World: Europe, 1100-1350*** (Mentor); and S. Painter, **The Rise of the Feudal Monarchies*** (Cornell) are excellent syntheses. See also C. Brooke, **Europe in the Central Middle Ages, 962-1154,*** 2nd ed. (Longman, 1975).

H. Cam, **England Before Elizabeth*** (Torchbooks); G. Sayles, **The Medieval Foundations of England*** (A. S. Barnes); and C. Brooke, **From Alfred to Henry III, 871-1272*** (Norton) are valuable surveys of English history during the period covered in this chapter. See also F. Stenton, **Anglo-Saxon England,** 3rd ed. (Oxford, 1971), the standard account; and D. Kirby, **The Making of Early England** (Schocken, 1968).

R. Allen Brown, **The Normans and the Norman Conquest** (Crowell, 1970); H. Lyon, **The Norman Conquest*** (Torchbooks); and J. A. Matthew, **The Norman Conquest** (Schocken) are all outstanding treatments. H. Muntz, **The Golden Warrior** (Scribner's) is a first-rate novel dealing with the Norman conquest.

Works on English monarchs of the period include E. Duckett, **Alfred the Great: The King and his England*** (Phoenix); Amy Kelly, **Eleanor of Aquitaine and the Four Kings*** (Vintage); S. Painter, **The Reign of King John*** (Johns Hopkins); James A. Brundage, **Richard Lion Heart** (Scribner's, 1974); and W. L. Warren, **Henry II** (Univ. of Calif., 1973). See also R. Winston, **Thomas Becket** (Knopf, 1967); and T. M. Jones, ed., **The Becket Controversy*** (Wiley, 1970).

On English constitutional history see J. C. Holt, **Magna Carta: The Idea of Liberty*** (Wiley, 1972); G. L. Haskins, **The Growth of English Representative Government*** (A. S. Barnes); B. Lyon, **A Constitutional and Legal History of Medieval England** (Harper

& Row); and A. Pollard, **The Evolution of Parliament,** 2nd ed. (Russell).

For French history see R. Fawtier, **The Capetian Kings of France, 987-1328*** (St. Martin's), the best account. See also C. Petit-Dutaillis, **The Feudal Monarchy in France and England: From the Tenth to the Thirteenth Centuries*** (Torchbooks).

R. Merriman, **The Rise of the Spanish Empire in the Old World and in the New,** Vol. I, (Cooper Square) is the standard work on medieval Spain. Gabriel Jackson, **The Making of Medieval Spain*** (Harcourt Brace Jovanovich) is brief and highly readable with many illustrations. See also R. Menendez Pidal, **The Cid and his Spain** (Frank Cass, 1971).

J. Bryce, **The Holy Roman Empire*** (AMS Pr.) is an old masterpiece and should be supplemented by G. Barraclough, **The Origins of Modern Germany*** (Capricorn). See also the diverse scholarly opinions presented in R. Herzstein, ed., **The Holy Roman Empire in the Middle Ages: Universal State or German Catastrophe?*** (Heath). P. Munz, **Frederick Barbarossa: A Study in Medieval Politics** (Cornell, 1969); E. Kantorowicz, **Frederick the Second, 1194-1250** (Ungar); and T. van Cleve, **The Emperor Frederick II of Hohenstaufen** (Oxford, 1972) are instructive biographies.

William F. Butler, **The Lombard Communes: A History of the Republics of North Italy** (Haskell, 1969) is a reprint of a standard work. L. Salvatore, **A Concise History of Italy** (AMS Pr., 1976) is a good general survey.

*Indicates a less expensive paperbound edition.

CHAPTER 11

Medieval Religion,
Thought,
and Art: 600-1300

To the Glory of God

INTRODUCTION. In Paris, on a small island in the Seine, stands an edifice of weather-beaten stone, the Cathedral of Notre Dame. Dedicated to the glory of God and the veneration of Our Lady, this cathedral offers a fascinating glimpse into the life and spirit of medieval Europe. Notre Dame de Paris was built by cooperative community action between 1163 and 1235, during some of the most epoch-making years of the Middle Ages. While workmen were supporting the cathedral's vault with flying buttresses and carefully fitting the multicolored windows into place, churchmen and students lolled on the Petit Pont, a bridge that led to the Left Bank. The students wrangled over theology, accused one another of heresy, and occasionally composed blasphemous poems that parodied the sacred liturgy. Some of these students were one day to occupy episcopal thrones as princes of the Church; one of the mightiest occupants of the papal throne, Innocent III, once studied in Paris.

The underlying difference between our medieval ancestors and ourselves would appear to be one of perspective. To them theology was the "science of sciences," whereas today there are those who say that we have made science our theology. Yet this difference is not due exclusively to the extension of knowledge during the intervening centuries. It also lies in the fundamental premise governing the lives of our medieval forefathers. They believed in a world order, divinely created and maintained. For them, the universe possessed an inner coherence and harmony, which it was the function of the theologian and the scientist alike to discover. Revelation and knowledge, faith and reason, Church and state, spirit and matter—these dualities could be reconciled in a great spiritual and social synthesis.

In this chapter we will examine the methods by which medieval men sought to realize this synthesis and the measure of their success. As a first step, we shall trace the institutional growth of the one universal organization of medieval Europe, the Church. Next we shall watch its progressive assumption of secular powers, culminating in the triumphs of Innocent III. Finally, we shall see how, under the sponsorship of the Church, scholars and philosophers, scientists and inventors, and artists and artisans labored for the glory of God and the salvation of man.

THE CHURCH IN THE EARLY MIDDLE AGES

Gregory the Great and the early medieval papacy (600-1050). While Europe gradually recovered from the shock of the Roman Empire's demise, the Church—the papacy and Benedictine monasticism in particular—became the mainstay of European civilization. During the pontificate of Gregory I, the Great (590-604), the medieval papacy began to take form. Gregory's achievement was to go beyond the claim of papal primacy in the Church (see p. 128) to establish the actual machinery of papal rule, temporal as well as spiritual.

A Roman aristocrat by birth, Gregory witnessed and commented on the devastation of Rome as the city changed hands three times during Justinian's long struggle to retake Italy from the Ostrogoths:

Ruins on ruins. . . . Where is the senate? Where the people? All the pomp of secular dignities has been destroyed. . . . And we, the few that we are who remain, every day we are menaced by scourges and innumerable trials.[1]

Concluding that the world was coming to an end, Gregory withdrew from it to become a Benedictine monk. In 579 the pope drafted him to undertake a fruitless mission seeking Byzantine aid against the Lombards, who had invaded Italy a few years before. After the people of Rome elected Gregory pope in

590, he assumed the task of protecting Rome and its surrounding territory from the Lombard threat. Thus Gregory was the first pope to act as temporal ruler of a part of what later became the Papal States.

Gregory the Great also laid the foundations for the later elaborate papal machinery of Church government. He took the first step toward papal control of the Church outside of Italy by sending a mission of Benedictine monks to convert the heathen Anglo-Saxons. The pattern of Church government Gregory established in England—bishops supervised by archbishops, and archbishops by the pope—became standard in the Church.

The task of establishing papal control of the Church and extending the pope's temporal authority was continued by Gregory the Great's successors. In the eighth century English missionaries transferred to Germany and France the pattern of papal government they had known in England; and the Donation of Pepin (see p. 190), by creating the Papal States, greatly increased the pope's temporal power. The papacy's spiritual and temporal power suffered a severe setback, however, with the onset of feudalism. Beginning in the late ninth century, the Church, including the papacy, fell more and more under the control of feudal lords and kings.

Missionary activity of the Church. The early Middle Ages was also a vital period of missionary activity. By disseminating Christianity, the missionaries aided in the fusion of Germanic and classical cultures. Monasteries served as havens for those seeking a contemplative life, as repositories of learning for scholars, and often as progressive farming centers.

One of the earliest Christian missionaries to the Germans was Ulfilas (c. 311-383), who spent forty years among the Visigoths and translated most of the Bible into Gothic. Ulfilas and other early missionaries were followers of Arius, and thus the heretical creed of Arianism (see p. 128) came to be adopted by all the Germanic tribes in the empire except the Franks and Anglo-Saxons. As we saw in Chapter 8, the Franks' adoption of Roman Catholicism produced an alliance between Frankish rulers and the papacy that was important for European history.

Another great missionary, St. Patrick, was born in Britain about 389 and later fled to Ireland to escape the Anglo-Saxon invaders. As a result of his Irish missionary activities, monasteries were founded and Christianity became dominant. From these monasteries in the late sixth and seventh centuries a stream of monks went to Scotland, northern England, the kingdom of the Franks, and even to Italy. The Irish monks eagerly pursued scholarship, and their monasteries were repositories for priceless manuscripts.

Beginning with the pontificate of Gregory the Great, the papacy joined forces with Benedictine monasticism to become very active in the missionary movement. Gregory, as we saw, sent a Benedictine mission to England in 596. Starting in Kent, where an archbishopric was founded at Canterbury ("Kent town"), Roman Christianity spread through England, and finally even the Irish Church founded by St. Patrick acknowledged the primacy of Rome.

The English Church in turn played an important part in the expansion of Roman-controlled Christianity on the Continent. St. Boniface, the greatest missionary from England in the eighth century, spent thirty-five years among the Germanic tribes. Known as the "Apostle to the Germans," he established several important monasteries, bishoprics, and an archbishopric at Mainz before he turned to the task of reforming the Church in France. There he revitalized the monasteries, organized a system of local parishes to bring Christianity to the countryside, and probably was instrumental in forming the alliance between the papacy and the Carolingian house. Roman Catholic missionaries also worked among the Scandinavians and the Western Slavs.

The monks as custodians of knowledge. One of the great contributions of the monasteries was the preservation of learning. Writing in the sixth century, Bishop Gregory of Tours lamented:

A monk copies a manuscript in the *scriptorium*, surrounded by other manuscripts and such tools of his trade as inkpots, pens, and brushes.

In these times . . . there has been found no scholar trained in the art of ordered composition to present in prose or verse a picture of the things that have befallen.[2]

Learning did not entirely die out in western Europe, of course. Seeing that the ability to read Greek was fast disappearing, the sixth-century Roman scholar Boethius, an administrator under the Ostrogothic king Theodoric, determined to preserve Greek learning by translating all of Plato and Aristotle into Latin. Only Aristotle's treatises on logic were translated, and these remained the sole works of that philosopher available in the West until the twelfth century. Unjustly accused of treachery by Theodoric, Boethius was thrown into prison, where he wrote *The Consolation of Philosophy* while awaiting execution. This little classic later became a medieval textbook on philosophy.

Cassiodorus, a contemporary of Boethius who had also served Theodoric, devoted most of his life to the collection and preservation of classical knowledge. By encouraging the monks to copy valuable manuscripts, he was instrumental in making the monasteries centers of learning. Following his example, many monasteries established scriptoria, departments concerned exclusively with copying manuscripts.

During the early Middle Ages most education took place in the monasteries. In the late sixth and seventh centuries, when the effects of the barbarian invasions were still being felt on the Continent, Irish monasteries provided a safe haven for learning. There men studied Greek and Latin, copied and preserved manuscripts, and in illuminating them produced masterpieces of art. *The Book of Kells* is a surviving example of their skill.

The outstanding scholar of the early Middle Ages, the Venerable Bede (d. 735), followed the Irish tradition of learning in a northern England monastery. Bede described himself as "ever taking delight in learning, teaching, and writing." His many writings, which included textbooks and commentaries on the Scriptures, summed up most knowledge available in his age. Through Alcuin later in the century, Bede's learning influenced the Carolingian Renaissance (see p.

192). Bede's best known work, the *Ecclesiastical History of the English People*, with its many original documents and vivid character sketches, is our chief source for early English history.

THE CHURCH MILITANT

The Church-state rivalry. In the last quarter of the eleventh century a resurgent and militant papacy entered into a bitter and prolonged struggle with what was then Europe's strongest state, the German or Holy Roman Empire. By 1200 the papacy had emerged triumphant; under Pope Innocent III, the most powerful man ever to sit on St. Peter's chair, the theory and the practice of papal power coincided.

Medieval political theory begins with the concept of a universal community divided into two spheres, the spiritual and the temporal—a view based upon Christ's injunction to "Render therefore to Caesar the things that are Caesar's, and to God the things that are God's" (Matthew 22:21). As Pope Gelasius I declared in the fifth century, God had entrusted spiritual and temporal powers to two authorities—the Church and the state—each supreme in its own sphere. At first the question of ultimate superority between these authorities did not arise, although Gelasius had implied that the Church was superior to the state in the same way that the soul was superior to the body. The issue could not be permanently shelved, however; a fight for supremacy was in the long run inevitable.

When the German king Otto the Great revived the Roman empire in the West in 962 (see p. 235), his act reemphasized the concept of the dual leadership of pope and emperor. Otto claimed to be the successor of Augustus, Constantine, and Charlemagne, although his actual power was confined to Germany and Italy. At first the papacy looked to the German king for protection against the unruly Italian nobles who for a century had been making a prize of the papacy. From the Church's viewpoint, however, this ar-

During the fourteenth century the Church-state struggle produced a great amount of rival political theory, with the Church making much use of symbolism and allegory. In this illumination Christ hands the sword of temporal power to a worldly king, while St. Peter, as pope, receives the key to heaven, symbol of spiritual power. Christ's gaze is fixed on St. Peter, thus indicating that the Church was more important than the state.

rangement had its drawbacks, for the German kings continued to interfere in ecclesiastical affairs—even in the election of popes.

During the eleventh century controversy arose between Church and state over the problem of lay investiture. Theoretically, on assuming office a bishop or abbot was subject to two investitures; his spiritual authority was bestowed by a Church official and his feudal or civil authority by a layman—a feudal lord or a king. In actual fact, however, feudal lords and kings came to control both the appointment and the installation of church prelates. As noted earlier (p. 234), this practice was most pronounced in Germany, where control of the Church was the foundation of the king's power. The German Church was in essence a state Church.

The Cluniac reform. A religious revival— often called the medieval reformation—began in the tenth century and reached full force in the twelfth and thirteenth. The first far-reaching force of the revival was the reformed Benedictine order of Cluny, founded

in 910. From the original monastery in Burgundy, there radiated a powerful impulse for the reform of the feudalized Church. The Cluniac program began as a movement for monastic reform, but in time it called for the enforcement of clerical celibacy and the abolition of simony, the purchase or sale of a Church office. (The term *simony* comes from Simon the magician, who tried to buy the gift of the Holy Spirit from the apostles.) The ultimate goal of the Cluniac reformers was to free the entire Church from secular control and subject it to papal authority. Some three hundred Cluniac houses were freed from lay control, and in 1059 the papacy itself was removed from secular interference by the creation of the College of Cardinals, which henceforth elected the popes.

Gregory VII. The most ambitious proponent of Church reform was Pope Gregory VII (1073-1085), who claimed unprecedented power for the papacy. Gregory held as his ideal the creation of a Christian commonwealth under papal control. Instead of conceding equality between the Church and the state, he drew from the Gelasian theory the conclusion that the spiritual power was supreme over the temporal. In the *Dictatus Papae* ("Dictate of the Pope") Gregory claimed:

> That the Roman pontiff alone can with right be called universal.
> That he alone may use the imperial insignia.
> That of the pope alone all princes shall kiss the feet.
> That it may be permitted to him to depose emperors.
> That he himself may be judged by no one.
> That he who is not at peace with the Roman Church shall not be considered catholic.
> That he may absolve subjects from their fealty to wicked men.[3]

The Investiture Struggle. In 1075 Gregory VII formally prohibited lay investiture and threatened to excommunicate any layman who performed it and any ecclesiastic who submitted to it. This drastic act virtually declared war against Europe's rulers, since most of them practiced lay investiture. The climax to the struggle occurred in Gregory's clash with the emperor Henry IV. The latter was accused of simony and lay investiture in appointing his own choice to the archbishopric of Milan and was summoned to Rome to explain his conduct. Henry's answer was to convene in 1076 a synod of German bishops which declared Gregory a usurper and unfit to occupy the Roman See:

Wherefore henceforth we renounce, now and for the future, all obedience unto thee—which indeed we never promised to thee. And since, as thou didst publicly proclaim, none of us has been to thee a bishop, so thou henceforth wilt be Pope to none of us.[4]

In retaliation Gregory excommunicated Henry and deposed him, absolving his subjects from their oaths of allegiance.

At last, driven to make peace with the pontiff by a revolt among the German nobles, Henry appeared before Gregory in January 1077 at Canossa, a castle in the Apennines. Garbed as a penitent, the emperor is said to have stood barefoot in the snow for three days and begged forgiveness until, in Gregory's words: "We loosed the chain of the anathema and at length received him into the favor of communion and into the lap of the Holy Mother Church."[5]

This dramatic humiliation of the emperor did not resolve the quarrel, nor do contemporary accounts attach much significance to the incident—public penance was not uncommon in those days even for kings. Yet the pope had made progress toward freeing the Church from interference by laymen and toward increasing the power and prestige of the papacy. The problem of lay investiture was settled in 1122 by the compromise known as the Concordat of Worms. The Church maintained the right to elect the holder of an ecclesiastical office, but only in the presence of the king or his representative. The candidate, such as a bishop, was invested by the king with the scepter, the symbol of his administrative jurisdiction, after which he performed the act of homage and swore allegiance as the king's vassal. Only after this ceremony had taken place was the candidate consecrated by the archbishop, who invested him with his spiritual functions, as symbolized by the ring and pastoral staff. Since the kings of England and France

had earlier accepted this compromise, the problem of lay investiture waned.

The struggle between Church and empire continued for more than a century, sparked by the papacy's resentment at the emperors' continued interference in Italian affairs. We have already seen how the prosperous cities of northern Italy formed the Lombard League, defeated Frederick Barbarossa and Frederick II, and achieved the pope's aim of keeping the emperors out of Italy.

THE CHURCH TRIUMPHANT

The papacy's zenith: Innocent III. As demonstrated by Urban II's leadership of the First Crusade in 1095, the papacy emerged from the Investiture Struggle as the most powerful office in Europe. A century later the zenith of papal power was reached under Innocent III (1198-1216), a new type of administrator-pope. Unlike Gregory VII and other earlier reform popes, who were monks, Innocent and other great popes of the late twelfth and thirteenth centuries were lawyers, trained in the newly revived and enlarged Church, or canon, law. Innocent was like Gregory VII, however, in holding an exalted view of his office:

The successor of Peter is the Vicar of Christ: he has been established as a mediator between God and man, below God but beyond man; less than God but more than man; who shall judge all and be judged by no one.[6]

Innocent III told the princes of Europe that the papacy was as the sun, whereas the kings were as the moon. As the moon derives its light from the sun, so the kings derived their powers from the pope. So successful was the pontiff in asserting his temporal as well as spiritual supremacy that many states, both large and small, formally acknowledged vassalage to the pope. In the case of King John of England, a struggle developed over the election of the archbishop of Canterbury, and Innocent placed England under interdict and excommunicated John. Under attack from his barons, John capitulated to Innocent by becoming his vassal, receiving England back as a fief, and paying him an annual monetary tribute. Innocent forced Philip Augustus of France to comply with the Church's moral code by taking back as his queen the woman he had divorced with the consent of the French bishops. As for the Holy Roman Empire, Innocent intervened in a civil war between rival candidates for the throne, supporting first one, then the other. In the end Innocent secured the election of his ward, the young Hohenstaufen heir Frederick II, who promised to respect papal rights and to go on a crusade.

Within the Church itself, nothing better illustrates the power of the papal monarchy under Innocent III than the Fourth Lateran Council, which he called in 1215 to confirm his acts and policies. More than four hundred bishops, some eight hundred abbots and priors, and representatives of all leading secular rulers answered Innocent's call. The Council dealt with a wide range of subjects; for example, it outlawed trial by ordeal, required Jews to wear distinctive yellow badges, declared clergymen exempt from state taxation, and formally defined the Christian sacraments, setting their number at seven.

The sacramental system. Christian theology held that salvation was won only with the grace of God, and that God bestowed His grace on man by means of sacraments through the Church and its officials. Thus the Church was the necessary intermediary between God and man, a position strengthened when the Fourth Lateran Council decreed that every adult Christian must confess his sins and attend communion at least once a year.

The sacraments have been defined as outward or visible signs instituted by Christ to signify and to give grace. Until fixed at seven by the Fourth Lateran Council, as many as eleven sacraments had been accepted.

In the first of the seven sacraments, Baptism, the taint of original sin was washed away, and the person was given a Christian name, hence "christening." Confirmation strengthened the character of the recipient and confirmed his membership in the Church. The sacrament of Matrimony was instituted to give the married couple spiritual help—although celibacy was prescribed for those who entered the Church as a career. Holy Orders, or ordination into the priesthood, was administered by a bishop. This sacrament conferred the power and grace to perform the sacred duties of the clergy; the ordained priest was capable of administering all sacraments except Confirmation and Holy Orders. Penance enabled sins committed after Baptism to be forgiven through the absolution of the priest. Extreme Unction was administered when death appeared imminent; it forgave remaining sins and bestowed grace and spiritual strength on the dying Christian.

The most important and impressive sacrament was the Holy Eucharist, defined as "both a sacrament and a sacrifice; in it Our Savior, Jesus Christ, body and blood, soul and divinity, under the appearance of bread and wine, is contained, offered, and received." The significance of this sacrament as the core of Christian worship can be fully appreciated only when the doctrine of transubstantiation is understood. According to this doctrine—a subject of dispute until formally defined by the Fourth Lateran Council—when the priest performing the mass pronounces over the bread and wine the words Christ used at the Last Supper, "This is My Body . . . . This is the chalice of My Blood . . . ," a miracle takes place. To all outward appearances, the bread and wine remain unchanged, but in "substance" they have been transformed into the very body and blood of the Savior.

Church administration. The universality and power of the Church rested not only upon a systematized, uniform creed but also upon the most highly organized administrative system in the West. At the head was the pope, or bishop of Rome (see Chapter 5). He was assisted by the Curia, the papal council or court, which in the twelfth and thirteenth centuries developed an intricate administrative system. Judicial and secretarial problems were handled by the papal Chancery, financial matters by the Camera, and disciplinary questions by the Penitentiary.

Special emissaries called legates, whose powers were superior to those of local prelates, carried the pope's orders throughout Europe.

The Church was ahead of secular states in developing a system of courts and a body of law. Church or canon law was based on the Scriptures, the writings of the Church Fathers, and the decrees of Church councils and popes. In the twelfth century the Church issued its official body of canon law, which guided the Church courts in judging perjury, blasphemy, sorcery, usury (the medieval Church denounced the taking of interest), and heresy. Heresy was the most horrible of all crimes in medieval eyes. A murder was a crime against society, but the heretic's disbelief in the teachings of Christ or His Church was considered a crime against God Himself.

The papacy's chief weapons in support of its authority were spiritual penalties. The most powerful of these was excommunication, by which people became anathema, "set apart" from the Church and all the faithful. "They could not act as judge, juror, notary, witness, or attorney. They could not be guardians, executors, or parties to contracts. After death, they received no Christian burial, and if, by chance, they were buried in consecrated ground, their bodies were to be disinterred and cast away. If they entered a church during Mass, they were to be expelled, or the Mass discontinued. After the reading of a sentence of excommunication, a bell was rung as for a funeral, a book closed, and a candle extinguished, to symbolize the cutting off of the guilty man."[7]

Interdict, which has been termed "an ecclesiastical lockout," was likewise a powerful instrument. Whereas excommunication was directed against individuals, interdict suspended all public worship and withheld all sacraments other than Baptism and Extreme Unction in the realm of a disobedient ruler. Pope Innocent III successfully applied or threatened the interdict eighty-five times against refractory princes.

In the last analysis the Church's effectiveness depended upon the parish priest, whose importance was enhanced by the required confession and communion decreed by the Fourth Lateran Council. Although the priest

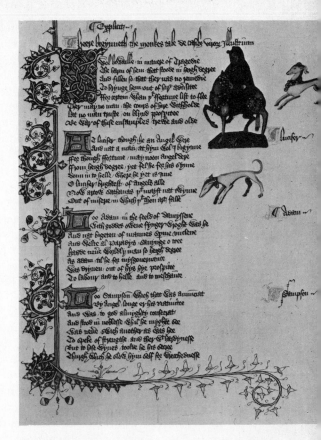

This detail from a fifteenth-century manuscript of Chaucer's *Canterbury Tales* shows the good parson.

was very likely of humble birth and little education, he was father confessor, social worker, policeman, and recreation director, all rolled into one. In most cases he was a credit to his Church. The "poor town Parson" in Chaucer's *Canterbury Tales* is a sympathetic portrayal.

He was a kind man, full of industry,
Many times tested by adversity
And always patient. . . .
Wide was his parish, with houses far asunder,
But he would not be kept by rain or thunder,
If any had suffered a sickness or a blow,
From visiting the farthest, high or low,
Plodding his way on foot, his staff in hand.
He was a model his flock could understand.
For first he did and afterward he taught.[8]

From the reign of Innocent III until the end of the thirteenth century, the Church radiated power and splendor. It possessed perhaps one third of the land of Europe, and all secular rulers and Church prelates acknowledged the power of Christ's vicar. Innocent III and his successors could and did "judge all and be judged by no one."

Yet while the Church's wealth enabled it to perform educational and charitable functions that the states were too poor and weak to provide, this wealth also encouraged abuses and worldliness among the clergy. Cracks were appearing in the foundation even while the medieval religious structure received its final embellishments. Weaknesses were evident in the lessening of religious zeal in the later crusades, in the need for renewed internal reform, and in the growth of heresy.

New monastic reforms. The medieval reformation gained momentum late in the eleventh century with a second movement of monastic reform brought on by the failure of the Cluniac reform to end laxity in monastic life. Among the new orders were the severely ascetic and hermit-like Carthusians and the very popular Cistercians.

The Cistercian movement received its greatest impetus from the zealous efforts of St. Bernard of Clairvaux in the twelfth century. The abbeys were situated in solitary places, and their strict discipline emphasized fasts and vigils, manual labor, and a vegetarian diet. Their churches contained neither stained glass nor statues, and the puritanical Bernard denounced the beautification of churches in general:

> Oh! vanity of vanities! but not more vain than foolish. . . . What has all this imagery to do with monks, with professors of poverty, with men of spiritual minds? . . . In fact, such an endless variety of forms appears everywhere that it is more pleasant to read in the stonework than in books, and to spend the day in admiring these oddities than in meditating on the Law of God.[9]

Spurred on by this militant denouncer of wealth and luxury in any form, the Cistercian order had founded 343 abbeys in western Europe by the time of Bernard's death in 1153 and more than double that number by the end of the century. Yet in one important sense these austere new monastic orders were failures. Being exclusively agricultural and dwelling apart from society, these orders were unfitted to cope with religious discontent in the towns and the consequent rise of heresy.

Heresies. Heresy, defined as "the formal denial or doubt by a baptized person of any revealed truth of the Catholic faith,"[10] flourished particularly in the towns, where an increasing consciousness of sin and a demand for greater piety went largely unheeded by old-style churchmen. This fertile ground produced many heresies, among which the Albigensian and Waldensian were major ones.

Harking back to an early Christian heresy, the Cathari ("Pure") or Albigensians—so called because Albi in southern France was an important center—went to extremes in thinking of the world as the battleground of the opposing forces of good and evil. The Albigensians condemned many activities of the state and the individual, even condemning marriage for perpetuating the human species in this sinful world.

The Waldensians derived their name from Peter Waldo, a merchant of Lyons who gave his wealth to charity and founded a lay order, the Poor Men of Lyons, to serve the needs of the people. He had parts of the New Testament translated into French, held that laymen could preach the Gospel, and denied the efficacy of the sacraments unless administered by worthy priests. Because the Waldensian church still exists today in northern Italy, it has been called the oldest Protestant sect.

For ten years Innocent III tried to reconvert these heretical groups. Failing, in 1208 he instigated a crusade against the prosperous and cultured French region of Toulouse, where the Albigensian heresy was widespread. The crusade began with horrible slaughter to the cry of "Kill them all, God will know His own." Soon the original religious motive was lost in a selfish rush to seize the wealth of the accused. In time the Albigensian heresy was destroyed, along with the flourishing culture of southern France, and the Waldensians were scattered. Until the rise of Protestantism, the Church was generally successful in its efforts to crush heresy.

The Inquisition. In 1233 a special papal court called the Inquisition was established to cope with the rising tide of heresy and to bring about religious conformity. The accused was tried in secret without the aid of legal counsel. If he confessed and renounced his heresy, he was "reconciled" with the Church on performance of penance. If he did not voluntarily confess, he could be tortured. If this failed, the prisoner could be declared a heretic and turned over to the secular authorities, usually to be burned at the stake.

In any evaluation of the Inquisition, it should be remembered that the soul was considered incomparably more important than the body—therefore torturing a suspected heretic was justifiable if confession could save his soul from the greater torments of hell. Furthermore, the use of torture, secret testimony, and the denial of legal counsel prevailed in all courts that followed Roman law procedure.

The Franciscans and Dominicans. As a more positive response to the spread of heresy and the conditions which spawned it, Innocent III approved the founding of the Franciscan and Dominican orders of friars ("brothers"). Instead of living a sequestered existence in a remote monastery, the friars moved among their brother men, ministering to their needs and preaching the Gospel.

The Franciscans were founded by St. Francis of Assisi (1182?-1226), who, like Peter Waldo, rejected riches and spread the gospel of poverty and Christian simplicity. Love of one's fellow men and all God's creatures, even "brother worm," were basic in the Rule of St. Francis, which was inspired by Jesus' example:

Jesus called the twelve disciples together and gave them power and authority to drive out all demons and to cure diseases. Then he sent them out to preach the Kingdom of God and to heal the sick. He said to them: "Take nothing with you for your trip: no walking stick, no beggar's bag, no food, no money, not even an extra shirt. . . ." The disciples left and traveled through all the villages, preaching the Good News and healing people everywhere.[11]

The second order of friars was founded by St. Dominic (1170-1221), a well-educated Spaniard whose early career had been spent fighting the Albigensian heresy in southern France. There he decided that to combat the strength and zeal of its opponents, the Church should have champions who could preach the Gospel with apostolic fervor. Dominic's order of friar-preachers dedicated themselves to preaching as a means of maintaining the doctrines of the Church and of converting heretics.

The enthusiasm and sincerity of the friars in their early years made a profound impact upon an age which had grown increasingly critical of ecclesiastical worldliness. But after they took charge of the Inquisition, became professors in the universities, and served the papacy in other ways, the friars lost much of their original simplicity and freshness. Yet their message and zeal had done much to

The simple piety preached by St. Francis is reflected in this altarpiece, painted only nine years after his death, which shows the characteristically austere saint surrounded by six scenes from his life. The marks on St. Francis' hands and feet are stigmata—symbolic wounds representing his identification with Christ—which he received after a period of prayer and meditation.

provide the Church with moral and intellectual leadership at a time when such leadership was badly needed.

Veneration of saints and relics. Neither the Church's concern for theology nor its claims to universal authority appealed to ordinary men; they wanted solace on this earth and assurance of salvation in the next life. Such concerns enhanced the veneration of the Virgin Mary, one of the most potent forces in the medieval reformation. In an age when even the most educated persons believed that thunderstorms, plagues, and famines were the devil's work and that hell loomed perilously close, it seemed natural to pray to the Mother of Christ for protection and comfort. As an earthly mother supplicates for mercy on behalf of her erring child, so the Virgin Mary would supplicate her Son in heaven for her children on earth. Many magnificent Gothic cathedrals, such as Notre Dame (Our Lady) in Paris, were dedicated to Mary as symbols of the people's devotion.

Medieval people believed that relics of saints had miraculous powers. The bone of a saint, for example, supposedly would halt disease or create abundant harvests. The manner in which unscrupulous venders of fake relics sometimes duped Christians has been vividly recounted by Chaucer in his description of the Pardoner:

No pardoner could beat him in the race,
For in his wallet he had a pillow case
Which he represented as Our Lady's veil;
He said he had a piece of the very sail
St. Peter, when he fished in Galilee
Before Christ caught him, used upon the sea.
He had a latten cross embossed with stones
And in a glass he carried some pig's bones,
And with these holy relics, when he found
Some village parson grubbing his poor ground,
He would get more money in a single day
Than in two months would come the parson's way.
Thus with his flattery and his trumped-up stock
He made dupes of the parson and his flock.[12]

The crusades, and especially the sack of Constantinople in 1204, so flooded the West with relics that the Fourth Lateran Council prohibited, with little effect, the sale of relics and required papal approval of all new relics.

THE INTELLECTUAL SYNTHESIS

The medieval renaissance. "The meeting of Roman decrepitude and German immaturity was not felicitous."[13] This concise commentary on the character of early medieval civilization is especially relevant to the intellectual side of the period, and it remains a moot question among modern scholars whether the seventh century or the tenth was "the darkest of the Dark Ages." By the close of the sixth century even the most influential of early medieval popes, Gregory the Great, was contributing to the growing intellectual murkiness by voicing strong disapproval of secular literature, insisting that "the same mouth cannot sing the praises of Jupiter and praises of Christ." So feeble had the light of learning become by the end of the eighth century that Charlemagne found it necessary to order the monasteries to revive their schools and resume instruction in the rudiments of "singing, arithmetic, and grammar" (see p. 192).

In sharp contrast to the fate of his political achievements, Charlemagne's modest educational revival survived his death. At least partly as a result of this stimulus, western Europe by the late eleventh century was on the threshold of one of the most productive and energetic periods in the history of western thought—the medieval renaissance.

What was revived first of all during the medieval renaissance was intellectual curiosity, plainly evident from contemporary accounts, such as the following concerning an eleventh-century scholar from Liège:

Olbert was not able to satiate his thirst for study. When he would hear of some one distinguished in the arts he flew there at once, and the more he thirsted the more he absorbed something delightful from each master. At Paris he worked at Saint-Germain and studied the Holy Faith which glowed there. In Troyes he studied for three years, learning gratefully many things. . . . He felt obliged to listen to Fulbert of Chartres who was proclaimed in the liberal arts throughout France. Afterwards just like the bees among flowers, gorged with the nectar of learning, he returned to the hive and lived there studiously in a religious way, and religiously in a studious manner.[14]

Scholasticism. Living "religiously in a studious manner" aptly characterizes the scholars of the medieval renaissance and points up an essential difference between medieval thought on the one hand and early Greek philosophy and modern scientific thought on the other. With but few exceptions, medieval man did not think of truth as something to be discovered by himself; rather, he saw it as already existing in the authoritative Christian and pagan writings handed down from antiquity. Spurred on by a new zest for employing reason (called logic or dialectic), medieval scholars of the twelfth and thirteenth centuries succeeded in understanding and reexpressing those elements in the Christian and pagan heritage that seemed significant to them. Since this task was carried out largely in the schools, these scholars are known as schoolmen—or scholastics—and the intellectual synthesis they produced is called scholasticism.

Each scholar formed his own judgments and earnestly sought to convince others. This led to much debate, often uncritical but always exuberant, on a wide range of subjects. Most famous was the argument over universals known as the nominalist-realist controversy.

Nominalists and realists battled over the problem of universal Ideas, basing their arguments on indirect evidence, transmitted by Boethius and others, that Plato and Aristotle did not agree on the subject. Plato had argued that Ideas had reality apart from their existence in men's minds. A specific object was *real* only insofar as it represented the nature of its Idea (see p. 52). Thus Plato himself, for example, was real inasmuch as he partook of the Idea of Man. Aristotle, taking an opposite view, maintained that individuals existed as individuals—a human being was a real entity, not just a reflection of the universal Idea of Man. To the realists in the Middle Ages, only universal Ideas could be real and exist independently. To the nominalists, abstract concepts such as universal Ideas were only names (*nomina*) and had no real existence.

Both realism and nominalism—if carried to their logical extremes—resulted in conclusions equally abhorrent to the Church.

Realism became pantheism (the universe as a whole is God), and nominalism became materialism (the universe is composed solely of matter).

The contribution of Abélard. The extreme views of nominalists and realists, along with other examples of the sterile use of logic ("whether the pig is led to the market by the rope or by the driver"), outraged a brilliant young student named Pierre Abélard (1079-1142), later a popular teacher at the cathedral school of Notre Dame in Paris. Like many bright students in all ages, Abélard succeeded in antagonizing his teachers, both realist and nominalist. "I brought him great grief," he wrote of one, "because I undertook to refute certain of his opinions." Another teacher was mercilessly ridiculed:

He had a miraculous flow of words, but they were contemptible in meaning and quite void of reason. When he kindled a fire, he filled his house with smoke and illumined it not at all. He was a tree which seemed noble to those who gazed upon its leaves from afar, but to those who came nearer and examined it more closely was revealed its barrenness.[15]

Abélard's great contribution to medieval thought was freeing logic from barrenness and rerouting it to become again a means to an end rather than an end in itself. Conceptualism, his common-sense solution to the nominalist-realist controversy, held that universals, while existing only in the mind as thoughts or concepts, are nevertheless valid (real) since they are the product of observing the similar qualities that exist in a particular class of things. Thus, by observing many chairs and sitting in them, we arrive at the universal concept "chair."

In addition to redefining the purpose of scholastic thought, Abélard perfected the scholastic method. Like others before him, Abélard emphasized the importance of understanding, but whereas the former had begun with faith, Abélard started with doubt. We must learn to doubt, he insisted, for doubting leads us to inquire, and inquiry leads us to the truth. Abélard's intellectual skepticism was not that of modern experimental science, however; he never transcended superimposed authority. He aimed to arouse intellectual curiosity in his students and turn it into useful channels, bringing reason to bear on inherited truths in order to achieve understanding.

In an epoch-making work, *Sic et Non* (*Yes and No*), Abélard demonstrated his method. Listing 158 propositions on theology and ethics, he appended to each a number of statements pro and con taken from the authoritative writings of the Church. Abélard did not go on to reconcile these apparent contradictions, but he urged his students to do so by rational interpretation. Abélard's methodology was used by his successors to assimilate and reexpress the pagan as well as the Christian heritage of the past. The resulting scholarly compilations, which bear such apt titles as *concordantia* (concordance), *speculum* (mirror), and *summa* (sum total), constitute the crowning achievement of the medieval intellectual synthesis.

Abélard is remembered as a great lover as well as a great scholar—a rather uncommon combination. His ill-starred romance with his pupil, the learned and beautiful Héloïse, niece of the canon of Notre Dame, cut short his promising career as a teacher. The two lovers were married in secret, but Héloïse's uncle, falsely believing that Abélard planned to abandon Héloïse, hired thugs who attacked and emasculated the scholar. Both Abélard and Héloïse then sought refuge in the Church—Pierre as a monk and Héloïse as the abbess of a nunnery.

The new material and the task of reconciliation. In the twelfth century the study of Greek learning with its Muslim additions was undertaken by western scholars who flocked to Spain and Sicily and there translated Muslim editions of ancient writings. As a result of these translations a host of new ideas, particularly in science and philosophy, were introduced to western scholars. Western knowledge was expanded to include not only Arabic learning but also such important classical works as Euclid's *Geometry*, Ptolemy's *Almagest*, Hippocrates' and Galen's treatises in medicine, and all of Aristotle's extant writing except the *Poetics* and the *Rhetoric*.

As his works became known, Aristotle became, in Dante's words, "the master of those who know," and his authority was generally accepted as second only to that of the Scriptures. But because the Church's teachings were considered infallible, Aristotle's ideas, as well as those of other great thinkers of antiquity, had to be reconciled with religious dogma. Using Abélard's methodology, the scholastic thinkers of the thirteenth century succeeded in this task of reconciliation.

Scholasticism reached its zenith with St. Thomas Aquinas (1225?-1274). In his *Summa Theologica* this brilliant Italian Dominican dealt exhaustively with the great problems of theology, philosophy, politics, and economics. After collecting the arguments pro and con on a given problem—for example, "Whether it is lawful to sell a thing for more than its worth?"—he went on to draw conclusions. (His answer to the problem cited reflects the great influence of Christian ethics upon medieval economic thought: "I answer that, it is altogether sinful to have recourse to deceit in order to sell a thing for more than its just price, because this is to deceive one's neighbour so as to injure him."[16])

St. Thomas' major concern was to reconcile Aristotle and Church dogma—in other words, the truths of natural reason and the truths of faith. There can be no real contradiction, he argued, since all truth comes from God. In case of an unresolved contradiction, however, faith won out, because of the possibility of human error in reasoning. St. Thomas was so convincing in settling this conflict—the first clash between science and religion in the history of our western civilization—that his philosophy still has its followers today.

The decline of scholasticism. Having reached its zenith, scholasticism declined rapidly. The assumption that faith and reason were compatible was vigorously denied by two Franciscan thinkers, Duns Scotus (d. 1308) and William of Occam (d. c. 1349), who elaborated on Aquinas' belief that certain religious doctrines are beyond discovery by the use of reason. They argued that if the human intellect could not understand divinely revealed truth, it could hope to comprehend only the natural world and should not intrude upon the sphere of divine truth. Such a position tended to undermine the Thomistic synthesis of faith and reason. Realism and nominalism revived, the one promoting an increase in mystical, nonrational religion, the other contributing to the growing scientific spirit and to individualism and worldly concerns in general. For better or for worse, this trend toward the emancipation of human knowledge and action from the unifying authority of religion and the Church became a characteristic feature of western civilization.

After the thirteenth century scholasticism increasingly became a term of reproach, for its adherents were obsessed with theological subtleties, discouraged independent thought, and in general lost touch with reality. But it should be remembered that the scholastics sought to appropriate and make subjectively their own the store of Christian and pagan knowledge left to them by a more advanced civilization. In terms of their needs and objectives—an intelligible and all-embracing synthesis of faith, logic, and science—the scholastics were eminently successful, and people of our own age should not look askance at their accomplishments. Ironically, we today increasingly recognize the importance of reconciling science and faith in an age which has so much of the former and so little of the latter.

Medieval science. Because of the emphasis upon authority and the all-pervasive influence of the Church, the medieval atmosphere was not conducive to free scientific investigation. Those who studied science were churchmen, and their findings were supposed to illuminate rather than contradict the dogmas of the theologians. During the early Middle Ages scientific knowledge was limited to such compilations as the *Etymologies* of Isidore, bishop of Seville. Written in the seventh century, this naive and uncritical scrapbook of information remained a standard reference work in the West for three centuries. Isidore believed that the real nature of a thing was to be found in its name, and so he usually introduced each item with an often fanciful etymological explanation:

The liver [*iecur* in Latin] has its name because there is resident the fire [*ignis*] which flies up into the brain. . . . and by its heat it changes into blood the liquid that it has drawn from food, and this blood it supplies to the several members to feed and nourish them.[17]

The *Etymologies* has been called "the fruit of the much decayed tree of ancient learning."

When Greek and Arabic works were translated in the twelfth century, the West inherited a magnificent legacy of mathematical and scientific knowledge. Algebra, trigonometry, and Euclid's *Geometry* became available, and Arabic numerals and the symbol *zero* made possible the decimal system of computation. Leonard of Pisa (d. 1245), the greatest mathematician of the Middle Ages, made a great original contribution to mathematics when he worked out a method to extract square roots and to solve quadratic and cubic equations. On the other hand, Ptolemy's belief that the earth was the center of the universe—a fallacious theory destined to handicap astronomy for centuries—was commonly accepted.

Physics was based on Aristotle's theory of four elements (water, earth, air, and fire) and on his theories of dynamics—doctrines which took centuries to disprove. Some fourteenth-century nominalists were the first to challenge Aristotle's theory that a heavy object falls faster than a light one. Chemistry was based on Aristotelian concepts, mixed with magic and alchemy. Like the Muslim alchemist, his European counterpart tried in vain to transmute base metals into gold and silver and to obtain a magic elixir that would prolong life; in both cases the attempts did much to advance chemistry.

Frederick II and Roger Bacon. Two notable exceptions to the medieval rule of subservience to authority were the emperor Frederick II (see also p. 237) and the English Franciscan Roger Bacon. Frederick had a genuine scientific interest in animals and was famed for his large traveling menagerie, which included elephants, camels, panthers, lions, leopards, and a giraffe. He wrote a remarkable treatise, *The Art of Falconry*, which is still considered largely accurate in its observations of the life and habits of various kinds of hunting birds. "We discovered by hard-won experience," he wrote, "that the

In this picture from a fifteenth-century manuscript the university students oppose one another in "disputation," the class debates which went on for hours.

deductions of Aristotle, whom we followed when they appealed to our reason, were not entirely to be relied upon."[18] At his Sicilian court Frederick gathered about him many distinguished Greek, Muslim, and Latin scholars (including Leonard of Pisa), and he wrote to others in distant lands seeking their views on such problems as why objects appear bent when partly covered by water. He indulged in many experiments; one was a test to determine what language children would speak if raised in absolute silence. The experiment was a failure because all the children died.

Roger Bacon (1214-1292) also employed the inductive scientific method—he coined the term "experimental science"—and boldly criticized the deductive syllogistic reasoning used by scholastic thinkers. His *Opus Maius* contains this attack on scholasticism:

There are four principal stumbling blocks to comprehending truth, which hinder well-nigh every scholar: the example of frail and unworthy authority, long-established custom, the sense of the ignorant crowd, and the hiding of one's ignorance under the show of wisdom.[19]

Bacon never doubted the authority of the Bible or the Church—his interest lay only in natural science—yet his superiors considered him a dangerous thinker because of his criticism of scholastic thought.

Medieval medicine. By the thirteenth century learned Muslim commentaries on Galen and Hippocrates and on Aristotle's biology were available in the West. This knowledge, coupled with their own discoveries and improved techniques, made medieval doctors more than just barbers who engaged in bloodletting. Yet the overall state of medical knowledge and practice was, by our standards at least, still primitive. This can be seen in the prevalence of superstitious beliefs and the resort to magical practices, the general lack of concern for public sanitation, the periodic decimation of entire populations by epidemics such as the Black Death, and that significant indicator of the state of public health—the infant mortality rate, which was staggeringly high.

Origin of universities. Roman schools had a curriculum of seven liberal arts, separated into two divisions: a *trivium* consisting of grammar, rhetoric, and dialectic; and a *quadrivium* of arithmetic, music, geometry, and astronomy. When the Roman empire in the West fell, the task of education went to the Church; and the liberal arts were adapted to prepare youths for the ministry. Through the work of Cassiodorus in the sixth century (see p. 243), monasteries became important centers of learning. By 1100, however, monastic schools were overshadowed by the more dynamic cathedral schools established by bishops in such important centers as Paris, Chartres, Canterbury, and Toledo.

The renaissance of the twelfth century, with its revival of classical learning, its unprecedented number of students flocking to the schools, and its development of professional studies in law, medicine, and theology, led to the rise of organized centers of learning—the universities, which soon eclipsed the monastic and cathedral schools. Originally the word *university* meant a group of persons possessing a common purpose. In this case it referred to a guild of learners, both teachers and students, analogous to the craft guilds with their masters and apprentices. In the thirteenth century the universities had no campuses and little property or money, and the masters taught in hired rooms or religious houses. If the university was dissatisfied with its treatment by the townspeople, it could migrate elsewhere. The earliest universities—Bologna, Paris, and Oxford—were not officially founded or created, but in time the popes and kings granted them and other universities charters of self-government. The charters gave legal status to the universities and rights to the students, such as freedom from the jurisdiction of town officials.

Two systems: Bologna and Paris. Two of the most famous medieval universities were at Bologna in northern Italy and at Paris. The former owed its growth to the fame of Irnerius (d. 1130), who taught civil law. Because of his influence, Bologna acquired a reputation as the leading center for the study of law. The students soon organized a guild for protection against the rapacious townspeople, who were demanding exorbitant sums for food and lodging. Because the guild went on to control the professors, Bologna became a student paradise. In the earliest statutes we read that a professor requiring leave of absence even for one day first had to obtain permission from his own students. He had to begin his lecture with the bell and end within one minute of the next bell. The material in the text had to be covered systematically, with all difficult passages fully explained. The powerful position of the students at Bologna developed as a result of the predominance of older students studying for the doctorate in law.

At the university in Paris conditions developed differently. This university, which had grown out of the cathedral school of Notre Dame, specialized in liberal arts and theology and became the most influential intellectual center in medieval Europe. Its administration was far different from Bologna's. The chancellor of Notre Dame, the bishop's officer who exercised authority over the cathedral school, refused to allow the students or the masters to obtain control of the burgeoning university. Charters issued by the French king in 1200 and by the pope in 1231 freed the university from the bishop's authority by making it an autonomous body controlled by the masters.

The collegiate system. Universities owned no dormitories, and students lived in rented rooms or pooled their resources to obtain housing on a cooperative basis. With masters' fees and living expenses to pay, the impoverished student labored under decided handicaps. A philanthropic patron, however, sometimes provided quarters where poor scholars could board free of charge. One such patron was Robert de Sorbon, the royal chaplain to the saintly Louis IX. About 1257 Robert endowed a hall for sixteen needy students working for their doctorates in theology, thus founding the College de Sorbonne; the University of Paris is still popularly known by the name of its great benefactor.

As more colleges were established, the large universities became collections of colleges in which the students lived and studied. Although organization by colleges finally disappeared in the University of Paris where the system originated, at both Oxford and Cambridge the collegiate system has remained an integral part of the university to this day.

Curriculum and degrees. The degrees available at medieval universities were similar to those offered today. The bachelor's degree, which could be obtained after studying from three to five years, was not considered very important. For a master of arts degree, which admitted the holder into the guild of masters and was a license to teach, particular emphasis was placed on the works of Aristotle. In theology, law, and medicine the master's degree was commonly called a doctorate. It was no easy matter to get a master's degree (or doctorate) from a medieval university; many years of preparation were required, and at the final examination the candidate had to defend his thesis publicly for hours against the learned attacks of the masters. If successful in his defense, the candidate then stood the cost of a banquet for his examiners.

Latin literature. During the entire Middle Ages Latin served as an international means of communication. This common tongue provided much of the cohesion of the Middle Ages, for virtually all the crucial communications of the Church, governments, and schools were in Latin. Undoubtedly the most splendid medieval Latin is found in the Church liturgy, which was chanted by the priest.

Any misconception that the Middle Ages were simply "other-worldly" and long-faced will be rudely shattered by glancing at the Latin poetry written during the twelfth and thirteenth centuries by students. Known as Goliardic verse because its authors claimed to be disciples of Goliath, their synonym for the devil, it unhesitatingly proclaimed the pleasures of wine, women, and song:

'Tis most arduous to make
  Nature's self-surrender;
Seeing girls, to blush and be
  Purity's defender!
We young men our longings ne'er
  Shall to stern law render,
Or preserve our fancies from
  Bodies smooth and tender. . . .

In the public house to die
  Is my resolution;
Let wine to my lips be nigh
  At life's dissolution:
That will make the angels cry,
  With glad elocution,
"Grant this toper, God on high,
  Grace and absolution!"[20]

The Goliardic poets were brilliant at parodying and satirizing the ideals of their elders. They substituted Venus for the Virgin, wrote masses for drunkards, and were guilty of other blasphemies. Yet many of these poets later became respected officials in the Church.

In contrast, the great Latin hymns such as the *Dies Irae* and the *Stabat Mater Dolorosa* show the genuineness of the religious spirit of the twelfth and thirteenth centuries. The latter hymn movingly describes the Virgin Mary standing beside the cross:

By the cross, sad vigil keeping,
Stood the mournful mother weeping,
While on it the saviour hung;
In that hour of deep distress
Pierced the sword of bitterness
Through her heart with sorrow wrung.[21]

Vernacular literature. A rising tide of literature in the vernacular tongues began to appear by the twelfth century, with the epic as the earliest form. The greatest of the French epics, or *chansons de geste* ("songs of great deeds"), is the late eleventh-century *Song of Roland*, which recounts the heroic deeds and death of Count Roland in the Pyrenees while defending the rear of Charlemagne's army (see p. 191). The great Spanish epic, the *Poema del Mio Cid* (see quoted selection, p. 232), is a product of the twelfth century. These stirring epic poems, with their accounts of prowess in battle, mirror the masculine warrior virtues of early chivalry (see p. 202).

By the twelfth century in the feudal courts of southern France, poets called troubadours were composing short, personal lyrics dealing mainly with romantic love. "The delicacy and romanticism of the troubadour lyrics betoken a more genteel and sophisticated nobility than that of the feudal north—a nobility that preferred songs of love to songs of war. Indeed, medieval southern France was the source of the entire romantic-love tradition of Western Civilization, with its idealization of women, its emphasis on male gallantry and courtesy, and its insistence on embroidering the sex drive with an elaborate ritual of palpitating hearts, moonlight, and sentimental ties."[22] Typical are these lines written in adoration of the lovely Eleanor of Aquitaine:

When the sweet breeze
Blows hither from your dwelling
Methinks I feel
A breath of paradise.[23]

Nothing comparable to these lines exists in the *chansons de geste*, but during the last half of the twelfth century this new interest in love fused with the purely heroic material of the early epics. The result was the medieval romance, an account of love and adventure, to which was often added a strong coloring of religious feeling. Examples are Chrétien de Troyes' *Perceval* (see p. 202) and the tales concerning King Arthur and his Round Table of chivalrous knights who variously pursue adventure, charming ladies, and the Holy Grail. In Germany about the beginning of the thirteenth century, the old saga material dealing with Siegfried, Brunhild, and the wars against the Huns was recast into the *Nibelungenlied* (*Song of the Nibelungs*).

All the foregoing literary types were written for the aristocracy. The self-made burgher preferred more practical and shrewd tales. His taste was gratified by the bawdy *fabliaux*, brief, humorous tales written in rhymed verse; and the animal stories about Reynard the Fox, the symbol of the sly bourgeois lawyer who easily outwits King Lion and his noble vassals. In England during the fourteenth century the Robin Hood ballads celebrated robbing the rich to give to the poor and *Piers the Plowman* condemned the injustices of a social system that had brought on the peasant revolt in England (see p. 217 and quoted selection, p. 201).

Dante Alighieri. The vernacular was also used by two of the greatest writers of the period—Dante and Chaucer. Combining a profound religious sense with a knowledge of scholastic thought and the Latin classics, the Italian Dante (1265-1321) produced one of the world's greatest narrative poems. The *Divine Comedy*, which Dante said described his "full experience," is an allegory of medieval man (Dante) moving from bestial earthiness (hell) through conversion (purgatory) to the sublime spirituality of union with God (paradise). Dante describes how

Midway this way of life we're bound upon,
  I woke to find myself in a dark wood,
  Where the right road was wholly lost and gone.[24]

Dante then accepts the offer of Virgil, symbol of pagan learning, to be his "master, leader, and lord" to guide him through hell and purgatory. But it is Beatrice, the lady whom he had once loved from afar and who is now the symbol of divine love, who guides him through paradise. At last Dante stands before God, and words fail him as he finds peace in the presence of the highest form of love:

Oh, how fall short the words! . . .
The Love that moves the sun and every star.[25]

The wit of Chaucer. In the *Canterbury Tales*, Geoffrey Chaucer (1340?-1400), one of the greatest figures in medieval literature, reveals a cross section of contemporary English life, customs, and thought (see quoted selections, pp. 247, 250). The twenty-nine pilgrims who assembled in April 1387 at an inn before journeying to the shrine of St. Thomas à Becket at Canterbury were a motley group. The "truly perfect, gentle knight," just returned from warring against the "heathen in Turkey," was accompanied by his son, a young squire who loved so much by night that "he slept no more than does a nightingale." The clergy was represented by the coy prioress who "would weep if she but saw a mouse caught in a trap,"[26] the rotund

This fresco by Domenico di Michelino, an Italian painter of the Florentine school, has as its subject the early Renaissance poet and humanist, Dante Alighieri. The fresco is a method of painting which uses pigments mixed in water and applied to freshly laid wet plaster so that the colors become incorporated. Here Domenico has depicted the Cathedral of Florence, in which the fresco is located. Also shown are scenes from Dante's *Divine Comedy*, the allegory in which medieval man moves from hell (left detail), through purgatory, to heaven and union with God (center detail).

monk who loved to eat fat swan and ride good horses, the friar who knew the best taverns and all the barmaids in town, and the poor parish priest who was a credit to his faith. Also included in the group were the merchant who could talk only of business, the threadbare Oxford student, the miller with a wart on his nose, and the worthy wife of Bath, who had married five times and was now visiting Christian shrines in search of a sixth husband.

Chaucer's fame rests securely upon his keen interest in human nature and his skill as a storyteller. The Midland dialect he used was the linguistic base for the language of future English literature, just as Dante's use of the Tuscan dialect fixed the Italian tongue.

Rebirth of drama. Like Greek drama, medieval drama developed out of religious ceremonies; it was used by churchmen to instruct the faithful. The earliest forms were the mystery plays, which naively but forcefully dramatized Biblical stories, and the miracle plays, which described the miraculous intervention of saints in human affairs. At first the plays supplemented the regular service and were performed inside the church proper. As their popularity grew, they were presented either on the church steps or on a separate stage. By the fourteenth century another type, the morality play, had become popular. The actors personified virtues and vices, and the plot of the drama usually centered on a conflict between them. *Everyman*, an excellent example of a morality play, is still occasionally produced.

THE ESTHETIC SYNTHESIS

Artistic correlation. The *Summa Theologica* of St. Thomas Aquinas and the *Divine Comedy* of Dante represent the best intellectual expressions of the medieval spirit. Similarly, the Gothic cathedral is the ultimate artistic expression of the age. Each of these masterpieces represents a different aspect of the attempt to organize everything into an overall pattern that would glorify God.

The order and form of scholastic thought find their counterparts in the structure and style of the Gothic edifices. A scholastic treatise was systematically arranged in logical parts; the cathedral was similarly articulated in space. The main sections, the nave, transept, and apse, were individually distinctive yet integrated into a coherent structure.

Early Christian churches. Early Christian churches imitated the plan of the Roman basilicas. In this design a rectangle is divided into three aisles: a central aisle, or nave, ending in a semicircular apse, and a lower-ceilinged aisle on each side. Parallel rows of columns separated the nave from the side aisles. The roof over the nave was raised to provide a clerestory—a section pierced by windows to illuminate the interior (see illustration, p. 127). In the fourth century the basilica plan was modified by the addition of a transept across the aisles between the apse and the nave. This essentially "T" shape added Christian symbolism to the basic plan of the pagan-style building. Graceful bell-towers were erected separate from the church building; the "leaning tower" of Pisa is a famous later example.

Romanesque architecture. In the eleventh century occurred a tremendous architectural revival, marked by the recovery of the art of building in stone rather than in wood, as was common during the early Middle Ages. At a much later date the name *Romanesque* came to be applied to this new style, because, like early Christian architecture, it was based largely on Roman models. Although details of structure and ornamentation differed with locality, the round arch was a standard Romanesque feature (see Color Plate 9). Both barrel and cross vaults were used, particularly in northern Europe, where the need to build fireproof churches made it impractical to follow the common Italian practice of using flat wooden roofs. While there was often one long barrel vault over the nave, the aisles were divided into square areas or bays with a cross vault over each bay. Thick outside walls and huge interior piers were necessary to support the heavy stone barrel and cross vaults. (In time diagonal ribs were built along the groins of the cross vault, transforming it into the ribbed-groin vault; see diagram.) Because the walls would be weakened by large window apertures, the clerestory windows were small or nonexistent. Thus the northern Romanesque interior was dark and gloomy, the exterior massive and monumental.

Gothic architecture. Actually, no clear-cut cleavage exists between Romanesque and Gothic. There was a gradual evolutionary process, which reached its culmination in the thirteenth and fourteenth centuries. The architects of the Gothic-style cathedral developed ribbed-groin vaults with pointed rather than round arches. This enabled them to solve the technical problem of cross-vaulting the nave, which, being wider than the aisles, could not easily be divided into square bays covered by Romanesque cross vaults (see diagram of floor plan, p. 261). Thus light ribbed-groin vaults, whose sides were of different length to fit the rectangular bays of the nave, replaced the heavy barrel vault, and the roof of the nave could be raised to permit the use of large clerestory windows. The thrust of the vaults over both the nave and the aisles was concentrated on a few strong structural supports. Part of the weight was carried down to the ground by columns within the building, and part by flying buttresses at points along the walls. With such vaulting and buttresses, the weight of the roof was largely shifted off the walls (see diagram of cross section, p. 261). Large stained-glass windows were set into the walls between the buttresses. The dark, somber interior of the Romanesque churches gave way to the jeweled light of the Gothic interiors.

Sculpture and stained glass. Most Romanesque and Gothic sculpture served an archi-

At the bottom of this detail of the "Last Judgment" scene at Autun Cathedral the dead rise from their graves in fear; at the top their souls are weighed in the balance. While the saved cling to the angels, the damned are seized by grinning devils and thrown into hell.

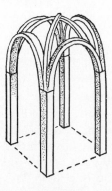

The ribbed-groin vault developed by Romanesque architects derived from the Roman intersecting vaults. The ribbed vault is made up of arches which span the sides of a square bay, with groin arches crossing diagonally from corner to corner.

tectural function by being carved to fit into the total composition of a church. To use sculpture to the best architectural advantage, the subject was often distorted to achieve a particular effect. Yet many thirteenth-century Gothic statues are masterpieces both in their fully developed craftsmanship and the grace and nobility of their content (see photos, pp. 261, 224). The relationship of the earlier Romanesque sculpture (see photo above) to the later Gothic reduplicates in large part that of archaic and classical sculpture in ancient Greece (see pp. 56-57).

Like sculpture, medieval painting in the form of stained-glass windows was an integral part of architecture. Composed of small pieces of colored glass held together in a

The Gothic age was the culmination of the Middle Ages, and the cathedral was the concrete synthesis of Gothic ideals. With his knowledge of weights and thrusts, the Gothic architect was able to raise his building to unprecedented heights and open it dramatically to light. The result, as evident in the cathedral at Cologne, is one of the most compelling unities of form and feeling in all of architecture.

pattern by metal strips which both braced the glass and emphasized the design, stained glass was an art whose excellence has not been duplicated in modern times. By adding various minerals to molten glass, thirteenth-century craftsmen achieved brilliant hues. Details such as hair were painted on the glass. The object, however, was not realism but the evoking of a mood—to shine with the radiance of heaven itself.

Secular architecture. What the cathedral was to religious life, the castle was to every-day living. Both were havens, and both were built to endure. The new weapons and techniques of siege warfare, which the crusaders brought back with them, necessitated more massive castles. By the thirteenth century castle building in Europe reached a high point of development. The towers were rounded, and bastions stood at strategic points along the walls. The castle as a whole was planned in such a skillful manner that if one section was taken by attackers, it could be sealed off from the remaining fortifications. Whole towns were fortified in the same way, with walls, watchtowers, moats, and drawbridges.

Toward the end of the Middle Ages there was less need for fortified towns and castles. At the same time the wealth accruing from the revived trade and increased industry encouraged the development of secular Gothic architecture. Town and guild halls, the residences of the rich, and the chateaux of the nobles all borrowed the delicate Gothic style from the cathedrals.

SUMMARY

The traditional division of history into "ancient," "medieval," and "modern" is fundamentally arbitrary and artificial in that history is a continuous process. Applying the same common denominator—"medieval" —to the thousand turbulent years between the fifth and fifteenth centuries obscures the wide variations that existed during the period. For five centuries after the fall of Rome, Europe experienced a long period of decline sometimes called the "dark ages." But between 1050 and 1300 the West began a rapid recovery. In the words of a contemporary poet, "This long dead land now flames with life again." This renewed life in religion and culture has been the subject of this chapter. (Economic, social, and political recovery were described in earlier chapters.)

Emerging out of feudal decentralization ahead of the state, the Church developed the first unified system of law and administration in medieval Europe and intimately affected the life of every person. It gave man a sense of security against the dangers on earth and those beyond. To perform its historical mission, the Church required a hierarchy of clergy and an elaborate doctrine,

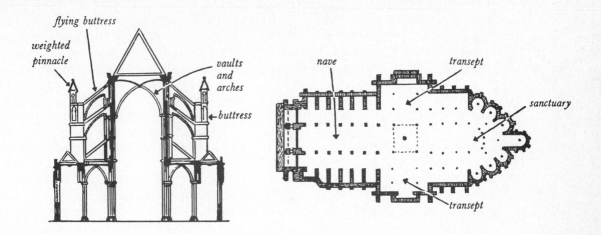

flying buttress

weighted pinnacle

vaults and arches

buttress

nave

transept

sanctuary

transept

The fusing of sculpture and architecture is apparent in this detail of one of the doorways of Amiens Cathedral. Medieval cathedrals were rich in sculptures of saints and great men of antiquity, episodes from history and the Old and New Testaments, and allegorical representations of science, philosophy, and theology. The unified effect of the fully developed Gothic style is one of awesome, but ordered, intricacy, as the photograph of the entire front of Amiens Cathedral demonstrates. Above is a drawing of the cross section and floor plan of the same cathedral. Vaults, arches, buttresses, and weighted pinnacles were important structural elements in the Gothic style of architecture.

accompanied by methods for enforcing its will. We have followed the areas of reform, watched the Church's power reach its apex in the age of Innocent III, and noted signs of its eventual decline.

Within the Church, thinkers wrestled with philosophical issues, such as the realist-nominalist controversy. In the thirteenth century such famous scholastics as St. Thomas Aquinas made herculean attempts to reconcile faith and reason, Church authority and classical thought.

Stimulated by the acquisition of Greek and Arabic knowledge, education established new frontiers. The earliest universities grew from unorganized groups of scholars and students to important centers of learning. Bologna and Paris, in particular, directly affected other universities. In literature, Latin, the international language of the educated, slowly gave way to the vernacular tongues. Chaucer and Dante, giants in the literary field, both wrote in their native languages and did much to develop modern English and Italian respectively.

Evolving from Romanesque patterns, the splendid Gothic cathedrals were the greatest artistic achievement of the medieval period. The rounded arches and massive walls of Romanesque architecture were replaced by pointed arches, ribbed-groin vaults, and the flying buttresses of the soaring Gothic cathedrals. This style carried over from churches to castles, town halls, and urban dwellings.

SUGGESTIONS FOR READING

R. W. Southern, **The Making of the Middle Ages*** (Yale) is a brilliant topical treatment of the eleventh and twelfth centuries. F. Heer, **The Medieval World*** (Mentor) vividly pictures the society of the twelfth and thirteenth centuries.

M. W. Baldwin, **The Mediaeval Church*** (Cornell) is a perceptive essay on Church development. See also Jeffrey Russell, **A History of Medieval Christianity: Prophecy and Order*** (AHM); and M. Deanesly, **A History of the Medieval Church, 590-1500,*** 9th ed. (Barnes and Noble, 1969).

G. Barraclough, **The Medieval Papacy*** (Harcourt Brace Jovanovich) is brief and lavishly illustrated. S. R. Packard, **Europe and the Church Under Innocent III** (Russell, 1968) is short and admirable. For greater detail see W. Ullmann, **A Short History of the Papacy in the Middle Ages*** (Harper & Row, 1974); and R. W. Southern, **Western Society and the Church in the Middle Ages*** (Penguin). On Church-state political theory see K. Morrison, **Tradition and Authority in the Western Church, 300-1140** (Princeton, 1969).

D. Knowles, **The Monastic Order in England,** 2nd ed. (Cambridge) is considered to be the best introduction to medieval monasticism. See also H. Workman, **The Evolution of the Monastic Ideal*** (Beacon); and E. Duckett, **The Wandering Saints of the Early Middle Ages*** (Norton).

A. Turberville, **Medieval Heresy and the Inquisition** (Shoe String) is a standard account. Religious radicalism, particularly that inspired by the love ethic, is treated in N. Cohn, **The Pursuit of the Millennium*** (Galaxy).

C. H. Haskins, **The Renaissance of the Twelfth Century*** (Harvard) is the basic study of the medieval intellectual revival. C.

Brooke, **The Twelfth Century Renaissance*** (Harcourt Brace Jovanovich) surveys all aspects of culture and is well illustrated. See also P. Wolff, **The Pelican History of European Thought,** Vol. I, **The Awakening of Europe*** (Penguin); and Colin Morris, **The Discovery of the Individual, 1050-1200*** (Torchbooks). D. Knowles, **The Evolution of Medieval Thought*** (Vintage) is an excellent introduction. Recommended for greater detail are W. Ullmann, **Medieval Political Thought*** (Penguin, 1976); and C. McIlwain, **The Growth of Political Thought in the West** (Cooper Square). See also J. Sikes, **Peter Abailard** (Russell, 1965); F. Copleston, **Aquinas*** (Penguin); and John H. Smith, **St. Francis of Assisi*** (Scribner's, 1974), a perceptive essay.

C. H. Haskins, **The Rise of Universities** (Gordon) is a brief survey. See also G. Leff, **Paris and Oxford Universities in the Thirteenth and Fourteenth Centuries** (Krieger, 1975).

William T. Jackson, **The Literature of the Middle Ages** (Columbia Univ.) and **Medieval Literature: A History and a Guide** (Collier) are recommended surveys. Outstanding also are Brian Stock, ed., **Mediaeval Latin Lyrics*** (Godine); C. S. Lewis, **The Allegory of Love*** (Galaxy); and E. Curtius, **European Literature and the Latin Middle Ages*** (Princeton).

Excellent on Romanesque and Gothic art are C. Morey, **Christian Art*** (Norton); O. von Simson, **The Gothic Cathedral*** ((Princeton); and A. Temko, **Notre-Dame of Paris*** (Viking). Stimulating interpretations of the interrelationship of medieval art, thought, and spirit are Henry Adams, **Mont-Saint-Michel and Chartres*** (Anchor); E. Mâle, **The Gothic Image*** (Torchbooks); and E. Panofsky, **Gothic Architecture and Scholasticism*** (Meridian).

*Indicates a less expensive paperbound edition.

This is the profile of members of a scholar-official's extended family. They live in Hsing-tsai (Quinsai in Marco Polo's account), the capital of the Southern Sung dynasty, which the Venetian traveler described as "the most noble city and the best that is in the world." The time is 1271, five years before its capture by the Mongols.

Hill beyond green hill, pavilion behind pavilion — at the West Lake, will the singing and the dancing never cease?
It's the warm wind that lulls them and beguiles them
    into thinking
That *this* place is the other one we knew in times of peace.

Perhaps the sunset on the lake on this festival day has caused Wang Ch'eng-ta to recite Lin Sheng's lines from the previous century — or is it the presence on the barge of his cousin the general, who has come south from the frontier that separates civilization from the barbarians' occupation of the Wangs' traditional homeland? The general is always worried — that's his job — nevertheless Wang Ch'eng-ta has sufficiently overcome the long-held antipathy of scholars towards the military to convey to fellow administrators his cousin's concerns about the mounting Mongol buildup. However, they reply that enough money has been spent on coastal forces, the defense of the Yangtze towns, and equipping both the navy and army with new catapults for hurling molten metal and explosive bombs. Meanwhile, the general is being good-naturedly accused of undue pessimism by his other cousin, the merchant, who feels that today's festival calls for celebration. Certainly his own business affairs have never gone so well. He had originally made his fortune in the river trade, and had his home at the mouth of the Yangtze; then had expanded into overseas commerce. Now he has a fleet of compass-equipped junks — two of which can carry 500 people and several dozen tons of goods — which sail regularly to Japan and make occasional voyages as far south as Malaya and Java. Silks, brocades, and porcelain fetch a good price in Japan, while spices, rare woods, and ivory are much sought-after imports from the lower latitudes. Now, at his wife's insistence, he has moved to the capital and built a handsome house on Phoenix Hill, to the west of the Imperial Palace.

Wang Ch'eng-ta agrees: it has been a splendid day, one that fully justifies his renting of the *Seven Jewels*, built to hold 20 persons below a flat roof on which the crew stand and pole the boat slowly along the Western Lake. For much of the day, however, the *Seven Jewels* has been anchored near Thunder Point, a small promontory at the southern end of the lake from which rises an octagonal pagoda, about 170 feet high, built of blue brick in

975. At the stern of the boat, the three youngest males are being given a fishing lesson by their maternal grandfather, while at the prow are Wang Ch'eng-ta's son and daughter together with the merchant's son, waving at friends in neighboring craft — and with the young men also making indecorous calls to the pretty singing-girls being ferried in small boats to other barges. Meanwhile, at one of the cabin tables, WangTse-t'ien, his wife, is serving tea to her husband's mother and the wife of the merchant, with a servant bringing in a fresh supply of hot water and dishes with sweet cakes. They have serious matters to discuss: the forthcoming marriage that will further cement the ties between the official and merchant sides of the family.

Today, the Wangs have been celebrating the Festival of the Dead. Officials, merchants, and the general populace have gathered round Western Lake and on the surrounding hills. The Wangs arrived early at the family graves to sweep them, burn sticks of incense, and place offerings of food, for it is proper to honor one's ancestors who have provided the family and each of its members with both an identity and destiny. Moreover, the Wangs are proud that their illustrious forebears include the famous statesman, Wang An-shih (see p. 176), and Wang Ch'eng-ta has sought to instill in his son, Wang Kuo-chung, the ambition to serve his emperor as still another memorable scholar-official.

But Wang Ch'eng-ta has all but given up that hope. With the growth of population in the Sung dominions, now over sixty million, and of public education, the competition for higher office has become fierce. Of course the Wangs enjoy important advantages. Since Wang An-shih's service two centuries ago, there has always been a member of the family in the upper rungs of the imperial administration stationed in the capital. Gazing at the Thunder Point pagoda, Wang Ch'eng-ta realizes that his own upbringing had seldom been out of sight of that landmark. As a child, he had been particularly close to all his grandparents and happy with his tutor. Then, he had attended at Phoenix Hill the special school for the children of the upper classes where he had learned his twenty characters a day — which never gave him the trouble that his son, with his lack of concentration, always had. At college, instruction had been aimed at forming candidates suitable for the official examinations. Wang Ch'eng-ta remembers the trial of stamina involved in sitting for each successively harder examination, and his family's pride when he passed near the top in the final doctorate of letters examination held at the Imperial Palace. Promotion had been rapid—instead of being sent as a subprefect to some distant province, he was assigned a comparatively high administrative post in the imperial secretariat. He had once seen his own dossier; his superiors had commented favorably on his capacity for work, judgment, and conduct; he had given proof of filial piety and integrity. Wang Ch'eng-ta has a secure career; he has every chance for further promotion, though it is too much to expect an appointment to the emperor's council during the next decade before he retires around age 66. Still . . .

No such chain of thought enters his son's mind as he watches the conclusion of the jousts among the dragon-boats. Wang Kuo-chung envies the strength and agility of the athletes, but of course it is a sport for the common people. He has been missing classes and frequenting one of the capital's pleasure grounds. These are places "where no one stands on ceremony," acrobats and jugglers perform, singing, dancing, and the dramatic arts are taught, and they are staffed with women musicians and singing-girls. (Little wonder that a contemporary author writes that these establishments "have become places of debauch and perdition for society people and young men of good social standing.") Wang Kuo-chung has been making contingency plans against his expected failure in the examinations. It is not unusual for well-to-do families to buy a business in one of the luxury trades for sons who have failed as scholars. Wang Kuo-chung hasn't dared raise the matter with his father, but has already discussed it with his mother.

For her part, Wang Tse-t'ien has been busy these past few days. As the daughter of a scholar-official, and the wife of another, she shares her class's disdain for people born in trade—including her husband's merchant cousin and his wife. But they are useful. She wants the merchant to suggest the best type of business for her son, to use his influence in obtaining it, and to provide much of the capital for its purchase. In return Wang Tse-t'ien will use her husband's influence to buy a petty title of nobility that should gratify the merchant and his greedy wife—and which would pass in time to the merchant's son and her own daughter, soon to be married.

Some years earlier, at the time of the Festival of the Dead, Wang Ch'ing-chao's coming of age at fifteen had been celebrated by the placing of hairpins in her hair. This was an important milestone in her early life which had been spent in the family household where she had learned to spin and embroider. She had also been taught to read and write—and had even written some inconsequential poetry—but the attainment of literary skills served no practical purpose in her case. Wang Ch'ing-chao has always known that her primary function is to marry and have children, and thus perpetuate the family—and that marriages serve as alliances between families. Actually, she quite likes her fiancé, while he is captivated by the extent to which she exemplifies the Sung ideal of feminine beauty: she is slender, petite, and dainty. In addition to the political advantages which the marriage will bring, her future parents-in-law feel that she has her fair share of the feminine virtues most admired: modesty, chastity, conjugal fidelity, and filial piety towards themselves as her husband's parents. After marriage, Wang Ch'ing-chao will continue to lead a life of luxury and leisure. She will seldom appear in public, and will usually stay confined to her own apartment. But she will exert authority in a large household—and her mother has already discerned in her daughter elements of her own shrewdness, business acumen, and ambition.

The sun has long set, so that the clouds are no longer reflected on the lake. The *Seven Jewels* lies moored near Thunder Point and the Wangs are ashore among the jostling crowd. The young men have set out for the pleasure ground near one of the bridges over which the Imperial Way runs; the boys and their grandfather are going home on foot; the ladies are returning in curtained carry-chairs; and the senior Wangs are on horseback astride their splendid saddles. The general and the merchant have gone ahead, while Wang Ch'eng-ta stops by the pagoda, outlined against the new moon. All this beauty . . . this harmony of water and human skills . . . this legacy of centuries of cultivated living . . . He wonders if the general is right—will the barbarians pierce the northern defenses? And if so, will all be over? Or will the dragon in some cunning way devour its captor? Surely whatever fortune has in store, other springs will appear . . . the great cycle will never cease to turn, maintaining order and balance between Heaven and Earth, between *yang* and *yin*, between the Universe and the Sons of Han.

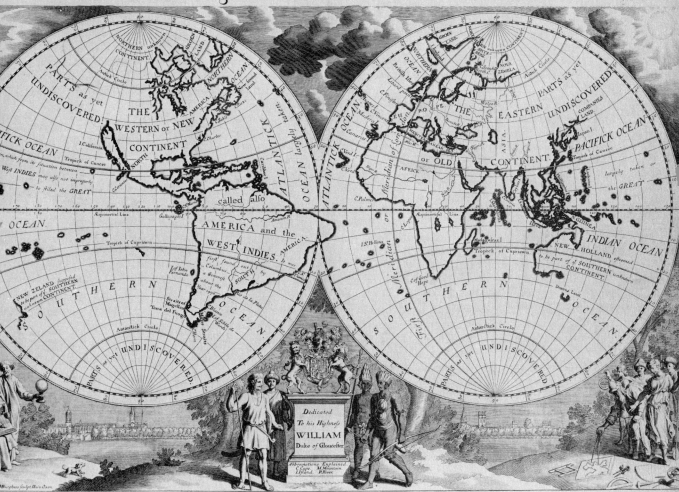

PART THREE
The Transition to Modern Times

■ So far in our study of history, we have encountered a number of societies which emphasized the group at the expense of the individual—societies such as that of ancient Egypt, for example, or of medieval Europe. In other societies, such as that of classical Greece, individualism counted for more than collectivism. During the period which historians speak of as early modern times, the interests and rights of the individual were again in the ascendant. In the political sphere, this emphasis upon individualism was manifested by the creation of nation-states; in the realm of thought and art, it produced the Renaissance; in the area of religion, it split Christendom through the Reformation; and in the field of exploration, it resulted in the discovery and colonization of the Americas and the reopening of the East to western trade.

By the end of the fifteenth century the medieval ideal of universal political unity had been shattered as national monarchies gained supremacy in England, France, and Spain. Despite opposition from popes and nobles alike, vigorous monarchs in these countries succeeded in their attempts at nation-making—a process that fostered and was in turn supported by a growing national consciousness among the common people. In Germany and Italy, however, unification was hampered by many obstacles, and in eastern Europe nation-making proceeded slowly, though Russia emerged as a powerful state after throwing off the Mongol yoke.

In the realm of thought, Italian scholars known as humanists discovered in the manuscripts of ancient Greece and Rome the same emphasis on individual freedom which was rapidly gaining momentum in their own day, and with this spirit of individualism sprang up an unashamed delight in the beauties and joys of life. Heeding Protagoras' ancient maxim that "Man is the measure of all things" and revolting against medieval authority and asceticism, Renaissance man was impelled by a new spirit of independence, a new hunger for experience. The creative vigor of the Italian Renaissance in literature, thought, and the fine arts surged throughout Europe, resulting in one of the most fruitful epochs in the cultural history of mankind.

Carried into the religious sphere, the resurgence of individualism shattered the universal supremacy of the Church and gave rise to the religious diversity of the modern western world. The followers of Luther, Calvin, and Zwingli substituted the authority of the Scriptures for that of the Roman Church and interposed no priestly mediator between the individual and his God. The Roman Church, which launched a vigorous reform movement of its own, nevertheless continued to be a potent force.

Finally, the economic structure of western Europe was transformed radically in early modern times. The quickening of town life abetted the rise of a new and forceful middle class, whose members were the chief supporters and benefactors of the system of economic individualism known as capitalism. Furthermore, overseas expansion stimulated trade, increased wealth, and introduced to European markets an abundance of products previously scarce or unknown. So important was the new trade and its many influences on European life and manners that it is referred to as the Commercial Revolution. The barter economy of the Middle Ages was superseded by one of money, banks, and stock exchanges; and Europe rapidly became the economic center of the world.

Up to the fifteenth century, Asia had been equal or superior to Europe in military power and cultural attainments. But as the West advanced, China and India declined in power and creativity. The European scramble for empire had serious consequences. In Asia, important trading concessions were wrung from the natives; in the New World, indigenous peoples were decimated and their cultures all but erased; in tropical Africa, the Europeans established a lucrative slave trade and reaped rich profits from this callous exploitation of human lives. From the mid-point of the seventeenth century to our own day, European civilization—the most creative, expansive, and aggressive on earth—was to be the dominant and pervasive influence in world history.

CHAPTER 12

Religion and Politics: 1300-1500

Europe in Transition

INTRODUCTION. In Europe the fourteenth and fifteenth centuries were marked by a decline of those institutions and ideas which we think of as typically "medieval" and which had reached their high point during the preceding two centuries. In thought and art an empty formalism replaced the creative forces which had given the Middle Ages such unique methods of expression as scholasticism and the Gothic style. Economic and social progress gave way to depression and social strife, with peasant revolts a characteristic symptom of instability.

The universal Church experienced a disintegration similar to that which had already fatally weakened its great medieval rival, the Holy Roman Empire. The Church's prestige was gravely weakened from within by the reformers and heretics, while external factors, chiefly political and economic, undermined its power and authority. By the sixteenth century these forces would be strong enough to bring about the Protestant and Catholic reformations.

Despite crises and setbacks—the Hundred Years' War came close to wiping out the gains made earlier by French and English monarchs—the process of nation-making continued during the fourteenth and fifteenth centuries. In western Europe the contrasting political trends clearly evident at the end of the thirteenth century—unification in England, France, and Spain, and fragmentation in Germany and Italy—reached their culmination. And in Slavic eastern Europe significant progress in nation-making was made in Russia. In much of Europe by the end of the fifteenth century, the conflicting aims of what are sometimes called the "new monarchies" were superseding the quarrels of feudal barons.

THE DECLINE OF THE MEDIEVAL CHURCH

Dangers facing the papacy. The history of the medieval Church divides roughly into three periods—dissemination, domination, and disintegration. In the initial period, which lasted from about the fifth through the eleventh centuries, Roman Christianity spread throughout the West. The advent of feudalism in the tenth century destroyed the Church's administrative apparatus centered on the papacy, but late in the eleventh century the Church revived under strong popes and became the most powerful institution in the West. The period of domination—the twelfth and thirteenth centuries—reached its zenith in the pontificate of Innocent III, who made and deposed temporal princes at will. The Church then seemed unassailable in its prestige, dignity, and power. Yet that strength soon came under new attack, and during the next two centuries the processes of disintegration were to run their course.

Papal power was threatened by the growth of nation-states, which challenged the Church's temporal pretensions. Joined by some of the local clergy, rulers opposed papal interference in state matters and favored the establishment of general Church councils to curb papal power. In addition, the papacy was criticized by reformers, who had seen the medieval reformation and the crusades transformed from their original high-minded purposes to suit the ambitions of the pontiffs, and by the bourgeoisie, whose realistic outlook was fostering growing skepticism, national patriotism, and religious self-reliance. During the fourteenth and fifteenth centuries these factors took their toll, and papal influence rapidly declined.

Boniface VIII. A century after the papacy's zenith under Innocent III, Pope Boniface VIII (1294-1303) was forced to withdraw his fierce opposition to taxes levied on the great wealth of the Church by Edward I in England and Philip IV in France. Emulating Innocent, Boniface threatened to depose the "impious king," as he termed Philip, but he gave way when Philip with the support of the Estates-General prohibited the export of money to Rome.

A final and more humiliating clash with the French king had long-range implications for the papacy. When Boniface boldly declared, in the most famous of all papal bulls, *Unam Sanctam* (1302), that "subjection to the Roman pontiff is absolutely necessary to salvation for every human creature," Philip demanded that the pope be tried for his "sins" by a general Church council. In 1303 Philip's henchmen broke into Boniface's summer home at Anagni to arrest him and take him to France to stand trial. Their kidnaping plot was foiled when the pope was rescued by his friends. Shocked and humiliated, Boniface died a month later.

The Avignon papacy. The success of the French monarchy was as complete as if Boniface had been dragged before Philip. Two years after Boniface's death, a French archbishop was chosen pope. Taking the title of Clement V, he not only exonerated Philip but praised his Christian zeal in bringing charges against Boniface. Clement never went to Rome, where feuding noble families made life turbulent, but moved the papal headquarters to Avignon in France, where the papacy remained under French influence from 1305 to 1377. During this period, the so-called "Babylonian Captivity" of the Church, papal prestige suffered enormously. All Christendom believed that Rome was the only rightful capital for the Church. Moreover, the English, Germans, and Italians accused the popes and the cardinals, who were also French, of being instruments of the French king.

The Avignon papacy added fuel to the fires of those critics who were attacking Church corruption, papal temporal claims, and the apparent lack of spiritual enthusiasm. Deprived of much of their former income from England, Germany, and Italy, and living in splendor in a newly built fortress-palace, the Avignon popes expanded the papal bureaucracy, added new Church taxes, and collected the old taxes more efficiently. This produced denouncements of the wealth of the Church and a demand for its reformation.

The Great Schism. When the papacy took heed of popular opinion and returned to Rome in 1377, it seemed for a time that the fortunes of the Roman Church would improve. But the reverse proved true. A papal election was held the following year, and the College of Cardinals, perhaps influenced by a shouting mob milling around the Vatican, elected an Italian pope. A few months later the French cardinals declared the election invalid and elected a French pope, who returned to Avignon.

The Church was now in an even worse state than it had been during the Babylonian Captivity. During the Great Schism, as the split of the Church into two allegiances was called, there were two popes, each with his college of cardinals and capital city, each claiming universal sovereignty, each sending forth papal administrators and taxing Christendom, and each excommunicating the other. The nations of Europe gave allegiance as their individual political interests prompted them. In order to keep that allegiance, the rival popes had to make concessions to their political supporters and largely abandoned the practice of interfering in national politics.

The Great Schism seemed to be permanent after the original rival popes died and each camp elected a replacement instead of working to heal the breach in the Church. Reli-

gious life suffered, for "Christendom looked upon the scandal helpless and depressed, and yet impotent to remove it. With two sections of Christendom each declaring the other lost, each cursing and denouncing the other, men soberly asked who was saved."[1] Heresy flourished as doubt and confusion caused many to break away from the Church.

The Conciliar Movement. Positive action came in the form of the Conciliar Movement, a return to the early Christian practice of solving Church problems by means of a general council of prelates (see p. 128). In 1395 the professors at the University of Paris proposed that a general council, representing the Universal Church, should meet to heal the Schism. A majority of the cardinals of both camps accepted this solution, and in 1409 they met at the Council of Pisa, deposed both pontiffs, and elected a third man. But neither of the two deposed popes would give up his office, and the papal throne now had three claimants.

Such an intolerable situation necessitated another Church council. In 1414 the Holy Roman emperor assembled at Constance the most impressive Church gathering of the period. For the first time voting took place on a purely national basis. Instead of the traditional assembly of bishops, the Council included lay representatives and was organized as a convention of "nations" (German, Italian, French, and English, the Spanish entering later). Each nation had one vote. The nationalistic structure of the Council was highly significant as an indication that the new tendency toward such alignments was being recognized by the Church's hierarchy. Finally, through the deposition of the various papal claimants and the election of Martin v in 1417, the Great Schism was ended, and a single papacy was restored at Rome.

Failure of internal reform. The Conciliar Movement represented a reforming and democratizing influence in the Church, aimed at transforming the papacy into something like a limited monarchy. But the movement was not to endure, even though the Council of Constance had solemnly decreed that general councils were superior to popes and that they should meet at regular intervals in the future. Taking steps to preserve his posi-

In this contemporary sketch of John Huss being led to execution, the reformer wears the headgear which branded him as a heretic condemned by the Council of Constance in 1415.

tion, the pope announced that to appeal to a Church council without having first obtained papal consent was heretical. The restoration of a single head of the Church, together with the inability of later councils to bring about much-needed reform, enabled the popes to discredit the Conciliar Movement by 1450. Not until almost a century later, in 1545, did the great Council of Trent meet to reform a Church which had already irreparably lost many countries to Protestantism.

Unfortunately, while the popes hesitated to call councils to effect reform, they failed to bring about reform themselves. The popes busied themselves not with internal problems but with Italian politics and patronage of the arts. Thus, "the papacy emerged as something between an Italian city-state and a European power, without forgetting at the same time the claim to be the vice-regent of Christ. The pope often could not make up his own mind whether he was the successor of Peter or of Caesar. Such vacillation had much to do with the rise and success . . . of the Reformation."[2]

Heresy: Wycliffe and Huss. Throughout the fourteenth century the cries against Church corruption became louder at the same time that heretical thoughts were being voiced. In England *Piers the Plowman* (see p. 257) mercilessly upbraided the corruption, ignorance, and worldliness of the clergy, and a professor at Oxford named John Wycliffe (1320?-1384) assailed not only Church abuses but Church doctrines. Because of his beliefs that the Church should be subordinate to the state, that salvation was primarily an individual matter between man and God, that transubstantiation as taught by the Church was false, and that outward rituals and veneration of relics were idolatrous, Wycliffe has been called the dawn-star of the Protestant Revolt. He formed bands of "poor priests," called Lollards, who taught his views; and he provided the people with an English translation of the Bible, which he considered the final authority in matters of religion. Although Wycliffe's demands for reform did not succeed, the Lollards, including the famous John Ball (see p. 217), spread a more radical version of Wycliffe's ideas until the movement was driven underground early in the next century.

In Bohemia—where a strong reform movement, linked with the resentment of the Czechs towards their German overlords, was under way—Wycliffe's doctrines were propagated by Czech students who had heard him at Oxford. In particular, his beliefs influenced John Huss (1369?-1415), an impassioned preacher in Prague and later rector of the university there. Huss' attacks on the abuses of clerical power led him, like Wycliffe, to conclude that the true Church was composed of a universal priesthood of believers and that Christ alone was its head. But Huss, who was more preacher and reformer than theologian, did not accept Wycliffe's denial of the validity of transubstantiation.

Huss' influence became so great that he was excommunicated. Later the emperor gave him a safe-conduct to stand trial for heresy at the Council of Constance. Huss refused to recant his views, and the Council ordered him burned at the stake in spite of his safe-conduct. This action made Huss a martyr to the Czechs, who rebelled against both the German emperor, who was also king of Bohemia, and the Catholic Church. The Czechs maintained their political and religious independence for more than a generation before they were crushed. In the sixteenth century the remaining Hussites merged with the Lutherans.

Reasons for Church decline. The reasons for the Church's decline during the fourteenth and fifteenth centuries can be divided into those that existed within the Church itself and those that were weakening it from the outside. By the early sixteenth century these forces were strong enough to bring about the Reformation.

As we have seen, trenchant criticisms of the clergy had come from a variety of sources, and the Conciliar Movement had gone so far as to challenge the supreme power of the pope himself. And while criticisms increased, the Church continued to decline in spiritual leadership. The worldly concerns of the fourteenth- and fifteenth-century popes—including their deep involvement in Italian politics—pushed the Church further in the direction of secularization.

Among the outside pressures that led to the Church's decline, the new spirit of inquiry encouraged by the Renaissance (see Chapter 13) resulted in a new critical attitude toward religious institutions. And the newly invented printing press provided the means for the rapid dissemination of ideas. In the socioeconomic field, the medieval Church was slow in adapting itself to the new environment of the towns. The problems arising from town life too often went unanswered by the Church, which failed to provide enough parish priests to keep pace with the growth of urban population. It is no accident that the towns became centers of heresy. Finally, the development of nationalism and the growing reluctance of kings to obey any opposing institution, including the Church, were evident in the encounters between Boniface VIII and the French ruler Philip IV.

CRISIS IN ENGLAND AND FRANCE

The Hundred Years' War. Nation-making in both France and England was greatly affected by the long conflict that colored much of their history during the fourteenth and fifteenth centuries. In both lands the crisis of war led to a resurgence of feudalism. Another deterrent to the rise of royal power was the increase in the power of the representative assemblies, Parliament and the Estates-General. Nevertheless, in the long run the increasing anarchy and misery of the times stimulated nationalistic feelings and a demand for strong rulers who could guarantee law and order. Thus by the late fifteenth century the French and English kings were able to resume the task of establishing the institutions of the modern nation-state.

The Hundred Years' War sprang from a fundamental conflict between the aims of the English and the French monarchies. The English kings wanted to regain the large holdings in France that had been theirs in the days of Henry II. The French kings, on the other hand, were determined not only to keep what had been taken from John of England but to expand further. Their ultimate goal was a centralized France under the direct rule of the monarchy at Paris.

Another factor was the clash of French and English economic interests in Flanders. This region was coming more and more under French control, to the chagrin of the English wool growers who supplied the great Flemish woolen industry, and of the English king whose income came in great part from duties on wool (see Reference Map 4).

The immediate excuse for the Anglo-French conflict was a dispute over the succession to the French throne. In 1328, after the direct line of the Capetians became extinct, Philip VI of the House of Valois assumed the throne. The English king, Edward III, maintained that he was the legitimate heir to the French throne because his mother was a sister of the late French king. The

French nobility disputed this claim, which became a pretext for war. Interrupted by several peace treaties and a number of truces, the conflict stretched from 1337 to 1453. At the naval battle of Sluys (1340) the English gained command of the Channel and thus were able to send their armies to France at will. Thereafter England won a series of great victories—at Crécy (1346), Poitiers (1356), and Agincourt (1415), where the French lost some 7000 knights, including many great nobles, and the English only 500.

The English armies were much more effective than those of the French. With no thought of strategy, the French knights charged the enemy at a mad gallop and then engaged in hand-to-hand fighting. The English learned other methods. Their secret weapon was the longbow, apparently taken over from the Welsh. Six feet long and made of special wood, the longbow shot steel-tipped arrows which were dangerous at four hundred yards and deadly at one hundred. The usual English plan of battle called for the knights to fight dismounted. Protecting them was a forward wall of bowmen just behind a barricade of iron stakes planted in the ground to slow down the enemy's charge. By the time the enemy cavalry reached the dismounted knights, only a few remained to be taken care of; the "feathered death" had done its work.

English military triumphs stirred English pride and what we now think of as nationalism—love of country, identification with it, and a sense of difference from, and usually superiority to, other peoples. However, patriotism was stirring in France also. The revival of French spirit is associated with Joan of Arc, who initiated a series of French victories.

Impelled by inward voices which she believed divine, Joan persuaded the timid French ruler to allow her to lead an army to relieve the besieged city of Orléans. Clad in white armor and riding a white horse, she inspired confidence and a feeling of invincibility in her followers, and in 1429 Orléans was rescued from what had seemed certain conquest. But Joan met a tragic end. Captured by the enemy, she was found guilty of bewitching the English soldiers and was burned at the stake, while the French king remained indifferent to her fate.

The martyrdom of the Maid of Orléans was a turning point in the long struggle. The nucleus of a permanent standing army was developed and the use of gunpowder to propel missiles began to transform the art of war. English resistance crumbled as military superiority now turned full circle; the English longbow was outmatched by French artillery. Of the vast territories they had once controlled in France, the English retained only Calais when the war ended in 1453.

Aftermath of war in England. The Hundred Years' War exhausted England, and discontent was rife in Parliament and among the peasants. (On the peasants' revolt of 1381, see p. 217.) Richard II (1377-1399), the last Plantagenet king, was unstable, cruel, and power hungry, and he foreshadowed modern absolute monarchs in believing that the king should control the lives and property

This illumination depicts a scene of late medieval warfare typical of the Hundred Years' War. Note the suits of armor, crossbows, longbows, and the early form of cannon.

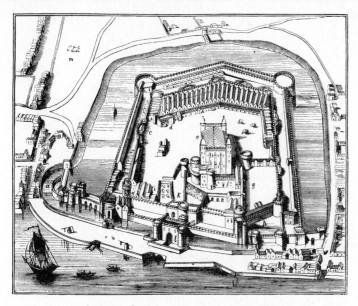

A sixteenth-century engraving of the Tower of London, long used as a prison for those accused of crimes against English monarchs, shows the complex network of walls, towers, living quarters, and fortress which was continually added to and modified from the time of William the Conqueror until well into modern times.

of his subjects. His seizure of the properties of Henry, the duke of Lancaster, led to a revolt in which Henry was victorious.

Henry IV established the House of Lancaster, which ruled England from 1399 to 1461. He was given the support of Parliament, which had deeply resented Richard's autocratic reign and was determined that its authority should not again be slighted. Hard-pressed for money to suppress revolts at home and carry on the war in France, the Lancastrian kings became more and more financially dependent upon Parliament. In return for money grants, Parliament acquired such gains as the guarantee of freedom of debate, the right to approve the appointment of the king's chief officials and members of his council, the stipulation that money bills must originate in the House of Commons, and the rule that the king's statutes should duplicate exactly petitions presented by the Commons. Not until 1689, when England became a constitutional monarchy, would Parliament again exercise such powers.

Baronial rivalry to control both Parliament and the crown flared up during the reign of the third Lancastrian king, and when he went completely insane in 1453, the duke of York, the strongest man in the kingdom, became regent. Two years later full-scale civil war broke out between the House of York and the partisans of the Lancaster family. The struggle became known as the Wars of the Roses; the white rose was the badge of the House of York, and the red rose that of the House of Lancaster. In 1461 the Yorkists managed to have their leader, Edward IV, crowned king. Ten years later Edward had succeeded in cowing the nobles and in winning the support of the middle class, who saw a strong monarchy as the only alternative to anarchy. Edward's power became practically absolute, foreshadowing the strong rule of the Tudors that soon followed.

The promise of the House of York ended in 1483 when Edward IV died, leaving two young sons as his heirs. Their uncle, Richard, bribed and intimidated Parliament to declare his nephews illegitimate and took the throne. The two boys were imprisoned in the Tower of London, where they were secretly murdered. The double murder was too much for the nation, and support was thrown to the cause of Henry Tudor, who, in his lineage and later marriage to Edward IV's daughter, united the Houses of Lancaster and York. At Bosworth Field in 1485 Richard died fighting as his army deserted him. According to tradition, his crown was found in a bush on the battlefield and placed on the head of Henry VII, the first of the Tudor line, which ruled England from 1485 to 1603.

Beginning of Tudor rule. Under Tudor rule England achieved the full status of a national state. During the reigns of the shrewd Henry VII (1485-1509) and his successor, Henry VIII (1509-1547), strong, almost absolute government was reintroduced into England, with the people supporting the monarchy because it held the nobility in check. The Court of Star Chamber, established by Edward IV, was the most effective royal instrument in suppressing the unruly barons; it bypassed the established common law courts, whose judges and juries were too often intimidated and bribed by powerful nobles, and operated secretly and swiftly without benefit of juries. Because the Tudor rulers restored order and promoted trade at home and abroad, they won the support of the people of middle rank—the burghers and landed gentry—and upon this support their power was primarily built. Though often high-handed, Tudor kings always worked through Parliament.

France after the Hundred Years' War: Louis XI. The Hundred Years' War left France with a new national consciousness and a royal power that was stronger than ever before. In 1438 the king had become the virtual head of the church in France by decreeing that it be run by a council of French bishops whose appointment was to be controlled by the monarch. Furthermore, the *taille*, a land tax voted during the war to support a standing army, became permanent, making the king financially independent of the Estates-General. Thus the purse strings, which the English Parliament used to gain concessions from the king, were kept firmly under royal control in France.

After the war the process of consolidating royal power was continued by Louis XI (1461-1483), son of the king aided by Joan of Arc. Physically unattractive and completely lacking in scruples, Louis earned himself the epithet, the "universal spider." In his pursuit of power he used any weapon—violence, bribery, and treachery—to obtain his ends. When the French nobles rose in revolt, dignifying themselves as the League for the Public Welfare, Louis outfoxed them by agreeing to their Magna Carta-like demands and then ignoring his pledged word.

Louis XI's most powerful antagonist was the duke of Burgundy, Charles the Bold, whose possession of Flanders and the other Low Countries or Netherlands (modern Holland, Belgium, and Luxemburg) made him one of Europe's richest rulers. After Charles' death in 1477, Louis seized most of Burgundy, while the remainder of the duke's possessions passed to his daughter Mary. When she married the German emperor Maximilian I, the Netherlands came into the hands of the House of Hapsburg (see map, p. 327). Like Henry VII of England, Louis XI was one of the "new monarchs" who created the absolute states which were to dominate Europe in the early modern period.

THE POLITICAL UNIFICATION OF SPAIN AND PORTUGAL

Ferdinand and Isabella: "One king, one law, one faith." Another "new monarchy" emerged in 1479 when Isabella of Castile and Ferdinand of Aragon, who had married ten years earlier, began a joint rule that united the Iberian peninsula except for Granada, Navarre, and Portugal. The "Catholic Sovereigns," to use the title the pope conferred on Ferdinand and Isabella, set out to establish an effective royal despotism in Spain. The Holy Brotherhood, a league of cities which had long existed for mutual protection against unruly nobles, was taken over by the crown, and its militia was used as a standing army and police force. The powerful and virtually independent military orders of knights, which had emerged during the *Reconquista*, were also brought under royal control.

Ferdinand and Isabella believed that the Church should be subordinate to royal government—a belief they shared with the other "new monarchs" of Europe. By tactful negotiations, the Spanish sovereigns induced the pope to give them the right to make Church appointments in Spain and to establish a Spanish Court of Inquisition, largely free of papal control. The Inquisition confiscated the property of most Jews and Muslims and terrified the Christian clergy and laymen into accepting royal absolutism as well as religious orthodoxy. Although the Inquisition greatly enhanced the power of the Spanish crown, it also caused many talented people to flee the land of persecution. About 150,000 Spanish Jews, mainly merchants and professional people, fled to Holland, England, North Africa, and the Ottoman empire. Calling themselves Sephardim, these exiles retained their Spanish language and customs into the twentieth century.

A final manifestation of Spanish absolutism, defined by Isabella herself as "one king, one law, one faith," was the virtual ignoring of the Cortes of Castile and Aragon. These representative assemblies had emerged in the twelfth century and were thus older than the English Parliament.

The most dramatic act of the Catholic Sovereigns was the conquest of Granada in 1492, the same year that Columbus claimed the New World for Spain. Before Ferdinand died in 1516, twelve years after Isabella, he seized that part of Navarre which lay south of the Pyrenees Mountains. This acquisition, together with the conquest of Granada, completed the national unification of Spain.

Results of Spanish unification. Royal absolutism and unification, coupled with the acquisition of territory in the New and Old Worlds, made Spain the strongest power in sixteenth-century Europe. But the process of unifying Spain had some unfortunate results: (1) Centuries of fighting against the Muslims left a legacy of warlike spirit and inordinate national pride. (2) Religious enthusiasm was whipped up as a means to an end, and the sequel was a heritage of religious bigotry and the death of that tolerance, intellectual curiosity, and sense of balance which had been characteristic of Muslim culture in Spain. (3) Spanish contempt for the Muslims created a scorn for those activities in which the unbelievers had engaged—trade, crafts, manual labor, and agriculture. This attitude hampered Spanish economic development in subsequent centuries.

Portugal. The nucleus of the area which eventually became Portugal was a part of Castile until 1095. In that year the king of Castile gave his daughter to Count Henry of Burgundy, one of many French knights who had helped take Toledo (see p. 208). Her dowry was the county of Portugal, named after its chief town Oporto ("The Port") at the mouth of the Duero River. The son of this marriage organized a revolt against his overlord, the king of Castile, and in 1139 proclaimed himself king of Portugal.

Attempts by Castile to regain Portugal ended in 1385 when John I, aided by English archers, decisively defeated the invader. The following year John signed an alliance with England which has been reaffirmed down the centuries and remains the oldest alliance in existence. In 1415 John took Ceuta in North Africa (see Reference Map 7), thus initiating Portuguese overseas expansion. Carried on by his son, Henry the Navigator, this policy eventually led to the creation of a great overseas empire (see Chapter 18).

DISUNITY IN GERMANY

The early Hapsburgs and the Golden Bull. Between 1254 and 1273 the German monarchy was made virtually nonexistent by the election of two rival foreign princes, neither of whom received wide recognition. Then in 1273 the imperial crown was bestowed upon the obscure Count Rudolf (1273-1291) of the House of Hapsburg—from Habichtsburg (Castle of the Hawk), their home in northern Switzerland. During the remainder of the Middle Ages and in modern times, the Hapsburgs had amazing success in adding to their ancestral lands. Rudolf himself acquired Austria through marriage, and thereafter the Hapsburgs ruled their holdings from Vienna. In the sixteenth century they obtained Bohemia and part of Hungary (see p. 276).

For the time being, however, the Hapsburg hold on the imperial crown proved to be brief. After Rudolf's reign it was passed from one family to another. Then in 1356 the nobility won another significant victory. The Golden Bull, a document which served as the political constitution of Germany until early in the nineteenth century, laid down the procedure for election of the emperor by seven German dignitaries—three archbishops and four lay princes. The electors and other important princes were given rights that made them virtually independent rulers, and the emperor could take no important action without the consent of the imperial feudal assembly, the Diet, which met infrequently. It has been said that the Golden Bull "legalized anarchy and called it a constitution"; in reality it stabilized the political situation in Germany by recognizing the independence of the princes, thereby encouraging them to emulate the new national monarchs and create stable governments in their principalities. It also ended disputed elections and civil wars over the succession. But with the emperor virtually powerless, people thereafter commonly referred to the welter of duchies, counties, bishoprics, and free cities as the Germanies, not Germany.

The imperial crown of Germany was returned to the Hapsburg family in 1438. From this time until 1806, when the Holy Roman Empire disappeared, the Hapsburgs held the imperial crown almost without a break. Maximilian I (1493-1519) helped make the Hapsburgs the most potent force in sixteenth-century Europe by taking as his wife Mary of Burgundy (see p. 272), heiress of the rich Low Countries, and by marrying his son to the heiress of Spain.

Inspired by the rise of the "new monarchies," Maximilian attempted to strengthen his power. His program for a national court system, army, and taxation was frustrated by the German princes who insisted on jealously guarding what they called "German freedom." The emperor continued to be limited in power; nor did the empire have

an imperial treasury, an efficient central administration, or a standing army. And so the phantom Holy Roman Empire lived on as Voltaire later characterized it: "Neither Holy, nor Roman, nor an Empire."

ITALY: WEALTHY BUT DIVIDED

The northern city-states. The virtual ending of German imperial influence after 1250 left the three major divisions of Italy—the city-states of northern Italy, the Papal States, and the Kingdom of Naples (see map, p. 283)—free to follow their own devices. Such city-states as Venice, Florence, Milan, Genoa, and Pisa had grown wealthy from their thriving industries, lucrative trade, and banking houses that handled papal revenues and made loans to European monarchs.

Within each city there were intense rivalries and feuds. Unlike the situation in northern Europe, where the bourgeoisie inhabited the towns and the nobles lived on country manors, the Italian nobility had city houses as well as country villas. In some Italian cities arcaded streets enabled the townsmen to go about their business safe from the arrows which from time to time flew between the towered houses of feuding nobles.

In both the intracity rivalries and the struggles between city-states, mercenary soldiers under the command of leaders called *condottieri* were employed. Coming from all over Europe, these adventurers sold their swords to the highest bidder, but, in order to live and fight another day, they carried on their fighting with a minimum of bloodshed. Far different from the twentieth-century wars of annihilation, these petty conflicts did not hinder the spectacular progress in art and learning called the Italian Renaissance (see Chapter 13).

Civic patriotism advanced rapidly under the influence of the prosperous burghers, who finally succeeded in ousting the restless feudal aristocrats from positions of power. Ingenious city charters and civic constitutions were drafted, and there was much trial

A view of the Italian city of Siena looking toward several medieval towers built in the thirteenth and fourteenth centuries. In the center is the Mangia Tower of the Palazzo Pubblico, over three hundred feet high, and an excellent example of pointed Gothic architecture. Towers such as these were built to convey civic pride; often one community or noble family tried to outdo another in the grandness of the tower's construction.

and error in the art of government. Until the end of the thirteenth century the prevailing political trend in the cities was toward republicanism and representative government.

Two city-state republics were of unusual interest. Venice, the "Pearl of the Adriatic," was one of the richest cities of its time, controlling an empire of ports and islands in the eastern Mediterranean and carrying much of Europe's maritime trade in its great fleets. The government of this rich republic had been in the hands of a doge (duke), together with a popular assembly, but beginning in the thirteenth century the rich merchants gradually took over the reins of power. They alone sat in the Great Council, which replaced the popular assembly. This oligarchic council appointed the doge and the members of smaller councils which administered the government. Most famous among the smaller councils was the secret Council of Ten, which dealt swiftly with suspected enemies of the government. The merchant oligarchy of Venice provided good government and, unlike other Italian city-states, resolutely squashed internal strife.

Florence—the center of flourishing wool, leather, and silk industries—boasted merchants and bankers who were among the most prosperous in Europe, and its gold florin circulated in many lands as a standard coin. With its many checks and counterchecks of power, the Florentine constitution was bewilderingly complex. For example, the head of the state held office for two months only, and all measures needed a two-thirds majority in five different committees or assemblies to become laws. In theory Florence was a democracy but, as in Venice, real political power was wielded by wealthy businessmen.

During the fourteenth century republicanism declined and most Italian city-states came under the rule of despots. Conspiracy, confusion, and incompetence caused many citizens to welcome a strong leader as political boss or despot. Although Venice maintained the benevolent oligarchy of its merchants with the doge as a figurehead, Florence went under the thumb of the Medici family, and its republican institutions became largely empty forms. The Medici had

no aristocratic antecedents; their status was based on commerce and finance. The significance of the family emblem—six red balls on a field of gold—is unknown, but we are all familiar with the later modification of this insigne—the three balls of the pawnbroker.

The Papal States and the Kingdom of Naples. The Papal States, extending from fifty miles south of the mouth of the Tiber to the northeast across Italy as far as the mouth of the Po River, were poorly organized. The popes found it difficult to force their will upon various petty despots who defied their political authority. Although they headed the great international Church, in Italy the popes acted little differently from the rulers of the other states in the matter of hiring troops, waging wars, and making treaties.

The Kingdom of Naples covered the southern half of the Italian peninsula as well as Sicily. After 1250 the houses of Aragon and Anjou disputed over the kingdom (see p. 238) until Aragon won out early in the fifteenth century. Impoverished by the warfare of foreign armies, with its powerful nobles rebellious, and with brigandage rampant, southern Italy and Sicily sank into a backwardness that was to continue into the twentieth century.

EASTERN EUROPE

German eastward expansion. Since the early tenth century German barons and churchmen had been founding bishoprics and colonizing the land east of the Elbe. The German settlements, however, remained precariously isolated in the midst of large Slavic populations. Then, shortly after 1200, a new development occurred. The Teutonic Knights, a military-religious order founded at the time of the Third Crusade, transferred their operations to eastern Europe. Within fifty years the Knights had conquered the pagan Slavs in Prussia, and by 1350 they ruled the Baltic coastlands as far north as the Gulf of Finland. Assuming the role of a colonial aristocracy, the Knights built castles and towns, and a steady stream of German settlers moved into the conquered lands.

Poland and Lithuania. To the south of Prussia lived the Slavic Poles. They were first united into a state late in the tenth century, but the Polish nobility seldom allowed their monarch to exercise much power. Also in the late tenth century the Poles were converted to Roman Christianity, thus linking Poland to western European culture.

The continued threat of the aggressive Teutonic Knights caused the Polish nobles in 1386 to offer the Polish crown to the king of the neighboring Lithuanians, a pagan people who had expanded into a Russia weakened and fragmented by the Mongol conquest (see p. 277). Converted to Latin Christianity, the Lithuanians joined with the Poles in defeating the Teutonic Knights in the great battle of Tannenberg in 1410. The Knights never regained their former power, and in 1466 they turned West Prussia over to the Poles, retaining East Prussia as a fief of the Polish crown. This settlement was a great blow to German expansion, for the Poles obtained control of the Vistula River and a corridor north to the Baltic Sea, including the important port of Danzig. East Prussia was now cut off from the rest of Germany. In the history of modern Europe, the Polish corridor and Danzig have played an important role.

The Polish state, united with Lithuania in 1386 under a common sovereign, was the largest in Europe, but its promise was never realized. The nobility succeeded in keeping the monarchy elective and weak, and the middle class, composed largely of German settlers and Jewish refugees from persecution in western Europe, remained small and powerless. Above all, Poland faced the hostility of the ambitious tsars of Moscow who sought to rule over all Russians, including those in the huge Polish-Lithuanian state.

Bohemians and Magyars. Two other peoples appeared in the east European family in the Middle Ages. During the ninth and tenth centuries the Slavic Czechs established a kingdom on the Bohemian plain. German influence became strong in Bohemia, which was a part of the Holy Roman Empire, and the Golden Bull of 1356 made the Bohemian king one of the seven imperial electors. Living southeast of Bohemia in the wide and fertile plain known as Hungary were the Magyars, an Asiatic people. Originally the terror of eastern Europe because of their brutal raids (see p. 233), they became civilized, adopted Christianity, and in the eleventh century expanded their state.

The promise of both these rising nations—Bohemia and Hungary—was blighted by a common disaster. The king of Hungary, who was also king of Bohemia, met his death fighting against the Turks in 1526. Terrified at the prospects of Muslim rule, both the Czechs and Hungarians elected the same man to their vacant thrones—Ferdinand, the Hapsburg archduke of neighboring Austria. The Turks, however, occupied most of Hungary (which they would hold until the end of the seventeenth century), leaving Ferdinand only a narrow strip along the western border (see map at left). This intertwining of national fortunes explains how the Haps-

CENTRAL AND EASTERN EUROPE 1526

burgs at Vienna came to rule a polyglot empire of Bohemians, Hungarians, and German Austrians.

South Slavs and Turks in the Balkans. The outstanding political development in southeastern Europe at the close of the Middle Ages was the disappearance of the Byzantine empire and the emergence of the Ottoman Turks as a threat to Europe. Before the end of the fifteenth century the Turks had extended their control over the Balkans and were pushing on toward Vienna. This huge new empire, with its center at Constantinople, was in no sense a national state but rather a bewildering mixture of Turks, Serbs, Hungarians, Bulgarians, Rumanians, Armenians, Greeks, and Jews.

Turkish rule delayed the rise of national states in southeastern Europe until the nineteenth century. The multiplicity of small countries in the Balkans in modern times and the resultant tensions and conflicts have made the peninsula a European danger zone, a source of constant worry to diplomats, and, as in 1914, the direct or indirect cause of wars.

The Mongol conquest of Russia. In Chapter 7 we followed the amazing career of Genghis Khan, who united the unruly tribesmen of Mongolia and then launched them like a thunderbolt on a campaign of world conquest. By 1240 the Mongols had conquered Kiev and other Russian principalities, and in 1242 they penetrated to the outskirts of Vienna. Western Europe seemed theirs for the taking, but the death of the great Khan in far-off Mongolia caused the Tatar, or Mongol, armies to return to the lower Volga pending the election of a new khan.

Central Europe was not molested again, but the Mongols continued to dominate Russia from their capital at Sarai on the Volga not far from the modern city of Volgograd. The various Russian principalities were allowed to govern themselves as long as they paid tribute to the Golden Horde, as the Tatars in Russia were called. The khanate of the Golden Horde was only one of the Mongol states, however; the successors of Genghis Khan ruled an empire stretching from Korea on the east to Poland on the west. On the south their holdings included Persia and Afghanistan, as well as the area north of what is now India and Burma. Only since the Second World War has an empire arisen—that of Soviet Russia and its satellites—which could rival the vast expanse of contiguous territory controlled by the Mongols. In fact, the Russian empire together with Communist China not only rivals but nearly duplicates that of the Mongol khanates.

Mongol domination changed the whole course of Russian history; it completed the break between Russia and western European civilization initiated by the decline of Kiev. Asian cultural influences were strong—the status of women was lowered as they accepted the veil and oriental seclusion. Mongols and Russians intermarried freely; hence the saying, "Scratch a Russian and you will find a Tatar." Many authorities believe that the Mongol conquest was a wholesale calamity. Russia was cut off from Europe, and a new Russia north and east of Kiev began to develop. Its nucleus was the grand duchy of Moscow.

Alexander Nevski: pioneer of Russian greatness. Following the Mongol conquest, the most important Russian leader was the prince of Novgorod, Alexander Nevski, who also became the ruler of Vladimir. In 1238 and 1240, during the Mongol advance, this staunch warrior had won great victories over the Swedes and the Teutonic Knights. To the Orthodox Church and most princes, the westerners seemed a greater threat to the Russian way of life than the Mongols. Indeed, Nevski accepted Mongol domination and assistance in fighting invaders from the west, who, hoping to profit from the Russian collapse under the Mongol impact, tried to annex territory. Meanwhile, Nevski may have looked forward to the day when his successors would be strong enough to challenge Tatar rule.

Moscow, challenge to Tatar rule. Daniel, the youngest son of Nevski, founded the grand duchy of Moscow, which eventually expelled the Tatars from Russia. Well situated in the central river system of Russia and surrounded by protective forests and marshes, Moscow was at first only a vassal of Vladimir, but it soon absorbed its parent

GROWTH OF THE DUCHY OF MOSCOW

- ■ Moscow c.1300 □ Acquisitions: c.1300-1462
- ■ Acquisitions Through Reign Of Ivan III, 1505
- ■ Acquisitions Through Reign Of Ivan IV, 1584

Ivan the Great. The Muscovite prince who laid the foundations for a Russian national state was Ivan III, the Great (1462-1505), a contemporary of the Tudors and other "new monarchs" in western Europe. Ivan more than doubled his territories by placing most of north Russia under the rule of Moscow, and he proclaimed his absolute sovereignty over all Russian princes and nobles by taking the title of "Great Prince and Autocrat of All Russia." Refusing further tribute to the Tatars, Ivan initiated a series of attacks that opened the way for the complete defeat of the declining Golden Horde, now divided into several khanates.

Ivan married Sophia Palaeologus, the niece of the last Byzantine emperor, and she brought with her to Moscow a number of gifted Italians. Among them were architects who designed an enormous walled palace called the Kremlin. Ivan not only adopted the double-headed eagle and court ceremonies of the Byzantine emperors but also claimed to be their legitimate successor. Thus Ivan sometimes used the title of *tsar*, derived from "Caesar," and he viewed Moscow as the Third Rome, the successor of New Rome (Constantinople).

"Two Romes have fallen, and the third stands." The doctrine that the Russian tsar was the successor of the Byzantine emperors was expressed by the monk Philotheos of Pskov late in the fifteenth century. "Two Romes have fallen," he wrote, "and the third stands, and a fourth one there shall not be." On the basis of the conviction that they were heirs of the Byzantine tradition, Russian rulers were later to press claims to the Dardanelles and parts of southeastern Europe. Moreover, as in the idea expressed by Philotheos when he said, "you are the only tsar for Christians in the whole world,"[3] the Russian tradition would henceforth encompass a great imperial mission.

Some historians see this Russian sense of destiny still operating in a new manifestation—communism—with the same fervor of the earlier Russian dedication to Orthodox Christianity. "Five centuries ago the words of Philotheos of Pskov may have sounded arrogant and foolhardy; but for us today, in the new constellation of world-

state. A major factor in the ascendency of Moscow was the cooperation of its rulers with their Mongol overlords, who granted them the title of Grand Prince of Russia and made them agents for collecting the Tatar tribute from the Russian principalities. Moscow's prestige was further enhanced when it became the center of the Russian Orthodox Church. Its head, the metropolitan, fled from Kiev to Vladimir in 1299 and a few years later established the permanent headquarters of the Church in Moscow.

By the middle of the fourteenth century the power of the Tatars was declining, and the Grand Princes felt capable of openly opposing the Mongol yoke. In 1380, at Kulikovo on the Don, the khan was defeated, and although this hard-fought victory did not end Tatar rule of Russia, it did bring great fame to the Grand Prince. Moscow's leadership in Russia was now firmly based, and by the middle of the fifteenth century its territory had greatly expanded through purchase, war, and marriage (see map).

forces after 1945, they echo through the centuries as the prophetic expression of the most momentous consequence of the fall of Constantinople . . . . on the wider stage of world-history the effects of the events of 1453 are only now making themselves felt."[4]

Ivan the Terrible. The next great ruler of Moscow was Ivan III's grandson, Ivan IV (1547-1584), called "the Terrible." Russia became more despotic as Ivan ruthlessly subordinated the great nobles to his will, exiling or executing many on the slightest pretext. With no consideration for human life, Ivan ordered the destruction of Novgorod, Russia's second city, on suspicion of treason. Another time, in a rage, he struck and killed his gifted eldest son. Yet Ivan was also a farseeing statesman who promulgated a new code of laws, reformed the morals of the clergy, and built the fabulous St. Basil's Cathedral that still stands in Moscow's Red Square.

During Ivan's reign eastern Russia was conquered from the Tatars, and Cossack pioneers then crossed the Ural Mountains in their push to the Pacific—a movement which can be compared with the simultaneous expansion of western Europe across the Atlantic. Ivan's efforts to reach the Baltic and establish trade relations with western Europe were forcibly stopped by Sweden and Poland. Later, however, he was able to inaugurate direct trade with the West by granting English merchants trading privileges at the White Sea port of Archangel (Arkhangelsk) in the far north.

Ivan's death in 1584 was followed by the Time of Trouble, a period of civil wars over the succession and resurgence of the power of the nobility. Both Poland and Sweden intervened in Russian affairs, and their invasions across an indistinct frontier which contains no major natural barriers demonstrated again the danger from the West and contributed to Russia's growing tendency to withdraw into her own distinctive heritage. Order was restored in 1613 when Michael Romanov, the grandnephew of Ivan the Terrible, was elected to the throne by a national assembly that included representatives from fifty cities. The Romanov dynasty ruled Russia until 1917.

SUMMARY

The medieval ideal was unity—a Europe united as a Christian commonwealth and ruled by dual powers, the universal Church and an all-embracing Holy Roman Empire. In theory the emperor would rule in the temporal or earthly realm, and the pope in the affairs of the spirit. Because papal authority was not constricted to national boundaries, the Church was nearly all-encompassing. By contrast, the emperor's authority was limited for the most part to Germany and Italy, and even there imperial power was intermittent.

During the fourteenth and fifteenth centuries, forces were at work which threatened and ultimately undermined the medieval

St. Basil's Cathedral in Moscow, begun in 1554 by Ivan the Terrible, was consecrated in 1557 but not completed until 1679. It is polygonal in plan with richly ornamented onion-shaped domes. The building is a fine example of Byzantine architecture adapted to the Russian tradition.

ideal and the edifices stemming from it. The Church was badly weakened from within as a result of the Babylonian Captivity, the Great Schism, and the demands of reformers. And despite continuous opposition from both the Church and the feudal nobles, the national state had become a reality in Europe by the end of the period discussed in this chapter.

Influencing nation-making in both France and England was the Hundred Years' War, which stimulated nationalism in the hearts of Englishmen and Frenchmen alike. Other significant changes resulted from that conflict: in England, the power of Parliament was increased, and the upsurge in the power of the nobility led to the Wars of the Roses, which ended finally with the accession of the Tudors; in France, royal power was consolidated under Louis XI, and further progress in national unification was made. Ferdinand and Isabella completed the creation of a national state in Spain and laid the foundations for its future greatness. On the other hand, Germany and Italy continued divided and weak; their day of national unification would not arrive until the nineteenth century.

Eastern and southern Europe were on the periphery of most of the dynamic currents of change that were transforming western Europe. There was much movement of peoples, and the rise and fall of states culminated in the emergence of Poland, Lithuania, Bohemia, and Hungary. Russia, effectively isolated on its frozen plains, languished for years under the rule of the Mongols. But when the dukes of Moscow assumed leadership of the Russians, a long campaign was initiated against the alien Mongols—a historical movement somewhat similar to the *Reconquista* in Spain.

Truly, the late Middle Ages was an era of nation-making. The nation-states this period produced—in particular England, France, and Spain—would assume new roles in the stirring international drama that is the story of Europe from about 1500 to 1650, a story which will be taken up in Chapter 15.

SUGGESTIONS FOR READING

W. K. Ferguson, **Europe in Transition, 1300 to 1520** (Houghton Mifflin, 1963) is a comprehensive work. See also D. Hay, **Europe in the Fourteenth and Fifteenth Centuries** (Harcourt Brace Jovanovich); and E. Cheyney, **The Dawn of a New Era, 1250-1453*** (Torchbooks). R. E. Lerner, **The Age of Adversity: The Fourteenth Century*** (Cornell); and Jerah Johnson and W. Percy, **The Age of Recovery: The Fifteenth Century*** (Cornell) are lively, interpretative essays. M. Aston, **The Fifteenth Century: The Prospect of Europe*** (Harcourt Brace Jovanovich) is a well-illustrated, popular introduction.

A good account of Church history during this period is L. Elliott-Binns, **History of the Decline and Fall of the Medieval Papacy** (Shoe String, 1967). See also G. Leff, **Heresy in the Later Middle Ages**, 2 vols., (Barnes and Noble, 1967); K. McFarlane, **John Wycliffe and the Beginnings of English Nonconformity** (Verry); and M. Spinka, **John Hus: A Biography** (Princeton, 1968).

E. Perroy, **The Hundred Years' War*** (Capricorn) is the standard account.

A. R. Myers, **England in the Late Middle Ages*** (Penguin); and George Holmes, **The Later Middle Ages, 1272-1485*** (Norton) are excellent surveys of English history during the period. See also Faith Thompson, **A Short History of Parliament, 1295-1642** (Minnesota).

P. S. Lewis, **Later Medieval France** (St. Martin's, 1968) covers government and society in the late Middle Ages. Also recommended are two biographies: J. Michelet, **Joan of Arc*** (Michi-

gan); and John H. Smith, **Joan of Arc** (Scribner's, 1973).

Gabriel Jackson, **The Making of Medieval Spain** (Harcourt Brace Jovanovich) is brief and highly readable with many illustrations. Other excellent surveys are F. Fernandez-Arnesto, **Ferdinand and Isabella** (Taplinger, 1975); J. H. Elliott, **Imperial Spain, 1469-1716*** (Penguin); and C. Roth, **The Spanish Inquisition*** (Norton).

G. Barraclough, **The Origins of Modern Germany*** (Capricorn) is the best account of this period of German history. J. A. Symonds, **The Renaissance in Italy,** Vol. I, **The Age of the Despots** (Peter Smith) is a celebrated account of Italian politics in the fourteenth and fifteenth centuries. D. Waley, **The Italian City Republics*** (McGraw-Hill); and D. S. Chambers, **The Imperial Age of Venice, 1380-1580*** (Harcourt Brace Jovanovich) are brief and well-illustrated.

Good introductions to Slavic eastern Europe are O. Halecki, **Borderlands of Western Civilization: A History of East Central Europe** (Ronald); and F. Dvornik, **The Slavs in European History and Civilization** (Rutgers, 1975).

N. Riasanovsky, **History of Russia,** 2nd ed. (Oxford, 1969); and G. Vernadsky, **History of Russia,*** rev. ed. (Yale) are excellent surveys. See also I. Grey, **Ivan III and the Unification of Russia*** (Collier); and S. Graham, **Ivan the Terrible** (Shoe String, 1968).

*Indicates a less expensive paperbound edition.

CHAPTER 13

The Renaissance: 1300-1600

Man Is the Measure

INTRODUCTION. In Italy during the fourteenth and fifteenth centuries men began to view the thousand years that had elapsed since the fall of Rome as the "dark ages"—a time of stagnation and ignorance—in contrast to their own age which appeared to them resplendent in wisdom and beauty. They exuberantly proclaimed that they were participating in an intellectual and esthetic revolution sparked by the "rebirth" *(renaissance)* of the values and forms of classical antiquity. Modern historians have accepted the term *Renaissance* as a convenient label for this exciting age of intellectual and artistic revival. But since the Middle Ages also made rich contributions to civilization, in what ways can the Renaissance be said to signify a "rebirth"?

First of all, there was an intense new interest in the literature of classical Greece and Rome. This Classical Revival, as it is called, was the product of a more worldly focus of interest—a focus on man rather than God, and on this life as an end in itself rather than as a temporary halting place on the way to eternity. Renaissance scholars searched the monasteries for old Latin manuscripts and translated hitherto unknown works from Greek antiquity into Latin. Thus the humanists, as these scholars were called, added more of the classical heritage to the mainstream of western thought. Second, while the humanists found a new significance in classical literature, artists in Italy were stimulated and inspired by classical sculpture and architecture.

But the spirit of the Renaissance was not characterized by a mere cult of antiquity, a looking backward into the past. The men of the Renaissance were the harbingers of the modern world, energetically and enthusiastically engaged in reshaping their political, economic, and religious environment, in pushing back geographical boundaries and extending the limits of human knowledge. Renaissance culture strikingly exhibits belief in the worth of man and his desire to think and act as a free agent and a well-rounded individual. The Renaissance spirit was admirably summed up by a versatile genius of the fifteenth century, Leon Battista Alberti, when he declared, "Men can do all things if they will."[1]

In some respects every age is an age of transition, but it may be fair to state that the Renaissance marks one of the turning points in western civilization. The dominant insti-tutions and thought systems of the Middle Ages were becoming devitalized; scholasti-cism, Church authority, and conformity were on the wane, and a more modern culture which depended on individualism, skepti-cism, and ultimately on science was taking its place.

We must be cautious in our analysis, how-ever. The Renaissance did not burst forth simultaneously in all parts of Europe, and some medieval habits and institutions per-sisted for a long time; throughout the Renais-sance the vast majority of illiterate common people clung to the ways of their forefathers.

The Renaissance originated with a rela-tively small, educated group dwelling in the cities of central and northern Italy. We shall begin with the Revival of Learning and the flowering of art in this locality and conclude with a discussion of other facets of the Re-naissance as its ideas crossed the Alps to France, Germany, and England. It was in England that the underlying optimism and dynamism of the entire Renaissance period was epitomized by Shakespeare when he said:

O, wonder!
How many goodly creatures are there here!
How beauteous mankind is! O brave new world,
That has such people in't![2]

THE ITALIAN RENAISSANCE: THE BACKGROUND

The waning of the Middle Ages. By the fourteenth century there was a marked de-cline in medieval institutions and ideas. The feudal social structure was weakening before the growing power of the middle class, which sided with the new monarchs and thrived on the revival of trade and the growth of towns. The threat of armies using gun-powder was revolutionizing warfare at the expense of armor-clad knights. Heresy and schism racked the Church, and its temporal power was increasingly being challenged by aggressive national monarchs.

An empty formalism replaced the creative-ness that had given the twelfth and thir-teenth centuries their unique forms of ex-pression. Although asceticism remained a pious ideal, it gained few adherents among the acquisitive townspeople and was openly flouted by many of the clergy. Scholars still held learned disputations at the universities, but scholasticism was unable to satisfy the growing interest in man and society. In art the Gothic style of the twelfth and thirteenth centuries, superb in its balance and restraint, had given place to exaggeration and flam-boyance. Decoration and ornamentation be-came ends in themselves.

Meanwhile, sophisticated Italian urban society no longer found medieval ideals of other-worldliness and asceticism satisfactory. Pious religious themes were not so engaging as satires directed against a sometimes corrupt clergy and the outworn conventions of chivalry. Searching for new modes of expression, thinkers and artists found what they wanted in the classical legacy of Greece and Rome.

Individualism and tradition in the Renaissance. In a sense, the Renaissance is the history of individual men expressing themselves brilliantly, and often tempestuously, in art, poetry, science, religion, and exploration. While the medieval way taught the unimportance of this life, stressed its snares and evils, and smothered the individual with a host of confining rules and prohibitions, the Renaissance beckoned man to enjoy beauty, to savor the opportunities of this world, and to be himself, regardless of restraints. Above all, the new spirit called upon its followers to adopt the concept of *l'uomo universale* ("the universal man" or "the complete man"). Life was best lived when the human personality showed its versatility by expression in many forms: advancement of the mind, perfection of the body, cultivation of the social graces, and appreciation and creativity in the arts.

Like any other movement, however, individualism had its negative aspects and its excesses. The lawlessness and political confusion of the Italian Renaissance and the strongly amoral character of its society were due in no small measure to the tendency of men to regard themselves as above the law.

Despite the prevalence of individualism, however, most men continued to share in the corporate life of the Church and the guilds, and many medieval customs and habits of thought persisted for centuries. In their love for Greek and Roman authors, Renaissance thinkers appear as subservient to the ancients as their medieval scholastic predecessors. Similarly, the artists of the Renaissance, who found inspiration in antiquity and whose works reflected a renewed interest in classical mythology and in the beauties of the human body, did not break completely with the subject matter and

RENAISSANCE EUROPE ABOUT 1500

→ Northward Spread of Renaissance

artistic techniques of their medieval predecessors. Although their interest in rendering secular subjects increased, Renaissance artists still looked to the Church as their greatest single patron. Building churches, sculpturing saints and Madonnas, and painting religious murals continued to occupy the genius of hundreds of artists during this period.

Renaissance patrons. In the Italian cities the newly wealthy class of traders, bankers, and manufacturers conspicuously displayed their wealth and bolstered their social importance by patronizing artists and scholars. While leading commissions for artists in the fifteenth century were still obtained from such communal bodies as guilds and churches, individual patronage began to play a more important role.

Among the most famous patrons were members of the Medici family who, by acting as champions of the lower classes, ruled Florence for sixty years (1434-1494) behind a facade of republican forms. Lorenzo de' Medici, who was first citizen of Florence from 1469 until his death in 1492, carried on

Among the Renaissance concepts which superseded the hierarchic medieval view of the world was the notion of man as a free individual, capable of fashioning his own destiny. A prime incarnation of this idea was the vibrant Florentine nobleman, statesman, and patron of the arts, Lorenzo de' Medici, portrayed here by the sculptor Verrocchio.

his family's proud traditions and added so much luster to Florence that he became known as Lorenzo the Magnificent. His career signifies the zenith of Florentine leadership in the arts.

Other princes and despots of Italian city-states patronized the arts, and the popes were eager to sponsor artists. In the sixteenth century the popes outdid secular rulers in the splendor of their court. Pope Alexander VI (1492-1503), the father of the unscrupulous poisoners Cesare and Lucrezia Borgia, was a target for criticism because he devoted more time and thought to furthering the fortunes of his family than he did to religious matters. Wealthy families actively sought to control the papacy, and the Medici succeeded in placing two of their members, Leo X (1513-1521), son of Lorenzo, and Clement VII (1523-1534), nephew of Leo, in this office. Leo's pontificate, in particular, was one of great activity in the arts and learning in Rome.

A Renaissance artist had the benefit of the security and protection offered by his patron and enjoyed a definite advantage from working exclusively on commission. The artist knew where his finished work would repose, in cathedral, villa, or city square; this situation contrasts with some later periods, when artists painted when and as they wished and then attempted to sell the work to anyone who would buy it.

Manners and morals. During the Renaissance the newly wealthy citizens of the Italian cities sought refinement in every aspect of their culture. Believing that the mark of nobility was an elegance of manner as well as a cultivated mind, they eagerly read etiquette books to learn the rules of correct social behavior.

The most famous book on Renaissance manners, published in 1528, was *The Courtier* by Baldassare Castiglione (1478-1529), which established a model for the Renaissance gentleman. To Castiglione, good manners and deportment were essential to the ideal courtier, but his central idea was that a courtier's true worth was more commensurate with his strength of character and excellence of intellect than with his hereditary social position. The courtier should be a well-

Leonardo da Vinci, who had a wide knowledge of many fields besides painting, typifies the Renaissance ideal of the "universal man." Throughout his life Leonardo carried a sketchbook which he would fill with drawings and notes in his unusual handwriting, written inverted from right to left and best deciphered with a mirror. Although approximately two thirds of his original writings have been lost, nearly 5000 pages of his notes and drawings were compiled after his death. Leonardo would often follow grotesque-looking people, making numerous caricatures and studies like those in the sketch at the right. His interest in anatomy led to amazingly accurate subjects like the drawing of an embryo (far right). His detailed plans for tools of war (below) such as an armored tank which would not be built until centuries later, exemplify his seemingly limitless engineering skills.

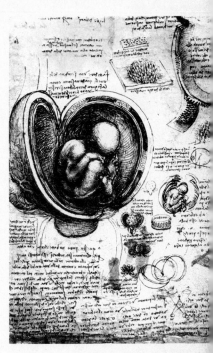

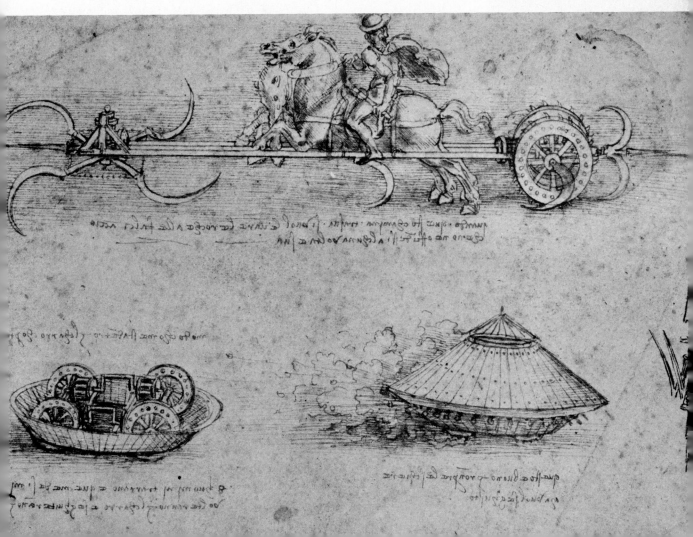

rounded individual, capable in the arts both of war and of peace.

The *Autobiography* of Benvenuto Cellini (1500-1571) gives us a vivid insight into Renaissance manners and morals, but it is no book of etiquette. Cellini was a bold and worldly adventurer, constantly embroiled in excitement and adventure—duels, love affairs, and prison terms. But he was also a fine sculptor (see Chapter 19). Vigorous and energetic, Cellini possessed *virtù,* a term used in the Renaissance to characterize a man of natural ability and abounding vitality. *Virtù* should not be confused with virtue; in fact, a man possessing *virtù* often appeared to be singularly deficient in virtue, as Cellini's life story reveals. He casually boasts of the number of personal enemies he has killed and quotes a pope as excusing him on the ground that "men like Benvenuto, unique in their profession, stand above the law."

THE CLASSICAL REVIVAL

Humanism and the classical revival. During the Middle Ages, Virgil, Cicero, and Caesar were popular authors; Aristotle was venerated much as though he were a Church Father; and Roman law greatly influenced Church, or canon, law. But in medieval times the writers of antiquity had been interpreted within the framework of the Christian religion and often cited as authorities to bolster Church dogma. Although many aspects of antiquity were avoided because of their disturbingly pagan quality, churchmen did make use of pagan literature for allegorical narratives which were Christian in character. Consequently, the true nature of the classical world was often distorted or obscured.

In fourteenth-century Italy, however, a new perspective was attained and a fresh appreciation of classical culture emerged. Successors to a small group of medieval teachers of grammar and rhetoric, the representatives of this new movement called themselves humanists, a name derived from the *studia humanitatis,* or "humanities,"

which Roman authors had used in the sense of a liberal or literary education.

Medieval scholastic education had emphasized the sciences and professional training in law, medicine, and theology at the expense of the "arts," or literary side of the curriculum. Hence the scholastics had centered their attention on Aristotle's scientific writings and other ancient works on astronomy, medicine, and mathematics. Stimulated by a rebirth of men's interest in the problems and values of human living, the humanists reversed this medieval emphasis and called attention to the importance of an education in the humanities—history, grammar, rhetoric, poetry, and moral philosophy. The humanists disdained the sciences because, as Petrarch—the first of the Italian humanists—wrote:

. . . they help in no way toward a happy life, for what does it advantage us to be familiar with the nature of animals, birds, fishes, and reptiles, while we are ignorant of the nature of the race of man to which we belong, and do not know or care whence we come or whither we go?[3]

Thus, despite the fact that both the humanist and the scholastic looked to the past and venerated its heritage, they differed widely in their choice of the ancient material to be revered.

Humanists and scholastics also differed in the manner in which they saw themselves in relation to the writers of ancient times. While the scholastic always felt himself inferior to the ancients and looked up to them as son to father or pupil to teacher, the typical humanist in his exultant individualism saw himself equal to the ancients and boldly hailed them as man to man and friend to friend. At the beginning of his *Divine Comedy* Dante described medieval man's reliance upon the authority of the ancients in allegorical terms. Dante (medieval man) is lost in the "dark wood" which is this life until he is rescued by Virgil (a favorite medieval symbol of ancient wisdom), who thereafter guides him along the right path. "Losing me," Virgil is made to say to Dante, "ye would remain astray."

The noticeably different attitude of the humanists was well expressed by one of their few medieval forerunners, John of Salisbury (d. 1180): "Most delightful in many ways is the fruit of letters that, banishing the irksomeness of intervals of place and time, bring friends into each other's presence. . . ."[4] It was in this spirit that Petrarch wrote his *Letters to Ancient Authors*, addressing Homer, Plato, Cicero, and others in familiar terms and sharing with them his own thoughts and experiences. This feeling of equality with ancient authors was also behind the humanists' practice of stuffing their own writings with apt quotations from the classics. The humanists' purpose, however, differed from that of the scholastics, who also quoted extensively from the ancients; as the humanist Montaigne explained in his essays (see p. 300), he quoted the ancients not because he agreed with them but because they agreed with him!

Petrarch, the "father of humanism." The "father of humanism" is a title that has been given to Francesco Petrarca, better known to us as Petrarch (1304-1374). Resentful as a youth of his father's desire to have him become a lawyer, he turned to reading Virgil and Cicero for consolation; and though he studied law at Bologna, he dreamed constantly of the glories of the classical age.

In 1327 he met the lady Laura and fell in love with her. Little is known of Laura or of the true nature of her relationship to Petrarch. But inspired by his love of her, Petrarch wrote sonnets which made him one of the greatest lyric poets of all time. In the love poetry of the age, his portrayal of Laura represents a fresh approach. Earlier poets had woven about their heroines an air of courtly love and religious idealization which made the characters quite unreal. Petrarch's Laura was a flesh-and-blood creature whom all readers could recognize as human.

The ancients wrote of the joys of this world, and their attitude toward life struck a sympathetic chord in Petrarch. In his *Secret* Petrarch has an imaginary conversation with St. Augustine which forcibly brings out the conflict between new ideas and those of medieval times. Petrarch concluded that, despite the importance of the world to come, the world of here and now held many delights which should not be shunned.

This inner conflict between his love of earthly things and his loyalty to the traditional medieval ideal of self-denial and otherworldliness exemplifies the transitional position Petrarch occupied in western culture. A product of medieval beliefs and attitudes, he nevertheless could not accept a depreciation of man's importance in the scheme of things or a constriction of his mental horizons. And thus he condemned the rigidity and arid logic of scholasticism and the extent to which medieval education was governed by dead tradition. He himself was not a careful scholar and never learned Greek, yet this versatile rebel had profound influence and gave humanism its first great impetus.

Boccaccio and the Decameron. Another early humanist was Giovanni Boccaccio (1313-1375), who began his career as a writer of poetry and romances. In 1348 the calamitous Black Death struck—a disaster which wiped out nearly two thirds of Florence's population. Boccaccio used this event to establish the setting of his masterpiece, the *Decameron*. To escape the pestilence, his characters—three young men and seven young women—sought seclusion in a country villa, where they whiled away the time by telling each other stories. Boccaccio suffused the hundred tales of the *Decameron*, based on the old *fabliaux* (see p. 257) and on chivalric accounts, with a new and different spirit. Recounted by sophisticated city dwellers, the tales satirize the follies of knights and other medieval types and express clearly the contempt which had developed for the old, and by then threadbare, ideals of feudalism. Many tales are bawdy and even scandalous—a charge which Boccaccio undertook to refute:

Some of you may say that in writing these tales I have taken too much license, by making ladies sometimes say and often listen to matters which are not proper to be said or heard by virtuous ladies. This I deny, for there is nothing so unchaste but may be said chastely if modest words are used; and this I think I have done.[5]

Nevertheless, the *Decameron* offers a wealth of anecdotes, portraits of flesh-and-blood characters, and a vivid (although one-sided) picture of Renaissance life.

The *Decameron* closed Boccaccio's career as a creative artist. Largely through the influence of Petrarch, whom he met in 1350, Boccaccio gave up writing in the Italian vernacular and turned to the study of antiquity. He attempted to learn Greek, wrote an encyclopedia of classical mythology, and went off to monasteries in search of manuscripts. By the time Petrarch and Boccaccio died, the study of the literature and learning of antiquity was growing throughout Italy.

The search for manuscripts. The search for manuscripts became a mania, and before the middle of the fifteenth century works by most of the important Latin authors had been found. The degree of difference between humanist and scholastic is indicated by the ease with which the early humanists recovered the "lost" Latin literary masterpieces: they were found close at hand in monastic libraries, covered by the undisturbed dust of centuries. The books had always been there; what had been largely lacking was a mature and appreciative audience of readers. In addition to these Latin works, precious Greek manuscripts were brought to Italy from Constantinople during the fifteenth century.

Individual scholars had their favorite classical authors, both Greek and Roman, but the highest universal praise was reserved for Cicero. Compounded of moral philosophy and rhetoric, his work displayed a wide-ranging intellect which appealed to many humanists. The revival of the art of writing classical Latin prose was due largely to the study and imitation of Cicero's graceful, eloquent, and polished literary style.

Revival of Platonism. As a result both of their rebellion against the Aristotelian emphasis upon natural science and of their search for a classical philosophy that stressed moral purpose and religious and mystical values, many humanists gravitated to Platonism during the fifteenth century. A factor in this revival was the study of Plato in the original Greek, particularly at Florence where Cosimo de' Medici, one of the great patrons of the Renaissance, founded the informal club that came to be known as the Platonic

Academy. Its leader, Marsilio Ficino (1433-1499), who always kept a candle burning before a bust of Plato, made the first complete Latin translation of Plato's works.

Ficino also sought to synthesize Christianity and Plato, much as St. Thomas Aquinas had done with Aristotle. In his principal work, *Theologia Platonica*, Ficino viewed Plato as essentially Christian and Plato's "religious philosophy" as a God-sent means of converting intellectuals. He coined the expression "Platonic love" to describe an ideal, pure love, and this concept found its way into much of Renaissance literature.

Aristotelianism. Despite its great attraction for many humanists, Platonism still had a formidable rival in Aristotelianism. Concerned chiefly with natural philosophy, logic, and metaphysics, Aristotelian commentators still dominated teaching in the Italian universities.

The most influential Aristotelians were the Latin Averroists, followers of the Muslim philosopher Averroës (see p. 165). The Averroists followed Aristotle in teaching that matter is eternal and in denying the immortality of the soul. Since such views were contrary to the Biblical story of creation and the belief in personal immortality, the Averroists advocated the doctrine of "double truth"—a truth in philosophy need not be valid in religion.

By the fifteenth century Padua had become the center of Aristotelianism, which reached its peak in the next century. By championing a secular rationalism that kept philosophy separate from theology, its adherents helped create an environment necessary for the triumph of scientific thought in the seventeenth century. As we shall see in Chapter 19, the new developments that Aristotelianism encouraged were to overthrow Aristotle's own brilliant but outmoded theories in physics and other fields of science.

Evaluation of humanism. We owe the humanists a debt of gratitude for reintroducing the whole of Latin and Greek literature into the mainstream of western thought. From their reading of the classics, humanists came to understand the classical world in a true historical perspective and corrected many misconceptions about ancient times which had existed in the Middle Ages. Medieval scholars, for example, had pictured Alexander the Great's soldiers as knights, but Renaissance historians no longer made such naive mistakes.

On the other hand, although the humanists condemned medieval restrictions, they themselves were often subservient to the authorities of antiquity. Indeed, theirs was a closed culture whose boundaries had been set by ancient Greece and Rome, so that the only course open to them was to retravel the ground, not to explore uncharted territory. Intent on returning to antiquity, so to speak, the humanists resented the centuries separating them from the golden days of Greece and Rome. Unfortunately, this viewpoint resulted in their disparagement of the best works produced in the Middle Ages.

The cult of classical letters gave rise to other defects. Humanist scholars were so dominated by Roman and Greek forms that they tended to imitate rather than to create for themselves. Their passion for Ciceronian Latin became pernicious; too often their writings were rich in form but barren in content. Worse still, their preoccupation with classical authors retarded the growth of a much more vital vernacular literature—as in the case of Boccaccio, who gave up writing prose and poetry in Italian to devote himself to Latin studies.

The humanists' contributions to philosophy were not extensive; they did little original thinking. Nevertheless the spread of humanistic influence resulted in a renewed and valuable emphasis upon the freedom and dignity of man as an individual and the importance of his place in the cosmos. This interest was manifested not only in literature but also in the fine arts.

ITALIAN RENAISSANCE ART

Transitional period in sculpture and painting. North of the Alps during the fourteenth and fifteenth centuries there was a continuation of "Gothic" art—in painting and sculpture, the same emphasis on realistic detail (see illustrations, pp. 230, 261); in architecture, an elaboration of the Gothic style. Fourteenth-century Italy, however, produced innovations in painting and sculpture that mark the beginnings of Renaissance art. Influenced by the humanistic spirit in thought and religion, a new society centered in rich cities, and a revived interest in antique art, Italian Renaissance art reached its zenith early in the sixteenth century.

The greatest figure in the transitional art of the fourteenth century was the Florentine painter Giotto (1266-1336), who, it was said,

Renaissance artists presented traditional subject matter in novel ways. Giotto's "Lamentation over the Dead Christ," one of thirty-eight frescoes painted for the Arena Chapel in Padua, lends a new drama and a new credibility to a familiar Biblical story.

"achieved little less than the resurrection of painting from the dead." While earlier Italian painters had copied the unreal, flat, and rigidly formalized images of Byzantine paintings and mosaics, Giotto observed from life and painted a three-dimensional world peopled with believable human beings dramatically moved by deep emotion (see ill., p. 289 and Color Plate 10). He humanized painting, as St. Francis humanized religion.

Quattrocento painting. The lull in painting that followed Giotto, during which his technical innovations were retained but the spirit and compassion that make him one of the world's great painters were lost, lasted

"St. James on the Way to His Execution," a fresco by Andrea Mantegna, is innovative in its perspective and use of classical models. St. James, at the left, is shown blessing a Roman soldier and healing a paralytic. Mantegna's interest in historical detail is obvious in both the classical buildings and the costumes of the soldiers.

until the beginning of the *quattrocento* (Italian for "four hundred," an abbreviation for the 1400's). In his brief lifetime the Florentine Masaccio (1401-1428) completed the revolution in technique begun by Giotto. As can be seen in his various works, Masaccio largely mastered the problems of perspective, anatomical naturalism of flesh and bone, and the modeling of figures in light and shade (*chiaroscuro*) rather than by sharp line. Masaccio was also the first to paint nude figures whose counterparts can be found in classical, but not in medieval, art.

Inspired by Masaccio's achievement, most *quattrocento* painters constantly sought to improve technique. This search for greater realism culminated in such painters as Andrea Mantegna (1431-1506), whose "St. James on the Way to His Execution" well shows the results of his lifelong study of perspective.

While Masaccio and his successors were intent upon giving their figures a new solidity and resolving the problem of three-dimensional presentation, a later Florentine painter, Sandro Botticelli (1447-1510), proceeded in a different direction, abandoning the techniques of straightforward representation of people and objects. Botticelli used a highly sensitive, even quivering, line to stir the viewer's imagination and emotion and to create a mood in keeping with his subject matter, frankly pagan at first but later deeply religious. Movement and the patterning of hair and drapery in such allegorical and mythological works as the "Birth of Venus" are particularly sensitive (see illustration, p. 291).

Quattrocento sculpture. In the meantime progress was being made in sculpture, and it, like painting, reached stylistic maturity at the beginning of the *quattrocento*. In his two sets of bronze doors for the baptistery in Florence, on which he labored for forty-four years, Lorenzo Ghiberti (1378-1455) achieved the goal he had set for himself: "I strove to imitate nature as closely as I could, and with all the perspective I could produce." These marvels of relief sculpture (p. 292), which drew from Michelangelo the declaration that they were worthy to be the gates of

The Renaissance emulation of the ideals of classical Greece and Rome extended to large-scale treatments of mythological subjects in painting and sculpture. The "Birth of Venus" by Sandro Botticelli contains the first important image since Roman times of the nude goddess in a pose similar to classical statues of Venus. This painting, done by Botticelli for the Medici family, was opposed to the Florentine artistic tradition of the period.

paradise, depict skillfully modeled human figures—including some classically inspired nudes—which stand out spatially against architectural and landscape backgrounds.

Although Ghiberti was a superb craftsman, he was less of an innovator than his younger contemporary in Florence, Donatello (1386-1466), who visited Rome to study the remains of antique statuary. Divorcing sculpture from its architectural background, Donatello produced truly freestanding statues based on the realization of the human body as a functional, coordinated mechanism of bones, muscles, and sinews, maintaining itself against the pull of gravity. His "David" is the first bronze nude made since antiquity, and his equestrian statue of Gattamelata the *condottiere* is the first of its type done in the Renaissance. The latter clearly reveals the influence of classical models and was probably inspired by the equestrian statue of Marcus Aurelius in Rome.

More dramatic than either of these equestrian statues is that of the Venetian *condottiere* Bartolomeo Colleoni (see p. 293), the creation of Andrea del Verrocchio (1435-1488). A versatile Florentine artist noteworthy as a sculptor, painter, and the teacher of Leonardo da Vinci, Verrocchio designed the statue of Colleoni to permit one of the horse's forelegs to be unsupported—a considerable achievement. The posture and features of the *condottiere* convey dramatically a sense of the supreme self-confidence and arrogance usually associated with Renaissance public figures.

Quattrocento architecture. Renaissance architecture, which far more than sculpture reflects the influence of ancient Roman models, began with the work of Filippo Brunelleschi (1377-1446). As a youth Brunelleschi

In 1403 the sculptor Lorenzo Ghiberti won a competition to design the bronze doors for the baptistry of the Florence Cathedral. His subject was scenes from the Old Testament; the panel shown is from the story of Esau and Jacob. The magnificently decorated doors well deserve the title given them by Michelangelo—the "Gates of Paradise."

accompanied Donatello to Rome where he employed measuring stick and sketchbook to master the principles of classical architecture. Returning to Florence, Brunelleschi constructed the lofty dome of the cathedral, the first to be built since Roman times. Although strongly influenced by classical architecture, Brunelleschi's buildings in Florence, which include churches and palaces, were not just copies of Roman models. Employing arcades of Roman arches, Roman pediments above the windows, and engaged Roman columns and other decorative motifs, Brunelleschi re-created the Roman style in a fresh and original manner.

The High Renaissance, 1500-1530. During the High Renaissance the center of artistic activity shifted from Florence to Rome and Venice, where wealthier patrons lived and where consequently greater opportunities were available to artists. The popes were lavish patrons, and the greatest artists of the period worked in the Vatican at one time or another. It did not seem inconsistent to popes and artists to include representations of pagan mythological figures in the decorations of the papal palace, and thus the Vatican was filled with secular as well as religious art.

The great architect of the High Renaissance was Donato Bramante (1444-1514) from Milan. Bramante's most important commission came in 1506 when Pope Julius II requested him to replace the old basilica of St. Peter, built by the emperor Constantine, with a monumental Renaissance structure. Bramante's plan called for a centralized church in the form of a Greek cross surmounted by an immense dome. The exterior of St. Peter's exemplifies the spirit of High Renaissance architecture—to approach nearer to the monumentality and grandeur of Roman architecture. In Bramante's own words, he would place "the Pantheon on top of the Basilica of Maxentius." Bramante died when the cathedral was barely begun, and it was left to Michelangelo and others to complete the work (see illustrations, p. 294).

High Renaissance architects also produced magnificent palaces and other secular buildings. Their decorative features show how classical details blended in a new fashion resulted in an impressive and refined structure. From the sixteenth century on, all Europe began to take to the new architecture.

The painters of the High Renaissance inherited the solutions to such technical problems as perspective space from the *quattrocento* artists. But whereas the artists of the earlier period had been concerned with movement, color, and narrative detail, painters in the High Renaissance strove to eliminate nonessentials and concentrated on the central theme of a picture and its basic human implications. By this process of elimination, many High Renaissance painters achieved a "classic" effect of seriousness and serenity and endowed their works with idealistic values.

Leonardo da Vinci. The great triad of High Renaissance painters consists of Leonardo da Vinci, Raphael, and Michelangelo. An extraordinary man, Leonardo da Vinci (1452-1519) was proficient in a variety of fields: engineering, mathematics, architecture, geology, botany, physiology, anatomy, sculpture, painting, music, and poetry. He was always experimenting, with the result that few of the projects he started were ever finished.

A superb draftsman, Leonardo was also a master of soft modeling in full light and shade and of creating groups of figures perfectly balanced in a given space. One of his most famous paintings is the "Mona Lisa," a portrait of a woman whose enigmatic smile has intrigued art lovers for centuries. Another is "The Last Supper," a study of the moment when Christ tells his twelve disciples that one will betray him. When he painted this picture on the walls of the refectory of Santa Maria delle Grazie in Milan, Leonardo was experimenting with the use of an oil medium combined with plaster, and, unfortunately, the experiment was unsuccessful. The painting quickly began to disintegrate and has had to be repainted several times. Last of the great Florentine painters, Leonardo combined an advanced knowledge of technique with deep psychological insight into many facets of human nature (see p. 285).

Raphael. The second of the great triad of High Renaissance painters was Raphael (1483-1520). By the time he was summoned to Rome to aid in the decoration of the Vatican, Raphael had absorbed something of Leonardo's intellectuality and Michelangelo's "body dynamics" and grandeur. His Stanze frescoes in the Vatican display a magnificent blending of classical and Christian subject matter and are the fruit of careful planning and immense artistic knowledge. Raphael possessed neither Leonardo's great range of knowledge nor Michelangelo's power, but an appealing serenity, particularly evident in his lovely Madonnas, characterizes his work (see illustration, p. 296).

Michelangelo. The individualism and idealism of the High Renaissance have no greater representative than Michelangelo

In Verrocchio's "Monument to Colleoni" the spirit of the great military leader is captured in the face, which is individual and very human rather than classical.

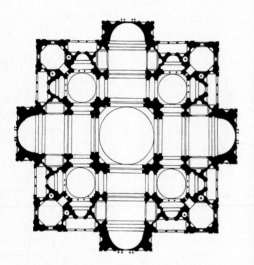

Bramante designed St. Peter's in the shape of a Greek cross with a dome similar to that of the Pantheon (see his architectural drawing). After his death, however, his plan was modified. Michelangelo redesigned the dome—which has been called the greatest achievement of Renaissance architecture—and later a long nave was added to the front of the church, giving it the form of a Latin cross rather than of a Greek cross. The courtyard view of the Palazzo Farnese in Rome shows the classical simplicity and symmetry which marked late Italian Renaissance palaces. The even spacing of the windows, the equal height of the three stories, and the repetition of decorative motifs all contribute to a feeling of unity in design.

Buonarroti (1475-1564). Stories of this stormy and temperamental personality have helped shape our ideas of what a genius is like. Indeed, there is something almost superhuman about both Michelangelo and his art. His great energy enabled him to complete in four years the entire work of painting the ceiling of the Vatican's Sistine Chapel, an area of several thousand square yards, and his art embodies a superhuman ideal of man. With his unrivaled genius for rendering the human form, he devised a wealth of expressive positions and attitudes for his figures in scenes from Genesis. Their physical splendor is pagan, but their spirit is Christian (see p. 296).

Michelangelo considered himself first and foremost a sculptor, and this *uomo universale*, who also excelled as poet, engineer, and architect, was undoubtedly the greatest sculptor of the Renaissance. The glorification of the human body, particularly the male nude, was Michelangelo's great achievement. Fired by the grandeur of such newly discovered pieces of Hellenistic sculpture as the Laocoön group (p. 61) and strongly influenced by Platonism, he expressed in art his idealized view of man's dignity and majesty (see Color Plate 11). Succeeding Bramante as chief architect of St. Peter's, Michelangelo designed the great dome (see p. 294), and was in the midst of creative activities when he died, almost in his ninetieth year, in 1564. He had long outlived the High Renaissance.

The Venetian school. Venice offered a congenial environment to artists. A prosperous merchant-prince could well afford to play the role of patron of the arts; trade with the East provided Venetians with luxuries and comforts which added splendor and color to daily life; and the beauty of the city itself would attract the eye of any artist.

This wealthy, sophisticated milieu produced a secular rather than a devotional school of painting. Most Venetian artists were satisfied with the here and now; they were not overly concerned with antiquity or classical canons. While they sometimes painted exquisite Madonnas, they more often painted wealthy merchants and proud doges, attired in rich brocades, jewels, and precious metals and grouped with beautiful young women who scarcely looked like Madonnas. There is a sensuousness in the Venetian painting of this period which is evident in the artists' love of decoration, rich costumes, radiant light and color, and striking nude figures.

Giorgione (1477-1510), like Botticelli, rejected the *quattrocento* concern to be scientific and realistic and substituted a delicate and dreamingly poetic lyricism. Common to all of his paintings is a mood of languor and relaxation that is called Giorgionesque.

The pictures of Titian (1485?-1576) contain sensuous beauties of color and atmosphere. During his long working life he proved himself a master of a wide variety of subjects ranging from religion to pagan mythology. His portraits, which earned him the greatest fame among his contemporaries, show the Venetian love of color and texture of rich fabrics (see p. 296).

High Renaissance music. In contrast to the single-voiced or homophonic music—called plain song or Gregorian chant—of the early Middle Ages, the late medieval composers wrote many-voiced, many-melodied, or polyphonic music. Polyphony often involved a shuttling back and forth from one melody to another—musical counterpoint. By the fifteenth century as many as twenty-four voice parts were combined into one intricately woven musical pattern. The composers of the High Renaissance continued to produce complicated polyphonic music, but in a calmer and grander manner. Compared with the style of his predecessors, that of Josquin des Près (d. 1521), the founder of High Renaissance music, "is both grander and more simple. All stark intervals of early polyphony are ruled out; few dissonances are used, and the rhythms and forms used are based on strict symmetry and mathematically regular proportions. Josquin handled all technical problems of complicated constructions with the same ease and sureness one finds in the drawings of Leonardo and Raphael."[6] During the sixteenth century, also, instruments such as the violin, spinet, and harpsichord developed from more rudimentary types.

The Renaissance in Italy stimulated many

Michelangelo's "Creation of Adam" (top), one of the major scenes on the ceiling of the Sistine Chapel, depicts God, with Eve protected under His left arm, instilling life in Adam by merely pointing His finger. The frescoed figures have a sculptural quality that creates an illusion of roundness and depth. While Michelangelo used the human figure as an expression of spirituality and sublime beauty, Raphael's works stressed the earthly qualities of natural human beauty. Although the subject matter is religious, his "Madonna of the Chair" (bottom left) is endowed with a warm, human quality. This painting also demonstrates Raphael's concern for form and equilibrium within a composition. Titian's paintings are marked by their sensuousness and intense, jewel-like colors. His "Young Woman at Her Toilet" (bottom right) typifies his favorite theme of warm feminine beauty.

new forms of secular music, especially the madrigal, a love lyric set to music. The madrigal found favor in England, while French *chansons* and German *lieder* added to the growing volume of secular music.

THE NORTHERN RENAISSANCE

The northward spread of the Renaissance. The Italian Renaissance had projected man once more into the center of life's stage and permeated the intellectual and artistic environment with humanistic values. In time the stimulating ideas current in Italy spread to other areas and combined with indigenous developments to produce a French Renaissance, an English Renaissance, and so on.

Throughout the fifteenth century the records of Italian universities listed hundreds of northern European students. While their chief interest was the study of law and medicine, many were influenced by the new Italian enthusiasm for the classics and carried home the manuscripts of classical and humanist writers.

The influence of printing. Perhaps even more important in the diffusion of the Renaissance and later in the success of the Reformation was the invention of printing in Europe. The essential elements—paper and block printing—had been known in China since the eighth century. During the twelfth century the Spanish Muslims introduced papermaking to Europe; in the thirteenth century Europeans were in close contact with China (see Chapter 7) and block printing became known in the West. The crucial step was taken in the 1440's at Mainz, in Germany, where Johann Gutenberg and other printers invented movable type by cutting up old printing blocks to form individual letters. Gutenberg used movable type to print papal documents and the first published version of the Bible (1454).

Within fifty years after Gutenberg's Bible had been published, all the major countries of Europe possessed the means for printing books. It is said that the prices of books soon sank to one eighth of their former cost, thus placing books within the reach of a multitude of people who formerly had been unable to buy them. In addition, pamphlets and controversial tracts soon were widely circulated, and new ideas reached a thousand times more people in a relatively short span of time. In the quickening of Europe's intellectual life, it is difficult to overestimate the effects of the printing press.

Erasmus and northern Humanism. The intellectual life of the first half of the sixteenth century was dominated by Desiderius Erasmus (1466?-1536). Born in Rotterdam, he passed most of his long life elsewhere—in Germany, France, England, Italy, and especially Switzerland. The most influential and cosmopolitan of the northern humanists, he corresponded with nearly every prominent writer and thinker in Europe and knew

Although printing was a far superior system of reproducing books than hand copying, it still was a slow, tedious, and expensive process. A copy of the Gutenberg Bible cost forty-two gulden, a price equivalent to that of fourteen oxen. Although large books were beyond the means of most common people, the presses turned out small books, pamphlets, and circulars in large quantities for common consumption.

The high level of European portraiture in the sixteenth century reflected the man-centered outlook of the time. The traditional meticulous realism of the north was employed by Hans Holbein the Younger, who recorded the likeness of the humanist Erasmus—as well as other famous contemporaries—with jewel-like accuracy and brilliance.

personally popes, emperors, and kings. He was *the* scholar of Europe, and his writings were read eagerly everywhere.

Perhaps the most famous and influential work by Erasmus was *In Praise of Folly*, a satire written in 1511. Folly, the term used in the Middle Ages as a synonym for human nature, is described by Erasmus as the source not only of much harmless enjoyment in life but also of many things that are wrong and need correcting. A historian has described the work in these words: "At first the book makes kindly and approving fun of the ways of action and the foibles and weaknesses of mankind. It is not mordant, only amused. But gradually from fools innocent and natural and undebased, it passes to those whose il-

lusions are vicious in their setting and results."[7] Among such are merchants ("they lie, swear, cheat, and practice all the intrigues of dishonesty"), lawyers ("they of all men have the greatest conceit of their own abilities"), scholastic philosophers ("that talk as much by rote as a parrot"), and scientists ("who esteem themselves the only favourites of wisdom, and look upon the rest of mankind as the dirt and rubbish of the creation"). Most roughly handled are churchmen, in particular monks, who are "impudent pretenders to the profession of piety," and popes, cardinals, and bishops, "who in pomp and splendour have almost equalled if not outdone secular princes." While his satire is indeed harsh, Erasmus was himself balanced, moderate, and intolerant only of bigotry, ignorance, greed, and violence.

In Praise of Folly points up a significant difference between the northern humanists and their Italian predecessors. While both were repelled by much that seemed to them wrong in the life of their day, their reactions took different forms. The typical Italian humanists followed the course set by Petrarch: "In order to forget my own time I have constantly striven to place myself in spirit in other ages. . . ."[8] Disdaining such escapism, the great majority of northern humanists faced up to reality and became reformers of their society's ills. They also went further in broadening their interest in ancient literature to include early Christian writings— the Scriptures and the works of the Church Fathers. This led them to prepare new and more accurate editions of the Scriptures (Erasmus' Greek edition of the New Testament became famous and was used by Luther) and to compare unfavorably the complexities of the Church in their own day with the simplicity of primitive Christianity. Since the northern humanists held that the essence of religion was morality and rational piety—what Erasmus called the "philosophy of Christ"—rather than ceremony and dogma, it is not surprising that the Church became a major target of their reforming zeal.

Sir Thomas More's Utopia. The most significant figure in English humanism was Sir Thomas More (1478-1535), the friend of Erasmus. More is best known for his *Utopia*, the first important description of the ideal state since Plato's *Republic*. In his epoch-making work More criticized his age by using as his spokesman a fictitious sailor who contrasts the ideal life he has seen in Utopia (The Land of Nowhere) with the harsh conditions of life in England. More's denunciations centered on the new acquisitive capitalism, which he blamed for the widespread insecurity and misery of the lower classes. More felt that governments

are a conspiracy of the rich, who, in pretence of managing the public, only pursue their private ends, . . . first, that they may, without danger, preserve all that they have so ill acquired, and then, that they may engage the poor to toil and labor for them at as low rates as possible, and oppress them as much as they please.[9]

In Utopia, by contrast, no man is in want because the economy is planned and co-operative and because property is held in common. Utopia is the only true commonwealth, concludes More's imaginary sailor:

In all other places, it is visible that while people talk of a commonwealth, every man only seeks his own wealth: but there, where no man has any property, all men zealously pursue the good of the public. . . . in Utopia, where every man has a right to every thing, they all know that if care is taken to keep the public stores full, no private man can want any thing; for among them there is no unequal distribution, so that no man is poor, none in necessity; and though no man has anything, yet they are all rich; for what can make a man so rich as to lead a serene and cheerful life, free from anxieties; neither apprehending want himself, nor vexed with the endless complaints of his wife?[10]

More was the first of the modern English socialists, but his philosophy should not be considered a forerunner of the socialism of our day. His economic outlook was a legacy from the Middle Ages, and his preference for medieval collectivism over modern individualism was of a piece with his preference for a Church headed—medieval style—by popes rather than by kings, a view that prompted Henry VIII to execute him for treason (see p. 315).

Rabelais. One of the best known of the French humanists was François Rabelais (1494-1553). A brilliant, if coarse, lover of all life from the sewers to the heavens, Rabelais is best remembered for his work *Gargantua and Pantagruel* (published 1533-1552). Centering on figures from French folklore, this work relates the adventures of Gargantua and his son Pantagruel, genial giants of tremendous stature and appetite, to whom were ascribed many marvelous feats.

In the course of his pungent narrative, Rabelais inserted his views on educational reform and his humanistic belief in man's inherent goodness and ability to solve his problems by reason. He made vitriolic attacks on the abuses of the Church and the shortcomings of scholastics and monks, but he had little patience with overzealous Protestants either. What Rabelais could not stomach was hypocrisy and repression; and for those guilty of these tendencies, he reserved his choicest invective. In the following excerpt he bids his readers to flee from that

rabble of squint-minded fellows, dissembling and counterfeit saints, demure lookers, hypocrites, pretended zealots, tough friars, buskin-monks, and other such sects of men, who disguise themselves like masquers to deceive the world. . . . Fly from these men, abhor and hate them as much as I do, and upon my faith you will find yourself the better for it. And if you desire . . . *to live in peace, joy, health, making yourselves always merry*, never trust those men that always peep out through a little hole.[11]

Von Hutten: German humanist and patriot. One of the outstanding German humanists was Ulrich von Hutten (1488-1523). In him was blended a hatred of ecclesiastical abuses with romantic nationalist feelings. This scion of an aristocratic family, who wanted to unite Germany under the emperor, led a tumultuous life as a wandering Greek scholar and satirist. He supported Luther as a rallying point for German unity against the papacy, to which Von Hutten attributed most of his compatriots' ills. Although he neither reconciled his humanistic philosophy with Luther's theology nor formulated a practical political program, Von Hutten reflected the tensions and aspirations of the German people in the early years of the sixteenth century.

This portrait of Michel de Montaigne, the originator of the modern essay, is ascribed to the French School of Corneille de Lyon.

Montaigne. The last notable northern humanist was the French skeptic Michel de Montaigne (1533-1592). At the age of thirty-eight he gave up the practice of law and retired to his country estate and well-stocked library, where he studied and wrote. Montaigne developed a new literary form and gave it its name—the essay. In ninety-four essays he set forth his personal views on many subjects: leisure, friendship, education, philosophy, religion, old age, death, and so forth. He did not pretend to have the final answer to the subjects he discussed. Instead, he advocated open-mindedness and toleration—rare qualities in the sixteenth century, when France was racked by religious and civil strife.

Montaigne condemned the pedantry into which humanism and humanistic education had largely degenerated by the end of the sixteenth century, arguing that "To know by heart is not to know; it is to retain what we have given our memory to keep."[12] Even today's student may have cause to listen sympathetically to the following words:

Our tutors never stop bawling into our ears, as though they were pouring water into a funnel; and our task is only to repeat what has been told us. I should like the tutor to correct this practice . . . I want him to listen to his pupil speaking in his turn.[13]

Montaigne's final essay, entitled "Of Experience," which developed the thought that "when reason fails us we resort to experience," is an acknowledgment of the bankruptcy of humanism and a foreshadowing of the coming triumph of science.

Cervantes, creator of Don Quixote. The transition from feudal knight to Renaissance courtier finds its greatest literary expression in a masterpiece of Spanish satire, *Don Quixote de la Mancha*, the work of Miguel de Cervantes (1547-1616). By Cervantes' day knighthood had become an anachronism, though its accompanying code of chivalry still retained its appeal. It remained for a rationalist like Cervantes to show up the inadequacies of chivalric idealism in a world that had acquired new, and intensely practical, aims. He did so by creating a pathetic but infinitely appealing character to serve as the personification of an outmoded way of life.

Don Quixote, the "knight of the woeful countenance," mounted on his "lean, lank, meagre, drooping, sharp-backed, and rawboned" steed Rozinante, sets out in the Spanish countryside to right wrongs and uphold his lady's and his own honor. In his misadventures he is accompanied by his squire, the much less gallant but infinitely more realistic Sancho Panza, whose peasant adages and hard-grained common sense serve as a contrast to the unpractical nature of his master's chivalric code. Tilting at windmills, mistaking serving wenches for highborn ladies and inns for castles, and lamenting the invention of gunpowder as depriving ardent knights of a chance to win immortality, Don Quixote is, on the surface at least, a ridiculous old man whose nostalgia for the "good old days" is a constant source of grief to him. Thus the story represents a superb satire directed against the outworn ideology of the Middle Ages; in particular, it laughed the ideal of chivalric romance into the world of make-believe.

And yet *Don Quixote* is still more. Cervantes instilled in his main character a pathos born in large measure of the author's own career of frustrated hopes and ambitions. As a result, Don Quixote becomes more than a romantic lunatic; he serves to embody that set of ideals which each of us would like to see realized but which we must compromise in a world that has other interests to serve.

Secular drama appears. Like Greek drama, medieval drama developed out of religious ceremonies (see p. 258). A complete divorce of the Church and stage did not occur until the middle of the fifteenth century when the Renaissance era of drama began in Italian cities with the performance of ancient Roman comedies. In the following century appeared the *commedia dell'arte*, reflections of everyday life in vulgar and slapstick fashion usually improvised by the players from a plot outline.

As secular dramas grew in popularity, theaters were built as permanent settings for their presentations. Great ingenuity was shown in the design of elaborate, realistic stage scenery as well as in lighting and sound effects. Theaters embodying these innovations only gradually appeared outside Italy. Not until 1576 was the first public theater erected in London; three years later, a similar theater was constructed in Madrid.

Imitating the ancient models they admired, French and Italian writers followed what they believed were the rigid conventions of the classical drama and, to a large extent, catered to the aristocracy. By contrast, Spanish and English playwrights created a theatrical environment that was at once more socially democratic, more hospitable to national themes, and less concerned with classical models.

William Shakespeare. The spring of lyric song that bubbled up in the England of Henry VIII formed a veritable stream of verse that sparkled through his daughter Elizabeth's countryside. Her reign (1558-1603) climaxed the English Renaissance and produced such a galaxy of talented writers that some scholars have felt it necessary to go back as far as Athens in the fifth century B.C. to find an age as prodigal of literary genius. Strongly influenced by the royal court, which served as the busy center of intellectual and artistic as well as of economic and political life, their writings were highly colored, richly romantic, and often wildly extravagant

in spite of all their poetic allusions to classical times.

The supreme figure in Elizabethan literature and perhaps in all literature is William Shakespeare (1564-1616). We can only touch briefly upon a few facets of this versatile genius. His rich vocabulary and poetic imagery were matched only by his turbulent imagination. He was a superb lyric poet, and numerous critics have judged him the foremost sonnet writer in the English language.

Shakespeare wrote thirty-eight plays—histories, comedies, and tragedies. His historical plays reflected the patriotic upsurge experienced by Englishmen as their country grew stronger and more prosperous. For his comedies and tragedies, Shakespeare was content in a great majority of cases to borrow plots from earlier works. His forte lay in his creation of characters—perhaps the richest and most diversified collection conceived by the mind of one man—and in his ability to translate his knowledge of human nature

An early 1600's illustration based on Claes de Visscher's *View of London* shows the Globe Theatre on the south bank of the Thames, a short distance west of London Bridge.

Northern Renaissance painting, with its original
Gothic realism, began to be affected by the Italian tendency toward naturalism and secularism at
the end of the fifteenth century. One of the first
German painters influenced by the Italian style
was Albrecht Dürer. His copper engraving
"Knight, Death, and the Devil" (lower left) is
typical of his combination of the new style with
medieval subject matter. In "The Harvesters"
(above), the Flemish artist Pieter Brueghel the
Elder has presented both a sweeping country
landscape along with a memorable scene of
peasant life.

into dramatic speech and action. Today his comedies are played to enthusiastic audiences: *The Taming of the Shrew, As You Like It, The Merchant of Venice, Merry Wives of Windsor,* to mention but a few. But it is in his tragedies that the poet-dramatist runs the gamut of human emotions and experience. Shakespeare possessed in abundance the Renaissance concern for man and the world about him. Hence his plays deal first and foremost with man's personality, passions, and problems. In such works as *Romeo and Juliet, Measure for Measure,* and *Troilus and Cressida,* the problems of love and sex are studied from many angles. Jealousy is analyzed in *Othello,* ambition in *Macbeth* and *Julius Caesar,* family relationships in *King Lear,* and man's struggle with his own soul in *Hamlet.* Shakespeare's extraordinary ability to build every concrete fact and action upon a universal truth makes his observations as applicable today as they were when first presented in the Globe Theater. Small wonder that next to the Bible, Shakespeare is the most quoted of all literary sources in the language.

Developments in painting. Before the Italian Renaissance permeated the artistic circles of northern Europe, the painters of the Low Countries had been making significant advances on their own. Outstanding was Jan van Eyck (1385?-1440), whose work has been called "the full flowering of the spirit of the late Middle Ages,"[14] for he continued to paint in the realistic manner developed by medieval miniaturists (see manuscript illuminations, pp. 215, 230). Van Eyck also perfected the technique of oil painting, which enabled him to paint with greater realism and also to devote more attention to detail.

The first talented German painter to be influenced deeply by Italian art was Albrecht Dürer (1471-1528) of Nuremberg. Dürer made more than one journey to Italy, where he was impressed both with the painting of the Renaissance Italians and with the artists' high social status—a contrast with northern Europe, where artists were still treated as craftsmen. Because he did not entirely lose many of the medieval qualities of the milieu in which he worked, his own work is a blend

of the old and the new; but among German artists he went farthest in adopting the rational standards of Italian art. His "Knight, Death, and Devil" fuses the realism and symbolism of the Gothic with the nobility of Verrochio's statue of Colleoni (compare p. 293). In the long run Dürer became better known for his numerous engravings and woodcuts than for his paintings.

Another German painter, Hans Holbein the Younger (1497-1543), was less imaginative than Dürer; but whereas the latter lived principally in Germany and interpreted its spirit, the younger artist worked abroad, especially in England, and as a result his painting acquired a more cosmopolitan character. In his portraits of Erasmus and Henry VIII (pp. 298, 328), northern realism and concern for detail continues evident.

While many Flemish painters lost their northern individuality in the rush to adopt Italian techniques, Pieter Brueghel the Elder (1525?-1569) retained a strong Flemish flavor in his portrayal of the faces and scenes of his native land. He painted village squares, landscapes, skating scenes, peasant weddings and dances just as he saw them, with a reporter's eye for detail. He also took Biblical or mythological themes and depicted them as if the events were taking place in the Flanders of his own day. The depiction of everyday scenes in realistic fashion is known as *genre* painting; and in this medium, Pieter Brueghel and the Flemish school as a whole remained unexcelled.

SUMMARY

In the Middle Ages man had thought and acted primarily as a member of a community —a manor, a guild, or, above all, the universal Christian community represented by the Church and the Holy Roman Empire. But gradually, for a variety of reasons, he began to attach importance to himself as an individual and to develop an interest in worldly things for their own sake without relation to the divine. This new individualistic and secular spirit, the period in which it became prominent, and the ways in which it manifested itself in art, literature, and learning we call the Renaissance.

The change took place earliest in Italy and first expressed itself in the great intellectual movement known as humanism. In its early stages humanism was a revival of classical learning. Scholars eagerly searched for ancient manuscripts and introduced the literature of Greece and Rome into schools and universities. This reverence for antiquity led to the copying of classical literary and artistic forms, and many humanists wasted on such imitation talents which might better have been employed in creating original literature in their native language.

But humanism was much more than sterile imitation. It provided the West not only with a comprehensive knowledge of classical literature and thought but also with a more accurate historical perspective. The humanists absorbed classical ways of thinking, as well as classical modes of expression, and

fostered an appreciation of the studies we know today as the "humanities." Above all, humanism reintroduced into western culture a much-needed emphasis on the dignity of man as an individual and on his place in the cosmos.

In its broader ramifications humanism stimulated a vital concern for the problems and challenges of the contemporary world. As we saw in this chapter and the one preceding, there was a progressive quickening of social life, resulting in sweeping changes in politics and economics and in men's minds. The common denominator of these changes was individualism.

Individualism manifested itself no less in the way in which the artist related his esthetic canons to the new man-centered view of the world. The extent to which the Renaissance sculptor, architect, and painter succeeded remains one of the glories of western civilization.

SUGGESTIONS FOR READING

P. L. Ralph, **The Renaissance in Perspective*** (St. Martin, 1973) is an excellent survey of all aspects of the period. W. K. Ferguson, **Facets of the Renaissance*** (Torchbooks) is an excellent survey of the Italian and Northern Renaissances. J. Huizenga, **The Waning of the Middle Ages*** (Anchor) is an influential study of "fading and decay" in the culture of northern Europe. J. Burckhardt, **The Civilization of the Renaissance in Italy*** (Mentor) is a classic study; it should be read in conjunction with W. K. Ferguson, **The Renaissance in Historical Thought: Five Centuries of Interpretation** (Houghton Mifflin); and T. Helton, ed., **The Renaissance: A Reconstruction of the Theories and Interpretations of the Age*** (Peter Smith).

F. B. Artz, **Renaissance Humanism, 1300-1550*** (Kent State) is a very brief introduction to humanism. P. O. Kristeller, **Renaissance Thought: The Classic, Scholastic, and Humanist Strains*** (Peter Smith) is an excellent analysis of Italian humanism. See also J. H. Whitfield, **Petrarch and the Renascence** (Haskell, 1969).

G. Brucker, **Renaissance Florence** (Wiley, 1969) contains much information as does F. C. Lane, **Venice: A Maritime Republic** (Johns Hopkins, 1973). See also C. Hibbert, **The House of Medici: Its Rise and Fall** (Morrow, 1975), from the emergence of this noted family to the end of the dynasty in 1743. Clemente Fusero, **The Borgias** (Praeger, 1973) is the role of another famous family in Renaissance Europe. See also E. R. Chamberlain, **Everyday Life in Renaissance Times*** (Capricorn); and F. W. Kent, **Everyday Life in Renaissance Florence** (Princeton, 1977).

Margaret M. Phillips, **Erasmus and the Northern Renaissance*** (Collier) is a valuable introduction. Outstanding studies of other Northern Renaissance figures include R. W. Chambers, **Thomas**

More* (Univ. of Michigan); J. H. Hexter, **More's Utopia: The Biography of an Idea*** (Torchbooks); D. B. Lewis, **Doctor Rabelais** (Greenwood, 1969); and M. Chute, **Shakespeare of London.** Two solid studies of England's Renaissance man are S. J. Greenblatt, **Sir Walter Raleigh: The Renaissance Man and his Roles** (Yale, 1973); and Robert Lacey, **Sir Walter Raleigh** (Atheneum, 1974).

On printing and its effect on culture see P. Butler, **The Origin of Printing in Europe** (Univ. of Chicago); and Marshall McLuhan, **The Gutenberg Galaxy*** (Mentor).

F. B. Artz, **From the Renaissance to Romanticism: Trends in Style in Art, Literature, and Music, 1300-1830*** (Phoenix) is a fine overall view of the arts through six centuries. E. Newton, **European Painting and Sculpture*** (Penguin) is brief and valuable. Also recommended are Creighton Gilbert, ed., **Renaissance Art*** (Torchbooks, 1970); and A. Hauser, **A Social History of Art,** Vol. II, **Renaissance to Baroque*** (Vintage). B. Berenson, **Italian Painters of the Renaissance*** (Meridian); and H. Wolfflin, **The Art of the Italian Renaissance*** (Schocken) are two classics of art history. On northern painting see O. Benesch, **The Art of the Renaissance in Northern Europe** (Phaidon). See also B. Lowry, **Renaissance Architecture*** (Braziller).

Two excellent biographies of Renaissance artists are D. Merejkowski, **The Romance of Leonardo da Vinci*** (Hart, 1976) and H. Hibbard, **Michelangelo** (Harper & Row, 1975).

On music see Alfred Einstein, **A Short History of Music*** (Vintage); and G. Reese, **Music in the Renaissance** (Norton).

*Indicates a less expensive paperbound edition.

CHAPTER 14

The Protestant and Catholic Reformations

Here I Take My Stand

INTRODUCTION. On October 31, 1517, a professor of theology named Martin Luther nailed some papers on the door of the castle church in Wittenberg, Germany. It was the custom of the day for a man who wanted to engage in a scholastic debate with another to post his propositions publicly. In this respect Luther's action was not unusual, yet the forces he set in operation altered the entire religious pattern of the western world. A religious movement was to be launched that would split Christendom into numerous factions and sects.

Until his death in 1546, Luther believed that it might be possible to reform Catholicism to the conditions existing in early Christian times. From this standpoint the religious upheaval which he did so much to set in motion can be logically designated as the Reformation. On the other hand, because the struggle shattered western Christendom permanently, it might be described from a broader historical viewpoint as a revolution or, alternatively, as the Protestant Revolt. The sixteenth century also witnessed a significant revival of Catholicism itself. This renewal of the traditional faith was not solely a Counter Reformation in the sense that it represented a belated response to the challenge of Protestantism. As modern scholars have demonstrated, a strong Catholic Reformation had been gathering momentum even before Luther posted his theses.

The Reformation had both its negative and its positive aspects. In the name of God, men persecuted and killed their fellow men. Rulers anxious for absolute power used the conflicts engendered by the religious upheaval to serve their own political ends. Yet, much as in the early centuries of Christianity, when the blood of the martyrs became the seed of the Church, so the struggles of the sixteenth century, led by men afire with conviction and ready to sacrifice their lives for what they believed, renewed and stimulated the religious consciousness of western Europe. Luther declared: "Here I take my stand"; and in a broad sense this affirmation was echoed by Zwingli in the Swiss cantons, by Calvin at Geneva, and by the Catholic Church at the Council of Trent. Such staunch and uncompromising assertions of honest differences of doctrine gave institutionalized Christianity the new religious vitality and intellectual diversity that were to leave their mark on almost every phase of life in the West and bequeath us a rich legacy of values.

THE PROTESTANT REFORMATION

Passing of the medieval order. The Church's dominant position in European society depended on the continuance of the medieval world order; during the late Middle Ages, however, forces were slowly modifying every aspect of that order. The spirit of the Middle Ages was fundamentally one of faith, devotion to established institutions—the feudal order, the guild, and the Church—and the subordination of the individual's interests to those of the group. It was this spirit which fed the power of the Church. When the Renaissance changed this spirit, the universalities of the Middle Ages were shattered. Man became assertive. He began to rebel against all institutions which prevented him from acting as he wished.

Broadly speaking, the ideal of the Middle Ages was other-worldliness; the ideal of the Renaissance was present-worldliness. The Church represented the older ideal. Thus it was not simply that the Church's financial and moral abuses stood in need of correction, but that the Church's ideals no longer commanded the same respect and allegiance among all the population. The European townsman, for example, found himself increasingly out of sympathy with the Church's economic concepts of the "just price" and anti-usury statutes, for they conflicted with the new capitalism.

The Church itself embodied a dangerous contradiction at this time. In dogma it was medieval, yet its highest officials, including the popes, were patrons of a Renaissance culture deriving its inspiration from pagan Greece and Rome. The Church might denounce usury, but at the same time it utilized the services of powerful moneylending families.

As we have seen in Chapter 13, the northern humanists directed searching criticisms against the Church, though for the most part they wished to remain within it. But because it was primarily an intellectual movement, humanism could not create the dynamic drive necessary to inspire widespread reform. Having laid the intellectual groundwork for the pending religious revolt, the humanists left to other men—the militant and the martyrs alike—the task of arousing action. The time was ripe for the rise of a religious leader who would employ as his weapon not the conflict of Renaissance ideology with that of the Church, for that was a philosophical problem of which few were conscious, but rather the financial and moral abuses of the Church, which were common knowledge.

Religious ferment in Germany. The religious issue first came to a head in Germany. Aided by the invention of printing, devout

Germans had been studying the Scriptures carefully and censuring the behavior of many of the German clergy. Whereas in Italy familiarity bred a tolerance and rationalization of papal corruption, the Germans fiercely resented papal abuses and expected practice and theory to coincide.

The political situation also had a bearing on the religious question. Divided into hundreds of states, Germany lacked unity except for the nominal rule of the elected emperor of the Holy Roman Empire. The failure of imperial administrative reform (see p. 274) encouraged the many German states to imitate the new nationalism of countries to the west. With the religious affairs of each principality increasingly under the control of its ruler, a greater diversity of religious opinion could exist in fragmented Germany than in a state ruled by a centralized authority.

Nor must economic factors be overlooked. Trade and banking flourished, and the German burgher found no conflict between piety and profits. On the other hand, his piety and profits were both affected by the draining of German revenues by the Roman Church, especially when unscrupulous means were used to gather them. In short, Germany was ripe for religious revolt.

Martin Luther. The son of a German peasant who by virtue of thrift and hard work had become a petty capitalist, Martin Luther was born on November 10, 1483. Young Martin received a sound education which included university studies, but he accepted as a matter of course the prevalent beliefs in witchcraft and other superstitions. To the end of his life Luther believed vividly in the existence of devils and witches. The story goes that he once threw an inkpot at a devil whom he thought he saw leering at him. In 1505 he became a member of the mendicant order of Augustinian monks, a move which met with scant favor from his practical father, who wanted his son to study law. In 1508 Luther received a temporary appointment as a lecturer at the new University of Wittenberg, and a few years later he became professor of theology.

In the meantime Luther had struggled with

The deterioration of monasticism was responsible for much disenchantment with the Church. Monks were accused of every possible vice, from drunkenness and adultery to the frequenting of brothels. Such charges fostered the contempt vividly illustrated in this early sixteenth-century woodcut.

and solved for himself the spiritual problem that confronted many people in his time: In view of God's absolute power and man's powerlessness, how can man be certain of salvation for his soul? For many years Luther probed deeply this problem of eternal salvation. Finally, in 1515, while contemplating St. Paul's Epistle to the Romans (1:17), he came upon these words: "For therein is the righteousness of God revealed from faith to faith: as it is written, The just shall live by faith." Luther believed that his quest for spiritual certainty had been solved:

Night and day I pondered until I saw the connection between the justice of God and the statement that "the just shall live by his faith." Then I grasped that the justice of God is that righteousness by which through grace and sheer mercy God justifies us through faith. Thereupon I felt myself to be reborn and to have gone through open doors into paradise.[1]

Man was saved only by his faith in the "sheer mercy" of God, which alone could wash away sin and save him from the grasp of the devil. Luther had come to his famous doctrine of justification by faith, as opposed to the Roman Church's doctrine of justification by faith and good works—the demonstration of faith through virtuous acts, acceptance of Church dogma, and participation in Church ritual. Later, in a hymn that reflects his vigorous style of expression, Luther described his spiritual journey from anxiety to conviction:

In devil's dungeon chained I lay
  The pangs of death swept o'er me.
My sin devoured me night and day
  In which my mother bore me.
My anguish ever grew more rife,
I took no pleasure in my life
  And sin had made me crazy.

. . .

Thus spoke the Son, "Hold thou to me,
  From now on thou wilt make it.
I gave my very life for thee
  And for thee I will stake it.
For I am thine and thou art mine,
And where I am our lives entwine,
  The Old Fiend cannot shake it."[2]

The implications of Luther's doctrine were enormous. If salvation could come only through a personal faith in God's mercy, then an interceding priesthood became superfluous, for each man would then be his own priest. But Luther himself had no idea as yet where his views would eventually lead him and half of Christendom. It required a financial abuse by the Church to bring on the religious revolt.

Tetzel and the indulgences. Leo X, a cultured scion of the Medici family, "who would have made an excellent Pope if he had only been a little religious,"[3] wanted to complete the magnificent new St. Peter's in Rome, but he lacked money for the costly enterprise. Several papal agents were sent out to sell indulgences as a means of raising money. One of these agents, named Tetzel, discharged his mission "in the German archbishopric of Mainz in a manner which would be recognized in America to-day as high-pressure salesmanship."[4]

The Church's position in regard to indulgences has often been misunderstood. Although the sacrament of Penance absolved the sinner from guilt and eternal punishment, some temporal punishment remained. An indulgence was a type of good work, to be compared with praying, visiting shrines, and contributing to worthy causes, and like all good works it was a means of remitting or pardoning the temporal penalty for sins. Theologically, the concept of indulgences rested on the theory of a "treasury of merits," which held that Christ and the saints had won merit far in excess of their own needs and had thereby created a vast storehouse of good works. By means of indulgences the Church was able to draw upon and distribute this surplus to help those who felt they had not rendered sufficient penance to extinguish the punishment which they deserved.

It was the abuse attending the sale of indulgences to raise money that was chiefly responsible for provoking Luther's resentment. The common folk did not understand theology and thought that a payment of money would buy God's grace and insure their salvation. Tetzel did nothing to enlighten the populace as to the true nature of indulgences but rather exhorted them to give liberally for themselves and for their dead relatives in purgatory who were "crying to them for help." Thus Luther's case against indulgences rested on moral as well as theological grounds.

Development of Luther's ideas. On October 31, 1517, Luther, following a university custom, posted ninety-five propositions (theses) on the subject of indulgences on the church door at Wittenberg, at the same time challenging anyone to debate them with him. The following are typical:

6. The pope has no power to remit guilt, save by declaring and confirming that it has been remitted by God; . . .

21. Therefore those preachers of indulgences are in error who allege that through the indulgences of the pope a man is freed from every penalty.

36. Every Christian who is truly contrite has plenary remission both of penance and of guilt as his due, even without a letter of pardon.[5]

An anonymous caricature of Johann Tetzel, the German hawker of indulgences, entitled "Johann Tetzel and His Indulgence-Junk." The last two lines of the notorious jingle here ascribed to Tetzel read: "As soon as coin in the coffer rings, Right then the soul to Heaven springs."

Luther wrote the ninety-five theses in Latin for the edification of his fellow theologians, but they were soon translated into the common tongue and six months later were well known throughout Germany. At first the Church at Rome did not seriously trouble itself. Heresy was anything but new, as the history of the Waldensians, Albigensians, and the followers of Wycliffe and Huss showed. But this particular "squabble among monks," as Leo x dismissed the matter, did not subside.

In 1519 Luther debated with the eminent Catholic theologian John Eck at Leipzig. Luther maintained that the pope ruled by virtue of human rather than divine authority and was not infallible; that Church councils did not exist by divine right either and could also err; and that Scripture constituted the sole authority in matters of faith and doctrine. When Eck pointed out that such views were similar to those of Wycliffe and Huss, Luther boldly declared that "among the opinions of John Huss and the Bohemians many are certainly most Christian and evangelic, and cannot be condemned by the universal church."[6] Yet in spite of these wide theological divergences, Luther continued to speak with affection of his "mother Church," which he hoped could be reformed

and remain unified. By basing his position squarely on the doctrine of justification by faith alone, however, Luther found himself propelled by its implications to a position far removed from that of the Church.

Following the Leipzig debate, Eck initiated proceedings at Rome to have Luther declared a heretic. Luther in turn decided to put his case before the German people by publishing a series of pamphlets. In his *Address to the Nobility of the German Nation*, Luther called on the princes to reform ecclesiastical abuses, to strip the Church of its wealth and worldly power, and to create, in effect, a national German Church. Among numerous other proposals contained in this influential treatise, Luther urged a union with the Hussites, claiming that Huss had been unjustly burned at the stake.

The Babylonian Captivity of the Church summarized Luther's theological views. He attacked the papacy for having deprived the individual Christian of his freedom to approach God directly by faith and without the intermediation of the priesthood, and he set forth his views on the sacramental system. To be valid, a sacrament must have been instituted by Christ and be exclusively Christian. On this basis Luther could find no justification for making a sacrament of matrimony, which was also observed by non-Christians, or for any of the other sacraments except Baptism and the Lord's Supper (his term for the sacrament known to Roman Catholics as the Holy Eucharist). Luther rejected the doctrine of transubstantiation on the grounds that a priest could not perform the miracle of transforming bread and wine into the Body and Blood of the Lord. Nevertheless, he believed in the real presence of Christ in the bread and wine of the sacrament. In Luther's view, the bread and wine coexist with the Body and Blood without a change of substance.

Luther's third pamphlet, *The Freedom of a Christian Man*, which was dedicated to the pope in the slight hope that reconciliation was still possible, set forth in conciliatory but firm tones Luther's views on Christian behavior and salvation. He did not discourage good works but argued that the inner spiritual freedom which comes from the certainty found in faith leads to the performance of good works. "Good works do not make a man good, but a good man does good works."[7]

The breach made complete. In June 1520 Pope Leo x issued the bull *Exsurge Domine* ("Arise, O Lord, . . . Arise all ye saints, and the whole universal Church, whose interpretation of Scripture has been assailed"[8]), which gave Luther sixty days to turn from his heretical course. When Luther publicly burned the bull amid the applause of students and townsmen, he propelled himself into the center of German politics and brought about a showdown with Rome. In January 1521 Leo x excommunicated Luther.

Meanwhile, Charles v, who had recently been crowned emperor, found himself in a difficult situation. He was aware of popular German feelings and was not anxious to see papal power reconsolidated in his domains, yet he was bound by his oath to defend the Church and extirpate heresy. Moreover, Charles was orthodox in his own religious beliefs. It was decided that Luther should be heard at the emperor's first Diet, which was held at Worms. Summoned under an imperial safe-conduct, Luther was asked whether he intended to stand by everything he had written. He stood before the assembly and replied firmly:

In this workroom in Wartburg castle Luther completed his translation of the New Testament into German.

Your Imperial Majesty and Your Lordships demand a simple answer. Here it is, plain and unvarnished. Unless I am convicted of error by the testimony of Scripture or (since I put no trust in the unsupported authority of Pope or of councils, since it is plain that they have often erred and often contradicted themselves) by manifest reasoning I stand convicted by the Scriptures to which I have appealed, . . . I cannot and will not recant anything, for to act against our conscience is neither safe for us, nor open to us.

On this I take my stand [*Hier stehe Ich*]. I can do no other. God help me. Amen.[9]

In May 1521 the Diet declared Luther a heretic and outlaw. He was, however, given protection by the elector of Saxony, in whose strongest castle he lived for almost a year under the guise of "Knight George."

During this period Luther began the construction of an evangelical church distinct from Rome. He wrote incessantly, setting forth his theological views in a collection of forceful sermons for use by preachers, in correspondence with friends and public figures, and in a treatise condemning monasticism. (In 1525 Luther married an ex-nun who had left the cloister after reading this treatise.) Luther also translated the New Testament into German, a monumental job accomplished in only eleven weeks. Later he translated the Old Testament. Luther's Bible was largely responsible for creating a standard literary language for all Germany.

Luther and the Peasants' War. Luther's teachings spread quickly through central and northern Germany. Pious persons who wanted the Church reformed embraced the new cause. Worldly individuals who believed that it would afford an opportunity to appropriate Church property also aided the movement, as did ardent nationalists like Von Hutten (see p. 299), who saw in it a means of uniting Germany. The emperor, meanwhile, was too deeply involved in a struggle with the French and the Turks to stamp out the new heresy (see p. 329).

Encouraged by Luther's concept of the freedom of a Christian man, which they applied to economic and social matters, the German peasants revolted in 1524. Long ground down by the nobles, the peasants included in their twelve demands the abolition of serfdom "unless it should be shown us from the Gospel that we are serfs"; a reduction of "the excessive services demanded of us, which are increased from day to day"; the fixing of rents "in accordance with justice"; and an end to "the appropriation by individuals of meadows and fields which at one time belonged to a community."[10] Luther recognized the justice of these demands, but when the peasants began to employ violence against established authority he turned against them. In a virulent pamphlet, *Against the Thievish and Murderous Hordes of Peasants*, Luther called on the princes to "knock down, strangle, and stab . . . and think nothing so venomous, pernicious, or Satanic as an insurgent."[11]

The revolt was stamped out in 1525 at a cost of an estimated 100,000 peasant dead, and the lot of the German peasant for the next two centuries was probably the worst in Europe. Luther had become a false prophet to the peasants, who either returned to Catholicism or turned to more radical forms of Protestantism. Politically and economically conservative, Luther believed that the equality of all men before God applied in spiritual but not in secular matters. This philosophy alienated the peasants but made allies of the princes, many of whom became Lutheran in part because it placed them in control of the church in their territories, thereby enhancing their power and wealth.

Local religious autonomy in Germany. At a meeting of the Diet of the Empire in 1529, the Catholic princes, with the emperor's support, pushed through a decree that the Mass must not be interfered with anywhere. This meant that while Lutheran activities were restricted in Catholic regions, those of the Catholics could be carried on even in Lutheran areas. In answer, the Lutheran leaders drew up a protest, and from this incident the word *Protestant* derives. The next Diet, meeting at Augsburg in 1530, was presented with a statement of Christian doctrine from the Lutheran viewpoint designed to conciliate the two parties. The Catholics refused to accept this statement, known as the Augsburg Confession, which became the official creed of Lutheranism.

The emperor now made public his intention to crush the growing heresy. In defense, the Lutheran princes banded together in 1531 in the Schmalkaldic League, and between 1546 and 1555 a sporadic civil war was fought. A compromise was finally reached in the Peace of Augsburg (1555), which allowed each prince to decide the religion of his subjects, gave Protestants the right to keep all Church property confiscated prior to 1552, forbade all sects of Protestantism other than Lutheranism, and ordered all Catholic bishops to give up their property if they turned Lutheran.

The effects of these provisions on Germany were profound. The Peace of Augsburg confirmed Lutheranism as a state religion in large portions of the Empire. Religious opinions became the private property of the princes, and the individual had to believe what his prince wanted him to believe, be it Lutheranism or Catholicism. Furthermore, by formally sanctioning state religion and thus enhancing a prince's power, the Peace of Augsburg added to Germany's political disintegration.

The death of Luther. In 1546, during the Schmalkaldic War, the founder of the new faith died. Martin Luther had been a born leader, genius, and zealot. His life had been molded by an absolute conviction of the rightness of his beliefs, which goes far to ex-

plain both his driving power and his limitations. "His weaknesses were manifest: intransigency in theological views, proneness to vehemence, narrowness of social concepts. . . . But Luther also had qualities to offset these: sincere desire for the truth, courage, determination, power of organization, an outstanding gift for identifying himself with the language and thought of the simple man. These were the qualities that permitted him to carry through what he had begun."[12]

In closing this account of Luther and the momentous movement which he set rolling, we might append an ironic footnote. The same sale of indulgences which furnished the money to build a fitting capital for a universal Church (St. Peter's in Rome) at the same time provided the occasion for destroying the unity of western Christendom.

Lutheranism in Scandinavia. In 1525 the Grand Master of the Teutonic Knights who ruled Prussia (see p. 275) turned Lutheran, dissolved the order, secularized its lands, and declared himself duke of Prussia. With this exception, outside Germany Lutheranism permanently established itself as a state religion only in the Scandinavian countries. Here emerging modern monarchs welcomed the opportunity to obtain needed wealth by confiscating church property and needed power by filling church offices with Lutherans who preached obedience to constituted authority. This was particularly the case in Sweden where Gustavus Vasa led a successful struggle for Swedish independence from Denmark. In 1523 he was elected king, and soon thereafter he declared himself a Lutheran and filled his empty treasury from the sale of confiscated Church lands. A century later his descendant, Gustavus Adolphus, would intervene in the religious wars in Germany and be instrumental in saving German Protestantism from extinction. In Denmark, which also ruled Norway, the spread of Lutheranism was encouraged by the king. In 1537 an ordinance, approved by Luther, established a national Lutheran church with its bishops as salaried officials of the Danish state.

Zwingli in Switzerland. Meanwhile, Protestantism had taken firm root in Switzerland.

Some of the giants of the Protestant Reformation are shown in this picture painted about 1530 by Lucas Cranach the Elder. At the far left is Luther, and at the far right his associate Melanchthon, who wrote the Augsburg Confession. Next to Melanchthon is Zwingli. In the center of the picture is John Frederick the Magnanimous, elector of Saxony, whose family supported Luther, John Frederick's uncle, Frederick III, once sheltered Luther in his Wartburg castle.

In the German-speaking area of that country —particularly in Zurich—the Reformation was led by Ulrich Zwingli (1484-1531). Like Luther, who was the same age, Zwingli repudiated papal in favor of scriptural authority, preached justification by faith, attacked monasticism and clerical celibacy, and drastically revised the sacramental system. But the differences between the two leaders proved irreconcilable when they met in 1529 at the University of Marburg, founded two years earlier as the first Protestant university in Europe. Whereas Luther looked on baptism as a means of helping to regenerate the individual, Zwingli considered it only a means of initiating a child into society. Nor did he believe with Luther that the real presence of Christ was found in the Lord's Supper. To Zwingli, who had been trained as a humanist and was therefore more of a rationalist than Luther, the bread and wine symbolized Christ's body and blood and the service was a commemoration of the Last Supper.

Zwingli was an ardent Swiss patriot who had once served as chaplain with Swiss mercenaries in Italy. The Swiss Confederation, comprising thirteen cantons, was a by-product of the weakness and disunity of the Holy Roman Empire. Originating in 1291 as a defensive union of three cantons, the confederation expanded and repulsed all attempts of the emperors to exercise jurisdiction over it. Switzerland's independence was won by the valor of its hardy peasant pikemen, whose prowess became so famed that foreign rulers and popes eagerly sought their services. Garbed in colorful Renaissance costumes, Swiss mercenaries still guard the Vatican.

In 1531 war broke out between Protestant and Catholic cantons, and Zwingli was slain in battle. The war ended in the same year with an agreement that anticipated by a quarter of a century the Peace of Augsburg in Germany—each canton was allowed to choose its own religion. This settlement was largely responsible for keeping Switzerland from taking sides in the great religious wars that subsequently engulfed Europe. Furthermore, it helped set the policy of neutrality which the Swiss have followed to our own day.

These pen and ink sketches of John Calvin in his later years were drawn by one of his students.

John Calvin. The most famous sixteenth-century Protestant leader after Luther was John Calvin (1509-1564). A Frenchman of the middle class, Calvin studied theology and law at Paris, where he became interested in Luther's teachings. About 1533 he had what he called a "conversion," whereby he abandoned Catholicism and fled to the Protestant city of Basel in Switzerland. Here in 1536 he published the first edition of his great work, the *Institutes of the Christian Religion*, unquestionably one of the most influential books of systematic theology ever written. His capacity for creative thinking was overshadowed by his ability as an organizer and synthesist. Influenced by his legal training as well as by humanistic scholarship and the doctrines of Luther, Calvin set forth a system that was a masterpiece of logical reasoning.

Whereas Luther's central doctrine was justification by faith, Calvin's was the sovereignty of God. "Both Calvin and Luther had an overwhelming sense of the majesty of God, but whereas for Luther this served to point up the miracle of forgiveness, for Calvin it gave rather the assurance of the impregnability of God's purpose."[13] God was omnipotent and for His own purposes had created the world and also man in His image. Since Adam and Eve had fallen from a state of sinlessness, man was utterly depraved and lost.

Carrying these doctrines to their logical conclusions, Calvin defined man's relation to God in his famous doctrine of predestination. Since God is omniscient, He knows the past, present, and future. Consequently, He must always know which men are to be saved and which men are to be damned eternally. Man's purpose in life, then, is not to try to work out his salvation—for this has already been determined—but to honor God. While Calvin did not profess to know absolutely who were to be God's chosen—the elect—he believed that the following three tests constituted a good yardstick by which to judge who might be saved: participation in the two sacraments, Baptism and the Lord's Supper; an upright moral life; and a public profession of the faith.

Calvin's emphasis upon the sovereignty of God led him to differ with Luther on the relationship of church and state. To Luther the state was supreme, but to Calvin the church and its ministers, as representatives of the sovereignty of God, must dominate. Calvinist church government in turn was democratically oriented in that it was based on the authority not of bishops but of synods or presbyteries, elected bodies composed of ministers and elders. Although Calvin upheld lawful political authority, he also approved of rebellion against a tyranny "which overrides private conscience." Thus, wherever Calvinism spread it carried with it the seeds of representative government and of defiance against despotism.

Calvinist Geneva. In 1536 the Protestants of Geneva invited Calvin to become their leader, and there he put his ideas on government into effect. Calvin believed it was the duty of the elect to glorify God by establishing a theocracy that would be governed according to scriptural precept. Although the Bible was the supreme authority, the chief instrument of government was the Consistory, or Presbytery, a council of ministers and elders which made and enforced the laws. Calvin in turn dominated the Consis-

tory, which showed great zeal in disciplining the community and punishing or removing any person found guilty of unseemly behavior. Although the regime was highminded, it carried its zeal to ridiculous lengths. Penalties were inflicted for being absent from sermons or laughing during the church service, for wearing bright colors, for swearing or dancing, for playing cards, or for having one's fortune told by gypsies.

In regard to more serious offenses, especially in the religious sphere, Calvin and his associates acted with a severity common to the Reformation age. They used torture to obtain confessions and banished citizens for heresy, blasphemy, witchcraft, and adultery. When the Spanish physician Servetus sought refuge in Geneva, having fled from Catholic persecution because he was a Unitarian who denied the doctrine of the Trinity, Calvin had him burned for heresy. "Because the Papists persecute the truth," Calvin explained, "should we on that account refrain from repressing error?"

The spread of Calvinism. From Geneva, Calvinism spread far and wide, imbued with its founder's spirit of austerity and a self-righteousness born of confidence in being among the elect of God. Many of its leaders studied at the Academy (today the University of Geneva), which trained students from other countries in Calvin's theology. In France, Calvinism made influential converts among both the bourgeoisie and the nobility. Known as Huguenots, the French Calvinists remained a minority but, as we shall see in the next chapter, their importance far outweighed their numbers. In Scotland the fiery Calvinist John Knox successfully challenged the authority of the Roman Church (see p. 316), and in Germany and the Netherlands Calvin's teachings formed the basis for the German and Dutch Reformed churches.

Henry VIII's quarrel with Rome. In Germany the revolt against the Church was primarily religious in nature, although it possessed political implications; in England the situation was reversed. There the leader was a monarch, Henry VIII (1509-1547), not a priest. Henry broke with Rome not for theological reasons but because the pope would not annul his marriage to Catherine of Aragon, daughter of Ferdinand and Isabella of Spain, whom he had married for dynastic reasons.

Catherine had given Henry a daughter, Mary, but no son, and Henry was convinced that a male heir was necessary if the newly established Tudors were to endure as a dynasty and England kept from reverting to anarchy. Catherine was the widow of his brother, and Church law forbade a man to marry his brother's widow. A special papal dispensation had been granted for the marriage, but Henry claimed the dispensation was not valid and in 1527 asked Pope Clement VII to revoke it.

Normally the pope might have acquiesced to Henry's wishes, for other popes had granted similar favors to monarchs and Henry had been loyal to the Church. In answer to Luther he had written a *Defense of the Seven Sacraments* (1521), in which he castigated Luther as a "poisonous serpent," the "wolf of hell," and the "limb of Satan." The pope gratefully bestowed on Henry the title "Defender of the Faith"—a title which English monarchs still possess. But much as he might have wished, the pope could not support Henry in his desires. There were two good reasons. First, the pope felt it would be dangerous for one pontiff to reverse the judgments of a predecessor. Second, the emperor Charles V, the most powerful monarch in Europe, was a nephew of Catherine and threatened the pope if he declared the marriage null and void. Clement decided to wait before giving his answer, hoping that in the meantime events would resolve themselves.

But Henry would not wait. He obtained from Parliament the power to appoint bishops in England without papal permission, designating Thomas Cranmer as archbishop of Canterbury—a willing tool who was sure to do his master's bidding. In 1533 Cranmer pronounced the king's marriage to Catherine invalid and legalized Henry's marriage to coquettish Anne Boleyn, whom he had secretly married three months earlier. At last goaded into action, Clement VII excommunicated Henry and maintained that Catherine alone was the king's true wife.

Establishment of the Anglican Church. In 1534 Henry severed all connections with Rome. A sympathetic Parliament passed the famous Act of Supremacy, which stated that the king "justly and rightfully is and ought to be supreme head of the Church of England." It also enacted the Treason Act, which declared liable to the death penalty anyone who called the king a "heretic, schismatic, tyrant, infidel, or usurper." Turning on his old friend, Henry had Sir Thomas More beheaded because he would not acknowledge the sovereign as head of the English Church. In recent years More has been canonized by the Catholic Church not only for his saintly life but also for his martyrdom in opposing Henry VIII's divorce and break with the Church.

To replenish the royal coffers and to gain popular support, Henry, working through Parliament, dissolved the monasteries and sold their lands to the nobles and gentry. Thus Henry acquired accomplices, in a sense, in his conflict with Rome. It must be remembered that Henry and Parliament could not perhaps have effected such sweeping changes if many Englishmen had not been anticlerical.

In the same year (1539) in which Parliament acted to dissolve the monasteries, it also passed the Six Articles, which reaffirmed the main points of Catholic theology. By this act, both the Catholic who denied the supremacy of the king and the Protestant who denied the validity of transubstantiation were to be punished severely. Thus England threw off the supremacy of the pope without at that time adopting the Protestant faith; the elements of Protestantism in the English Church crept in after Henry's reign.

After Henry's death in 1547, his frail ten-year-old son mounted the throne as Edward VI. During his reign the growing Protestant party in England became ascendant. The Six Articles were repealed; priests were no longer held to their vows of celibacy; and the old Latin service was replaced by Cranmer's Book of Common Prayer, written in English, which brought the service much closer to the people and exerted a powerful influence on the development of the language. In 1553 the Forty-Two Articles defined the faith of the Church of England along Protestant lines.

Under the devoutly Catholic Mary (1553-

The lives of Europe's monarchs were often interwoven through ties of marriage and kinship; those bonds were emphasized or ignored according to the monarchs' nationalistic aims. Until she was widowed at eighteen, Mary Stuart had ruled France for two years as the queen of the youthful Francis II.

preserved, along with the ecclesiastical government of bishops in apostolic succession.

Presbyterianism in Scotland. The religious revolt in Scotland was largely the work of the zealous reformer John Knox (1505?-1572), who had become a disciple of Calvin in Geneva, which he called "the most perfect school of Christ that ever was on earth since the days of the Apostles." After returning to his native Scotland in about 1559, Knox became the leader of a group of Protestant nobles who wished to overthrow both the jurisdiction of the Roman Catholic Church and the monarch—Queen Mary Stuart, whose husband was king of France (see p. 333). In 1560 the Scottish Parliament severed all ties with Rome and accepted Knox's Articles of the Presbyterian Church, modeled after Calvin's views on theology and church government. When the beautiful but ill-fated queen returned from France one year later she found her bleak kingdom alienated from her own Catholic views. Her scandalous behavior (see p. 333) and her steadfast Catholicism led the Scots to depose her in 1567 in favor of her Protestant son James.

The Anabaptists. The most radical among those who rejected the religious establishment of the time were the Anabaptists ("rebaptizers"), so called because they denied the efficacy of infant baptism. They formed many sects led by self-styled "prophets" who carried to extreme Luther's doctrines of Christian liberty, priesthood of all believers, and return to primitive Christianity. Centered in Germany and the Netherlands, Anabaptism was predominantly a lower-class movement; many of the peasants whose hopes for economic and social reform had been crushed by the Peasants' War turned from Luther to the Anabaptists. In communities of their own, they shared their worldly goods with one another and lived as they thought the primitive Christians had lived, working and praying together. On occasion they employed force to purify society and establish a New Jerusalem. Mainly, however, they believed in the separation of church and state and advocated pacifism and the love-ethic. Today some portion of their spirit lives on among such groups as the Mennonites, the Amish, and the Quakers.

1558), the unfortunate daughter of the still less fortunate Catherine of Aragon, Catholicism was reinstated, and three hundred Protestants, including Archbishop Cranmer, were burned at the stake. But with the accession to the throne of Anne Boleyn's red-headed and fiery-tempered daughter, Elizabeth I (1558-1603), the Anglican Church took on a strong Protestant character. Realizing the political necessity for religious peace, Elizabeth worked hard to achieve a compromise settlement. Although the Church of England remained a state church under the control of the monarch, Elizabeth astutely changed her title from "Supreme Head" to the more modest "Supreme Governor." In accepting the Bible as the final authority, and in recognizing only Baptism and Holy Eucharist as Christ-instituted sacraments, Elizabeth's Thirty-Nine Articles (1563) were essentially Protestant, although many articles were ambiguously phrased in an effort to satisfy both parties. Much Catholic ritual was

THE CATHOLIC REFORMATION

The background. The Catholic Reformation should not be viewed as only a retaliatory movement or a series of measures taken to stem the rising tide of Protestantism. The Roman Church had always retained latent forces of recuperation and strength which it could draw upon in challenging times. Before Luther had posted his ninety-five theses, evidence of renewed vitality and internal reform was visible in the Roman Church.

One of the prime examples of this resurgence occurred in Spain under Ferdinand and Isabella, ardent Catholics as well as autocrats. To deal with Moors, Jews, and heretics, the "Catholic Sovereigns" requested and got papal permission for a separate Spanish Inquisition under their control (see p. 272). The Inquisition soon came to dominate the Spanish Church, making it virtually a state church, and moved on to the problem of religious reform. Under the able Grand Inquisitor, Cardinal Ximenes (d. 1517), both the secular clergy and the monastic orders were invigorated by a renewal of spirit, discipline, and education—the latter including the scholarly study of the Bible at the University of Alcala, founded by Ximenes as a means of training able bishops. Thus Spain became a model Catholic state, where Protestantism would make few converts.

In a category of his own was the Dominican friar Savonarola (1452-1498), an ardent puritan, mystic, and reformer of Church and society. In 1494, when the Medici were expelled from Florence, Savonarola emerged as master of the city. For four years he ruled the Kingdom of God, as he called Florence, invoking the wrath of God upon worldly living and sinful luxuries. Bands of teenagers were organized to go about the city collecting and burning "vanities"—fashionable clothes, wigs, ornaments, and secular books and paintings. Savonarola also bitterly denounced the iniquities of the Borgia pope, Alexander VI, and called for a general council to reform the Church. But he lacked the power to reform the papacy and the Church, or even to maintain his hold on the fickle Florentines. Publicly humiliated by having his Dominican garb torn from him in the great square of Florence, Savonarola was hanged and burned, a victim of political intrigue. He was later hailed by Luther and the Protestants as a forerunner of their movement.

By the 1530's the inroads of Protestantism were apparent, and in retaliation the Church rallied its forces and prepared a powerful offensive. This renewal of strength, known as the Catholic Reformation—or, as some prefer, Counter Reformation—penetrated all areas of the Church. New monastic orders adapted monastic life to the needs of the time, the papacy headed a program of vigorous reform, and the Church regained much ground lost to the Protestants. Climaxing the whole movement was the Council of Trent, where the Church boldly reaffirmed its traditional doctrines and flatly refused to compromise in any way with the Protestants.

Reformist monasticism. In response to the same forces that had produced monastic reform during the earlier medieval reformation (see Chapter 11), a number of new monastic orders sprang up in the first half of the sixteenth century. Prominent among them were the Theatines, a body of devoted priests who undertook to check the spread of heresy by concentrating upon the regeneration of the clergy; the Capuchins, an offshoot of the Franciscan order inspired by the original spirit of St. Francis, who became notable for their preaching and for the care of the poor and the sick; and the Ursulines, whose special task was the education of girls. Reflecting both the reforming zeal of the new orders and the mystical reaffirmation of faith that characterized most reformers, Protestant as well as Catholic, was the order of barefoot Carmelites and their founder, the Spanish nun St. Theresa. These devout sisters slept on straw, ate no meat, and lived on alms. Quietistic mysticism, which teaches that spiritual peace can be attained by losing the sense of self in passive contemplation of God and His works, is well reflected in St. Theresa's written accounts of her ecstasies and visions.

Loyola and the Jesuits. The Society of Jesus, better known as the Jesuits, founded

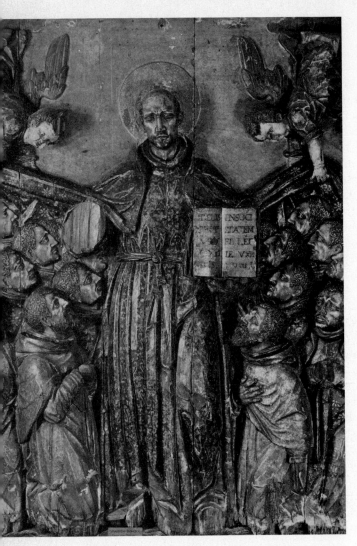

Ignatius Loyola, flanked by members of the Society of Jesus, is pictured in this intricate seventeenth-century Spanish woodcarving. The Jesuits, as they were called, were founded primarily to convert the Moslem world and carried out successful missionary activities. In Europe their intellectual and political skill often raised them to places of great influence.

by the Spanish nobleman and ex-soldier Ignatius Loyola (1491-1556), played a vital role in the Catholic Reformation. While recovering from a severe battle wound, Loyola experienced a mystical religious conversion and vowed to become a soldier of Christ and "serve only God and the Roman pontiff, His vicar on earth." His "Company [*Societas*] of Jesus," founded in 1534 and given papal authorization in 1540, was organized along military lines with Loyola as "general." Members were carefully selected, rigorously

trained, and subjected to an iron discipline. One of the classics in the field of religious literature, Loyola's *Spiritual Exercises*, a work of great psychological penetration based on his own mystical religious experience, was used to inculcate disciplined asceticism and absolute obedience to superior authority. In addition to the usual monastic vows of chastity, obedience, and poverty, the Jesuits took a special vow of allegiance to the pope. As preachers, confessors to monarchs and princes, and educators, the Jesuits had remarkable success in stemming and even reversing the tide of Protestantism, particularly in Poland, Bohemia, Hungary, Germany, France, and the Spanish Netherlands (modern Belgium). In addition, the Jesuits performed excellent missionary work in America and Asia.

Papal reform: Paul III. A new era was at hand for the Church when Paul III, who reigned from 1534 to 1549, ascended the papal throne. He chose outstanding men as cardinals and appointed a commission to look into the need for reform. Their report listed the evils requiring correction, including the appointment of worldly bishops and priests, the traffic in benefices and indulgences and other financial abuses, the venality of some cardinals, and the absence of others from the papal court. Ignoring the opposition of some high churchmen, Paul made plans to call a general council to carry out needed reforms.

The Council of Trent. The Catholic Reformation came to a climax in the Council of Trent, which met in three sessions between 1545 and 1563. Rejecting all compromise with Protestantism, the Council restated the basic tenets of Catholic doctrine. It declared salvation to be a matter of both faith and good works, and it affirmed the source of doctrine to be not only the Bible, as interpreted by the Church, but also the "unwritten traditions, which were received by the Apostles from the lips of Christ himself, or, by the same Apostles, at the dictation of the Holy Spirit, and were handed on and have come down to us. . . ."[14] The Council also reaffirmed the seven sacraments, with special emphasis on transubstantiation, decreed that only Latin be used in the Mass, and approved the spiritual usefulness of indulgences, pilgrimages, veneration of saints and relics, and the cult of the Virgin.

At the same time, the Council sought to eliminate abuses by ordering reforms in Church discipline and administration. Such evils as simony, absenteeism, the abuse of indulgences, and secular pursuits on the part of the clergy were strictly forbidden. Bishops were ordered to supervise closely both the regular and the secular clergy, appoint reputable and competent men to ecclesiastical positions, and establish seminaries to provide a well-educated clergy. The clergy, in turn, were requested to preach frequently to the people.

In addition to freeing the Church of its worst abuses and formulating its doctrines clearly and rigidly, the Council of Trent strengthened the authority of the papacy. The pope's party in the Council, ably led by Jesuit theologians, defeated all attempts to revive the theory that a general council was supreme in the Church. And when the final session of the Council voted that none of its decrees were valid without the consent of the Holy See, the Church became more than ever an absolute monarchy ruled by the pope.

EFFECTS OF THE RELIGIOUS UPHEAVAL

Religious division but renewed faith. By 1550 Christendom was composed of three divisions—Greek Orthodox, Roman Catholic, and Protestant. With Protestantism predominant in northern Europe, the unity of western Christendom was split irreparably. The Catholics placed their faith in the authority of the pope and the need for a mediatory priesthood. The Protestants placed their faith in the authority of the Bible and held that every Christian could win salvation without priestly mediation. But since they differed among themselves in their interpretation of the Bible and the methods of church organization, in time hundreds of separate Protestant sects arose.

Although the religious upheaval fostered the religious diversity of modern times, it also represented in some aspects a return to medievalism. It was a great religious revival, a renewal of faith. Renaissance emphasis on free and secular thought gave way again to authority—for Protestants it was the Bible; for Catholics, the Church. The Renaissance movement, having fostered doubt and criticism of medieval values, was now engulfed in a return to some of those values. Thus, temporarily at least, the Renaissance spirit was stifled. But it was to prove stronger than this intense religious revival and in time was to profit from the passing of the single religious authority of the universal Church.

Another by-product of the religious upheaval was a new interest in education, already broadened by the intellectual and moral concerns of the humanists. Each faith wanted its youth to be properly trained in its teachings. As part of its campaign to win Protestants back to the fold, the Jesuits in particular developed a school system so superior and so attractive that many Protestant as well as Catholic youths attended. One feature of Protestantism eventually stimulated education a great deal. Its emphasis upon the importance of Bible reading encouraged the promotion of universal education; Luther, for example, insisted not only that the state should establish schools but that "the civil authorities are under obligation to compel the people to send their children to school."[15]

On the debit side the Reformation era witnessed an intensification of religious intolerance. There seems little choice between Catholics and Protestants in the degree of their detestation for one another and for religious liberty in general. Each religious sect assumed that salvation came through it alone, and all were equally intolerant when they had the power to be so. In the words of Sebastian Castellio (d. 1563), a one-time follower of Calvin who wrote a protest against the execution of Servetus:

Although opinions are almost as numerous as men, nevertheless there is hardly any sect which does not condemn all others and desire to reign alone. Hence arise banishments, chains, imprisonments, stakes, and gallows and this miserable rage to visit daily penalties upon those who differ from the mighty about matters hitherto unknown, for so many centuries disputed, and not yet cleared up.[16]

How can we call ourselves Christians, Castellio asked in effect, if we do not imitate Christ's clemency and mercy?

O Creator and King of the world, dost Thou see these things? Art Thou become so changed, so cruel, so contrary to Thyself? When Thou wast on earth none was more mild, more clement, more patient of injury. . . . O blasphemies and shameful audacity of men, who dare to attribute to Christ that which they do by the command and at the instigation of Satan![17]

Unfortunate, too, was the break between the humanists and the Protestants, which began when Luther broke with the Church.

Although both groups wanted to reform the Church by removing its abuses and returning to the practices and faith of early Christianity, Erasmus could say of Luther's revolt: "I laid a hen's egg: Luther hatched a bird of quite different breed."[18] The humanists, in other words, desired reform, not revolution. Furthermore, because they exalted the rationality and innate goodness of man, the humanists disagreed with the strong Protestant emphasis on man's depravity and the necessity of salvation by superhuman means. As Luther saw it, "The human avails more with Erasmus than the divine."[19]

Protestantism and capitalism. The Renaissance had encouraged a new individualism in economic matters, which contributed to a breakdown of the guild system and to the rise of the individual entrepreneur. While

Both Catholics and Protestants were guilty of incredible atrocities in their respective attempts to achieve religious conformity. Processions such as this became common in French cities as members of a "holy league" paraded through the streets seeking out Huguenots to execute for heresy.

Luther continued to accept the medieval concept of the "just price" and the ban against usury (receiving interest on money loaned), with the Calvinists investment of capital and loaning of money became respectable. Calvin encouraged individual enterprise by teaching that a man's career was a "calling" assigned to him by God and success in his calling was a sign of election to salvation. Indeed, it has been asserted that:

Calvin did for the bourgeoisie of the sixteenth century what Marx did for the proletariat of the nineteenth, . . . the doctrine of predestination satisfied the same hunger for an assurance that the forces of the universe are on the side of the elect as was to be assuaged in a different age by the theory of historical materialism. He set their virtues at their best in sharp antithesis with the vices of the established order at its worst, taught them to feel that they were a chosen people, made them conscious of their great destiny in the Providential plan and resolute to realize it.[20]

The business classes were among those that encouraged the revolt from Rome; we can now see that they were also among those that gained most by it.

Union of religion and politics. In many cases the religious division of Europe followed political lines. In Germany the Peace of Augsburg gave the ruler of each state the right to decide the faith of his subjects, thus controlling the church in his realm. Similarly, rulers of other countries, both Catholic and Protestant, developed national churches, so that Europe was divided religiously into an Anglican Church, a Dutch Church, a Swedish Church, and so on.

In many countries one effect of such division was to strengthen the hand of the king in building a unified state. The authority and prestige of the Protestant monarch was increased as he became the spiritual as well as the political ruler of his subjects. Even in Catholic countries, though the pope remained the spiritual ruler, the Church became national in sentiment, and it was the king rather than the pope who enforced religious conformity among his subjects. Conversely, where the split between Protestants and Catholics was deep, as in the Holy Roman Empire, the power of the central ruler was limited and national unity impeded.

Freedom of religion, as we have noted, was still far from a reality. Persecution flourished, partly because the clash between faiths engendered intolerance but even more because religious uniformity was the ideal of the rulers of the rising national states. Just as he sought to create a uniform system of law and justice throughout his realm, so the strong monarch endeavored to establish a single faith to which his subjects owed complete obedience. An incidental result of this policy was the emigration of religious minorities to areas where they could worship freely, as in the New World.

Political and religious developments continued to be closely related throughout the sixteenth and early seventeenth centuries. In the Religious Wars to be described in the next chapter political duels were superimposed on religious quarrels, resulting in some of the bloodiest and most prolonged warfare in human history. The founder of the Christian religion had given as a primary command, "Thou shalt love thy neighbor as thyself." But there was no brotherhood between Catholic and Protestant nor between political rivals who played on religious antagonisms to serve their own ends.

SUMMARY

The Renaissance represented a new emphasis on man's individuality, an outlook which could not fail eventually to have its impact on religion. An appeal for religious reform came from the northern humanists who criticized ecclesiastical abuses and called for a Christianity based closely upon the New Testament. By means of the printing press, which vastly increased the number of books available, the new ideas spread rapidly throughout Europe. Already beginning to revolt against all institutions which hampered them in their new economic freedom, many men of the middle class were sympathetic to the cry for Church reform. The new spirit also found an ally in the new nationalism and in the growing power of the kings, who were reluctant to be thwarted by any force, even the Church. When a leader appeared with a religious message in keeping with the spirit of the age, the long bottled-up forces of reform exploded.

Luther's open breach with the Church encouraged such Protestant leaders as Zwingli, Calvin, and other reformers to form their own churches. The essence of the new movements was an emphasis on Biblical authority, a denial of the need for priestly mediation for salvation, and a repudiation of the pope as head of organized religion. After the Protestant Revolt, churches were firmly tied to the political administration of the states. Thus Calvin and Zwingli established theocracies in Geneva and Zurich in Switzerland. In Germany each prince chose between Lutheranism and Catholicism for the religion of his subjects. In the Scandinavian countries the national churches were Lutheran. Without repudiating the basic elements of Catholicism, the English king broke with Rome and assumed the headship of the Anglican Church.

The challenge flung at the Church did not remain unanswered. As the medieval Church had arrested decline by new zealous orders of monks, so once again the Church was invigorated by various new religious brotherhoods and a resurgence of mysticism and morality. Pope Paul III and his successors carried out an energetic program to excise the abuses which had plagued the Church for centuries. Without any compromise with the Protestants, the Council of Trent reaffirmed the fundamental doctrines of the Church. But there was no possibility of the Church reuniting Europe.

Europe was plunged into an epoch of intolerance and bigotry from which it slowly emerged when, after the prolonged and bloody struggles to be described in the next chapter, it became apparent that no one faith could exterminate the others. But if the clock was set back in some ways, in other ways the religious upheaval furthered the transition from a medieval to a modern pattern of life. The revolt from the universal Church shattered the medieval ideal of unity and gave us the religious diversity of the modern world.

SUGGESTIONS FOR READING

H. J. Hillerbrand, **The World of the Reformation*** (Scribner's, 1973) is a fresh interpretation. G. L. Mosse, **The Reformation,*** 3rd ed. (Peter Smith); E. H. Harbison, **The Age of Reformation*** (Cornell); R. H. Bainton, **The Reformation of the Sixteenth Century*** (Beacon); and A. G. Dickens, **Reformation and Society in Sixteenth-Century Europe*** (Harcourt Brace Jovanovich) are all good brief surveys. J. Hurstfield, ed., **The Reformation Crisis*** (Torchbooks) contains brief, perceptive essays by noted scholars on major aspects of the Reformation era. See also J. Russell Major, **The Age of the Renaissance and Reformation*** (Lippincott, 1970); and R. L. DeMolen, ed., **The Meaning of the Renaissance and Reformation*** (Houghton Mifflin, 1974). J. Huizenga, **Erasmus and the Age of the Reformation*** (Torchbooks); and E. H. Harbison, **The Christian Scholar in the Age of the Reformation*** (Scribner's) are excellent on the northern humanists' criticism of the Church.

R. H. Bainton, **Here I Stand: A Life of Martin Luther*** (Mentor) is the most readable account. See also E. Erikson, **Young Man Luther*** (Norton); R. Marius, **Luther** (Lippincott, 1974); and E. Schwiebert, **Luther and his Times** (Concordia).

Williston Walker, **John Calvin: The Organiser of Reformed Protestantism*** (Schocken) is probably the best introduction. J. T. McNeill, **The History and Character of Calvinism*** (Galaxy) is a standard work. See also E. W. Monter, **Calvin's Geneva*** (Krieger, 1975); and J. Ridley, **John Knox** (Oxford, 1968).

A. G. Dickens, **The English Reformation*** (Schocken); and T. M. Parker, **The English Reformation to 1558*** (Oxford) are excellent surveys.

On the "left wing" of Protestantism, see George H. Williams, **The Radical Reformation** (Westminster, 1962); and N. Cohn, **The Pursuit of the Millennium,*** rev. ed. (Galaxy).

A. G. Dickens, **The Counter Reformation*** (Harcourt Brace Jovanovich, 1969) is brief and richly illustrated. A sympathetic Catholic account is P. Janelle, **The Catholic Reformation** (Christian Classics). See also R. Ridolfi, **The Life of Girolamo Savonarola** (Greenwood); and J. Brodrick, **The Origin of the Jesuits** (Greenwood, 1976).

On the effects of the religious upheaval see R. H. Tawney, **Religion and the Rise of Capitalism*** (Mentor); R. Kingdon and R. Linder, eds., **Calvin and Calvinism: Sources of Democracy?*** (Heath, 1970); H. Kamen, **The Rise of Toleration*** (McGraw-Hill, 1967); E. Troeltsch, **Protestantism and Progress: A Historical Study of the Relation of Protestantism to the Modern World*** (Beacon); and E. W. Monter, **European Witchcraft*** (Wiley, 1969).

*Indicates a less expensive paperbound edition.

CHAPTER 15

Power Politics
and the New Diplomacy:
1500-1650

The Strife of States and Kings

INTRODUCTION. By acquiring a historical perspective we can do much to illuminate today's events and problems and bring them into focus. The period from 1500 to 1650 is particularly significant; it can serve as a laboratory in which we can watch the genesis and development of the statecraft of modern times.

The central factor in this troubled period was the rise of the competitive state system, involving the actions of independent and sovereign nations. These budding nations exhibited three fundamental features that contrasted sharply with the characteristics the same territories had possessed in earlier, feudal times: they had strong and effective central governments, their citizens displayed increased national consciousness, and their rulers claimed sovereignty—that is, supreme power within the boundaries of their own states. As we shall see in this chapter, these states were expansionist and aggressive, taking every opportunity to grow more powerful at the expense of weaker nations.

The decline of the medieval papacy and the religious revolt in the sixteenth century ended the Church's role as the arbiter of right and justice in disputes between secular rulers. The rulers of the sovereign states were thus completely free and untrammeled in the arena of international politics. Would one state be able to dominate all the rest? Would there be varying degrees of power among states without any one becoming supreme? Would these independent and sovereign nations be able to establish a pattern of cooperation, ensuring thereby a measure of peace and political amity in the western world? These fundamental questions were answered in Europe between 1500 and 1650. And the way in which they were an-swered set the pattern of international relations from that day to this.

The one hundred fifty years following 1500 are among the bloodiest and most complex in European history. The story of these years is chiefly one of battles, alliances, and treaties —in a word, drum-and-trumpet history. Yet running through the wars and complexities of this period two major threads can be discerned: the emergence of the modern diplomatic technique of the "balance of power" as a means of providing some degree of equilibrium to the new European state system, and the rise and fall of Spain as the dominant power in Europe.

THE COMPETITIVE STATE SYSTEM EMERGES

Sovereignty replaces suzerainty. Both the medieval ideal of universal empire and Church and the medieval actuality of decentralized feudalism were undermined by the rise of strong monarchs who defied popes and put down rebellious nobles. The century before 1500 had witnessed much disorder, civil conflict, and war; more and more, people looked to their kings to provide the state with a measure of stability and security. Rulers also took an active part in stimulating the economy of their nations, and in return they obtained from the bourgeoisie larger revenues which they used to expand administrative bureaus and government services. Of great importance was the fact that kings could now afford to hire soldiers for standing armies—monarchs were no longer feudal suzerains dependent upon the irregularly available feudal forces. Moreover, the king's army could easily squelch the retainers of a rebellious noble. Thus the power once distributed throughout the feudal pyramid was concentrated in the hands of the ruler.

The theory of centralized, unchallenged authority—that is, sovereignty—was given its first comprehensive expression by a French lawyer and university professor, Jean Bodin (1530-1596). Dismayed by the disorders of the religious wars in France (see p. 335), Bodin attacked both the feudal idea of contract and the universalism of empire and Church in his work *Concerning Public Affairs.* He supported the power of the monarch and his right of sovereignty, which he defined as "unlimited power over citizens and subjects, unrestrained by law."[1] According to Bodin, the king was free of all restraint save some rather shadowy limitation exercised by God and divine law.

The advent of power politics. Equipped with a standing army, royal courts, and new sources of revenue and backed by the growing support of the bourgeoisie, a European monarch was to a great extent master of his own state by the sixteenth century. And, equally significant, he was his own master in foreign affairs. The Church was no longer an international arbiter, and the factionalism of the Protestant Reformation was soon to reduce appreciably the Church's claim to universal influence. The international arena now consisted of a number of free agents who could keep what they could defend and take what they wanted if they had sufficient force. A nation-state depended for survival on the exercise of its power, and war was the chief instrument at hand. Thus statecraft became the politics of power, and the competitive state system emerged.

The rise of modern diplomacy. The development of the competitive state system gave rise to the practice of modern diplomacy. Rulers needed to be informed about the plans and policies of their rivals; states fearful of attack from stronger foes had to seek out allies; and, after wars had been fought, agreements between victor and vanquished required negotiations.

Medieval popes customarily sent envoys to reside at royal courts, but modern diplomatic practice had its real birth among the fiercely independent city-states of northern Italy. The republic of Venice—"the school and touchstone of ambassadors"—was particularly active; its authorities maintained diplomatic archives and sent their representatives throughout Europe with elaborate instructions. To act as a safeguard against poisoning, trusted cooks were part of a diplomat's retinue, but ambassadors' wives were forbidden to accompany their husbands on diplomatic missions for fear they might divulge state secrets. About 1455 the first permanent embassy in history was sent to Genoa by the duke of Milan. Within a short time most of the important nations of the day followed suit and posted representatives in European capitals.

On many occasions the new diplomacy encouraged negotiation and prevented war. Diplomatic methods so often involved deceit and treachery, however, that negotiations often fanned rather than diminished the fires of international hostility. A seventeenth-century Englishman defined an ambassador as "an honest man sent to lie abroad for the commonwealth."[2] Diplomacy during the past three hundred years often has done little to refute this definition.

Balance-of-power politics. One of the most important achievements of the new diplomacy was the technique known as the "balance of power," whereby a coalition of states could checkmate the swollen power of one or more rival states and thereby restore equilibrium. Balance-of-power politics then and later aimed not so much at preventing war as at preserving the sovereignty and independence of individual states from threatened or actual aggression. Yet as international relations more and more took the form of alignments aimed at preserving the balance of power, a sense of the interdependence of the European state system developed. The strong movement toward European unity in our day is the latest manifestation of this sense of interdependence.

The sixteenth century was the formative period for the behavior pattern of modern nations in international affairs. Unrestrained by religious or ethical scruples, the sovereign governments were about to begin an era of international strife with the quest for power as their only guide to success. With disunited Italy as a pawn in the game, the counters on the chessboard began to move.

ITALY: CASE STUDY IN POWER POLITICS

Charles VIII and the Italian Wars. Because of Louis XI's success as a statemaker (see p. 272), his son Charles VIII (1483-1498) entertained grandiose notions of imitating the exploits of Hannibal and Charlemagne by invading Italy, conquering Naples, and eventually wresting Constantinople from the Turks. In 1494 Charles crossed the Alps at the head of thirty thousand well-trained troops and initiated the Italian Wars that were to last intermittently until 1559. At first the expedition was little more than a holiday for the French. Charles' cavalry, pikemen, and light, quick-firing cannon won easy victories, and he soon took possession of Naples.

This quick conquest alarmed the rulers who had previously acquiesced to Charles' plan. Ferdinand of Spain suspected that Charles might next try to conquer the Spanish possession of Sicily, and the Holy Roman emperor became uneasy at the prospect of French dominance in Italy. In addition, Venice feared for its independence and took the lead in forming a league which also included the Papal States, the Holy Roman Empire, and Spain. Called the Holy League, it was the first important example of a coalition of states formed to preserve the balance of power in Europe. Its armies drove Charles out of Italy in 1495, thus halting French designs on the peninsula for the moment.

Machiavelli's works, which were translated into several different languages, had tremendous impact all over Europe.

cial in the Florentine republic. Outraged at the cavalier manner in which invaders had smashed their way into his beloved Italy, Machiavelli mourned his native land as being

more a slave than the Hebrews, more a servant than the Persians, more scattered than the Athenians; without head, without government; defeated, plundered, torn asunder, overrun; subject to every sort of disaster.[4]

Machiavelli's wide acquaintance with the unprincipled politics of the early Italian Wars produced his cynical and ruthless attitude toward men and politics. *The Prince*— one of a half-dozen volumes that have helped form western political thought—was written as a guide for an audacious leader who would use any means to win and hold power, free Italy from invaders, and end Italian disunity. A realist who wanted his leader-statesman to understand the political facts of life as they had been operating in Europe, Machiavelli wrote:

A prudent ruler . . . cannot and should not observe faith when such observance is to his disadvantage and the causes that made him give his promise have vanished. If men were all good, this advice would not be good, but since men are wicked and do not keep their promises to you, you likewise do not have to keep yours to them. Lawful reasons to excuse his failure to keep them will never be lacking to a prince.[5]

Machiavelli did not, of course, invent the precepts of ruthlessness in politics. Rulers had dishonored treaties and used force to attain their ends before *The Prince* was written. What Machiavelli did was to accept the politics of his day without any false illusions. He gave his prince many suggestions for survival and conquest in the brutal world of unrestrained power.

In the actions of all men, and especially those of princes, where there is no court to which to appeal, people think of the outcome. A prince needs only to conquer and to maintain his position. The means he has used will always be judged honorable and will be praised by everybody, because the crowd is always caught by appearance and by the outcome of events, and the crowd is all there is in the world. . . .[6]

End of the first phase of the Italian Wars. Following the death of Charles VIII in 1498, his successor, Louis XII, invaded Italy. The counters again moved on the chessboard: alliances were made and then broken, pledges went unhonored, and allies were deserted. Ferdinand of Spain offers a particularly good example of duplicity and treachery. Louis XII accused Ferdinand of cheating him on at least two occasions. Hearing this, Ferdinand scoffed: "He lies, the drunkard; I have deceived him more than ten times."[3]

In the first phase of the Italian Wars— which ended in 1513 with the French again ejected from Italy—one can see the new power politics at work, without benefit of rules and indeed without benefit of any moral or religious scruples. The only important objectives were glory, power, and wealth. In attaining these objectives "necessity knows no law," as Renaissance lawyers liked to observe. The conflict over Italy clearly prophesied the mode of future relations among modern sovereign states.

Machiavelli and Machiavellian politics. The primer for diplomacy and power politics was written by Niccolò Machiavelli (1469-1527), historian, playwright, and offi-

Although "Machiavellian politics" is generally a term of condemnation, it should be noted that Machiavelli had an idealistic end in view: to "bring good to the mass of the people of the land" of Italy.[7]

EUROPEAN EMPIRE OR SOVEREIGN STATES?

Charles v. The manner in which the rulers of Europe practiced power politics is shown clearly by the events in Europe during the first half of the sixteenth century, a period often referred to as the Age of Charles v.

Charles' grandfather, Maximilian I, Archduke of Austria and Holy Roman emperor, had added the Netherlands and Franche-Comté to his realm by marrying Mary of Burgundy. (Franche-Comté was that part of Burgundy not seized by Louis XI; see p. 272). Maximilian's son (Charles' father) had married a daughter of Ferdinand and Isabella of

Spain. This calculated policy of dynastic marriages was to elevate the Austrian Hapsburgs to a position no ruler since Charlemagne had held. Following his father's death in 1506, Charles became ruler of the Netherlands; in 1516 his maternal grandfather, Ferdinand, bequeathed him Spain and its overseas empire and Naples and Sicily. The death of his other grandfather, Maximilian, gave him Austria and left vacant the throne of the Holy Roman Empire, to which Charles was elected in 1519 as Emperor Charles v.

Charles' efforts in protecting his dispersed territories, together with his dream of restoring royal authority and religious unity in Germany, led many of his contemporaries to believe that he sought to dominate all of Europe. Although he was essentially conservative and moderate, Charles found himself with too many irons in the fire; he was constantly frustrating plots, crushing rebellions, and repelling invasions in his many dominions.

EUROPE IN THE EARLY 16TH CENTURY

- Holdings of Charles V, 1520
- Acquired by Ferdinand, Brother of Charles, 1526
- Holdings of Henry VIII of England
- Holdings of French Kings
- Suleiman's Empire
- Holy Roman Empire

Two prominent kings on the European chessboard were Francis I (left, portrait by Jean Clouet) of France and Henry VIII (right, portrait by Hans Holbein) of England.

Charles' problems were inextricably connected with the activities of Francis I of France, Henry VIII of England, and Suleiman, ruler of the Ottoman empire. Out of the interplay of their rivalries unfolded the bloody drama of the first half of the sixteenth century.

New moves on the chessboard. The basic cause of Franco-Hapsburg rivalry was the fact that Charles' possessions encircled the realm of Francis I (1515-1547). In 1515, just before Charles V came into his inheritance, Francis invaded Italy, occupied Milan, and so set the stage for the renewal of the Italian Wars. Across the English Channel, Henry VIII followed the events closely, aiming to use his state, with its small population of 2,500,000, as a counterweight in the Franco-Hapsburg rivalry. Believing Francis to be militarily stronger than Charles, Henry allied himself with the Hapsburg emperor in order to check French power.

The test of strength began as Charles' forces drove the French from Milan. Francis soon recaptured it, but at the battle of Pavia (1525) the French were defeated and Francis was taken prisoner. Realizing that he had

miscalculated, Henry VIII executed a sudden about-face, deserting Charles and supporting France and a coalition of lesser powers against the Hapsburgs. This use of England's power to equalize the strength of Continental rivals is a spectacular example of what now became the cornerstone of English foreign policy. Time and again in modern history, England has employed balance-of-power diplomacy to maintain European equilibrium.

Suleiman, ruler of the Turks. The Ottoman empire, which reached the height of its power under Suleiman the Magnificent (1520-1566), was far stronger than any European state. The outstanding feature of its efficient administrative and military system was the dominant role played by slaves. Although Christians were granted a separate religious and civil status under the leadership of their bishops, every five years between 2,000 and 12,000 Christian boys from the ages of ten to fifteen were enslaved and brought to Constantinople. There they were converted to Islam and trained to enter the administration, where even the post of grand vizier was open to them, or the army. In the latter instance they served as Janissaries, the elite 12,000-man core of the Turkish standing army, who were fanatical in their devotion to Islam.

The powerful Ottoman empire was still expanding. Suleiman's predecessor had given Europe a respite by turning eastward to conquer Syria and Egypt, but Suleiman resumed the advance westward. With the European states politically and religiously at odds, Suleiman faced no concerted resistance. In 1521 he captured Belgrade, the key fortress of the Hungarian frontier, and in 1526 on the plain of Mohacs the Janissary infantry crushed the cavalry of the Hungarian magnates. The Hungarian king and many of his magnates were killed, and Suleiman moved on to plunder Buda without organized resistance.

The king who perished at Mohacs had ruled both Hungary and Bohemia. Terrified by the prospect of new Turkish attacks, both the Bohemians and the Hungarians offered their vacant thrones to Ferdinand, brother-in-law of the dead king and brother of Charles v. Since most of Hungary had been occupied by the Turks, Ferdinand's rule extended only over the northwest portion of that country. Thus a Turkish victory placed the destiny of both Hungary and Bohemia in the hands of the Hapsburgs and established the Turks as a threat on Charles' Austrian borders.

Religion and politics on the chessboard. Following his release from captivity in 1526, after making promises he had no intention of keeping, Francis I decided upon an alliance with Suleiman. The enemies of the French king protested loudly against this "unholy alliance," but power politics took precedence over religion in both Paris and Constantinople.

Indirectly, the Turks aided the Protestant cause in Germany. In 1529 Suleiman's armies besieged Vienna, but supply difficulties and Hapsburg resistance forced the attackers to retire. To deal with the Turkish threat, Charles, who had been planning measures against the Lutherans, was forced to arrange a truce with the Protestant princes to gain their support against the Turks.

Suleiman now turned to the Mediterranean where Tunisia and Algeria became Ottoman vassal states and bases for Turkish pirates, known as corsairs, who preyed on Christian shipping and raided the coasts of Spain and Italy. The strength that Charles might have amassed to crush the French monarchy was diverted to his besieged lands bordering on the Mediterranean. A truce in 1544 halted the French-Hapsburg struggle, and Charles could at last concentrate his efforts on the German states, where in 1546 the Lutheran struggle flared into civil war. With France aiding the Lutherans and the Catholic princes

King Sapor of Persia Humiliating Emperor Valerian, School of Antwerp, ca. 1515-1525, oil on panel, 14$\frac{9}{16}$ × 11$\frac{1}{4}$ inches, 1934.64 (formerly believed to be a portrait of Emperor Charles V and formerly attributed to Cornelisz).

giving only half-hearted support to Charles lest he become powerful enough to dominate them, the Schmalkaldic War ended in 1555 with the compromise Peace of Augsburg (see p. 311). The Lutheran faith received official sanction, and Charles was thwarted in his cherished aim of restoring religious unity to Germany.

In 1556, five months after the Peace of Augsburg, the weary and discouraged emperor retired to a monastery. He turned over the Hapsburg possessions in central Europe to his brother Ferdinand, who was elected emperor, and gave Spain, the Netherlands, and his Italian possessions to his son Philip. Thereafter two Hapsburg dynasties, one Spanish and the other Austrian, ruled in Europe. A legend has it that Charles spent the two remaining years of his life trying to make several clocks keep exactly the same time—apparently an allegory suggesting that he was faced with so many problems that he could never settle all of them.

Significance for modern times. The eventful Age of Charles v had laid down much of the political and religious foundation for modern Europe:

1) It had been decided by force of arms that no single state was to dominate all of Europe. The balance of power was maintained.

2) German and Italian national growth was further stunted. Italy had been a battleground since 1494, and when the Italian Wars finally ended in 1559, Milan and Naples were Spanish possessions and Spain was to dominate Italy for nearly two hundred years.

3) Charles' wars with France and the Turks prevented him from applying pressure on the Lutherans and so saved the Reformation in Germany.

4) The Peace of Augsburg confirmed France's hold on the bishoprics of Metz, Toul, and Verdun in Lorraine, which the French had occupied during the Schmalkaldic War. French expansion toward the Rhine had begun, with momentous consequences for the future.

5) The advance of Ottoman power in Europe meant that Turkish control over the Balkans was handed down to later European statesmen as an explosive legacy. The alliance of France with Turkey, which also gave the French trading rights and a protectorate over the Holy Places in the Near East, became an enduring though irregular factor in European diplomacy.

6) The history of the first half of the sixteenth century made it quite clear that diplomacy a la Machiavelli was to be the order of the day. Deceit, treachery, surprise attacks, and broken promises were written into the record.

FAITH AND NATIONALITY IN WESTERN EUROPE

Era of the Religious Wars. While the threat of Hapsburg domination of Europe had been lessened after Charles v divided his lands, the Continent was still to witness convulsive rivalries and a century more of warfare. The period from roughly the middle of the sixteenth century to the middle of the seventeenth century is often referred to as the Era of the Religious Wars, for the religious issues which flamed forth from the Protestant upheaval—particularly that most international form of Protestantism, Calvinism—colored every political conflict.

Zenith of the Spanish state. The Era of the Religious Wars began in 1556 when Philip II, the son of Charles v, became king of Spain. Several factors made it seem that Philip's future would be impressive and successful. First, when his uncle Ferdinand received the Hapsburg Austrian lands together with the imperial crown of the Holy Roman Empire, Philip was freed of the political and religious complexities in middle Europe; that is, he had no "German problem." Second, the end of the Franco-Hapsburg wars over Italy in 1559 was followed by religious wars in France (see p. 335), leaving Spain without a rival on the Continent. Third, Philip inherited a new empire overseas which was more lucrative and more easily administered than his father's empire in the Germanies had been. From the New World came untold treasure to enrich the Hapsburg coffers at Madrid (see Chapter 18).

In addition to the riches of the Americas

and the Spanish possessions in Europe— the Netherlands, Franche-Comté, Naples, Sicily, and Milan—Philip had the best army of the time. The mercenary armies employed by other states could not rival the training and discipline of the native Spanish infantry. The dread of Spanish power caused people to say, as they had under Charles v, that "When Spain moves, the whole world trembles."

During his long reign (1556-1598) Philip sought three basic goals: to make his royal power absolute in all his possessions, to combat heresy and strengthen Catholicism, and to extend Spain's influence. Under Charles v the traditional parliaments, or Cortes, of Castile and Aragon had been largely superseded by a number of royal councils staffed by a well-trained civil service. Building on this foundation, Philip erected a centralized system of government in which every decision rested with the king and in which all agencies of government were subordinate to his will.

Philip was extremely devout and saw no distinction between the good of the Church and the interest of the Spanish state. At home the Spanish Inquisition both ferreted out heretics and strengthened royal power. Abroad, by championing the Counter Reformation Philip also justified his interference in the political and religious conflicts of other European nations.

One of Philip's great achievements was the uniting of the Iberian peninsula under the Spanish crown. In 1580 the direct line of the Portuguese royal family died out, and Philip claimed the throne through his mother, a Portuguese princess. When the Portuguese refused to accept him as their ruler, Philip invaded the country and seized the throne. The annexation of Portugal and its vast colonial empire brought new riches to Madrid from Brazil, Africa, and the East Indies.

Crusade in the Mediterranean. After Suleiman's death in 1566 the Turkish advance in the Mediterranean continued, and in 1570 the Turks captured the Venetian island of Cyprus, the last Christian outpost in the area. At the pope's urging, Christian Europe turned to Philip, the champion of the Catholic faith, to block Turkish expansion.

A Holy League was formed to raise a great fleet and destroy Ottoman naval power in the Mediterranean. Spanish and Venetian warships, together with the smaller squadrons of Genoa and the Papal States, made up a fleet of over two hundred vessels which was joined by volunteers from all over Europe. In 1571 the League's fleet and the Turkish navy clashed at Lepanto, on the western side of Greece. The outcome was a decisive victory for Christian Europe; Ottoman sea power was crushed, never to be restored as a major threat to Christendom. Lepanto is often considered the last crusade.

Unrest and revolt in the Netherlands. The conquest of Portugal and the defeat of the Turks were signal victories for Philip, but the specter of failure stalked him in the Netherlands. The seventeen provinces of the Low Countries (which included today's Holland, Belgium, and Luxemburg) had been restive under Charles v, who had imposed heavy taxes to help finance his wars. Yet he had continued to enjoy the confidence of the Netherlanders, who regarded him as one of themselves because he had been born in the city of Ghent. But the Netherlanders did not feel the same about Philip, whom they distrusted as a foreigner. Seeking to make his rule absolute in the Netherlands, Philip excluded the local nobility from the administration, maintained an army of occupation, and introduced the Inquisition to stop the advance of Calvinism.

Calvinism continued to spread, however, and in 1566 a series of violent anti-Catholic and anti-Spanish riots broke out. "The Council of Troubles"—soon dubbed "The Council of Blood"—was set up to stamp out treason and heresy. During the ensuing reign of terror some 8,000 were slain, 30,000 were deprived of their property, and 100,000 fled the country. At the same time Philip proposed new and oppressive taxes, including a 10 percent sales tax, which antagonized most Netherlanders, Catholic as well as Protestant. Under the Dutch leader, William the Silent of the House of Orange, discontent flared into open revolt in 1568.

In the first years of the revolt the puny forces commanded by the tenacious William the Silent were dispersed again and again.

The Dutch turned to the sea to outfit privateers to prey on Spanish shipping. Then in 1576 the incident of the Spanish Fury electrified the entire Netherlands. Usually well-disciplined, the badly fed and unpaid Spanish soldiers mutinied and marched on Antwerp where they burned public buildings and murdered seven thousand citizens. The calamity settled the local differences between the seventeen provinces that had prevented them from making a concerted effort against Spanish tyranny. The Pacification of Ghent, which the provincial representatives signed in 1576, declared that all Spanish soldiers must be expelled from the land, after which the representative body, the Estates-General, would govern the country.

Unfortunately for the rebels' cause, the seventeen provinces did not long maintain the unity manifested in the Pacification of Ghent. The Spaniards were able to take advantage of the differences between the Protestant provinces in the north and the predominantly Catholic provinces in the south. Employing a combination of diplomacy and force, the Spanish succeeded in reuniting the ten southern provinces with Spain in 1579. The Dutch in the north, however, continued to fight on, and in 1581 the Estates-General of the Dutch United Provinces (also called Holland because of the preeminence of that province with its flourishing city of Amsterdam) issued a declaration of independence. One of its provisions stated:

The people were not created by God for the sake of the Prince . . . but, on the contrary, the Prince was made for the good of the people.[8]

The declaration of 1581 set the model for later declarations justifying revolution in England, France, and the English colonies in America. It also established another landmark in modern history by decreeing freedom of worship for the large Catholic minority in the new nation. The stability of the state had become a greater concern than religious conformity.

Three years later the cause of Dutch freedom was placed in serious jeopardy when William the Silent was assassinated by a young Catholic fanatic and the Spanish stepped up their efforts to destroy the new republic. At this critical moment Elizabeth I of England, fearing that Philip planned to use the Netherlands as a base for an invasion of England, rushed troops to the aid of the United Provinces. The destruction of Philip's Armada by England in 1588 (see p. 334) further weakened the ability of Spain to crush the Dutch.

In 1609 a twelve years' truce was signed, which recognized the partition of the Netherlands along the line where the fighting had stopped. Not until the end of the Thirty

The 1566 rioting in the Netherlands was instigated by mobs of Calvinists who invaded Catholic churches, toppling images, smashing windows, and looting valuable articles. The Spanish reacted to such riots with ferocity.

Year's War in 1648 did the Dutch Republic gain from the Spanish formal recognition of its independence. The ten southern provinces, however, remained in Hapsburg hands and were known first as the Spanish Netherlands and then after 1713 as the Austrian Netherlands. In 1830 they achieved independence as the state of Belgium.

The English throne: Protestant or Catholic? On more than one occasion during the reign of Philip II, it seemed that England would come under Spanish domination. In 1554, two years before he ascended the throne of Spain, Philip had married Mary Tudor, the older daughter of Henry VIII. Mary adored her husband, and as queen she was strongly influenced by him, although he had no official status in the governing of England. After a brief reign Mary died, and in 1558 her half-sister, Elizabeth I, assumed the throne.

Elizabeth's disputed succession provided the next occasion for possible Spanish domination of England. The daughter of Henry by his second wife, Anne Boleyn, Elizabeth was considered illegitimate by English Catholics, who recognized only Henry's first marriage as valid. Furthermore, in the eyes of Catholic Europe, the rightful heir to the throne was the great-granddaughter of Henry VII, Mary Stuart, Queen of Scotland.

Brought up in France as a Catholic, Mary had wed the heir to the French throne and reigned for two years as queen of France. After the death of her husband, she returned to her native Scotland, where her French mother had been ruling as regent with the aid of French troops. Mary found Scotland in the hands of rebellious nobles and vigorous Protestant preachers under the Calvinist reformer John Knox (see p. 316). A widow of eighteen, famous for her charm, beauty, and grace, Mary proceeded to alienate her subjects by a series of blunders: she was too frivolous for her straitlaced Calvinistic subjects, she was unsuccessful in concealing her pro-Catholic sympathies, and, finally, she was accused of being involved in the sordid murder of her weakling husband, Lord Darnley. The Scottish Presbyterians revolted, and in 1568 Mary was forced to seek refuge with her cousin Elizabeth in England. There,

During the brief marriage of Philip II of Spain and Queen Mary of England, it appeared that Spain might come to dominate the island kingdom.

her Catholicism and her good claim to Elizabeth's throne made her an unwelcome guest, potentially dangerous to the Tudor monarch and to English Protestantism.

For his part, Philip had no compunctions about plotting to place Mary on the throne of England. Philip's ambassador in London became the center of a web of intrigue.

The island fortress: obstacle to Spanish hegemony. As Philip became the chief enemy of Protestant England, Elizabeth gradually emerged as the foremost obstacle to Spanish power. Unlike the impetuous Mary Stuart, who was often the blind instrument of her emotions, Elizabeth was realistic, calculating, and thoroughly Machiavellian. As the Spanish ambassador wrote to Philip:

. . . what a pretty business it is to treat with this woman who I think must have a hundred thousand devils in her body, notwithstanding that she is forever telling me that she yearns to be a nun and to pass her life in prayer.[9]

Elizabeth resorted to every subterfuge and trick available to her in the duel with Philip of Spain. Using her sex as a diplomatic weap-

A sixteenth-century Dutch drawing shows the execution of Mary, Queen of Scots. The inscription in old Dutch on the drawing reads, "On the VIII of February, Mary Stuart, Queen of Scots, fervent Roman Catholic, was beheaded, having tried to cause much unrest (and) to make herself mistress of England, which was completely proved against her by the Council of the Parliament."

on, she carried on long flirtations with the brothers of the French king, thereby helping to prevent an alliance between France and Spain. In addition she sent covert assistance to the Dutch, aware that their rebellion was sapping Spanish strength.

Elizabeth also secretly encouraged her sea captains to prey upon Spanish shipping and to attack the rich Spanish settlements in the New World. The most famous of Elizabethan Sea Dogs, Sir Francis Drake, sailed into the Pacific, plundered the western coast of Spanish America, and, after circumnavigating the globe, arrived in England with a hold full of gold and silver.

Aware of Elizabeth's duplicity, Philip planned to gain control over England by placing Mary Stuart on the English throne. But a plot against Elizabeth's life, in which Mary was obliquely implicated, was discovered. Parliament was convinced that as long as Mary lived, Elizabeth's life would be endangered, and therefore, in 1587, Elizabeth signed Mary's death warrant. But in a sense Mary had not failed. She had left behind in Scotland a son, James, who was destined to become the common monarch of England and Scotland, not by conspiracy or force but by common consent.

Philip and Elizabeth at war. After the discovery of the plot against her life, Elizabeth sought to hinder Philip's plans by openly sending arms and soldiers to the Netherlands, by aiding the Protestant cause during the French religious wars, and by authorizing Drake to destroy Spanish shipping. Philip meanwhile was planning his "great enterprise"—an invasion of England, blessed by the pope, to gain the kingdom for himself and wean its people from heresy.

Philip's strategy was to have a fleet of 130 ships, called by contemporaries the "Invincible Armada," join a large Spanish army in the Netherlands and then land this force on the coast of England. The Dutch, however, prevented the rendezvous by blocking the main ports in the Low Countries, and Philip's designs were ruined completely when the Elizabethan Sea Dogs trounced the Armada in the English Channel. The small, swift English ships outmaneuvered the bulky Spanish galleons, and a severe storm, the famed "Protestant wind," completed the debacle. The Armada limped home after losing a third of its ships.

The defeat of the Armada meant that England would remain Protestant, that it would soon emerge as a dominant sea power, and that the Dutch rebellion against Spain would succeed. By building new ships, Spain quickly recovered from the material effects of the defeat of the Armada, but it never overcame the psychological effects of that disaster. The Spanish people had been told that the Armada was "the most important [enterprise] undertaken by God's Church for many hundreds of years. . . . we are defending the high reputation of our King and lord, and of our nation; . . . and simultaneously our peace, tranquility and repose."[10] The optimism engendered by Spain's great past achievements soon vanished; in the words of a modern scholar, "If any one year marks the division between the triumphant

In July 1588 the English completely routed Spain's "Invincible Armada."

Spain of the first two Hapsburgs and the defeatist, disillusioned Spain of their successors, that year is 1588."[11]

The Wars of Religion in France. Soon after France and Spain ended their long conflict over Italy in 1559, France underwent one of the most terrible civil conflicts in its history. Persecution of Protestants had been sporadic under Francis I (d. 1547) and his son Henry II (d. 1559), who were more fearful of the Hapsburgs than of heresy, but by 1560 the Calvinist Huguenots numbered about one million out of a population of sixteen million. Huguenots were numerous in the cities, except in Paris, but the most influential element was the 40 to 50 percent of the nobility that had been attracted to Calvinism. The French nobility had long been restless; its numbers were increasing and it was frustrated by the loss of its former military and political preeminence.

Because the three weakling sons of Henry II had no heirs, the Valois line that had ruled France since 1328 (see p. 269) was nearing its end. This situation led to ruthless factional rivalry between two noble houses in France, both of which aspired to the throne. The Bourbons, who espoused Protestantism, had the better claim because they traced their descent from St. Louis, the revered Capetian king of the thirteenth century. Champions of Catholicism were the powerful Guises, who claimed descent from Charlemagne. This was the setting for the series of civil wars, partly religious and partly political, that broke out in 1562.

During this period and until her death in 1589, the most powerful individual in France was Catherine de' Medici, the queen mother. Like her contemporary in London, Queen Elizabeth, Catherine was completely cynical and ruthless in statecraft. Even her youngest son referred to her as "Madame la Serpente." No matter how cruel or base, no technique was beneath her use; one of Catherine's political weapons was "'a flying squadron' of twenty-four maids of honor of high rank and low principles to help her seduce the refractory nobles on both sides."[12]

Determined to maintain the power of her sons, Catherine attempted to steer a middle course and to play one party off against the other. But as the Huguenots grew stronger, she resolved to crush them. Thus Catherine is blamed for the terrible Massacre of St. Bartholomew's Day. At dawn on August 24, 1572, with a signal from the bell of the Palace of Justice in Paris, the Catholics fell upon their Protestant rivals, and ten thousand Huguenots were slain.

The massacre did not destroy Huguenot power, however, and civil conflict continued. A new phase began in 1585, when Philip II entered the war on the side of the Catholics. He hoped first to extirpate Protestantism in France and then to control French policy, thereby gaining valuable support in crushing the Dutch revolt and in conquering England. In 1589, after assassins had eliminated both the Guise pretender and the last weakling Valois ruler, the Protestant Bourbon prince Henry of Navarre became King Henry IV of France by right of succession. Philip determined to crush the new king before he could consolidate his power. At this critical moment Queen Elizabeth intervened by sending Henry five thousand troops which turned the tide in his favor. Realizing that most Frenchmen were Catholic and sensing

that all were weary of civil war, Spanish intervention, and anarchy, Henry decided to place the welfare of France ahead of his own conscience and accepted the faith of Rome. "Paris is well worth a mass," he is supposed to have said, and soon Paris and other cities opened their gates to him. By 1595 the civil war was over and Philip was forced to withdraw his troops.

The Edict of Nantes. Although Henry IV changed his own faith, he sought to protect the liberties of the Huguenot minority in the Edict of Nantes (1598). When both Catholic and Protestant extremists denounced the measure, Henry refused to be intimidated: "I insist upon being obeyed. It is time that we all, having had our fill of war, should learn wisdom by what we have suffered."

The Edict of Nantes followed the example first set by the Dutch Republic of recognizing that more than one religion could be maintained within a state. To guarantee their religious freedom, Henry allowed the Protestants to fortify about a hundred French towns and garrison them with their own troops. As a result, the Huguenots in France constituted virtually a state within a state.

The failure of Philip II. Philip's failure in France was the last of his many setbacks. His final opponent, Henry IV, provided some fitting last words on Philip's hopes for Spanish dominance in Europe: while witnessing the departure of Spanish troops from Paris, Henry called out, "Gentlemen, commend me to your master, but do not come back."

While in the eyes of his Spanish subjects Philip was a wise, moderate, pious, and hardworking monarch, his enemies singled him out as a detestable example of trickery, cruelty, and religious intolerance. Yet Philip was not equal to Elizabeth in duplicity and diplomatic cunning, and it must be remembered that nearly all sixteenth-century European monarchs believed that the relentless persecution of noncomformists was essential to the welfare of the state. Philip's failures cannot be attributed to defects ingrained in his nature but to the fact that, in general, he was less skillful than his opponents in the game of power politics.

Most important, perhaps, is that Philip unwittingly pitted himself against the grow-

A contemporary drawing shows German cannoneers preparing to arm and fire a large mortar during the Thirty Years' War. During this period Gustavus Adolphus developed the tactical use of light and medium-weight artillery to be used in conjunction with infantry in open-field battles against the Hapsburg forces.

ing feelings of nationalism. Patriotism thwarted Philip's ambitions in the Netherlands and in England, and it also contributed to the failure of his intervention in the French religious wars.

Despite Philip's failures, Spain still enjoyed the reputation of being the first power in Europe. Spanish soldiers were the best on the Continent, and Spain's wealth from its vast overseas possessions seemed inexhaustible. Moreover, Spanish writers, scholars, and painters were outstanding; in fact, the last half of the sixteenth century and the first half of the seventeenth are usually regarded as the zenith of Spanish culture.

In the seventeenth century, however, Spanish power rapidly declined. Bad economic policies (see Chapter 18) coupled with continued overexertion in the game of power politics proved too great a burden for a nation of only eight or nine million people. The last of the so-called religious conflicts, the Thirty Years' War (1618-1648), accelerated the decline of Spain and left France the dominant state in Europe.

The issues of the Thirty Years' War. The Peace of Augsburg (see p. 311) failed to bring about a satisfactory religious settlement in the Germanies, and friction continued after 1555. The higher clergy and the princes who thereafter turned Protestant continued to take over Church lands within their jurisdiction. Furthermore, religious toleration for rapidly spreading Calvinism was now a burning issue, since the Peace of Augsburg had recognized only Lutheranism and Catholicism. A final religious factor was the progress being made by the Catholic Counter Reformation in the empire under the leadership of the Jesuits and the Jesuit-educated emperor, the Hapsburg Ferdinand II.

In addition to his deep antipathy toward heretics, Ferdinand wanted a united and subservient empire to strengthen his position in Europe. His desire to reassert imperial authority was opposed by the princes whose own power would remain strong with Germany divided and weak. Even the Catholic princes, who willingly supported Ferdinand as a Catholic leader against the Protestants, were opposed to any strengthening of imperial power. The papacy, too, was often lukewarm in its support, regarding a strong emperor as a threat to the freedom of the Church in Germany and fearing that a too close association with the Hapsburgs would alienate the rulers of other states. Ferdinand could hope for unquestioned support only from his cousin, the Hapsburg king of Spain, who was still considered the most powerful ruler in Europe.

The varied religious and political issues in the empire created an atmosphere of tension in which one slight incident might upset the precarious peace. A prelude to the contest of arms was the formation of a Protestant League of German princes in 1608 and a similar Catholic League in 1609.

Phases of the Thirty Years' War. The complexities of the Thirty Years' War, which soon became an international struggle, can be divided into four phases: (1) Bohemian, (2) Danish, (3) Swedish, and (4) French.

The first battleground was Bohemia, preponderantly Protestant and strongly nationalistic, which had enjoyed a large measure of toleration under its Catholic Hapsburg kings. When Ferdinand withdrew that tolerance on mounting the throne of Bohemia in 1617, he precipitated a rebellion in 1618 which became a general religious war when the Bohemians invited the Calvinist head of the Protestant League to rule them. By the end of the following year Ferdinand had crushed the Bohemians, and his kinsmen, the Spanish Hapsburgs, had defeated the German Protestants supporting the Bohemian insurrection. Protestantism was stamped out in Bohemia, and the Protestant League in Germany was dissolved.

The second phase of the conflict began in 1625 when the Lutheran king of Denmark, who as duke of Holstein (see Reference Map 5) was also a prince of the empire, invaded Germany. The Danes sought not only to champion hard-pressed Protestantism but also to gain additional German territory and to thwart Hapsburg ambitions. However, the Hapsburg armies soon crushed the Danes.

This second defeat of the Protestants threatened to undo the work of the Protestant Reformation and to create a unified Hapsburg-ruled Germany. This prospect drew the leading Lutheran power, Sweden, into the fight in 1630. King Gustavus Adolphus told his people that "the papal deluge is approaching our shores"; he also hoped to acquire territories along Germany's Baltic coast as "guarantees against the emperor." The Swedish king was the founder of a new technique of warfare which stressed discipline, mobility, and morale; in Germany his well-drilled, hymn-singing veterans and mobile cannon quickly scored a series of brilliant victories. But after Gustavus Adolphus was killed in battle, a compromise peace was arranged in 1635.

The peace never went into effect, however, for Cardinal Richelieu, the chief adviser of the French king and the actual head of the government, decided that France would be secure only when the Hapsburgs of Austria and Spain, whose lands ringed France on three sides, had been defeated. Richelieu earlier had given secret aid to the German Protestants, the Danes, and the Swedes; now, in 1635, he came out in the open and the struggle became primarily a dynastic contest between Bourbons and Hapsburgs. The Swedes and the German Protestants kept the Austrian Hapsburg armies busy in Germany while French arms were concentrated against the Spanish Hapsburgs. In 1643 at the battle of Rocroi in the Spanish Netherlands the legend of the invincibility of the Spanish infantry came to an end, and the French turned to the Germanies. Although Richelieu had died in 1642, his successor, Cardinal Mazarin, continued his designs for weakening the power of the Hapsburgs.

The Peace of Westphalia. Peace negotiations began in 1644 without a cease-fire agreement, but they proceeded slowly. The delegates wrangled endlessly over such questions of protocol as who was to enter the conference room first and where they were to sit, and the fortunes of war frequently altered the bargaining power of the rival diplomats. Finally, in 1648, the longest peace negotiation on record ended in a series of treaties collectively known as the Peace of Westphalia. (Spain, however, stubbornly refused to make peace with France until 1659.)

A recapitulation of the various provisions of the peace would be very complex; suffice it to say that France moved closer to the Rhine with the acquisition of much of Alsace; Sweden and the Protestant state of Brandenburg made important territorial gains along Germany's Baltic coast; and Holland and Switzerland—the latter having successfully resisted its Hapsburg overlords since 1291—were granted independence. The Calvinists were given recognition in Germany, and Protestants were allowed to retain the Church lands they had taken before 1624.

The Peace of Westphalia permanently ended Hapsburg dreams of reviving the authority of the emperor in Germany. The sovereignty of the more than three hundred German states was recognized, with each state having the right to coin money, make war, maintain armies, and send diplomatic representatives to foreign courts. Henceforth the Hapsburg emperors worked to form a strong Danubian monarchy out of their varied Austrian, Bohemian, and Hungarian possessions.

The great significance of the Peace of Westphalia was that it symbolized the emergence and victory of the sovereign state which acknowledged no authority higher than its own interests and was prone to assume what Thomas Hobbes three years later called "the position of gladiators." More specifically, the conference established the basic principle underlying the modern state system—the essential equality of all independent sovereign states. It also instituted the diplomatic procedure of convening international congresses in order to settle the problems of war and peace by negotiation.

Thus the struggle against the Hapsburg encirclement of France begun by Francis I against Charles V early in the sixteenth century ended more than a century later. Changes had been wrought in the relative powers of nations. Both England and Holland had become great sea powers, and their commercial prosperity was increasing rapidly. The golden age of Spain was over, and France emerged as the greatest power in Europe. Although reports of devastation, population decline, and cultural retrogression in the Germanies have perhaps been exaggerated, the Thirty Years' War left a grievous legacy and thwarted German progress for a century. But by demonstrating that Protestants and Catholics were unable to exterminate each other, the Thirty Years' War—indeed, the entire Era of the Religious Wars—greatly promoted the cause of religious toleration in Europe.

THE CONTINUING SENSE OF EUROPEAN INTERDEPENDENCE

Proposals for keeping the peace. The irresponsible use of power was the outstanding feature of international politics in the late sixteenth and early seventeenth centuries. But gradually powerful rulers and diplomats realized that frequent wars threatened the growth of European trade and commerce and menaced even the existence of civilized society in the West. We have seen some of the early steps taken to improve international relations—the establishment of consular and diplomatic services, the formation of alignments to preserve the balance of power, and the first use of a general European peace congress to adjust conflicting interests after a great war. In addition, trade agreements and treaties formed the crude beginnings of a system of international law. Although these varied measures all too often had a negligible effect on the continued use of war as the means of settling disputes among nations, they reflect a continuing sense of the interdependence of the European state system—the Concert of Europe, as it would later be called.

The increased destructiveness of modern warfare had aroused the protests of many sixteenth-century humanists—Erasmus, for example, asserted that "war is sweet only to the inexperienced." In the early seventeenth century students of international affairs made some specific recommendations that are of particular interest today.

In 1623, Emeric Crucé, an obscure French monk, published a plan to eliminate war by means of an international organization which, he claimed, would be "useful to all nations, and agreeable to those who have some light of reason and the sentiment of humanity." The central idea in his work was that all wars were harmful and their abolition would allow governments to devote themselves to the arts of peace. To this end he proposed that a permanent corps of ambassadors from all over the world be maintained at Venice as an international assembly for the settlement of all disputes through negotiation and arbitration. Crucé acknowledged that his plan for a seventeenth-century "United Nations" was in advance of his time, but added:

I have wished, nevertheless, to leave this testimony to posterity. If it serves nothing, patience. It is a small matter to lose paper and words. I have said and done what was possible for the public good, and some few who read this little book will be grateful to me for it, and will honor me, as I hope, with their remembrance.[13]

Either the first Bourbon monarch, Henry IV, or his chief minister, the Duke of Sully, devised the plan known as the Grand Design, which called for the establishment of a European federal union headed by a council of representatives from all states. The council was to secure disarmament and to control an international police force which would back its decisions by force. Each state was to contribute troops and money according to its strength. Despite its theoretical and utopian character, the Grand Design "shows that at the very moment when the modern national state, centralized within and dividing Europe into mutually hostile camps, emerged from the ruins of medieval unity, the ablest minds realized that eventually a new unity would have to be built out of these distinct entities, a United States of Europe. . . ."[14]

Grotius and international law. A number of European scholars were also at work laying the foundation for a science of international law by developing the principle that the nations formed a community based upon natural law. The first to obtain a hearing outside scholarly circles was Hugo Grotius (1583-1645), a gifted Dutch historian, theologian, practicing lawyer, and diplomat. In 1625 appeared *On the Law of War and Peace*, the work which gained Grotius instant fame and lasting recognition as the founder of international law. "Such a work," he declared, "is all the more necessary because in our day, as in former times, there is no lack of men who view this branch of law with contempt as having no reality outside of an empty name." And he continued:

I have had many and weighty reasons for undertaking to write upon this subject. Throughout the Christian world I observed a lack of restraint in relation to war, such as even barbarous races should be ashamed of; I observed that men rush to arms for slight causes, or no cause at all, and that when arms have once been taken up there is no longer any respect for law, divine or human; it is as if, in accordance with a general decree, frenzy had openly been let loose for the committing of all crimes.[15]

War and Peace are reconciled in the allegorical title page from the 1689 edition of Grotius' *De Jure Belli ac Pacis.* Four years before he wrote this great work, Grotius had escaped from a Dutch prison, where he had been sentenced to life imprisonment as a result of his campaign against the harsh Calvinist doctrine of predestination and for a more liberal regime in his own country, Holland.

Grotius endeavored to set forth a new code of international conduct based not upon the authority of the Church but on what he termed the fundamental idea of the law of nature. The law of nature was in turn founded on the dictates of reason, morality, and justice. If civilization was to endure, Grotius argued, humane considerations should prevail in the councils of the mighty, and rules of conduct binding all men should be established.

More realistic than his contemporaries Crucé and Sully, Grotius did not propose to eliminate war entirely. He sought instead to outlaw "unjust" wars and limit the effects of "just" wars. Wars were justified only to repel invasion or to punish an insult to God. Grotius' appeal fell largely upon deaf ears. Machiavelli's *The Prince* enjoyed more popularity in European palaces than *On the Law of War and Peace.*

SUMMARY

By the middle of the seventeenth century the pattern of politics in western Europe had changed significantly. Gone was the ideal of unity, whether based on empire or on universal Church; and sovereignty had replaced suzerainty. The new monarchies were largely absolute in authority within their own frontiers and free agents in the domain of international affairs. Following the principles of political behavior systematized by Machiavelli, these sovereign states pursued power, prestige, wealth, and security. No moral or religious scruples were allowed to interfere with these objectives. It was considered axiomatic that a nation had no permanent enemies or friends—only permanent interests. This maxim was illustrated by the manner in which alliances based on the new diplomatic technique of balance of power were formed on the European chessboard. We shall see in our study of later eras how the great powers have continued to alter their alliances in deference to the exigencies of the balance of power. It is also noteworthy that since balance-of-power diplomacy was the product of a felt need to preserve the security and independence of the new sovereign states, it

10. Giotto: "The Raising of Lazarus" (c. 1305). In 1300 a wealthy merchant from Padua, Enrico Scrovegni, acquired the ruins of an ancient Roman arena as the site for his palace and chapel. He engaged the Florentine artist, Giotto, to decorate the interior. Giotto painted a series of murals using the fresco technique of applying watercolors to a freshly plastered wall. In this powerful scene,

Christ stands silhouetted against the blue background, calling Lazarus from the dead by a simple gesture of His hand. The scene is composed simply and clearly, divided into blocks of figures by broad diagonals, verticals, and curves. The figures have a three-dimensional quality, and a good sense of balance and depth. The whole work becomes a powerful religious statement.

11. (left) **Michelangelo: "Moses"** (c. 1515). The High Renaissance, more than any other period, developed the idea of artistic genius—of greater creative, even "divine" talent—in a single individual, who, by its possession, stood above the rules governing ordinary men. No one represented this concept more convincingly than Michelangelo—sculptor, painter, architect, and poet, who dominated the period like a colossus. The eight-foot-high statue of Moses, part of a vast sculptural program for the tomb of Julius II, was meant to be viewed from below and to project an awesome force and energy. The idealization and exaggeration of the human form expresses divine presence and conveys the sculptor's own deep religious feelings. **12.** (above) **George Gower: "Armada Portrait of Elizabeth I"** (c. 1588). This painting which is attributed to George Gower, a fashionable portrait painter in London, is probably the most magnificent Elizabethan costume portrait in three-quarter length, a popular style promoted to glorify the aging queen. It is a full-blown costume piece, using brilliant mosaics of color, and emphasizing delicate lines and details. The result is a distinctive style more medieval than Renaissance in origin. The details of the Spanish Armada prior to and after its defeat commemorate the stunning English victory.

13. Caravaggio: "The Lute Player" (c. 1595). Michelangelo de Caravaggio, one of the masters of the Italian Baroque, was a revolutionary artist who directed much of his work against the serenity of the Renaissance and the studied artificiality of his Mannerist contemporaries. Although a large portion of his work was in a religious vein, he also painted many secular subjects. Caravaggio was stubborn and often egocentric; he managed to scandalize the artistic Italian world by claiming that classical art and the great masters were not suffcient examples for the artist and that the natural world was the best teacher. "The Lute Player" is among the works Caravaggio produced while in Rome whose subjects are young boys ornamented by flowers, fruit, and musical instruments. Every detail of its story reveals the strength of its composition, with its sensitivity to color, accentuated by the severity of the surrounding outlines, and the emphasis on the central figure in relation to a neutral background.

reflected an early recognition of the interdependence of the European state system. The present-day movement toward European unity can be viewed as the latest expression of this recognition.

Power politics between 1500 and 1650 developed amid complex happenings, especially the so-called Religious Wars. Just what was religion and what politics was often difficult to determine, especially since religion was often used as a cover for political intrigue. With Philip II of Spain, for example, Catholic conviction appropriately coincided with Spanish national interests; to champion the Catholic Church was, in Philip's mind, to build a strong Spain. In other instances expediency, not religious principles, governed international politics: witness Francis I's alliance with the Turks and Richelieu's support of the German Protestants.

The revolt of the Dutch from Spain was the first large-scale example before 1650 of a successful countertrend to the increasing centralization of the monarch's power. The establishment of the Dutch Republic in the name of people's rights foreshadows the later and more famous revolts against absolutism which would establish constitutional government in England during the last half of the seventeenth century and in North America and France by the end of the eighteenth.

In the survey of European affairs in this chapter, two opposing principles were discussed: one, the right of a state to conduct its foreign affairs—even to waging war—without hindrance; the other, the concept that nations should accept some limitation of their freedom of action in international affairs. Ever since the early seventeenth century, when scholars began to think of limiting wars and the need for international law, national sovereignty and internationalism have been in competition. Sovereignty has gotten the best of it by far. But we will see that since Grotius' time, much effort has been devoted to a study of averting conflicts and subordinating disputes to the rule of law.

SUGGESTIONS FOR READING

The following are crisp, purposeful, and readable political surveys of all or part of the century and a half following the beginning of the Protestant Reformation: M. L. Bush, **Renaissance, Reformation, and the Outer World, 1450-1660*** (Torchbooks); H. Koenigsberger and G. Mosse, **Europe in the Sixteenth Century** (Longman, 1973); J. H. Elliott, **Europe Divided, 1559-1598*** (Torchbooks); T. Aston, ed., **Crisis in Europe: 1560-1660*** (Torchbooks); A. Moote, **The Seventeenth Century: Europe in Ferment*** (Heath, 1970); and J. R. Strayer, **On the Medieval Origins of the Modern State** (Princeton, 1970).

J. H. Whitfield, **Machiavelli** (Russell, 1965) is a sympathetic account. The older, unfavorable view is well presented in H. Butterfield, **The Statecraft of Machiavelli*** (Collier). S. Anglo, **Machiavelli: A Dissection** (Harcourt Brace Jovanovich, 1970) is a perceptive study with new insights. See also the brilliant study by G. Mattingly, **Renaissance Diplomacy*** (Sentry).

J. Lynch, **Spain Under the Hapsburgs,** Vol. I, **Empire and Absolutism, 1516-1598*** (Rowman, 1973) is an authoritative treatment. Also recommended are A. D. Ortiz, **The Golden Age of Spain, 1516-1659** (Basic Books, 1971); and R. Trevor-Davies, **The Golden Century of Spain, 1501-1621*** (Torchbooks). Fernand Braudel, **The Mediterranean and the Mediterranean World in the Age of Philip II,** 2 vols. (Harper & Row, 1975) is a masterful survey. See also K. Brandi, **Emperor Charles V: The Growth and Destiny of a Man and a World Empire*** (Humanities, 1968); and R. B. Merriman, **Suleiman the Magnificent** (Cooper Square, 1966).

G. Mattingly, **The Armada*** (Sentry) is the classic account. Popular and profusely illustrated is Jay Williams, **The Spanish Armada** (Harper & Row, 1966).

K. H. Haley, **The Dutch in the Seventeenth Century** (Harcourt Brace Jovanovich, 1972) is an excellent account. C. Wedgwood, **William the Silent*** (Norton) is a beautifully written biography.

Elizabeth Jenkins, **Elizabeth the Great*** (Capricorn) is short and lively. J. Neale, **Queen Elizabeth I*** (Anchor) is the most authoritative biography. Antonia Fraser, **Mary, Queen of Scots** (Delacorte, 1969) is a best-seller. See also J. Hurtsfield, **Elizabeth I and the Unity of England*** (Torchbooks); W. C. Richardson, **Mary Tudor, the White Queen** (Univ. of Washington); A. L. Rowse, **The England of Elizabeth*** (Macmillan); S. Bindoff, **Tudor England*** (Penguin); and R. Wernham, **Before the Armada: The Emergence of the English Nation, 1485-1588** (Norton, 1972).

J. Neale, **The Age of Catharine de' Medici*** (Torchbooks) describes the religious and political troubles of sixteenth-century France. For a briefer account see F. Palm, **Calvinism and the Religious Wars** (Fertig, 1972).

C. V. Wedgwood, **The Thirty Years' War*** (Anchor) is a vigorous account as is G. Pages, **The Thirty Years' War*** (Torchbooks). See also H. Holborn, **A History of Modern Germany,** Vol. I, **The Reformation** (Knopf) and Victor L. Tapié, **The Rise and Fall of the Hapsburg Monarchy** (Praeger, 1971) about the royal family that dominated central Europe and the Balkans.

*Indicates a less expensive paperbound edition.

CHAPTER 16

India, China, and Japan: 1300-1650; Southeast Asia: 100-1650

Old Worlds Beyond the Horizon

INTRODUCTION. In this chapter, we once more pick up the narrative of the "old worlds" of the East begun in Chapter 4 and continued in Chapter 7. We now view the civilizations of India, China, Japan, and Southeast Asia during the period when they were at their peak of cultural accomplishment. Outside influences, such as the intrusion of the Europeans, were yet to come. At the same time when Europe was just beginning its rebirth of art, thought, and cultural values, these societies were continuing to build and develop their own rich heritage that had started some two thousand years before.

India expanded upon its period of flourishing growth that had developed in the age of the Guptas (see Chapter 7), an age which had played a major role in diffusion of culture and creative thought throughout the East. Under the influence of the Mughuls, who established a powerful dynasty which would reach its zenith in the sixteenth century, accomplishments in government, learning, and the arts continued their advance under the leadership of the great statesman,

Akbar. The Mughul empire came to compare favorably in its wealth and power with any of its contemporaries in the West.

In Southeast Asia and the Pacific, notable kingdoms influenced by contact with India and China over a long period had risen and fallen. This area in general presented a complex picture of ethnic and political flux resulting from diverse migrations of peoples and unstable governments.

In the period up to the seventeenth century, China and Japan continued to develop their indigenous cultures by following traditional patterns; these patterns were barely touched by European culture and grew in almost complete ignorance of the West. Indeed, repelled by what little they had seen of Europeans, both China and Japan sought to cut themselves off entirely from western influence. The great civilizations of the East were therefore left to pursue their own courses, unaware of the impending collision of cultures that would soon take place under the impetus of the Industrial Revolution, a collision that was to set the breakdown of China's culture into motion and from which Japan was to save itself by its swifter and more integrated response.

THE GLORY OF THE MUGHULS IN INDIA

Babur, founder of the Mughul empire. At the end of the twelfth century Hindu power in India was eclipsed by invading Muslims who established a powerful dynasty in Delhi. By 1500, however, a new Muslim force from the north was preparing to invade India. Two years after Columbus sailed westward toward what he hoped would be India, a descendant of Genghis Khan and Tamerlane mounted the throne of a little principality in Turkestan (see map, p. 175). The youthful ruler was Babur (the Tiger), an able general with the strength of a giant, who was to be the founder of the Mughul empire in India. In his memoirs Babur says that he used to think ceaselessly of the capture of Hindustan. At length he set out with an army of no more than twelve thousand men to achieve his goal. Defeating the large forces of the sultan of Delhi, who then ruled all Hindustan, Babur made himself sultan in 1526. A year later he subdued the Rajputs, who were trying to restore Hindu supremacy in northern India. The submission of the Rajputs placed the Mughul dynasty securely on the Delhi throne. (The name *Mughul* is a corruption of *Mongol*, a word much dreaded in India because of its association with Tamerlane, the ruthless destroyer of Delhi.) Babur himself did not live long to enjoy the fruits of his victory; worn out by his campaigns and adventures, he died in 1530.

Akbar, conqueror and administrator. Babur's grandson was Akbar, meaning "Very Great." In 1560 Akbar's empire consisted of a strip of territory some three hundred miles wide, extending from the northwest frontier eastward to Bengal. Sixteen years later Akbar had extended his rule over all of India north of the Vindhya Mountains, the natural boundary between Hindustan and the Deccan. Continuing southward, Akbar invaded part of the Deccan. When he died in 1605, his dominions ran from Kashmir in the far north well into the Deccan in the south, and his heirs were to extend them even farther.

Akbar's greatness should not be measured by his military conquests alone, however. He instituted innovations and reforms in the government and fostered cultural growth and religious toleration. As an administrator he had few equals. He divided his empire into twelve provinces (later increased to fifteen), ruled by governors whom he appointed and who were paid monthly salaries from the imperial treasury. Each province was divided into districts, and each district into smaller units.

Law was similarly well administered. In each village the headman was responsible for keeping law and order, while in the larger cities special officials were in charge of the administration of justice. Akbar himself often acted as a judge, for everyone in his do-

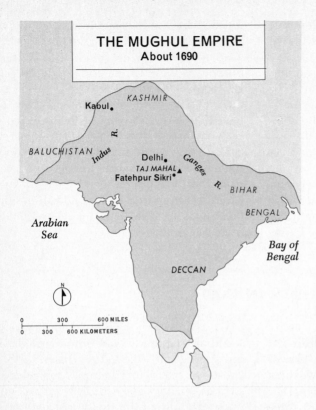

THE MUGHUL EMPIRE
About 1690

KASHMIR

Kabul•

Indus R.

BALUCHISTAN

Delhi•
TAJ MAHAL
Fatehpur Sikri•

Ganges R.

BIHAR

BENGAL

*Arabian
Sea*

*Bay of
Bengal*

DECCAN

N

0   300   600 MILES
0   300   600 KILOMETERS

gious debates which often lasted far into the night. When the Jesuits arrived in India, Akbar had them stay at his court for periods of several years and treated them with every courtesy.

But the sultan never accepted any one religion completely; instead he created his own religion, called *Din Ilahi*, the "Divine Faith," which incorporated what he considered the best features of the other existing religions. By promulgating this new faith, he hoped to bring all India into common agreement on religious matters. But the older faiths were too strongly entrenched, and Akbar's religious theories died with him.

Monuments of Mughul architecture. At the crest of their power in the reigns of Akbar and his immediate successors, the Mughuls displayed one of the most magnificent civilizations of their time. In military strength, government efficiency, and patronage of the arts, they had few equals. Above all, they were great builders.

The Indo-Islamic style of architecture which the Mughuls developed for tombs, mosques, forts, and palaces was a blend of Indian and Persian elements characterized by a lavish use of mosaics, bulbous domes, cupolas, and lofty vaulted gateways. The Mughuls were also fond of formal gardens in which pools and fountains, architecture and greenery were carefully harmonized.

The Mughul style began with Akbar, an avid builder. Not far from the modern city of Agra, he erected a new capital, Fathpur Sikri, which he occupied for only fourteen years before abandoning it for Lahore. Fathpur Sikri is still preserved intact today, and a tourist strolling through its splendid buildings can feel the power of the great empire that made this city possible:

main had the right to appeal to him personally. The practice of *suttee* (burning a wife on her husband's funeral pyre), which had come into use during the Gupta age, was forbidden, and widows were permitted to remarry. Akbar prohibited child marriages and trial by ordeal, although he permitted such tortures as impalement, amputation, and death by elephant dragging. Nevertheless, in contrast to the barbaric punishments permitted in Europe at this time, the Mughul emperor probably had the most enlightened criminal code in the sixteenth century.

Despite the Mughul dynasty's allegiance to the Muslim faith, Akbar allowed complete freedom of religious belief in his empire, because he realized that religious strife made for political and social disintegration. Akbar's views were not based simply on political expediency, however; his own temperament was the chief reason for his enlightened policy. He felt that every faith had something of truth to offer but that all were untrue when they denied each other's sincerity of purpose. Every Thursday, Muslims, Brahmins, and members of smaller sects congregated in his Hall of Worship for reli-

Nothing sadder or more beautiful exists in India than this deserted city—the silent witness of a vanished dream. It still stands with its circuit of seven miles, its seven bastioned gates, its wonderful palaces, peerless in all India for noble design and delicate adornment; its splendid mosque and pure marble shrine . . . its carvings and paintings—stands as it stood in Akbar's time, but now a body without a soul.[1]

The Mughul rulers brought to India a rich Islamic style of art and architecture. Their court was magnificent with thousands employed to provide luxuries for them. In a contemporary painting (right) the great ruler Akbar is overseeing the construction of his new capital at Fathpur Sikri. A miniature painting (below) depicts an audience in the court of a Mughul ruler, while Hindu pilgrims (above) bathe at a shrine of the god Siva.

During the reign of Shah Jahan, Akbar's grandson, Mughul architecture reached its zenith. Shah Jahan had the red sandstone buildings of Akbar at Delhi demolished and erected a huge capital of marble containing fifty-two palaces. The famous Hall of Private Audience had ceilings of solid silver and gold and a Peacock Throne encrusted with costly gems. On the walls can still be seen the inscription by a Muslim poet: "If anywhere on earth there is a Paradise, it is here, it is here, it is here." Besides making Delhi a site of unrivaled splendor, Shah Jahan erected at Agra the famous Pearl Mosque and the Taj Mahal, the marble mausoleum built as a final resting place for himself and his favorite wife (see illustration below).

Signs of Mughul decline. The blend of Hindu-Islamic cultural elements under the Mughuls brought civilization in India to the highest point yet achieved there. It is unfortunate for world culture that the union of Muslim and Hindu genius could not continue to flower. But Akbar's tolerance and wisdom were lost in the fanaticism of his successors.

Shah Jahan, who came to the throne in 1628, held none of Akbar's views on religious

toleration. He officially promoted the Muslim faith, destroyed Hindu temples, and forcibly opposed the spread of Christianity. In 1630 Shah Jahan began the conquest of the Deccan; eventually it was subjugated and divided into four provinces. After Shah Jahan's health began to fail in 1657, a ruinous civil war broke out among his four sons, each of whom became an almost independent ruler. The last eight years of Shah Jahan's life (d. 1666) were spent as a prisoner of his son and successor, Aurangzeb. Despite his ignominious end, the reign of Shah Jahan marked the summit of the Mughul empire.

CHINA TURNS INWARD

Rise and fall of the Ming dynasty. The Ming (1368-1644) followed a pattern typical of Chinese dynasties, arising out of and ending in rebellion. With the weakening of Mongol power, the concentration of land in the hands of small numbers of wealthy landlords, and resentment against alien rule, the conditions were set by the middle of the fourteenth century for dynastic breakdown. Such a pattern, known as a dynastic cycle, was a feature of Chinese history common to most dynasties. Dynasties tended to rise while exercising a clean sweep of the political broom, beginning in strength and prosperity but succumbing to rebellions or invasions as the lands of the peasants fell into the hands of rich landowners. The final result was the overthrow of the dynasty. Rebellion broke out in southern China, Nanking falling in 1356 to forces led by a young monk, Chu Yuan-chang. It took Chu another twelve years before he at last drove the Mongol army out of Peking and established the dynasty in 1368, adopting the reign title, Hung-wu. (Chinese emperors were known by their reign titles rather than their personal names.)

The Hung-wu emperor, with Nanking as his capital, took a firm hand in reconstruction and in the restoration of traditional Chinese culture. A new code of law based on T'ang and Sung precedents was compiled, the examination system for selecting civil and military officials was reestablished, ir-

With its arches, decorations, domes, minarets, and formal gardens, the Taj Mahal, built about 1640 as a mausoleum, is a fine example of Islamic architecture influenced by the Indian imagination.

rigation systems were repaired, and secret societies, so often breeding grounds for rebellion, were harshly suppressed. When Hung-wu died in 1398, he was succeeded by a grandson, who after a brief reign was overthrown in 1403 by his uncle Chu Ti, the Yung-lo emperor. It was under Yung-lo that the capital was transferred, in 1421, to Peking and the persistent attempts by the Mongols to retake China were at last stopped.

The Ming has been described as having been far more despotic than its predecessors. While harsh punishments for both the people and the members of the bureaucracy were characteristic of Ming rule, at the highest levels of government there was a progressive shift of power from the imperial house to the bureaucracy that ran parallel to the decline in Ming power. In 1380 Hung-wu took a major step in consolidating political power by abolishing the offices of chief councilor and the secretariat. By this move, he took full authority for decision-making into his own hands. Yung-lo, however, went back to relying on his grand secretaries (high court officials) for advice so that power began to shift toward the bureaucracy again. Under later emperors, the grand secretaries took over more and more of the initiative of government, with the emperors exerting a merely passive authority in accepting or rejecting their proposals. Other emperors relinquished their power to their eunuch attendants, whose growing influence contributed to the severe corruption that arose at the court and to the weakening of dynastic power.

Ming foreign policy followed a similar pattern of early strength and later decline. In 1403, Yung-lo sent missions of eunuchs to Tibet, Java, Siam, and Bengal. This venture was followed by a series of spectacular naval expeditions ranging from the South Seas to India and the Persian Gulf that began in 1405 and ended suddenly in 1431. Although historians are not sure why they were begun or why they were halted, at about this time an isolationist spirit took over the court and Chinese subjects were forbidden to leave the coastal waters of China. In the early Yung-lo period, the Chinese also exerted an aggressive military policy, bringing Annam (the

present Vietnam) back under Chinese domination in 1406. In 1421, Yung-lo led an expedition against the Mongols that culminated in successful drives across the Gobi desert. With their involvement in Annam, however, the Chinese armies became involved in long and bitter guerrilla warfare with which they could not cope, and, in 1427, the decision was made to withdraw. The breakdown of naval strength following the retreat to coastal waters opened the way for attacks by Japanese pirates, often aided by Chinese brigands, on the coastal provinces. In spite of this evident weakness, Chinese armies were able to stop the Japanese attempt to subdue Korea and then China by defeating the Japanese fleet in 1592.

The Ming dynasty was brought down by a combination of factors—military weakness, the corruption of the court under eunuch domination, and the exorbitant taxes and pitiable circumstances of the peasants typical of end-of-dynasty periods. Peasant uprisings broke out throughout China, and, had history followed its usual course, the dynasty would have fallen to the strongest of the rebel leaders. Instead, it fell, as had the Sung

The picture above demonstrates two methods of irrigation used in Ming China which were established earlier—a chain pump worked by treadmill operators contrasted with the more traditional style of a suspended rod with a bucket at one end and a weight at the other. Additional details of life in Ming China are shown in the sketch of a magistrate at work (left) and a spring river festival (below) in the midst of a busy commercial district.

before it, to an alien people, the Manchu from Manchuria in the north. Taking advantage of the disruption and weakness of the Chinese empire, they brought the dynasty to a close with the capture of Peking in 1644.

Foreign influences under the Ming. Although China turned inward under the Ming, influences from the outside world continued to filter in. Cotton culture, introduced earlier in the thirteenth century, was promoted by government edicts so that China had become, by the fifteenth century, a major cotton-producing nation. Western agricultural crops, corn, the sweet potato, and peanuts in particular were brought in. The Spanish peso and silver were also introduced, the latter replacing the copper currency to a great extent. Contact with the South Seas regions was maintained by an illegal trade that the government could not control.

Thus, China was not cut off from the material culture of the outside world. Nor was the governing class completely ignorant of western science and culture. The sixteenth century saw the arrival in China of the Jesuits, who through their writings and translations brought a knowledge of European sciences to the court and to China's intellectuals. In the end, however, these foreign intellectual influences were inconsequential. Rather, the Chinese remained turned inward to the traditional culture and ignored western thought until it was forcibly thrust upon them in the nineteenth century.

Ming society and culture. One reason for this inward turn of mind was the superiority of Chinese culture to other world cultures. At the beginning of the Ming dynasty, the Renaissance in Europe had not yet begun, while Confucianism provided a complete system of philosophy and ethics. Another key factor leading to the lack of Chinese receptivity to outside influences was the intellectual conformity fostered by Hung-wu's reinstitution of the examination system in a form that endured almost up to the fall of the Manchu in 1912. The examinations, which were given in a series beginning at the local level and continuing on to a final "palace" examination given under the supervision of the emperor himself, tested the candidates on their knowledge of the Confucian classics

as interpreted by the Sung philosopher Chu Hsi. Success in the examinations, which was the primary means to upward mobility open to ambitious young men, not only made a man eligible for appointment as a government official but also brought him into a position of prestige and influence in his home locality. To this goal, the candidates devoted years of study. As a consequence, there was fostered among the intellectual and governing class a conformity of thought and an indoctrination into Confucianism, a philosophical orientation which supported this type of hierarchical social structure and was conducive to the maintenance of imperial power.

Although the humanistic course of Confucian thought tended to discourage development of the sciences, the Ming period was rich in the amateur writings of scholar-bureaucrats on topics ranging over the fields of zoology, botany, astronomy, mathematics, geography, agriculture, and medicine. A major work, the *Pen-ts'ao Kang-mu*, completed by the physician Li Shih-chen in 1578 after twenty-six years of research and field work, represented the most complete compilation of medical knowledge in China up to that time. However, in keeping with the spirit of Confucianism, the Chinese potential for scientific analysis was turned to the literary field in which impressive strides were made.

The bulk of intellectual activity under the Ming was directed toward traditional studies. Yung-lo commissioned extensive compilations of encyclopedias and dictionaries. Most notable was the *Yung-lo Ta-tien (Encyclopedia of the Yung-lo Period)*, a work of 11,095 volumes, now largely lost, that comprised all knowledge up to that time. Many Chinese scholars occupied themselves with philosophical writing, much of which was devoted to opposing or defending the views of a new school of Confucian thought developed by Wang Yang-ming. Wang, whose thought derived from one of the contending Neo-Confucian schools of the Sung period, held that knowledge was intuitive and should be sought through meditation. Aside from the writings of Wang, there was little that was new or creative in Chinese philoso-

The Temple of Heaven at Peking, built during the Ming dynasty, is a typical example of the pagoda form of Chinese architecture. Its cylindrical construction with three roofs is characteristic of the early pagoda style, introduced into China with the spread of Buddhism.

phy during the Ming. Government officials and local gentry took the responsibility for compiling gazetteers providing detailed accounts of local customs, history, geography, and political and social institutions.

In the arts, Ming painters produced many excellent works. Ming artisans tried to duplicate the standards of Sung pottery, but instead of emphasizing the beauty of form of the vessel, they concentrated on brilliant coloring and elegant decoration.

The Forbidden City, the imperial family's area of palaces and temples at Peking, was constructed in the early years (1403-1424) of the Ming dynasty. With its series of courtyards, brilliant lacquer work, and tile, marble, and alabaster decorations, it is typical of a period of richly ornamented architecture.

In literature, there was a significant new development. While the T'ang and Sung were the golden ages of poetry, popular fiction came to prominence during the Ming. Written in the colloquial speech of the time, which differed from the antiquated literary language of serious literature and philosoph-

ical discourse, it had its origins in the tales told by the oral storytellers who had been entertaining city dwellers since Sung times. Because of the complex twists of the plots, devised to string the audiences along, the storytellers often kept prompt books, some of which contain the earliest versions of such famous tales as the *Romance of the Three Kingdoms* and *All Men Are Brothers*. Although, from a moralistic Confucian standpoint, it was thought hardly proper for a serious scholar to demean himself with this form of writing, many did take up and elaborate on these stories, producing such popular tales as *Monkey* and the partially pornographic novel the *Chin P'ing Mei*. Later in the Ch'ing dynasty, this genre was to reach its culmination in the superb *Dream of the Red Chamber*. However, Ming fiction was not honored in its own time and serious works continued to be written in literary Chinese until the literary revolution of the 1920's, when use of the colloquial language in literature at last became accepted.

Thus, Chinese culture in the Ming period was integral and self-sufficient and it did not appear to the Chinese that the European "barbarians" had much to offer beyond more efficient means of warfare. Although the examination system was certainly responsi-

Glazed porcelain pieces, such as this ewer, were among the most highly prized trade items in the world.

ble for fostering a conservatism and intellectual sterility that were to serve China badly with the coming of the West in the nineteenth century, the self-sufficiency and superiority of Chinese culture itself perhaps played as great a part in hardening the Chinese mind against new ways of thought and new ideas. So it was that China's intellectuals came to look to their own past rather than to the future for their golden age.

JAPAN'S SELF-IMPOSED ISOLATION

Ashikaga state and culture. The decline of the Kamakura shogunate in Japan resembled the end of a dynasty in China. It was accompanied by economic difficulties, political and military strife, and the erosion of the bonds of feudal loyalty. Although the successors to the Kamakura shogunate, the Ashikaga, retained the shogunal office from 1338 to 1573, their government was so different from that of its predecessor that it represented a new stage in the history of Japanese feudalism.

Following the destruction of the Kamakura, Ashikaga Takauji set up a new emperor in Kyoto in 1336, a succession dispute arising when the former emperor escaped to the south and established a rival court. After Takauji became shogun in 1338, the Ashikaga family struggled for dominance over the contending feudal barons. In 1392, the succession dispute came to an end and the country settled into an unstable but relatively long period of peace. The Ashikaga, however, lacked the authority of the former Kamakura government and their effective control never extended far beyond Kyoto. Thus it was that the local lords, or *daimyo*, rather than the shoguns, were the key figures during this period. Furthermore, the warrior or samurai class had broken up into separate groups of lords and retainers, a relationship differing from past social arrangements in that it was based on vassalage.

Sporadic fighting among feudal lords persisted and spread until a civil war broke out between rival Ashikaga houses, lasting from

The Golden Pavilion, built at Kyoto in 1397, was the elegant home of the Ashikaga shoguns. The Japanese architectural style utilized here placed important emphasis on the setting and surrounding gardens of its buildings.

1467 to 1474. The civil war ended in a redistribution of feudal power but warfare continued in the provinces. The central government at last collapsed and by 1500 warfare had spread throughout the entire country.

Despite wars and political decentralization, the Ashikaga period was one of economic growth. The feudal lords encouraged trade and commerce in their own domains, and as the money economy grew, various merchants and even some Buddhist monasteries organized themselves into a kind of guild system to protect their interests and encourage trade across feudal boundaries. Towns began to develop at important geographical points and around castles and monasteries. Trade with China grew, inspired by the need for money to support the pretentious way of life of the Ashikaga shoguns, who, devoid of real power, still lived in elegance. The actual business of trade was undertaken by priests of the Zen sect, which was highly favored by the Ashikaga shoguns. This trade was extremely profitable and led to the development of seaports, one of the most important of which was Sakai, which was located just south of present-day Osaka and which became a strategic and financial center.

During the Ashikaga period the greatest art form of the Zen cultural influence was landscape painting. Here the artist portrays the spirit of nature by eliminating minor details and uses bold brush strokes to emphasize what he feels is essential. In these paintings, people and houses, bridges and boats, often appear as subordinate, blending into the great pattern of nature. This detail, from a screen by Sesshu done in ink on paper, is a fine example of painting in this tradition.

A major social development of the period resulting from the breakdown of the old feudal system was the emergence of the family as a social unit, with the interests of the family taking precedence over those of the individual. Women, who had enjoyed high political, social, and cultural status during earlier periods, gradually lost their rights and became both socially and legally inferior to men—a situation that was to continue well into Japan's modern period.

The roughly seventy-year period up to the beginning of the civil wars in 1447 was one of great artistic and cultural vitality. With ancient Kyoto as their capital and living in luxury and elegance in their Golden Pavilion, the shoguns promoted a distinctive new culture, fusing the once separate courtier and warrior cultures. It was to the Buddhist church and to Zen Buddhism in particular that the arts owed their survival in this age of turmoil, for the Zen monasteries were havens for artists. Perhaps for this reason, the Zen spirit exerted a strong influence on Japanese culture, which came to be pervaded by an urbane taste for things elegantly simple: the restrained and quiet contemplation of the tea ceremony, new architectural styles, monochrome painting, and landscape gardening. Among the masters of ink painting was Sesshu, whose works are felt to reflect Zen taste. In poetry, there was a passion for Chinese styles, and poets, writing in Chinese, strove to imitate and outdo their predecessors of the T'ang and Sung. The most enduring artistic development of the period was a form of lyric drama, the *No*, which combined stately mimetic dancing, music, and song.

Western influence first made itself felt with the arrival of the Portuguese in 1542. Francis Xavier, a Jesuit missionary, began to preach Christianity in western Japan and Kyoto in 1549. By the end of the century he may have converted as many as 300,000 persons to Christianity, including some of the feudal lords of Kyushu, who took up the new religion in order to gain commercial advantages and advanced military technology. Many feudal lords, for the same reasons, ordered the conversion of their vassals and just as promptly ordered them to give up Christianity when the expected advantages did not materialize. However, apart from Christianity and military technology, the Japanese took little interest in European culture and science and failed to adopt the new methods of scientific inquiry that were to shape the modern world.

Changes toward unification. Warfare among Japanese feudal lords sharpened following the civil war of 1467-1474, with the roughly 260 *daimyo* that existed before 1467 being reduced to about a dozen by 1600. During this long period of almost constant warfare, increasing economic burdens fell on the peasants and townfolk, so that riots and local uprisings became frequent. Between 1560 and 1600, however, a series of three able leaders, Oda Nobunaga, Toyotomi Hideyoshi, and Tokugawa Ieyasu, progressively established a single military power over all the *daimyo*. At first, this drive toward unification was conducted in the name of the last Ashikaga shogun, but Nobunaga, who had been his supporter, drove him out of Kyoto in 1573, bringing the line to an end. Nobuna-

ga still had powerful enemies to contend with and next set himself to bringing the Buddhist church under submission. Once this was accomplished, he moved to subdue central and western Japan and by 1582 his armies under Hideyoshi had driven the powerful Mori family out of central Japan. Following the death of Nobunaga, Hideyoshi became regent in 1584. A series of battles against the remaining *daimyo* finally united Japan under a single government in 1590, creating a dictatorial power unique in Japanese history. Although theoretically the chief minister of the emperor, Hideyoshi ruled Japan through the feudal institution of vassalage. He disarmed the populace, and in attempting to create social change he tried to define more sharply than ever the various social classes and to prevent people from changing their class status. While Nobunaga had been personally attracted to the Jesuits and had allowed them to go about their religious activities unhampered, Hideyoshi in 1587 issued an edict banning the foreign missionaries. Nevertheless, perhaps out of a fear of alienating the Portuguese traders who were then the agents of the lucrative China trade, he did little to enforce the ban, although in 1597 there was a series of persecutions in which nine missionaries and seventeen Japanese converts were killed.

The arrival of Portuguese traders in Japan was initially greeted with interest by the Japanese who were intrigued by their odd style of dress. This screen painting portrays the strange foreigners who arrived from the south and became known in Japan as the "southern barbarians."

Scenes of life in Tokugawa Japan include a contemporary painting of people crossing a river by raft and on the backs of coolies (left), and a game being played in the teahouse (right). The sixteenth-century screen painting (below) depicts scenes from the *Tale of Genji*, a literary classic.

The Tokugawa shogunate. Hideyoshi, who died in 1598, was succeeded by Tokugawa Ieyasu. A brief period of dissension arose as a number of powerful families again vied for control of the nation. A decisive battle took place in 1600 at Sekigahara, out of which Ieyasu emerged victorious. He became shogun in 1603, but because of opposition to his plans to redistribute fiefs, he did not secure complete domination until his victory at the siege of Osaka in 1615. From his personal headquarters at Edo (Tokyo), he set up a rigid system of laws and institutions designed to perpetuate his family's position indefinitely. In this he was successful, for the Tokugawa family was supreme in Japan for the next two hundred and fifty years.

Like his predecessors, Ieyasu at first took a tolerant view of the Christian missionaries, and in his desire to maintain Japan's foreign trade, decided not to enforce the previous bans against Christianity. However, as he learned more about how missionary activities and the colonial aspirations of the European nations often went hand in hand, his suspicions grew. In 1612, 1613, and 1614, he issued edicts prohibiting Christianity and thousands of loyal Japanese Christians suffered martyrdom. Finally, the regime expelled European missionaries and traders and excluded all foreigners except the Dutch, who were not interested in missionary activity. They were allowed limited and rigidly controlled trade at Nagasaki. At the same time, all Japanese were forbidden to go abroad or even to build ships capable of navigating beyond coastal waters. Thus Japan, like China, chose to cut itself off from the West just as the fruits of the Renaissance were about to transform European culture and to lay the foundations for the dominance of the West.

This raises the intriguing question as to why in later years Japan responded so much more swiftly and effectively and with less internal dissension to the western challenge than did China. The contrast in the responses of the two countries is made even more striking by the fact that China by Ming times possessed a far more advanced technology in many fields than that of the West before the Renaissance.

One important factor was education. While education in China was very sophisticated, it was confined to a relatively small elite segment of society. The peasants, who made up the overwhelming majority of the population, were illiterate. In Japan, by contrast, there had grown up in Ashikaga times a type of school known as the *terakoya*, which became even more widespread during the Tokugawa period. Through the *terakoya* and similar schools, children from commoner families throughout all of Japan learned the basic skills of reading, writing, and computation. With a large literate population, Japan was in a better position for rapid modernization when confronted by the sudden western challenge.

But the Japanese had one other characteristic that was to serve them in good stead, a willingness to borrow and learn from foreign cultures. As inhabitants of a small island nation, the Japanese were conditioned to looking out and responding to the outside world. In earlier times, the Japanese had taken in the best of Chinese culture and had transformed it into uniquely Japanese forms. Japan's isolation during the Tokugawa period was, then, an aberration from the typical pattern of their culture. China, by contrast, was a vast, continental country with a rich indigenous culture. The Chinese saw China as the center of civilization and themselves as bearers of civilization to the inferior "barbarians" who came upon their shores or harassed their inner Asian frontiers. As a consequence, they had developed a spirit of self-sufficiency that has persisted even to the present day. No better examples can be found of how the prevailing attitudes among a people can affect the course of their history and civilization.

SOUTHEAST ASIA: BACKGROUND OF CONFLICT

The geographical foundations of disunity. At the southern tip of the Asian mainland, wedged between India and China and including a multitude of islands in both the Indian and Pacific oceans, lies Southeast Asia. Stretching over a combination of land and sea far greater in size than the United States, Southeast Asia is geographically, culturally, and politically one of the most complex regions in the world.

The Irrawaddy, Salween, and Mekong rivers, which flow south from the Tibet-Burma-China border region, provided avenues for the southward migration of distinctive ethnic groups from South China. North-south mountain chains, which divide Burma from Thailand and Thailand from Vietnam, provided barriers to communication that further emphasized the cultural and political differentiation between the peoples occupying the river valleys. Moreover, later migrants pushed earlier inhabitants out of the valleys and into the mountainous regions, making for further ethnic complexities. Unlike China, where some form of political unity and cultural homogeneity developed, Southeast Asia has always been characterized by political and cultural balkanization. The thousands of islands that make up the Philippine and Indonesian archipelagoes were also subject to natural division rather than unity. Pervasive influences exerted by the great civilizations of India and China added to the confusion.

Chinese, Islamic, and Christian influences in Southeast Asia. In addition to Hindu cultural penetration (discussed in Chapter 7), Chinese influence and on occasion political sovereignty has been a factor in Southeast Asia. During the past five hundred years especially, Chinese settlers migrated to urban centers in this region, where as merchants they came to dominate both local and foreign trade.

The spread of Islam to the Far East started only after the conquest of India by Turkish Muslims during the eleventh and twelfth centuries. As Muslim political and military power began to become dominant, many local rulers found it to their political and commercial advantage to become Muslims. During the fifteenth century, as Hindu rulers were driven from their thrones, Java was completely converted to Islam, which also spread to Sumatra, the Malay peninsula, and

the other islands of the Indonesian archipelago. The one exception was the fabled island of Bali, which became the refuge of the former ruling family and has retained its basically Hindu culture into modern times.

In the fifteenth and sixteenth centuries Malayan and Indonesian merchants and settlers carried Islam into the Philippines particularly to the large southern island of Mindanao. But its influence was too late and too weak to spread further north, where Christianity was beginning to make significant inroads.

Spain began a concerted attempt to occupy the Philippines in the middle of the sixteenth century and established its colonial capital at Manila in 1571. By 1581, when Manila was made a bishopric, no fewer than four Catholic orders were active in the islands, and the Catholic university of Santo Tomàs was founded in 1611. By 1622 there were half a million Catholic converts in the Philippines, and this number increased to almost a million within a century. With the exception of Mindanao and some minor peripheral islands, the Philippines were destined to become the only Christian country in Southeast Asia.

The birth of nationhood. The heritage of geographical and ethnic complexity, of conflict between lowland immigrants and older settlers in the hills, and the waves of distinctive cultural influences from outside Southeast Asia, all made for uneven political development throughout the area in the centuries before the arrival of the West and it is almost impossible to make any generalizations that are valid for the entire region.

What is now Burma was occupied in successive waves and regions by various ethnic groups. Constantly at war with each other and with the neighboring Thais, and often in conflict with the Chinese to the north, the Burmese never succeeded in developing a unified kingdom with a centralized bureaucracy. There was often little continuity in succession from king to king, and though often successful in war, the Burmese kings were more given to raids and brief occupations than to the painstaking business of nation-building and statecraft.

The Thai, or Siamese, on the other hand,

A bas-relief from the temple of Angkor Wat in Cambodia details the *Davatas*, a minor type of genii. There are nearly 2000 of these figures reproduced throughout the structure, which is considered a superb example of Hindu architecture as combined with the influence of Southeast Asia (see Color Plate 15).

early developed a sense of nationhood and a durable administrative system. Furthermore, the Thais were culturally more homogeneous than the Burmese. By the early seventeenth century the Thai monarchs were already in active contact with the West, sending embassies to Holland and the court of Louis XIV. They were also in early contact with China, whose merchants purchased rice in Thailand. Chinese merchants and their families settled in Thailand early and in such numbers that they became a significant part of Thai society and were not even considered foreigners. Because the Chinese community was an important source of attractive women for the royal harem, many Thai monarchs were at least half Chinese, and the present dynasty and its capital, Bangkok, were founded by a half-Chinese general in the latter part of the eighteenth century.

Laos, lying in the northwestern part of the Indochinese peninsula, was a congeries of petty princedoms fought over by the Thais, Vietnamese, and Cambodians. The modern Cambodians are largely descended from the Khmer builders of the great empire which centered on Angkor Wat. Indonesia and Malaya remained the realm of petty Muslim princes and European colonies, which fought to control the rich resources of these lands

and the trade routes between eastern and southern Asia.

In the islands of the Indonesian archipelago, one kingdom and empire succeeded another on the great islands of Sumatra and Java. The sea was their thoroughfare, and the important Strait of Malacca, which controlled the trade routes between the Indian Ocean and the Far East, was a major prize of war. But the successive waves of cultural influence that traveled along the trade routes were not a sufficient basis for unification when faced with the geographical and ethnic divisions that plagued both continental and island Southeast Asia. The religious and political thought and institutions of *Hinayana* Buddhism, superimposed on early Brahminic Hindu influence, dominated, and continue to dominate today, Burma, Thailand, Laos, and Cambodia. Islam today pervades Indonesia, the southern Philippines, and the Malay peninsula.

The only region in Southeast Asia to come under Chinese cultural and political domination was what today constitutes North and South Vietnam. The Vietnamese people are the product of the integration of early migrants from South China with local populations, and their language, closely resembling Chinese, has marked Khmer and Thai elements. Spending over a thousand years of their history, beginning with the Han dynasty, under Chinese rule, and even longer under Chinese influence, Vietnam so closely resembled China culturally and politically that it has been called "The Lesser Dragon." Adopting *Mahayana* Buddhism, Confucian political thought, Chinese institutions, and the Chinese written language, the Vietnamese constructed a Confucian state on the Chinese model, complete with an emperor, a civil service bureaucracy recruited through the traditional Confucian examination system, a mandarin class, and court records and a literature in the Chinese style. Even the imperial palace at the capital at Hue in central Vietnam was built on the Chinese model. Sometimes more conservative than the Chinese themselves, the Vietnamese held onto tradition longer. For instance, Confucian examinations which were abolished in China in 1905, remained in force in Vietnam until the mid-1920's. But despite the amazingly strong Chinese influence on Vietnam and its culture, the Vietnamese throughout their history remained strongly conscious of themselves as Vietnamese. They constantly struggled for independence from China and, once independence was achieved, for the continuity and integrity of their own state.

SUMMARY

The great civilizations of the East—those of India, China, Japan, and Southeast Asia— seemed to reach their height in the period corresponding to Europe's Middle Ages and before the period of European domination. The alien Mughuls gave India its most brilliant period, surpassing the glories of the Guptas. The Mughul ruler Akbar is regarded as one of the greatest statesmen of all time. All facets of culture flourished under Mughul rule, but the noblest legacy was in architecture; the Taj Mahal and the buildings of Fathpur Sikri are ample evidence of the genius of Mughul builders.

As we have seen, China and Japan during this period were beset by internal changes that would in the end bear heavily on how these nations would respond to the coming challenge of the West. The overthrow of the yoke of Mongol oppression by the Ming led to a revival of traditional Chinese culture. Although touched by European influences, the Chinese tended to turn more and more inward, convinced of the superiority of their own culture. The result was a lack of preparedness for the challenge of the West and a set of attitudes that was to stand in the way of modernization in western terms.

In the fifteenth and sixteenth centuries, Japan underwent a long period of internal dissension and warfare that finally culminated in the formation of a closely knit state under the Tokugawa. Here too, a pattern of foreign exclusion was set that was to endure until the arrival of Admiral Perry's "black ships" in the nineteenth century. Nevertheless, the social and political stability and the great homogeneity of Japanese culture, with the widespread basic literacy of the time, as well as the Japanese willingness to learn from other countries, were to make Japan's response to the western impact more decisive than that of China. This allowed Japan to fend off the encroachments of the imperialist West that were to befall a China immersed in itself and lacking in homogeneity and political stability.

Although strongly influenced by Indian and Chinese cultures, the incredible political and ethnic complexities that characterized Southeast Asia inhibited the growth of the kind of cultural and national self-consciousness that marked China and Japan. Moreover, geographical considerations contributed to the inability of the peoples of this region to develop political unity and stability. These factors were to make Southeast Asia a relatively easy prey for Europe's expanding empires.

In following the detailed accounts of events in Europe and in the colonies that Europe would soon establish in Asia, we must not lose sight of the rich heritage of the peoples of the Asian continent. In the centuries to follow, they would move ever closer to the center of the stage of world history.

SUGGESTIONS FOR READING

W. T. de Bary, ed., **Introduction to Oriental Civilizations: Sources of Japanese Tradition,** 2 vols., **Sources of Chinese Tradition,** 2 vols., and **Sources of Indian Tradition,** 2 vols. (Columbia). These texts consist of brief introductory passages followed by translations of relevant documents. The best large-scale general survey of the Far East is E. O. Reischauer, J. K. Fairbank, and A. Craig, **History of East Asian Civilization,** Vol. I, **East Asia: The Great Tradition** (Houghton Mifflin, 1960). See also N. Peffer, **The Far East: A Modern History** (Univ. of Michigan, 1968), a good general text; and W. Bingham, *et al.,* **A History of Asia,** 2nd ed., 2 vols. (Allyn and Bacon, 1974).

M. Biardeau, **India** (Viking, 1960) is a well-illustrated introduction. See also Donald Lach, **India in the Eyes of Europe: The Sixteenth Century** (Univ. of Chicago); and S. M. Ikram, **Muslim Civilization in India** (Columbia, 1964). J. M. Shelat, **Akbar** (Verry) is an important biography.

Dun J. Li, **The Ageless Chinese: A History** (Scribner's) is a well-written full account. See also Donald Lach, **China in the Eyes of Europe: The Sixteenth Century** (Univ. of Chicago). On Sino-European contacts see G. F. Hudson, **Europe and China** (Gordon Pr., 1976).

Essays on Confucian thought include Arthur F. Wright, ed., **The Confucian Persuasion** (Stanford, 1960); D. S. Nivison and Arthur F. Wright, eds., **Confucianism in Action** (Stanford); and Arthur F. Wright and Denis Twitchett, eds., **Confucian Personalities** (Stanford, 1969). On Chinese literature see Chi-chen Wang, trans., **Dream of the Red Chamber** (Twayne); and Liu Tieh-yun, H. Shadick, trans., **The Travels of Lao Ts'an** (Cornell).

E. O. Reischauer, **Japan: The Story of a Nation,** rev. ed., (Knopf, 1974) is lucid and authoritative. A well-written account is D. Lach, **Japan in the Eyes of Europe: The Sixteenth Century** (Univ. of Chicago); and John W. Hall, **Japanese History,** (Greenwood). G. B. Sansom, **A History of Japan,** 3 vols., (Stanford, 1958-1963) is a detailed account. Other titles by the same author are **The Western World and Japan** (Knopf); and **Japan: A Short Cultural History** (ACC, 1962). More specialized books on Japan include T. C. Smith, **The Agrarian Origins of Modern Japan** (Stanford); R. P. Dore, **Education in Tokugawa Japan** (Univ. of Calif., 1965); and Robert Bellah, **Tokugawa Religion** (Free Press). On Japanese literature see Donald Keene, ed., **Japanese Literature: An Introduction for Western Readers** (Grove); and Donald Keene, ed., **Anthology of Japanese Literature: Earliest Era to the Mid-Nineteenth Century** (Grove).

Excellent general surveys on Southeast Asia are D. G. Hall, **A History of South-East Asia,** 3rd ed., (St. Martin's); Donald Lach, **Southeast Asia in the Eyes of Europe: The Sixteenth Century** (Univ. of Chicago, 1968); J. F. Cady, **Southeast Asia: Its Historical Development** (McGraw-Hill); and B. Harrison, **Southeast Asia: A Short History** (St. Martin's, 1966). See also R. C. Lester, **Theravada Buddhism in Southeast Asia** (Univ. of Michigan, 1973).

*Indicates a less expensive paperbound edition.

CHAPTER 17

Precolonial Africa:
3000 B.C.-1800 A.D.;
Native Cultures
in the Americas:
1000 B.C.-1500 A.D.

Before
the European
Impact

INTRODUCTION. Europe's isolation from Asia and its ignorance of sub-Saharan Africa and the Americas ended in the fifteenth century when a multitude of European explorers, traders, conquerors, and missionaries secured footholds in territories far from their homelands. Reaching out to trade, to conquer, and to spread the gospel of Christianity, they encountered civilizations and ways of life which dramatically revealed the limitations of their own knowledge and experience. The story of their explorations and discoveries will be taken up in Chapter 18; this chapter is concerned with the civilizations in Africa and the Americas prior to the arrival of the Europeans.

In describing the early history of sub-Saharan Africa and the Americas, we will introduce to the stage of world history peoples we have not previously encountered. In a number of instances we will take a giant step backward several thousand years, for both Africa and the Americas had inhabitants who, in the eighteenth century, were not so technologically advanced as some of their European and Asian counterparts had been two thousand years before. Yet both continents had fascinating cultures, some of which were to make important contributions to the civilization we know today. The variety of these contributions — from cotton, coffee, and Indian corn to the rhythms upon which jazz is based and sculpture which strongly influenced the development of modern art — reflects the remarkable diversity of the peoples of these lands, peoples who hunted, farmed, built cities, worshiped gods, and waged wars for centuries while Europeans remained totally ignorant of their existence.

Today a significant aspect of our world is the reawakening of old centers of civilization in the newer independent nations of Africa. Nationalistic fervor and brave hopes for the future have been built on pride in the past. For example, the former British colony known as the Gold Coast adopted the name of a long-dead African empire, Ghana, when it was granted independence in 1957. Rhodesia will once more be known as Zimbabwe when it is granted black majority rule. In the New World, Mexican artists take their themes and motifs not from their Spanish colonial heritage but from pre-*conquistadore* Indian cultures.

Thus, if we are to understand the new dynamic spirit that now moves many of these regions, we must know something of the sources of inspiration upon which their people draw. Some of these sources are outlined in the history of Africa and the Americas in the centuries covered by this chapter.

AFRICA: A CONTINENT OF MANY CULTURES

Records of Africa's past. Extending south from the southern fringes of the Sahara Desert to the Cape of Good Hope is sub-Saharan Africa. The terms "Africa" and "Africans" are often used to refer solely to this part of the African continent and its inhabitants who are mostly Negroid in physical characteristics. Africans are often thus distinguished from the Arab and Berber people of North Africa (north of the Sahara) who are mostly Semitic in physical characteristics and have been culturally involved in the Mediterranean world. Nevertheless, the Sahara has never been an impenetrable barrier, and the earliest written sources about sub-Saharan Africa come from North Africa: writings on Egyptian tombs, references in Greek and Roman histories, and trade manuals for North African merchants.

The Nile Valley was one of the original cradles of civilization and here, recorded on the tomb of a noble of the sixth dynasty of Egypt (c. 2340 B.C.), is the story of a trader named Harkhuf who made four long journeys south from Egypt along the Nile River, returning with African products. Conquest followed trade and soon the people of Nubia, as the lands south of ancient Egypt were called, were sending annual tributes of ivory, frankincense, gold, timber, hides, and black recruits for the Egyptian army. These tributes are recorded in pictures and written inscriptions in the temples and tombs of Egyptian royalty and constitute, with the story of Harkhuf, some of the earliest references available to historians about sub-Saharan Africa.

By the first millennium B.C. the thriving trade of the Mediterranean world led traders and travelers into better contact with Africa south of the Sahara, and surviving accounts provide more bits of information for historians. For example, a fifth century B.C. account by the Carthaginian admiral Hanno tells of a long journey taken by sea around the west coast of Africa. The Greek historian Herodotus, writing c. 430 B.C., described North Africans proceeding south into the Sahara with four-horse chariots. This account was thought to be false until the twentieth century, when ancient rock drawings of horse-drawn chariots were found in caves in the middle of the Sahara. The geographer Ptolemy (c. 150 B.C.) described the source of the Nile River as rising in the "Mountains of the Moon." This account was also thought to be imaginary until the nineteenth century when European explorers saw for themselves that the source of the Nile was the huge Lake Victoria fed by streams from the mist- and snow-covered mountains of East Africa.

By the end of the first century after Christ, a sailors' guide to the ports of the East African coast had been written. Ships from the Red Sea nosed their way along this coast exchanging iron tools and weapons for African ivory, tortoise shell, and some slaves. This was the period of the growth of Axum, a kingdom in what is now Ethiopia, whose busy ports along the Red Sea provided a crossroads for trade with India, Africa, and the Graeco-Roman world. Historians know much of Axum because the Axumites had their own written language which can be read easily today. That language, Ge'ez, is the parent of Amharic, the present-day Ethiopian language, and numbers of documents and inscriptions remain from the early Christian era.

Following the eleventh century A.D., documents concerning Africa became more numerous because much of West and East Africa had by then been drawn into the trading world of Islam. Arab travelers and scholars wrote a great deal about Africa. In West Africa the courts and traders of the great African kingdoms used Arabic for keeping some records. But the scholarship of Islam was not available to the Christians of Europe until after the Crusades and the Renaissance. Thus it was only after 1500 that Europeans became vitally concerned with Africa. Then for over three centuries that interest was primarily coastal and concerned the slave trade. Not until the nineteenth century did traders, missionaries, and explorers progressively penetrate what to Europe was a virtually unknown continent.

Europe's penetration of Africa came at a time when the West was experiencing remarkable advances in technology and the arts, stemming from the Renaissance and its subsequent scientific and industrial revolutions. To the intrusive Europeans, Africa south of the Sahara appeared static and many of its peoples backward. The absence of writing in many African societies and the fact that most Africans were not Christians mold-ed western stereotypes of them. Preliterates and non-Christians were considered barbaric, a people without history and a people without civilized morals. In their rush for the ivory, gold, and slaves that Africans had to offer, the Europeans did not take time to study the epic poems and ancient rituals that many African societies had preserved for generations by memorization. They did not bother to examine the complex laws and morals that formed the "unwritten" constitutions of African political systems, and in most cases they would not and could not read the numerous Arabic manuscripts that could have informed them of much African history.

Rediscovery of Africa's past. Since 1945 however, great advances have been made in the approach to the study of Africa and in the recovery of the African past. The new view of Africa as an integral part of world history is one of the most exciting and rewarding events in contemporary historical studies.

This progressive rediscovery of Africa's past has been aided by the newly independent sub-Saharan states' interest in archaeological and historical research. In addition historians are now collecting and developing new criteria for interpreting oral tradition, i.e., the histories, poems, genealogies, and rituals which are memorized, often with great accuracy, by generation after generation of Africans. Oral traditions can sometimes relate accurate genealogies as far back as 700 years. Specialists from other fields such as geology, botany, biology, and linguistics are also working at revealing more and more the richness and importance of Africa's once unappreciated past.

Africans and geography. Africa has roughly four major ecological regions which run like bands across the continent. Beginning at the very north and south ends of the continent are two narrow strips of fertile coastline. Both these coastlines give way to deserts—the huge Sahara in the north (as large in area as the continental United States) and the smaller Kalahari in the south. The deserts merge into grassy plains called savanna which become more and more wooded as they near the equator. In the center and extending also along the West African coastline is the African forest of towering trees and abundant rainfall. As it approaches the East African coast, the forest gives way in places to wooded and grass savanna. East Africa is one of the continent's more interesting geological settings for in addition to broad sweeping plains there are also the highest mountains in Africa, and huge inland lakes.

The geography of Africa affects the way people live their lives and the progress of their history. The ecology of the northern coast is capable of supporting a large population and consequently it has been heavily settled for thousands of years. The Sahara is dry and forbidding, in parts even plants are unable to live in it. Only nomadic peoples can and do survive there. The camel has especially adapted to these dry conditions, while in the savanna donkeys, oxen, sheep, goats, and cattle are used both as beasts of burden and for meat. Many grain crops such as rice and millet can be raised as well; in this way large populations have been supported by the ecology of the savanna for the past two thousand years with farming villages scattered across the plains and large cities arising at key points of trade. Over one-half of the African continent is savanna and it is here where most Africans have lived and where many historical African states and governments have been located. It should be noted, however, that the lack of trees in the savanna has meant a shortage of wood for building, and this has prevented the adoption of many technological skills, particularly the construction of large storied buildings.

Many nutritious crops such as bananas, yams, and oranges which do not tolerate the drier conditions of the savanna thrive in the ecology of the African forest. All East Asian foods, they were introduced to Africa some time ago in the early centuries after Christ and created the potential for larger populations to live in the forest. However, an insect known as the tsetse fly lives in and near the forest, carrying a disease called trypanosomiasis, better known as sleeping sickness, which kills cattle, horses, and sometimes people. This precludes a plentiful supply of meat, and communication is often limited because of the absence of the horse and donkey and because of the difficulty of keeping large roads cleared of dense undergrowth.

Peoples of Africa. A large variety of types of people inhabit Africa. Today there are over 850 ethnic (or tribal) groups and some 1000 different languages. The peoples can, however, be grouped into four major linguistic families.[1] The Afro-Asiatic speakers live between the Sahara and the Mediterranean in North Africa. This area has been peopled for at least five thousand years by the ethnic group known as Berbers. In addition there is in North Africa a prominent Semitic element, introduced through the immigration of both Jews and Arabs during the period of the Roman Empire and the era of Muslim expansion. Nilo-Saharan languages are spoken by black, Negroid type peoples in the central savanna south of the Sahara and by the tall, slender, lighter-skinned Nilote peoples in the lake region of East Africa. Niger-Kordofanian languages are spoken over most of Africa south of the Sahara and include the widely used Bantu languages. The Bushmen and Hottentots of southern Africa and a few hunting groups in East Africa, brown skinned but non-Negroid in physical characteristics, all speak the older Khoisan family of languages.

Language classification, however, while useful to scholars, can sometimes seem academic and not always practical. For example, the Masai of Kenya speak a Nilo-Saharan dialect but they still cannot be understood by their neighbors, the Luo, who speak a different Nilo-Saharan dialect. Perhaps more instructive is a classification of peoples according to their life-styles and their environment. The Pygmies and the Bushmen, though separated by many miles and speaking different languages, support themselves with primarily the same techniques: they use bows and arrows to hunt for meat and they collect wild roots and fruits. People living in this manner are called hunting and gathering societies, and their mode of existence traces far back into antiquity. Another type of society in Africa is the pastoral society in which the entire wealth and sustenance of the members comes from raising cattle. People living in these societies, such as the Fulani and Masai, organize their daily lives, work patterns, marriages, and politics around their herds of cattle. Farming societies represent another type of life-style followed by the majority of Africans, though this type can be broken down into two groups: those who must farm in the forest areas where they make clearings and those who farm the vast, more easily cultivated but less fertile areas of the savanna. Finally, there are urban societies in Africa and in these people live in large cities, producing and trading small products for their livelihood. Many large urban centers of Africa date back to 1000 A.D., and there is evidence that some such as Meroë and Nok existed in the first millennium B.C. Today many of these ancient cities have disappeared and large modern industrial cities have grown up on different sites. Yet archaeologists and historians know that urban life is nothing new to certain areas of Africa.

The formative period of Africa. It is now believed that during the Old Stone Age, Africa was among the most advanced areas in the world, a leader in the slow march toward civilization. In addition to developing the hand-ax, Africa produced the first true weapon of attack, the bolas, and its tool-making techniques may have been diffused to other continents by streams of migration.

The technique of plant domestication is thought by many scholars to be the next major step in people's effort to control their surroundings, after mastering weapon and toolmaking. According to present evidence, Africa was not the site of the earliest plant domestication. It appears that this first occurred in western Asia and then spread to the Middle East. Under the pharaohs, farming was flourishing in the lower Nile valley at least by the fifth century B.C. and possibly spread from there to sub-Saharan Africa. Some scholars believe, however, that Africans living in the upper Niger River valley independently developed domestic agriculture about 2000 B.C. Regardless of which theory is correct, crops of grains, mostly African rice and millet, were grown in the savanna by 2000 B.C. One of the earliest Neolithic farm cultures in Africa that has been excavated by archaeologists in detail is that of Nok, in central Nigeria, dating from 800 B.C. to 200 A.D. Its people were not only skilled farmers, but artisans who produced iron and tin tools and

This stylized terra-cotta head, dating from about 500 B.C., is an outstanding example of the highly developed level of sculpture reached by the Nok culture. The head represents a human face and was probably used for religious purposes.

decorations. The vitality of African neolithic culture can be sensed by examining Nok's most distinctive accomplishment, the production of strikingly beautiful terra-cotta (baked clay) sculpture.

During the first millennium B.C. the tempo of Africa began to quicken. Iron was introduced, and its use spread over much of the continent between 300 B.C. and 900 A.D. In West Africa, in the northwestern area of present-day Cameroun, Bantu-speaking peoples who farmed and worked iron began to increase in numbers. This "population explosion" led to historic expansion southward into the forest and eastern savanna regions. Bantu expansion in central and eastern Africa was supported by new types of crops, particularly a more nutritious type of banana called plantain, brought in the early centuries A.D. by Indian sailors who followed the wind currents from Asia to East Africa in search of trade. In addition, peoples moving south from the Nile Valley were bringing cattle and the techniques for raising them into East Africa and so provided increased protein supplies for the growing population. The Bantu increased rapidly and, as they pushed southward and eastward, they absorbed or displaced most of the hunting and gathering peoples they encountered, the latter being no match for the Bantu iron hoes and spears. By the eighth century A.D. the Bantu had reached the area of present-day Rhodesia, and by the sixteenth century they were nearing the tip of South Africa.

Africa's earliest civilizations. The first contacts with sub-Saharan Africa made by outsiders were probably by the ancient Egyptians. They sailed far up the Nile River and down the east coast of Africa in search of new markets and new conquests. The most famous expedition was sent by Queen Hatshepsut in c. 1470 B.C. to the land of "Punt" which probably was located in what is now Somaliland. Illustrations on Egyptian tombs show her sailors returning with live baboons, ivory, leopard skins, exotic trees, and bags of incense. Phoenicians also made contact with sub-Saharan Africa. The most famous of their several voyages was that of a fleet of sixty ships which in 520 B.C. was sent by the Phoenician colony at Carthage to explore northwestern Africa and to establish trading posts. There is evidence that the expedition sailed as far south as the modern nation of Sierra Leone, but today there is no indication of any trade post they may have established.

Along the valley of the Nile the pharaohs had extended their control well into Upper Egypt by 2000 B.C., and five hundred years later they gained mastery of the area known as Kush in the northern part of the modern state of the Sudan. In 750 B.C. this former colony of Egypt became so strong that it invaded and conquered Egypt. The Kushite kings, probably very dark-skinned peoples, made themselves the twenty-fifth dynasty of the pharaohs of Egypt, dominating their former masters until 600 B.C. when they were pushed back to their own land by the dissatisfied Egyptians. However, the Kushite kings continued to rule independently at their capital of Meroë, located not far from the modern city of Khartoum.

Meroë carried on lively trade with Egypt, Arabia, India, Ethiopia, and portions of Afri-

ca to its south. Its trade goods of hides, ivory, and ebony indicate that the trade to sub-Saharan Africa was as substantial as that to Egypt and the Middle East. Most important for trade were Meroë's valuable iron ore deposits which the Kushites learned to smelt. Kush thus supplied Egypt and other African lands with tools and weapons. Today Meroë is uninhabited, but the extensive heaps of iron refuse and ruins of brick palaces, pyramids, temples, and homes can still be seen. Although Kush was influenced by Egyptian culture, as the Meroë pyramids show, it assuredly developed its own distinct culture influenced by sub-Saharan Africa. Its own system of writing has not yet been translated and this makes it difficult to know exactly what occurred in Kush during its centuries of power and what caused its gradual decline. Although not so famous as a result, Meroë can be considered along with Carthage and Egypt as one of the great civilizations of ancient Africa.

Kush was gradually superseded by a rival trading state to its east, Axum, in modern-day Ethiopia. Eventually the peoples of Kush became weaker, yet they began to raid the borders of Axum. King Ezana of Axum in 350 A.D. decided to crush his weak and worri-

Near the junction of the White and Blue Nile in the Sudan, the Kushites founded their fabulous capital, Meroë, building massive monuments, palaces, and sculptured gods. Their remains give a vivid impression of the city's former grandeur.

some rival and a lively description of his expedition remains today engraved on a monument in Axum. It reads:

And as I had warned them, and they would not listen but refused to cease from their evil deeds and betook themselves to flight, I made war on them . . . They fled without making a stand and I pursued them for 23 days, killing some and capturing others . . . I burnt their towns, both those built of bricks and those built of reeds, and my army carried off their food and copper and iron . . . and destroyed the statues in their temples, their granaries, and cotton trees and cast them into the river [Nile].[2]

Axum supplanted Meroë's importance and came to control a large share of the trade between Africa and the Mediterranean world, the Arabian peninsula, the Persian Gulf, and the Indian Ocean. Greek and Roman merchants lived at Axum, with Greek being the language of official records for some time, though this later was replaced by Ge'ez.

By the sixth century A.D., the documents indicate a high standard of living. Most people lived in stone houses and the king resided in a huge palace. He had chariots pulled by elephants and wore luxurious robes and splendid jewels; he was followed by a group of flute players. Axum's wealth was such that in the fields around Axum today one can still find its distinctive gold coins.

Axum's role in trade brought it into contact with Christianity at an early date. In 330 A.D. two young Byzantine Christian scholars were brought to the court of King Ezana where they converted the king to Christianity and persuaded him to make it the state religion. A large number of churches were then built throughout the countryside, and an archbishop was sent from Alexandria. At this time the Bible was translated into Ge'ez.

When the Arab empire began to expand in the seventh century A.D., its Muslim warriors were unable to conquer Axum and convert its Christians to Islam. Nevertheless Axum was surrounded by the Islamic world and cut off from ties with the outside for several centuries thus causing its decline. In the fourteenth century the descendants of the people of Axum reorganized and began to build the state that has grown to be Ethiopia today.

They trace the ancestry of their royal family back to ancient Axum, a historical tradition of unusual length.

The trans-Saharan trade. The kingdom of Axum had become prominent at the time of the Roman Empire, but the Romans were also interested in expanding trade all along the North African coast. Their chief competitors for a while were the people of Carthage who, as already mentioned, had explored the coast of Africa in search of new markets. Carthage was apparently aware of the rich gold deposits located in West Africa near the source of the Niger River. Although they probably did not reach this gold area, called Wangara, they did have trade contacts with it through local peoples across the Sahara. The Sahara is not the great barrier that first glance may make it seem. It is much more like an ocean which, though one cannot live there, one can cross rather quickly with the proper means, in ancient Roman times the horse, later the camel. Thus contact between the peoples on either side of this great desert has never ceased. This contact has been maintained partly because of the nature of the items that are traded across the Sahara, gold and salt. The gold of West Africa has always been valued and in exchange for it the people of North Africa have traded salt, an item essential for human health, particularly in warm climates, and painfully lacking as a natural resource in West Africa. Large supplies of salt are found in the ground in the northwestern part of the Sahara.

When Carthage was destroyed by the Romans in 146 B.C. the Romans fell heir to the trade routes across the Sahara, as their imports of gold, ivory, hides, and black slaves testify. Roman North Africa reached its peak in the third century A.D. and it was at this time that the camel was permanently introduced to the area from the Middle East. Thereafter, although Roman North Africa's prosperity declined along with the Roman Empire, the trans-Saharan routes became much more practical and permanent (see map, p. 367). After the amazingly rapid spread of the Islamic Arabs across North Africa in the seventh and eighth centuries, the trans-Saharan trade routes became more important. From this period on, written ac-

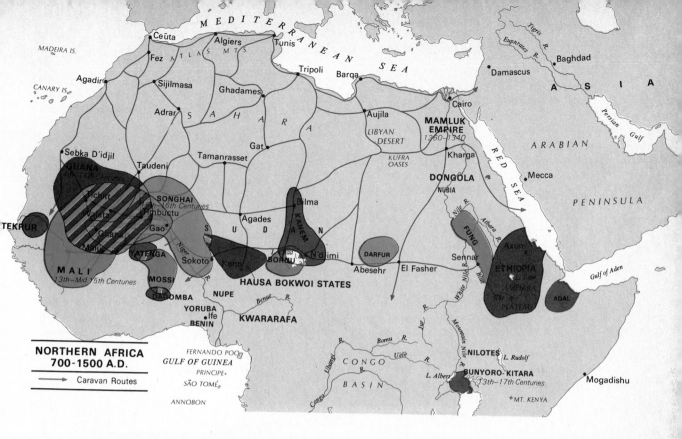

The following labels appear on the map:

MADEIRA IS.

CANARY IS.

MEDITERRANEAN SEA

Ceuta
Algiers
Tunis
Fez
ATLAS MTS.
Tripoli
Barqa
Agadir
Sijilmasa
Ghadames
Adrar
SAHARA
Aujila
Cairo
Tamanrasset
Gat
LIBYAN DESERT
MAMLUK EMPIRE 1260-1340
KUFRA OASES
Kharga
Sebka D'idjil
Taudeni
GHANA
Tichit
SONGHAI 14th-16th Centuries
Timbuctu
Bilma
KANEM
DONGOLA
NUBIA
Walata
Gao
Agades
TEKRUR
SUDAN
Niger R.
N'djimi
Mecca
MALI 13th-Mid 15th Centuries
KATENGA
Sokoto
Kano
BORNU
DARFUR
Abesehr
El Fasher
Sennar
FUNG
Axum
ETHIOPIA
MOSSI
DAGOMBA
NUPE
HAUSA BOKWOI STATES
Benue R.
YORUBA
Ife
BENIN
KWARARAFA
ADAL
ASIA
Tigris R.
Euphrates R.
Baghdad
Damascus
Persian Gulf
ARABIAN PENINSULA
RED SEA
Gulf of Aden
Nile R.
Atbara R.
White Nile R.
Blue Nile R.
Mountain Nile R.
L. Tana
ABYSSINIAN PLATEAU
Bomu R.
Uele
Ubangi R.
CONGO BASIN
Congo R.
FERNANDO POO
GULF OF GUINEA
PRINCIPE
SÃO TOMÉ
ANNOBON
NILOTES
L. Rudolf
L. Albert
BUNYORO-KITARA 13th-17th Centuries
MT. KENYA
Mogadishu

NORTHERN AFRICA
700-1500 A.D.
→ Caravan Routes

counts by Arab geographers and traveling traders make historical reconstruction easier.

Empires of the western savanna. The dangers of the desert—bandits, risks of being lost and dying of thirst—meant that preparations for a trading expedition across the Sahara were made with great care. Traders traveled in large groups of up to 10,000 camels, and the journey could take from eight to twelve weeks to complete with as much as three weeks between oases. The first site of ample water and rest, the Niger River, was a convenient stopping place. Here were located peoples who knew the African savanna better than the desert travelers and who could penetrate more easily the still distant gold-producing areas. Thus the Africans living near the bend of the Niger River became important middlemen in the trade of gold for salt across the Sahara. It was just west of the Niger that Ghana, the first of the great western Sudanic kingdoms developed. (The Sudan is a geographical term for the savanna lands of western Africa and should be distinguished from the modern nation of Sudan, south of Egypt.)

According to tradition, about 400 A.D. the kingdom of Ghana (not to be confused with the modern state of that name) began to develop. Little is known about the early centuries of Ghana's growth, but by the eighth century, when Arab geographers began to write about it, Ghana had become a large empire based on lively trade and savanna-type agriculture. The government was strongly centralized, with the king being able to appoint and demote the main officers and advisers of the empire. Considered to be partly divine and able to intercede with the gods for the good of the empire, the king was also the ultimate judge of all court cases. When appearing in public he was surrounded by retainers holding gold swords, horses with gold-cloth blankets, and dogs with gold and silver collars. All the princes and advisers of the empire sat around him splendidly dressed as well.

The Arab writer al-Bakri was so impressed with Ghana that he wrote in 1067 that its army comprised 200,000 warriors with which to control the large variety of peoples in its territory. Although the primary occupation of most people in Ghana was agriculture, trade brought the kingdom its great wealth. The king claimed the right to every gold nugget coming from the mines of Wangara, though citizens could own as much gold dust as they could afford to buy. Taxes were levied on all goods entering and leaving Ghana. The wealth of this kingdom is evidenced by al-Bakri's description of the capital of Ghana, Kumbi-Saleh. It was really comprised of two towns about six miles apart, one occupied by the king and his officers and the other by merchants and strangers. In between were the dwellings of the inhabitants who grew food to supply the capital. The king's town was built like a fortress and the merchants' town, wrote al-Bakri, was even larger, with twelve mosques, two-storied stone houses, and public squares. The ruins of this latter town have been uncovered in modern-day Mauritania. Many *imama* (Muslim theologians), legal experts, and scholars lived there. Regarding the religion of the king of Ghana and his people, al-Bakri wrote:

The king's town is surrounded by huts and clumps of trees and copses, in which dwell the magicians of the nation, entrusted with the religious cult; it is there that they have placed the idols and tombs of their sovereigns.[3]

Although the king of Ghana was tolerant of the religion of Islam, he and the majority of his subjects never converted. In the eleventh century one section of the Almoravids, a group of zealous Muslim reformers living in the desert northwest of Ghana attacked Kumbi-Saleh. Ostensibly crusaders pledged to rid Ghana of its pagan practices, the Almoravids overran Ghana in 1076 and ruled for about ten years, enjoying the profits of the trans-Saharan gold trade as well as attempting religious reform. The people of Ghana, however, soon began to rebel against their conquerors and this in turn disrupted the

In this 1375 map from the Catalan Atlas, Mansa Musa, the wealthy king of Mali, awaits the arrival of a Musilim trader. The king—sometimes called Musa Mali, as in the following inscription—is holding a nugget of gold. The legend beside him reads: "This Negro lord is called Musa Mali, lord of the Negroes of Guinea. So abundant is the gold which is found in his country that he is the richest and most noble king in all the land."

security of the long trade routes. Many traders moved away to other parts of West Africa, and many small states which had owed their allegiance to Ghana became independent.

One of the provinces which declared itself independent at this time was the kingdom of Mali. In 1235 its greatest leader, Sundiata, even succeeded in conquering its former suzerain, Ghana. Sundiata's eleven brothers had been murdered by the king of Ghana, according to the oral traditions concerning this period, but Sundiata miraculously survived this purge and his praises are sung by Malian historians today as the glorious founder of the Mali empire. Sundiata and his successors conquered vast territories, with the result that Mali became larger than Ghana had ever been. Although Sundiata was not himself Muslim, his descendants were. One of the most famous kings of Mali, Mansa Musa, is well known to historians for his pilgrimage to Mecca in 1324. The splendor of his caravan with thousands of retainers, gifts of gold and ivory, horses, camels, and slaves certainly deserves its fame.

Mali's, and Mansa Musa's, wealth was based on the gold mines of Wangara and the trans-Saharan trade, just as Ghana's had been. Its major commercial city, Timbuktu, succeeded Ghana as the main point of convergence for the caravan routes and became a great metropolis and center of Muslim learning. Muslim scholars from all over the world came to Timbuktu to study and to use its huge library. The famous Muslim traveler Ibn Batuta visited Mali in 1352 and wrote a detailed description of the country. He was most impressed by its security:

Among the admirable qualities of these people, the following are to be noted: 1) The small number of acts of injustice that one finds there; for the Negroes are of all peoples those who most abhor injustice. The sultan pardons no one who is guilty of it. 2) The complete and general safety one enjoys throughout the land. The traveler has no more reason than the man who stays at home to fear brigands, thieves, or ravishers.[4]

Ibn Batuta was surprised to find that the women of Mali were often educated and had more privileges and freedom of movement

No European ever saw Timbuktu until 1828, when René Caillé, disguised as a Muslim pilgrim, made the journey. The mixture of Muslim and native architecture is apparent in his drawing of the city. Caillé was most impressed by the difficulties the builders must have encountered in setting up a great city "in the midst of the sands."

than those he had observed in all his other travels. He admitted that he did not like the food very much during his stay, but was impressed with the wealth, comfortable living, and great amount of trade that was evident there. His only disappointment was to find that many Malians were not Muslim.

Mali at its height, c. 1350, controlled an area as large as western Europe, but the descendants of Mansa Musa were less and less able to control the huge empire. Many of the segments of the empire rebelled. One of these provinces, Songhai, with its capital of Gao further down the Niger River had reestablished its independence in the fourteenth century. One of the greatest of the Songhai rulers, Sonni Ali, captured Timbuktu in 1468 and proceeded to conquer much of Mali.

To some extent Sonni Ali merely conquered the empire of Mali and substituted himself as its ruler, though Songhai eventually was larger than Mali. After thirty years of ruthless military dictatorship and cruel warfare, this great conqueror died and was replaced by one of his generals, Askia Muhammad, who chose to institute major organizational changes. He set about reorganizing the entire empire so that it might be administered peacefully and not kept under control by force. He bureaucratized the government by appointing ministers and regional administrators who were directly responsible to him and no local intermediaries. He established a professional army and expanded the naval fleet of canoes which constantly patrolled the Niger River, supplying, policing, and keeping communications open with the different parts of the empire. Taxation was regularized and attempts were made to impose more consistent judicial standards, especially Islamic ones. Askia Muhammad also encouraged Islamic scholars and revitalized Timbuktu, which had been harassed for lack of cooperation by the militaristic Sonni Ali. A traveler writing after 1520 noted:

In Timbuktu there are numerous judges, professors, and holy men, all being handsomely maintained by the king who holds scholars in much honor. Here too they sell many handwritten books from North Africa. More profit is made from selling books in Timbuktu than from any other branch of trade.[5]

At the height of his power Askia Muhammad's influence reached from the Atlantic Ocean throughout much of the northern and western sections of the continent.

Songhai was supplying great quantities of gold across the Sahara in order to satisfy the demands of wealthy Italian city-states who were financing and inspiring the Renaissance. Once again Africa's neighbors to the north coveted the wealth of the rich middleman role of the West African empires and saw no reason to continue to pay the taxes of Songhai for its services. Hence, in 1590, the king of Morocco equipped an army of 5000 men to cross the Sahara and attack Songhai. Only about 1000 Moroccan soldiers were alive at the end of the desert crossing but they had brought guns with them. The superiority of these weapons over the swords and spears of Songhai was such that the Moroccans, although greatly outnumbered, were victorious in battle. Yet they were not powerful enough to take over the complex government of Songhai and during the following years large numbers of provinces, cities, and small kingdoms broke away, and the conquerors could do little about it. The historian Abderrahman es-Sadi was born in Timbuktu at this time and as he grew up he observed the progressive decay of the Songhai empire. His experiences later motivated him to write the *Tarikh es-Sudan (History of the Sudan)*, which is the source of much information about Songhai and which he introduced with the following comment:

When the Moroccan army arrived in the Sudan they found one of God's most favored countries in richness and fertility. Peace and security reigned throughout all its provinces . . . [but] . . . now all that has changed: Danger has replaced security; misery has replaced opulence; tranquility has been succeeded by trouble, calamities, and violence.[6]

Smaller states such as Kanem-Bornu, the Hausa city-states, and the Mossi kingdoms survived independently in the century after the Moroccan invasion.

The Sudanic empires of Ghana, Mali, and Songhai had a number of common features that incline historians to group them together. Their boundaries were ill-defined and embraced a variety of ethnically and culturally diverse peoples. Often established by conquest, these empires depended in many cases on military force and personal leadership for their perpetuation. But even the most stable systems of succession cannot guarantee that strong leadership will always be available for the throne, and thus incompetent rulers usually meant a rapid weakening of the empires. Ghana, Mali, and Songhai each endured for over two centuries, but they succeeded each other as empires rather than existing alongside each other in competition. For this reason historians consider them weak and illusive.

In addition, there was in all three empires an overlay of Islamic culture represented by the scholars, merchants, urban dwellers, clerics, and administrators of the government. This culture often clashed with the non-Muslim masses who were the labor force and suppliers of food to the wealthy and professional classes. Thus, despite its hold on West Africans, Islam never took deep root in the countryside. Customs, laws, and life-styles in rural areas for the mass of the people remained radically different from those of the towns, and this was an inherent weakness in the Sudanic empires.

However, the vast empires of the Sudan existed in order to manage the long-distance trade routes, to make them secure for travelers, to maintain order and consistency in the marketplaces—in short, to ensure that the lucrative gold and salt trade went as smoothly as possible and was not interrupted by quarrels and capricious laws in every little chiefdom en route. If this was accomplished and if peace was maintained, taxes paid, and sufficient foodstuffs and troop requisitions provided, then the provinces, chiefdoms, and kingdoms that made up the empires were left alone by the central government to follow their own customs, religion, and local rulers. Therefore a period of relative peace and gradual centralization endured in the Sudan from the tenth to the seventeenth centuries. But the overall lack of cultural unity had the potential of causing the whole system to dissipate into its separate parts when exposed to a major disruption, specifically, the Moroccan invasion of 1590.

The collapse of the system was hastened not only by Moroccan inability to govern, but by the simultaneous reorientation of the trade routes. The latter was the result of the appearance in the sixteenth century of Europeans for the first time on the southern West African coast trading for gold and slaves. These first Europeans were seeking, just like the Moroccan invaders, to avoid the Sudanic middlemen in obtaining gold. But the Europeans came around by sea and so began to draw the Wangara gold trade to the south and west rather than across the desert, thus sapping the prosperity of the Sudan. After the sixteenth century there was never again to be an empire in West Africa as territorially large as Songhai had been, though eventually others just as wealthy and efficiently governed were to arise.

The impact of trade in East Africa. From the beginning of the Christian era traders from India and Arabia followed coastlines and favorable winds to the coast of East Africa in search of ivory and tortoise shell. The trade continued and grew, as Greek and Roman coins found along the coast testify. Population also grew, for the plantain was introduced to Africa from Asia about this time and made possible its support.

As Roman trade waned in the fifth century, Arab and Indian trade expanded. By the time of Muhammad the trade routes and coastal towns were very familiar to the Arabs.

By the fourteenth century the trade of the East African coast had expanded tremendously, for the 1331 travelogue of the widely traveled Muslim, Ibn Batuta (who also visited West Africa) describes numerous trade cities and bustling ports all along the coast. One in particular, Kilwa, struck Ibn Batuta as the most beautiful and well-constructed town he had seen in the world. Archaeological excavations today, which bear out some of Ibn Batuta's description, reveal the stone ruins of enormous palaces, complex mansions and peaceful mosques, arched walkways, town squares, and public fountains. Coral and wood were used to make carved arches, doors, and windows. The main palace of Kilwa was built on the very edge of a cliff overlooking the ocean and contained over 100 rooms, as well as an eight-sided bathing pool in one of its many courtyards. The remains of at least thirty-seven cities along the East African coast have been uncovered today.

Through some written records from China we know, for example, that there were extensive trade contacts between China and East Africa. The city of Malindi even sent a giraffe as a gift to the emperor of China in 1415, and the emperor responded with a fleet of Chinese sailors and numerous gifts which accompanied the Malindi traders back to Africa. Chinese desire for large quantities of ivory coupled with East African demand for Chinese porcelain found in many of the ruined cities today accounts for much of this contact.

The trading cities of East Africa spread their influence and control along the coast, but there is as yet no evidence that their influence spread very far into the interior of the continent. Each city was a unit unto itself, usually in fierce competition with the other city-states. Each had its own government, laws, taxes, police force or army, and rulers. They rarely united for defense even in the face of severe outside threat, as the arrival of Europeans would subsequently be.

The ruins in the valley of Zimbabwe, meaning "the sacred graves of the chiefs," are dominated by the massive stone wall of the temple.

The peoples and rulers of the city-states were predominantly Bantu, with a minority being Arab, Persian, and Indian who soon intermarried with the local inhabitants. The Portuguese, arriving in 1500, described the coastal people as either black, tawny, or light—in all various stages of intermarriage. The language of the coast was Swahili, a Bantu language with some Arabic, Persian, and Indian word-borrowing. It was written in Arabic script, and by the seventeenth century poems, ballads, and letters, as well as trade and government documents, were commonly composed in Swahili. The architecture of the city-states was greatly influenced by Arab architecture of the Middle East but, although some Bantu converted to Islam, indigenous religious customs were common and Islam never spread far beyond the coast. The term "Swahili" can refer to the peoples of the coast and their cosmopolitan culture as well as to their language.

Zimbabwe. Partly in response to the active coastal trade, the prosperous Bantu state of Zimbabwe emerged in what is now Rhodesia. The rulers of this kingdom built the stone city of Great Zimbabwe over a long period of time, from as early as the eighth century until the early eighteenth. Constructed of granite blocks without mortar or cement, and often in elaborate patterns, the massive walls of its temple ruins measure from ten to fifteen feet thick and from twenty to thirty feet high. The remains of the acropolis—built to be an impregnable fortress—can be seen on a nearby hill. Close by is the Valley of Ruins, the former site of a flourishing religious and administrative center.

Zimbabwe grew with the expanding coastal trade, even though it was 300 miles from the ocean, because it was the site of important gold mines. The trade of its gold with the coast was important, and many of the common people of Zimbabwe were involved in gold mining. Remains of over 7000 gold-working sites have been found, and much more gold was collected from streams. The mines were simple pits dug into the earth but some were as deep as fifty feet, and both men and women participated in the actual labor.

The Monomotapa, or king of Zimbabwe at this time, was thought by his subjects to be semidivine. He had the authority to judge the cases of the land, yet only his closest advisers were allowed to see him. He was expected to commit suicide if he became ill in order to maintain the health of the country. The main building in the Valley of Ruins was the palace of the king. Archaeologists estimate that about 1000 people occupied the site at one time; cooks, servants, farmers, and soldiers were housed with their families in smaller stone buildings that surrounded the main palace structure. Ruined stone buildings of the type found at Zimbabwe are much in evidence throughout the region. Some of the larger sites are thought to have been the sites of provincial administrative headquarters.

Early European contact. For some eight hundred years, beginning about 700 A.D., Islam was the most important outside influence in Africa and an important stimulant of trade between Africa, the Middle East, and India. Throughout this same period Islam was a dominant source of worry in Europe, as Christian enthusiasm for the Crusades against Islam demonstrates. In the fifteenth

14. Ch'iu Ying: "Peach Blossom Spring" (1530). The entire length of this hand scroll painting (detail shown) is over thirteen feet. It is done in ink and colors on silk in a precise, brilliantly refined style by one of the Ming dynasty's finest artists. It contains a careful blend of delicate and subtle colors with major attention devoted to detail. Landscape paintings such as this one are China's leading contribution to world art. Although limited in subject matter to mountains, forests, lakes, and sometimes agricultural scenes, their variations in mood are magnificently carried out. Landscape paintings of the Ming dynasty use bolder strokes, yet maintain the gentle lyricism of their predecessors.

15. (above) **Angkor Wat, Cambodia** (early twelfth century). Indian art styles spread far beyond the borders of India and in many cases not only retained vitality but increased it. Angkor Wat, the immense temple city of the Khmers in Cambodia, is considered by many to be the most perfectly realized example of Indian architectural technique. The gigantic size of the complex (its moat is two and one half miles long and one of its courtyards contains a half mile of sculptured reliefs) is matched by the brilliant spatial ordering of its profusion of galleries, sanctuaries, pavilions, and towers.

16. (right) **Aztec mural: "Rain God's Heaven"** (fifteenth century). Aztec art, as exemplified by this mural, is marked by strength and brutality. The work is painted in vivid colors and has no sense of spatial relationships, yet its strong emotional message is unmistakable. Much of the subject matter of Aztec art concerns human sacrifice which in itself was an integral part of their religion. The Aztecs believed that all their gods sprang from two deities, one male and one female. These gods in turn created the sun, the earth, and all creatures on the earth. The sun was created by one of the gods immolating himself, and to give it the energy necessary to move through the heavens, the other gods sacrificed themselves. Humanity then assumed this obligation for the gods and sacrifice to the sun became a sacred duty and necessary in order for the world to go on. Every time a human being was sacrificed, the disaster that always threatened to engulf the earth was postponed for a while. The conviction that human sacrifice was the key to life as opposed to death was so strong that it was considered a great honor to be chosen as one to be sacrificed.

17. (left) **Oni (king) of Ife** (thirteenth century). Characterized by a high degree of technical skill and a restrained, but stately realism, this bronze head is one of the masterpieces of an impressive collection of bronzes and terracottas discovered at Ife, Nigeria. The casting technique, called the *cire perdue* (lost wax) process, was possibly imported from the Mediterranean region. The modeling was done in wax over an earthen core, with another layer of earth packed around the head. The head was then heated to melt out the wax, and molten bronze was poured into the hollow form. Another theory, however, is that ancient Egypt may have been the source of Ife art, for terracottas dating from before the birth of Christ have been found in North Nigeria. Still other archaeologists believe that Ife art has neither European nor Oriental precedents. Although harmonious and noble in expression like the classical art of Greece and Rome, this head is related to other primitive art by the tribal scars on the face, the holes for attaching hair for realism, and its use in ancestor worship.

century, therefore, the Portuguese, who were in close geographical proximity to Muslim Spain and North Africa, decided that it might be possible to avoid traveling through Muslim lands to reach the spices and gold of India by sailing around them. With this in mind, they set about systematically exploring the coast of Africa, establishing several trading stations along the west coast. In 1498 Vasco da Gama succeeded in sailing around the southern tip of Africa, passed through the harbors of the East African city-states, and finally reached India.

The Portuguese explorers, a rather rough lot of sailors, were overwhelmed with the wealth and luxurious living they discovered along the East African coast. On the other hand, the suave Swahili peoples scorned the Portuguese for their lack of manners, unclean habits, and tawdry trade goods. However, the Swahili coast had been prosperous and peaceful for so long that there were few actual military defenses, and the Portuguese, certain that they could capture vast gold reserves quickly, attacked the cities, taking them by surprise and often without opposition. In most cases the towns were looted and burned. Kilwa, for example, was burned in 1505 after the Portuguese had marched ashore, said a mass, and removed all the cotton and silk stored there for trade to Zimbabwe. In the same year at Mombassa, Portuguese sailors broke into houses with axes, looted and killed, and then set the town on fire. In a letter of warning to the sultan of Malindi up the coast, the sultan of Mombassa wrote about the Portuguese:

He raged in our town with such might and terror that no one, neither man nor woman, neither the old nor the young, nor even the children however small was spared to live. His wrath was to be escaped only by flight. Not only people, but even the birds in the heavens were killed and burnt. The stench from the corpses is so overpowering that I dare not enter the town, and I cannot begin to give you an idea of the immense amount of booty which they took from the town. Pray harken to the news of these sad events, that you may yourself be preserved.[7]

Although the Portuguese built their own trade fort at Mombassa in 1590, they were unable to replace the functioning governments and complex trade networks they destroyed with anything of their own. The insecurity and fear which they instigated among the people caused the centuries-old Indian Ocean trade to wither. Swahili language and culture survived, but the trade did not revive until the early nineteenth century.

Interior East Africa. Throughout this period (500 to 1500) there were societies of peoples forming in the interior of East Africa as well. People such as the Kikuyu were organized in clans based on kinship ties and these clans in turn determined the division of land and farms which were the basis of their livelihood. Numbers of clans speaking the same language and acknowledging the same distant ancestors united to form tribes, or ethnic groups, as they are now called. But the rise and fall of these ethnic groups are barely known to historians, for no written and little archaeological evidence has survived concerning them. Oral traditions record that around 1300 A.D., tall, handsome, godlike warriors known as the Chwezi arrived in the area of Lake Victoria. They brought with them sophisticated knowledge of cattle-raising and state organization which they shared with the already present Bantu and stimulated the beginnings of the kingdom of Bunyoro-Kitara and its successor Buganda. The Chwezi disappeared as suddenly and mysteriously as they came, according to the epic poems of East Africa which immortalize them. However, the Bantu kingdoms influenced by the Chwezi continued to develop, many still being in existence in the early twentieth century.

Europeans and the slave trade. The Portuguese also made contacts with people along the west coast of Africa. Here they encountered some African kingdoms already centuries old whose prime interests were in trading with the empires of the savanna. One of these kingdoms was Benin, located in the forest of what is now southern Nigeria. The kings of Benin, called obas, had begun to rule over the area as early as the eleventh century. By the time the Portuguese arrived in 1472, the oba was very powerful with central religious and political responsibilities, living in a huge palace protected by a surrounding maze of courtyards. Benin had a powerful army and prosperous trade with the Sudan, exchanging forest products for items of the trans-Saharan trade.

The Portuguese, and the French, Dutch, and English traders who followed on their heels after 1500, were favorably impressed with the city and life-style of the Benin people. Benin was powerful enough not to suffer the fate of the East African city-states. Europeans were not allowed to live in Benin, but had to remain with their ships on the coast. They had to pay taxes and import duties and could trade only with the chosen representatives of the oba. The obas were powerful enough to enforce these rules.

Another kingdom encountered by the Portuguese was that of Kongo located near the mouth of the Congo River. The people of the Kongo, the Bakongo, responded differently to the arrival of the Europeans than had either the Swahili or Benis. Portuguese advisers and Catholic priests were welcomed by the Bakongo and invited to stay at the court of the king where their technical expertise was used to the best advantage and where

This drawing from Thomas Astley's *A New and General Collection of Voyages and Travels* depicts an audience given to Dutch traders in 1642 by Don Alvaro, king of Kongo. By this time so many Kongolese were taken into slavery that the population had become dangerously small.

large numbers of people were soon converted to Christianity. Letters of friendship and alliance passed between the Manikongo (king) and King Manuel of Portugal. Portuguese became the language of the court and many Kongolese learned to read and write it as well as church Latin. A Catholic cathedral was built and the people were encouraged by their king to adopt European dress and manners. The capital was renamed São Salvador and the king, Nzinga Myemba, took the name Dom Afonso. Schools were opened and by 1516 there were said to be over a thousand students in them.

But by the mid-sixteenth century the Portuguese had an ever increasing need for cheap labor to work in the mines and on the sugar plantations in their New World colonies and on the island of São Thome. Interest in furthering friendly relations with Kongo soon waned, except to gain slaves. At first Dom Afonso delivered his prisoners of war and criminals to the Portuguese traders and received in payment European cloth and metal. This trade was the precursor of what was to become the Atlantic slave trade, which endured into the nineteenth century. Soon Portuguese and Kongolese traders began to ignore the laws of the Kongo and developed the business of selling any person, not just criminals or prisoners of war.

The slave trade increased in Kongo rapidly. Eventually Dom Afonso wrote the king of Portugal protesting what was happening:

There are many traders in all corners of the country. They bring ruin to the country. Every day people are enslaved and kidnapped, even nobles, even members of the King's own family.[8]

Dom Afonso gradually curbed the slave trade in his country and hence the Portuguese began to engage in slave trade in other parts of Africa. Finally in 1540 Dom Afonso was shot by some disgruntled Portuguese traders while he was attending mass. This ended the good relations between Kongo and Portugal and to what many historians see as the first unsuccessful attempt to westernize and modernize an African kingdom.

By the seventeenth century, the slave trade had become the dominant commerical enter-

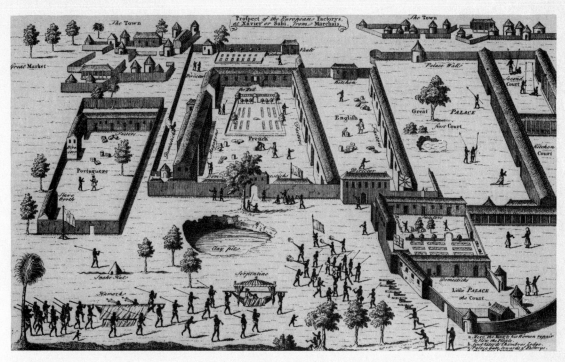

Slave compounds were often constructed on the West Coast of Africa where the captives were held before being shipped off to America or the West Indies. In this sixteenth-century map, a native king maintains "factorys" consisting of separate quarters for slave traders from Portugal, France, England, and the Netherlands.

prise along the West African coast. Domestic slavery had been practiced in Africa since ancient times, but the slave in African society was considered a part of the family, could marry, own property, own a slave of his own, and even inherit from his master. Slaves could achieve freedom, usually over several generations, by merging with the master family. Slaves might also be sold or beaten depending on the society and the individual. More harsh than this domestic slavery was the ancient slave trade which dates back at least to the time when the Egyptians sought African slaves for their armies. Over the centuries several hundred thousand slaves were exported from the coast of East Africa and across the Sahara to the Middle East. When European trade began, however, West African slaves were brought to the Americas in numbers approaching ten million from the period 1450–1850.[9] Furthermore, for every slave sold in the Americas, another is said to have lost his or her life in the cruel roundup in Africa or on the crowded slave ships.

The stimulant of the European-African slave trade was the plantation economy, es-

pecially sugar, of the West Indies and, much later, the cotton economy of the American South. Sugar was in great demand in sixteenth- to eighteenth-century Europe, and the West Indies was one of the few climates suitable for its growth. The sugar and cotton were exported to Europe where they were manufactured into goods such as rum, brandy, and cotton cloth. These, added to other manufactured items as guns and iron tools, were then shipped to the west coast of Africa. Here they were exchanged for the slaves who were packed in large numbers into the ships and taken to the West Indies where their cheap labor was essential for the production of the raw materials. This sequence is sometimes referred to as the triangular trade because all three points were needed to make it operate. The transport of the slaves across the Atlantic is called the "middle passage" and it was during that crossing that the most suffering and death occurred, for conditions on the ships were cramped and unsanitary.

Both Europeans and Africans accepted the trade and cooperated in it. It was a very lu-

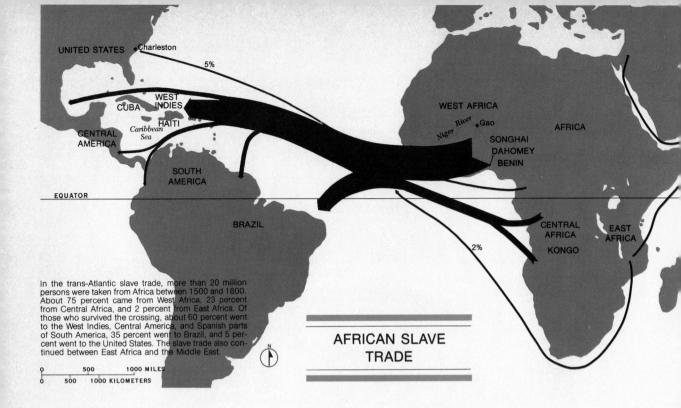

In the trans-Atlantic slave trade, more than 20 million persons were taken from Africa between 1500 and 1800. About 75 percent came from West Africa, 23 percent from Central Africa, and 2 percent from East Africa. Of those who survived the crossing, about 60 percent went to the West Indies, Central America, and Spanish parts of South America, 35 percent went to Brazil, and 5 percent went to the United States. The slave trade also continued between East Africa and the Middle East.

AFRICAN SLAVE
TRADE

crative enterprise, bringing as much as 200 percent profit to some European and African traders. Slaves were obtained in the hinterland by Africans who then delivered the victims to the slave ships on the coast. African rulers and middlemen were very jealous of their trading rights and privileges. Hence Europeans were rarely permitted by Africans to penetrate into the interior of Africa. They were forced to live on ships anchored offshore, in special locales in the coastal towns, or in forts built on the shoreline.

The rise of West African forest states. Until the late fifteenth century all commercial contacts in West Africa had been north across the Sahara. With the arrival of Europeans the pattern of trade was revolutionized, routes shifting to the west and south by sea. As the trans-Saharan trade dwindled and the trans-Atlantic trade increased, the states along the savanna became less important, though they did not die out completely. Instead other kingdoms in the forest along the west coast of Africa developed. On the basis of the traffic in human beings, new West African states such as Dahomey, Oyo, and Asante rose to power and wealth. Dahomey, for example, was dependent and prospered on the slave trade until it decreased in the early

nineteenth century. Other states such as Oyo were adversely affected by the demoralizing experience of continuous slave raiding. Oyo's otherwise sound and fascinating system of complex government degenerated into a century of civil war which left it bitterly divided.

On the other hand, the state of Asante which developed in the late seventeenth century was able to diversify its economy such that it was not dependent on the slave trade alone. It had gold deposits for which Europeans and Arabs traded more eagerly than for slaves. It also had forest products which it deliberately cultivated, such as the kola nut, a type of chewy nut highly valued by Muslims. Thus Asante traded as much with the savanna-Muslim states to the north as with the European traders to the south. Asante was able to build up a highly centralized system of government, and even a certain sense of nationalism and patriotism emerged. Therefore it had a strength which, coupled with its economic advantage, helped it to resist the European imperialist attacks of the nineteenth century.

Historians continue to study and debate the long-term effects of the slave traffic, and researchers are reluctant to make sweeping generalizations about its effects in West Africa where it peaked in about 1790 and was outlawed by the British in 1807. Though its ultimate inhumanity and cruelty must not be ignored, the slave trade also resulted in a new type of contact with the outside world that was not completely evil. The slave trade helped introduce new medicines and tools, and it has led to the development of new, constructively organized state systems. The introduction of crops from the Americas such as maize, cassava, pineapples, and coffee was also a result. Depopulation caused by the slave trade was in many instances more than offset by an increase in population made possible by the more productive crops and by the stability and security of centralized states like Asante. It was in fact not until the end of the slave trade in the nineteenth century, and the subsequent recession in the African economy, that Europeans began to attempt serious geographic exploration and political domination of Africa's interior.

Some historians feel, however, that the origins of modern western racism lie in the years of participation in this dehumanizing activity—that Europeans developed theories of the blacks' inferiority in order to justify their participation in the slave trade. If this is so, it is indeed the most tragic legacy the slave trade has left.

The peopling of South Africa. One area of Africa which remained almost completely unaffected by the trans-Saharan trade, Islamic expansion, and even Portuguese greed, was the southern tip of the continent, from the Limpopo River to the Cape of Good Hope. Here the Khoisan people continued their hunting and pastoral existence, as yet unaffected by the Bantu expansion. In 1652, however, the Dutch chose the Cape of Good Hope as a site for a colony to serve as a supply station for their ships to India. As the colony of white settlers expanded, they slowly overwhelmed the native Khoisan, most of whom died off. The Bantu expansion of central and eastern Africa continued through the years and by the seventeenth century had reached the southeastern tip of the African continent. As the Bantu turned west, they and the expanding Dutch settlers, called Boers, encountered each other for the first

time in numbers at the Fish River in 1736. Then began a competition for land and livelihood between Boer and Bantu.

The Bantu response to the new competition for land was to become more militant. The Zulu people particularly, under their great leader Shaka (1787–1828), organized their various clans into a strict military society. Males and females served in the army from puberty until they were released for marriage. The military unit, not the village, came to be the focus of identity and organization. The Zulu made fierce warfare on their fellow Bantu starting in the eighteenth century, driving enemies back north and sending a wave of violence, insecurity, and population pressure through East Africa. Yet their greatest enemy was the ever expanding Boer coming from the west. Caught between the Boers and the sea, the Zulu and other Bantu groups were defeated again and again by the Boers as all parties struggled for the land—a struggle that continues in less overt forms to this day (see Chapter 36).

Indigenous culture of black Africa. What can be said of the collective achievement of the African before the European impact? The extent of control over nature and technological development certainly varied greatly from place to place in Africa. Hundred-ton barges moved goods up and down the Niger River, and Swahili *dhows* (large sailing vessels) plied the eastern coast while reed canoes alone were used by fishermen on some of Africa's interior rivers and lakes. Large stone houses in Zimbabwe, arched palaces in Kilwa, and multistoried houses in Asante and Timbuktu contrasted sharply with small mud and thatch huts scattered across the savanna where poor farmers labored for their meager crops. Shifting hoe cultivation, growing crops on a plot for only two or three years and then leaving it fallow for ten or twenty, was practiced by most African farmers. Yet Ethiopians plowed their fields with oxen, and the Kikuyu farmers terraced and irrigated their lands. In some parts of Africa the poor clothed themselves at best with the skins of animals. But in many areas, particularly in the savanna where cotton was grown, thread was spun and elaborate designs were woven into beautiful and colorful cloth on large looms. Some towns even had municipal dye vats for the use of the inhabitants. Although some very remote areas of Africa still used only stone tools, metalworking was highly developed throughout most of the continent, and weapons, shields, bridles, even chain mail, as well as utensils, containers, money, and exact weights and measures were produced. Later the blacksmiths were able to produce guns and ammunition modeled after European imports.

The skilled workers of African societies often organized themselves into tightly knit groups which tried to keep the secrets of their skill within their own families. Men were not permitted near where women fired the pots they sold, and blacksmiths were such a secretive group that people often attributed magical abilities to them. The miners, weavers, masons, shipwrights, and tanners all guarded the knowledge of their skills, demanding a fair value for their labor. Strikes were not unknown to historical Africa.

The type of manufacturing and technology that developed indigenously in Africa is called cottage industry, and as such it was not able to compete with the mass manufacturing and industrialized techniques of the Europeans in the eighteenth and nineteenth centuries. African-made guns and iron hoes for example could not be produced as quickly or consistently as those from English foundries. African-produced brass and leather jewelry could not compete with the flood of European glass beads. Thus African technology is often ignored or denigrated, even though Europe herself did not progress beyond cottage industry until the seventeenth and eighteenth centuries. Europe's amazing development of industrialization is indeed its major contribution to the centuries-old interaction of European and African culture, and industrialization will continue to be the one aspect of European culture that Africans feel they must acquire.

African cultures, however, have much to offer westerners who wish to study them. African societies in their laws, governments, education, and codes of social conduct were complex and efficiently regulated long before the European impact. Rules and conventions regarding the role of parents, worship of gods, education of children, and laws concerning land occupation and possession of property were carefully worked out. Effective social methods were at hand to compel the individual to conform without often resorting to use of a police force.

In political organization the basic unit for many Africans was the ethnic group, consisting of many clans who recognized a chief but often only as the first among equals. Hundreds of these ethnic units, microscopic or large, still exist in Africa today. Yet one of the most fascinating aspects of African society is the vast variety of forms of political organization it had. The people of Zimbabwe had a semidivine king while the Zulus organized themselves into a military state. The East African cities developed independently around trade and profit, the names of their leaders in many cases being unimportant and forgotten. The empires of Ghana, Mali, and Songhai became more and more bureaucratically organized, and yet more vast in size, incorporating a variety of peoples and life-styles. Other groups like the Asante achieved a centralized bureaucratic state, compact in area, and compelled by a sense of nationhood. Dahomeans had strict, statewide economic planning, with an annual census in order to determine what the taxes would be, how much food should be planted, and how many people could become traders or soldiers. Moreover, in almost all these cases, the African rulers, be they chiefs or kings or merchants, were rarely despots. They had to govern within the framework of accepted law and custom and seek and obey the advice of their council of elders, the representatives of the people.

Religion played an essential role in African life, touching every phase of it. While religious practices varied from tribe to tribe, they shared some aspects in common. Animism, as traditional religion is sometimes called, centered around the belief that the dead depart from this life but continue to observe and influence it. One had an obligation to honor and remember one's dead relations regularly, such as when eating, and to appease them if they became angry. Most African societies also believed in some sort of supreme being or highest power, but this power was far removed from this world.

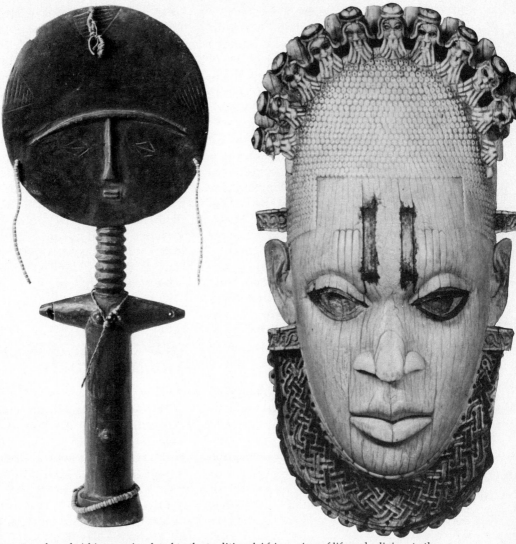

The purpose of much African art is related to the traditional African view of life and religion; to the powers and prejudices of the spirit world; and to symbolize the might and prestige of the kings and rulers. The doll from Asante (left) is carved of blackened wood; its round face is attached to a cylindrical body by a long neck. Fertility symbols such as these were carried by pregnant women and were considered to bring good luck and healthy children. The ivory mask of the king of Benin (right) was carved in the sixteenth century and features heads of Portuguese traders as its crown. It is thought to symbolize the divine kingship of its subject.

Rather, lesser spirits such as those of thunder or war or smallpox have the ability to affect directly such occurrences in life, and these gods must also be remembered and dealt with when necessary. The strict monotheism of Islam introduced another variation into the quite varied religious beliefs of Africans, at times conflicting with them, and at times converting them.

African arts are an integral part of African cultures and societies. They are not removed from life and hung in isolation in museums nor preserved under glass. African music, for

example, is part of everyday life. African songs, much like western traditional folk songs, are about real-life situations: hunting, planting, cattle, love affairs, money, and famous heroes. Unlike the case of musical events in the western world where there are usually two parties—the artist and the audience, all Africans participate in the rendering of music. There are of course certain songs sung only on special occasions such as funerals, weddings, or coronations. Musicians were often kept at the courts of ancient kings such as in Mali and Axum to play whenever the king appeared. But on the whole African music is more communal than individual and audiences usually join in with clapping and dancing.

African visual art par excellence is sculpture. It is an ancient skill in Africa, with sculpted terra-cotta heads found in Nigeria dating to as early as 500 B.C. Sculpture is carved of wood, ivory, or soapstone, or cast in terra-cotta and bronze. Some of the bronze work has been compared to the best produced by Renaissance artists. A naturalistic bronze head found at the site of the ancient city of Ife in Nigeria, a forerunner of Benin, has been pronounced by art historians the finest surviving example of African art.

Sculpture often served a functional role too. For example, the kingdom of Benin not only created portraits of its kings and nobles but left a record of important events such as specific wars, alliances, good harvests, and the arrival of the Portuguese in plaques of bronze which were mounted on the walls of the oba's palace.

A rich body of folk tales and oral tradition attests to the artistry and imagination of Africans. Important literary and historical sources were produced written in Arabic, but not in the native languages. A perceptive reason for writing and studying history was given by the African historian es-Sadi of seventeenth-century Timbuktu in the preface to his Songhai *History of the Sudan:*

I saw the ruin of learning and its utter collapse and because learning is rich in beauty and fertile in its teaching, since it tells men of their fatherland, their ancestors, their annals, the names of their heroes and what lives these led, I asked divine help and decided to record all that I myself could gather on the subject of the Songhai princes of the Sudan, their adventures, their history, their achievements and their wars.[10]

African culture has indeed had a long tradition. While it would not compare materially with later European industrialization, and while it was uneven in development across the continent, it could boast outstanding sculpture, complicated and vital music, functional and well-organized political forms, prosperous commerce, crafts and cottage industry, and in some areas its own litera-

ture. Some tribes paid careful attention to family planning and population control. Capital punishment was rare, only the habitual murderer or thief being put to death. The rights of women—in relation to property, custody of children, and protection from abuse from the husband—were often more carefully spelled out than in western societies until very recent times. One of the most admirable traits of African society was the prevalence of the ideal of community. A built-in system of social security took care of the needy, the mentally ill, the old, the orphan, and the widow. Unlike the westerner with his emphasis on individual advance (often at the expense of the group), the African has always placed the group and family interests above his own.

OLD CIVILIZATIONS IN THE NEW WORLD

The earliest American immigrants. The question of when the Western Hemisphere was first settled remains uncertain. It is generally agreed that man did not originate in the Americas, for no bones of humans earlier than *Homo sapiens* have been found there. Man was already fully developed when he became the earliest immigrant to seek his fortune in the New World.

Making their way from Asia to Alaska via the Bering land bridge, nomadic groups spread out in various directions on the American continents. Until the 1920's it was thought that the Amerinds (American Indians) came to the Western Hemisphere as recently as three thousand years ago. The date of their arrival, however, has been progressively modified. Significant research in the 1960's has dated the Bering crossing as far back as 15,000 B.C. The most spectacular claim, not yet fully substantiated, is the discovery in central Mexico of crude tools dating back 40,000 years ago. It is apparent that the chronology of the Amerind migrations will be substantially rewritten in the near future.

The cultural levels achieved by different groups of Amerinds before the arrival of the

PACIFIC

OCEAN

M E X I C O

Rio Las Balsas

Tula AZTEC
• Teotihuacan
• Tenochtitlán

Mayapan • Chichén Itzá
• MAYA
Uxmal

YUCATAN
PENINSULA

BRITISH
HONDURAS

Tikal
MAYA
GUATEMALA HONDURAS
• Copan

EL
SALVADOR NICARAGUA

COSTA RICA
PANAMA

**AZTEC AND MAYAN
CIVILIZATIONS**

Europeans varied. Most of the Indians of North America and of the Amazon region never progressed further than the Neolithic stage, with its dependence upon hunting, primitive agriculture, and village life. By contrast, the Mayas and the Aztecs in Mexico and Central America and the Incas in the Andes of Peru created advanced civilizations on a par with those which arose in Asia and the Near East. Perhaps the major reason for the more advanced cultures of the Mayas, Aztecs, and Incas was the efficient domestication of the all-important maize, or Indian corn, known as the "food of the gods." This former wild grass, skillfully bred into a basic crop, was capable of supporting large populations.

Unfortunately, we probably know less about these remarkable civilizations than about any great civilization of the Old World. In their fanatical zeal, many early Spanish *conquistadores* and missionaries destroyed libraries, dismantled cities, and suppressed as much of the native tradition as possible. The historical record of the Americas was damaged beyond repair.

The splendid culture of the Mayas. At its height, Mayan civilization was much more advanced than any other on the western continents. At least a thousand years before the birth of Christ, the Mayan Indians migrated into northern Central America. At the time that the Roman Empire and the classical civilization of the Mediterranean were collapsing, the Mayas had built wonderful cities in the southern part of their territory. Later, the

southern cities of what is called the Mayan classical period sank into decay, and the center of the Mayan civilization shifted northward to the Yucatán peninsula. From about 980 to 1200 a confederacy of independent city-states held sway; and during that period there occurred a splendid Mayan renaissance in architecture and art.

Within the city-states strict social stratification existed: the highest classes were the priests and nobles; below them were the farmers, craftsmen, and merchants; the last two levels included the lowest freemen and the slaves making up the bottom rank. The slaves performed the drudgery and heavy work; their lot was especially arduous, for until the arrival of the Spaniards there were no beasts of burden or wheeled vehicles in North and Central America.

Most of the populace labored in the fields surrounding the cities. The rich soil laid bare when the jungle was cleared away was made more productive by irrigation. The Mayas raised squash, pumpkins, chili peppers, and many grains and vegetables. But maize—the mainstay of their civilization—was the chief crop, supplying 80 percent of their food.

Religion permeated all phases of Mayan life. Dominated by a powerful priesthood, the government was a form of theocracy. Education was concerned primarily with religion, and reading and writing were the private domain of the clergy. The numerous gods of the Mayas were divided into three general groups: the deities of the sky, the earth, and the underworld. To maintain an accurate schedule of religious observances, which were intimately linked to their agricultural way of life, the Mayas constructed a calendar which approaches our own in accuracy. They also built several observatories, which were run by the priests; exactness in astronomical calculations was possible because of the excellent numerical system the Mayas devised.

Of all the Amerinds, the Mayas came the closest to developing an efficient system of writing. They used an advanced system of pictographs rather than alphabetic letters or

Tikal, located in what is now northern Guatemala, is the oldest and one of the largest of the Mayan temple centers. The Mayas lived close to their fields and only came to their cities for religious ceremonies and to work on necessary construction.

a syllabic system, but no Rosetta Stone has yet been discovered to give us a key to the hieroglyphics which adorned their monuments, buildings, jewelry, pottery, and books.

In architecture and sculpture the Mayas produced work of the highest quality. In the plaza of a Mayan city was a terraced mound or pyramid, topped by a temple. The highly stylized sculpture which decorated the temple terraces is regarded by some art experts as among the world's best, despite the fact that Mayan sculptors did their intricate carving without the aid of anything better than stone tools. Almost completely religious in inspiration, Mayan art depicted the deities and the animals connected with them—snakes, frogs, jaguars, and hummingbirds. Minor arts such as weaving, jade sculpture, ceramics, and gold and silver work were also highly developed and showed an extremely sophisticated sense of design which compares favorably with the best of Egyptian art.

Eventually the Mayan cities fell victim to internal strife, in which petty chieftains fought for supremacy. In addition to civil war, inroads were made by Toltec and Aztec invaders, who eventually conquered the Mayas. After the conquest, the Mayan population and culture declined. When the *conquistadores* came upon the scene, the country was in chaos; and the Spaniards found it a simple matter to subdue the Mayan peoples.

The warlike Aztecs. In the early centuries A.D. the peoples of the Mexican plateau were also advancing in civilization. They built cities, pyramids, and temples, which can be seen at Teotihuacán, near Mexico City. As warlike peoples came in from the north, empires arose, for example, the Toltec empire. The last and best known migrants, the Aztecs, entered central Mexico and, about 1325, founded a lake settlement called Tenochtitlán on the site of the present Mexico City. Then, allying themselves with other Mexican Indian tribes, they created a confederacy which in the fifteenth century ruled an area extending across Mexico from the Gulf of Mexico to the Pacific Ocean. Like the ancient Assyrians, the Aztecs glorified war, maintained a superb fighting force, and plundered the lands of their neighbors.

Dominating the one-quarter-square-mile Great Temple precinct in the Aztecs' capital city of Tenochtitlán was the huge double pyramid sacred to Uitzilopochtli, sun god and god of war, and Tlaloc, the rain god. The precinct was separated by a "serpent wall" and a moat from the rest of the city.

However, Aztec power lasted less than a century, for the arrival of Cortés in 1519 brought about its collapse.

Scholars have held different opinions concerning the Aztec form of government. Earlier writers looked upon it as an empire, ruled by an absolute king. Many historians today feel that the Aztec government was essentially a democracy. In Aztec society the main controller of rank was ability. As in our own society, a man could rise to any position if he had the requisite ability. Thus, through personal talent and initiative, a craftsman or farmer might become a priest or a member of the tribal council. Among the soldiers, rank was determined mainly by success in war. Chiefs were elected from powerful families and could be removed; sons or brothers of chieftains succeeded them only if they were capable.

While the Aztecs worshiped a pantheon of gods, their devotion to the sun was particu-larly important and unusually barbaric. In every city of their domain, great pyramids were built, topped by temples to the sun and rain. There, stone altars were set up, on which thousands of people were sacrificed to Uitzilopochtli, the god of war and the sun. Victims included men, women, and children, who were stretched out on a sacrificial stone where the priests tore out their hearts as offerings to the god. Aztec military superiority assured a large number of captives for these sacrifices.

Like the Romans, the Aztecs borrowed many aspects of their culture from their predecessors or captives. In fact, a fair analogy may be drawn between the Mayas and Aztecs in the New World and the ancient Greeks and Romans. Generally speaking, the Mayas were more artistic and intellectual than the Aztecs and remind us somewhat of the Greeks. The brusque and brutal characteristics of the Aztecs can be likened to the

A natural fortress, Machu Picchu was built by the Incas probably after 1440 on a narrow ridge between two mountain peaks. It appears to have been the residence and stronghold of the last Incan ruler after the Spanish conquest had begun. When the ruler died, the city was abandoned and lost until it was rediscovered in 1911.

tendencies which the Romans sometimes displayed.

The Incas. About the eleventh century some people known as Incas (children of the sun) settled in the heartland of the Andes. Some archaeologists believe that they wandered northward from the Lake Titicaca region until they came to the valley of Cuzco. From there they began to extend their dominion over the mountain peoples and the coastal dwellers. From 1438 until the arrival of the *conquistador* Pizarro in 1532, a vast Inca empire flourished, extending for about 2700 miles along the western coast of the continent and including an estimated population of ten million at the time of the Spanish conquest. Even today the bulk of the peoples on the Peruvian coast and in the highlands are descended from Inca stock.

The Inca form of government was a hereditary absolute monarchy, ruled by a king called the Inca, who exercised the power of life and death over his subjects. Actually, it was a true theocracy, for the people were sun worshipers who believed that the Inca was an offspring of the sun.

The power of the ruler depended largely on an excellent military organization based on compulsory and universal military training. Another source of power was control by the Inca of all the food throughout the empire. If any district produced more than it needed, he had the surplus stored for future use or transferred to a district which through drought or other misfortunes had failed to produce enough food.

The absolute control which the Inca exercised over his subjects made possible the magnificent construction projects in the empire. Immense slabs carved out of the mountain sides were trimmed at the quarry to fit exactly into a specific niche in a temple or fortress wall; no mortar was used by the Incas. Despite their lack of wheeled vehicles, the Incas transported the giant blocks for miles through the mountains. A splendid system of roads and trails radiated from Cuzco to every part of the Inca realm.

Why did the wealthy, powerful Inca and Aztec empires fall so easily before a handful of European conquerors during the sixteenth century? A primary reason is that both the great Indian empires of the Western Hemispheres were weakened by internal strife; the tribes ruled by the Incas and the Aztecs were restive under the control of their conquerors. Thus the Spanish with their firearms—weapons completely unknown to the Indians—were able to hasten a process of political dissolution perhaps already under way.

SUMMARY

Most of the Indians of North America never achieved what is usually called "civilization," but in Mexico and Central and South America a number of brilliant civilizations emerged—those of the Aztecs, Mayas, and Incas. The Aztecs have been compared to the Romans; they were practical, martial people, skillful at conquest and at governing subject peoples. By contrast, the Mayas have been likened to the Greeks; they were great builders and artists, and they were also scholars and scientists who invented a remarkable calendar, studied astronomy, and pursued mathematics. Of all the Indian nations of the Americas, the Incas should be remembered for developing one of the first totalitarian states in history.

During the many centuries covered by this volume, little has been seen of Africa south of the Sahara. This vast region lay on the periphery of great world movements; therefore much of African history was unknown and the achievements of its people usually dismissed as inconsequential. A more accurate evaluation, however, has developed in recent times. The continent of Africa has several different ecological regions. In the north and south are narrow regions of fertile coast. Farther inland are deserts—the Sahara and the Kalahari. The deserts of Africa merge into large regions of savanna where populations have prospered because of the farming and pastoralism that are possible there. In the west-central section of the continent is the rain forest. The rivers of Africa connect the villages and cities and are a means for transporting goods for trade.

Throughout the centuries many great empires have risen and fallen. One of the earliest ironworking centers in Africa gave rise to the ancient kingdom of Kush. Axum was another rich empire that existed at this time and even supplanted Kush in its wealth and greatness. Ancient Ghana, Mali, and Songhai were three wealthy empires in the western savanna that existed from the ninth to the sixteenth centuries. They were based on the gold and salt trade across the Sahara, and their armies and governments controlled large areas. Their cities, such as Timbuktu, became centers of scholarship. From the seventh through the fourteenth centuries, trading ships from Arabia, India, and China carried on much trade with the East African coast. Thriving city-states grew there until the Portuguese destroyed much of the East African trade after 1500. Another great state that developed in the East African interior was Zimbabwe. The extensive ruins of large stone buildings are evidence of the power and wealth of this kingdom. Forest states, such as Benin, Dahomey, and Asante developed in conjunction with the arrival of the Europeans in search of trade and slaves. However, the slave trade did much damage to many African communities until it ended in the nineteenth century.

Throughout its long history, Africa has always maintained its own unique culture. Its sculpture, for instance, follows complex traditions and is comparable to the best work produced by European artists (see Color Plate 17). In recent decades, scholars, recognizing that Africans may not have attained the technological and industrial achievements of Europeans and Asians, have nevertheless pointed out the Africans' significant advances in social and political organization and in the arts.

SUGGESTIONS FOR READING

Basil Davidson, **Africa: History of a Continent** (Macmillan, 1972) is a superbly illustrated survey. E. J. Murphy, **History of African Civilization*** (Dell, 1974) is a good introductory general history of precolonial Africa. See also Harry A. Gailey, **History of Africa: From Earliest Times to 1800*** (Holt, Rinehart and Winston, 1970); and Robert July, **A History of the African People,** rev. ed. (Scribner's, 1974), two widely used surveys.

Margaret Shinnie, **Ancient African Kingdoms*** (St. Martin's, 1965) covers the early period of African history, discussing and illustrating archaeological findings. Easily read histories by regions are: Basil Davidson, **History of West Africa*** (Doubleday, 1966); and **History of East and Central Africa*** (Doubleday, 1969). See also Derek Wilson, **A History of South and Central Africa*** (Cambridge, 1975).

For additional facets of African history see J. D. Fage and R. A. Oliver, eds., **Papers in African Prehistory*** (Cambridge, 1970); Philip Curtin, ed., **Africa Remembered: Narratives by West Africans from the Era of the Slave Trade*** (Wisconsin, 1968). Other topics of interest are R. Oliver and C. Oliver, **Africa in the Days of Exploration*** (Prentice-Hall); F. Willett, **African Art: An Introduction*** (Praeger, 1971); and J. Maquet, **Civilizations of Black Africa*** (Oxford, 1972).

J. D. Fage, ed., **Africa Discovers Her Past*** (Oxford, 1970) contains essays evaluating new approaches to African history. Basil Davidson, **The African Genius: An Introduction to Social and Cultural History** (Little, Brown, 1970) is a sympathetic and scholarly analysis of indigenous cultures.

S. G. Morley, **The Ancient Maya** (Stanford) is the best general survey. V. W. von Hagen, **The World of the Maya*** (Mentor) is a brief survey.

F. Peterson, **Ancient Mexico*** (Capricorn) is a valuable account. Brief, lucid surveys of Aztec civilization are V. W. von Hagen, **Aztec: Man and Tribe*** (Mentor); and G. C. Vaillant, **The Aztecs of Mexico*** (Penguin). See also A. Caso, **Aztecs, People of the Sun** (Oklahoma Pr., 1970), a lavishly illustrated work; R. McC. Adams, **The Evolution of Urban Society: Early Mesopotamia and Prehispanic Mexico** (Aldine, 1966); and J. Soustelle, **Daily Life of the Aztecs on the Eve of the Spanish Conquest*** (Stanford).

J. A. Mason, **Ancient Civilization of Peru*** (Peter Smith) is an anthropological history of the culture and peoples of pre-Columbian Peru. See also V. W. von Hagen, **Realm of the Incas*** (Mentor); and B. Flornoy, **The World of the Inca*** (Anchor), a scholarly account of the Inca empire at its height.

*Indicates a less expensive paperbound edition.

This is the profile of a representative family of the influential *pochteca* class, merchants in charge of foreign trade who also played a strategic political role in Aztec society. The family lived at Tlaltelolco, the center of Mexico's commercial institutions. The time is 1519, immediately prior to the arrival of the Spaniards under Cortés.

Acamapichtli is restless and unable to sleep. Too much spiced iguana? Or is it tomorrow's festivities, in which the family will celebrate both Atototl's marriage and his own birthday? His daughter seems happy, and the young man's prospects are excellent. But the household won't be the same, and besides, birthdays make Acamapichtli pensive. He's getting old — 44 tomorrow — and still no grandchildren. What lies ahead for his family and himself?

From his second-story bedroom, he can see in the moonlight across much of Tlaltelolco to the twin city of Tenochtitlán. These two centers occupy a square of some 2500 acres on Lake Texcoco. Two centuries of labor have transformed the area into a network of raised earthworks and canals, and urban life is organized around the two principal centers, each possessing its pyramidal temple and square, together with palaces, residential districts, and government buildings. From the platform atop the 114-step pyramid at Tlaltelolco one can see the aqueduct bringing fresh water from Chapultepec as well as the causeways leading to the island capital. One axis runs from Tlaltelolco to the great temple at Tenochtitlán, and the capital's principal thoroughfares are wide and straight. Half of each street is surfaced with beaten earth, while the other half is occupied by a canal, along which ply boats and barges. Every day a thousand men clean the streets of the capital.

Acamapichtli belongs to an increasingly important class, the Pochteca, traveling merchants comprising a hereditary guild with its own gods, judges, and privileges. A level below the ruling class of chief priests, soldiers, and civil servants, the Pochteca were preoccupied not with prestige but with the power that wealth creates. Their essential role derived from the way that towns had developed — each specialized in certain goods, such as metalwork, woven cloth, and pottery; trade was regularly carried on between centers hundreds of miles apart. It was the Pochteca who organized and led the caravans of porters which journeyed from the central valley of Mexico to remote areas on the Pacific and Gulf coasts.

They bought and sold throughout the Aztec possessions and even beyond, exchanging the manufactured goods of the capital — embroidered clothes, golden jewels, and rabbit-hair blankets —

for such luxury items as jade, amber, jaguar skins, and exotic plumes. Valuable as these exchanges were, however, they accounted only partly for the Pochteca's strategic role. Aztec rule had been created by conquest, and it existed by virtue of tribute levied on the conquered provinces. They had to provide annual taxes in the form of raw materials: gold discs and gold dust or vast amounts of cotton, corn, cacao, and rubber. This tribute was borne to the capital on the shoulders of porters led by the Pochteca.

These traders lived in their own urban districts — the most important was at Tlaltelolco, which had the largest marketplace in Mexico. There Acamapichtli felt secure in his wealth and status. He was a guild officer and no longer traveled himself, but supplied the younger traders with their material. He helped supervise the departure of the caravans and presided over the ceremonies on their return, represented the guild before the emperor, and served in the guild's own law courts.

Acamapichtli thought of his son who was already justifying his birth name, Quauhtlatoa (speaking eagle). As a young trading merchant, he had proved adept in learning the language of distant, and often hostile, tribes and had led caravans that were no less political than mercantile in their objectives. Quauhtlatoa and his young associates led a life of high adventure, spearheading alike the commercial and strategic campaigns of the state. Commerce preceded conquest, and the traveling Pochteca acted as spies, reporting on the strengths and weaknesses of still unconquered tribes, and even stirring up trouble so that the emperor could become "personally insulted" and undertake reprisals that culminated in territorial gains. Quauhtlatoa had quickly proved his ability as both merchant and warrior. On his second expedition to the north, he had personally captured three prisoners and had been present at the temple at Tlaltelolco when they were sacrificed to Yacatecutli, the god of commerce and merchants. He had thus proved his manhood and soon claimed his right of marriage which took place when he was twenty-two to the daughter of another merchant.

All Aztec children were entitled to an education, but the Pochteca were also allowed to send their male offspring to either the *calmecal* or *telpochcalli* type of school. One of Quauhtlatoa's cousins had shown a scholarly disposition and had gone to the *calmecal*. By its severe standards, requiring continuous fasts, penances, working on the temple's lands, and drawing blood from one's own ears and legs to sacrifice with incense to the gods, the *calmecal* prepared its students for the highest offices of state and the priesthood. Much less austere had been Quauhtlatoa's education at the *telpochcalli*, "the house of the young men." They had for their masters, not priests, but experienced warriors. Here they concentrated on learning the arts of warfare. As a student at the shool. Quauhtlatoa enjoyed a communal existence, enlivened by dancing and songs, and by the company of young women, the *auianime*, officially provided courtesans. Among his other amusements were *tlachtli*, the ancient Mexican ballgame played on courts marked by two carved stone rings on their side walls; *patolli*, a dice game where he could indulge the national passion for gambling; and hunting, for which his trading expeditions into the hinterland offered him scope. To other peoples, the Aztecs could give the impression of excessive zeal in warfare and atonement by human sacrifice, yet in personal behavior they instilled the virtues of restraint in manners, dress, and deportment and the sanctity of family life. So from childhood, Quauhtlatoa had been warned against alcoholic excesses and the stringent laws against public drunkenness. Similarly, he knew that not even the highest dignitaries would escape the punishment of death for both parties caught in adultery.

Acamapichtli's thoughts now returned to his daughter and tomorrow's wedding. He had always indulged her, and for good reason. As a little girl she had been bright and shown an aptitude for spinning, and subsequently had learned to spin cotton, grind corn efficiently, and use the loom to weave cloth of superior quality. Like other girls of her class, Atototl had been consecrated to the temple when young and for several years had stayed there for instruction from the elderly priestesses. She had become expert in making intricately embroidered materials and temple vestments, took part in the rituals, and offered incense to the gods several times a night. Prior to her marriage Atototl had little or no contact with the opposite sex. But now her girlhood was at an end—tomorrow a complicated marriage ceremony involving the two families and lasting some five days would begin. At its conclusion, she would enter into her full status in Aztec society: wife, mother, matron attending the many ceremonies open to her, matchmaker—and, when old, free to make speeches at the family feasts, as befits a society which honors longevity in both sexes.

The moonlit waters of the lake of Texcoco stretch eastward into darkness. Acamapichtli compares the gleaming temple to his left with its pyramidal twin in Tenochtitlán, their tops glowing from the ever-tended hearths. From them come the roll of drums and the piercing cries of the conches to mark yet another of the nine divisions of the day. While the priests are casting incense into the hearths and intoning their prayers, perhaps the emperor himself has risen in the palace to offer his own blood in the darkness. For the Aztecs are the "people of the sun"—and when the world was created, the sun itself was born from sacrifice and blood. In order to move, it required blood, and so some of the gods immolated themselves to provide the solar deity with the life to begin his course across the sky. Humanity had assumed the role of the gods. To keep the sun moving and prevent the darkness from overwhelming the world forever, they must provide their god every day with "the precious water" (*chalchiuatl*)—human blood. By means of this alchemy, the disaster that always threatened to engulf the cosmos could be averted for yet another day. Again the drums roll and the conches call from the temples. Humanity has come safely through the night and dawn is breaking. The state will endure. Acamapichtli can celebrate his birthday and Atototl's wedding.

CHAPTER 18

Exploration and
Colonization: 1450-1650;
The Commercial Revolution:
1450-1750

Seek Out, Discover, and Find

INTRODUCTION. One of the most potent forces molding modern world history was the thrust of European political power, commerce, and culture over the globe. Before 1500 the people of Europe existed largely on their own resources, supplemented by a slender trade with Africa and Asia. But within the next 150 years the picture was dramatically altered through the discoveries of new continents and trade routes. The riches of the entire world were funneled into Europe's economy, and the horizons of Europe's people were immensely widened—socially and intellectually as well as geographically. The discovery of hitherto unknown and unsuspected parts of the globe was probably more revolutionary than the space explorations of our own day.

Who wrought this miracle? First, there were the sea captains—da Gama, who made the first ocean voyage from Europe to India; Columbus, who introduced Europe to a New World; and Magellan, whose expedition ventured ever westward until its weary survivors had sailed completely around the world and dropped anchor once more in their home port. Close on the heels of such captains came the *conquistadores*—the "conquerors"—resourceful and ruthless soldiers like Cortés and Pizarro, who laid the foundations for a vast European empire by overwhelming flourishing native cultures in the New World.

Then came the task of exploiting what had been found and won. The European powers took advantage of the claims of their discoverers and explorers in one of two basic ways—through trade or by colonization. In Africa and Asia the emphasis was on trade; Europeans carried on their business from forts, acting as foreign merchants rather than as settlers. While in Africa their dealings were mostly with tribal peoples, in the Far East they faced venerable civilizations and urban cultures. There, they were the barbarians, and when their activities proved offensive by native standards, reprisals could be swift and severe.

The story of European expansion in the New World, on the other hand, is largely that of colonization, of the transplanting of European civilization to a new and exotic environment. Politically, the territories in the Americas were treated as extensions of the mother countries. The Spanish colonies, for example, were ruled directly by the king of Spain; the colonial economy was geared to supplement that of the homeland; and the Spanish priests set out to bring the Indians into the spiritual fold with their Spanish masters. Similarly, the English and French who settled in North America brought with them the economic, political, and social institutions they had known at home.

For the native peoples of the New World, the arrival of the Europeans was cataclysmic. And the impact of the New World on the Old, while obviously quite different, was no less significant. As new stores of wealth were tapped by the immensely lucrative transatlantic trade, Europe's economic center of gravity shifted from the Mediterranean to the Atlantic seaboard; and the rapid influx of gold and silver made possible an unprecedented expansion of the economy. Nor was the revolution confined to economics: new medicines, foods, and beverages became available to Europeans, and even styles of dress were altered. Thus a handful of adventurers, ranging beyond the horizon in quest of El Dorado, the legendary city of gold which symbolized their hopes and dreams, set in motion a train of events which brought significant changes to European society and which ultimately influenced the very history of civilization.

CAPTAINS AND CONQUISTADORES

Medieval maps and adventurers. Early medieval maps were curiosities rather than documents of fact. They included lands which no man had ever seen; the oceans were shown abounding in sea dragons, while drawings of elephants and more fanciful animals were used to fill up empty land spaces, thereby adding to the picturesqueness of the map as well as conveniently concealing the ignorance of the map maker. Arabic works on astronomy and geography, acquired in the thirteenth century, proved that the earth was a sphere and greatly expanded geographical knowledge. Of greatest significance for the development of scientific geography, however, was the recovery in 1409 of Claudius Ptolemy's *Geography* (see p. 87) with its elaborate map of the world. Although this second-century work added greatly to current knowledge, it contained a number of errors, two of which encouraged Columbus and other fifteenth-century explorers to sail boldly across the uncharted oceans. Ptolemy exaggerated the size of the known continents so that the distance between western Europe and eastern Asia appeared much smaller than it really is, and he underestimated the circumference of the world by five thousand miles.

Medieval adventurers also contributed to geographical knowledge, much of which influenced Columbus and his fellow explorers. The earliest prime examples were the Norsemen, who reached Iceland in the last half of

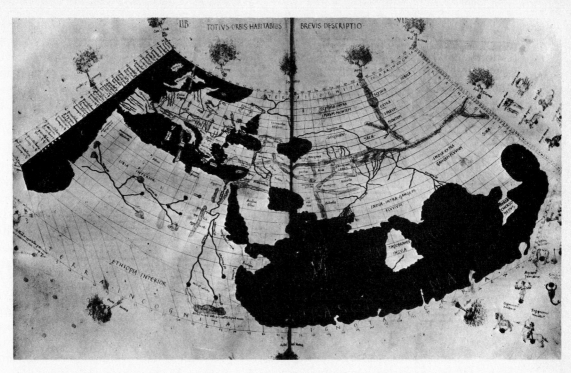

This map, published in the fifteenth century but based on one designed by Ptolemy in the second century, represents the first attempt to project the curved surface of the earth on a flat surface. The outline of the European continent (upper left) is fairly accurate.

the ninth century (see p. 195). In about 982 Eric the Red, son of a Norwegian noble, was banished from the Norse settlements in Iceland and sailed west to Greenland, which may have been discovered earlier in the century by Celtic refugees from Ireland, fleeing Viking raids on their homeland. Eric founded two settlements on the western coast of Greenland, which existed until about 1500 when they mysteriously vanished. It now appears that the first European to set foot on the North American coast was Bjarni Herjolfson. In 985 Bjarni was blown off course while sailing from Iceland to Greenland and made a landfall in Newfoundland. About fifteen years later Leif, son of Eric the Red, retraced Bjarni's route and named the country *Vinland* (Wineland) because of its wooded, vine-covered shore. A number of other voyages were made to Vinland, whose lumber was highly prized in treeless Greenland. Apparently no permanent settlement was made in Vinland, although archaeologists have recently discovered what appears to be the remains of a Viking camp in New-

foundland at L'Anse au Meadow.[1] But monumental as these voyages were, their implication were lost on contemporary Europeans, and they added little or nothing to European knowledge of geography.

In the thirteenth and fourteenth centuries a number of Europeans, many of them Christian missionaries, journeyed overland to the Far East. The most famous of these travelers was Marco Polo (see p. 180). But these exploits had little permanent effect because of political changes in Asia in the last decades of the fourteenth century. The Mongol dynasty in China, which had been friendly to European missionaries and merchants, was overthrown, and the succeeding Ming rulers proved anti-Christian. Meanwhile, the belligerent heathen Turks stood astride the eastern Mediterranean. These two developments put an end to further European penetration into the Orient, although trade continued at certain terminals controlled by the Muslims.

The search for new routes. The three major routes by which trade flowed from the

Far East to Europe had existed since Roman times (see map, p. 116). The northern one cut across Central Asia and the Caspian and Black seas to Constantinople (Byzantium); the middle route went by sea along the coasts of India and Persia through the Persian Gulf and the Euphrates valley to Antioch; and the southern route utilized the monsoon winds to strike across the Indian Ocean and up the Red Sea to Alexandria in Egypt. During the fifteenth century the commerce that flowed westward to Europe was rich indeed, even though the expansion of the Turks greatly reduced the importance of the northern route across Asia. The most important imports into Europe were spices—pepper, cinnamon, nutmeg, ginger, and cloves— highly valued as condiments and preservatives for food. Also in great demand were Chinese silk, Indian cotton cloth, and various precious stones.

The Mediterranean carrying trade in oriental goods was in the hands of Venice and other Italian city-states, which wielded an extensive and lucrative monopoly. Since the Arabs held a similar monopoly east of the Mediterranean, oriental goods were sold in the West at many times their price in India. As the demand for the products of the East increased during the latter half of the fifteenth century, the rulers of the new nations of western Europe became aware that an adverse balance of trade was draining their coined money away to Italy and the East. They determined to find new trade routes of their own, and, as rulers of powerful nation-states, they had the resources to support the stupendous feats of discovery and conquest that were needed.

Prince Henry the Navigator. It was the Portuguese who spearheaded the drive to find oceanic routes that would provide cheaper and easier access to oriental products. The man who set in motion the brilliant Portuguese achievements in exploration and discovery was Prince Henry the Navigator (1394-1460), whose original goal was to tap at its source the gold of Guinea and the African Gold Coast (see Reference Map 6), which came to Europe through Muslim middlemen (see illustration p. 368).

Henry employed skilled cartographers and navigators to construct accurate maps, and under his direction the caravel, the finest vessel afloat for long voyages, was developed. By utilizing the lateen rig, the triangular sail developed by the Arabs, the caravel revolutionized sailing by being able to tack into the wind. Augmenting Henry's innovations were other navigation aids. In the twelfth century the Europeans set their course with the aid of a magnetic needle floating on a straw in a bowl of water. By the time Henry's sailors were setting sail, the compass consisted of a needle which pivoted on a card showing the points of the compass. During the fifteenth century another great aid to navigation came into general use— the astrolabe, a graduated brass circle by which the altitude of stars could be estimated and latitudes more accurately measured.

The African voyages. Although Henry died before any of the numerous expeditions he sent forth had explored the entire length of Africa, his mariners did not fail him. In 1488 Bartholomew Diaz rounded the southern tip of Africa, from which point he noticed that the coast swung northeast. But his disgruntled crew forced him to turn back. Pleased with the prospect of soon finding a direct sea route to India, King John II of Portugal named the great cape rounded by Diaz "Cape of Good Hope."

Vasco da Gama commanded the first Portuguese fleet to reach India. Three ships left Lisbon in 1497 and, after rounding the Cape, crossed the Indian Ocean to Calicut in twenty-three days. The Arab merchants in Calicut sought to preserve their trading monopoly by delaying the return voyage, and it was not until 1499 that da Gama dropped anchor in Lisbon. He had lost two of his ships and one third of his men through scurvy and other misfortunes, but his one cargo of pepper and cinnamon was worth sixty times the cost of the expedition.

Lured by such fantastic profits another expedition set sail the following year and established a permanent base south of Calicut at Cochin. The Portuguese soon acquired a monopoly over trade in the Indian Ocean, and by 1516 their ships had reached Canton in China. The king of Portugal assumed the impressive title "Lord of the Conquest,

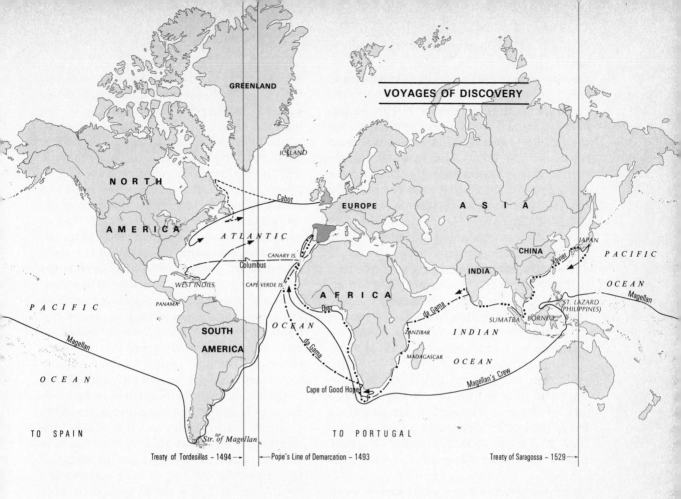

GREENLAND

VOYAGES OF DISCOVERY

ICELAND

NORTH

AMERICA

Cabot

EUROPE

A S I A

ATLANTIC

CHINA

JAPAN

PACIFIC

Columbus

CANARY IS.

INDIA

Xavier

OCEAN

PACIFIC

WEST INDIES

CAPE VERDE IS.

A F R I C A

Magellan

PANAMA

Diaz

da Gama

ST. LAZARD
(PHILIPPINES)

SOUTH
AMERICA

OCEAN

SUMATRA

BORNEO

da Gama

I N D I A N

ZANZIBAR

Magellan

MADAGASCAR

OCEAN

Magellan

Cape of Good Hope

Magellan's Crew

OCEAN

TO SPAIN

Str. of Magellan

TO PORTUGAL

Treaty of Tordesillas – 1494 → ← Pope's Line of Demarcation – 1493   Treaty of Saragossa – 1529 →

Navigation, and Commerce of Ethiopia, Arabia, Persia, and China.''

Columbus discovers the New World. Meanwhile, Spanish ambitions for riches and prestige were realized through the exploits of a Genoese sailor named Christopher Columbus (1451?-1506). Influenced by Marco Polo's overestimate of the length of Asia and Ptolemy's underestimate of the size of the world, Columbus believed that Japan was less than 3000 miles from Europe (the actual distance is 10,600 nautical miles) and that it could be reached in one or two months by sailing westward. He tried unsuccessfully to interest the rulers of Portugal, England, and France in his enterprise before Queen Isabella of Castile agreed to sponsor his voyage. On August 3, 1492, Columbus set sail from Spain with three small ships and ninety men. On October 12 he landed on a small island in the West Indies. After he returned to Spain, Columbus announced that he had found the route to Asia, and the Spanish monarchs proclaimed him ''Admiral of the

Ocean Sea, Viceroy and Governor of the Islands that he has discovered in the Indies.''

Even after da Gama's voyage had opened up the eastward route to India, Columbus steadfastly refused to acknowledge that what he himself had discovered was in fact a massive obstacle on the route to the Far East. Although he made three more voyages to the New World in a vain attempt to find a direct opening to the Asian mainland, Columbus had already changed the course of history, though he did not know it. A New World had been revealed; old geographical views had been shattered; and the entire history of Europe was soon to be affected by the discovery of the new lands.

Spain and Portugal divide the new lands. An immediate repercussion of Columbus' first voyage was the destruction of Portugal's monopoly over discovery. Some sort of compromise had to be worked out between the two countries, and the Spanish monarchs invited the pope to define the pagan areas which Spain and Portugal might claim. In

1493 the pope issued the Bull of Demarcation, which drew a line from north to south running one hundred leagues west of the Azores and proclaimed that all heathen lands west of this line as far as the Indies were reserved for Spain. The Portuguese protested, claiming that this arrangement would confine their operations too closely to the African coast. By the Treaty of Tordesillas (1494) Spain agreed to have the line moved farther west. This new demarcation later enabled Portugal to claim Brazil after Pedro Cabral's sighting of South America in 1500 while sailing to the Indies. In 1529 another treaty fixed a similar demarcation line in the Eastern Hemisphere.

Balboa and Magellan. The search for riches drove the Spaniards to organize many expeditions to chart the coastlines and to penetrate the interior of the New World. One such enterprise was particularly successful. Having heard from Indians of a vast ocean only a short distance to the west, Vasco de Balboa led a band of 190 Spaniards across the Isthmus of Panama. On September 25, 1513, Balboa climbed to the summit of a hill from

The Spanish troops, aided by Indian allies, storm the main gate of Tenochtitlán in this illustration from a sixteenth-century Aztec manuscript.

which he beheld the Pacific Ocean—and in that act paved the way for European exploration of the largest single portion of the world's surface.

Ferdinand Magellan, a Portuguese navigator in the service of Spain, found a sea route into the Pacific. Encouraged by Balboa's discovery of the short distance between the two oceans, Magellan believed it was possible to sail around South America just as Diaz had rounded Africa. In August 1520 Magellan made his memorable discovery of the strait which bears his name. His five small ships made their way between huge ice-clad mountains and through tortuous passages. After a terrifying thirty-eight days they sailed out upon the western ocean, which looked so calm after the stormy straits that Magellan termed it "Pacific." Then followed a harrowing ninety-nine day voyage across the Pacific to Guam, during which rats had to be eaten for food. Magellan was slain by natives in the Philippine Islands, and only one of his ships returned to Spain in 1522 by way of India and the Cape of Good Hope. Its cargo of spices paid for the cost of the entire expedition. Magellan's tiny vessel had taken three years to circumnavigate the world, but henceforth no one could doubt that the earth was round and that the Americas constituted a New World.

Cortés conquers Mexico. While the Portuguese soon profited from their hold on the rich oriental trade, the Spaniards found that the islands and coasts of the New World did not immediately produce the harvest of riches which they had eagerly sought. Such wealth was not to be found along the seashore but in the unknown hinterland, where rich indigenous cultures flourished. Penetration of inland areas was the work of the *conquistadores*, the courageous but independent-minded and often brutal conquerors who looted whole native empires and planted the Spanish flag from California to the tip of South America.

In the same year that Magellan set forth (1519), the Spanish governor of Cuba dispatched Hernando Cortés on an expedition to Mexico, from which had come rumors of a great Aztec empire, flowing with gold. Montezuma, ruler of the Aztecs, had thousands of warriors, while Cortés had about six hundred men. But the Spaniards were equipped with horses, armor, and gunpowder, all unknown to the Aztecs. Two other factors aided the Europeans: the discontent of many subject tribes, which looked for a chance to break the Aztec rule; and an ancient Mexican legend which prophesied that the Aztecs would one day be conquered by the white-skinned descendants of an ancient god-king who had been repudiated by their ancestors.

Having made the fateful decision to march inland on the Aztec capital, Tenochtitlán, Cortés destroyed his ships to prevent his men from turning back. Crossing the coast lands and the mountains, the Spaniards entered the valley of Mexico. Cortés treacherously made a virtual prisoner of Montezuma and through his cooperation ruled peacefully until a popular uprising gave the Spaniards an excuse to plunder and destroy the capital. Yet Cortés was more than a plunderer; he built a new City of Mexico on the site of Montezuma's capital and demonstrated administrative skills in adapting the former Aztec confederacy to Spanish rule.

Pizarro in Peru. The conquest of the Incas in Peru was carried out with less skill and more enduring ill effects than Cortés' exploit in Mexico. Obsessed by tales of a rich and mighty empire in South America, a tough, illiterate peasant's son named Francisco Pizarro determined to explore and conquer it. In 1531 Pizarro sailed from Panama with 180 men and 27 horses. Landing on the Peruvian coast, the small band made its way across the barren mountains into the interior, where they seized the Incan monarch Atahualpa.

Attempting to buy his freedom by paying a huge ransom, Atahualpa offered to have a room measuring seventeen by twelve feet filled to a height of some seven feet with plates and vessels of gold and to have it filled twice over with silver. Despite this magnificent ransom, the Spaniards did not release the emperor but instead sentenced him on trumped-up charges to be burned to death. In the end, because Atahualpa accepted Christian baptism, he was merely strangled. The imprisonment and death of its ruler

rendered the highly centralized Incan government incapable of effective, organized resistance; and Pizarro soon captured the capital.

Within a decade civil war broke out among the conquerors, and Pizarro was murdered. When the Spanish royal government sought to protect the oppressed Indians from their colonial masters, Gonzalo Pizarro, a brother of Francisco, set up a government independent of Spain. But Madrid dispatched officials and soldiers to arrest the unruly *conquistadores* and to pacify the area so that silver could be mined for Spain and conversion of the natives to Christianity could proceed. Not until near the end of the sixteenth century was Spanish authority securely established over Peru. In time Spanish dominions in South America formed a huge, uninterrupted semicircle, while the Portuguese took possession of the vast hinterland of Brazil (see Reference Map 6).

Spanish penetration into North America. Using Mexico and the West Indies as bases, the Spanish explorers searched what is now the southern part of the United States for the treasures which rumors planted there. That the expeditions failed to find gold or other riches does not detract from the tremendous progress they made in opening up new and potentially wealthy areas. Not only mythical treasure but an equally mythical Fountain of Youth attracted Spanish *conquistadores*. In 1521 Juan Ponce de León lost his life trying to find the Fountain of Youth in Florida.

Eighteen years later Hernando de Soto, whose participation in the conquest of Peru had gained him a fortune, landed in Florida with a company of some six hundred adventurers. His search for treasure took him through the southern United States, and De Soto was possibly the first white man to sight the Mississippi River. He died without finding any treasure, and his followers buried him in the Mississippi.

Marvelous tales had persisted of a fabled land north of Mexico containing seven cities with golden towers, and in 1540 Francisco de Coronado set out from Mexico with a large band to find them. But the fabled cities turned out to be only adobe pueblos. In his vain search Coronado appears to have penetrated as far as Kansas, becoming the first European to behold the vast herds of buffalo roaming the American plains. The adventurer returned embittered by failure, and the Spanish authorities concluded that there was little to be gained in occupying the area north of the silver mines of Mexico.

English search for the Northwest Passage. The division of the overseas world between Spain and Portugal, as set forth by the Bull of Demarcation and the Treaty of Tordesillas, aroused little enthusiasm among other European powers, and it was not long before France, England, and Holland encroached on the private preserves of both Portugal and Spain.

In 1497—the same year in which da Gama embarked for India—John Cabot, an Italian mariner financed by the merchants of Bristol in England, sailed across the North Atlantic in a small ship manned by only eighteen men. After a turbulent six weeks' voyage, the expedition dropped anchor off the northern coast of the New World. When Cabot returned to England, Henry VII rewarded him with £10, the title of Grand Admiral, and the

right to make another voyage. Cabot made his second voyage in 1498, coasting along the eastern shore of America in a vain attempt to find a passage to the Orient.

Cabot was the first European after the hardy Norse sailors to land on the mainland of North America; and, what was most important, his discovery laid the foundation for England's claim to the whole rich continent. Thus for £10 and a title England eventually acquired all of Canada and the territory along the Atlantic coast which constituted the thirteen American colonies—certainly an excellent business transaction.

For the next hundred years English seamen tried in vain to reach China through the illusive Northwest Passage, a sea route believed to exist north of Canada. Although similar expeditions trying to reach China by way of the Northeast Passage above Russia also failed, one of them reached Archangel and was granted trading privileges by Tsar Ivan the Terrible.

French explorations of inland America. France also joined in the search for the Northwest Passage. In 1523 Francis I commissioned the Florentine mariner Giovanni da Verrazzano to investigate the coast from North Carolina to Newfoundland. Eleven years later Jacques Cartier was sent on the first of three voyages that explored the St. Lawrence River as far as the present city of Montreal. These expeditions gave France its claim to sovereignty over eastern North America, a claim which duplicated England's.

Not until after its Wars of Religion did France resume its activities in the St. Lawrence region. Sponsored by the energetic first Bourbon ruler, Henry IV, Samuel de Champlain not only founded the first successful French overseas colony at Quebec (1608) but also journeyed over the lake which bears his name and westward to the Great Lakes. In 1673 Louis Joliet, a fur trader, and Father Marquette, a Jesuit missionary, reached the Mississippi River and followed it as far south as Arkansas in the hope of finding a short route to the Pacific. Nine years later René de La Salle explored the Mississippi to its mouth, taking possession of the entire territory and naming it *Louisiana* in honor of Louis XIV.

Drawn by Sir Humphrey Gilbert in 1582, this polar map shows a clear northwest route to the East. The belief in the existence of such a route helped stimulate the exploration of North America.

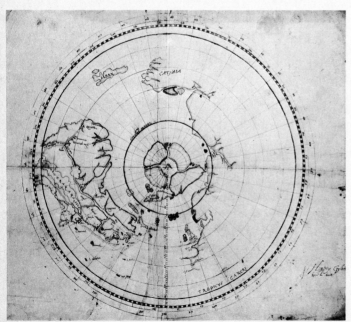

Pictured above is New Amsterdam (New York) as it appeared around 1640. In the center foreground are the gallows, to the right the West India Company stores (G), and to the left the governor's house (D), a church (B), the jail (C), and the fort (A).

The Dutch in America. Dutch interest in the New World coincided with the rise of the United Provinces (Holland) to a position of political independence and great economic strength during the first half of the seventeenth century. Dutch ambitions to find a shorter route to the Far East caused them to hire the English explorer Henry Hudson, who in 1609 sailed up the river that now bears his name. In 1621 the Dutch West India Company was founded for the purpose of trading in western Africa and the Americas. As part of its work, the company founded New Amsterdam on Manhattan Island in 1624 and permanently colonized Guiana, Curaçao, and Aruba in the Caribbean area.

EUROPE INVADES THE EAST

Portugal's eastern empire. Before the exciting era of exploration began to wane, the Europeans were faced with the problem of exploiting their newly found territories. In virtually every case, the natives suffered. Only in a few instances, notably in the Far East, were the indigenous people able to enforce their own policies. In most extreme contrast was Africa, where millions of natives were enslaved.

To ensure their toehold in Africa, the Por-

tuguese built fortified posts along the coast, began to develop a colony in Angola, and settled traders on the island of Zanzibar. Early in the sixteenth century Afonso de Albuquerque, the greatest of all Portuguese viceroys (1509-1515), resolved to consolidate his country's position in Africa and in the East. As a realist, he saw that Portugal could wrest commercial supremacy from the Arabs only by force, and he therefore devised a plan to establish forts at strategic sites which would dominate the trade routes and also protect Portuguese interests on land. The western end of the Arab trade routes was partially sealed off: Ormuz at the mouth of the Persian Gulf (see Reference Map 6) was captured, but the attempt to close the entrance to the Red Sea at Aden was only temporarily successful. To obtain a major base for a permanent fleet in the Indian Ocean, Albuquerque in 1510 seized Goa on the coast of India, which the Portuguese held until 1961. From Goa the Portuguese dominated the Indian ports that had supplied the Arab traders.

Albuquerque next set about securing control of the trade with the East Indies and China. His first objective was Malacca, which controlled the narrow strait through which most Far Eastern trade moved. Captured in 1511, Malacca became the springboard for further eastward penetration. The first Portuguese ship reached Canton on the south coast of China in 1516, but it was not until 1557 that the Portuguese gained a permanent base in China at Macao, which they still hold. About 1516, also, the first trading post was established in the rich Moluccas, or Spice Islands, source of the finest spices.

Thus Portugal, through its control of most of the traffic between India and Europe as well as the trade between India and the Far East, developed the first European commercial empire. Portugal's greatest poet, Luis de Camoëns, in 1572 celebrated his compatriots' overseas achievements in a memorable epic poem, *The Lusiads* ("The Portuguese"):

In golden treasures rich, distant Cathay,
And all the farthest Islands of the East,
And all the seas, to them shall homage pay.[2]

An already lucrative trade was vastly augmented when the Portuguese began to export slaves from Africa about 1500. Envying the rich profits, other nations—England, Holland, France, and Sweden—began to send in rival expeditions, and Portugal was forced on the defensive. In 1642 the Dutch drove the Portuguese out of the Gold Coast, and this rich trade and slaving area was left to other Europeans, especially the Dutch and English.

Dutch inroads in the East. Portugal's star was destined to set for many reasons, not the least of which was attacks on their commercial empire launched by the Dutch and the English—the beginning of a world-wide struggle over empire that lasted until 1763. Two events facilitated Dutch encroachment on the Portuguese monopoly of oriental trade. One was the Netherlands revolt against Spanish rule, and the other was the Spanish acquisition of Portugal. The Dutch looked on Spain's trade and colonies as fair game, and when the two crowns of the Iberian peninsula were joined in 1581, they felt free to attack Portuguese territory in eastern waters. Furthermore, the Dutch had previously enjoyed a rich trade carrying oriental goods from Lisbon to the ports of northern Europe; this traffic ceased when Spain took control of Portuguese ports. If Dutch trade was to survive, the Hollanders had to capture its source in the East.

In the 1590's a number of Dutch companies were formed to finance trading expeditions to the Far East. Because competition lowered their profits, in 1602 the companies amalgamated into the Dutch East India Company which received from the government the right to trade and rule in the area stretching from the Cape of Good Hope eastward to the Strait of Magellan. It was the Dutch East India Company that broke the power of the Portuguese in the islands of the Malay archipelago.

The governor-general of the East Indies who was appointed in 1618, Jan Pieterszoon Coen, laid the foundations for the Dutch empire in the East Indies. Whereas Albuquerque had felt that it was sufficient to occupy strategic points along the sea routes, Coen believed that the Dutch had to control the actual areas of production as well. He built a fortified trading station at Batavia on Java, a site which eventually became the capital of the Dutch East Indies, including Sumatra and the Moluccas. Dutch monopoly of the spice trade became complete after they drove the Portuguese from Malacca (1641) and Ceylon (1658), the latter the main source of cinnamon. In 1652 the Dutch established a colony at Cape Town on the southern tip of Africa as a port of call on the long journey to the Far East.

The English gain a foothold in India. The English meanwhile were staking out claims in India at the expense of the Portuguese. In 1600 Queen Elizabeth incorporated the English East India Company, granting it a monopoly of trade from the Cape of Good Hope eastward to the Strait of Magellan. By 1622 the company had put the Portuguese posts on the Persian Gulf out of business, and in 1639 it acquired Madras on the east coast of India. Through political stratagems, bribes, diplomacy, and exploitation of weak native rulers, the company prospered in India, where it became the most powerful political force in the subcontinent.

Europeans unwelcome in China. When the Portuguese first arrived in Canton in 1516, they were given the same privileges that Arab merchants had enjoyed for centuries. In response, the Portuguese behaved very badly, scorning the customs of the sophisticated inhabitants, and treating the "heathen" with arrogance and cruelty.

However, because trade was mutually profitable to both Chinese and foreign merchants, in 1557 the Portuguese were granted the right to trade at Macao. There, under close surveillance and subject to many strict regulations, the "ocean devils" conducted business. Stemming from this period is the mutual suspicion and hostility which characterized Sino-European relations in the nineteenth and early twentieth centuries.

A somewhat friendlier contact occurred when Jesuit missionaries arrived in China during the second half of the sixteenth century. They converted many important persons at the imperial court and in the provinces, thereby gaining protection for Christians generally.

Japan rejects European contacts. About 1542 three Portuguese ships from Macao were driven far off their course and landed at one of the southern Japanese islands. Before long, others visited the islands and began trading. Hearing about Japan after he had sailed from Lisbon for the Far East, St. Francis Xavier went there and started to convert the inhabitants. After Xavier's death in 1552, his work was carried on by other missionaries. By 1600 Japanese converts to Christianity numbered perhaps 300,000.

Suspicion on the part of the Japanese rulers that Christianity was endangering the status quo was reinforced by the bigotry of many Christians and by economic exploitation on the part of various unscrupulous Portuguese merchants. As we have seen in Chapter 16, the Japanese began persecution of the

Portuguese ships are shown anchored at the port of Macao on the Chinese coast in this sixteenth-century engraving.

AMACAO.

Jesuits and their converts, and in 1638 Japan cut itself off from the outside world:

For the future, let none, so long as the Sun illuminates the world, presume to sail to Japan, not even in the quality of ambassadors, and this declaration is never to be revoked on pain of death.[3]

Except for a small, closely watched Dutch post at Nagasaki, the islands were closed to western contact until 1853.

The Philippines. In the Far East, Spanish energies were concentrated primarily on the Philippine Islands. After 1565, cargoes of Chinese goods were transported from the Philippines to Mexico and from there to Spain. By this complicated route, Spain enjoyed some of the oriental commerce about which Columbus had dreamed. Spanish officials and missionaries brought Christianity and a degree of European civilization to the islands, which were henceforth a corner of the Far East fundamentally oriented toward the West, in contrast to Japan and China.

Renewal of the East-West contact. The remarkable series of geographical discoveries beginning in the fifteenth century which carried intrepid European explorers, soldiers, traders, and missionaries to the ends of the earth recalls a similar movement in the second and third centuries A.D. when rich contacts in commerce and culture existed among three intercommunicating empires—the Graeco-Roman, the Indian, and the Chinese. But the decline of Rome and other factors (discussed in Chapter 4) weakened and ultimately destroyed the lines of contact. For nearly a thousand years there was little exchange or communication between East and West.

Until the fifteenth century civilizations in the Near East, India, and China had been fully as advanced as those in Europe; and in some eras and in some aspects of culture they had surpassed the West. In the late Middle Ages, however, western Europe began to experience an astonishing resurgence—a "rebirth" which was reflected in the rise of powerful and well-administered nation-states, the increase of wealth and trade, the growing importance of the bourgeoisie, and

the intellectual and artistic achievements of humanist scholars and artists. In contrast to the energetic West, the empires of India and China (as we saw in Chapter 16) were less dynamic both culturally and politically. And in Japan, isolation was the keynote of the Tokugawa shogunate—a regime no longer dynamic. Therefore, when the contact between East and West was renewed in the fifteenth century, it was not a meeting of equals. The discrepancies in effective political organizations, in disciplined armies, in energy and ambition prevented the resumption of East-West contacts on the same equal footing as had prevailed a thousand years earlier.

Europe's dominance begins. The same imbalance was readily apparent in both Africa and the Americas. In the Western Hemisphere promising civilizations among the Incas, the Aztecs, and the Mayas were no match for armed invaders. African potentialities had been restricted by isolation and harsh environmental forces, so that the natives fell an easy prey to the Europeans. Progress in sub-Saharan Africa was probably cut short by the effects of the slave trade.

The natural result of the impact of the strong upon the weak was that Europe took advantage of the other continents; the wider world became the servant of the West. The expansion of Europe and its mastery of much of the world is generally referred to as imperialism. Many of the conflicts and tensions in modern world politics find their source to a large degree in the imperial systems created by the West.

VICEROYS AND COLONISTS IN THE NEW WORLD

Spain consolidates its empire in the Americas. The *conquistadores* who carved out a mighty Spanish empire in the New World had been allowed to embark on their expeditions only after having secured royal permission. The crown's ultimate purpose was to replace these brilliant but erratic men of action with staid but reliable civil servants who would consolidate the territorial gains into a centralized colonial regime.

In theory, all overseas dominions were the personal property of the king, who made the major administrative decisions aided by one of his advisory councils, the Council of the Indies. Holding almost unrestricted power during the reigns of weak monarchs, the Council of the Indies formulated legislation, appointed colonial officials, and heard important colonial law cases. Before the end of the sixteenth century Spain possessed an American empire twenty times its own size, comprising in 1574 some 200 towns and about 160,000 Spanish settlers. For most of the colonial period the Spanish empire in the Americas was divided into two kingdoms: New Spain, which was made up of the West Indies, Venezuela, and the lands north of the Isthmus of Panama; and Peru, which consisted of all Spanish territory south of those lands.

Each kingdom had a viceroy who lived in splendor in Mexico City or Lima. Although the viceroys were the kings' representatives in America, they enjoyed only the appearance of great power. The Council of the Indies kept a tight rein on imperial affairs, judging the viceroys chiefly by their effectiveness in sending back treasure to Madrid. Under orders from the Spanish crown, the colonial regimes sharply restricted self-government. In the ten largest cities of the empire lawyers sent from Spain were in charge of courts called *audiencias*, which not only heard appeals against the decisions of viceroys and governors but also advised them in administrative matters. The crown levied head taxes, customs on imports, and excise charges on goods exchanged within the colonies, as well as demanding one fifth of all the gold and silver mined. The colonists were left no voice in the taxation. Membership in town councils was the only regular political outlet for the Spanish settlers, and there only the richest could participate. The Spaniards born in the Americas (Creoles) were regarded as potential rebels against the mother country, as indeed they proved to be in the nineteenth century.

For three centuries Spain was a potent agent in transmitting European culture and institutions to the New World. Its most important contributions were its language and literature. Also of lasting significance was the establishment of schools of higher learning. In 1551, eighty-five years before the founding of Harvard College, the first two universities in the New World—one at Lima, the other at Mexico City—were established. By the end of the seventeenth century no less than seven universities had been founded in Spanish America.

Mercantilism guides economic life. The economic theory current in the nation-states of Europe during this period was mercantilism, a doctrine which stressed the need of governmental intervention to increase the wealth and power of the state. Mercantilism had ramifications for the colonies as well as for the mother country. It postulated that a nation should be as economically self-sufficient as possible and that the colonies should be exploited for the gain of the ruling country. Each European nation wanted to export more than it imported, and the colonies provided ready-made markets for the finished products of the homeland. Thus Spain sent wines and finished goods to the New World but forbade the colonists to produce goods that would compete with those produced in Spain.

Under the mercantile system a nation's wealth was measured by the amount of precious metal it had accumulated, and the New World was a source of fantastic riches for Spain. Transporting the silver and gold to Spain was a perilous business. Each spring two well-guarded fleets left Seville or Cádiz, one heading for Mexico and the other for Panama. Laden with silver from the Andes and Mexico, the convoys returned to Spain in the autumn at great risk. After a rendezvous at Havana the combined fleets ran the gantlet back to Spain. Pirates and buccaneers were ever ready to swoop down on stragglers, as were warships of rival powers. Yet most of the treasure usually reached Spain, where the crown received its royal fifth.

In return for exploiting the virgin wealth of the New World, the Spanish introduced new products and methods which revolutionized agriculture, the mainstay of the American economy. To obtain farms, settlers often banded together to found a town in exchange for a royal grant of land, which was apportioned among the citizens. On the large estates of the aristocrats and the clergy, the forced labor of Indians and, later, African slaves was employed in the cultivation of cotton, vanilla, indigo, cacao, and other crops for export. The Spanish brought with them wheat, barley, rye, and rice, as well as coffee, sugar cane, and a variety of fruits. The importation of cattle and other livestock not only drastically modified the native diet but also stimulated such valuable new industries as breeding animals and exporting their hides. Originally the Indians had been their own pack animals, for the New World lacked beasts of burden except for the llamas domesticated by the Incas. The *conquistadores* introduced horses and mules and further revolutionized transportation by the introduction of the wheel. Through these imports and many more, the cultural state of certain areas in the Americas was abruptly jerked from a Neolithic level to a position approaching that of the Old World.

Indian plight eased by the Church. The desire to extend Christianity among the heathen had been one of the avowed objectives of every *conquistador*, but it was generally overlooked in the mad scramble to acquire gold and silver, jewels and slaves. In the islands of the Caribbean the forced labor and even enslavement of the Indians on the plantations proved so injurious that most of them died off. They were replaced by African slaves, who were imported to the islands about 1503 and to the American mainland a few years later. From the middle of the sixteenth century to the middle of the eighteenth century, some three thousand African slaves were imported annually, eventually transforming the racial composition of the Caribbean islands.

The work of the Church in establishing missions and persuading the crown to enact safeguards enabled the natives to survive in other areas of Spanish America. Early in the sixteenth century some clerics began to upbraid the Spaniards for their cruelties in exploiting the labor of the Indians. The most famous of these reformers was a Dominican friar, Bartolomé de Las Casas (1474-1566),

who insisted that the Indians, as subjects of the Spanish king, enjoyed the same rights as the Spaniards. He obtained royal permission to establish missions and settlements where the Indians and Spaniards could live on civilized terms. Las Casas' efforts also led to the promulgation of the New Laws of the Indies, directed at the greed of the plantation owners. But the attempt to improve the lot of the Indians was a losing battle, since the reforms ran counter to the economic interests of the settlers.

In order both to convert and to protect the Indians, a number of religious orders established mission towns. There, a few friars shielded the natives from white exploitation and taught them Christianity along with European habits and skills. The missionaries followed Las Casas in believing that the Indians should be converted not by force but by patient persuasion, "as rain and snow falls from heaven, not impetuously, not violently, not suddenly like a heavy shower, but gradually, with suavity and gentleness, saturating the earth as it falls."[4]

Portuguese activity in South America. Already burdened by its sprawling African and Asian interests, Portugal managed to establish a local administration in Brazil by the middle of the sixteenth century. In the 1570's Brazil's surge forward began as great numbers of African slaves were imported to cultivate sugar. This forced immigration continued for almost three centuries. During this period the crown imposed a highly centralized control on Brazil through its own officials, and a mercantilist policy was pursued in economic affairs.

After the Spanish king acquired control over Portugal, the Dutch and English regarded Portuguese possessions as lawful prizes to be won from their Spanish enemies. The Dutch took over land north of the mouth of the Amazon and founded Dutch Guiana. Subsequently, the English and French gained control over other parts of Guiana.

French colonization of North America. In 1608, as we noted earlier in this chapter, the city of Quebec was founded by Samuel de Champlain. To exploit the infant colony, a joint-stock company headed by Cardinal Richelieu was formed about twenty years

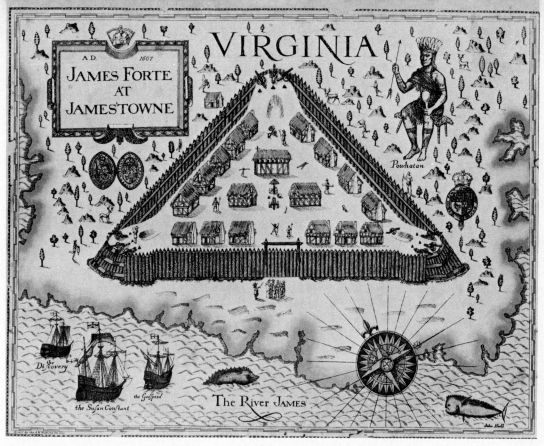

An early map details the Jamestown colony as it looked in 1607. Three ships, the *Discovery*, the *Sarah Constant*, and the *Godspeed* shown anchored in the James River were the ones that brought the original settlers from England. Also featured prominently is Powhatan, chief of an Indian confederation that was hostile to the early colonists.

later. In return for a perpetual monopoly on the fur trade and the title to certain lands, this company was supposed to bring several thousand settlers to Canada. But the company was unable to attract colonists. Stories of the severe Canadian winters frightened away most potential settlers; and the Huguenots, who would have been glad to escape religious restrictions, were not allowed to leave France.

By the middle of the seventeenth century New France had survived the initial, dangerous stages of an infancy marked by parental neglect. After La Salle in 1682 had explored the Mississippi River to its mouth, France also claimed the entire Mississippi valley. The French were at last firmly established in North America, ready to do battle with the English for the northern half of the continent and the Mississippi basin and prepared to resist any encroachment by the Spaniards from the Gulf of Mexico.

English colonies on the Atlantic seaboard. Like France, England was slow in following

up the valuable work of its explorers. Cabot had given it the means of claiming an entire continent, yet it was not until the days of Queen Elizabeth that Englishmen began to interest themselves in the potentialities of the New World. The defeat of the Spanish Armada in 1588 and the building of a strong English navy ensured safer passage from the Old World to the New. Reports of the wealth garnered by the Spaniards whetted the appetites of Englishmen to look for El Dorado. More important, the economic difficulties accompanying the spread of the enclosure movement—the diverting of land from food growing to sheep raising—brought unemployment and with it the desire by many to try their luck overseas. Added to these factors was the religious question. Although the Spanish and French governments forbade nonconforming religious elements to move to the New World, the English government saw emigration as an excellent means of getting rid of dissident sects. For their part, these strong-willed, God-fearing people were eager to migrate to a new land where they could worship freely.

Actually, the first successful English settlement was founded by a joint-stock company, called the London Company, whose shareholders hoped for substantial profit. (They were told that the lands to be developed were so rich that pots and pans were made of solid gold.) The company's charter, issued by James I, permitted it to act as a miniature government, even to the extent of coining money, levying taxes, and annexing territory.

In 1607 the London Company landed its first colonists at Jamestown in Virginia. For a number of years the colonists suffered from lack of food and other privations, but they were tided over this initial period by the dauntless Captain John Smith, whose motto was "It is less perilous to go forward than to go backward," and whose romantic rescue by the beautiful Pocahontas is one of the legends most cherished by Americans. Recent scholarship suggests that this story, like other of Smith's improbable tales, may have a basis in fact.

The first example of the transplantation to the New World of English common law and representative government is found in the royal charter to the London Company:

All and every the Persons, being our Subjects, which shall dwell and inhabit within every and any of the said several Colonies and Plantations, and every of their children . . . shall have and enjoy all Liberties, Franchises and Immunities within any of our Dominions . . . as if they had been abiding and born within this our Realm of England.[5]

In 1619 the governor of the Jamestown colony called a representative assembly to assist in the tasks of government. This body, which later became the legislature of the state of Virginia, is one of the oldest representative assemblies in existence.

Another great landmark in American history was the landing of the Pilgrims at Plymouth in 1620, after James I had granted them permission. This momentous royal decision in effect opened English North America to settlement by religious dissenters. Ten years later another Puritan group,

organized as the Massachusetts Bay Company, settled around Boston. Both groups had secured royal charters which allowed them to be virtually self-governing.

Between 1629 and 1642, as a result of increased hostility toward religious dissenters in England, some 25,000 Puritans migrated to New England. This movement, called the Great Migration, had important consequences for the future. It brought to the New World a number of educated and responsible people whose courage and intellectual attainments greatly stimulated the process of colonization. By the middle of the seventeenth century the English language and law and the religious and cultural institutions of England had become firmly rooted in North American soil.

THE COMMERCIAL REVOLUTION

The transformation of Europe's economic life. In the period between 1450 and 1750 Europe underwent a great economic transformation which is associated with the rise of capitalism and the shift from the town to the territorial state as the center of the economy. The period is often termed the Commercial Revolution because commerce and the activities of merchants were central to the great economic progress of the age.

The nature of capitalism. Capitalism is commonly defined by economists as an economic system in which capital, or wealth, is invested in order to produce more capital. Thus capitalism is an expanding economic system, ever producing more wealth. Other important characteristics are the private ownership of the means of producing wealth (such as land, raw materials, and factories) and the separation of capitalists and wage workers, which is not found in medieval guilds and manors or modern socialism. Also essential is the existence of the profit motive.

Four phases of capitalism. Much of the history of the five hundred years between the midpoint of the fifteenth century and the present day is concerned with the virtues and sins of capitalism, its defense and condemnation, and its development (as in the United States) or rejection (as in the Soviet Union). Its history can be traced in four distinct stages.

The first stage—commercial capitalism—is associated with geographical discoveries, colonization, and the astounding increase in overseas trade. These early capitalists, protected and encouraged by governmental controls, subsidies, and monopolies, made most of their profits from the buying and selling of goods.

Beginning about 1750, the second phase—industrial capitalism—was made possible by the accumulation of vast amounts of capital and its investment in machinery and the factory system of manufacturing. During the resulting Industrial Revolution the industrialist replaced the merchant as the dominant figure in the capitalistic system.

In the last decades of the nineteenth century, when the ultimate control and direction of large areas of industry came into the hands of financiers, industrial capitalism gave way to finance capitalism. The establishment of mammoth industrial empires and the ownership and management of their assets by men completely divorced from production were the dominant features of this third phase.

Since the great world depression of the 1930's, the state has played an increasingly dominant role in the capitalistic system, one well-known manifestation in the United States being the New Deal and its successor programs. This fourth phase is commonly known to economists as state capitalism and to its opponents by such terms as "creeping socialism."

Mercantilism. The body of economic theory and practice that accompanied commercial capitalism is called mercantilism. As previously noted (p. 399), mercantilism was a system of governmental regulation of economic matters in order to increase the wealth of the nation. In the words of Francis Bacon, its purpose was "the opening and well-balancing of trade; the cherishing of manufactures; the banishing of idleness; the repressing of waste and excess by sumptuary laws; the improvement and husbanding of the soil; the regulation of prices . . ."[6] A

similar program of stimulation and regimentation had characterized the economic life of medieval towns; now, under mercantilism, the new territorial state superseded the town and its guilds as the regulator of the economy.

Among the major tenets of mercantilism was bullionism, a doctrine which stressed the importance of accumulating precious metals. Mercantilists emphasized state power as the chief objective of economic policy, and "money," they liked to say, "is the sinews of war."

A second and corollary tenet of mercantilism was that a nation should maintain the most favorable balance of trade possible: it should export more than it imported so that foreign nations would have to pay the difference in precious metals. Only raw materials that could not be obtained at home were to be imported; after these materials had been manufactured into finished articles, they were then to be exported. Government subsidies, such as the granting of monopolies and the use of protective tariffs, encouraged the home production of manufactured goods.

Mercantilists believed that when raw materials were native, the profit to the home country was 100 percent. Therefore, if a country could not supply its own materials, it should acquire colonies from which they could be procured. Furthermore, colonies constituted not only sources of supply for raw materials but also markets for finished products. Because the mother country did not want competition for its infant industries, colonies were prevented from engaging in manufacturing. In addition, the colonies were prohibited from trading with foreign powers.

Mercantilism declined after 1750, when a new group of economic theorists challenged such basic mercantilist doctrines as the belief that the amount of the world's wealth remains constant and a nation can increase its wealth only at the expense of another. The more backward economic powers such as Russia and Prussia, however, still favored mercantilism long after other nations had turned to newer doctrines.

Decline of the early commercial centers. During the Middle Ages the central agency of European trade was the city-state. In northern Europe trade had been dominated by the confederacy of towns in the Baltic area known as the Hanseatic League. After the fifteenth century, however, the League rapidly declined, a victim of mercantile rivalry from the rising nation-states of Denmark, Sweden, and Russia. The absence of a strong central government in Germany left the League without adequate protection.

In southern Europe the merchants of the Italian city-states, with Venice in the lead, had for centuries acted as the great middlemen of Europe because they controlled the lucrative Asiatic trade. But the Portuguese smashed the Italian monopoly by discovering a new sea route to India and by obstructing the Red Sea and Persian Gulf routes that led to the Mediterranean ports. In addition, the Italian Wars of the sixteenth century had a disastrous effect upon the prosperity of the Italian city-states.

Portugal, temporarily paramount. With its limited population, Portugal could not permanently administer and protect an empire scattered over three continents. During the sixteenth century emigration, plague, and famine reduced the country's population from one and a half million to less than one, and the Portuguese were unable to man their ships and fortresses adequately. In 1580 Portugal came under the Spanish crown, and when it regained its independence in the following century, it retained only a few small possessions in the Far East, some islands in the mid-Atlantic, Brazil, and Mozambique and Angola in Africa. The economic power of Portugal ebbed away, not from lack of initiative so much as from lack of resources to support so great a task.

The economic decay of Spain. The decline of Spain's commercial might cannot be explained so simply. This nation apparently had everything—and failed. During the sixteenth century Spain had far more gold and silver than any of its rivals; and to this wealth was added that of Portugal and its possessions. Yet the wealth and power lavishly displayed during the reign of Philip II (1556-1598) were only surface deep. Farming was neglected, and industry was overburdened with governmental regulations. Religious

persecution and the expulsion of the Jews and Moors had deprived Spain of many of its skilled financiers and craftsmen. Since the Church and the upper classes were exempt from certain forms of taxation, the tax burden fell disproportionately on the classes engaged in trade, commerce, and industry.

An outward symbol of wealth, the rich flood of bullion from the Americas wreaked havoc in the Spanish economy by causing inflation. From 1500 to 1600 Spain experienced a fivefold rise of prices, a condition which attracted a stream of lower-priced products from Holland, France, and England, to the detriment of Spanish manufacturers. Spain's riches were drained off to purchase foreign manufactured goods—and even grain—and to pay the costs of Philip II's wars.

Antwerp's period of glory. As Spain and Portugal declined, the commercial center of Europe moved northward to Antwerp. To this great Flemish port came Europe's merchants and bankers. Antwerp was made a toll-free port, and the city fathers set up a merchants' exchange—the bourse—which, unlike the medieval fairs, operated continuously as an international commercial and financial center. It was said that Antwerp did as much business in one month as Venice in two years. Various institutions of modern capitalism evolved at Antwerp. Its bourse developed into the first stock exchange, trading in the shares of joint-stock companies. Life and property insurance came into use. But the spectacular prosperity of Antwerp was short-lived; in 1576, during the wars of the Netherlands against Spain, the city was sacked, and in 1585 the Dutch occupied the mouth of the Scheldt River and cut off the city's access to the sea. Henceforth Antwerp's trade and finances were largely appropriated by the Dutch city of Amsterdam.

Holland's golden age. During most of the seventeenth century Holland was the principal commercial, financial, and manufacturing country in Europe. Both the Dutch East India Company and the West India Company were markedly successful. The Dutch built better ships than their rivals and operated them more efficiently; their lower freight rates gained for them a monopoly on the carrying trade of Europe. The Dutch policy of religious toleration attracted artisans from abroad, and Holland became the leading industrial nation of Europe. Dutch exports included textiles, salted herring, glazed pottery, fine jewelry, and printed books. Trade, in turn, made Amsterdam the center of banking and credit.

Nevertheless, like Portugal, Holland was a comparatively small nation, and larger neighbors were presently to overtake it. Rivalry with England and France led to a series of wars during the latter half of the seventeenth century, and the Dutch lost much of their carrying trade to the English. Yet Dutch skill, together with the retention of the East Indies, enabled Holland to remain a significant factor in world commerce and finance.

France's rise and decline. With a population of about fifteen million in the seventeenth century, France was the premier nation of Europe. Its abundant economic resources were assiduously cultivated by Colbert (1619-1683), Louis XIV's astute minister of finance, who sponsored the colonization of Canada and chartered a number of trading companies which established slaving stations in Africa and trading posts in both India and the Caribbean sugar islands. Colbert also subsidized French industry by protecting it with high tariffs and granting monopolies, tax reductions, and loans without interest. In particular, Colbert subsidized the manufacture of those luxury items which the upper classes had habitually imported—tapestries, porcelains, laces, mirrors, glass, and fine woolens. There is no doubt that French commerce and industry gained much from Colbert's aggressive mercantilist policies.

After the death of Colbert in 1683, his mercantilistic system began to develop creaks and strains. Lacking Colbert's guiding genius, his followers added all kinds of minute and irksome regulations. The system's weaknesses also became apparent when, in retaliation for Colbert's restrictions against foreign imports, other nations refused to purchase French farm products and wines. Furthermore, the big governmental monopolies were increasingly unpopular with businessmen, who demanded the removal of governmental regulations and of controls by the old medieval guilds.

In addition, it has been estimated that between 1685 and 1715 France lost a million subjects through warfare, the surrender of colonies, and the drain of emigration. The revocation of the Edict of Nantes in 1685 resulted in the flight from France of a large group of industrious Huguenots, who took their capital and skills as artisans to neighboring countries. And the rivalry between France and England during the Seven Years' War (see Chapter 20) culminated in French disaster. Thus France lost to England the commercial supremacy which it might have had.

Rise of England's sun. Although England was inferior to France in area, fertility of soil, and population (between four and five million inhabitants), this island kingdom had many compensating factors in its favor. Geographical isolation discouraged military conquest from the Continent—the last successful invasion by a foreign power had taken place in 1066—and the English economy had not been burdened by the cost of maintaining large standing armies. After the union of England and Scotland in 1707, internal trade flourished in the largest customs-free area in western Europe. The aristocracy and middle class which controlled Parliament also controlled the principal trading and banking companies so that the growth of new enterprises was more peaceful and steady than anywhere else in Europe. The gradual control of the seas, the establishment of trading posts in exotic lands, and the shrewd policy of taking overseas territory as its booty from successful European wars enabled England to gain commercial benefits and to build the world's largest empire.

An important step in the rise of England's sun came in 1651 with the passage of the first Navigation Act forbidding the importation of goods into England or its dependencies except in English ships or in ships of the country producing the goods. The act was aimed at the Dutch carrying trade, and it provoked the first of three maritime wars with Holland noted previously. England soon outstripped Holland and by 1750 had laid the

On the Atlantic crossing, slaves were packed in so tightly that there was little room to stand, or even sit. When the weather permitted, they were allowed on the main deck for food and fresh air. An eyewitness drawing details slaves on the *Wildfire* on the way to Key West, Florida.

foundation for its economic domination of the world in the nineteenth century.

We shall see that England's textile industry was no small factor in accounting for its overall growth. Daniel Defoe, the author of *Robinson Crusoe*, maintained that the woolen industry in England was "the richest and most valuable manufacture in the world,"[7] of greater value to England than the rich mines of Peru and Mexico were to Spain.

More imports in Europe's markets. The discovery of sea routes to both Asia and the Americas provided an unparalleled impetus to the expansion of Europe and its commerce. The spice trade was especially profitable because there was no refrigeration for foods at this time, and slightly spoiled food could be made palatable by seasoning it with cloves, cinnamon, or pepper. Cloths from the East— calicoes, chintzes, and ginghams—became popular. The textile workers of England became so incensed at the foreign competition that they demanded a prohibition on the import of these inexpensive cotton fabrics, which they maintained were "made by a parcel of heathens and pagans that worship the Devil and work for 1/2*d*. a day."[8] Among other imports from Asia were silks, carpets, and rugs, precious stones, porcelain, brassware, and the all-important beverages tea and coffee.

From the New World came a variety of products which revolutionized the eating and drinking habits of the Europeans. The food supply of Europe was greatly improved by the addition of potatoes, maize (Indian corn), and tomatoes. From the Caribbean came sugar, which soon became so popular that it supplanted honey. An abundant supply of fish, primarily cod, came from Newfoundland's Grand Banks; and warm furs were obtained by trappers penetrating the interior of North America. The sacred beverage of the Aztecs, cocoa, found its way to Spain and thence throughout Europe.

The use of one commodity—tobacco— spread rapidly among rich and poor alike. It was used mainly in the form of snuff or for smoking in pipes. The medicinal qualities of tobacco were strongly recommended; even schoolchildren were forced to smoke during the Great Plague in London. Seventeenth-century claims for tobacco were as extravagant as some we hear today:

Divine Tobacco! which gives Ease
To all our Pains and Miseries;
Composes Thought, makes Minds sedate,
Adds Gravity to Church and State . . .[9]

Gold and ivory came to Europe from Africa, but the most important African export enriched the European powers indirectly. This export was that most misery-ridden produce —slaves. To obtain slaves to labor in the mines and on the plantations of the New World, slavers sailed to the Guinea coast, where they bought or stole their human freight. "A woman slave might change hands for a gallon of brandy, six bars of iron, two small guns, one keg of powder, and two strings of beads; a man slave might cost eight guns, one wicker-covered bottle, two cases of spirits, and twenty-eight sheets."[10] The voyage across the Atlantic to America cost the lives of from 10 to 25 percent of the Africans—inhumanly packed as they were in evil-smelling, suffocating quarters below deck—but the remainder were profitably disposed of at their destination. It is estimated that in three centuries some thirty million Africans were brought to the Americas.

The price revolution. The gold and silver brought to Europe from the New World in enormous quantities may have had a more direct effect on Europe's economy than any of the other products of Africa, Asia, or the Americas. By the middle of the fifteenth century Europe was confronted with a severe gold and silver shortage, caused both by the depletion of European mines and by increasing demands for currency to finance the new standing armies and navies and to pay for spices and other luxury commodities. The critical situation was partially relieved by the development of new European mines, by imports of gold from West Africa, and, above all, by the unprecedented quantities of precious metals from mines of Spanish America. The bonanza of bullion upset price levels throughout western Europe; between 1500 and 1650 commodity prices more than tripled.

This price revolution affected all classes. Merchants and manufacturers were benefited, but laborers were harmed because wages lagged behind prices. Except in parts of England, the landowners of western Europe, most of whom rented their land to peasants on long-term leases, suffered because their incomes were fixed. The peasants, on the other hand, benefited from rising prices for their farm products. In Europe east of the Elbe River, however, the situation was reversed. Here the landowners benefited from the rising price and growing market for grain in the West by the twofold process of increasing production and enserfing their peasants, who during the Middle Ages had been freer than those in western Europe. The subjection of the east European peasantry—as a means of obtaining a cheap labor force—contrasts sharply with the freedom of western Europe's peasant renters and farmers. Through the centuries the Elbe would continue to divide Europe economically and socially, and today it divides communist and capitalist Europe.

Banking becomes big business. One indicator of the resurgence of commerce was the growth of banking and related business practices. The word *bank* derives from the Italian *banca*, meaning "bench," on which medieval Italian moneylenders sat in the marketplace to carry on their business. When a man failed, the people broke his bench, and from this custom came the word *bankrupt*, or "broken bench." During the late Middle Ages moneylending became indispensable to the administration of both national monarchies and the Church so that traditional prohibition on usury was often ignored.

Large-scale banking was first developed in Italian cities, where merchant bankers arranged bills of exchange and negotiated loans. By 1350 some eighty banking houses were in business in Florence alone. In the fifteenth century the most illustrious of these families was the Medici, who established branch offices all over western Europe and acted as financial agents for the popes. Loans also were made to rulers who were continually in need of funds to carry on their wars.

The greatest of the sixteenth-century bankers were the Fuggers of Augsburg in Germany. They repeated the pattern set by the Medici, loaning money to the Church (half of the money collected by Tetzel from the sale of indulgences went to repay a Fugger loan), to Charles v to finance his election as emperor, and to the Spanish and Austrian Hapsburgs. The Hapsburg loans were secured by mining concessions, and the Fuggers gained a virtual monopoly on silver and copper mining in central Europe and silver and mercury mining in Spain. For decades the Fuggers realized an average yearly profit of over 30 percent, but they went bankrupt in 1607 when Spain for the third time defaulted on its loans.

By the seventeenth century the resources of banking families like the Fuggers were inadequate to meet the needs of the time, and private banks were superseded by public banks chartered by the government. The first of these great public institutions was the Bank of Amsterdam, chartered in 1609. Its main purpose was to facilitate trade by the conversion of various currencies into credits called bank money, which because of its standard value came to be preferred to coins. In 1694 the Bank of England was chartered as a means of financing England's wars. In return for a large loan to the government at 8 percent, the bank was granted a monopoly on such banking operations as issuing paper bank notes and marketing the government's securities. With banking there naturally evolved new financial techniques. Despite the increase in precious metals after 1500, the supply could not keep pace with the increase in trade, and the Bank of Amsterdam began the practice of issuing loans against its deposits. Because it could safely loan larger sums than had been deposited, the Bank of Amsterdam initiated a new, effective means of expanding credit. Bank notes also came to replace gold and silver currency.

Progress was also made in commercial arithmetic and in bookkeeping. Simple single-entry bookkeeping had been developed as early as the thirteenth century. Soon afterwards, double-entry bookkeeping came into use; it was well known in Italy by 1500 and in western Europe a century later. By listing a transaction either as a *debit* (meaning, "he owes") or a *credit* ("he believes" a promiser will carry out his promise), a businessman could readily determine his status in terms of profit and loss.

New methods of financing companies. Not only banks but also modern corporations were developed in response to needs arising from the expanded commerce of early modern times. Unprecedented difficulties resulted from trading at long distances overseas in strange lands. It was natural that those engaged in overseas trade should seek to combine their efforts both to provide mutual protection and to share losses as well as profits.

The companies were of two main types—regulated and joint-stock—and both were chartered, regulated, and granted monopolies by the state. In the regulated company individuals financed their own businesses and abided by the rules the group had accepted to protect the trade in which the members had a mutual interest. The earlier companies were of this nature.

The joint-stock companies involved an association of capital as well as of men. The members put their money into a common fund and gave over the management to a board of directors. Because of its advantages, the joint-stock company became almost universal. It had a permanent legal personality that did not expire, whereas the regulated company was not a legal entity, and in case of damages each member had to sue or be sued individually. As many people as wanted could contribute capital. Stock might be transferred as the owner saw fit, and at the same time, the company's policy underwent no serious change. The vast corporations of today grew out of this early type of business organization.

Stock exchanges and insurance. The creation of joint-stock companies gave impetus to the growth of stock exchanges, because the shares could be easily transferred from one person to another like any other commodity. A stock exchange made it easier to accumulate capital from many different sources, thereby enabling very large commercial companies to be formed. We have seen that the first stock exchange, the bourse at Antwerp, was primarily a commodity exchange. Later the two functions were separated.

Another method of sharing losses besides the joint-stock company was insurance. Since the loss of his vessel might well ruin an individual merchant, it came to be the practice to distribute losses among a group of traders by means of insurance. Interested merchants drew up an agreement by which each was responsible for a percentage of any possible loss. Because the merchants signed their names at the bottom of this document, the practice came to be known as underwriting.

The most famous of all marine insurance groups, Lloyd's of London, came into being about 1688. Lloyd's was not a stock company but an association of shipowners, merchants, and underwriters who first met together in a London coffee house owned by Edward Lloyd. Since its modest beginnings, Lloyd's has grown steadily and branched out into other forms of insurance. Today it is the world authority on matters of ship classification, and it publishes *Lloyd's List*, a daily paper which indicates the whereabouts of all registered vessels.

After the disastrous London fire of 1666,

fire insurance companies were started, and in the same period companies specializing in life insurance were also formed. In 1684 the Friendly Society was organized. This society was the first mutual company—an association in which policyholders received a share of the company profits.

Speculation and business bubbles. Toward the end of the seventeenth century, the accumulation of capital brought about a mania for speculation in the shares of joint-stock companies in England, France, and Holland. One authority comments on the fantastic nature of the wildcat schemes, "which promised to earn great dividends by trading in human hair, making square cannon balls, getting butter from beech trees, marketing an air pump for the brain, perfecting a wheel for perpetual motion, searching for rich wrecks off the Irish coast, or importing jackasses from Spain."[11] The two most notorious speculative companies were the South Sea Company in England and the Mississippi Company in France.

The financiers of the South Sea Company assumed the British national debt of about £9,000,000 in return for a 6 percent annual interest payment and a monopoly of British trade with South America and the islands in the South Seas. The price of company stock rose rapidly until it was far above the value of the company's earnings. In 1720, with a £100 share selling for £1,060, the huge speculative bubble burst when shareholders lost confidence and began to sell. Many lost not only their savings but also property they had mortgaged in the hope of getting rich quickly.

The Mississippi Company had a similar history. Formed to promote trade with France's Louisiana territory, where it founded New Orleans in 1718, the company soon acquired a monopoly on all French colonial trade. In addition, the company assumed the national debt and was granted the right to collect all indirect taxes in France and to establish a central bank with the privilege of issuing paper money. Speculative fever combined with currency inflation to bid up the company's stock to fantastic heights. Thousands suffered losses when shareholders began to unload and the company went bankrupt in 1720.

The demoralizing failure of these schemes left a legacy in both countries. In England Parliament passed the "Bubble Act," which drastically restricted the right of incorporation. In France distrust of paper money and the government's credit and solvency continued for generations.

The domestic system. In the Middle Ages manufacturing had been carried on under the guild system. The impetus of commercial expansion caused an important change in the organization of industry. The domestic, or putting-out, system evolved in the sixteenth century and reached its widest application in the textile industry of England. It operated in this fashion: a merchant capitalist would buy raw materials, assign them to artisans to be worked on in their own homes, take the finished product, and sell it to his customers. Thus, between producer and customer, a middleman intervened—an entrepreneur who accumulated capital by selling his goods at a profit. Because work was no longer planned and conducted by master and apprentice under one roof, this

The famous insurance association known as Lloyd's of London took its name from Lloyd's coffee house, where the insurance underwriters used to meet with merchants and shipowners. This satirical scene at Lloyd's dates from the late eighteenth century.

system widened the gulf between employer and employee, capitalist and worker.

The domestic system had many advantages. The accumulation of capital in the hands of the entrepreneur made possible the purchase of raw materials in greater bulk and allowed for marketing of finished products on a larger scale than had been possible under the guild system. The domestic system also contributed to an increased specialization of skills within an efficient system of overall production; an employer could have his raw wool sent to spinners, then to weavers, and finally to dyers. From the workers' point of view, it was now possible for agricultural tenants to augment the bare subsistence they eked from the soil by working at home. The capitalist employer, on the other hand, could operate without the restrictions imposed by the urban guilds.

The domestic system persisted for two hundred years in England, although in some trades workers were brought together in central shops long before the beginning of the machine age and the factory system proper. On the Continent, however, where the guilds were retained as agents of the mercantilist state in controlling industry, the guild system remained strong. Hence industrial production on the Continent lagged behind that in England, where industry was less restricted by guild practices.

Innovation in agriculture. The condition of agriculture was a basic socioeconomic factor in the life of the period, for agriculture provided the majority of Europeans with their livelihood. In England, especially, the advent of commercial capitalism wrought significant changes. The profit-making potentialities in farming attracted enterprising entrepreneurs, who bought up large tracts of land. Because the possession of land had always been the mark of nobility, the *nouveaux riches* consolidated their position in polite society by acquiring estates and marrying into the landed gentry. The alliance between land and trade created a powerful new group in Parliament—a class which promoted legislation favorable to its own needs and desires, often at the expense of the national good. But the satisfaction of the profit motive had a beneficial effect upon agriculture; the

new commercial landowners applied efficient business methods to the management of their estates. They encouraged the use of new tools and crops and were sympathetic to new ideas in stock breeding and soil development.

A pioneer agronomist was Jethro Tull (1674-1741), who advocated careful plowing of the land, planting seeds in neat rows by the use of a drill he invented, and keeping the plants well cultivated as they grew to maturity. By mixing clay and lime into the soil, Viscount Charles Townshend (1674-1738) restored the fertility of land that had once been worthless swamp and sand. He also suggested crop rotation as a method of soil restoration superior to the wasteful custom of allowing good farm land to lie fallow. He was so enthusiastic over turnips, his pet crop for livestock feed, that he was nicknamed "Turnip Townshend."

Robert Bakewell (1725-1795) was responsible for attacking the problem of livestock breeding. Haphazard breeding had resulted in sheep weighing only from twenty-five to forty pounds and cattle of about four hundred pounds. Through the select breeding of choice animals, Bakewell raised larger livestock, improved the quality of the meat, and increased the quantity of milk available from his dairy cattle. His methods attracted attention, especially from the wealthy farmers, but most of the rank and file were suspicious of his innovations and too poor to adopt them.

While the tempo of agricultural reform was much faster and more general in England than on the Continent, there was evidence of some progress in farming methods there also. In fact, the great advances in English agriculture owed much to Continental techniques and improved seeds, but these achievements were applied much more systematically in England.

The enclosure movement. The practice of enclosing open lands, a development which had begun in England even before Tudor times, was accelerated by the changes in farming methods. Aided by special acts of Parliament, members of the new commercial landowning class seized the opportunity to enclose the common lands, where for hundreds of years English villagers had grazed their cattle, and to purchase and fence in the small farms owned and operated by the sturdy, independent yeomen. These lands were consolidated into holdings which were, in effect, large-scale business enterprises requiring substantial capital for operation and upkeep. The demand for wool in the textile industry resulted also in the enclosure of large tracts of arable land for sheep raising.

The controversy over the enclosure movement reached its climax between 1750 and 1810. The advocates of enclosure justified amalgamation of small agricultural holdings by claiming that new methods of stock breeding and crop rotation could not be practiced on unfenced land. From an economic standpoint, enclosure was inevitable, and some historians believe that the enclosure movement resulted ultimately in a more careful use of a greater amount of land than had been available before. Better and more food was thus made available for a population on the verge of rapid increase. Like most drastic economic changes, however, the enclosure movement spelled misery and dislocation to a large number of countryfolk. The destruction of the yeoman class and the depopulation of many villages was ruefully pondered by Oliver Goldsmith in his poem, "The Deserted Village":

Ill fares the land, to hastening ills a prey,
Where wealth accumulates, and men decay.
Princes and lords may flourish, or may fade;
A breath can make them, as a breath has made;
But a bold peasantry, their country's pride,
When once destroyed can never be supplied. . . .
Ye friends to truth, ye statesmen, who survey
The rich man's joy increase, the poor's decay,
'Tis yours to judge how wide the limits stand
Between a splendid and a happy land.

The saga of the yeoman's misfortunes did not end with their departure from the villages; its finale took place in the cities. When the story of industrial capitalism is taken up in Chapter 22, we will view the bleak and harsh environment of displaced rural people as they labored long and hard in grimy factories and lived as best they could in ugly, disease-ridden slums.

SUMMARY

Braving the terrors of uncharted seas and the dreadful hardships of long voyages, a few daring sea captains opened up rich trade routes to the East and discovered new lands in the Western Hemisphere. In the New World the feats of the explorers were followed by the bold, and often cruel, exploits of the *conquistadores*, who carved out vast empires for their homelands.

Meanwhile, various European countries had erected forts on the African coast for the purpose of exploiting the slave trade. In the teeming lands of Asia, European penetration was secured only by the establishment of strongly fortified trading settlements at strategic sites. Using this system, the Portuguese controlled trade in the East during the 1500's but gradually lost out to the English and Dutch, who garnered most of the profits in the next century. While the Dutch concentrated more and more on the East Indies, the English East India Company built up a commercial stronghold in India. In China and Japan the behavior of the Portuguese caused native officials to restrict the westerners to a narrow theater of operations. In the East, European ways of life were successfully and permanently imposed only in the Philippines.

In sharp contrast to their failures in Japan and China, the western European powers were able to transplant not only their authority but also their institutions and culture to the sparsely populated lands of the Americas. The government and economics of the Spanish and Portuguese colonies were directly—and minutely—controlled by royal decrees and officials, whereas the development of the French, English, and Dutch colonies was left largely to private companies.

The impact of the New World upon the Old was so far-reaching as to intensify the Commercial Revolution, the name given to the first phase of our capitalistic economic system. The capitalism of this period, during which the economy in western Europe became nation-centered instead of town-centered, is called commercial capitalism because of the dominant part played by commerce as a producer of wealth. With the spectacular outburst of geographical discoveries and the creation of new trade routes, the areas which had thrived on the Mediterranean trade lost their leading roles to those along the Atlantic seaboard. The first great colonial empires were built up by Portugal and Spain, only to be superseded through the dynamism of Holland and later England and France. New products poured into Europe to augment diet, clothing, and the general standard of living, while the influx of gold and silver completed the change from a barter to a money economy and produced a price revolution.

This era also saw the development of large-scale banking and commercial practices. By the seventeenth century important banking institutions had been founded throughout western Europe. Because overseas trading ventures required large amounts of capital and entailed great risks, merchants pooled their resources by forming companies, the earlier ones of the regulated type, the later and more successful ones joint-stock companies—forerunners of present-day corporations. To serve as marketplaces for stock that could change hands readily, stock exchanges developed.

The geographical, political, and commercial expansion of Europe between the years 1450 and 1650 was so immense that it transformed the basic pattern of global existence. With it we enter the formative period of modern times. For the next three centuries the civilization of western Europe—carried to the four corners of the earth and stimulated by new and dynamic forces—was to dominate world culture.

SUGGESTIONS FOR READING

C. Nowell, **The Great Discoveries and the First Colonial Empires***** (Cornell); J. H. Parry, **The Establishment of the European Hegemony, 1415-1715***** (Torchbooks) and **The Age of Reconnaissance***** (Mentor) have excellent brief coverage. See also Robert L. Reynolds, **Europe Emerges: Transition Toward an Industrial World-Wide Society, 600-1750***** (Wisconsin, 1961); and D. Lach, **Asia in the Making of Europe,** Vol. 1, **The Century of Discovery** (Univ. of Chicago, 1965).

S. E. Morison, **The European Discovery of America: The Northern Voyages** (Oxford, 1971) and **The Southern Voyages** (Oxford, 1974) are engrossing surveys. The best book on Columbus is S. E. Morison, **Admiral of the Ocean Sea** (Little, Brown) condensed as **Christopher Columbus, Mariner***** (Mentor). On exploration in America before Columbus see H. Holand, **Norse Discoveries and Explorations in North America***** (Dover); and Carl Sauer, **Northern Mists***** (Univ. of California). On Portuguese explorations see S. E. Morison, **Portuguese Voyagers to America in the Fifteenth Century***** (Octagon); and E. Sanceau, **Henry the Navigator: The Story of a Great Prince and his Times** (Shoe String).

F. A. Kirkpatrick, **The Spanish Conquistadores***** (Meridian) is a colorful treatment. W. H. Prescott, **History of the Conquest of Mexico***** (Phoenix) and **The Conquest of Peru***** (Mentor), both abridged, are historical classics. On the same subject see Jorge E. Hardy, **Pre-Columbian Cities** (Walker, 1973); and J. E. Thompson, **The Rise and Fall of Maya Civilization,** 2nd ed. (Univ. of Oklahoma, 1973).

Good accounts of individual explorers are as follows: William W. Johnson, **Cortes** (Little, Brown, 1973); C. M. Parr, **Ferdinand Magellan, Circumnavigator** (Crowell); J. C. Beaglehole, **The Life of Captain James Cook** (Stanford, 1974); and G. M. Thomson, **Sir Francis Drake** (Morrow, 1972).

C. Boxer, **The Dutch Seaborne Empire, 1600-1800** (Knopf); and K. Haley, **The Dutch in the Seventeenth Century***** (Harcourt Brace Jovanovich, 1972) are lively portraits of Dutch society.

C. H. Haring, **The Spanish Empire in America***** (Harbinger) is the best introduction. See also J. H. Parry, **The Spanish Seaborne Empire** (Knopf, 1966); and L. Hanke, **The Spanish Struggle for Justice in the Conquest of America***** (Little, Brown).

A. L. Rowse, **Elizabethan Renaissance***** (Scribner's, 1974) is a highly readable account. C. Bridenbaugh, **Vexed and Troubled Englishmen, 1590-1642** (Oxford) describes the factors influencing English migration to America. Also recommended are Grace Woodward, **Pocahontas** (Oklahoma, 1970); and G. D. Langdon, Jr., **Pilgrim Colony: A History of New Plymouth, 1620-1691***** (Yale).

M. Dobb, **Studies in the Development of Capitalism,***** 2nd ed. (New World) is a useful introduction. The following are excellent special studies: R. De Roover, **The Rise and Decline of the Medici Bank, 1397-1494***** (Norton); R. Ehrenberg, **Capital and Finance in the Age of the Renaissance: A Study of the Fuggers and Their Connections** (Kelley); and V. Barbour, **Capitalism in Amsterdam in the Seventeenth Century***** (Harcourt Brace Jovanovich, 1972).

A. P. Thornton, **Doctrines of Imperialism***** (Wiley, 1965) contains good short accounts of early modern imperialism and mercantilism. On other aspects of the Commercial Revolution see E. J. Hamilton, **American Treasure and the Price Revolution in Spain, 1501-1650** (Octagon); R. H. Tawney, **The Agrarian Problem in the Sixteenth Century***** (Torchbooks); and B. H. van Bath, **Agrarian History of Western Europe, A.D. 500-1850** (St. Martin's).

On the African slave trade see D. Mannix and M. Cowley, **Black Cargoes***** (Compass); and J. Pope-Hennessy, **Sins of the Fathers: A Study of the Atlantic Slave Traders, 1441-1807** (Knopf). David B. Davis, **The Problem of Slavery in Western Culture***** (Cornell) is a historical review of ideas on slavery.

*****Indicates a less expensive paperbound edition.

In the 1540's, as the reign of Henry VIII drew to a close, John Johnson and his family settled in at Glapthorn Manor in Northamptonshire. Compared to the noblemen's estates of the region, Glapthorn was small, with only a hundred acres of cultivated land and pasture and another hundred and fifty acres of meadowland and wooded hills. The manor was a few miles southeast of the old market town of Oundle, near the marshy Fen Country, in a belt of rich farmland and lush pasture encircled by deep forests of oak and beech. More than a thousand sheep grew fat in the enclosed grazing lands, whose wool John Johnson sent to his brother Otwell in London to be weighed and packed in the woolhouse and then sold to clothmakers in England and on the continent.

John and Otwell Johnson were partners in the firm of Johnson and Company, a loose association of woollen merchants who dealt in the fleeces and fells (skins) of English sheep. In the early 1540's their business was flourishing; the drapers of Calais and Bruges always wanted more wool than the English merchants had to sell, and as a result prices were rising higher and more rapidly than ever before. It was because his profits were so great that John Johnson had been able to rent Glapthorn Manor. Every merchant dreamed of living the life of a country gentleman on an estate far from the crowds of "the Street"—Lombard Street, where merchants met in the open air to transact business, find out international news and learn the latest rates of exchange on the currency of France, the Low Countries, Italy, and Spain.

The rent at Glapthorn was £8 a year, but with careful management and good luck in his business ventures John could afford it. As a merchant he had no fixed income; he was entirely dependent on the fortunes of the marketplace, the honesty of the traders he dealt with, and the soundness of the currencies that changed hands in the London counting houses. In a good year, John and his family lived well. His wife Sabine could spend £7 on cauldrons, pans, and kettles for the kitchen, and £11 on six silver goblets, and still have plenty of money to buy herself some of the sweet-smelling gloves that sold for six shillings the dozen. But in a bad year Sabine Johnson was hard pressed to keep the cellars stocked with the barrels of beer that cost four shillings tenpence, or to pay the hogsherd his five shillings a year in wages.

Sabine Johnson ran Glapthorn Manor whenever her husband was away, which was perhaps half the year. She was a lively, capable woman and the marriage was a happy one. Their letters—and they wrote often when John was abroad—were full of lighthearted endearments. John called Sabine his "loving heart"; "with all my heart, entirely beloved," she answered. "Would ye were in my bed to tarry me!" he wrote to her at the end of a long business day in Antwerp.

John had known Sabine since he was a young apprentice in his early twenties. She was the niece of his master, a wool merchant in London, and was then a child of nine or ten. While Sabine was still a girl, the young merchant had worked out the details of the marriage settlement with her father. She had a dowry of a hundred marks, and a good supply of sheets and blankets and furnishings. The dowry would help to set John up in business, the linens and furnishings would supply his first household, and the marriage would make the bond between John and his father-in-law more intricate and more enduring. Such were the practicalities of Tudor marriage; that John and Sabine loved one another was an unexpected dividend.

Sabine Johnson had been educated to serve as a dutiful helpmeet to her future husband. She had learned to read the Bible and devotional books, and to model herself on the perfect housewife— "of chaste thought, stout courage, patient, untired, watchful, diligent, witty, pleasant, constant in friendship, full of good neighborhood." She was taught to suppress her anger, to do as her husband told her, to endure his displeasure with a "mild sufferance," while remaining "ever unto him pleasant, amiable and delightful." Since her marriage at twenty, she had borne four children: three girls, Charity, Rachel, and Faith, and a boy, Evangelist. Another child, a boy, had lived only a few weeks and was buried in a tiny coffin in a nearby village churchyard.

The three Johnson daughters were sent at an early age to be educated in the home of their uncle Otwell Johnson. The son, however, was trained to carry on his father's profession. As soon as he was old enough Evangelist traveled with his father through the sheep farms of Northamptonshire and Buckinghamshire, watching John Johnson bargain with the wool growers and inspect the wool the shepherds showed him, learning to tell good fleeces from bad and to calculate in advance what price the wool might bring in the market at Calais. Several times he went up with his father to London, striding beside him through the confusion of bales and carts and coaches that choked the narrow streets and listening to the haggling of the merchants in Flemish, Italian, and French.

It was John Johnson's good fortune that, at a time when food prices were doubling, Glapthorn Manor was almost completely self-sufficient. Except for the delicacies sent up from London from time to time—hard white sugar, packed in chests, from the Canary Islands, boxed candies from the confectioners of Antwerp, ripe lemons and oranges bought at dockside from Spanish ships each autumn—all food eaten at Glapthorn was produced there. The bread was made from home-grown wheat and rye, stone-ground in the manor's own mill and risen with yeast from the ale vats in the brewhouse. The dairy yielded more than enough milk, butter, and cheese; the hens laid so abundantly that the surplus eggs had to be taken to Oundle market to be sold.

In more settled times the cook at Glapthorn would have sent four to six meat and fish dishes to the table at the noon dinner, but as things were, there were no more than two or three. (Noble households in the Tudor age were often served beef, mutton, veal, lamb, kid, pork, rabbit, capon, deer, and several varieties of ocean and freshwater fish at a single meal, with preliminary courses of poultry and game birds.) A salad began the Johnsons' meal, and fruit and sweets rounded it out, and with every course there was wine, preferably Bordeaux but sometimes lighter vintages from Orleans or Auxerre. At other times the family washed down a light meal of cheese and brawn (meat from baited bulls) with firkins of foaming beer—either the strong normal brew or the "double beer" that was twice as potent.

Meals were eaten in the great hall, a cavernous room with high ceilings filled with a long table for the family and guests and low benches for the servants. The manor house, a fifteenth-century stone and timber building set in a large garden, had three floors. On the ground floor the kitchen, pantry, and storage rooms led off the great hall. The bedrooms were on the second floor, and the third floor or attic contained the children's and servants' bedrooms. Every year at the hiring fair Sabine Johnson hired "mean drudges," servant girls who rose at dawn to light the fires, then spent their long days cleaning, washing, spinning, making candles, and beating the laundry clean with wooden bats. Sabine felt responsible for shaping her servants' characters as well as their work habits. She watched them carefully, and subtracted a few pence from their wages when they were late or slow in their work, or when they swore.

The Johnsons were a devoutly religious family. Along with his brother John Johnson held the Calvinist belief that only the elect of God would be saved, and was as eager to hear a good sermon as he was to condemn the pope as the "Antichrist of Rome." Both brothers took Bibles with them in their business travels, and would go miles out of their way to see a play on "the battle betwixt the Spirit, the Soul, and the Flesh." The religious enthusiasm of the family was evident at Glapthorn. The pictures on the walls (besides a portrait of the Supreme Head of the Church, Henry VIII) were of figures from the Bible. The books in the parlor were devotional books and stories from scripture, and the friends that came to visit there were almost exclusively Lutheran or Calvinist in their opinions.

But the family had other amusements as well. There was a chess set in the parlor, and an "old great Venice lute" that John played. In the summer there was hunting, hawking, and coursing hares. In spring came the festival of the sheep shearing, and village fairs with their entertainments of racing, wrestling, and morris dancing.

In 1551 a series of reverses struck the Johnson household. The sweating sickness, a virulent form of influenza with pulmonary complications, swept through southern England, reaching London and the merchant quarter in July. Otwell Johnson fell ill early one evening and was dead within eight hours. John Johnson barely had time to mourn his brother before he was caught up in the vast financial crisis brought on by the disastrous government policy of debasing the coinage. Johnson & Co. dealt daily with the merchants of Antwerp and Calais, and relied for its profits on a favorable rate of exchange between English pounds and foreign currencies. When the king and his council cut the value of English coins by half, continental creditors refused to accept payment in English money. Wool sales dropped drastically, and with no large reserves to fall back on, Johnson & Co. was forced to declare bankruptcy.

Immediately everything of value was seized by creditors—clothes, furniture, iron pots, and even the books off the shelves. Out of kindness the landlord allowed the family to stay on at Glapthorn rent free until such time as John could rebuild his fortunes, but his chances of recovery were slim, and he would in any case be encumbered with debt for the rest of his life. Two years later, with the accession of the Catholic Queen Mary Tudor, the Johnson family left England to join the colony of Protestant exiles in Geneva.

Notes

PROLOGUE: PERSPECTIVE ON HUMANITY

1. David G. Mandelbaum, "Concepts of Civilization and Culture," *Encyclopaedia Britannica*, 1967 ed., Vol. 5, p. 831A.
2. See A. J. Toynbee, *Civilization on Trial* (New York: Oxford University Press, 1948), p. 11.
3. Quoted in *The New York Times* (July 15, 1973, Section 10), p. 16.
4. See P. Gardiner, *The Nature of Historical Explanation* (London: Oxford University Press, 1952), p. 98.
5. We are indebted to Professor James A. Brown of Northwestern University for updated information about the Koster site, which was closed in 1979.

CHAPTER 1: ALONG THE BANKS OF RIVERS

1. R. E. F. Leakey, "Evidence for an Advanced Plio-Pleistocene Hominid from East Rudolph, Kenya," *Nature* (April 13, 1973), p. 449. See also "News and Views: More Questions Than Answers at East Rudolph," same source, p. 431.
2. R. Braidwood, *Prehistoric Men*, 7th ed., (Glenview, Ill.: Scott, Foresman and Co., 1967), p. 34.
3. G. S. Hawkins in collaboration with John B. White, *Stonehenge Decoded* (New York: Dell Publishing Co., 1966), pp. 117-118.
4. V. Gordon Childe, *New Light on the Most Ancient East* (London: Routledge & Kegan Paul Ltd., 1954), p. 114.
5. Tom B. Jones, *Ancient Civilization* (Chicago: Rand McNally & Co., 1960), p. 10.
6. V. Gordon Childe, *What Happened in History* (New York: Pelican Books, 1946), p. 74.
7. The ancient Mesopotamian chronology followed here is that presented in *The Cambridge Ancient History*, rev. ed. (1962) Vol. I, Ch. 6.
8. H. Frankfort, *The Birth of Civilization in the Near East* (London: Williams and Norgate, Ltd., 1951), p. 60.
9. "Les reformes d'Urukagina," trans. by M. Lambert in *Revue d'Assyriologie*, L (Paris, 1956), p. 183.
10. James B. Pritchard, ed., *Ancient Near Eastern Texts Relating to the Old Testament*, 2nd ed., trans. by E. A. Speiser (Princeton: Princeton University Press, 1955), p. 119.
11. *Sumerische und Akkadische Hymnen und Gebete*, trans. by A. Falkenstein and W. von Soden (Zurich: Artemis-Verlag, 1953), p. 188. For a partial translation and full discussion of this text, see S. N. Kramer, *From the Tablets of Sumer* (Indian Hills, Colo.: The Falcon's Wing Press, 1956), pp. 267-271.
12. H. de Genouillac, trans., in *Revue d'Assyriologie*, XXV (Paris, 1928), p. 148.
13. Quoted in Kramer, p. 50.
14. R. F. Harper, *The Code of Hammurabi* (Chicago: University of Chicago Press, 1904), p. 3.
15. *Ibid.*, p. 49.
16. *Ibid.*, p. 101.
17. From *Epic of Gilgamesh*, trans. by E. A. Speiser, in Pritchard, p. 90.
18. Nels Bailkey, ed., *Readings in Ancient History from Gilgamesh to Diocletian*, 2nd ed. (Lexington: D. C. Heath & Co., 1976), p. 27.
19. Quoated in *City Invincible: A Symposium on Urbanization and Cultural Development in the Ancient Near East*, ed. by Carl H. Kraeling and Robert McC. Adams (Chicago: University of Chicago Press, 1960), p. 163.
20. Quoted in M. A. Murray, *The Splendour That Was Egypt* (London: Sidgwick & Jackson, Ltd., 1949), p. 67.
21. Trans. by John A. Wilson, *The Burden of Egypt* (Chicago: University of Chicago Press, 1951), p. 117.
22. *Ibid.*, p. 164.
23. Adolf Erman, *The Literature of the Ancient Egyptians*, trans. by Aylward M. Blackman (London: Methuen & Co., Ltd., 1927), pp. 190, 196, 197.
24. From "The Instruction of Meri-ka-Re," trans. by John A. Wilson, *The Burden of Egypt*, p. 120.
25. *Ibid.*, p. 119.
26. Quoted in George Steindorff and George Hoyningen-Huene, *Egypt* (Locust Valley, N.Y.: J. J. Augustin Inc., 1943), p. 23.
27. Trans. by George Steindorff and Keith E. Seele, *When Egypt Ruled the East* (Chicago: University of Chicago Press, 1942), p. 125. Copyright 1942 by the University of Chicago Press.
28. Quoted in J. H. Breasted, *The Dawn of Conscience* (New York: Charles Scribner's Sons, 1939), p. 284.
29. Ezekiel 27:33-34. Revised Standard Version of the Bible.
30. B. W. Anderson, *Understanding the Old Testament* (Englewood Cliffs, N.J.: Prentice-Hall, Inc., 1957), p. 537.
31. I Samuel 8:6, 20. Revised Standard Version of the Bible.
32. I Kings 4:20 ff.; 10:14 ff. Revised Standard Version of the Bible.
33. II Kings 25:14. Revised Standard Version of the Bible.
34. Micah 6:8. Revised Standard Version of the Bible.
35. D. D. Luckenbill, *Ancient Records of Assyria and Babylonia*, I (Chicago: University of Chicago Press, 1926), p. 147.
36. Quoted in Georges Roux, *Ancient Iraq* (Baltimore: Penguin Books, Inc., 1966), p. 278.
37. Nahum 3:8. Revised Standard Version of the Bible.
38. Herodotus, *History*, I, 181; trans. by George Rawlinson.
39. Daniel 5:27. Revised Standard Version of the Bible.
40. Herodotus, IX, 122; trans. by A. R. Burn, *Persia and the West* (New York: St. Martin's Press, 1962), p. 61.
41. Herodotus, VIII, 98; trans. by Rawlinson.

CHAPTER 2: THE GLORY THAT WAS GREECE

1. Plutarch's *Lives*, II, trans. by Sir T. North (London: J. M. Dent & Sons Ltd., 1898), p. 144.
2. See Leonard R. Palmer, *Mycenaeans and Minoans: Aegean Prehistory in the Light of the Linear B Tablets* (New York: Alfred A. Knopf, Inc., and London: Faber and Faber, Ltd., 1961), Chapter 5, "The Last Days of Pylos."
3. Quoted in Werner Jaeger, *Paideia: The Ideals of Greek Culture*, I (New York: Oxford University Press, 1939), p. 70.
4. "Laws," V, 735; in *The Dialogues of Plato*, II, trans. by B. Jowett (New York: Random House, 1937), p. 503.
5. Plutarch's *Lives*, "Solon" 16, trans. by the authors.
6. Trans. by A. R. Burn, *The Pelican History of Greece* (Baltimore: Penguin Books, Inc., 1966), p.186.
7. C. E. Robinson, *Hellas: A Short History of Ancient Greece* (New York: Pantheon Books, 1948), p. 68.
8. From Thucydides, *The History of the Peloponnesian War*, II, 65, edited by Sir Richard Livingstone, by permission of the Oxford University Press, p. 130.
9. *Ibid.*, 37, 40, pp. 111, 113.
10. Thucydides, II, edited by Sir Richard Livingstone, pp. 40-41.
11. *Ibid.*, I, 23, p. 46.
12. *Ibid.*, II, 65, p. 130.
13. *Ibid.*, V, 105, p. 270.
14. *Ibid.*, VI, 90, p. 325.
15. Herodotus, *History of the Persian Wars*, VII, p. 10.
16. Quoted in M. Cary and T. J. Haarhoff, *Life and Thought in the Greek and Roman World* (London: Methuen & Co., Ltd., 1951), p. 200.
17. "Apology," in *The Four Socratic Dialogues of Plato*, trans. by B. Jowett (Oxford: Clarendon Press, 1924), pp. 91-92.

18. ''Phaedrus,'' 247; quoted in *The Greek World*, edited by Hugh Lloyd-Jones (Baltimore: Penguin Books, Inc., 1965), pp. 137-138.
19. Quoted in Cary and Haarhoff, p. 192.
20. Thucydides, I, 22, edited by Sir Richard Livingstone, pp. 44-45.
21. Excerpt from a poem by Archilochos cited in *The Lyric Age of Greece* by Andrew Robert Burn. London: Edward Arnold Publishers Ltd., 1960.
22. Excerpt from a poem by Sappho cited in *The Lyric Age of Greece* by Andrew Robert Burn. London: Edward Arnold Publishers Ltd., 1960.
23. From Agamemnon, trans. by Gilbert Murray in *Ten Greek Plays*, ed. by Lane Cooper (New York: Oxford University Press, 1929), p. 96. Reprinted by permission of George Allen & Unwin Ltd. for the Estate of Gilbert Murray.
24. Quoted in *The Cambridge Ancient History*, XI (Cambridge: The University Press, 1936), p. 696.
25. Excerpt from *Theocritus, Bion and Moschus* trans. by Andrew Lang. London: MacMillan and Company Limited, 1941.
26. G. Murray, *Hellenism and the Modern World* (Boston: Beacon Press, 1953), pp. 56-57.

CHAPTER 3: THE GRANDEUR THAT WAS ROME
1. Polybius, *Histories*, I, 10, trans. by Evelyn S. Shuckburgh (Bloomington: Indiana University Press, 1962), Vol. I, p. 10.
2. Livy, *Roman History*, XXXIII, 33, trans. by E. T. Sage in The Loeb Classical Library (Cambridge: Harvard University Press, 1945), Vol. IX, p. 367.
3. Plutarch's *Lives*, ''Tiberius Gracchus,'' IX, 5, trans. by Bernadotte Perrin in The Loeb Classical Library (Cambridge: Harvard University Press, 1945), Vol. X, pp. 165, 167.
4. M. Hammond, *City-State and World State in Greek and Roman Political Theory Until Augustus* (Cambridge: Harvard University Press, 1951), p. 153.
5. Tacitus, *Annals*, XV, 44; trans. by Michael Grant (Baltimore: Penguin Books, Inc., 1959), p. 354.
6. Tertullian, *Concerning the Soul*, quoted in S. Katz, *The Decline of Rome and the Rise of Medieval Europe* (Ithaca, N.Y.: Cornell University Press, 1955), p. 7.
7. Virgil, *Aeneid*, VI, 847-853, in *Roman Civilization: Selected Readings*, II, ed. by Naphtali Lewis and Meyer Reinhold (New York: Columbia University Press, 1955), p. 23.
8. Aelius Aristides, *To Rome* (Oration XXVI), trans. by S. Levin (Glencoe, Ill.: The Free Press, 1950), p. 126.
9. R. C. Trevelyan, *Translations from Horace, Juvenal and Montaigne* (New York: Cambridge University Press, 1941), p. 129.
10. Quoted in Grant Showerman, *Century Readings in Ancient Classical Literature* (New York: The Century Co., 1925), p. 386.
11. Lucretius, *On the Nature of the Universe*, Book III, line 70, trans. by Ronald Latham (Baltimore: Penguin Books, Inc., 1951), p. 98.
12. Horace, *Odes*, III, 29 (in Part), trans. by John Dryden.
13. From *Juvenal's Satires*, translated by William Gifford, revised by John Warrington. An Everyman's Library Edition (New York: E. P. Dutton & Co., Inc., 1954), p. 5. Reprinted by permission of the publishers, E. P. Dutton & Co., Inc. and J. M. Dent & Sons Ltd.
14. Lucretius, *On the Nature of Things*, Book III, lines 830 ff., translated by John Dryden.
15. Pliny, *Natural History*, II, xiv, 117-118; translated by H. Rackham, the Loeb Classical Library (Cambridge: Harvard University Press, 1938), Vol. I, pp. 259, 261.
16. Quoted in *Caesar and Christ* by Will Durant (New York: Simon & Schuster, Inc., 1944), p. 506. Copyright 1944 by Will Durant, Copyright renewed © 1971 by Will Durant. Reprinted by permission of Simon & Schuster, Inc.

CHAPTER 4: THE ASIAN WAY OF LIFE
1. Quoted in H. G. Rawlinson, *India: A Short Cultural History* (New York: Appleton-Century, 1938), pp. 51-52.

2. Quoted in Vincent Smith, *The Oxford History of India* (Oxford: Oxford University Press, 1958), p. 131.
3. Quoted in Charles Drekmeier, *Kingship and Community in Early India* (Stanford: Stanford University Press, 1962), p. 175.
4. R. Grousset, *The Rise and Splendour of the Chinese Empire* (Berkeley: University of California Press, 1953), p. 26.
5. Quoted in Jack Finegan, *The Archeology of World Religions* (Princeton: Princeton University Press, 1952), p. 351.

CHAPTER 5: THE CITY OF GOD
1. St. Jerome's *Commentary of Ezekiel*, I, Prologue.
2. E. Wilson, *The Scrolls from the Dead Sea* (New York: Oxford University Press, 1955), p. 60.
3. Frank M. Cross, Jr., *The Ancient Library of Qumran and Modern Biblical Studies*, rev. ed. (Garden City, N.Y.: Doubleday Anchor Books, 1961), p. 242.
4. John 18:33-38. From the *Good News Bible—New Testament*. Copyright © American Bible Society 1966, 1971, 1976, p. 258. Used by permission.
5. Acts 22:6-10. From the *Good News Bible—New Testament*, Copyright © American Bible Society 1966, 1971, 1976, p. 324. Used by permission.
6. Galatians 2:16, 3:28. From the *Good News Bible—New Testament*, pp. 421, 424.
7. Tertullian, *Apology*, Ch. 50, trans. by A. Souter (Cambridge: Cambridge University Press, 1917), p. 145.
8. Quoted in Henry Bettenson, ed., *Documents of the Christian Church* (London: Oxford University Press, 1943), p. 28.
9. *Ibid.*, p. 9.
10. Tacitus, *Germania*, Ch. 14, trans. by H. Mattingly. *Tacitus on Britain and Germany* (Harmondsworth: Penguin Books, Ltd., 1948), p. 112.
11. S. Katz, *The Decline of Rome and the Rise of Medieval Europe* (Ithaca, N.Y.: Cornell University Press, 1955), p. 7.
12. E. Gibbon, *The History of the Decline and Fall of the Roman Empire* (London: Methuen & Co., Ltd., 1896), Ch. XXXVIII, ''General Observations on the Fall of the Roman Empire in the West.''
13. A. E. R. Boak, *Manpower Shortage and the Fall of the Roman Empire in the West* (Ann Arbor: University of Michigan Press, 1955), p. 115.
14. Katz, p. 98.

CHAPTER 6: CITADEL AND CONQUEROR
1. Procopius, *History of the Wars*, Book I, trans. by H. B. Dewing (London: William Heinemann, Ltd., 1914), pp. 231, 233.
2. Geoffrey de Villehardouin, *The Conquest of Constantinople*, trans. by Sir Frank T. Marzials, Memoirs of the Crusades (New York: Everyman's Library, E. P. Dutton & Co., Inc., 1933), pp. 51, 65.
3. Quoted in J. F. C. Fuller, *A Military History of the Western World*, I (New York: Funk & Wagnalls, 1954), p. 522.
4. ''The Book of the Prefect,'' trans. by A. E. R. Boak, *Journal of Economic and Business History*, I (1929), p. 600.
5. Quoted by C. Diehl, ''Byzantine Art,'' in *Byzantium: Introduction to East Roman Civilization*, ed. by N. H. Baynes and H. St. L. B. Moss (New York: Oxford University Press, 1948), p. 166.
6. Procopius, *Buildings*, I, i, 33-34, trans. by H. B. Dewing (Cambridge: Harvard University Press, 1940), p. 17.
7. D. Talbot Rice, *Byzantine Art* (Harmondsworth: Penguin Books, Ltd., 1954), pp. 150-151.
8. Quoted in Alfred Guillaume, *Islam* (Harmondsworth: Penguin Books, Ltd., 1954), pp. 28-29.
9. See T. P. Hughes, *A Dictionary of Islam* (London: W. H. Allen and Co., 1885).
10. Quoted in E. H. Palmer, *Haroun Alraschid, Caliph of Bagdad* (London: Marcus Ward and Company, 1881), p. 76.
11. H. A. R. Gibb, ''Literature,'' in *The Legacy of Islam*, ed. by T. W. Arnold and A. Guillaume (Oxford: Clarendon Press, 1931), p. 182.
12. *Rubáiyát of Omar Khayyám*, trans. by Edward Fitzgerald, Stanzas 12, 13, 71, 72.

13. Ibn Khaldun, *The Mugaddimah: An Introduction to History*, trans. by Franz Rosenthal, Vol. I (London: Routledge & Kegan Paul Ltd., 1958), p. 71.

CHAPTER 7: THE GUPTAS AND THE T'ANG: TWO GOLDEN AGES

1. Quoted in H. H. Gowen and J. W. Hall, *An Outline History of China* (New York: D. Appleton & Co., 1926), p. 117.
2. From *The Works of Li Po*, translated by Shigeyoshi Obata. Copyright, 1922, renewal, 1950, by E. P. Dutton & Co., and reprinted with their permission.
3. Quoted in Gowen and Hall, *An Outline History of China*, p. 127.
4. Obata, *The Works of Li Po*, p. 39.
5. Quoted in Gowen and Hall, *An Outline History of China*, p. 142.
6. K. S. Latourette, *The Chinese: Their History and Culture*, II (New York: The Macmillan Company, 1934), p. 264.
7. Quoted in I. Nitobé, *Bushido, the Soul of Japan* (Tokyo: Maruzen, 1935), p. 592.

CHAPTER 8: EUROPE'S SEARCH FOR STABILITY

1. Gregory of Tours, *History of the Franks*, II, 30; quoted in Eleanor S. Duckett, *The Gateway to the Middle Ages* (New York: The Macmillan Company, 1938), p. 231.
2. Quoted in C. Dawson, *The Making of Europe* (London: Sheed & Ward Ltd., 1932), p. 76.
3. Quoted in M. L. W. Laistner, *Thought and Letters in Western Europe, A.D. 500 to 900* (Ithaca, N.Y.: Cornell University Press, 1931), pp. 196-197.
4. *Ibid.*, p. 390.
5. *Piers the Plowman*, quoted in G. B. Adams, *Civilization During the Middle Ages* (New York: Charles Scribner's Sons, 1941), p. 222.
6. Quoted in E. M. Hulme, *History of the British People* (New York: Century Co., 1929), pp. 121-122.
7. Quoted in Sidney Painter, *French Chivalry: Chivalric Ideas and Practices in Medieval France* (Baltimore: Johns Hopkins Press, 1940), p. 169.

CHAPTER 9: THE WEST TAKES THE OFFENSIVE

1. Trans. by D. C. Munro, *Translations and Reprints from the Original Sources of European History*, Vol. I, No. 2(Philadelphia: University of Pennsylvania Press, 1897), pp. 6-7.
2. Quoted in A. C. Krey, *The First Crusade* (Princeton: Princeton University Press, 1921), p. 261.
3. Quoted in R. H. C. Davis, *A History of Medieval Europe: From Constantine to Saint Louis* (London: Longmans, Green & Co., Ltd., 1957), p. 290.
4. E. P. Cheyney, *The Dawn of a New Era, 1250-1453* (New York: Harper & Bros., 1936), p. 132.

CHAPTER 10: NATIONS IN THE MAKING

1. Quoted in Dorothy Whitelock, *The Beginning of English Society* (Baltimore: Penguin Books, Inc., 1952), p. 66.
2. Quoted in E. P. Cheyney, *Readings in English History Drawn from the Original Sources* (Boston: Ginn and Co., 1908), p. 112.
3. D. C. Douglas and G. Greenaway, *English Historical Documents, 1042–1189* (New York: Oxford University Press, 1953), p. 200.
4. W. S. Churchill, *The Birth of Britain*, Vol. I of *A History of the Engish-Speaking Peoples* (New York: Dodd, Mead & Co., 1965), pp. 222-223.
5. Quoted in Churchill, I, p. 210.
6. Quoted in Cheyney, pp. 157-158.
7. Quoted in *ibid.*, pp. 183, 185.
8. Quoted in J. H. Robinson, *Readings in European History*, I (Boston: Ginn and Co., 1904), p. 202.

9. *Ibid.*, p. 204.
10. Jonathon F. Scott *et al.*, *Readings in Medieval History* (New York: F. S. Crofts and Company, 1933), pp. 464-465.
11. From *The Lay of the Cid*, trans. by Sheldon R. Rose and Leonard Bacon, pp. 25-26. Published in 1919 by The Regents of the University of California; reprinted by permission of the University of California Press.
12. R. H. C. Davis, *A History of Medieval Europe: From Constantine to Saint Louis* (London: Longmans, Green & Co., Ltd., 1957), p. 315.

CHAPTER 11: TO THE GLORY OF GOD

1. Quoted in R. H. C. Davis, *A History of Medieval Europe: From Constantine to Saint Louis* (London: Longmans, Green & Co., Ltd., 1957), p. 80.
2. Quoted in S. M. Brown, *Medieval Europe* (New York: Harcourt, Brace & Co., 1935), pp. 382-383.
3. Harry J. Carroll, Jr., *et al.*, *The Development of Civilization: A Documentary History of Politics, Society, and Thought*, I (Chicago: Scott, Foresman and Co., 1961), p. 304.
4. Henry Bettenson, ed., *Documents of the Christian Church* (London: Oxford University Press, 1943), p. 144.
5. Quoted in J. H. Robinson, *Readings in European History*, I (Boston: Ginn and Co., 1904), p. 283.
6. Quoted in S. R. Packard, *Europe and the Church Under Innocent III* (New York: Henry Holt & Co., 1929), p. 35.
7. Summerfield Baldwin, *The Organization of Medieval Christianity* (New York: Henry Holt & Co., 1929), p. 35.
8. From *The Portable Chaucer* edited by Theodore Morrison. Copyright 1949 by Theodore Morrison. Reprinted by permission of The Viking Press, Inc.
9. Quoted in J. Evans, *Life in Medieval France* (New York: Oxford University Press, 1925), p. 87.
10. From *A Catholic Dictionary*, 3rd ed., edited by Donald Attwater. Copyright 1931, 1949 and renewed 1959, 1977 by Macmillan Publishing Co., Inc. © Macmillan Publishing Co., Inc., 1958. Reprinted by permission of Macmillan Publishing Co., Inc. and Cassell & Collier Macmillan Ltd.
11. Luke 9:1-6. *Good News for Modern Man: The New Testament in Today's English* (New York: American Bible Society, 1966), p. 158.
12. Morrison, pp. 80-81.
13. Robert S. Lopez, *The Tenth Century: How Dark the Dark Ages?* (New York: Rinehart and Co., 1959), p. 1.
14. Quoted in Urban T. Holmes, Jr., "Transitions in European Education," in *Twelfth-Century Europe and the Foundations of Modern Society*, ed. by Marshall Clagett, Gaines Post, and Robert Reynolds (Madison: University of Wisconsin Press, 1961), p. 17.
15. *The Story of My Misfortunes: The Autobiography of Peter Abélard*, trans. by Henry Adams Bellows (Glencoe, Ill.: The Free Press, 1958), pp. 3, 10.
16. Quoted in *Introduction to Contemporary Civilization in the West: A Source Book*, I (New York: Columbia University Press, 1946), p. 85.
17. *An Encyclopedist of the Dark Ages: Isidore of Seville*, trans. by E. Brehaut (New York: Columbia University Press, 1912), pp. 218-219.
18. *The Art of Falconry . . . of Frederick II of Hohenstaufen*, trans. by Casey A. Wood and F. Marjorie Fyfe (Boston: Charles T. Branford Co., 1943), pp. 3-4.
19. Quoted in H. O. Taylor, *The Mediaeval Mind*, II (London: Macmillan & Co., Ltd., 1938), p. 524.
20. J. A. Symonds, *Wine, Women and Song* (New York: Oxford University Press, and London: Chatto & Windus Ltd., 1931), pp. 67-69.
21. From "Stabat Mater Dolorosa" quoted in Frederick B. Artz, *The Mind of the Middle Ages, A.D. 200-1500*, 2nd ed. (New York: Alfred A. Knopf, Inc., 1954), p. 332.
22. C. W. Hollister, *Medieval Europe: A Short History* (New York: John Wiley & Sons, Inc., 1964), p. 230.
23. Quoted in Amy Kelly, *Eleanor of Aquitaine and the Four Kings*, from F. J. M. Raynouard, *Choix des Poesies Originales des Troubadours*, Vol. III (Paris, 1816-1821), p. 86. Copyright 1952 by the President and Fellows of Harvard College. Reprinted by permission.

24. *L'Inferno*, Canto I, lines 1-3, trans. by Dorothy L. Sayers, *Dante, The Divine Comedy, I: Hell* (Harmondsworth: Penguin Books, Ltd., 1949), p. 71. Reprinted by permission of A. Watkins, Inc. as agents for the Estate of Dorothy L. Sayers and David Higham Associates Limited.
25. *Paradise*, Canto XXXIII, lines 121, 144 in Sayers, *Dante, The Divine Comedy*.
26. Geoffrey Chaucer, *Canterbury Tales*, trans. by J. U. Nicolson (New York: Crown Publishers, Inc., 1936), pp. 3-5.

CHAPTER 12: EUROPE IN TRANSITION
1. A. C. Flick, *Decline of the Medieval Church*, I (London: Kegan Paul, Trench, Trubner and Co., Ltd., 1930), p. 293.
2. R. H. Bainton, *The Reformation of the Sixteenth Century* (Boston: Beacon Press, 1952), p. 15.
3. Quoted in M. Cherniavsky, " 'Holy Russia': A Study in the History of an Idea," *The American Historical Review*, LXIII, No. 3 (April 1958), p. 625.
4. G. Barraclough, *History in a Changing World* (Oxford: Basil Blackwell, 1955), p. 134.

CHAPTER 13: MAN IS THE MEASURE
1. Quoted in J. Burckhardt, *The Civilization of the Renaissance in Italy*, trans. by S. G. C. Middlemore (London: George Allen & Unwin Ltd., 1921), p. 138.
2. William Shakespeare, *The Tempest*, Act V, Scene i.
3. Quoted in J. H. Randall, Jr., *The Making of the Modern Mind* (Boston: Houghton Mifflin Co., 1940), p. 213.
4. Quoted in F. B. Artz, *The Mind of the Middle Ages A.D., 200-1500*, 2nd ed. (New York: Alfred A. Knopf, Inc., 1954), p. 307.
5. *The Decameron of Giovanni Boccaccio*, trans. by Richard Aldington (New York: Garden City Publishing Co., 1949), p. 559.
6. F. B. Artz, *From the Renaissance to Romanticism: Trends in Style in Art, Literature, and Music, 1300-1830* (Chicago: University of Chicago Press, 1962), p. 102.
7. H. O. Taylor, *Thought and Expression in the Sixteenth Century*, I (New York: The Macmillan Company, 1920), p. 175.
8. Quoted in Randall, p. 118.
9. From the 1684 translation by Gilbert Burnet, in *Introduction to Contemporary Civilization in the West: A Source Book*, I (New York: Columbia University Press, 1946), p. 461.
10. *Ibid.*, p. 460.
11. Quoted in Taylor, pp. 328–329.
12. Montaigne, "Of the Education of Children," in *The Complete Works of Montaigne*, trans. by D. M. Frame (Stanford: Stanford University Press, 1957), p. 112.
13. *Ibid.*, p. 110.
14. J. van der Elst, *The Last Flowering of the Middle Ages* (New York: Doubleday & Co., Inc., 1946), p. 59.

CHAPTER 14: HERE I TAKE MY STAND
1. Quoted in R. H. Bainton, *Here I Stand: A Life of Martin Luther* (New York and Nashville: Abingdon-Cokesbury Press, 1950), p. 65. Copyright 1950.
2. *Ibid.*, pp. 66-67.
3. Quoted in R. H. Bainton, *The Reformation of the Sixteenth Century* (Boston: Beacon Press, 1952), p. 27.
4. Quoted in C. Hayes, *A Political and Cultural History of Modern Europe*, I (New York: The Macmillan Company, 1933), p. 154.
5. Quoted in H. Bettenson, ed., *Documents of the Christian Church* (London: Oxford University Press, 1943), p. 261 ff.
6. Quoted in P. Smith, *The Age of the Reformation* (New York: Henry Holt & Co., 1920), p. 69.
7. Quoted in George L. Mosse, *The Reformation*, 3rd ed. (New York: Holt, Rinehart and Winston, Inc., 1963), p. 31.
8. Quoted in Bainton, *The Reformation of the Sixteenth Century*, p. 58.
9. Quoted in Bettenson, pp. 282-283.

10. From *The Twelve Articles* in A. Schrier *et al.*, *Modern European Civilization: A Documentary History of Politics, Society, and Thought from the Renaissance to the Present* (Chicago: Scott, Foresman and Co., 1963), pp. 105-106.
11. Quoted in H. J. Grimm, *The Reformation Era, 1500-1650* (New York: The Macmillan Company, 1956), p. 175.
12. R. Fife, *The Revolt of Martin Luther* (New York: Columbia University Press, 1957), p. 693.
13. Bainton, *The Reformation of the Sixteenth Century*, p. 114.
14. Bettenson, p. 365.
15. Quoted in F. Eby and C. F. Arrowood, *The Development of Modern Education* (New York: Prentice-Hall, Inc., 1936), p. 91.
16. *Concerning Heretics . . . . An anonymous work attributed to Sebastian Castellio*, ed. by R. H. Bainton (New York: Columbia University Press, 1935), pp. 122-123.
17. *Ibid.*, pp. 134-135.
18. Quoted in V. H. H. Green, *Luther and the Reformation* (New York: Capricorn Books, 1964), p. 141.
19. *Ibid.*, p. 142.
20. R. H. Tawney, *Religion and the Rise of Capitalism* (Baltimore: Penguin Books, Inc., 1947), p. 99.

CHAPTER 15: THE STRIFE OF STATES AND KINGS
1. Quoted in B. Reynolds, *Proponents of Limited Monarchy in Sixteenth Century France: Francis Holman and Jean Bodin* (New York: Columbia University Press, 1931), p. 182.
2. Quoted in G. Mattingly, *Renaissance Diplomacy* (London: Jonathan Cape, 1962), p. 239.
3. Quoted in M. Guizot, *The History of France from the Earliest Times to 1848*, II (New York: Thomas Y. Crowell & Co., n.d.), p. 428.
4. *Machiavelli: The Prince and Other Works*, trans. by A. H. Gilbert (Chicago: Packard and Co., 1941), p. 177 (Ch. 26).
5. *Ibid.*, p. 148 (Ch. 18).
6. *Ibid.*, p. 150 (Ch. 18).
7. *Ibid.*, p. 177 (Ch. 26).
8. Quoted in R. Ergang, *Europe from the Renaissance to Waterloo* (Boston: D. C. Heath & Co., 1954), p. 296.
9. *Ibid.*, p. 246.
10. Quoted in J. H. Elliott, *Imperial Spain, 1469-1716* (New York: St. Martin's Press, 1964), p. 282.
11. *Ibid.*, p. 283.
12. Quoted in P. Smith, *The Age of the Reformation* (New York: Henry Holt & Co., 1920), p. 215.
13. Quoted in Carl L. Becker, *Modern History* (Chicago: Silver Burdett Co., 1942), pp. 204, 205.
14. Carl J. Friedrich, *The Age of Baroque, 1610-1660* (New York: Harper & Bros., 1952), p. 129.
15. See "Grotius: *Law of War and Peace, Prolegomena*," in *The American Journal of International Law*, XXXV, No. 2 (April 1941), pp. 206, 217.

CHAPTER 16: OLD WORLDS BEYOND THE HORIZON
1. S. Lane-Poole, *Medieval India* (New York: G. P. Putnam's Sons, 1903), p. 271.

CHAPTER 17: BEFORE THE EUROPEAN IMPACT
1. Based on Joseph Greenberg, *The Languages of Africa*, 2nd ed. (Bloomington: Indiana University Press, 1966).
2. "Africa Speaks" in *The Horizon History of Africa* (New York: American Heritage, 1971), p. 80.
3. From David Killingray, *A Plague of Europeans* (New York: Penguin Books, Inc., 1973), p. 14.
4. *Ibid.*, p. 14.

5. Basil Davidson, *History of West Africa* (Garden City, N.Y.: Doubleday Anchor Books, 1966), p. 166.
6. Robert Rotberg, *A Political History of Tropical Africa* (New York: Harcourt Brace Jovanovich, 1965), p. 100.
7. *Ibid.*, pp. 85-86.
8. Killingray, p. 20.
9. See Phillip Curtin, *The Atlantic Slave Trade: A Census* (Madison: University of Wisconsin Press, 1969).
10. Cited in Basil Davidson, *The African Past: Chronicles* (Boston: Little, Brown and Company, 1965).

CHAPTER 18: SEEK OUT, DISCOVER, AND FIND

1. See H. Ingstad, "Vinland Ruins Prove Vikings Found the New World," *National Geographic Magazine*, Vol. 126, No. 5 (November 1964), pp. 708–734.

2. Quoted in Sir Percy Sykes, *A History of Exploration* (New York: Harper Torchbooks, Harper & Row, 1961), p. 108.
3. Quoted in H. H. Gowen, *An Outline History of Japan* (New York: D. Appleton Co., 1927), p. 255.
4. Quoted in H. Herring, *A History of Latin America*, 3rd ed. (New York: Alfred A. Knopf, Inc., 1968), p. 173.
5. Quoted in H. Robinson, *The Development of the British Empire* (Boston: Houghton Mifflin Co., 1922), p. 38.
6. Quoted in Sir George Clark, *The Seventeenth Century* (New York: Oxford University Press, 1961), p. 24.
7. Quoted in H. Heaton, *Economic History of Europe* (New York: Harper & Row, 1948), p. 315.
8. Quoted in *ibid.*, p. 238.
9. Quoted in J. B. Botsford, *English Society in the Eighteenth Century, As Influenced from Overseas* (New York: The Macmillan Company, 1924), p. 70.
10. Heaton, p. 239.
11. *Ibid.* (published in 1936), p. 363.

List of Illustrations

LIST OF CHARTS AND DRAWINGS

LIST OF MAPS

Chronological Tables

Chronological Table 1

NEAR EAST AND EGYPT	INDIA AND CHINA
Neolithic revolution c. 7000	
Sumerian city-states emerge c. 3500	
B.C. 3000 Menes unites Egypt c. 3100	
Old Sumerian period c. 2800-2370	
Old Kingdom in Egypt c. 2700-2200	
Akkadian empire c. 2370-2230	
Neo-Sumerian period c. 2113-2006	
Middle Kingdom in Egypt c. 2050-1800	Indus valley civilization c. 2300-1800—capitals at Mohenjo-Daro and Harappa
2000 Hittites enter Asia Minor c. 2000	
Hammurabi rules lower Mesopotamia 1760	
Hittites sack Babylon 1595	
New Kingdom or Empire in Egypt c. 1570-1090	
1500 Thutmose III c. 1490-1436—the "Napoleon of Egypt"	Invasion of India by Aryans from Black and Caspian seas c. 1500
	Vedic Age c. 1500-900—beginning of three pillars of Indian society; autonomous village, caste system, joint-family
Hittite empire c. 1450-1200	*Vedas*—oldest Sanskrit literature
Akhenaton c. 1369-1353	Shang dynasty 1500-1027—China's first civilization
Era of small states 1200-700	
Phoenician and Aramean traders; the alphabet	Chou dynasty 1027-256—China's "classical age"—Mandate of Heaven promulgated
Period of Decadence in Egypt c. 1090-332	
1000 United Hebrew kingdom (1020-922): Saul, David, Solomon	Later Vedic Age in India c. 900-500—caste system becomes more complex:
Divided Hebrew kingdom: Israel (922-721); Judah (922-586)	priest, warrior, merchant, serf, "untouchable"
The great Hebrew prophets 750-550	
Assyrian empire 745-612	*Upanishads* 800–600—foundation of Hinduism
Lydians and Medes	
Chaldean empire (604-539): Nebuchadnezzar	
Zoroaster, early 6th century	
Persian empire (550-330): Cyrus; Darius (522-486)	Guatama Buddha 563?-483—founder of Buddhism
End of the Babylonian Exile of the Jews 538	Confucius 551-479—most famous and influential Chinese philosopher
500	
	Chinese poetry collected in *Shih Ching*, or *Book of Odes*
	Two greatest Indian epics composed: the *Mahabharata* (including the
400	*Bhagavad-Gita*) and the *Ramayama*
	Lao-tzu and Taoism—aim: intuitive approach to life; *Tao te Ching*
	Mencius c. 372-289 links theory of Mandate of Heaven to democratic concept of the will of the people in government
Conquests of Alexander the Great 334-331	Alexander the Great crosses Indus valley 326
300 Death of Alexander (323); Ptolemy siezes Egypt; Seleucus rules Asia	Chandragupta Maurya founds Mauryan dynasty in India 322-c. 185
	Ashoka 273-232—"the first great royal patron of Buddhism"
	Period of Warring States in China—Ch'in defeat Chou 221
	China reunited under First Emperor, Shih Huang-ti 221-210
	Han dynasty of China 202 B.C.-220 A.D.
200	Tamil kindgoms—Hindu states, chief trading area with the West
	Mauryan empire falls 185; Bactrian rule extends to
	India and Punjab; Graeco-Bactrian kingdom created
Maccabean revolt wins independence for Judea 142 (see Chapter 5)	Han emperor Wu Ti 141-87
100	Kushan empire in India (first century B.C.-220 A.D.)
	Kanishka, Kushan ruler c. 78-128, sponsors *Mahayana*
Dead Sea Scrolls	("Great Vehicle") school of Buddhism, which spreads north and east;
Pompey annexes Syria and Palestine 63	*Hinayana* ("Lesser Vehicle") Buddhism spreads south and east
Herod the Great, king of Judea 37-4	
Jesus Christ c. 4 B.C.-30 A.D.	
Paul (d. c. 65)	
A.D. 100 Jews revolt from Rome (66-70)—end of the ancient Hebrew state	

GREECE   **ROME**

                                                                                                    3000 B.C.

Aegean civilization c. 2000-1200   Indo-Europeans invade Italian peninsula 2000-1000; Latins settle in lower
Achaean Greeks invade Peloponnesus c. 2000   Tiber valley (Latium)   **2000**

Zenith of Minoan culture 1700-1450

Mycenaean Age 1450-1200   **1500**

Dorian invasion c. 1200

Greek Dark Ages c. 1150-750 and Homeric Age

                                                                   Etruscans settle on Italy's west coast
                                                                   Carthage founded in North Africa by Phoenicians c. 800
                                                                   Rome founded 753   **1000**
Hellenic Age c. 750-338   Greeks colonize southern Italy and Sicily
Age of Oligarchy (c. 750-500): Hesiod; colonization
Athens—growth of democracy: Solon (594), Pisistratus (560),
Cleisthenes (508)
Sparta—militaristic totalitarian state, Spartan League   Etruscans conquer Rome c. 600

                                                                   Roman Republic established 509
Persian Wars (490-479): Marathon, Thermopylae   **500**
Delian League (478) and Athenian imperialism   Plebeians vs. patricians (509-287)—tribunes and *Concilium Plebis*
Athen's Golden Age under Pericles (461-429)
Peloponnesian War (431-404)—Athens vs. Sparta   Laws of the Twelve Tables c. 450
                                                                                                                           400
Philip II of Macedonia conquers Greece 338
Hellenic culture: Thales, Pythagoras, Democritus, Hippocrates, Socrates,
Plato, Aristotle, Herodotus, Thycydides, Sappho, Aeschylus, Sophocles,
Euripides, Aristophanes, Phidias, Praxiteles
Alexander the Great conquers Persia 331
Hellenistic Age 323-31—Ptolemaic Egypt, Seleucid Asia,
Macedonia; Greek federal leagues   Roman expansion in Italy (338-270): Latins, Etruscans, Samnites, Greeks

Hellenistic culture: Epicurus, Zeno, Eratosthenes, Aristarchus, Euclid,   Roman expansion in western Mediterranean 270-146—Punic wars: **300**
Archimedes, Hipparchus, Polybius, Theocritus   Hannibal

                                                                   Roman expansion in eastern Mediterranean 200-133—wars with   **200**
                                                                   Macedonia and the Seleucids; Macedon and Greece annexed (146);
                                                                   first Roman province in Asia (133)
                                                                   Reform movement of the Gracchi 133-121

                                                                   Civil wars 88-30   **100**
                                                                   Marius vs. Sulla (88-82): dictatorship of Sulla (82-79)
                                                                   Pompey vs. Caesar (49-46): dictatorship of Julius Caesar (46-44)
                                                                   Antony vs. Octavian (32-30)
                                                                   Augustus' reconstruction—the Principate 30 B.C.-180 A.D.
                                                                   Golden Age of literature: Cicero, Catullus, Lucretius, Virgil, Horace
                                                                   Julio-Claudian and Flavian emperors 14 A.D.-96 A.D.
                                                                   Antonine emperors (96-180): Hadrian, Marcus Aurelius
                                                                   Silver Age of literature: Juvenal, Tacitus, Seneca, Plutarch   **100** A.D.

Chronological Table 2

EUROPE

B.C. **100**

A.D. **1**

100 End of the *Pax Romana* 180-285—civil wars, economic decline, invasions
Reconstruction by Diocletian (285-305)—the Dominate
300 Constantine (306-337)—Edict of Milan (313), Council of Nicaea (325), founding of Constantinople (330)
Ulfilas (d. 383), missionary to the Goths
Theodosius divides Roman Empire 395
Battle of Adrianople (378)—German invasions begin
400 Alaric sacks Rome 410
Western Church Fathers: Jerome, Ambrose, Augustine
St. Patrick in Ireland c. 450
Attila crosses the Rhine—battle near Troyes 451
Pope Leo the Great (440-461)
Odovacar deposes last western emperor 476
Clovis (481-511) unites Franks, and rules Gaul
500 Theodoric (493-526) rules Italy; Cassiodorus and Boethius
St. Benedict establishes Benedictine Order 529
Lombards invade Italy 568
Merovingian decline, sixth-seventh centuries
600 Pope Gregory the Great (590-604)
Isidore of Seville (d. 636)—the *Etymologies*

700 Charles Martel (714-741) rules the Franks; defeats Muslims at Tours 732
Bede (d. 735)
St. Boniface (d. 755), "the apostle to the Germans"
Pepin the Short (741-768) ends rule of Merovingian kings; "Donation of Pepin" to pope
Charlemagne (768-814) revives Roman Empire in the West (800); fosters Carolingian Renaissance

800 Treaty of Verdun divides Carolingian empire into West Frankland, East Frankland, and Lorraine 843
Magyar, Muslim, and Viking invasions terrorize Europe (ninth-tenth centuries)
Alfred the Great (871-899) establishes strong Anglo-Saxon kingdom in England
Kievan Russia emerges
900 Feudalism well established in France c. 900
Henry I, the Fowler (919-936), founds Saxon dynasty in Germany
Otto I, the Great (936-973)—alliance of crown and Church; routs Magyars at battle of Lechfeld 955; crowned emperor by pope 962
Ethelred the Unready 978-1016—power of English government lags; invasion by Canute, Viking king
Hugh Capet (987) founds Capetian dynasty
1000 Peace and Truce of God (eleventh century)
Normans arrive in Italy 1016
Yaroslav the Wise 1019-1054—peak of Kievan Russia; Byzantine influences in art and literature
Salian House succeeds Saxon kings in Germany 1024
College of Cardinals formed to elect pope 1059
Pope Gregory VII (1073-1085) supports Cluniac religious reform; Investiture Struggle
Norman Conquest of England 1066
Fall of Bari to Normans 1071—last Byzantine stronghold in Italy
The *Reconquista* gains Toledo from Muslims 1085
First Crusade—Jerusalem captured; Latin kingdom of Jerusalem established 1099
1100 Renaissance of the twelfth century; revival of trade and towns
Welf-Hohenstaufen rivalry (1106-1152) wrecks structure for a strong German State
Louis the Fat 1108—first strong Capetian ruler in France
Concordat of Worms 1122
Second Crusade 1147
Frederick Barbarossa (1152-1190)—centralized feudal monarchy; struggle with popes and Lombard League
Henry II (1154-1189) reforms English judicial system; Thomas à Becket
St. Dominic (1170-1221); St. Francis of Assisi (1182?-1226)
Philip II Augustus (1180-1223) extends royal power
Third Crusade 1189—the "Crusade of Kings"
Frederick II 1194-1250—end of the medieval German empire
1200 Pope Innocent III 1198-1216—zenith of the medieval papacy
Fourth Crusade 1202-1204—crusaders sack Constantinople
King John of England signs Magna Carta 1215
Kiev destroyed by Mongols 1240
St. Thomas Aquinas (1225?-1274) reconciles faith and reason in *Summa Theologica*; zenith of scholasticism
Louis IX (1226-1270) brings dignity to the French crown
Edward I (1272-1307)—rise of Parliament; power of nobility curtailed
Philip IV, the Fair (1285-1314), centralizes French government; humiliates Pope Boniface VIII
Acre, last Christian stronghold in Holy Land, conquered by Muslims 1291
1300 Dante (d. 1321)
Hundred Years' War between France and England 1337-1453
1400 Chaucer (d. 1400)

NEAR EAST AND BYZANTINE EMPIRE

INDIA, CHINA, AND JAPAN

	Rule by Yamato clan in Japan · **100 B.C.**
(See also Chronological Table 1)	Kanishka ruler in India (c. 78-128) · **1 A.D.**
Christian missionaries	Expansion of Indian culture into Southeast Asia begins (second century) · **100**
	Fall of Han dynasty in China 220
Eastern Church Fathers: Clement of Alexandria	Buddhism gains popularity in China (third century) · **300**
Council of Nicaea 325—Nicene Creed	Chandragupta I founds Gupta dynasty in India 320
Constantine establishes New Rome (Constantinople) 330	
St. Basil (330-379) establishes Rule of St. Basil	Chandragupta II (c. 380-c. 413)—zenith of Gupta power
	Kalidasa (c. 400-450), lyric poet, the "Indian Shakespeare" · **400**
	Buddhism enters Japan (sixth century) · **500**
Justinian (527-565)—reconquests; *Corpus Juris Civilis*; Hagia Sophia	
Muhammad 570-632—the Hijra	Harsha (606-647) rules northern India · **600**
Heraclius (610-641)—regains Syria, Palestine, Egypt from Persians	T'ang dynasty founded 618; golden era of China
First four caliphs (632-661)—conquest of Syria, Iraq, most of Egypt and Persia	T'ai Tsung (627-650)—first great T'ang ruler
Rise of the Shia	Taika reform in Japan 646; ruler considered divine
Umayyad dynasty 661-750—expands in North Africa, Turkestan, Indus valley, Spain; defeated by Franks at Tours 732	T'ang poets: Li Po and Tu Fu · **700**
Leo III (717-741) repulses Muslims 718; administrative and military reforms; iconoclastic controversy	Japanese court established at Nara 710
Abbasid dynasty 750-1258—end of Arab predominance; peak of Islamic power, civilization, and prosperity	
Harun-al-Rashid 768-809—relations with Charlemagne	Fujiwara period in Japan (857-1160); capital at Kyoto · **800**
Cyril and Methodius—missionaries to the Slavs	*Diamond Sutra* printed 868
Golden age of Muslim learning 900-1100—advances in medicine, mathematics, literature, philosophy, architecture, decorative arts; geniuses of this period and later: Al-Razi, Avicenna, Alhazen, Al-Khwarizmi, Omar Khayyám, Averroës, ibn-Khaldun	T'ang dynasty falls 906 · **900**
	Expansion of Indian culture into Southeast Asia ends (tenth century)
	Sung dynasty founded in China 960
Basil II (976-1025) defeats Bulgars	Gunpowder used by Sung c. 1000 · **1000**
	Wang An-shih (1021-1086), Chinese socialist reformer
Final separation of the churches 1054	Muslims invade India, Turks and Afghans annex Punjab 1022
Seljuk Turks seize Persia and Iraq, conquer Baghdad (1055)	
Battle of Manzikert 1071—loss of Asia Minor to Seljuks	
Alexius Comnenus and the First Crusade 1096	Angkor Wat built c. 1100 · **1100**
Kingdom of Jerusalem (1099-1291) and crusader states	
	China divided between empires of Sung (south) and Chin (north) 1127
	Yoritomo (1147-1199) rules Japan as *shogun* from Kamakura 1192
	Genghis Khan (1162-1227) unites Mongols
Saladin regains Jerusalem 1187	
Fourth Crusade 1202-1204—Constantinople sacked	Hojo period in Japan 1199-1333 · **1200**
Latin Empire 1204-1261	Delhi sultanate established 1206; Indian culture divided into Hindu and Muslim
Fall of Abbasid dynasty—Baghdad conquered by Mongols 1258	Mongols conquer China 1234; *Pax Tatarica* links East and West via trade routes
Michael Palaeologus regains Constantinople 1261	Kublai Khan (1260-1294), Yüan emperor of China
	Marco Polo arrives at Kublai Khan's court c. 1275
	"The Divine Wind" 1281
Ottoman Turks invade Europe 1356	Kamakura destroyed 1333; Ashikaga shogunate founded in Japan 1338 · **1300**
	Ming dynasty established in China 1368
Constantinople falls to Ottoman Turks 1453	Tamerlane (Timur the Lame) destroys Delhi 1398 · **1400**

Chronological Table 3

THE EUROPEAN SCENE

300

900

1000

1100

1200 Mongols conquer Kiev 1240
Transitional period in Italian art c. 1250-c. 1400—Giotto d. 1336
Rudolf of Hapsburg becomes Holy Roman emperor 1291
Pope Boniface VIII (1294-1303) feuds with Philip IV

1300 Avignon papacy 1309-1376
Hundred Years' War (1337-1453) begins
Golden Bull 1356
Petrarch 1304-1374
Great Schism 1378-1417
John Wycliffe d. 1384
Grand Prince of Moscow defeats Mongols at Kulikovo 1380

1400 The *quattrocento* (fifteenth century) of Italian Renaissance
Council of Constance 1414
Commercial Revolution 1450-1650
Gutenberg used movable type to print Bible 1454
Early Renaissance masters in Italy—Brunelleschi, Ghiberti, Donatello, Masaccio, Montegna, Botticelli
Wars of the Roses 1455-1485
Louis XI (the "universal spider") of France (1461-1483)
Ivan III (the Great) of Russia (1462-1505)
Ferdinand and Isabella begin joint rule in Spain 1479
Henry VII (1485-1509) founds Tudor dynasty in England
Reconquista ends with conquest of Granada 1492; unification of Spain completed
Maximilian I (1493-1519), Holy Roman emperor
Italian Wars (1494-1513) begin
Leonardo da Vinci 1452-1519

1500 Northern Renaissance (sixteenth century)—painters Jan van Eyck, Albrecht Dürer, Hans Holbein the Younger, Brueghel the Elder
Late Renaissance in Italy c. 1500-1530—Bramante, Michelangelo, Da Vinci, Raphael, Giogione, Titian, Castiglione, Cellini
Henry VIII of England 1509-1547
Luther posts ninety-five theses 1517; excommunicated, declared heretic at Diet of Worms 1521
Charles V elected Holy Roman emperor 1519
Suleiman rules the Turks 1520-1566
Peace of Augsburg 1555 ends Schmalkaldic Wars (1546-1555)
The Prince (1532) by Machiavelli
Henry VIII founds Anglican Church 1534
Loyola establishes Jesuit order 1534
John Calvin published *Institutes of the Christian Religion* 1536
Erasmus d. 1536
Council of Trent 1545-1563
Ivan IV (the Terrible) of Russia 1547-1584

1550 Mary Tudor reinstates Catholicism in England 1553-1558
Philip II of Spain 1556-1598
Era of Religious Wars (1556-1650) begins
Elizabeth of England 1558-1603
St. Bartholomew's Day Massacre 1572
Shakespeare 1564-1616
Battle of Lepanto 1571
Dutch United Provinces declare independence 1581
Time of Trouble in Russia 1584-1613
Spanish Armada 1588
Henry IV (1589-1610) founds Bourbon dynasty in France
Edict of Nantes 1598

1600 James I (1603-1625) founds Stuart dynasty in England
Bank of Amsterdam founded 1609
Thirty Years' War (1618-1648)—Peace of Westphalia 1648
De Jure Belli ac Pacis (1625) by Grotius
Colbert d. 1683
Lloyd's of London founded c. 1688
Bank of England chartered 1694

FAR EAST

AMERICAS AND AFRICA

	Ghana empire in Africa c. 300-1200	**300**
	Mayan city-states in Yucatan peninsula 980-1200	**900**
	Eric the Red discovers Greenland c. 982	
Muslims invade India; Turks and Afghans annex Punjab 1022	Mali empire in Africa c. 1000-c. 1400	**1000**
	Zenj empire in Africa c. 1000-1497	
China divided into two empires: Sung and Chin 1127	Incas settle Cuzco valley in Andes (eleventh century)	**1100**
Yoritomo (1147-1199) rules Japan as *shogun* from Kamakura 1192	Ghana captured by Berbers 1076	
Hojo period in Japan 1199-1333	Toltecs dominate Mexican plateau (twelfth century)	
Delhi sultanate established 1206		**1200**
Mongols conquer China 1234	Fall of Ghana state 1240	
Kublai Khan 1260-1294—Marco Polo arrives at his court c. 1275		
	Aztec confederacy in Mexico (fourteenth century)	**1300**
Kamakura destroyed 1333; Ashikaga shogunate founded in Japan 1338		
Fall of Mongol China; Ming dynasty founded 1368		
Timur the Lame (Tamerlane) destroys Delhi 1398	Songhai empire in the African Sudan c. 1400-c. 1600	**1400**
Chinese naval expeditions to India, Near East, Africa (fifteenth century)	Atlantic slave trade begins (fifteenth century)	
	Zenith of Inca empire 1438-1532	
	Prince Henry the Navigator (1394-1460)	
	Diaz rounds Cape of Good Hope 1488	
	Columbus discovers New World 1492	
	Bull of Demarcation 1493; Treaty of Tordesillas 1494	
	North America claimed by Cabot for England 1497	
	Da Gama reaches India 1498	
Portuguese trade monopoly in Far East (sixteenth century)		**1500**
	Albuquerque captures Goa (1510) and Malacca (1511)	
Chinese edict bans foreign merchants in Chinese waters 1522	Balboa sights Pacific Ocean 1513	
Babur (the Tiger) defeats Delhi sultanate and Rajputs 1526-1527; founds Mughul empire in India	Cortés arrives in Mexico 1519; Aztec empire falls	
	Magellan rounds South America 1520	
Akbar (1556-1605) expands Mughul empire; promotes religious tolerance	*Conquistadores* in New World	**1550**
Portuguese granted right to trade with Chinese at Macao 1557	Jacques Cartier explores St. Lawrence River 1534	
Spanish use Philippines as trading stop c. 1565	Bartolomé de Las Casas c. 1560	
Japanese attempt invasion of China and Korea 1592		
Hideyoshi persecutes Christians in Japan 1592	Jamestown founded 1607; Quebec 1608	**1600**
English East India Company incorporated 1600	Henry Hudson attempts to find shorter route to Far East 1609	
Dutch East India Company formed 1602		
Tokugawa period begins in Japan 1603		
Foundations for Dutch East Indies laid by Coen 1618	Plymouth founded 1620	
Shah Jahan (1628-1658) promotes Muslim faith; height of Mughul empire in India	Dutch West India Company founds Manhattan 1624	
Europeans forbidden entry to Japan 1639	René La Salle takes possession of Louisiana territory for France 1681	
Manchu invade Ming China; establish Manchu dynasty 1644		
Aurangzeb (1658-1707); decline of Mughul power		

Chronological Table 4A

SCIENCE AND TECHNOLOGY, THOUGHT AND ART: 1500–1700

1500 Revolution in astronomy—Copernicus proposes heliocentric theory of universe, publishes *Concerning the Revolutions of Heavenly Spheres* 1543; Brahe attempts compromise between geocentric and heliocentric theories; Kepler coordinates Brahe's data; Galileo confirms Copernican theory

1550 Pioneers in medicine: Paracelsus experiments with new drugs; Vesalius, founder of modern anatomy; Harvey describes circulation of blood in *Anatomical Exercise on the Motion of the Heart and Blood* 1628
El Greco (1541?–1614), master of Mannerist style in painting

Francis Bacon (1561–1626) champions deductive method of philosophical inquiry; *Novum Organum* 1620; *New Atlantis* 1627

Descartes (1590–1650) proposes deductive method of philosophical inquiry; develops analytical geometry; proposes theory of philosophical dualism
1600 Gilbert's *De Magnete* 1600

Neoclassical dramatists in France—Corneille, Racine, Moliere
Inventions of seventeenth century: telescope, microscope, thermometer, pendulum clock, micrometer, barometer, air pump
Baroque style: Rubens, Velázquez, Vermeer, Hals, Rembrandt, Bernini; opera originates in Italy

1650 Defenders of absolutism—Hobbes of England, author of *Leviathan* 1651, and Bossuet of France

Scientific societies founded: Academy of Experiments at Florence 1657; Royal Society of London 1662; French Academy of Science at Paris 1666
Boyle's law is formulated 1660
Spinoza expresses his pantheistic philosophy; publishes *Ethics* 1663

Newton expounds theory of gravitation in *Philosophiae Naturalis Principia Mathematica* 1687

Locke, publishes *An Essay Concerning Human Understanding* 1690; advances doctrine of popular sovereignty as argument against absolutism in "Of Civil Government" 1690
Rococo style exemplified in works of Watteau; English portrait painting by Reynolds, Gainsborough

POLITICS

James of England (1603–1625) and successor Charles I antagonize Parliament; Petition of Right denies king's right of taxation with parliamentary consent 1628
Richelieu 1624–1642 becomes real authority behind French throne

Frederick William, the Great Elector (1640–1688), makes Brandenburg the most important Protestant state in Germany
English Civil War (1642–1648); the Commonwealth and the Protectorate (1649–1660)
Mazarin (1643–1661) governs France during minority of Louis XIV; triumphs over enemies during civil war 1648–1653

Restoration of Stuart kings in England—controversy between Charles II and Parliament 1660–1685; secret Treaty of Dover with Louis XIV 1670; Whig and Tory parties organized; Habeas Corpus Act 1679
Louis XIV (1661–1715) transforms French state into an absolute monarchy; invades Spanish Netherlands and German border districts 1667–1697; halted by William of Orange and allied nations
Peter the Great 1682–1725, absolutist tsar of Russia, attempts to westernize realm
James II of England (1685–1688) attempts to impose absolute rule
Louis XIV revokes Edict of Nantes 1685
Glorious Revolution—Whigs and Tories invite William of Orange to rule England; Bill of Rights passed; Parliament becomes dominant agency in government 1688

Index

Suggested pronunciations for difficult or unusual words are respelled according to the table below, which is repeated in simplified form at the bottom of each right-hand page of the INDEX. The local pronunciations of many foreign words are too unusual for persons untrained in linguistics, and pronunciations given here are those commonly acceptable in unaffected, educated American speech.

a	hat, cap	j	jam, enjoy	u	cup, son
ā	age, face	k	kind, seek	u̇	put, book
ã	care, air	l	land, coal	ü	rule, move
ä	father, far	m	me, am	ū	use, music
		n	no, in		
b	bad, rob	ng	long, bring		
ch	child, much				
d	did, red	o	hot, rock	v	very, save
		ō	open, go	w	will, woman
		ô	order, all	y	you, yet
e	let, best	oi	oil, toy	z	zero, breeze
ē	equal, see	ou	out, now	zh	measure, seizure
ėr	term, learn				
		p	pet, cup		
f	fat, if	r	run, try	ə	represents:
g	go, bag	s	say, yes	a	in about
h	he, how	sh	she, rush	e	in taken
		t	tell, it	i	in pencil
i	it, pin	th	thin, both	o	in lemon
ī	ice, five	ᴛH	then, smooth	u	in circus

FOREIGN SOUNDS

Y as in French *lune*. Pronounce ē with the lips rounded as for English ü in *rule*.

Œ as in French *deux*. Pronounce ā with the lips rounded as for ō.

N as in French *bon*. The N is not pronounced, but shows that the vowel before it is nasal.

H as in German *ach*. Pronounce k without closing the breath passage.

hat, āge, cãre, fär; let, ēqual, tèrm; it, īce; hot, ōpen, ôrder, oil, out; cup, pùt, rüle, ūse; ch, child; ng, long; th, thin; ŦH, then; zh, measure; ə represents *a* in *a*bout, *e* in tak*e*n, *i* in penc*i*l, *o* in lem*o*n, *u* in circ*u*s.

hat, āge, cãre, fär; let, ēqual, tèrm; it, īce; hot, ōpen, ôrder, oil,
out; cup, pùt, rüle, ūse; ch, child; ng, long; th, thin; ᴛʜ, then;
zh, measure; ə represents *a* in about, *e* in taken, *i* in pencil, *o* in
lemon, *u* in circus.

hat, āge, cāre, fär; let, ēqual, tėrm; it, īce; hot, ōpen, ôrder, oil, out; cup, pút, rüle, ūse; ch, child; ng, long; th, thin; ᴛʜ, then; zh, measure; ə represents *a* in *a*bout, *e* in tak*e*n, *i* in penc*i*l, *o* in lem*o*n, *u* in circ*u*s.

hat, āge, cãre, fär; let, ēqual, tėrm; it, īce; hot, ōpen, ôrder, oil; out; cup, pût, rüle, ūse; ch, child; ng, long; th, thin; ᴛʜ, then; zh, measure; ə represents *a* in *a*bout, *e* in tak*e*n, *i* in penc*i*l, *o* in lem*o*n, *u* in circ*u*s.

Reference Maps

The Reference Maps

History accounts for man's activities in time, and maps depict them in space. Therefore, to understand mankind's experiences, knowledge of the planetary environment is essential. These reference maps show key areas at significant periods; they include basic physical features which affect man's attempts to control his environment as well as his fellow man.

Map 1: The Ancient Near East and Greece. In the area displayed we can trace the progressive expansion of man's environmental control resulting from his invention of new tools and social institutions. Thus the transition from food collecting to farming occurred in well-watered sites bordering the Syrian, Arabian, and Iranian deserts—such as at Jericho in the Great Rift Valley of the Jordan and at Jarmo in uplands to the east of the Tigris. The breakthrough from Neolithic barbarism to civilization, i.e., to societies sufficiently complex to permit the emergence of urban centers, occurred in two important river basins, the Tigris-Euphrates and the Nile—linked by a Fertile Crescent with minimal natural obstacles to impede the movement of peoples and goods.

Employing primitive craft, Neolithic seafarers had hugged the Mediterranean coasts and slowly pushed westward—as attested by Neolithic sites in Cyprus, Rhodes, and Crete. Improvements in maritime technology permitted the emergence of a splendid Aegean civilization centering at Knossos in Crete, and Pylos on the Greek mainland, and Troy in northwest Asia Minor. Civilization's center of gravity shifted progressively northward across the eastern basin of the Mediterranean, culminating in Hellas with its sea-oriented city-states: Corinth, Thebes, and, above all, Athens. Continued advances in maritime technology enabled the Greeks to master the eastern Mediterranean and Black seas and establish colonies, while the Phoenicians carried their mercantile ventures from their port cities of Tyre and Sidon along the North African coast. What the Tigris-Euphrates had been to the Babylonians, and the Nile to the Egyptians, the Mediterranean became to the Greeks, the Phoenicians, and eventually to the Romans—the "middle of the earth."

Map 2: The Roman Empire c. 117 A.D. This map underscores the importance of physical features in the creation of the Roman world-state. From its east-west maritime axis, the Roman *imperium* stretched into the hinterland, which was linked by rivers and roads to strategically located ports that provided transshipment to other parts of the empire.

The expansion of the Roman world followed a logical sequence. It began with Rome's conquest of the Italian peninsula and Great Greece (including Sicily). The Punic Wars opened up the entire western basin of the Mediterranean, while subsequent intrusion into the eastern basin made Rome mistress of the Hellenistic world. The first century B.C. saw the consolidation of Roman control in Asia Minor, the conquest of transalpine Gaul by Julius Caesar, and the annexation of Egypt, Numidia, and Cyrenaica. The territorial domain was rounded out later by the acquisition of Mauretania, Dacia, Armenia, and Mesopotamia.

Here we see the Roman world at its broadest expanse, encompassing almost 100 million diverse peoples and linked by the greatest communications network then devised. However, the world-state soon entered its time of troubles, attended by decline of population, of administrative efficiency, and of military power. The empire then found itself overextended and had to reduce its territorial perimeter. Armenia, Mesopotamia, and Dacia were abandoned, and eventually the Roman legions were recalled from Britain.

In the fourth century the once majestic Roman empire was polarized into two unequal segments—the western section administered from Rome and having the weaker but spatially larger area; and the eastern section controlled from New Rome (Constantinople) and having a larger population, more compact territory, and a stronger economy. At last the two segments, each centering on one of the major basins of the Mediterranean, were split asunder by the barbarian invasions. The classical world then gave way to the medieval world.

Map 3: The Ancient East. Here we encounter the homelands of the two major fluvial civilizations (societies originating in river basins) centering on the Indus-Gangetic and the Huang Ho drainage basins. The remarkable longevity of Indian and Chinese societies owes much to physical factors which inhibited alien intrusion. The Indian triangle was protected by the Indian Ocean and the Himalayas, though invasion was possible through the western passes; as for China, the obstacles posed by the Pacific Ocean, the forbidding Taklamakan and Gobi deserts, and a series of mountain ranges effectively limited entrance into the Huang Ho valley.

The map also shows the boundaries of three empires: the Han in China, the Mauryan in India, and the Parthian in western Asia. Note that they are contemporary with the Roman world-state at its zenith. After centuries of feudal fragmentation, China was reunited, and under Shih Huang-ti, the Great Wall was rebuilt and lengthened to keep the nomadic tribes in the north and west from pillaging the sedentary farmers tilling the "good earth" to the south. The centuries marked by the Han dynasty were stable and prosperous. So too were the centuries of Mauryan rule in India. Under Ashoka, a single administration extended from the Himalayas across the Narbada River and included the Deccan—leaving only the southernmost part of the subcontinent outside its rule. Meanwhile, to the northwest lay Bactria, where Hellenistic and Indian culture interfused, producing the Gandharran art found in Taxila.

This is the era, too, when the western and eastern segments of the Eurasian land mass were in commercial and cultural contact. Ships plied the Indian Ocean, taking advantage of the recently discovered monsoon mechanism while a tenuous but profitable Silk Route stretched from Ch'ang-an through Kashgar, Samarkand, and across Parthian lands to Ecbatana, Ctesiphon, and Seleucia. In addition, the movement of goods from both China and India westward enriched the "caravan cities" such as Palmyra (see Map 2).

Map 4: Medieval France, Spain, and the British Isles 1328. We can perceive here the emerging outlines of the national state system in western Europe. For example, in 1328 Edward II had to officially recognize Scotland as independent, while across the Channel, the extinction of the Capetian line set the stage for a protracted struggle over the succession to the French throne. Known as the Hundred Years' War (1337–1453), it was marked by the loss of large English holdings obtained in Plantagenet days. Meanwhile, ambitious French kings enlarged their domain from the Ile de France around Paris southward to the Mediterranean and then sought to expand their territory eastward at the expense of the feudal-fragmented Holy Roman Empire. The Iberian peninsula was also fragmented, but here the Christian kingdoms were girding to clear the peninsula of those Moors still entrenched in Granada.

Certain areas are noteworthy for their economic importance at this juncture: the Low Countries, where the textile industry enriched such towns as Bruges, Lille, Ghent, Ypres, and Cambrai; Champagne in northeastern France, where the most famous medieval fairs in all Europe were held; and southern France, with its thriving commercial centers at Narbonne and Marseille.

Note, too, that whereas in classical times urban centers predominated on the coast, in medieval Europe a large number of river-oriented towns were founded or acquired increasing importance. Roads were poor, and river transport was both economical and efficient. Rivers such as the Thames, Meuse, Seine, Loire, Rhone, Garonne, Tagus, Guadalquivir, and Po were being constantly utilized, while the Rhine and Danube, important as political and military boundaries in Roman times, were vital waterways throughout medieval times.

Map 5: Europe 1648. The year 1648 is a crucial one, for the Thirty Years' War, started as a religious conflict, ended with the victory of the national state which acknowledged no authority higher than its own sovereignty and interests. The map indicates the further territorial consolidation of the national state system (as compared with Map 4). Thus Scotland and England are now one political entity; the Iberian peninsula is demarcated as Spain and Portugal (though neither is any longer a first-class power); France has acquired bishoprics in Lorraine and a foothold in Alsace. The map also shows the emergence of Switzerland, the three Scandinavian countries, Poland, and Russia.

Germany and Italy remain territorially fragmented and politically unstable, as the Holy Roman Empire has vanished in everything but name and pretensions. The situation in the flat north European plain remains fluid; the boundaries of Brandenburg, Poland, and Russia were always subject to change on that plain, reflecting the fluctuating power relations of those states. Meanwhile, the Ottoman Turks continue to threaten central Europe despite their defeat at sea at Lepanto in 1571.

Map 6: European Empires c. 1700. With the age of exploration, western Europeans set out to explore the unmapped portions of the globe, spreading their religion, cultures, and languages wherever their questing galleons made a new landfall. In the wake of the explorer went the missionary, merchant, and musketeer so that in time Europeans controlled most, or all, of the land surface of every other continent. The age of exploration both intensified and territorially expanded European national rivalries.

This map has much to tell us. The European states bordering the Atlantic attempted to explore and colonize lands in the New World in latitudes roughly comparable to their own. Thus the Danes proceeded northwestward to Iceland and Greenland, the English and French competed for lands north of the Gulf of Mexico, and Spain and Portugal laid their claims in more southerly latitudes. Following Portuguese initiative, other Europeans sought out—and fought over—islands, coastal strips, and spheres of interest around the African and Indian coasts and in the archipelagoes of Southeast Asia.

The contrasting depths of European penetration of the New and Old Worlds at this juncture are significant. In the Americas, Europeans encountered either Stone Age Amerinds or pre-Columbian civilizations incapable of assimilating, much less fighting off, the newcomers. Consequently, the European acquisition of North and South America—and later of Australia—was complete. This resulted in the establishment of colonial empires in which the language, laws, religion, and cultural values of the respective metropolitan nations were brought *in toto* to the New World. In contrast, in sub-Saharan Africa as well as South and East Asia, the Europeans were invariably outnumbered. Hence, though they managed to establish trading settlements along the coast, and eventually acquire political ascendency in most of these regions, they did not succeed in replacing the indigenous culture patterns.

Map 7: Europe 1815. This map can best be examined by comparing it with Map 5—the European landscape 167 years earlier. The fewest territorial-political changes have occurred in western Europe, though some further consolidation has taken place. Thus Ireland is now part of the United Kingdom; Sweden has been allowed by the major powers to annex Norway (in compensation for its loss of Finland to Russia); while what had formerly been Holland and the Spanish Netherlands are now included in the Kingdom of the Netherlands. France, though deprived of some of Napoleon's earlier territorial conquests, has by this time acquired Alsace and Lorraine, and Franche Comté (to the immediate west of Switzerland).

A comparison of Maps 4 and 7 would seem to point to greater fragmentation of the defunct Holy Roman Empire. Actually the German people have now to give their allegiances to only thirty-nine states, as compared with some three hundred in the old Empire, and are loosely organized in a confederation. Most striking is the growth of Prussia from its nucleus in Brandenburg, due to its superb army, to dynastic inheritances, and to astute diplomacy. Italy remains highly fragmented; in Metternich's disdainful phrase, it is only a "geographical expression."

Further east, the political and territorial changes that occurred between 1648 and 1815 are more dramatic. The Austrian empire has expanded into northern Italy and also includes parts of Poland and territory formerly conquered by the Ottoman empire. Meanwhile, due to the partitions of 1772, 1793, and 1795, Poland has ceased to exist, while the corruption-ridden Turks are being forced back toward their home base in Asia Minor.

The most spectacular of all territorial gains has been registered by Russia, advancing westward toward the heart of Europe and southward in the general direction of Constantinople. Moscow has acquired Finland, Estonia, the bulk of Poland, the Ukraine, and Bessarabia.

Map 8: Europe August 1939. This map can be profitably compared with the map on page 687. The most noticeable changes result from the defeat of the Central Powers in World War I and also from alterations in what had formerly been tsarist Russia. Germany was shorn of its overseas colonies, while in Europe it lost Alsace-Lorraine, half of Schleswig, three western districts to Belgium, the Polish Corridor, and a zone in the Rhineland, which was demilitarized. The Austrian empire was dismembered; the nationalist movements of the Czechs, Poles, and Slavs achieved formal territorial recognition; and the remnant of the empire was converted into the separate states of Austria and Hungary. The Ottoman empire was in turn dissected: Greece obtained nearly all of European Turkey, Syria was mandated to France, Palestine and Iraq to Great Britain. After the Bolshevik Revolution, Russia lost much of its western territory, resulting in the establishment of Finland, Estonia, Latvia, and Lithuania, as well as the major portion of reconstituted Poland, while Bessarabia was ceded to Rumania.

Important changes also took place during the interwar years. Under Hitler, Nazi Germany reoccupied the Rhineland in 1936, seized Austria and occupied Sudetenland in 1938, and the following year seized other Czech territory as well as Memel. In 1939, too, Hungary annexed part of Slovakia, while Mussolini's Italy defeated and annexed Albania. The stage was also set for Russia to reannex territory lost after the Bolshevik Revolution.

Map 9: Africa 1914. Four major cultural environments of Africa, each with its unique historical development, may be partially explained by two physical features of the continent—the Sahara Desert and the Great Rift Valley, which runs from the Jordan Valley in Palestine to Western Tanzania. Separated from the rest of the continent by more than 1000 miles of the Sahara, most of the peoples of northwest Africa live close to the Mediterranean, which connects them with Europe from which has long come a flow of people, goods, and ideas. Northeast Africa, partly cut off from the rest of the continent by the Sahara, has long been linked with southwest Asia. Moreover, the Red Sea has always facilitated movement between northeast Africa and Arabia. Africa east of the Great Rift Valley has long been oriented to the Indian Ocean, to the Arab trader, and, since, the last century, to the European who has farmed the plateaus of Kenya, Uganda, and Tanzania.

The lands in the southern section of the Great Rift Valley also form part of sub-Saharan Africa. In this huge area the Sudanese savanna lands, equatorial rain forest, and the steppes and deserts of southern Africa succeed each other from north to south. In these lands occurred Europe's great scramble for empire in the nineteenth century.

Map 10: Africa. Profound political and territorial changes have occurred in Africa since 1914—undoubtedly the most spectacular to be found in any continent during the past half century. From being a vast collection of colonial holdings, Africa has emerged as an agglomeration of national states, virtually all having minimal political stability or economic viability. During the interwar years some major changes took place on the political landscape. German Togoland and the Cameroons were mandated to Great Britain and France; German East Africa was divided into two mandates: Ruanda-Urundi (Belgium) and Tanganyika (Great Britain); and German Southwest Africa was mandated to South Africa. Egypt became an independent kingdom, but Italy's possessions in East Africa were enlarged by the conquest of Abyssinia. Since World War II, however, a spectacular alteration has occurred. The entire continent has passed into indigenous political control, with the exception of Rhodesia, still under white minority control, and South Africa, where European domination remains entrenched.

Map 11: U.S.S.R. and Asia. Dominating Eurasia, the greatest land mass on earth, is the enormous area of the Soviet Union (more than 8 million square miles), extending on a west-east axis for 5000 miles. European Russia, largely a continuation of the north European plain, is drained by the Dvina, Dnieper, Don, and Volga, the last three flowing southward. East of the Urals virtually all rivers flow north to the Arctic, save the Amur,

which in its eastward journey also serves as a boundary with China. As the river pattern indicates, Soviet Asia tends to be separated from middle- and low-latitude Asia by physical obstacles, in this case steppes, deserts, mountains. The highest population and urban densities are found in Soviet Europe, while in Siberia, which is rapidly growing, the population is located along the major waterways or the Trans-Siberian Railroad.

As a result of their eastward expansion, the Russians had settled on the Pacific by 1649. In the next two centuries they penetrated east of the Caspian in what is now the Kazakh, Uzbek, and Turkmen Soviet Socialist Republics. In their expansion they collided with the Chinese in Sinkiang, Mongolia, and Manchuria. These border regions today constitute areas of tension and jockeying between the two major Communist powers.

For its part, China has continued to develop south of the Great Wall and Gobi Desert and east and north of such massive mountain ranges as the Tien Shan, Pamirs, and Himalayas. The vast majority of its estimated 750 million people live in the fertile Huang Ho and Yangtze basins or along the coast. Similarly, Indian society has continued to multiply within the confines of its triangular subcontinent, while influencing the culture patterns of neighboring lands to the east and south.

Southeast Asia has long been subject to recurrent cultural and military intrusions alike. Its highly indented coastline and physical terrain have contributed to a fragmentation of cultures and languages. Offshore in East and Southeast Asia are three archipelagoes: the Philippines; Japan, which is the most highly industrialized and prosperous of nonwestern countries; and Indonesia, whose estimated 110 million people make it the world's fifth largest country.

Map 12: Latin America. Latin America was first colonized by Southern Europeans, notably the Spaniards and Portuguese. Exploiting the mountain ranges, running the length of Central and South America, for their precious metals, the Spaniards increased their holdings until the close of the eighteenth century. They created several viceroyalties: New Spain, including Mexico and Central America; Peru, at first embracing all of Spanish South America; New Granada, in what is now Colombia and Venezuela; and La Plata, which subsequently became Bolivia, Paraguay, Uruguay, and Argentina. Brazil, discovered by the Portuguese Cabral in 1500, was made a viceroyalty in 1714.

In half a century (1776–1826) of colonial revolutions in the New World, Spanish and Portuguese

America became independent (except for Cuba and Puerto Rico which remained Spanish until 1898); but each of the Spanish viceroyalties split into more than one political entity.

The tropical regions of Latin America, including Mexico, Central America, and the lands drained by the Magdalena, Orinoco, and Amazon rivers, have predominantly Amerind populations. In contrast, temperate South America, comprising southern Brazil, Uruguay, Argentina, and Chile, finds Europeans in the majority. In 1960 Latin America had some 200 million people, roughly equivalent to the population of Anglo-America. But Latin America is the fastest-growing region in the world and within forty or fifty years may have a population of perhaps 600 million—or about double that of the United States and Canada.

Map 13: The Middle East. This region—segmented by deserts and seas, but with the latter providing interconnecting routes of travel—has long permitted maximal movement of peoples, goods, and ideas in virtually all directions. In this area, which is unique for the convergence of three continents, we find the birthplace of "civilization" and of three major religions, as well as a continuous succession of dynasties and empires. For centuries Islamic political authority and cultural vitality were bound up with the fortunes of the Ottoman empire, and when the latter was defeated by European powers, the Muslim peoples of this region were in turn subordinated in status and made to feel inferior. The twentieth century, however, has witnessed a resurgence of Islamic culture and political strength—attended by the creation of numerous independent states, including Morocco, Algeria, Libya, Egypt, Sudan, Syria, Lebanon, Jordan, Iraq, and Pakistan; and this resurgence has capitalized upon the strategic value of the region in the geopolitical programs of the superpowers, as well as upon its massive oil resources.

The region has also been in a state of continuous tension and intermittent conflict since the end of World War II, because of Arab-Israeli animosities. When the British mandate of Palestine was terminated in 1948, the area proclaimed itself the new state of Israel—a step sanctioned by the United Nations as well as both the United States and the Soviet Union. But the Arab states remained implacably opposed to any such recognition, and several campaigns were mounted in an effort to regain Palestine for the Muslim Arabs.

Two other Arab-Israeli conflicts occurred in 1967 and 1973. An Israeli victory resulted in occupation of the west bank of the Jordan River; the Sinai peninsula and east bank of the Suez Canal have since been returned to Egypt.

Map 14: Europe. This map can profitably be compared with Map 8 in order to obtain a clearer picture of territorial changes resulting from the outcome of World War II. As after World War I, defeated Germany and its allies were deprived of territory, with the Soviet Union emerging as the greatest single territorial beneficiary.

In 1945 Germany was stripped of East Prussia, while its eastern boundary was set at the Oder-Neisse rivers—the farthest line west achieved by the Slavs since the twelfth century. Moreover, postwar Germany was both ideologically and territorially split, its western segment associated in military and economic pacts with the western world, its eastern section integrated in the Communist world and a member of the Warsaw Pact. While faring better, defeated Italy lost its overseas colonies and Albania.

Conversely, the Soviet Union expanded westward, annexing part of Finland, all of Estonia, Latvia, and Lithuania, and the eastern portion of Poland, shifting that country's center of gravity westward at the expense of Germany. Stalinist policies and power also created a series of "people's democracies" from the Baltic to the Black seas, resulting in the iron curtain. Yet the region was to prove far from monolithic. Shortly after the war Tito declared Yugoslavia an independent Communist state, tiny Albania was later to ally itself with Peking in the great split within the Communist world, while the 1950's and 1960's also witnessed abortive attempts in Hungary and Czechoslovakia to gain greater freedom from Moscow's control.

The contemporary map of Europe differs markedly from earlier maps of the continent not only because of its ideological division but also because of the emergence of new economic groupings. To break down traditional trade barriers, the European Economic Community (the "Common Market") was formed. Another such community is the European Free Trade Association, or "Outer Seven." In an effort to keep pace, the Communist countries organized the Council of Mutual Economic Assistance. It will be interesting to watch the long-term effects of these economic groupings upon the traditional political forces —and boundaries—of Europe.

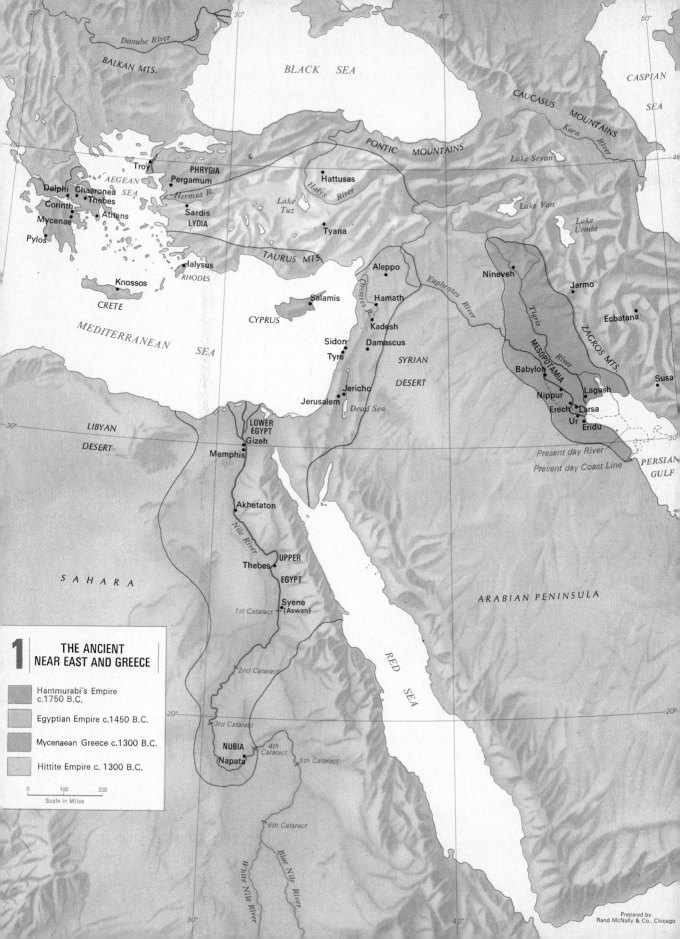

THE ANCIENT
NEAR EAST AND GREECE

Hammurabi's Empire
c.1750 B.C.

Egyptian Empire c.1450 B.C.

Mycenaean Greece c.1300 B.C.

Hittite Empire c. 1300 B.C.

0   100   200
Scale in Miles

Prepared by
Rand McNally & Co., Chicago

ATLANTIC
OCEAN

NORTH
SEA

IRELAND

Antoninus' Wall
(C. 140 A.D.)

Hadrian's Wall
(C. 122 A.D.)

IRISH
SEA

PENNINES

York

Chester

Lincoln

BRITAIN

Colchester

Bath

London

Thames R.

ENGLISH CHANNEL

GERMANIA

Elbe

Oder

Cologne

BELGICA

Mainz

Rhine River

Seine River

Paris

Meuse

Loire River

Saône R.

GAUL

BAY OF
BISCAY

Bordeaux

Garonne R.

CENTRAL
MASSIF

Rhône

Lyons

ALPS

CISALPINE GAUL

Po River

Genoa

Ravenna

ADRIATIC

CANTABRIAN MTS.

Douro River

Segovia

Tagus River

SPAIN

Toledo

Guadiana River

SIERRA MORENA

Cordova

Guadalquivir R.

Cádiz

SIERRA NEVADA

Tangier

Strait of Gibraltar

Pillars of Hercules

Ebro River

PYRENEES

Saguntum

Valencia

New
Carthage

Marseilles

Pisa

CORSICA

SARDINIA

BALEARIC
ISLANDS

MEDITERRANEAN

Salo

ITALY

APENNINES

Rome

Naples

Pompei

TYRRHENIAN
SEA

Messina

SICILY

Syrac

MALTA

MADEIRA
ISLANDS

MAURETANIA

ATLAS MOUNTAINS

Moulouya R.

Cheliff

CANARY
ISLANDS

ATLAS

Medjerda R.

Utica

Carthage

Chott
Djerid

NUMIDIA

Oea

Leptis
Magna

GRAND ERG OCCIDENTAL

GRAND ERG ORIENTAL

2 | **THE ROMAN EMPIRE C. 117 A.D.**

0   100   200   300
Scale in Miles

AHAGGAR
MOUNTAINS

SAHARA

GOTHS

HUNS

Lake Ladoga

Western Dvina River

Volga River

Kama River

URAL MOUNTAINS

Vistula R.

Bug River

Dnieper River

Dniester River

River

SARMATIA

Volga River

Ural River

Tobol R.

ARAL SEA

CARPATHIANS

•Olbia

SEA OF AZOV

•Apulum

TRANSYLVANIAN ALPS

DACIA

River

BALKAN MTS.

•Naissus

BLACK SEA

CAUCASUS MOUNTAINS

Kura River

CASPIAN SEA

Don River

Lake Sevan

THRACE

Byzantium•

•Sinope

•Trapezus

Aras River

•Artaxata

PONTIC MOUNTAINS

ARMENIA

ELBURZ MTS.

MACEDONIA

Sea of Marmara

PONTUS

River

Lake Van

Lake Urmia

Daryācheh-ye Namak

PINDUS MTS

EPIRUS

AEGEAN SEA

•Pergamum

ASIA

Lake Tuz

Kizil

ASSYRIA

PLATEAU

PARTHIAN EMPIRE

OF IRAN

Thebes•

•Ephesus

MESOPOTAMIA

Ecbatana•

ZAGROS

Corinth•

•Athens

Tarsus•

Tigris

•Sparta

CILICIA

RHODES

CYPRUS

•Palmyra

SYRIA

•Dura Europos

Euphrates River

•Ctesiphon

River

MTS.

PERSIAN GULF

Knossos•

•Damascus

CRETE

Sidon•

Tyre•

SEA

PALESTINE

•Jerusalem

Dead Sea

•Cyrene

Alexandria•

CYRENAICA

Memphis•

ARABIA

EGYPT

LIBYAN

DESERT

Nile River

•Thebes

RED SEA

•Berenice

•Syene

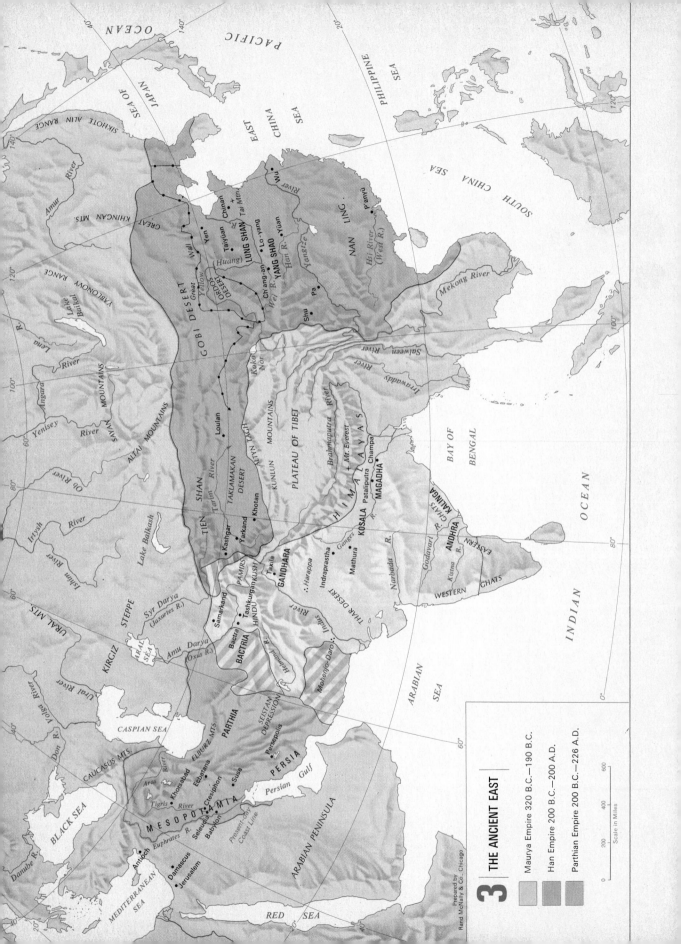

PACIFIC OCEAN

SEA OF JAPAN

SIKHOTE ALIN RANGE

EAST CHINA SEA

PHILIPPINE SEA

SOUTH CHINA SEA

KHINGAN MTS.

Amur River

YABLONOVY RANGE

GREAT KHINGAN MTS.

Great Wall

GOBI DESERT

ORDOS DESERT

Yellow (Huang) River

Yen

Taiyüan Chinan

Tai Mtn.

LUNG SHAN

Lo-yang

Ch'ang-an

Wei R. YANG SHAO

Han R.

Shu

Pa

Yangtze River

Wu

Yüan River

NAN LING

Hsi River (West R.)

P'anyü

Mekong River

Lena River

Angara River

Lake Baikal

SAYAN MOUNTAINS

ALTAI MOUNTAINS

Yenisey River

Ob River

Irtysh River

Lake Balkash

TIEN SHAN

Tarim River

TAKLAMAKAN DESERT

Loulan

Khotan

Yarkand

Kashgar

Koko Nor

ALTYN TAGH

KUNLUN MOUNTAINS

PLATEAU OF TIBET

Brahmaputra River

Mt. Everest

HIMALAYAS

Salween River

Irrawaddy River

BAY OF BENGAL

OCEAN

Ishim River

URAL MTS.

KIRGIZ STEPPE

Syr Darya (Jaxartes R.)

Aral Sea

Amu Darya (Oxus R.)

PAMIRS

HINDU KUSH

Tashkurgan

Samarkand

Bactra

BACTRIA

Taxila

GANDHARA

Indus River

Helmund R.

Mohenjo-Daro

.·. Harappa

Indraprastha

Mathura

Ganges R.

KOSALA

Pataliputra

MAGADHA

Champa

Narbada R.

Godavari R.

Kistna R.

ANDHRA

KALINGA

EASTERN GHATS

WESTERN GHATS

THAR DESERT

ARABIAN SEA

INDIAN OCEAN

Volga R.

Don R.

Ural River

CASPIAN SEA

CAUCASUS MTS.

Aras R.

BLACK SEA

Tigris River

Khorsabad

Ecbatana

ELBURZ MTS.

PARTHIA

SEISTAN DEPRESSION

Susa

PERSIA

Persepolis

Persian Gulf

Danube R.

Antioch

Damascus

Jerusalem

MEDITERRANEAN SEA

Euphrates R.

Seleucia

Ctesiphon

Babylon

MESOPOTAMIA

Present-day Coast Line

RED SEA

ARABIAN PENINSULA

3 | THE ANCIENT EAST

Maurya Empire 320 B.C.—190 B.C.

Han Empire 200 B.C.—200 A.D.

Parthian Empire 200 B.C.—226 A.D.

Scale in Miles

0   200   400   600

Prepared by
Rand McNally & Co., Chicago

ATLANTIC

OCEAN

NORWAY

SWEDEN

DENMARK

Copenhagen

NORTH

SEA

SCOTLAND
Aberdeen

Glasgow
Edinburgh

Durham

IRELAND
Galway
Limerick
Shannon
Wexford
Cork
St. David's

Dublin
Chester
Lincoln
York

Severn R.

WALES

ENGLAND

London
Bath
Winchester   Hastings
Thames River

ENGLISH CHANNEL

Brest

NORMANDY
Mont St. Michel
BRITTANY
Champeaux
ANJOU
Carnac

Chartres

Loire R.
Tours

POITOU
Poitiers

Haarlem   Amsterdam
Rotterdam
Bruges   Ghent   Louvain
FLANDERS
Ypres   Brussels
Agincourt   Lille
Crécy   Cambrai   Cateau-
Cambrésis
Amiens   Vervins   Rocroy   LUXEMBOURG
Rouen   Soissons   Verdun
Compiègne   **LORRAINE**
Paris   Toul
Seine   **CHAMPAGNE**   **ALSACE**
Clairvaux   Luxeuil
Orléans
Molesme   **ROMAN**
Vézelay
BURGUNDY
Cluny   SWITZERLAND

HOLY

Brandenburg

Elbe River
Weser River
Rhine River
Meuse R.
ARDENNES
Danube River

50°

FRANCE

Saône R.

Lyons

EMPIRE   **VENICE**

ALPS

Po River
**PAPAL
STATES**

BAY

OF

BISCAY

Cognac

AQUITAINE
Bordeaux
Dordogne
Garonne River

GASCONY

CENTRAL

MASSIF

Rhône R.

Nîmes

Marseilles
THE CORNICHE
Toulon

Toulouse   Carcassonne   Narbonne
Perpignan

CORSICA

SARDINIA

Cagliari

Santiago de
Compostela
Miño R.
ASTURIAS
Oviedo   Cave of
Covadonga
CANTABRIAN MTS.
Ebro
León
PORTUGAL   *Douro River*
Porto
Salamanca
Segovia
KINGDOM OF
Madrid
Toledo
CASTILE AND
Lisbon
Tagus River
Guadiana River
Segura R.
LEON
Las Navas
de Tolosa
Cordova
Seville   *Guadalquivir River*
Granada
Cádiz   **KINGDOM OF GRANADA**
Strait of Gibraltar   Pillars of Hercules
Tangier

Roncesvalles
Pass
**KINGDOM
OF
NAVARRE**
PYRENEES

Saragossa
**KINGDOM
OF
ARAGON**

Barcelona

Palma

Valencia

BALEARIC ISLANDS

MEDITERRANEAN

SEA

MUSLIM   STATES

40°

10°

10°

40°

0°

10°

10°

Prepared by
Rand McNally & Co., Chicago

4 MEDIEVAL FRANCE,
SPAIN, AND THE
BRITISH ISLES 1328

England and possessions

France

Kingdom of Navarre

Kingdom of Castile and Leon
and dependencies

Kingdom of Aragon
and dependencies

Kingdom of Granada

Portugal

0   100   200
Scale in Miles

EUROPE 1648

Prepared by
Rand McNally & Co., Chicago

Austrian Hapsburgs

Spanish Hapsburgs

Holy Roman Empire

Anglican	Islamic
Calvinist	Lutheran
Greek Orthodox	Roman Catholic

Scale in Miles
0   100   200   300   400

URAL MOUNTAINS

KAZAKH

RUSSIA

PERSIA

ARABIA

SYRIA

CYPRUS

EGYPT

Nile Delta

Alexandria

Tigris River

Euphrates River

CAUCASUS MTS.

+ Mt. Elbrus

CASPIAN SEA

L. Urmia
L. Van

TAURUS MTS.

Kizil River
TAURUS MTS.

PONTIC MOUNTAINS

L. Tuz

BLACK SEA

Sea of Azov

Don River

Volga River

Kama River
Ural River

Northern Dvina R.

Sukhona River

Vychegda R.

Tura R.

L. Onega
Lake Ladoga

Vyg River

FINLAND

Moscow

Novgorod
Pskov

INGRIA

VALDAI HILLS

Western Dvina R.

LIVONIA
ESTONIA
Riga
COURLAND

LITHUANIA
Vilna

Königsberg
EAST PRUSSIA

POLAND

Warsaw
Vistula River

Bug R.

Dnieper River
Kiev

Dniester River

Danube River

TRANSYLVANIAN ALPS

CARPATHIAN MTS.

Bucharest

BALKAN MTS.

OTTOMAN EMPIRE

Constantinople
Sea of Marmara
Dardanelles
Bosporus

PINDUS MTS.

Salonica

Athens

AEGEAN SEA

CRETE (Venice)

RHODES

CYRENAICA

Bengasi

MEDITERRANEAN SEA

Naval Battle of Lepanto 1571

IONIAN SEA

Ragusa

ADRIATIC SEA

TRIPOLITANIA

Tripoli

MALTA

SICILY
Messina
Palermo

NAPLES
Naples

TYRRHENIAN SEA

SARDINIA

CORSICA

Bona (Fr.)

TUNIS
Tunis

ALGIERS
Algiers

Oran
Melilla (Sp.)
(Sp.)

FEZ AND MOROCCO
Fez

Tangier (Sp.)
Strait of Gibraltar

BALEARIC ISLANDS

Barcelona

SPAIN
Madrid
Saragossa

Oviedo
CANTABRIAN MTS.
Duero R.

SIERRA MORENA
Ciudad Real
Cordova
Granada
Seville
SIERRA NEVADA
Cádiz

Lisbon
PORTUGAL
Tagus R.

PYRENEES

BAY OF BISCAY

Bordeaux
Garonne R.
Toulouse

Nantes
Loire R.

Brest

Bristol
Southampton
English Channel

IRELAND
ULSTER
Dublin

SCOTLAND
Edinburgh
PENNINES

ENGLAND
London
Thames R.

ORKNEY IS.
SHETLAND IS. (Scot.)
FAEROE IS. (Den.)

ATLANTIC OCEAN

NORTH SEA

NORWAY

SWEDEN
Stockholm
GOTLAND

L. Vänern
L. Vättern

DENMARK
Copenhagen
Kattegat
Skagerrak

Oslo

Gulf of Bothnia

BALTIC SEA

Gulf of Finland

HOLLAND
Amsterdam

SPANISH NETHERLANDS
Antwerp
Brussels

FRANCE
Paris
Orléans
Seine R.
Marseilles
Rhône R.
CENTRAL MASSIF

Avignon
ORANGE
FRANCHE COMTÉ

Verdun
Toul
METZ

GERMAN STATES

Cologne
Münster
Osnabrück

Bremen
Hamburg
HOLSTEIN

BRANDENBURG
Berlin
POMERANIA
Elbe R.

SAXONY
Wittenberg

BOHEMIA
Prague

AUSTRIA
Vienna

HUNGARY
Buda

Bavaria
Munich
Augsburg
Stuttgart
PALATINATE

Worms
Rhine R.

Basel
SWITZERLAND
Zürich

ITALIAN STATES

Milan
Turin
Genoa
Po R.

Venice

PAPAL STATES
Rome

APENNINES

Mont Blanc
Mont Cenis

Danube R.

Main R.

CYRENAICA

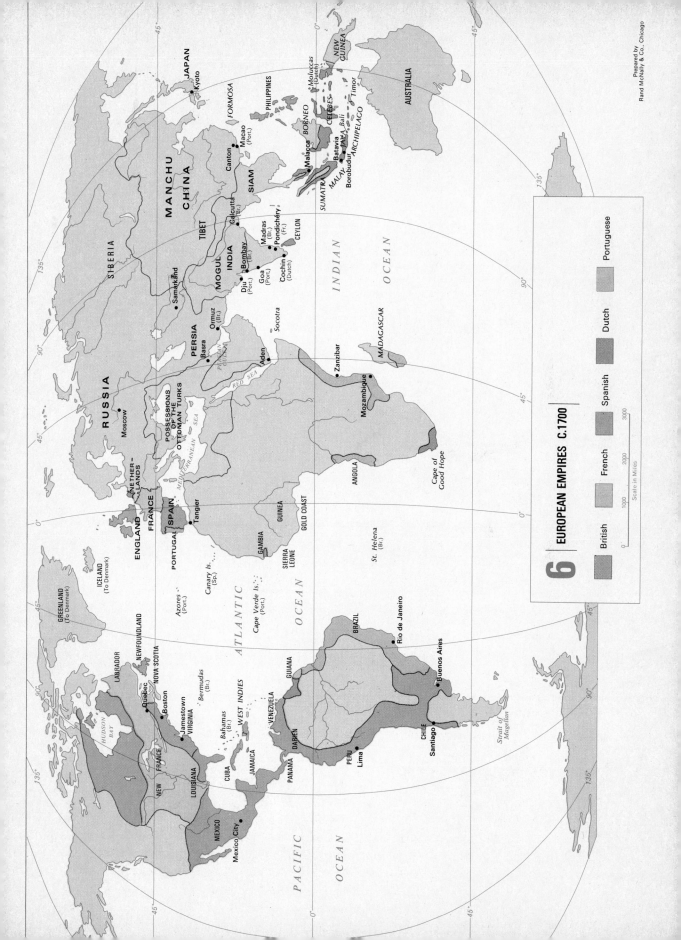

URAL MOUNTAINS

Tavda R.
Tura R.
Ural River

CASPIAN SEA

PERSIA

30°

SYRIA

Jerusalem

Beirut

PONTIC MOUNTAINS

CAUCASUS MTS.

Mt. Elbrus

Kura R.

L. Urmia

L. Van

Araks R.

Tigris River

Euphrates River

40°

Prepared by
Rand McNally & Co., Chicago

CYPRUS

Ankara

Smyrna

TAURUS MTS.

L. Tuz

Constantinople

Bosporus

Sea of Marmara

Dardanelles

AEGEAN SEA

CRETE

Athens

Navarino 20°

IONIAN ISLANDS (Br.)

Ionian Sea

Alexandria

EGYPT

30°

Bengasi

TRIPOLITANIA

Tripoli

MALTA (Br.)

MEDITERRANEAN SEA

TUNIS

Tunis

ALGERIA

ATLAS MOUNTAINS

Oran

Algiers

MOROCCO

Melilla (Sp.)
Ceuta (Sp.)
Casablanca

Strait of Gibraltar
Gibraltar (Br.)
Cape Trafalgar

URAL RIVER
RUSSIAN EMPIRE

Northern Dvina
White Sea
Arkhangelsk

Sukhona R.
Vologda R.

L. Onega
L. Ladoga

Moscow

Kharkov

Poltava

Kiev

Dnieper River

Don R.

Don

Sea of Azov
Azov

CRIMEA
Sevastopol

Odessa

BLACK SEA

CIRCASSIA

San Stefano
Adrianople
BULGARIA
Varna

FINLAND
Gulf of Bothnia

St. Petersburg
Novgorod
L. Ilmen
Narva
Reval
L. Peipus
Riga

Helsinki
Nystad

Åland Is.

Gotland

Öland

BALTIC SEA

LITHUANIA
Tilsit
Königsberg
Danzig

POLAND
Warsaw
Vistula R.
Bug R.

Pest
Buda
HUNGARY

CARPATHIANS

BESSARABIA
MOLDAVIA
Dniester River
Bug R.

WALLACHIA
RUMANIA
Bucharest
Danube River
SERBIA
Belgrade
Karlowitz

TRANSYLVANIA
TRANSYLVANIAN ALPS

BALKAN MTS.

MONTE NEGRO
VINA
ALBANIA

GREECE

KINGDOM OF NORWAY AND SWEDEN

Bergen
Oslo

Göteborg
L. Väner
L. Vätter

Stockholm

Skagerrak
Kattegat

KINGDOM OF DENMARK

Copenhagen

NORTH SEA

KINGDOM OF THE NETHERLANDS
Amsterdam
Utrecht
The Hague
Antwerp
Brussels
BELGIUM
Waterloo

SCHLESWIG
HOLSTEIN
Hamburg
Bremen
HANOVER
BRANDEN- BURG
Berlin
MECKLEN- BURG
PRUSSIA
Breslau
Oder R.
Sadowa
Troppau

EMPIRE OF AUSTRIA

BOHEMIA
Prague
Carlsbad
Austerlitz
Vienna
Buda
KINGDOM OF HUNGARY

CROATIA- SLAVONIA
Laibach
BOSNIA
HERZEGO- VINA
DALMATIA

Adriatic Sea

THE UNITED KINGDOM OF GREAT BRITAIN AND IRELAND

Edinburgh
IRISH SEA
Dublin
Liverpool
Manchester
Birmingham
London
Dover
Thames

ENGLISH CHANNEL

Le Havre
Sedan
Valmy
Paris
Versailles

FRANCE

Seine River
Loire River

Nantes
Lorient

BAY OF BISCAY

La Rochelle
Bordeaux
Garonne R.

CENTRAL MASSIF

Marseilles

PYRENEES
ANDORRA

Barcelona

BALEARIC ISLANDS

SPAIN
Madrid

Ebro River
Tagus River
Douro River
Guadalquivir R.
Guadiana R.

SIERRA MORENA
SIERRA NEVADA

CANTABRIAN MTS.

PORTUGAL
Lisbon
Cádiz

FAEROE IS. (Den.)

SHETLAND IS. (Br.)
ORKNEY IS. (Br.)

ATLANTIC OCEAN

SAXONY
Leipzig
Frankfurt
Aix-la-Chapelle
Cologne
BERG
WÜRTEM.
BADEN
ALSACE
BAVARIA
Augsburg
Munich
Ulm
Carlsbad

SWITZER- LAND
LIECHT.
NEUCHÂTEL
Geneva
Rhône R.
SAVOY
Nice
MONACO

PIEDMONT
LOMBARDY
Milan
VENETIA
Venice
Verona
PARMA
MODENA
LUCCA
TUSCANY
Florence
PAPAL STATES
SAN MARINO
Rome
Corsica (Fr.)
Elba
Genoa

APENNINES

KINGDOM OF SARDINIA

Tyrrhenian Sea

KINGDOM OF NAPLES AND SICILY

Naples
Palermo

0°
10°
20°
30°
40°
50°
60°

7 | EUROPE 1815

Boundary of German Confederation

Small German States

0   100   200   300   400
Scale of Miles

8 | EUROPE AUGUST 1939

German aggression

Military reoccupation of the Rhineland 1936

Seizure of Austria 1938

Seizure of Memel 1939

Occupation of Sudetenland 1938

Seizure of other Czech territory 1939

Other territorial aggressions

Czech territory annexed by Hungary 1938-1939

Italian seizure of Albania 1939

Prepared by Uni-Map, Inc. Palatine, Ill.

ATLANTIC

OCEAN

MADEIRA IS.
(Port.)

CANARY IS.
(Br.)

• London
• Amsterdam • Berlin
• Brussels • Warsaw
• Paris

E U R O P E

Danube R.

• Vienna
• Budapest
• Belgrade

BLACK SEA

Aral
Sea

CASPIAN SEA

A S I A

Dnieper R.

• Rome

• Madrid
• Lisbon

Tangier • SP. MOROCCO
Casablanca •

Algiers •
Tunis •
TUNISIA

M E D I T E R R A N E A N
S E A

Tripoli •
Bengasi •

• Athens

• Constantinople

• Damascus
Jerusalem •

Euphrates R.

Tigris R.

• Tehran

• Baghdad

MOROCCO
ATLAS MOUNTAINS

ALGERIA

IFNI

RIO DE ORO

Villa
Cisneros •

S A H A R A

AHAGGAR MTS.

L I B Y A

Alexandria •
Cairo •

Suez
Canal

Aswan •

E G Y P T

LIBYAN
DESERT

RED SEA

• Mecca

A R A B I A N

P E N I N S U L A

PERSIAN GULF

Gulf of Aden

TIBESTI
MASSIF

NUBIAN
DESERT

FRENCH WEST AFRICA

Timbuktu •

S U D A N

A N G L O -

Omdurman •
Khartoum •

Asmara •

ERITREA

Aden •

Dakar •
GAMBIA
Bissau •
PORT.
GUINEA
FRENCH GUINEA
Freetown •
SIERRA
LEONE
LIBERIA
Monrovia •

SENEGAL R.

Bamako •

Niger R.

L. Chad

CHAD

Ft. Lamy •

Kano •

Shari

NIGERIA

Benue R.

IVORY
COAST

GOLD
COAST

TOGO
DAHOMEY

Lagos •

Lome •
Accra •

FERNANDO PO
(Sp.)

PRINCIPE
(Port.)

SAO TOME
(Port.)

ANNOBÓN
(Sp.)

GULF OF
GUINEA

CAMEROONS

Douala •

RIO
MUNI

Libreville •

GABON

EQUATORIAL AFRICA
UBANGI-SHARI

Brazzaville •

CABINDA

Léopoldville •

FRENCH

Ubangi R.

CONGO
BASIN

Congo R.

Stanleyville •

Uele R.
Bonu R.

L. Albert

E G Y P T I A N

S U D A N

White Nile

Blue Nile

Atbara R.

Tana

FR. SOM.
Djibouti •
Addis
Ababa •

ABYSSINIA
(ETHIOPIA)

Berbera •
BR. SOM.

ITALIAN SOMALILAND

• Mogadishu

B E L G I A N

C O N G O

L. Rudolf

UGANDA

Entebbe •

Lake
Victoria

Mt. Kilimanjaro ×

Lake
Tanganyika

KENYA
(BR. EAST AFR.)

• Nairobi

Tabora •

• Mombasa

ZANZIBAR (Br.)
Dar-es-Salaam •

GERMAN
EAST
AFRICA

INDIAN

OCEAN

ALDABRA IS.
(Br.)

COMORO IS.
(Fr.)

Kasai R.

Kwango R.

Luanda •

Benguela •

ANGOLA
(PORT. WEST AFR.)

Cunene R.

Kwanza R.

Zambezi R.

Lake
Nyasa

RHODESIA

NORTHERN RHODESIA

Livingstone •

Victoria
Falls

SOUTHERN
RHODESIA

Salisbury •

Beira •

NYASALAND
• Blantyre

MOZAMBIQUE
(PORT. EAST AFR.)

MADAGASCAR

• Tamata
Tananarive •

GERMAN

SOUTHWEST

AFRICA

Windhoek •
Walvis Bay •

NAMIB DESERT

KALAHARI
DESERT

BECHUANALAND

Mafeking •

Limpopo R.

Pretoria •
Johannesburg •

SWAZILAND

Lourenço Marques •

Lüderitz •

Orange R.

U N I O N O F

BASUTOLAND

Durban •

Cape Town •
Cape of Good Hope

SOUTH AFRICA

East London •
Port Elizabeth •

---

9 **AFRICA 1914**

British

French

German

Belgian

Portuguese

Italian

Spanish

0   400   800

Scale in Miles

Prepared by Uni-Map, Inc.   Palatine, Il.

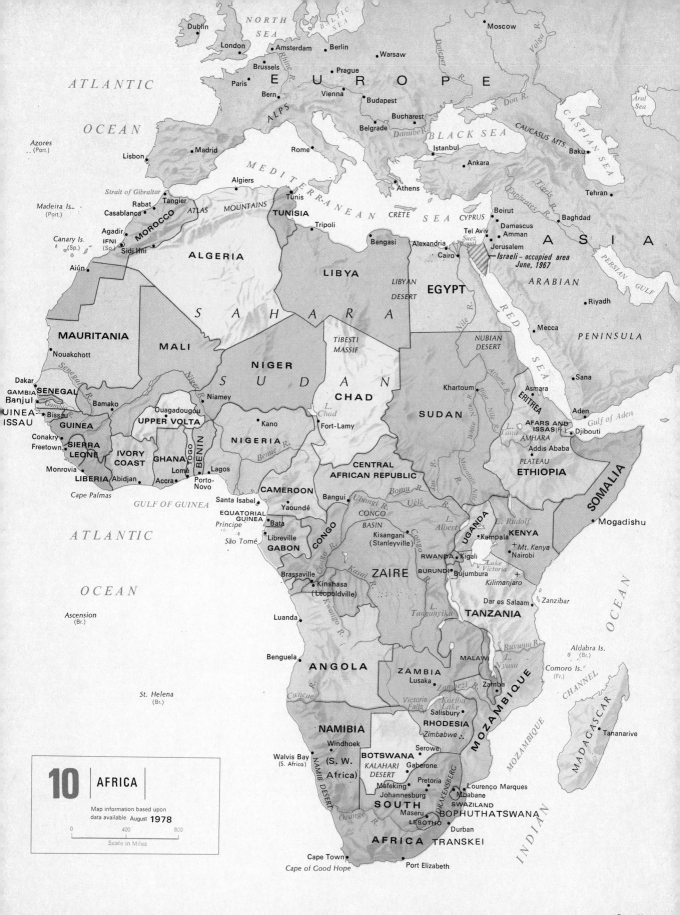

ATLANTIC

OCEAN

Azores
(Port.)

Madeira Is.
(Port.)

Canary Is.
(Sp.)

NORTH SEA

BALTIC SEA

• Dublin

• London   • Amsterdam   • Berlin   • Warsaw   • Moscow

• Brussels   • Prague

• Paris   Bern   E U R O P E

• Vienna   • Budapest

• Belgrade   • Bucharest

Volga

Don R.

Aral Sea

CAUCASUS MTS.

• Baku

CASPIAN SEA

Dnieper R.

BLACK SEA

• Madrid   • Rome

ALPS

• Istanbul

• Ankara

• Tehran

M E D I T E R R A N E A N   CRETE   SEA

CYPRUS

• Beirut

• Damascus   • Baghdad

Euphrates R.   *Tigris R.*

• Lisbon

Strait of Gibraltar

Rabat • Tangier   ATLAS   • Tunis

Casablanca   MOROCCO   MOUNTAINS   TUNISIA

Agadir   • Tripoli

IFNI   Sidi Ifni

(Sp.)

Aiún

MAURITANIA

• Nouakchott

Dakar •

GAMBIA   SENEGAL

Banjul

GUINEA   Bissau

BISSAU   GUINEA

Conakry

Freetown   SIERRA
LEONE

Monrovia •   IVORY
COAST   GHANA

LIBERIA   Abidjan   Accra

Cape Palmas

ALGIERS

A L G E R I A

LIBYA

• Bengasi

Tel Aviv   • Amman

Jerusalem

Suez Canal

*Israeli – occupied area
June, 1967*

• Alexandria

• Cairo

EGYPT

Nile R.

*LIBYAN
DESERT*

*TIBESTI
MASSIF*

*NUBIAN
DESERT*

ARABIAN

PENINSULA

• Riyadh

• Mecca

• Sana

RED SEA

• Aden

Gulf of Aden

S A H A R A

MALI

N I G E R

C H A D

SUDAN

S   U   D   A   N

• Khartoum

• Asmara   ERITREA

Atbara R.

Blue Nile R.   *White Nile R.*

AFARS AND
ISSAS (F.)   • Djibouti

AMHARA

• Addis Ababa

PLATEAU

ETHIOPIA

PERSIAN GULF

A S I A

Senegal R.

• Bamako   • Niamey

UPPER VOLTA

Ouagadougou

• Kano

Niger R.

N I G E R I A

Benue R.

Lomé   Lagos

TOGO   BENIN

Porto-
Novo

L.
Chad

Fort-Lamy

CENTRAL
AFRICAN REPUBLIC

Bangui

CAMEROON

• Yaoundé

EQUATORIAL
GUINEA

Santa Isabel

Principe

Bata

São Tomé   Libreville

GABON   CONGO

Brassaville

• Kinshasa
(Léopoldville)

Ubangi R.   *Uélé R.*

*CONGO
BASIN*

Congo R.

Kisangani
(Stanleyville)

*L.
Albert*

RWANDA   • Kigali

BURUNDI

Bujumbura

ZAIRE

Kasai R.

Kwango R.   *Kwilu R.*

UGANDA

• Kampala

L. Rudolf

KENYA

+ Mt. Kenya

• Nairobi

*Lake
Victoria*   +
Kilimanjaro

• Dar es Salaam   • Zanzibar

T A N Z A N I A

*L.
Tanganyika*

• Mogadishu

S O M A L I A

INDIAN

OCEAN

*Aldabra Is.
(Br.)*

*Comoro Is.
(Fr.)*

MOZAMBIQUE CHANNEL

MADAGASCAR

• Tananarive

ATLANTIC

OCEAN

*Ascension
(Br.)*

*St. Helena
(Br.)*

• Luanda

• Benguela

A N G O L A

Cunene R.

NAMIBIA

Windhoek •

Walvis Bay
(S. Africa)   (S. W.
Africa)

NAMIB DESERT

Orange R.

ZAMBIA

• Lusaka

Zambezi R.

Ruvuma R.

*L.
Nyasa*

MALAWI

• Zomba

MOZAMBIQUE

*Victoria
Falls*   *Kariba
Lake*

• Salisbury

RHODESIA

Zimbabwe

BOTSWANA

• Serowe

*KALAHARI
DESERT*   Gaberone •

Mafeking •   • Pretoria

Johannesburg •   • Mbabane

SWAZILAND

SOUTH   Maseru

LESOTHO

AFRICA   TRANSKEI   • Durban

BOPHUTHATSWANA

DRAKENSBERG

• Lourenço Marques

GULF OF GUINEA

Cape Town •

Cape of Good Hope   • Port Elizabeth

Prepared by
Rand McNally & Co., Chicago

OCEAN

NEW SIBERIAN ISLANDS

Wrangel I.

180°

CHERSKIY MTS.

VERKHOYANSK

Verkhoyansk

Zhigansk

MOUNTAINS

Vilyuy River

Yakutsk

Seymchan

Markovo

ANADYR RANGE

CIALIST   REPUBLIC

Aldan River

Magadan

60°

BERING SEA

KAMCHATKA PENINSULA

SEA OF OKHOTSK

Petropavlovsk

Aleutian Islands

180°

REPUBLICS

Irkutsk

L. Baikal

Ulan-Ude   Chita

YABLONOY RANGE

Aleksandrovsk

SAKHALIN

Kuril Islands

Amur River

Khabarovsk

MOUNTAINS

MONGOLIA

Ulan Bator

GREAT KHINGAN MTS.

Harbin

Korsakov

GOBI DESERT

NAN SHAN

Paotow

Kalgan

Mukden

Vladivostok

HOKKAIDO

Koko Nor

Peking (Peiping)

Port Arthur

NORTH KOREA

SEA OF

JAPAN

ILUN MOUNTAINS

Lanchow

Tientsin

Pyongyang

Seoul

KOREA

SOUTH KOREA

JAPAN

HONSHU

TEAU

Sian

Yellow River (Huang)

YELLOW SEA

Pusan

Osaka

Tokyo

PACIFIC

OF

CHINA

BET

TIBET

Lhasa

Yangtze River

Wuhan

Shanghai

Kitakyushu

SHIKOKU

KYUSHU

HIMALAYAS

Chungking

EAST CHINA SEA

Ryukyu Islands

30°

Everest

BHUTAN

Brahmaputra

Foochow

NAN LING

Taipei

OCEAN

es R.

anasi

Dacca

BANGLADESH

Calcutta

Kunming

Si River

Canton

Kowloon

Macao (Port.)

Victoria

HONG KONG (Br.)

TAIWAN (FORMOSA)

BURMA

Hanoi

NORTH VIETNAM

HAINAN

GHATS

Irrawaddy R.

Rangoon

Vientiane

LAOS

VIETNAM

SOUTH CHINA

LUZON

Quezon City

Manila

PHILIPPINES

PHILIPPINE

BAY OF BENGAL

THAILAND

Bangkok

SOUTH VIETNAM

SEA

Guam I. (U.S.)

as

CAMBODIA

SEA

LON

SRI LANKA

mbo

Phnom Penh

Saigon

Celebes Sea

MINDANAO

MALAYA

MALAYSIA

BRUNEI (Br.)

SABAH

Kuala Lumpur

SARAWAK

MOLUCCA ISLANDS

SINGAPORE

BORNEO

SUMATRA

CELEBES

Jayapura

NEW IRELAND

TERRITORY OF NEW GUINEA (Austl.)

NEW GUINEA

EAN

0°

Jakarta

INDONESIA

Surabaya

JAVA

FLORES

Dili

PORT.TIMOR

OCUSSI (Port.Timor)

TIMOR

PAPUA (Austl.)

NEW BRITAIN

Port Moresby

AUSTRALIA

90°

120°

ROCKY MOUNTAINS

Columbia R.

Snake River

Missouri River

New York

Chicago

Washington

Denver

St. Louis

UNITED STATES

Dallas

SIERRA MADRE OCCIDENTAL

GULF OF CALIFORNIA

Conchos

Rio Grande

SIERRA MADRE OR.

New Orleans

Mississippi R.

Miami

ATLANTIC

OCEAN

Bermuda Is.
(Br.)

OCEAN

Monterrey

Tampico

MEXICO

Laredo

Sta. Maria

GULF OF

MEXICO

BAHAMAS

Havana

Guadalajara

Mérida

Chichen Itza

Balsas R.

Mexico City

Veracruz

Uxmal

Acapulco

Oaxaca

MADRE ORIENTAL

WEST

CUBA

Santo Domingo

DOMINICAN REPUBLIC

PUERTO RICO
(U.S.)

Guadeloupe
(Fr.)

Martinique
(Fr.)

Port-
au-Prince

HAITI

JAMAICA

Kingston

INDIES

BELIZE
Br.

Belize
City

GUATEMALA

Guatemala

HONDURAS

Tegucigalpa

EL
SALVADOR

San Salvador

NICARAGUA

Managua

CARIBBEAN SEA

BARBADOS

TRINIDAD AND TOBAGO

Port of Spain

COSTA RICA

San José

Colón

Panamá

PANAMA

Barranquilla

Lake
Maracaibo

Caracas

Orinoco R.

VENEZUELA

Georgetown

GUYANA

Paramaribo

SURINAME

FRENCH GUIANA

Cayenne

GUIANA HIGHLANDS

Bogotá

COLOMBIA

Buenaventura

Quito

ECUADOR

Guayaquil

GALÁPAGOS IS.
(Ec.)

Iquitos

Marañón R.

Japurá R.

Rio Negro

Manaus

Amazon River

Purús R.

Madeira River

Tapajós River

Xingú River

Tocantins River

Belém

BRAZIL

Recife

PERU

Lima

PACIFIC

OCEAN

Guaporé R.

Mamoré R.

Lake
Titicaca

La Paz

Arequipa

BOLIVIA

Sucre

PLATEAU OF
MATO GROSSO

BRAZILIAN

Brasília

São Francisco R.

Salvador

HIGHLANDS

Belo
Horizonte

Rio Grande

Antofagasta

ATACAMA DESERT

GRAN CHACO

PARAGUAY

Pilcomayo River

São Paulo

Iguassú Falls

Rio de Janeiro

Santos

Tucumán

Mt.
Aconcagua

Córdoba

Asunción

Salado R.

Santa Fé

Rosario

Paraná R.

Uruguay R.

URUGUAY

Montevideo

Valparaíso

Mendoza

ANDES MTS.

ARGENTINA

Santiago

Buenos
Aires

Rio de la Plata

ATLANTIC

Colorado R.

PAMPA

Valdivia

Bahía Blanca

Chubut R.

PATAGONIA

OCEAN

FALKLAND IS.
(Br.)

Punta Arenas

TIERRA DEL FUEGO

SOUTH GEORGIA
(Br.)

Cape Horn

Drake Passage

SOUTH
ORKNEY IS.
(Br.)

12 LATIN AMERICA

Map information based upon
data available March 1981

0   400   800

Scale in Miles

THE MIDDLE EAST

13

Map information based upon
data available July 1978

Scale in Miles

0   100   200   300   400

SOVIET UNION

KYZYL KUM DESERT

Amu Darya R.

Chardzhou

Maimana

AFGHANISTAN

Kandahar

Herat

PAKISTAN

Helmand R.

KARA KUM DESERT

Ashkhabad

Krasnovodsk

Meshed

KOPET MTS.

Birjand

DASHT-I-KAVIR (DESERT)

Kerman

Yezd

I R A N

PLATEAU OF IRAN

CASPIAN SEA

Baku

Resht

ELBURZ MTS.

Tehran

Shiraz

Isfahan

ZAGROS MOUNTAINS

Bushire

ARABIAN SEA

Muscat

Sur

OMAN

GULF OF OMAN

KURIA MURIA IS. (Br.)

Boundary

Sayhut

PEOPLE'S DEM. REP. OF YEMEN

Undefined

Mukalla

UNITED ARAB EMIRATES

Sharja

RUB' AL KHALI (EMPTY QUARTER)

BAHREIN

Doha

QATAR

PERSIAN GULF

Abadan

Dhahran

Hofuf

Riyadh

KUWAIT

Kuwait

NEUTRAL ZONES

Basra

Buraida

S A U D I   A R A B I A

N E J D

Hail

AN NAFUD

Taima

Medina

Yenbo

HEJAZ

Mecca

Jiddah

ASIR

San'a

YEMEN

Hodeida

Aden

RED SEA

Tbilisi

MTS.

Kura R.

L. Sevan

MT. ARARAT

Erzurum

Trabzon

Diyarbekir

Tabriz

L. Urmia

KURDISTAN

Mosul

Kirkuk

Baghdad

Karbala

An Najaf

I R A Q

Tigris

Euphrates R.

SYRIAN DESERT

Aleppo

Hama

SYRIA

Homs

Damascus

Amman

JORDAN

Elath

Gulf of Aqaba

SINAI

Gulf of Suez

Port Said

ISRAEL

Tel-Aviv

Jerusalem

Cairo

Suez

LEBANON

Beirut

CYPRUS

Nicosia

Samsun

Trabzor

Gaziantep

Kayseri

Adana

Konya

T U R K E Y

Ankara

Eskisehir

Bursa

Üsküdar

Istanbul

Sea of Marmara

Izmir

RHODES

MEDITERRANEAN SEA

CRETE

AEGEAN SEA

Thessaloniki

Athens

GREECE

ALBANIA

Bengasi

Tobruk

L I B Y A

LIBYAN DESERT

Siwa

EGYPT

El Alamein

Alexandria

El Faiyum

El Minya

Asyut

Kharga

Qena

Aswan

Wadi Halfa

S U D A N

Dongola

Omdurman

Khartoum

El Obeid

Kassala

Atbara

Port Sudan

Asmara

ETHIOPIA

Blue Nile

White Nile

Nile

Kermanshah

Hamadan

20°

30°

40°

50°

20°

30°

40°

50°

Prepared by Uni-Map, Inc., Palatine, Ill.

EUROPE

14

Map information based upon data available March 1981

Prepared by
Rand McNally & Co., Chicago

Scale in Miles
0   100   200   300   400